PUBLIC FINANCE

PUBLIC FINANCE

Charles F. Bastable

Simon Publications, Inc.
2003

Originally published in 1892 by Macmillan & Co. London and New York

Library of Congress Card Number: 08013176

ISBN: 1-932512-12-8

Published by Simon Publications, Inc. P. O. Box 910455, San Diego, CA 92191-0455

PREFACE

THE subject of Public Finance, as distinct from that of Political Economy, has not of late years attracted much attention in Great Britain. The very excellence of English financial institutions and management has contributed to this result by making the need of theoretic study as a basis for practical reforms less pressing. Though our financial literature is not quite so poor as some critics imagine, it must be allowed to be deficient in works dealing with the subject as a whole. Since the well-known book of McCulloch—first published in 1845 and now out of print—there has been no manual available for the student.

Such a want is specially felt in the work of teaching. A lecturer who desires to deal with financial questions has no text-book—like those at the service of his French, German, and Italian colleagues—to use as the groundwork of his instruction, and is therefore compelled to make constant reference to foreign treatises not readily accessible to, or easily read by, his class.

In the present work I have sought to temporarily supply this need by going over the whole field of Public Finance and presenting the results in a systematic form, so that a student may at least obtain a general knowledge of the leading facts and present position of this branch of political science. The selection of topics and the space assigned to each have been determined under the influence of this guiding idea, which has led to limitation of the treatment in two respects.

In the first place, I have not sought to specially discuss matters of temporary or local political interest, or to decide on the merits of the conflicting arguments of party advocates. For the purpose of scientific study it is the general and permanent aspects of finance that most require elucidation. None the less, however, do conditions that underlie existing political controversies frequently come into view. In every department of Finance questions of real and practical importance are to be found. The 'purely academic discussion' of to-day will be the 'burning question' of a twelvemonth hence. This explanation is necessary to account for the apparently curt treatment of certain prominent questions—such as that of compulsory insurance (p. 85)—which I had disposed of long before the present situation had arisen.

Again, I have not thought it advisable to devote space to discussion of the financial bearings of the latest economic theories. Admitting fully the great ability and vigour with which the supporters of the Austrian school have urged its claims, I feel that the controversy is as yet unclosed and that the complete acceptance of the new theory seems at the utmost to involve a translation rather than a reconstruction of the older views on Finance, while the practical deductions to be drawn from it are not at all clear or universally accepted even by its upholders. A full examination of its influence on Finance would, from both the length and the difficulty of the inquiry, be altogether unsuited for a work like the present. Where necessary—as in the case of progressive taxation (p. 284)—I have, however, noted its bearing.

In acknowledging my many and heavy obligations I feel

bound first to mention M. P. Leroy Beaulieu, whose *Traité de la Science des Finances* is probably the best-known and most generally valued work on the subject. It was in his full and admirably lucid treatise that I first studied the science, and I have always used it with pleasure and profit. Next, I would place the elaborate work of Wagner, who supplies his readers alike with ingenious, if often disputable doctrines, and carefully collected masses of material. The manuals of Cohn, Roscher, and (though in a less degree) Stein I have also found very serviceable. On questions of administration and control I owe most to M. Stourm's *Le Budget.* The same writer's *Les Finances de l'Ancien Régime et de la Révolution* threw most light on that important part of French financial history. I used with advantage Clamageran's *Histoire de l'Impôt en France* for the earlier periods. In respect to England Mr. Dowell's instructive and entertaining volumes have been my chief guide. Besides the usual books of reference—amongst which I would specially name the successive issues of *The Statesman's Yearbook*, the *Annuaire de l'Économie Politique*, *The Statistical Abstract*, and *The Victorian Yearbook*—the two *Dictionnaires* of M. Léon Say, and the works of Vignes, Fournier de Flaix, Alessio, and Professor Ely gave me most information on existing conditions.

In dealing with financial statistics—which have been kept within the narrowest possible limits—I have in most cases rounded the figures in order to fasten attention on the really important facts expressed by them. For the same reason in the conversion of foreign money into English I have been satisfied with the approximate equation of £1 = $5 = 25 francs or lire = 20 marks. The fluctuations of the rupee, the Austrian florin, and the rouble have generally made their conversion undesirable, but I have sometimes taken them at their exchange value.

Finally, I should explain that the references are, unless where otherwise stated, to the volume and page of the particular author. In order to prevent any mistake I have added a list of the chief works referred to and the editions used.

C. F. BASTABLE.

TRINITY COLLEGE, DUBLIN.
May, 1892.

CONTENTS

INTRODUCTION.

Part I.

PAGES

§§ 1–5. Nature and scope of Public Finance. §§ 6, 7. Its relations to economics. § 8. To history and statistics. § 9. Its appropriate method; must combine induction and deduction. § 20. Outline of present work 1–15

Part II.

§ 1. Need for studying the development of financial theory. § 2. Reasons for its absence in ancient times. § 3. And in the Middle Ages. § 4. Its commencement. Bodin. § 5. The Cameralists—Vauban, Montesquieu, Hume. § 6. The Physiocrats: their influence. § 7. Adam Smith's *Wealth of Nations*: its position and merits. § 8. His English successors. Modern French writers. § 9. The German followers of Adam Smith. Later financial theories in Germany. § 10. Italian writers. § 11. Recent English and American works on Finance 15–33

BOOK I.

PUBLIC EXPENDITURE.

CHAPTER I.

State Economy. General Considerations.

§ 1. Expenditure necessary in all economies. § 2. Peculiarities of the public economy. § 3. Classification of public wants by J. S. Mill and Roscher. § 4. Theories of State functions. Paternal government. *Laissez-faire.* Adam Smith's statement. J. S. Mill. Modern position. § 5. The development of State functions in the several social stages. § 6. Permanence of certain wants. § 7. Commodities and services both required 37–53

CHAPTER II.

The Cost of Defence.

PAGES

§ 1. Increase of expenditure for this object. § 2. Partly in preparation, partly for actual warfare. §§ 3, 4. Development of the military organization. Its dependence on economic conditions. § 5. Volunteer service. § 6. Cost of navies. § 7. Growing cost of war *matériel*, possible alleviations. § 8. Cost of warfare. § 9. Summary. Note 54–68

CHAPTER III.

Justice and Security.

§ 1. Importance of the function, its extent. § 2. Its development. The fee theory. §§ 3, 4. Compulsory and voluntary services. § 5. Police expenditure. § 6. The prison system . . . 69–76

CHAPTER IV.

Administrative Supervision. Poor-Relief.

§ 1. Decay of state regulation; its revival. § 2. Reasons for this new growth. § 3. Tests of its expediency. § 4. The problem of poor-relief. Conflicting arguments. § 5. Practical result. § 6. Other modes of assistance 77–85

CHAPTER V.

Education. Religion.

§ 1. The State in relation to education. § 2. In primary education. § 3. In secondary education. § 4. In University education. § 5. Technical education. § 6. Other means of culture. § 7. Voluntary aid. § 8. Religious endowments 86–94

CHAPTER VI.

Expenditure on Industry and Commerce. Constitutional and Diplomatic Expenditure.

§ 1. All expenditure is partly for economic ends. § 2. Action of the State to encourage industry generally. § 3. Assistance to special branches of industry and commerce. § 4. Over-expenditure for this object rare. §§ 5, 6. Maintenance of the Government. § 7. Cost of public debt and revenue collection 95–103

CHAPTER VII.

Central and Local Expenditure.

PAGES

§ 1. Real unity of general and local government. § 2. Differences in local government the result of historical conditions. § 3. But yet conform to general principles. § 4. Opposing tendencies. § 5. Greater complexity of local government in modern times. Its causes. § 6. Division of financial duties between the State and local bodies. § 7. Application to the several heads of expenditure. § 8. Some special cases. § 9. Central control expedient . . . 104–122

CHAPTER VIII.

Some General Questions of Expenditure.

§ 1. Ordinary and extraordinary expenditure. Various uses of these terms. § 2. Productive and unproductive expenditure. §§ 3, 4. Relation of public to national revenue. Proper limit of the former. § 5. Growth of expenditure in modern times. Its causes. § 6. Influence of public expenditure on the national economy . 123–138

BOOK II.

PUBLIC REVENUE.

THE ECONOMIC OR QUASI-PRIVATE RECEIPTS.

CHAPTER I.

The Forms and Classification of Public Revenues.

§ 1. Expenditure and revenue correlative. § 2. Complexity of the forms of revenue. Attempted classifications. § 3. Criticisms. § 4. The true arrangement. § 5. Divisions of the economic revenue . 141–151

CHAPTER II.

The State Domain. Lands and Forests.

§ 1. The origin of the domain. §§ 2, 3. Its present position in the several countries of the world. § 4. Land nationalization. § 5. Arguments for and against the retention of public lands. § 6. Methods of management. § 7. Increase of public lands undesirable. § 8. Exception in the case of forests. § 9. The actual position of public forests. § 10. Division of management between central and local governments 152–173

CHAPTER III.

The Industrial Domain.

PAGES

§ 1. Contrast between agricultural and industrial domain. § 2. State mines. § 3. State manufacture of fine products and for its own use. § 4. Monopoly of manufacture for taxation. §§ 5, 6. Municipal industries. Water-supply, lighting, drainage. § 7. The Post Office, its history and present position. § 8. It is a combination of several distinct industries. § 9. Its financial bearings. § 10. State telegraphs. § 11. Roads and canals. § 12. Treatment of railways. § 13. French railway policy. § 14. German state railways. § 15. Other European railways. § 16. Railway policy of non-European countries. § 17. Objections to the system of state railways. § 18. Municipal tramways. § 19. The management of state railways. § 20. Treatment of state employees. § 21. Financial importance of the industrial domain. 174–212

CHAPTER IV.

The State as Capitalist. Administrative Revenue.

§ 1. Decline of state trading. § 2. State banks. § 3. Public lotteries. § 4. The State as lender. § 5. Fixed charges on land. § 6. Dues. § 7. The fee system. § 8. Juridical fees. § 9. Administrative and miscellaneous fees. § 10. Heterogeneous character of the revenue from fees 213–226

CHAPTER V.

State Property.—General Considerations on Quasi-private Revenue.

§ 1. Growth of public property that does not yield revenue. § 2. Contrast between economic and tax receipts. § 3. Division of the former between central and local government. § 4. Difficulty of laying down general rules on the subject. § 5. Proportion of economic receipts to total revenue. § 6. Much smaller in the net than in the gross revenue 227–238

BOOK III.

PUBLIC REVENUE.

THE PRINCIPLES OF TAXATION.

CHAPTER I.

Definition and Classification of Taxation.

§ 1. Prominence of taxation in Finance. § 2. Need of definitions. § 3. Definition of taxation. §§ 4, 5. Other definitions; errors in this connexion. § 6. Etymological meaning of terms. § 7. 'Subject' and 'source' of taxation. § 8. Use of terms, 'direct' and

PAGES

'indirect,' 'real' and 'personal,' 'rated' and 'apportioned.' § 9. Economical classification of taxes. § 10. Empirical classifications. § 11. Grouping adopted in the present work . . . 241–259

CHAPTER II.

The General Features of Taxation.

§ 1. Study of the broader features of taxation essential. § 2. Taxation means a deduction of wealth and therefore is an evil; fallacies on this head. § 3. Taxation hardly ever increases production. § 4. It is often uneconomical. § 5. Income the normal source of taxation, but wealth may also contribute. § 6. Theory of net produce; Physiocratic view. § 7. Later German theories. § 8. Importance of the preceding discussions 260–273

CHAPTER III.

The Distribution of Taxation.

§ 1. Distribution an ethical question, but involves economic considerations. § 2. The theory of payment for state service; its error. § 3. Equal payment by all. Ability as a measure of taxation. § 4. Proportional taxation advocated by the classical economists. § 5. Progressive taxation; reasons for its popularity. § 6. Objections to its use. § 7. Arguments in its support. § 8. The results of experience. § 9. Degressive taxation. § 10. Exemption of the minimum of subsistence. § 11. Treatment of (*a*) temporary incomes; (*b*) savings. § 12. Summary of preceding sections. § 13. Taxation of speculation and unearned increment. § 14. International double taxation. § 15. Politico-social view. § 16. McCulloch's theory 274–307

CHAPTER IV.

The Tax System. Its Forms.

§ 1. Single and multiple taxation. § 2. Proposals of Vauban and Deckker. § 3. The *Impôt unique* of the Physiocrats. § 4. Objections to the single tax. § 5. Evils of multiple taxation. § 6. Variety in taxation desirable. § 7. Meanings of direct and indirect taxation. § 8. Merits and defects of direct taxation. § 9. And of indirect taxation. § 10. Other taxes. § 11. Combination of the three classes desirable. § 12. And likely to continue . 308–328

CHAPTER V.

The Incidence of Taxation.

§ 1. Importance of the question. § 2. Development of the economic theory of incidence; the Physiocrats, Adam Smith, Ricardo, J. S. Mill. § 3. Criticism of this theory. § 4. The diffusion theory of taxation; its defects. § 5. The incidence of a tax on commodities.

PAGES

§ 6. The incidence of taxes on rent and the shifting of taxation to rent. § 7. Taxes on capital and employer's gain; their varied incidence. § 8. Taxes on wages not always shifted. § 9. Complicated nature of shifting 329–353

CHAPTER VI.

The Principles of Local Taxation.

§ 1. Reasons for separating local from general taxation. § 2. The history of local institutions helps to determine their revenue. § 2. What taxes should belong to the central government. § 4. Those that are best for local governments. § 5. Just distribution in local taxation. § 6. Relations between general and local Finance. § 7. The amount of liberty to be granted to local bodies . . . 354–371

Appendix. The maxims of Taxation. 372–376

BOOK IV.

PUBLIC REVENUE.

TAXATION. THE SEVERAL KINDS OF TAXES.

CHAPTER I.

Taxes on Land.

§ 1. Antiquity of land taxes. § 2. Their development. § 3. *Cadrastral* surveys. § 4. English taxes on land. § 5. The *Impôt foncier* in France. § 6. Land taxes in Italy, Spain, Portugal and Belgium. § 7. In Germany and Austria. § 8. General features of land taxation. § 9. Its incidence 379–394

CHAPTER II.

Taxes on Capital and Business.

§ 1. Development of taxes on buildings. § 2. In England. § 3. House and building taxes in other countries. § 4. Further considerations. § 5. Incidence of these taxes. § 6. Taxation of floating capital. § 7. Profits more readily dealt with. § 8. Taxation of profits in England. § 9. The *Patente* in France. § 10. Taxation of profits in Italy, Germany, &c. § 11. Characteristics of continental taxation of profits. § 12. The incidence of taxes on business profits . 395–413

CHAPTER III.

Personal and Wages Taxes.

§ 1. Origin of poll taxes. § 2. Illustrations in England, France, Russia and Prussia. § 3. Decline of poll or wages taxes; their unfairness. 414–417

CHAPTER IV.

TAXES ON PROPERTY AND INCOME.

PAGES

§ 1. General abandonment of the property tax. § 2. Its survival in Switzerland ; peculiarities of the system. § 3. Property taxes in the United States ; their defects. § 4. Superiority of the income-tax. § 5. The English Income-tax. § 6. The income-tax in Italy. § 7. In the German States. § 8. General considerations on the income-tax. § 9. Its incidence 418–437

CHAPTER V.

TAXES ON CONSUMPTION : THEIR CLASSIFICATION. DIRECT CONSUMPTION TAXES.

§ 1. Secondary or consumption taxes. § 2. Their classification. § 3. Origin and decline of direct taxes on consumption. § 4. English taxes of this class. § 5. These taxes in other countries. § 6. Best reserved for local purposes 438–446

CHAPTER VI.

INTERNAL TAXES ON COMMODITIES.

§ 1. Importance of excise taxes; their development. §§ 2, 3. Problems of excise taxation. § 4. It must be suited to the particular country. § 5. History and present position of the British Excise. § 6. History of the French indirect taxes. § 7. The existing French system: its principal features, its defects. § 8. Italian taxation of commodities. § 9. History of the German Excises ; small return under the present system. § 10. Internal taxation in other countries. § 11. General features of modern internal taxation. § 12. The history of *Octrois*. § 13. Their present use. § 14. Criticism of the *Octroi* system. § 15. Incidence of excise duties 447–488

CHAPTER VII.

CUSTOMS DUTIES.

§ 1. The early forms of customs taxation. Its gradual development. § 2. Customs to be considered in connexion with the Excise. § 3. The English customs system, its history and chief features. § 4. French customs duties, their financial defects. § 5. Customs duties in Italy, Germany, and other countries. § 6. Intrusion of political motives into the customs system. Prominence of import duties. § 7. The incidence of customs duties. Complicated nature of the problem 489–509

CHAPTER VIII.

TAXES ON COMMUNICATIONS, ACTS AND SUCCESSIONS.

§ 1. Different elements that contributed to the establishment of taxes on circulation. § 2. Taxes on communication and transport.

PAGES

§ 3. Stamps as a form of taxation. § 4. Taxation on acts and transactions. § 5. Stamp and registration duties in England, France, Italy, and Germany. § 6. Incidence of taxes on acts. § 7. Succession duties. § 8. The English death duties. § 9. Succession duties in other countries. § 10. The incidence of succession duties . 510–532

BOOK V.

THE RELATIONS OF EXPENDITURE AND RECEIPTS.

CHAPTER I.

INTRODUCTORY. STATE HOARDING.

§ 1. Impossibility of keeping complete equality between expenditure and receipts. § 2. Ancient and mediaeval state treasures. § 3. Reasons for state hoarding. The present German reserve. Objections to the system of keeping a reserve. § 4. Public debts more important at present 535–542

CHAPTER II.

PUBLIC INDEBTEDNESS. ITS MODERN DEVELOPMENT.

§ 1. No state borrowing in classical times. § 2. Mediaeval state borrowing. § 3. Causes of modern public debts. § 4. Their rapid growth. § 5. Summary 543–550

CHAPTER III.

THE HISTORY OF THE ENGLISH DEBT.

§ 1. Commencement of the debt at the Revolution; its early progress (1692–1740). § 2. Chief features in that period. § 3. The second period (1740–1792). § 4. The English debt during the French war (1793–1815). § 5. The peace history of the debt. § 6. Reduction of debt by redemption and conversion. § 7. The continued existence of the debt due to war and to weak financial policy . . 551–561

CHAPTER IV.

HISTORY OF THE FRENCH DEBT. INDEBTEDNESS IN OTHER COUNTRIES.

§ 1. Borrowing under the *Ancien Régime*. § 2. The formation of the present debt (1793–1870). § 3. The Franco-German war. The actual position. § 4. Public debts in Italy and Germany. § 5. The history and present position of the United States debt. § 6. General increase of public debts 562–574

CHAPTER V.

THE THEORY OF PUBLIC CREDIT AND PUBLIC DEBTS.

PAGES

§ 1. Public credit is one species of credit in general and governed by the principles applicable to all credit. § 2. Peculiar features of public credit. § 3. Early theories as to advantages of public debts. § 4. The views of Montesquieu, Hume, and Adam Smith. Truth and error in their position. § 5. The theory of Chalmers and J. S. Mill. § 6. German doctrines: C. Dietzel's theory of reproductive borrowing. § 7. Criticism of Chalmers. § 8. Of the theory of reproductive borrowing. § 9. The real effect of borrowing. Taxation and borrowing contrasted. § 10. Borrowing sometimes desirable. General rules. § 11. Foreign loans. § 12. Modes of estimating the pressure of public debt 575–600

CHAPTER VI.

THE FORMS OF PUBLIC DEBTS.

§ 1. Forced, patriotic, and business loans. § 2. Temporary and perpetual debts. Advantage of the latter. § 3. Variety desirable. § 4. Methods of contracting loans. § 5. Loans should not be contracted under *par*. § 6. Floating debt: its treatment. § 7. Inconvertible paper 601–612

CHAPTER VII.

THE REDEMPTION AND CONVERSION OF DEBT.

§ 1. Redemption of debt desirable. § 2. Conditions to be considered in this process. § 3. All payment must be out of surplus revenue. The Sinking Fund: its error. § 4. Necessity of debt reduction. § 5. Conversion as a mode of relief. § 6. Redemption by a single property contribution. § 7. Automatic reduction of debt. § 8. Is there any distinction between home and foreign loans in respect to redemption? 613–625

CHAPTER VIII.

LOCAL INDEBTEDNESS.

§ 1. Danger in the increase of local debt. § 2. Instances of increase in England and abroad. § 3. Causes of this increase. § 4. Local borrowing often justifiable. § 5. Forms of local loans. § 6. Repayment also necessary in their case. § 7. Provincial and county borrowing. § 8. Necessity for central control over local borrowing 626–635

BOOK VI.

FINANCIAL ADMINISTRATION AND CONTROL.

CHAPTER I.

INTRODUCTORY. HISTORICAL DEVELOPMENT.

PAGES

§ 1. Administration and control a necessary part of financial science. § 2. Gradual development of financial regulation. Classical and mediaeval periods. § 3. Regulation under absolute monarchy. § 4. Constitutional system of English origin. § 5. Its extension to other countries. § 6. Modern financial systems admit of general treatment 639-647

CHAPTER II.

THE BUDGET: ITS PREPARATION. THE COLLECTION OF REVENUE.

§ 1. Meaning of the term 'Budget.' § 2. Preliminary estimates necessary. § 3. Period, form, and matter of the Budget. Should it be 'gross' or 'net'? § 4. Unity of the Budget. Should it deal with cash or transactions? Modes of estimating income and outlay. § 5. The collection of taxation. Farming of taxes. Apportionment. Direct state levy. Rules respecting it. § 6. Dealing with the funds received 648-658

CHAPTER III.

THE VOTE OF THE BUDGET. CONTROL AND AUDIT.

§ 1. Summary of budgetary rules. § 2. Method of examining the Budget. Right of proposing expenditure. § 3. Relative powers of the two chambers. Specialization of votes. § 4. Difficulty of adjusting income to outlay. Supplemental votes. Fixed expenditure and taxation. § 5. Comparison of English and French methods. § 6. Checks over issues. Their development in England, France, and Italy. § 7. Methods of audit. The English appropriation audit. The United States system. French *Cour des Comptes*. Other countries. § 8. Conclusion 659-672

LIST OF WORKS REFERRED TO

ALESSIO, *Saggio sul Sistema Tributario in Italia*, 2 vols., 1883–7.

BOLLES, *Financial History of the United States from* 1861 *to* 1885 (1886).

BRYCE, *The American Commonwealth*, 2nd ed., 2 vols., 1890.

BUXTON, *Finance and Politics*, 2 vols., 1888.

CLAMAGERAN, *Histoire de l'Impôt en France*, 3 vols., 1867–76.

COHN, *System der Finanzwissenschaft*, 1889.

DICEY, *The Law of the Constitution*, 1st ed., 1885.

DILKE, *Problems of Greater Britain*, 3rd ed., 1890.

DOWELL, *A History of Taxation and Taxes in England*, 2nd ed., 4 vols., 1888.

ELY, *Taxation in American States and Cities*, 1888.

FOURNIER DE FLAIX, *Traité de Critique et de Statistique Comparée des Institutions Financières*, 1889.

HAMILTON, *An Inquiry concerning the National Debt of Great Britain*, 2nd ed., 1814.

HOCK, *Öffentliche Abgaben und Schulden*, 1863.

HUMBERT, *Essai sur les Finances et la Comptabilité chez les Romains*, 2 vols., 1886.

LEROY BEAULIEU, *Traité de la Science des Finances*, 3me ed., 2 vols., 1883.

M'CULLOCH, *Treatise on Taxation and the Funding System*, 3rd ed., 1863.

MARSHALL, *Principles of Economics*, vol. I, 1st ed., 1890.

MEYER, *Die Principien der gerechten Besteuerung*, 1884.

PARIEU, DE, *Traité des Impôts*, 2me ed., 4 vols., 1866–7.

PARNELL, *On Financial Reform*, 2nd ed., 1830.

RICARDO, *Works* (ed. J. R. McCulloch), 1846.

ROSCHER, *System der Finanzwissenschaft*, 2nd ed., 1886.

SCHÄFFLE, *Grundsätze der Steuerpolitik*, 1880.

SCHÖNBERG, *Finanzwissenschaft und Verwaltungslehre* (the 3rd vol. of the *Handbuch der Politischen Oekonomie*), 2nd ed., 1885.

SIDGWICK, *The Principles of Political Economy*, 1st ed., 1883.

ADAM SMITH, *The Wealth of Nations* (ed. J. S. Nicholson), 1884.

STEIN, *Lehrbuch der Finanzwissenschaft*, 5th ed., 4 vols., 1885–6.

STOURM, *Les Finances de l'Ancien Régime et de la Révolution*, 2 vols., 1885.

STOURM, *Le Budget*, 1re ed., 1889.

TURGOT, *Œuvres* (éd. Daire), 2 vols., 1844.

UMPFENBACH, *Lehrbuch der Finanzwissenschaft*, 2nd ed., 1887.

VIGNES, *Traité des Impôts en France*, 4me ed., 2 vols., 1880.

VOCKE, *Die Abgaben, Auflagen und die Steuer*, 1887.

WAGNER, *Finanzwissenschaft*, vol. i, 3rd ed., 1883; vol. ii, 2nd ed., 1890; vol. iii, 1st ed., 1889.

ERRATA ET ADDENDA

Page 30, line 3, *for* and *read* with
,, 32 ,, 14, to the books on English taxation *add* Wilson's *National Budget* (1882).
,, 56 ,, 33, *for* puts *read* put
,, 159 ,, 6, *for* has *read* have
,, 182, note, line 3, *insert* to *before* quasi-public
,, 275 ,, 12, *for* is *read* are
,, 316 ,, 4, *insert* that of *after* is
,, 387 ,, 19, *for* £10,400,000 *read* £10,200,000
,, 388 ,, 17, *for* £9,200,000 *read* £9,600,000
,, 411, note, *add* Under the Prussian Law of 1891—to come into force in 1893—the *Gewerbesteuer* will be adjusted according to product and capital employed. The contributors are to be grouped in four classes, the highest consisting of those whose product is over £2000, or whose capital is over £50,000.

INTRODUCTION.

I.

§ 1. IN any society that has passed beyond the lowest stage of social development, some form of governmental organization is found to be an essential feature. The various activities or functions of this controlling body furnish the material for what are known as the 'Political Sciences' (*Staatswissenschaften*). Every governing body or 'State' requires for the due discharge of its functions repeated supplies of commodities and personal services, which it has to apply to the accomplishment of whatever ends it may regard as desirable. The processes involved in obtaining and using these supplies naturally vary much in the several stages of social advance: they are comparatively simple and direct in a primitive community, while in a modern industrial society they present a high degree of complication, and are carried out by elaborate regulations. For all States, however — whether rude or highly developed,—some provisions of the kind are necessary and therefore the supply and application of state resources constitutes the subject-matter of a study which is best entitled in English, PUBLIC FINANCE[1].

[1] For the various meanings of the term 'Finance,' see Roscher, § 1, also Garnier, 1–3. The original idea is that of paying a fine (*finare*). Unfortunately, in England the word has been used with a wider meaning, as including all monetary and even industrial facts. Thus we have Jevons' *Investigations in Currency and Finance*, Mr. Patterson's *Science of Finance*, and Mr. Giffen's *Essays in Finance*, all dealing mainly with those wider questions. An English

§ 2. The importance of the subject hardly requires much insistence. The collection of funds for state purposes and the use of the resources so obtained is such a vital part of the political organization, that it is almost certain to receive attention from all who are interested in political and social inquiries. But, if demanded, abundant evidence is at hand. The citizen of any civilized country need only reflect for a few minutes in order to satisfy himself of the number and importance of the actions of the State on its financial side. His letters are carried by a state agency which claims a monopoly, and in some cases realizes a large profit for the general revenue. The commodities that supply his table are in many cases taxed to create a fund for the payment of public services. Either his income or property or some of their elements is sure to be subjected to a charge of greater or less amount, and several of the most ordinary avocations are only open to him on obtaining a costly licence for permission to engage in them. The claims of the State do not cease here. In addition to the central body, the local authorities have to be considered. If the person of our supposition be the inhabitant of a town, his house may be lighted by public agency, while it is more than possible that for one of the first necessaries of life—water—he is dependent on his municipality. There is little need for further working out of details. The way in which the purely financial agencies of the State—and still more those which have some connexion with Finance—affect the members of the society in their every-day existence, is being always illustrated afresh by the ordinary course of social life.

§ 3. The importance of a subject is of itself a strong plea for its scientific study, but in the present case more special arguments may be urged. There is in Finance, as in all matters depending in some degree on human will, the possibility of choosing between different courses, some of which

writer is therefore compelled, in order to avoid misapprehension, to limit the word as in the text, when he is treating of what the Germans can without inconvenience call *Finanzwissenschaft* or the French *Science des Finances*.

are likely to prove better than others, and for the formation of a correct judgment as to the relative merits of the lines of action open to the State, careful examination of the conditions affecting the phenomena is indispensable. Such examination is, however, only possible by scientific study, or rather it is that study. More particularly is this true at present in consequence of the great expansion of the functions of the State, which is partly due to—and which in turn increases—the complications of modern societies. The effects of state action in a primitive community are far more easily followed ; the forms both of revenue and expenditure are reducible to a few simple kinds, directed by rude and partially developed agencies. The modern State, even when it allows an amount of individual liberty unknown in any former period is obliged to employ complicated machinery for the regulation and management of its outlay and receipts. The results, moreover, are not so readily perceived ; numerous interests and classes are affected by any change in the course of public expenditure or by readjustments of taxation. The many indirect results of financial processes must be considered before we can either understand their operation or fairly judge their merits ; but to trace the action of economic forces in their effects on the highly developed systems of modern industrial societies is a task of considerable difficulty, not to be accomplished without the aid of general principles, and careful reference to former experience. The case for a scientific study of Finance is so strong that it does not require much vindication, and the value of critical investigations has been already verified by the results obtained.

§ 4. The scope of our subject has been already indicated in a general way, but for clearness of thought and in consequence of the differing views of many writers of authority we must now determine it more precisely. State expenditure and state revenue at once occur to the mind as the two great heads of inquiry, standing opposed to each other as Production and Consumption, or Supply and Demand do in economic science. Closer examination shows that this simple grouping does not exhaust the field of investigation. Problems of revenue and of expenditure are indeed the most important. Adam Smith, who was, at least for England, the founder of the scientific study of Public Finance, as of Political Economy in general, devoted separate chapters of his Fifth Book to 'The Expenses of the Sovereign' and 'The Revenues of the Sovereign'; but by the nature of the subject he found himself forced to add a third section, in which the relation between expenditure and receipts is examined. He knew that many ancient and mediaeval sovereigns had accumulated treasures; it was apparent that most modern governments had heaped up debts—a process that has been carried much further since his day—and it followed that an enquiry into the balance between state incomings and outgoings was an essential—as it is also a difficult—part of Public Finance.

Nor is this the only addition. The phenomena to be dealt with do not admit of being conveniently grouped under Adam Smith's three heads. This difficulty is at once felt on calling to mind that the expenditure and revenue under consideration is *state* expenditure and *state* revenue. We must examine not the processes merely, but the mechanism by which those processes are carried on. The collection and application of wealth by the State require legislative and administrative action. The right of voting supplies and supervising expenditure—'the power of the purse'—is one of the leading privileges of a representative body; it is also the most effectual safeguard of constitutional rights. Methods of administrative control seriously affect the working of the national finances, and are deserving of attentive study. No financial treatise can be complete unless it considers the problems of 'the Budget' and 'financial administration' (*Finanzverwaltung*), and such has in late years been the almost invariable practice[1].

[1] That is with continental writers. In England these topics are generally relegated to works on 'Constitutional Law' and 'Parliamentary Usage.'

§ 5. In one respect the scope of Public Finance has been curtailed by some of its ablest expounders. French writers, more especially M. P. Leroy-Beaulieu, have refused to regard the problems of public expenditure as a part of their subject. The reason for this limitation is said to be the difficulty of scientifically determining the proper amount of state outlay, as that must depend on the functions assigned to the State. 'This kind of inquiry,' says M. Leroy-Beaulieu, 'does not in my opinion belong to the science of Finance . . . . . . A State has wants : it does not belong to us at present to know what they are, and what they ought to be, but how it is possible to satisfy them in the amplest manner with the least loss and sacrifice to individuals. If you engage a builder to build you a house, it is not his business to inquire if the building is too large for your income or your social position ; what does concern him is to build the house in question with the utmost possible solidity, convenience, and beauty, at the lowest cost to the owner. In like manner, a writer on Finance can sincerely lament that States spend too much, but his real task lies in showing how a State can obtain supplies, while treating the interests of individuals with due tenderness and respecting justice [1].'

English writers have gone further in this direction, and, by disregarding all forms of state revenue except that derived from taxation, have replaced the broader treatment of Adam Smith and the Germans by treatises on 'Taxation' and 'Public Debts [2].'

It nevertheless seems clear that the question of expenditure is just as much a financial problem as that of revenue. Neither in theory nor in practice is it advisable to separate them completely. The greatest finance

[1] Leroy-Beaulieu, i. 2, 3.

[2] Cf. the title of J. R. McCulloch's well-known work, *Taxation and the Funding System*. So strong is the disposition in England and America to limit the subject of Finance to Taxation, that in the recent American translation of Cossa's useful *Scienza delle Finanze*, the title is changed into *Taxation ; its Principles and Methods*.

ministers have made their reputations as much by judicious control of outlay as by wise reforms in revenue [1], while for theoretical discussion the principles and facts of expenditure are of considerable interest. M. Leroy-Beaulieu's suggested parallel of the builder is not in point, since the practical statesman is the only person to whom the illustration would apply, and he evidently does not act in conformity with it; the scientific student is only limited in his inquiries by the nature of the material that he is investigating. One admission may indeed be made. Questions of expenditure do not admit of quite as precise treatment as those referring to taxation, some parts of the latter subject permitting the use of lengthened deductions. This test of fitness for exact investigation would, however, exclude other large parts of the subject—e. g. 'the public domain'—which are nevertheless discussed by all recent writers, M. Leroy-Beaulieu included. For a complete inquiry into the theory of Finance some consideration of the conditions governing state outlay is indispensable, e. g. the increase of military expenditure in European States, its causes and limits, cannot be left wholly unnoticed by any thorough student of Public Finance. Such an inquiry is more especially needed owing to the fact that expenditure and revenue are connected. Public outlay is not something unchangeable and determined, to be met 'with the least loss and sacrifice to individuals.' Expenditure that would be legitimate in a lightly taxed State would be blameworthy in one that is heavily taxed. The aim of the statesman is not simply to distribute loss and reduce it to a minimum, it is rather to procure the maximum of advantage to the community, and to so balance expenditure and revenue as to attain that result.

The principal difficulty in the scientific examination of public expenditure is found when attempting to limit the

[1] The statement of Turgot's policy in his *Letter to the King* (ii. 165): *Point de banqueroute, point d'augmentation d'impôts, point d'emprunts*, is a striking example.

mode of treatment. Some writers enter into discussions as to the legitimacy of certain state functions, and their relative urgency. Others simply state the forms and facts of public outlay, leaving further inquiry to the political theorist. In the present work, in accordance with the precedent set by Adam Smith, the several items of expenditure will be treated on a positive basis, and at the same time the considerations naturally arising from their existence, and the financial questions that they suggest will be noticed, though no complete examination of state functions will be aimed at. Whatever theoretical questions may be raised, such seems to be the course that convenience suggests, and is one to which the subject naturally lends itself. Our object is to elucidate the principles of Public Finance; and the admission or exclusion of any special topic, as well as the extent of treatment in each case must be determined solely by reference to that end[1].

§ 6. Theoretical writers on Finance, especially in Germany, have very fully considered the relations of their subject to cognate branches of knowledge, i. e. to the various social and political sciences, and have in particular emphasized its close ties to Economics[2]. In its origin financial science was a product of economic study. It appears either as a special section or as the main subject of the older treatises of Political Economy, 'when considered as a branch of the science of a statesman or legislator,' to quote Adam Smith's phrase. In another aspect it may be regarded as belonging to administration, and as such formed a large part of the 'Chamber Science' (*Cameralwissenschaft*) which was in Germany the precursor of scientific Economics. The undue limitation of the scope of Finance by English writers has led to its inclusion under the title of 'taxation'

[1] The omission of public expenditure as a topic in 'Finance,' in the case of English writers, was perhaps in part caused by neglect of the economic theory of the 'Consumption of Wealth' with which it would be naturally connected.

[2] E g. Umpfenbach, 1–22; Roscher, § 5; Cohn, §§ 4–7; Wagner, i. 16–20.

in the various systematic expositions of Political Economy[1], and the more enlarged view taken by German writers has not prevented a similar result in that country, for since the time of K. H. Rau, Political Economy has been regarded as comprising, in addition to the general theory, the Economics of special industries, economic legislation and administration, as well as Public Finance[2]. This apparent absorption of Finance in Economics is really the result of a peculiar conception. If the latter science be limited, in the manner usual in England and France, to an investigation of the laws governing the phenomena of wealth, it is beyond dispute that Public Finance cannot form a part of it, as political and fiscal conditions have to be recognised to an extent impossible in a pure science of wealth. Moreover practical considerations have to be weighed in every department of Finance. That Political Economy in the most extended use of the term may fitly include Finance is indeed true, but then it would appear that this wider Political Economy is nothing more than a common name for the various social and political sciences; it is in fact a rudimentary Sociology and Art of Politics combined[3].

§ 7. Though the problems of Finance are really suited for treatment in a separate form, it does not follow that their relation to Economics should be disregarded. On the contrary there is a close connexion, or rather series of connexions between the two studies. State outlay is a part of the consumption of the society of which the State is the regulating organ, and for a knowledge of the con-

[1] The works of J. S. Mill, Fawcett, and Shadwell may be given as examples.

[2] The treatises of Rau, Roscher, Wagner, and Cohn on Finance are all in name sections of text-books of *Political Economy*. The collection of monographs on financial questions in the Schönberg *Handbuch* is another instance.

[3] Examination of the works referred to in the preceding note will support the statement in the text. The financial sections of the treatises there mentioned are in fact independent works, and may be studied quite apart from the other sections.

ditions that govern it we must have a theory of the consumption of wealth in general. Unhappily, questions relating to consumption have been too much neglected by economists, and thus there is no complete theory available for application to financial problems. Still, the leading truths on the matter are suggested in modern economic theories, and may be developed by their aid. The management of state property, again, requires a reference to various economic doctrines, and more especially the industrial enterprises carried on under a public monopoly illustrate and are explained by the general theory of monoplies. It is, however, when we reach taxation that the aid of Economics becomes most valuable. The merits of the general system of taxation, as also those of each special tax have to be tested by the aid of economic principles. The important problem of justice in taxation is indeed an ethical one, but until its economic efforts are known it is impossible to say whether any given form of taxation is just or the reverse. All the intricate points respecting the incidence of taxation can be handled successfully only by applying a sound theory of the distribution of wealth, and the effect of taxation on accumulation makes it necessary to constantly bear in mind the conditions of effective production. In another department of Finance, the nature and effect of public loans can be best explained by the economic theory of credit, and such is the course usually adopted. An acquaintance with economic science is, it may be said, an indispensable part of the equipment of the student of Finance.

§ 8. Close as is the relation between Economics and Finance, it is by no means exclusively to the former science that we have to look for aid when developing the latter. In a subject so inseparable from the State, it is in many cases necessary to recognise the action of political and administrative conditions. Financial problems are often the occasions on which constitutional issues are raised, and as noticed above, they may make a line of conduct desirable, that from the purely economic point of view would be very objectionable. The same statement holds good of administration[1]. The whole system of Finance must be kept in conformity with the general mode of managing the affairs of the State. This is, in fact, involved in the position that Public Finance belongs to the domain of Political Science.

The science of Finance has another important auxiliary in History, which illustrates, verifies, and in some instances affords data for its principles. The material of Public Finance is not confined to that afforded by modern societies, and even for a true knowledge of actual conditions it is often necessary to be acquainted with their growth. No pure *a priori* system of Finance can be successfully established. Each country has special features arising from its previous history, and the sentiments of its people—in great part the product of historical forces. The most violent revolution cannot really break this connexion with the past[2]. As a consequence, a system of Finance admirably suited for one country, may be quite unfitted for another. A comparison of the systems of the United Kingdom and of India shows at a glance extraordinary differences, and yet in each case the attainment of solid results. These obvious truths, however, suggest the need of a caution. The necessary varieties of financial practice do not show that general principles are unattainable, though they tend to render their application more difficult. The conclusions of financial theory ought to underlie all the special systems and regulations, but they require to be applied with most careful regard to the cir-

[1] The determination of the comparative advantages of raising supplies by loans or by fresh taxation, the choice between different methods of levying taxes, and the need in certain cases of resorting to issues of inconvertible paper are instances.

[2] French financial history is the best possible illustration. M. Stourm in his valuable work, *Les Finances de l'ancien Régime et de la Révolution*, has shown conclusively that the modern French system is developed from that existing before the Revolution. Stourm, *passim*, and especially ii. 501-2.

cumstances of time and place, and above all, to the sentiments and habits of the people. Any form of expenditure or taxation that is peculiarly obnoxious, has, by that fact alone, a strong presumption raised against it, to be rebutted only by very weighty reasons on the other side.

As history throws light on the evolution of Finance, and enables us to confirm or to limit our general propositions by the evidence derived from previous times, so do Statistics give us a firmer position in dealing with the present. Without correct information as to state revenue and expenditure, financial policy is little better than guesswork. In order to comprehend the effects of taxation it is indispensable to have full statistics as to the distribution of wealth among classes and among localities. Such materials as those collected by census agencies and statistical departments are necessary elements in any financial calculations, and their absence, of itself, suffices to explain the late origin of financial science. In no respect is modern administration so superior to that of ancient and mediaeval times, as in the improved data on which it bases its estimates and makes its practical suggestions.

§ 9. From an examination of the various sciences that may assist the study of Finance, we pass by a natural transition to the proper method of inquiry. In regard to all Social Science, and notably to Economics, this question has been vigorously discussed, even to the neglect of the positive matter of research The principles of scientific inquiry and the appropriate method of investigation belong in reality rather to Logic than to the special sciences; though the processes employed in discovery can only be adequately appreciated by those who are conversant with the particular branch in which they are used. At all events, it is clear that the disputes as to method have in many cases arisen from misapprehension as to the exact position of each of the contending parties. Protracted controversy has, however, finally led, if not to complete agreement, at least to a recognition of the common ground occupied by the disputants, and also, it may be said, to a belief that the whole question is, as has been often remarked, one of 'emphasis.' A difference in view is, in many cases, the result of personal tastes; one writer places much weight on a particular method, another on a different and apparently opposed one, though both, if interrogated, would probably allow that each form of inquiry was valid within limits, the exact fixing of which would be the only point in dispute[1].

The principal ground of debate was for a long period as to the claims of the 'inductive' and the 'deductive' methods to be regarded as *the* legitimate process of investigation. To that question it may be confidently replied that both are in particular cases valid and indeed indispensable. Without 'induction' in the wider sense of the term[2] no materials for study would be available: mere observation without arrangement and generalisation is evidently worthless for scientific use. The particular form of induction which proceeds by comparison is frequently serviceable. The simple juxtaposition of two financial systems will sometimes throw a great deal of light on the conditions governing each. In this process history, as we saw in the preceding section, plays a great part, and it is thus quite correct to maintain that the science of Finance is in one of its aspects 'inductive,' 'comparative,' and 'historical.'

But this, though the truth, is not the whole truth. The generalizations of Economics and the permanent facts of human nature enable us to draw important

[1] On this subject see Wagner, iii. 199, and his article in Conrad's *Jahrbücher*, 1886, i. 197 sq.; Dunbar in *Quarterly Journal of Economics*, i. 1 sq.; Marshall, *Principles of Economics*, Bk. i. ch. 5; also J. N. Keynes, *Method and Scope of Political Economy*.

[2] Cairnes' *Logical Method* (2nd ed.), 60 sq. The varying use of the term 'induction' by logicians has helped to increase the confusion as to the real relation of the inductive and deductive methods. Cf. J. S. Mill, *Logic*, Bk. ii. ch. 4, § 5; and Bk. iii. ch. 2, which contains his controversy with Whewell on this point.

conclusions as to the effects of certain forces in their bearing on Finance. The whole theory of the incidence and repercussion of taxation is and must be 'deductive,' i. e. it must be developed from simple conditions by logical trains of reasoning. Deduction, too, is needed in order to ascertain the effects of public indebtedness as well as to trace the ultimate results of public expenditure. It must be remembered that in all these cases verification by appeal to facts is required, but the process of verification is admittedly one of the component parts of the deductive method. On the whole, the study of Finance will force on us the conclusion that 'induction' and 'deduction' are not so much opposed as complementary methods, each remedying and making good the weakness of the other.

The preceding argument holds, to some extent, of even the most extreme forms of the two methods. Thus, some —as Macaulay—have maintained that experiment is the really fruitful form of social inquiry. Now, though it is evident that strictly speaking experiment is impossible in respect to any part of social life, since we cannot bring about that isolation of a particular phenomenon without which no experiment can be conclusive, it yet seems true that a modified form of experiment may give a *probable* result that will, in some cases, prove of great practical use. In Finance, for example, each change of taxation may be regarded as an experiment in the popular sense; if, to take an instance, it appeared that a reduction in the rates of taxation on commodities so stimulated consumption that the loss in revenue through the reduction was made up by the increase in the quantities used, it might fairly be said that the policy of reducing duties was experimentally justified, notwithstanding that the logical conditions for experiment were absent. We must, however, notice that a result of this kind cannot safely be extended to fresh cases unless it is supported by more general considerations[1].

[1] For this loose use of experiment, cf. Jevons' 'Experimental Legislation'

The advocates of the mathematical method stand at the other extreme. There is, at first sight, something absurd in suggesting so exact a mode of inquiry in a subject where very many complications exist, and where each fact is dependent on a number of circumstances, but in those parts of Finance in which deduction is the best instrument of research it may prove convenient to arrange the steps of reasoning in a mathematical form; the problem will perhaps be thereby more easily solved or its exposition more readily followed [1]. Where the conditions can be sufficiently simplified, and where it is important to develop the *quantitative* results, this procedure is probably advisable [2]. It is, however, at best confined to a very limited area and needs to have its conclusions tested by the best statistical results available. The more concrete problems of Finance are entirely unamenable to this rigid and precise method of treatment.

§ 10. Having thus briefly considered the questions preliminary to the study of Public Finance, it only remains to give an outline of the course of our further inquiries. After a very concise account of the historical development of financial science (Introduction, Part II) we shall take up the subject of Public Expenditure and its principal problems (Book I).

Next in order of treatment will come the Public Revenues, and first what may be described as the economic and industrial receipts of the State and their subdivisions (Book II). The examination of these more primitive forms of revenue will lead up to the discussion of Taxation. Owing to the great extent and complexity of

in *Methods of Social Reform*, 253 sq.; also Newmarch, *Address to British Association* (section F), 1861.

[1] It is interesting to notice that one of the earliest attempts to apply mathematical methods to social questions was in regard to the theory of taxation by Canard in his *Principes d'Économie Politique*, Paris, 1801.

[2] See for good examples of the method Auspitz und Lieben, *Untersuchungen über die Theorie des Preises*, and M. Pantaleoni, *Teoria della traslazione dei tributi*. Fleeming Jenkin, 'The incidence of Taxes' *Works*, ii. 107–121.

this topic it will be expedient to devote a separate book to the principles and operation of Taxation (Book III), reserving for distinct treatment the study of special taxes (Book IV).

The questions relating to revenue having been thus disposed of, Book V will deal with the balance of expenditure and receipts, or, in other words, with public treasures and public debts.

The only remaining part of the financial system, viz. its mechanism, administration, and control will form the subject of a final book (Book VI).

The principal features of 'local Finance' will be examined, each in its appropriate place,—local expenditure in Book I, local taxation in Books III and IV, and local indebtedness in Book V.

II.

§ 1. Some conception of the gradual formation of the modern theory of Finance, and of the steps by which it has assumed its present shape, will enable the student to form clearer ideas as to its relation to other branches of social inquiry, and the real meaning of those parts of earlier systems which at present seem to have little or no justification. It is only by tracing the history of speculative thought on the various problems of Public Finance that we can fully understand the way in which errors have been gradually eliminated, and incomplete doctrines have been so expanded as to embrace a larger portion of truth.

There is a more special reason for this preliminary historical inquiry in regard to social and political sciences. The particular stage of social development peculiarly affects such studies; their cultivators are not merely like those of all sciences influenced by the knowledge and ideas of their age, but the very phenomena to be interpreted are themselves produced by and dependent on the condition of society. It is this feature which alone can fully explain the absence of financial theory at periods of apparently high civilization and culture.

Our historical inquiry has at present to be limited to what is known as the 'external' history of the Science of Finance, i. e. to an outline of its general aspect and leading representatives at each stage of its growth. Its 'internal' history which considers the origin and growth of the separate doctrines of Finance will be more fitly treated in the systematic sections of the work.

§ 2. In classical antiquity, though the need of revenue was often a pressing one, and though at least under the Roman Empire financial administration was elaborately organized [1], there is no appearance of a scientific treatment of financial problems. The nearest approach to discussion of such questions is found in Xenophon's little work on *the Athenian Revenues* and modern research has succeeded in collecting stray passages from classical authors that incidentally deal with financial questions [2]. There is no great difficulty in accounting for this neglect. The causes which prevented the development of Economics equally hindered that of Finance. The whole constitution of the societies of Greece and Rome was based on conceptions directly opposed to those under which our modern doctrines have been formed. With them the State was placed above and before the individual, who was bound to sacrifice himself unreservedly for his country. To persons holding such a belief the question of just taxation would appear to be of trifling importance. That one man was asked for 20% of his income, while another

[1] The parts of the Theodosian Code dealing with administration are our principal source of information as to the financial system of the later Roman Empire. See, for a lucid exposition of the mechanism of Roman Finance, Humbert's *Essai sur les Finances et la Comptabilité publique chez les Romains* (Paris, 1886, 2 vols.). The standard work on Athenian Finance is Boekh, *Staatshaushaltung der Athener* (3rd ed. by Fränkel).

[2] E. g. Tacitus, *Ann.* 13. 31; Pliny, *Pan.* 37.

escaped with a payment of 10 % would not concern those who regarded all revenue as due in case of need to the State. The views of these ancient societies in respect to public expenditure and credit were vitiated by the same notion of State omnipotence[1]. The whole organization of classical society tended to confirm this belief: both in Greece and Rome war, and its product slavery, were regarded not simply as permissible, but as praiseworthy. Free industry was consequently placed at a disadvantage, and the retardation of economic development which inevitably resulted did not allow of the existence of those institutions through whose agency public revenue and credit can alone be successfully promoted. It requires some knowledge of economic forces to see that state Finances depend ultimately on the production of wealth by individuals, and that without security, and a just division of public burdens, it is impossible to expect the continuous growth of the source from which all income, public and private, comes, viz. the effective application of labour, natural agents, capital and invention to the task of production. The history of the fall of the Roman Empire is but one long illustration of the danger of neglecting a proposition so obvious to any modern[2].

§ 3. The mediaeval period shows quite as little trace of financial theory, while the actual organization of administrative agencies is much inferior to that of the later Roman Empire. On its financial side the so-called feudal system exhibited a surrender of the public claims in favour of the principal lords. Some parts of the Roman arrangements survived, but they were gradually transformed until

[1] See De Coulanges, *La Cité antique*, Bk. iii. ch. 18, for a powerful statement of the classical ideas respecting the relations of the individual and the State.

[2] For the causes hindering the rise of economic science, see Ingram, *Hist. of Pol. Economy*, 7–9; for Roman ignorance of the principles of taxation, cf. Merivale, *Romans under the Empire*, viii. 356; and for the obstructive effects of the methods employed by the Empire, Guizot, *Civilization in France*, Lect. 2; Clamageran, *Histoire de l'impôt en France*, i. 89 sq.

the sovereign at last had to depend on his own property for support, with whatever supplement might be derived from the fees that he obtained. It necessarily followed that —even were the intellectual conditions favourable—no theory of Finance was possible. The first traces of a revival of method in practical Finance are found in the German and Italian cities, which in many respects were free from external control. The administration of the royal income forced the officials of the feudal State to attend to the details of financial procedure, but of theory or even precise knowledge there is no appearance[1].

§ 4. The dissolution of the Middle Age economy both in state and private life, and its replacement by the modern system marks the time at which Finance as a theoretic study first became possible. The political writings of the preceding period were under theological influence, and even those of the fifteenth and the opening of the sixteenth century, more especially those of Macchiavelli and Sir Thomas More were limited by their dependence on the ideas of classical writers. But the firmer organization of the centralized monarchies of France, Spain, and England, the development of money dealings, and the revolution in economic relations produced by the supplies of the precious metals from the New World presented to reflective minds a series of problems which could not be solved without the aid of wider conceptions, and accordingly we find that the latter part of the sixteenth century exhibits a new development of social and political inquiry. The most prominent representative of this movement is the French writer Bodin (1530–1596) whose *Republic* appeared in French in 1576, and in a more complete form in Latin in 1586. Apart from its general treatment of political science the second chapter of the sixth book of the work contains an examina-

[1] For one example of mediaeval city finance see Schönberg, *Finanzverhältnisse der Stadt Basel im* 14. *und* 15. *Jahrhundert*. The *Dialogus de Scaccario* in Stubbs' *Select Charters*, 168–248, shows the processes of the English Exchequer.

tion of the various forms of the public revenue; they are grouped under seven heads, the most important being (1) the public domain, (2) import and export duties, and (3) direct taxation. In accordance with the ideas of the mercantile system he approves of customs both on imports and exports, but he distinguishes between 'raw materials' and 'manufactured articles,' advocating high export dues on the former, and high import ones on the latter. Direct taxes should, he thinks, be resorted to only in case of necessity, and then should be proportioned to 'faculty.' Taxes on luxury he regards with special approval. He condemns the many exemptions from direct taxation which existed in the France of his time, and advises a census to enable charges to be proportioned to property. His influence can be traced in the German financial writers of the next century [1].

§ 5. The predominance of the set of conceptions usually described as 'Mercantilism' is the principal condition affecting the growth of Finance in the seventeenth century. Political economy came into existence as a collection of practical rules for the guidance of statesmen [2]. In this aspect it is described by Adam Smith, who states that it 'proposes two distinct objects; first to supply a plentiful revenue or subsistence for the people . . . . ., and secondly to supply the State or Commonwealth with a revenue sufficient for the public service [3].' The latter or financial aim was particularly developed in Germany. Not to dwell on the writers on 'the Treasury' and 'on Taxes' in the seventeenth century, who show some advance on the views of Bodin [4], there is the 'Chamber Science' of the

[1] The fullest account of Bodin is in Baudrillart's *Jean Bodin et son Temps* (Paris, 1853). His views on taxation are described by Clamageran, ii. 314–330. For English readers, Hallam, *Literature of Europe*, Part II. ch. 4. § 2, may be noticed as giving a convenient summary.

[2] Such was the work of Antoine Montcrétien, *Traicté d'Économie Politique* (1615), a series of counsels addressed to Louis XIII.

[3] *Wealth of Nations*, 173.

[4] The most remarkable of these writers are Faust, Conring, and Klock. An

eighteenth century which presents its highest form in the works of Justi and Sonnenfels. The former writer discusses financial questions both in his *Staatswissenschaft* (1755) and his *Finanzwesen* (1766). He holds that taxation should be proportioned to property, and is credited with the creation of a theory of the so-called *Regalia*, but his real service seems to have been the placing in systematic order the views prevalent in his day on the various parts of Public Finance, and giving such matters a prominent place in an exposition of political science [1].

In France financial topics received a different treatment. The organization of the absolute monarchy, the wars which accompanied it, and the elaborate and many-sided commercial policy of Colbert's administration (1661–1683) brought about a state of things that effectively marked out the line of thought on such problems. The extraordinary brilliancy and apparent prosperity of the State contrasted so forcibly with the extreme misery of the people as to give reason for believing, either that the distribution of taxation was unjust, or that its amount was excessive. The French people, in fact, suffered from both these evils, and it was in the advocacy of a reformed tax-system that the first efforts of the dissentients from the prevailing mercantile doctrine were made. Vauban's *Dîme Royale* (1707) presents a melancholy picture of the condition of France, and suggests the reform of taxation by abolishing most of the existing taxes and their replacement by his proposed 'royal tithe'—a single direct tax of ten per cent. on all classes. Here we notice a complete departure from the more superficial view of the earlier writers, who especially approved of taxes on commodities as encouraging

attempt has been made by Stein (i. 125, and *Finanzarchiv*, i. 1 sq.) to prove that the last-named was 'the true founder of the theory of taxation,' but the bulk of his work seems not above the ordinary mercantile position, and his views on taxation are derived from Bodin. He has been further accused of copying from the earlier work of Faust. See also Roscher, *Geschichte*, 210 sq.

[1] For Justi see Roscher, *Geschichte*, 444–465; for his Finance, 461–65; also Cohn, §§ 9, 71; Meyer, 16–17; Wagner, i. 35–6.

industry, and a clearer appreciation of the real pressure of taxation. Boisguillebert, both in his *Détail de la France* (1697) and his *Factum de la France* (1707) maintains somewhat similar views, more particularly as to the superiority of direct taxation. Both may be regarded as precursors of the advocates of the direct single tax in the eighteenth century. In a different part of Finance and at a later time Montesquieu contributed some additions to the received views. The 13th book of the *Spirit of Laws* (1748) is devoted to an examination of the political side of taxation and to a criticism of several existing taxes. He is strongly in favour of progressive taxation, influenced probably, as M. Sorel has remarked [1], by the practice of the Athenians. It is, however, in showing the relation of the system of Finance to the political constitution of each country that Montesquieu is at his best; his views are evidently formed from his study of the English Constitution which provided more efficient safeguards for the interests of the subjects than were to be found in any continental State [2]. In other respects the study of financial problems had not claimed much attention in England. The pamphlet literature of the seventeenth century had handled certain special points, but the pressure of taxation was not such as to lead men to look for remedies against its evils. The rise of statistics under the name of 'political arithmetic' gave an impetus to the examination of the facts of Finance especially in the numerous works of Sir W. Petty, who, in company with Locke, considered the question of incidence in taxation. The question of public credit was discussed by Davenant, and the proposals of Dekker and Vanderlint for the establishment of a single tax are worthy of note as marking the tendency of thought [3]. Two of Hume's *Political Essays*

[1] *Montesquieu*, 108.

[2] See the texts of Vauban and Boisguillebert in *Les Économistes Financiers du XVIIIme Siècle* (ed. Daire). Also Ingram, 57–9. For Montesquieu cp. Stein, i. 131–2.

[3] On these minor writers see Ricca-Salerno, *Le Dottrine Finanziarie in Inghilterra*; also Vocke, *Finanzarchiv*, vii. 56.

(1752) are devoted to 'Taxes' and 'Public Credit.' They show traces of the teaching of Montesquieu on the political effects of financial regulations, but also a far greater knowledge of the economical influence of taxation and credit. The Physiocratic doctrine of the incidence of taxation is rejected by Hume, as is also the popular view that national debts were beneficial. A few years later than Hume's *Essays* appeared the *Principles of Political Economy* of Sir James Steuart (1767), embodying the teaching of the English mercantilists in a systematic form. The destruction of the system which it advocated prevented the work acquiring any influence or even general reputation, though some of its discussions of Finance are interesting and suggestive [1].

§ 6. The changes in the tone of thought on economic questions and the position of society facilitated the establishment of the first scientific school of social philosophy—the famous group or 'sect' of '*Économistes.*' Most of their views are to be found in germ in earlier writers, but they have the merit of presenting them in a definite form. It concerns us particularly to notice that one of their cardinal doctrines—the '*impôt unique*'—was a financial one, and that financial questions occupied a great deal of their attention. However widely modern writers on Finance may differ from the Physiocratic conclusions, they must at least allow that their selection of problems was a good one. With very defective information the '*Économistes*' sought to determine the question of justice in taxation; its real as opposed to its apparent incidence, and its effects on the growth of national wealth; their analysis of the sources of revenue and of the extent to which each could contribute to the public requirements, though not correctly worked out, yet indicated a fruitful line of research for later inquirers. The founder of the school—Quesnay—has discussed taxation in his *Second Problème Économique* and

[1] The most important parts of Steuart's *Principles* so far as Finance is concerned are—Book iv. part 4 (Public Credit), and Book v (Taxes).

several of his *Maximes* refer to Finance. The elder Mirabeau, one of his most ardent disciples, published a treatise on 'taxation,' and all the members of the group adopted the belief in the superiority of direct taxation on the net product of land though admitting the temporary use of other taxes[1]. By far the most illustrious member of the school—though in some particulars he dissented from their doctrines—was the statesman and philosopher Turgot (1727–1781), who in his numerous papers on questions of Finance has shown an amount of practical insight combined with theoretic power that his successors have rarely equalled[2].

The influence of the Physiocrats on practical Finance was slight, but it appears that the Constituent Assembly, (1789–91) under the guidance of Du Pont de Nemours, sought to partially realize their idea of a tax on the 'net product' from land. Their action on the progress of speculation has been much more powerful; the form of many financial problems in modern times can be traced back to their teaching, and their leading conceptions have affected the *Wealth of Nations*[3].

§ 7. The great reputation and the permanent merits of Adam Smith's economic and financial work have led to a perhaps undue depreciation of the services rendered by his predecessors, but it is hardly questionable that in Finance as in Economics the *Wealth of Nations* was far superior to any earlier work, and its superiority in each case was due to the same qualities. The fifth book—which considers 'the expenses and revenue of the Sovereign' shows com-

[1] See *Physiocrates* (ed. Daire), 128, for the *Second Problème*. Of the *Maximes*, Nos. 5, 27, 28, 29, 30, relate to Finance. For the latest views of Quesnay's position, see S. Bauer, 'Zur Entstehung der Physiocratie'; Conrad's *Jahrbücher*, August 1890; and *Quarterly Journal of Economics*, v. 100 sq.; also Schelle, *Du Pont de Nemours* (Paris, 1888).

[2] See *Œuvres de Turgot* (ed. Daire); for Finance more especially, i. 389-632, ii. 368–432, but financial questions are often noticed by him when treating of other matters. On his differences from Quesnay, see Schelle, 127 sq.

[3] For the influence of the Physiocrats on the financial system of the Revolution, see Stourm, i. 128–130, ii. 2–11; Schelle, 319 sq.

prehensiveness of view, felicity of illustration, and thorough understanding of the practical aspects of financial problems, while the looseness of arrangement, which has been so often censured, is less evident here than in the earlier parts of the work. It is quite possible for critics, irritated by the lavish praise bestowed on Adam Smith by the less intelligent of his followers, to show that most of his views have been set forth by others at an earlier time: the Physiocrats may have had a firmer grasp of the narrower premisses from which they reasoned: the technical side of Finance may have been more exhaustively handled by the trained officials of the German States; but the establishment of any or of all these propositions does not invalidate Adam Smith's claim to be the greatest of theorists on Finance. Not only does he stand in the centre of financial development, summing up and co-ordinating the work of the preceeding century in its various lines and determining the future course of scientific thought: he further contributed an important element to the science of Finance in his recognition of its close connexion with the theory of Economics. It was by bringing out clearly that the solution of such questions as the incidence of taxation depended on the economic theory of the distribution of wealth[1] that he affected the progress of the science. Moreover, it was a renovated political economy which he applied as a solvent for some of the most difficult of financial problems. His assaults on the mercantile system effectually deprived it of any claim to be the accredited economic doctrine of European thought, and replaced it by a more accurate body of principles influenced by far different views. The State appeared as but one among the several claimants on the national revenue, which was the product of individual energy and prudence not of the paternal wisdom of statesmen. This alteration of aim at once limited and rendered definite the province of Finance; instead of the constant

[1] Cp. Book i. chap. 6 (22) with Book v. chap. 2. part 2 (347).

regulation and encouragement which Colbert deemed necessary for national prosperity, the problem was narrowed down to maintaining the natural conditions of society, and applying state-revenue to that comparatively simple object. The question of Finance came thus to occupy a larger share of attention than could be bestowed on it, when industry, art and morals were also subjects for the sovereign's constant watchfulness and care. It may have been, as many German writers have argued [1], that this doctrine bears the marks of exaggeration usual in all reactions, though their view of the case is not completely established, but when a comparison is made of the work of those who came under Adam Smith's influence with the systems that preceded the appearance of his treatise, we can say that any possible loss through 'radical' or '*doctrinaire* dogmatism' is far outweighed by the removal of perplexing fallacies and the establishment in their place of broader and more philosophical principles. Finally, the value of each part of the *Wealth of Nations* is so bound up with that of the substance it contains that it is only in studying the actual doctrines of Finance that we can form a satisfactory judgment on its position.

§ 8. The *Wealth of Nations* was speedily translated into the leading European languages and exercised a powerful effect on the development of financial doctrine, but the nature of its influence varied with the condition of the different countries in which it was studied. In England where its action on practical Finance, at first great, was retarded by the outbreak of the French Revolution and the unreasoning conservatism which the excesses of the Jacobins confirmed in the minds of the ruling classes [2], the principal stimulus to speculative thought was found in his analysis of

[1] Cohn, §§ 11-12; also his *Grundlegung*, §§ 74-79; Geffcken, in Schönberg, 22; Wagner, i. 40-1; also Ingram, 107-9.

[2] The contrast between the liberal policy pursued by the younger Pitt in the earlier years of his administration and his later measures is very marked. The Commercial Treaty with France in 1786 and the consolidation of the Customs Laws are examples belonging to our subject.

the operation of taxation on national wealth. This part of his work was further developed in Ricardo's *Principles of Political Economy and Taxation*, where it naturally found a place as an application of the revised theory of distribution in a peculiarly rigorous and abstract manner[1]. This tendency to abstraction led to a division of the treatment of financial questions that proved very unfortunate for the progress of the science. Writers on political economy contented themselves with general and rather vague discussions as to the influence of taxes, while the facts of the existing system were criticised or defended in numerous pamphlets of ephemeral interest. Even works of greater merit, such as Parnell's *Financial Reform* (1830) and Sayer's *Income Tax* (1831) suffered by the separation. The nearest approach to a combination of the different aspects of Finance was made by McCulloch in his work on *Taxation and the Funding System* (1845, 3rd ed. 1863), in which the defects are more apparent to modern readers than the merits which at the time it undoubtedly possessed.

French economists and financial theorists were more impressed by the negative side of Adam Smith's teaching, a tendency that was much strengthened by the works of J. B. Say—*Traité d'Économie Politique* (1803), and *Cours Complet* (1828)—who was disposed to undervalue the services of the State even in the discharge of its necessary functions. The very complicated financial system of France has, however, led to its study from the administrative point of view, and special financial questions have received much more attention from French than from English economists. There are numerous treatises on 'Taxation' and 'Public Revenue,' marked by a general disposition to lay stress on the principles of natural right and justice as against economic expediency. Most French

[1] Ricardo, chaps. 8-18 inclusive. See Wagner, ii. 333, and Cohn, § 248, for recognition of his work in this respect. In another department of Finance, R. Hamilton, by his work on *The National Debt*, developed and added to the arguments of Adam Smith, and was followed by Ricardo.

writers also exhibit a strong feeling against any financial measures believed to savour of socialism, e.g. progressive taxation or even an income-tax. With rare exceptions, such as the work of Canard already mentioned, they show little taste for deductive reasoning or for the discussion of questions like that of the incidence of taxation which need its use. On the other hand they are prolific in historical and statistical works such as those of Vuitry, Clamageran, Stourm, De Parieu, Vignes, Audriffret, and others; the great but incomplete *Dictionnaire des Finances*, issued under M. Léon Say's superintendence, is a storehouse of materials on French financial administration. In the convenient work of Garnier, *Traité des Finances* (4me éd. 1883), and the more brilliant treatise of Leroy Beaulieu, *Science des Finances* (5me éd. 1892), they have text-books of a high order, the last-mentioned work in particular being remarkable for fulness of information and lucidity of style. Up to the present the dislike to State action is a distinctive note of French financial work, and in this respect it furnishes a useful corrective to the doctrines prevalent in Germany.

§ 9. The introduction of the doctrines of the *Wealth of Nations* into a country where the older traditions of the 'Chamber Sciences' were so strong as in Germany, brought about a re-casting rather than an abandonment of the earlier methods. The masses of material which writers in conformity with previous usage continued to bestow on their readers, were presented from the new point of view. Financial questions were either examined in special works, or were assigned a separate place in general economic treatises under the title *Finanzwissenschaft*. Passing over the less important works of the early part of this century[1], we come to the treatise of K. H. Rau on *Economics*, the third volume of which, devoted to Finance,

[1] Among those who may be mentioned are Harl, Krehl, Fulda, and more especially Jacob (*Finanzwissenschaft*, 1821) and Malchus (*Finanzwissenschaft*, 1830).

appeared in 1832 (5th ed. 1864). The merits of Rau's writings lay in the fulness of their information, and in their systematic arrangement, both of which admirably fitted them for use by students, who obtained a general view of the science as accepted at the time. His influence in promoting the study of Economics and Finance in Germany was great, though often forgotten by his successors [1]. Discussion of his doctrines belongs to the treatment of the science, but we may just note his separation of 'fees' (*Gebühren*) from 'taxes' (*Steuern*), and his recognition of the influence of administration in Finance. The monograph of Nebenius on *Public Credit* (2nd ed. 1829), is entitled to a place beside Rau's more comprehensive work, as giving a full treatment of one of the most disputed topics of Finance. Somewhat later in date is Hoffmann's *Theory of Taxation* (1840), which has been adversely criticised by Roscher and Wagner on account of its unsystematic character, but which nevertheless has had considerable effect on the progress of Finance. It appears to aim at giving a scientific justification of the contemporary fiscal policy of the Prussian State. Many other German writers will require attention in connexion with special doctrines, but the older school of Finance that was more or less closely limited by the traditions of Adam Smith's teachings in the shape in which they had been arranged by Rau, presents but one more writer for consideration at present, Von Hock, who examined in separate works the financial systems of France (1857), and of the United States (1867), and also wrote on *Public Revenue and Debts* (1863). This work includes in brief compass the leading questions of taxation and indebtedness; it is specially good, as might have been expected from the production of a trained official, in its discussion of administrative points [2].

[1] See Roscher, *Geschichte*, 847 sq.

[2] For fuller examination of the German writers of this period, see Wagner, i. 44-5, ii. 7-9, 11-12; Meyer, §§ 6-9, 13, 17, 18, 19; Vocke, 10-33; Falck, *Lehre von der Steuerüberwälzung*, 104-144.

So far the development of Finance in Germany had been carried on in conformity with the conceptions of Adam Smith and his followers, though modified in some degree by the peculiar conditions of the country; but towards the middle of the century, new forces began to act on the social sciences, which had considerable effect on their methods and doctrines. Among the agencies that more particularly influenced financial studies, we can indicate three, viz. (1) the rise of the 'historical' school, (2) the disposition to treat Finance as a part of administration (*Verwaltung*) in the newer sense of that term, and (3) the advocacy of politico-social, as opposed to purely financial aims in fiscal matters. The historical economists did not contribute much to the substance of financial doctrine, but the importance attached by them to distinctions between the different stages of social life, and their assertion of the impossibility of laying down universal precepts, were evidently applicable with peculiar force to the systems of taxation existing in different countries. Their belief that the present could be fully understood only in the light of the past made it desirable to study the history of financial arrangements, and some of the best work of German Finance has been in this direction[1]. Some supporters of the school, in particular Schäffle and Schmoller, went further and assailed such cardinal doctrines of received financial theory as that of 'net income being the sole fund on which taxation could fall,' and this questionable position was supported by arguments which led to a closer study of fundamental principles in Finance[2]. To Stein is due a movement towards regarding Finance as a problem of administration. His *Finanzwissenschaft* (5th ed. 4 vols. 1885–6), much modified and expanded in its later editions,

[1] Such as the already mentioned work of Schönberg, *Finanzverhältnisse der Stadt Basel* (1879); Schmoller, *Die Epochen der preussischen Finanzpolitik*; Zeumer, *die deutschen Städtesteuern*; Vocke, *Geschichte der Steuern der Brit. Reiche.*

[2] Schäffle, *Gesammelte Aufsätze*, i. 158–183, esp. 167 sq.; Schmoller, 'Die Lehre vom Einkommen' (*Zeitschrift für Gesammte Staatswissenschaft*, 1863)

contains, along with a great deal that is disputable and fanciful, a full treatment of financial organization. The State and its administrative organs is in his view the basis of Finance, and the history and statistics of European Finance receive considerable attention. More important, from a practical standpoint, than the influence of Stein is the tendency to regard the financial system as an agency for redistributing wealth. This position, supported most prominently by Wagner[1], is not fully accepted by other economists and financial writers, but in several works propositions are set forth which need this politico-social view of Finance as their logical basis.

The result of these several influences has been to give a special tone to German financial work, since even where the newer ideas are not accepted, they are present to the writer's mind. This change in attitude towards financial problems is the outcome of beliefs which may briefly be enumerated as follows: (1) Public Finance is a matter of national interest, it is not merely a distribution of burdens among the individual citizens, who owe duties to the State which it ought to be their privilege to discharge; (2) Financial administration is largely dependent on national peculiarities. Each country has or needs a system suited to itself, so that the idea of a single 'rational' system of taxation is absurd; (3) The same conception of relativity applies to the history of Finance; earlier systems, e. g. the Roman, have to be judged in relation to the circumstances of the age in which they existed.

Instead of attempting to criticise the opinions and tendencies just described, we have rather to notice the remarkable productiveness which has been the outcome of the study of Finance in Germany. Either in respect to general text-books and manuals or to monographs on the most complicated questions she holds the first place. Of the former, in addition to the previously noticed work of Stein, there are: the very extensive treatise of Wagner—

[1] Especially i. 48–50, ii. 449.

still incomplete—in which each aspect of Finance is handled at even undue length; the shorter and more lucid work of Cohn, where the evolution of financial systems is brought out by description rather than by brief and precise propositions; the less attractive manual of Roscher which, however, gives a collection of the various opinions and a mass of interesting historical detail; and lastly, the compact and conservative work of Umpfenbach, exhibiting some of the best qualities of the older writers. Almost reaching the character of general manuals are the more limited treatises of Schäffle, Neumann, Sax, and Vocke. Among special works there is the collection of monographs in the third volume of Schönberg's *Handbuch*—which had best be regarded in that light—and numerous smaller studies on such questions as 'progressive taxation' (Neumann), 'incidence of taxation' (Falck, Kaizl), 'justice in taxation' (Meyer), 'the exemption of the minimum of subsistence' (Schmidt). When the abundant periodical literature appearing in the journals of Conrad, Schmoller, and Schanz—the last devoted exclusively to Finance—is added, we can form some idea of the activity of German workers in Finance.

§ 10. At a comparatively early period questions relating to public revenue and expenditure had attracted attention in Italy. The work of Broggia (1743) is commended by Cossa, and several of the economists of the latter half of the eighteenth century, examined the effects of taxation, and especially of those taxes actually levied in their country. The influence of Adam Smith and J. B. Say, was for a long time predominant in Italy as elsewhere. The development of financial science in Germany has, however, deeply affected the more modern writers, who have zealously devoted themselves to an examination of financial subjects, bringing to bear on their selected topics considerable independence of mind, and at the same time, a thorough acquaintance with what has been already accomplished. More especially may be mentioned the brief and condensed manuals by Cossa (already referred to), and by Ricca-Salerno, with the latter author's writings on special parts of Finance; the recent works of Viti de Marco, Mazzola, and Zorli, on the more fundamental principles of the science in connexion with the Value theory of Jevons and Menger; the study of Pantaleoni on the 'repercussion' of taxation, the similar work of Conigliani, and the very complete investigation of Italian Finance by Alessio [1].

§ 11. There has been far less interest in financial studies in English speaking countries. Since the last edition of McCulloch's work no treatise has appeared that could even pretend to be a 'Manual of Finance.' English taxation has, indeed, been discussed in such books as those by Peto (1863), Levi (1860), and Noble, and special questions have received consideration from Jevons, Dudley Baxter, Cliffe Leslie, Thorold Rogers, and Mr. Palgrave [2]. In the last few years the historical aspects of the English system have been elucidated by Messrs. Sydney Buxton, Dowell, and Hall [3]. Some of the most valuable contributions to the statistics and theory of Finance are, however, buried in the volumes of Parliamentary papers, such as the Report on Import Duties (1840), the Inquiries on the Income Tax (1852–3, 1861), and on Local Taxation [4]. The speeches of finance Ministers, and the debates on financial measures are also instructive to the student, though practically unknown unless where, as in Mr. Gladstone's case, reprinted.

In the United States there has been till recently a similar neglect; but the rapid growth of economic science in that country has already extended to Finance. Thus we have

[1] For further details, Cossa, *Guida allo Studio dell' Economia Politica*, ch. 7; also his *Scienza delle Finanze* (Am. Trans.), 10 and 181–193 (a Bibliography); Ricca-Salerno, *Storia delle dottrine finanziarie in Italia* (1881).

[2] Prof. Nicholson's article on 'Taxation' in the *Encyclopaedia Britannica* should be added.

[3] S. Buxton, *Finance and Politics* (2 vols. 1888); S. Dowell, *A History of Taxation and Taxes in England* (2nd ed. 4 vols. 1888); H. Hall, *A History of the Custom Revenue in England* (1885).

[4] Goschen, *Local Taxation*, where his report is reprinted.

a valuable monograph on *Public Debts* by Professor Adams, Dr. Ely's *Taxation in American States and Cities*, the learned and instructive articles of Dr. Seligman, and a large number of minor contributions dealing with special points of history or theory in either federal or state Finance. America, like England, is rich in official reports and collections of evidence on financial matters, though this material is hardly available for the European student. With regard to both England and America, it may be predicted that there will be a much larger contribution to financial literature in the coming years.

BOOK I.

PUBLIC EXPENDITURE.

CHAPTER I.

STATE ECONOMY. GENERAL CONSIDERATIONS.

§ 1. THE question of the nature and amount of public outlay forms, as we have seen, one of the cardinal branches of Finance; it has an important influence on the other departments of the subject, and may be regarded as the final object of the financial system. In order to estimate correctly the expenditure of any given society for state or public purposes, it is desirable to see the general features of the agency which so applies this part of national wealth. Most persons are familiar with the conception of a state economy, and are even prepared to adopt the view prevalent among students of social science, that Society is an organism with an independent life, manifesting itself in the exercise of different functions, one set of which has been specialized in the regulating organ or the State. Without pressing this resemblance so far as is sometimes done[1], we may accept the evident fact that the state organization has certain points of analogy with the arrangements of the individual, and that in regard to economic action the comparison is particularly close. The individual and the State have each receipts and expenditure. Each endeavours, or should endeavour, to obtain the greatest result with the smallest effort; for each it depends on the relation between these economic categories, whether wealth is being accu-

[1] E. g. Mr. Spencer, *Principles of Sociology*, Part ii.

mulated or debt incurred; and for each a careful method of keeping accounts is needed as a safeguard against errors. There is, however, a still closer parallel to be found in the case of those associations formed for the accomplishment of certain special ends which are usually known as 'juristical persons' or corporations. From the ordinary private partnership, through the local trading company, the progression can be traced up to such a body as the East India Company, that in some respects was sovereign all but in name. In all these associations the principal financial phenomena are exhibited in a similar manner, and in a way that helps to explain the character of state Finance. The existence of such general resemblances should not, however, conceal from us the fact that public agencies are in some essential points distinct from the 'economy' of the individual or of the association. It is the presence of these special and peculiar features that renders the examination of state economy needful in treating of Public Finance.

§ 2. The first distinctive point in the public or state economy is its compulsory character. The individual or private association has to submit to limits other than those of his or its own will, but so far as legal restraints are concerned, the State stands above them in a position of independence. It is entitled to claim all the services and property of its subjects for the accomplishment of whatever aims it prescribes to itself. When stated in so rigid a form, the proposition is likely to awaken dissent, and yet from the strictly legal and administrative point of view, it is a commonplace since the time of Austin[1]. The effectual limits to state action depend, not on any legal or administrative rules, but on the difficulty of overcoming the obstacles set by external nature, and the sentiments of its subjects. Its expenditure and the objects to which it is directed, are bounded by the productiveness of the national

[1] See his *Province of Jurisprudence determined*, and for earlier statements of the same truth, Hobbes, *Leviathan*, ch. 18; Bodin, *De Republica*, Bk. i. ch. 7.

industries, and the facility with which the national wealth can be obtained through taxation for public use. The compulsory nature of state action is, then, a trait which marks it off from the individual or the private society.

A second point of difference appears in the ends to be attained through state agencies. They are mainly, as Roscher remarks[1], of an immaterial kind: the protection of the society against aggression, or internal disturbance, and the promotion of progress in civilization, are hardly capable of being definitely measured and assigned a precise value, nor even if they were, could the share of each individual be allotted to him in the exact proportion that he was willing to pay for it. The force of the State must prescribe what is to be paid by its subjects as a body, and the share that shall be borne by each. As regards expenditure, the absence of a strict standard makes it very hard to judge the extent to which the public resources should be applied for the satisfaction of the several wants. This vagueness is made still more apparent by confining our attention to a single public need in a given country—say, the amount of protection against foreign and home enemies required by England at present. How shall we determine the expenditure that is suitable for this object?

'Adequacy in such cases,' says Dr. Sidgwick, 'cannot be defined by a sharp line. Most Englishmen are persuaded that they at present enjoy very tolerable protection of person and property against enemies within and without the country, but it would be difficult to argue that our security would not be enhanced by more and better-paid judges and policemen, or more and better-equipped soldiers and sailors[2].'

The problem, it is evident, can only allow of an approximate solution, such as the actual circumstances will permit, and this finds its expression in the sentiment of practical statesmen, who say with Sir R. Peel, 'In time of peace you must, if you mean to retrench, incur some risk.'

[1] § 109. [2] *Political Economy*, 543–4 (1st ed.).

When the problem is widened so as to include the relations of the several wants of the public organs of the society, its difficulty is increased; the adjustment of the separate items of outlay and the proportion that the total amount shall bear to the sum of national revenue, is a task that tries the abilities of the most skilful administrator.

In connexion with the direction of public expenditure, a third feature of public economy comes into prominence; one which, it is true, may in some degree be found in private associations, but in a very restricted form. That is the existence of special-interests opposed to the general welfare. It goes without saying that the individual desires what he deems to be for his own good, and in most private companies the shareholders wish for the prosperity of the institution in which their capital is invested. There are, however, cases where the holder of a few shares may make a gain indirectly, through some action of his company, which will lower its dividends, and being so far 'an economic man,' he may vote for and advocate that course. Instances of the kind are not very common, and the power possessed by persons in the situation just described is so slight that it may be neglected. The state organization is differently placed. 'Sinister interests' exercise a good deal of control on its actions. There are large classes whose aim it is to increase, not to reduce, the public expenses. More particularly is this true of salaried officials, who readily advocate increased outlay, but offer a determined opposition to any savings[1]. Military and naval officers are extremely anxious to insist on the importance of increasing our land and sea forces in order to secure a better system of defence. Every additional outlay unfortunately fails to attain this object, which seems as far off as ever.

Reaction against the evils produced by these tendencies has, in England at least, raised up an opposite school of

[1] 'Each public department stands prepared to give the most confident reasons why it is absolutely necessary to keep up the scale of its expenditure to the exact point at which it now is.' Parnell, *Financial Reform*, 100.

extremists, who are opposed to even the outlay required for real efficiency. The inherent difficulties of the state economy are thus intensified by conflicts of interest and sentiment which, if not peculiar to it, at all events are most prominently exhibited in its working.

A fourth point of difference between the economy of the individual and that of the State, is shown in the determination of the area of work for each. The citizen will naturally adopt the most profitable employment open to him, or if it should seem expedient, he will combine several different occupations. The interest of others is a very secondary consideration; his activities, their sphere and extent, will depend on the 'net advantages' to be gained. His investments of capital will be similarly determined. Within the customary limits of law and morality he will seek to make his advantages as great as possible. The field of state action has to be mapped out on different grounds. The fact that a particular business or part of social action could be managed by the State without economic sacrifice, does not prove that it should be handed over to public agency. It is in general a sound practical rule that 'the State should not interfere with private enterprise,' and whatever be the theoretical qualifications needed, it is plain that even its partial truth limits the operations of the public power. The existence and constant working of individual and associated 'economies' (*Privatwirthschaften*) beside and under the protection of the great compulsory economy (*Zwangwirthschaft*) of the State, is a point which should never be forgotten.

Fifthly, a private economy differs from that of the State not only in the limitation of its area of action, but in the object of its working. It seeks to obtain a profit from its operations; in the language of Finance it aims at a 'surplus.' The individual or company who just makes ends meet at the close of the year[1] is not in a prosperous

[1] I.e. allowing only necessary expenses for the individual, anything above being manifestly profit.

condition. Something more is required to give a fund for expenses beyond the necessary minimum in the former and for dividends in the latter case. The greater the surplus the more successful is the result deemed to be. The ideal of state economy is, on the contrary, to establish a balance between receipts and expenditure. A State that has very large surpluses is as ill-managed as one with large deficits [1]. The practical rule is to aim at a slight excess of receipts over outlay in order to prevent the chance of a deficit. The position of the State as drawing its resources from the contributions of the several private economies under its charge is the reason for this course of conduct.

The last of the points of difference usually noted is rather apparent than real; it results from the mode adopted in regulating state Finance, but in fact state and private economy here fundamentally agree. The private person must, it is said, regulate his expenditure by his income; the State regulates its income by its expenditure. Such is in form the common mode of determination. The individual says, 'I can spend so much:' the finance minister says, 'I have to raise so much.' On looking more carefully into the matter, we discover that a certain amount of expenditure is necessary to support individual life, and that each person must procure that amount at least under peril of death. For all classes above the lowest this minimum of expenditure rises to a higher point and increased outlay is essential for the obtaining of increased income [2]. On the other side state expenditure is not definitely fixed, it has to be determined by various considerations, one of which is the pressure that its discharge will place on the national resources. We can easily conceive the United States wisely incurring expenditure that an Indian administration would as wisely avoid [3].

[1] Cp. the recent difficulties of the United States with their surplus revenue.

[2] Marshall, *Principles of Economics*, i. 134 (1st ed.).

[3] Roscher, § 109; Wagner, i. 9–16; Geffcken in Schönberg, 6.

§ 3. Though the several characteristics that we have been engaged in noticing, mark clearly the distinct and peculiar aspect of public economy, we have still to constantly bear in mind that the consumption of wealth for public ends is a part of the consumption of wealth in general. As a study of human wants must prove the basis of the economic theory of consumption, so must an examination of the number and order of state wants be an essential part of our present inquiry.

The classification most familiar to English readers is that of J. S. Mill who distinguishes between the 'necessary' and the 'optional' functions of government[1]. The value of this division is, however, much impaired by his subsequent admission that no employment of state agency can ever be purely optional, as also by the further concessions made in his examination of the limits of *laissez faire*. The arrangement suggested by Roscher is more in analogy with the case of private outlay, viz. that into (1) necessary, (2) useful, and (3) superfluous or ornamental expenditure[2], corresponding to the necessaries, decencies, and luxuries of individual consumption. It does not require much acumen to add, that the first head is unavoidable, that there is generally a presumption in favour of the second, while there is always one against the last. The formation of such general categories as the foregoing does not help to solve the real difficulties of the matter. The terms used to describe the groups just mentioned carry with them an already-formed judgment. By placing a particular form of expense under the heading of 'necessary' or of 'ornamental' outlay, we have pronounced an opinion on its merits or demerits. It still remains to settle—and this is by far the most troublesome part of our task—the several items to be placed under each head. In order to meet this difficulty we find it necessary to consider the proper functions of the State, and how far it

[1] *Principles*, Bk. v. ch. I. § I. Cp. ch. II. *passim*.

[2] § 109.

is bound to discharge each and all of those functions under circumstances of financial pressure. One of two possible lines of inquiry may be adopted. Starting from our conception of the State, we may seek to determine the proper sphere of its action, and the amount of its justifiable outlay within that sphere, using either general reasoning or appeals to specific experience as our guide. Or we may prefer to trace the development of public tasks and endeavour by following their direction in the past to form an estimate of their present position and probable future. It may even be expedient to combine the two courses of inquiry, using each as the corroborator or corrective of the other. Here, as often elsewhere, the historical or inductive method comes in to support and check the conclusions of deduction.

§ 4. The primitive theory of politics, if theory it can be called, accepted the omnipotence of the State as a leading principle. The legislator was to fashion the society in the mould which seemed to him best; the very idea of individual claims had no place in such a doctrine. In its passage through feudalism European society obtained the idea of private liberty, though, owing to the imperfect state organization of the period, the effect that might naturally be expected was not produced. The centralized monarchies which succeeded the mediaeval system claimed the privilege of regulating individual action in a mode that in some respects recalled classical antiquity. The religious and political struggles of the sixteenth and seventeenth centuries were the result of their undue activity in those domains of human life. Commerce and industry did not assert their right to freedom till a later period. State regulation of industry found its highest expression in the so-called mercantile system of the seventeenth century, and particularly in the administration of Colbert[1]. The reaction against this policy produced the first theory of state action that had an economic basis—the doctrine of

[1] *Supra*, Intr. Part ii. for the effect on financial theory.

laissez faire or as it was entitled by Adam Smith 'the simple and obvious system of natural liberty.' Its rise at the particular time was the result of powerful forces. It is true of humanity that 'it learns truth a word at a time' so that, as the problem of the sixteenth century had been religious liberty, that of the seventeenth political liberty [1], it was reserved for the eighteenth century to assert the claims of industrial and commercial liberty. The similarity in general features of these movements is remarkable. Each was the natural reaction against exaggerated pretensions; each perhaps attached too much importance to its special object, but all have profoundly affected European society for good. In examining this earliest scientific theory of the State it is most desirable to see exactly what its doctrines really were. The common opinion that the advocates of *laissez faire* were opposed to any state action is dissipated by a study of their writings. They lived in an age of restrictions in which the most pressing work was to get the many hindrances to effectual industrial activity removed. A body of thinkers, who included Quesnay, Turgot, and Du Pont de Nemours among its members, can hardly be said to be indifferent to the needed functions of the State. The real bearing of the *laissez faire* or 'natural liberty' system can be best appreciated by a consideration of the exposition given of it by Adam Smith. In a well-known passage of the *Wealth of Nations* he has set forth the functions of the ideal State in a manner that leaves no room for mistake as to his views.

'According to the system of natural liberty, the sovereign has only three duties to attend to; three duties of great importance indeed, but plain and intelligible to common understandings; first, the duty of protecting the society from the violence and invasion of other independent societies; secondly, the duty of protecting as far as possible, every member of the society from the injustice or oppression

[1] Strictly true only of England, and in a much less degree of France.

of every other member of it, or the duty of establishing an exact administration of justice; and thirdly, the duty of erecting and maintaining certain public works, and certain public institutions, which it can never be for the interest of any individual, or small number of individuals, to erect and maintain; because the profit could never repay the expense to any individual, or small number of individuals, though it may frequently do much more than repay it to a great society [1].'

It is only necessary to read this passage in order to see that the policy favoured by Adam Smith was not a purely negative one. The State has not merely non-economic functions; where private interest is likely to prove insufficient, it has economic ones also, and those, too, of great extent and importance, as will appear when considering his more detailed discussion.

The predominance in the domain of political speculation of the *laissez faire* view is a commonplace of the historians of political economy [2]. We need not repeat the account already given of the different effect of the Smithian doctrine on French and English thought. It will suffice to see the operation of newer tendencies, and for this purpose we may pass at once to J. S. Mill. His theory of state action is in fact a product or rather application of his utilitarianism, and thus we are led to expect what we do in fact find, viz. a close resemblance between his practical proposals and those of Bentham [3]. He declares emphatically that—

'The admitted functions of government embrace a much wider field than can easily be included within the ring fence of any restrictive definition, and that it is hardly possible to find any ground of justification common to them all except the comprehensive one of general expediency [4].'

[1] 286.

[2] Ingram, *History of Pol. Econ.*, ch. 5.

[3] See specially the latter's *Theory of Legislation* ('Principles of the Civil Code').

[4] *Principles*, Bk. v. ch. 1. § 2.

This extremely vague and general statement is, however, supplemented by a declaration in favour of *laissez faire* as a general rule.

'Letting alone, in short, should be the general practice: every departure from it, unless required by some great good, is a certain evil[1].'

In regard to state action, as in so many other respects, Mill occupied a transitional position. He had accepted the traditional creed of the economists which was strengthened by his own sympathies in favour of freedom, as well as by his study of the brilliant work of Dunoyer[2], which he frequently quotes with approbation. But other influences affected him; the writings of the French socialists and the social philosophy of Comte both tended to impress him with the advantages of state action in certain comparatively untried directions, and consequently his attitude as to the true policy of the State is in some respects not defined with sufficient precision.

Since his time the disposition to criticise the shortcomings of the doctrines of the Physiocrats and Adam Smith has become general. The possible theoretical difficulties and the conflicts of individual with general interest have been most forcibly stated in the minute and thorough examination of Dr. Sidgwick[3]. This natural tendency has been reinforced by the influence of German economists who repudiate the practical position of Adam Smith as a product of the 'shallow *a priori* rationalism' of the eighteenth century, which regarded the State as an agent for determining private rights and duties (*Rechtsstaat*) in opposition to the older system of paternal government (*Polizeistaat*). This newer and wider conception of the State's sphere is conveyed in the term 'civilizing State' (*Culturstaat*) or in the fuller description of Bluntschli who regards 'the proper and direct end of the State as the

[1] *Principles*, Bk. v. ch. 11. § 7. [2] *Liberté du Travail.*

[3] *Principles of Political Economy*, Bk. iii. ch. 2. See also his *Elements of Politics*, ch. 10.

development of the national capacities, the perfecting of the national life, and finally its completion[1].'

Admitting the force of some of the criticisms that have been urged against an exaggerated policy of *laissez faire*, it seems nevertheless possible to adhere to the substantial truth of the doctrine quoted above from the *Wealth of Nations*. The real ground for limitation of state functions is not the existence of an abstract rule forbidding various classes of acts. The rule itself is dependent on the results of experience. To the plea that in many cases state intervention would obviate evils to be found under a system of liberty, Adam Smith would reply that the legislator's 'deliberations ought to be governed by general principles,' that he must act by rules which in the supposed cases would do more harm than good, and that it is the balance of advantage which needs to be regarded.

This consideration duly weighed suggests the possibility of so modifying the older position as to include a class of cases that has appeared to be the greatest stumbling-block in its way, viz. the functions of the State in the lower stages of social development. Now it is beyond question plain that the province, and therefore the expenditure, of the regulating organs of society will vary at different stages of social progress. We may take it as indisputable that the duties of the Sovereign of a central African State and of the government of a European society are and must be very different, but the conclusion does not follow that there are no general principles to which the modes of state action may conveniently conform. The construction of a 'cut and dried' formula for the duties of the State is perhaps an impossible task, but a careful study of the nature and forms of state activity as determined by the character of its organization will help to elucidate the difficult problem of its suitable duties.

§ 5. For understanding the true position of the State it

[1] *Theory of the State* (Eng. Trans.) 301. Cp. also Wagner, i. 76; Cohn, §§ 34 sq.

is essential to see the way in which its functions have been gradually evolved. In the rudest forms of society each individual depends on his own resources. The Fuegians, e. g. have no conception of government and consequently, as Darwin notes [1], no chance of attaining to civilization. In the hunting tribe, where the first advance beyond the lowest stage of savagery has been made, the elder is leader in war and judge in peace, the 'warriors' are soldiers and administrators. The tribe hunts in common over its territory which it tries to protect from intruders, and it divides the game that is captured among its members. Thus we see that war, justice, or rather the administration of custom, and economic effort are the three forms of the rudimentary society's activity. The two former, and especially war, are, however, the kind of action in which regulation is needed and where the power of the chief is particularly manifested.

The domestication of animals, which is the characteristic of the pastoral stage, facilitates the further differentiation of the chief and ruling body. The accumulation of the peculiar wealth of the period is more an individual concern, but war and justice are public duties. Here, and even in the preceding stage, we can notice the primitive forms of public expenditure, viz. the services of the members of the clan, and commodities, in the form of weapons and supplies for those going on expeditions.

When the tribe settles down on the land and devotes itself to agriculture a further division of duties appears. The primitive agricultural community frequently tills its land by means of slaves; the freeman confining himself to warlike pursuits and the duty of attendance at the public assembly where he has to decide disputes and regulate matters of general interest.

Far later in historical order, but still presenting many points of resemblance so far as public functions are concerned comes the 'feudal' organization. Some of the

[1] *Voyage of the* 'Beagle,' 229, 230.

actuating sentiments are different, and the traditions of the Empire and the Church exercise a potent effect; but the same economic basis brings about a reversion to the phenomena of earlier periods. The 'feudal' society is essentially militant. State power is vested in the 'King' or 'Lord' who represents and personifies the community. In this capacity he contracts with the vassals for the supply of his (i. e. the State's) needs. The feudal army with its loose organization is one result of this arrangement. Justice is administered through the 'Lord's' Courts. The economic side of state activities appears in the management of the domain and the regulation of commerce. In this particular historical form we notice the rudiments of much that is important in the developed financial systems of the present time.

The City State as it is found in ancient Greece and Italy, or in Germany and Italy during the mediaeval period, presents a distinctly higher type of political life. There is no longer the tribe struggling dimly to attain to the conception of political unity. The disorganization and absence of the idea of political, as opposed to personal, duty which mark the 'feudal' epoch have disappeared. The free citizen of Athens or Florence had as firm a (perhaps a firmer) grasp of the truth that he owed duties to his city as the Englishman of to-day. An exaggerated conception of the State's powers, and a disregard of private rights were a natural consequence, but so far as the financial aspect of political life is concerned, we may note the close analogy in many respects to the modern State. More especially is this true of the objects of public outlay. The maintenance of military (and in some cases of naval) force, the administration of justice and police, the furtherance of certain economic ends are the principal claims on the public resources. Subordinate to these main parts of public service may be enumerated certain requirements, also represented in modern budgets, to wit, provision for religious service, for education and for matters affecting social well-being.

The later developments of state life, either in the Roman Empire or in modern European countries, present the same general groups of public wants. Many special points will require attention when we come to examine more closely the detailed heads of expenditure, but so far as the general outline goes there is in many respects a consensus of practice in all stages of society respecting the sphere of the State [1].

§ 6. The preceding survey of the actual development of state functions brief and imperfect as it is tends to confirm and yet in some degree to qualify the conclusions of theory. The forms of state outlay have arisen gradually in the course of history as the outcome of social conditions and sentiments, and they in turn influence the society. A community in which some special duty has been for a long period entrusted to the public power will not easily be able to dispense with this mode of supplying its need. The force of habit is as great here as in other cases. The conditions of social life are, however, subject to incessant change. The state outlay suited for the Middle Ages when war and religion were the great operating forces is almost necessarily unfit for the modern age concerned as well with industry and commerce. The ready acceptance of this truth must not lead us to ignore the equally important fact, that state wants in their main features are permanent to a surprising degree. It is not in the character of the public needs but in the modes of supplying them that the most remarkable changes occur. There is, moreover, a universal recognition of the superior claims of defence and justice as being the primary duties of the State.

Writers of all schools agree in this belief, and so far history and analysis are in accord. The disputable part of state outlay is that which more especially concerns economic and social administration, and even here a good deal of the matter of controversy lies outside the subject

[1] Cp. Cohn, Book i. chaps. 1, 2, for a general view of the financial relations of social development. Also Vocke, *Abgaben*, &c., Part i.

of pure Finance and belongs more fitly to economic policy. Some trifling amount may be expended, say, on the promotion of art. The advocate of *laissez faire* may object to the course as a matter of economic policy, but so far as Finance is concerned the smallness of the amount makes it a matter of comparative indifference. The question of public expenditure in its fiscal aspects is best considered in relation to each particular period of society. We may even accept the doctrine of Mill, that 'In the particular circumstances of a given age or nation, there is scarcely anything, really important to the general interest, which it may not be desirable, or even necessary, that the government should take upon itself[1],' while we at the same time remember that Adam Smith's determination of the Sovereign's duties can include these possible cases. Finan- heory in its application to the modern State is at all ts bound to recognise and indicate clearly the diffi- s which extension of state action is likely to produce. growing budgets of all modern societies have the ncy towards enlarging the sphere of the State as their ate cause, and it is important to see that a persistence policy is certain to lead to embarrassments in financial tration, but the very necessity for discussing this compels us to examine the forms of expenditure as have been, and are, while seeking to indicate what ought to be.

. Another aspect of State wants requires notice. All omic life depends on a due supply of two distinct es of objects, viz. commodities and services, or, in less nical language, material objects and human labour. public power cannot dispense with either of these ns of supply, and at each period of its existence we it demanding them both. The hunting tribe requires varriors *and* their weapons and food : either the men nout equipment, or the outfit without the men, would useless. This distinction runs through every phase of

[1] *Principles*, Bk. v. ch. 11, § 16.

social evolution, though it is much more complex in the higher stages. A very rude community can summon its members to act for the public good, and require them to fit themselves for their task. In such cases outlay and income are combined; the member of the tribe is at once paying his taxes and performing a public service. The opposite extreme is witnessed in a civilized State of the present age. The supply of public wants is obtained by the purchase of commodities and the hire of services; the power to carry out these transactions being procured through the possession of the public revenue. Intermediate stages show us the way in which personal service was commuted for money payment, and the delivery of commodities in kind was obviated by the development of a money economy. Survivals of the older order continue; in some cases they are too important to be regarded as mere relics of the past: they are rather 'revivals' under new and favouring conditions. When dealing with revenue we shall have to compare the direct with the circuitous method of satisfying public needs, and in the present Book we shall have to note some of the economic consequences of the adoption of one or other of these modes.

Having disposed of the more general aspects of public expenditure, we shall next consider the several details, commencing with the oldest and most enduring—the need for defence against outside enemies.

CHAPTER II.

THE COST OF DEFENCE.

§ 1. ADAM SMITH commences his examination of the cost of defence by the statement that it 'is very different in the different states of society,' and adds, as the result of his inquiry, that it 'grows gradually more and more expensive as the society advances in civilization [1].' A reference to the statistics of military and naval expenditure will show that the tendency to increased outlay has continued during the century that has elapsed since the above passage was written [2]. There is, moreover, no sign of change in this respect. It is as certain as any prediction in social matters can be, that no reduction in the military budgets of Europe will soon be made; on the contrary, there is every probability that this form of expenditure will go on increasing in the future as it has done in the past.

The causes that have produced this, at first sight, unfortunate state of things, must, it is clear, be deep-seated and persistent, and accordingly, when we scrutinise more closely the operating forces, it appears that the increased cost of warfare and of the preparations which it involves is closely connected with some of the normal features of social development. It is principally the result of two general tendencies, viz. (1) the increased division of labour which necessarily accompanies the advance of society, and (2) the

[1] 289, cp. 296.

[2] See tables at end of this chapter.

development of those inventions that are such a striking characteristic of modern civilization. The former makes it absolutely essential to set a specially trained section of the population apart for military service to the sacrifice of their assistance in the ordinary work of production, while they usually receive a higher reward than a similar body of labourers would be able to command in the market. The pay of the British army is a good illustration of this fact, and it is the most suitable instance to take, as enlistment in it is purely voluntary. The rapid progress of scientific discovery increases the cost of warlike material and equipment, since the constituents of this part of 'consumers' capital,' as it may be called, become much more elaborate and have to be more frequently replaced. If we compare the stock of weapons of a savage tribe with the equipment of a mediaeval army, and either of them with the war material now necessary for a single 'army corps' of any European State, we cannot fail to recognise the increase in complexity and in cost which the later organizations show. Even in the last quarter of a century the changes in warlike implements and supplies have been such as, while vastly increasing their cost, to render them very different from the appliances previously existing.

§ 2. The expenses of defence and agression have, it must be noticed, to be divided into two distinct parts. The former, which may be regarded as the normal and regular part—the peace establishment—meets the preparation for war. It is so well-recognised a feature of the modern budget, that it passes without comment. The other part of state outlay in this respect is that devoted to actual warfare; it is evidently irregular in amount and may so far be called 'abnormal,' though it is almost certain to recur at indefinite intervals[1].

The cost of preparation for war consists in obtaining a supply both of services and commodities, i.e. in the recruiting and training of troops, the provision for pensions,

[1] See infra, Bk. i. ch. 8. § 1. Cp. Wagner, i. 417 sq. Roscher, § 119.

and the selection and preparation of arms, ammunition, and stores generally. Actual war causes expenditure on campaigns and expeditions, and, further, in the replacement of losses alike in men and stores, incurred during its continuance. In estimating the loss to society through the persistence of the custom of war between nations, both the above-mentioned elements have to be combined in order to judge accurately of the real cost imposed.

§ 3. Preparation for war, as it appears in the successive stages of society, conforms to the general principle declared by Adam Smith. In a savage or barbarous community the cost of warlike preparation is insignificant. The ordinary course of life is of itself a training for times of conflict; the hunter or shepherd is ready at the shortest notice to transfer his exertions to a fresh and more exciting employment. Such rude societies are (with some rare exceptions) organized on a basis of militancy, all the adult males being available as 'warriors.' Similar conditions prevail with respect to commodities. Bows, spears, staves, &c., are useful either in peace or war; they are eminently non-specialized capital, and more elaborate contrivances are as yet unthought of. The introduction of agriculture has a modifying effect, in so far as it tends to retard the mobility of labour and commodities, but even in this stage the same general features recur. The ordinary husbandman easily becomes a soldier, and there is a recognised interchange between swords and plough-shares. An invasion is still carried out or opposed by a *levée en masse*, and usually takes place in the 'off-season' of agricultural work. The cost of preparation for such wars obviously cannot be very heavy.

The introduction of manufactures, and the establishment of urban life that accompanies it, puts an effectual check to the ruder forms of belligerency. A State possessing the varied elements of an industrial society—even in a rudimentary form—cannot permit the suspension of the normal economic processes during a period of hostilities, and it is therefore compelled to make adequate arrangements in time of peace in order to obviate the danger. The difficulty is met by the introduction of standing armies whose origin is thus easily explained. It, in fact, becomes necessary to carry the gradually increasing division of employments into the military art, and to form at least the nucleus of an army which can be readily increased in case of need. The difficulty of suddenly shifting the artisan from the workshop to the field of battle makes this imperative. Improvements in weapons and systems of discipline furnish additional reasons in favour of increased special training, to be given either to the whole efficient population, or to a selected portion of it, but in any case involving larger outlay.

The section of the *Wealth of Nations* devoted to this topic regards the adoption of either of the alternatives just mentioned as a cardinal point in the evolution of the military system. The former method—that of training the whole effective population—is described as the creation of a militia, the latter as the formation of a standing army, and a very strong judgment is pronounced in favour of the latter expedient. Admitting fully the truth of some of the views set forth on this point by Adam Smith it is nevertheless desirable to remember that they by no means exhaust the subject and the considerations relevant to it. His appeal to history more particularly strikes the reader as superficial. To support his contention that standing armies are always superior to militias—an idea evidently derived from his belief in the advantages of increased division of labour [1]—he brings forward the examples of the Macedonian army that overthrew the forces of the Hellenic commonwealths and the Persian Empire; the early successes of Hannibal and the ultimate triumph of the Romans, and finally the fall of the Western Empire before the barbarian invaders. The cases quoted, however,

[1] In some cases Adam Smith saw clearly enough that division of labour was not always desirable. Cp. 217 and 327.

fail to establish the doctrine asserted. It is surely contrary to fact to speak of the army of imperial Rome as 'a militia'; if ever there were a 'standing army' it was one. The whole discussion in short amounts simply to this: that the better disciplined and trained force will generally defeat its opponent, and that it ought to be called 'a standing army.' The historical summary is accurate if somewhat trite, but the interpretation results in a truism.

We have therefore to replace Adam Smith's account by one more consonant with facts while preserving those parts of his exposition that are substantially correct. It is certainly beyond dispute that the course of development tends to replace the rude levies described as 'militias' by the better-trained forces known as 'standing armies.' In addition to the instances given above, we may mention the introduction of permanent armies in every European State, so that the general tendency towards specialization is clearly operative in this as in other cases. An opposing tendency, however, comes into play. It is equally a principle of evolution that all organized bodies tend to lose their original plasticity; they become, as it were, crystallized into a rigid form, and from this condition armies are not exempted. But warfare is the struggle for existence in its intensest shape, and in that struggle, mobility and power of adjustment are important advantages. The natural result is that the most efficient military machine or organization of one period proves to be unsuitable for the changed requirements of another and later one. The history of war is, in fact, a series of illustrations of this truth. As convincing and well-known examples we need only note the Phalanx, the Legion, the man-at-arms of mediaeval times, the army system of Frederick the Great, and the French system of the present century. And it may well happen that a future European war will afford a further instance in the fate of the present German army. The essential condition of military efficiency is constant readjustment—incessant striving towards improvement in discipline, training, and equipment. Such efforts, necessary as they are, demand continuous intellectual strain on the part of the organizers, and heavy demands on the public purse.

§ 4. If, as we believe, Adam Smith failed to correctly interpret the past, he certainly did not succeed in forecasting the future. Up to his time there had been a steady movement towards the establishment and increase of permanent forces maintained at great cost. The effect produced on thoughtful persons by the growing European armaments can be best understood by considering the views of Montesquieu. In a remarkable chapter of the *Spirit of Laws*[1] he describes the position and its dangers to the future of Europe in the following terms :—

'A new disease has spread through Europe ; it has seized on our sovereigns and makes them maintain an inordinate number of troops. It is intensified and of necessity becomes infectious, for as soon as one State increases its forces the others at once increase theirs, so that nothing is gained by it except general ruin. Each monarch keeps on foot as many armies as if his people were in danger of extermination ; and this struggle of all against all is called peace! Thus is Europe ruined to such a degree that private persons in the present position of the three richest powers of that quarter of the globe would not have the means of living. We are poor with the wealth and commerce of the whole world ; and soon by dint of having soldiers we shall have nothing but soldiers and be like the Tartars. For that we need only make effective the new invention of militias established in most of Europe and carry it to the same excess as we have the regular troops.'

This vigorous statement has been largely justified by the actual course of events. The wars that resulted from the French Revolution proved the power of national sentiment to raise and maintain enormous forces during a

[1] Bk. xiii. ch. 17.

period of protracted conflict, and the reform of the Prussian army under Hardenberg's guidance after the disaster at Jena, carried the tendency towards the enrolment of the nation into periods of peace. The wars of the third quarter of the present century, and especially the Austro-Prussian war of 1866, and the Franco-German one of 1870–1, have greatly increased the popularity of the national army system which has been adopted by nearly all continental States[1], and has been approved by many English writers. The change of opinion in recent years is perhaps most instructively shown in a remarkable essay of Cairnes, where the respective merits of the older French, the English, and Prussian systems are estimated with a conclusion strongly in favour of the 'national army[2].'

We almost seem to have lost sight, for the moment, of economic and financial considerations, but they really underlie the whole military movement of modern times. The increase of permanent forces had reached its limit before the opening of the French Revolution when about one per cent. of the population was available for actual service. The prolonged conflicts which arose out of that event led to the *addition* (as Montesquieu apprehended) of a militia. The modern national army in its full force is the old 'standing army,' plus a *levée en masse*, the latter, it is true, being suitably organized and equipped. This system, though produced at first by a particular set of circumstances, was obviously necessitated by economic conditions. Military power had to be increased, and as the state revenues did not allow of increase in the permanent force, the only alternative was that actually adopted, by which the whole effective male population became a reserve, and was yet enabled, in times of peace, to carry on its ordinary industrial pursuits.

[1] See Wagner, i. 427, for a full list.

[2] Cairnes, *Political Essays*, 199–255. On this point his judgment is for once supported by the agreement of Cliffe Leslie, *Essays* (1st ed.), 128–147. Leslie's opinion is the more valuable, as it was formed after personal study of the Prussian system, and was in opposition to his earlier belief.

The question of cost is in the last resort decisive, and it is by it that the merits of the several military systems must be judged. One of the conditions to be included in our measurement of cost is efficiency. National defence is too important even from a purely economic standpoint to be placed in jeopardy through narrow ideas of economy. An ineffective and badly organized army is dear on any terms, though on the other hand large outlay will not of itself secure efficiency, and so far weakens the economic resources of the nation. The problem is, indeed, as remarked before [1], one of extreme difficulty, and only allows of an approximate solution. As regards the cost or sacrifice involved in the various methods of defence, the national army presents two great advantages: (1) it requires less direct outlay, and (2) its real pressure is not so acutely felt. It is plain that services obtained through legal compulsion will be cheaper than those that are hired in the labour market at the current rate. Moreover, when the duty of military service is general and enforced without favouritism the sacrifice entailed by it will probably be less felt than if the large amount of additional funds needed under voluntary enlistment had to be levied through taxation. Granting, however, both these positions, it yet remains doubtful whether the indirect losses may not be more than the gains just mentioned. The real cost of an army formed on the German type is hard to measure. Mere comparison of army estimates will not establish its superiority over a freely-enrolled force. Thus an able writer [2] compares the English and German outlay for 1883–4. The former was £16,600,000 for 199,273 men, the latter £18,325,000 for 445,392 men, i. e. an army much more than twice that of England was maintained by Germany at an increased cost of only 10 per cent. This estimate is supported by additional calculations, which make the cost per soldier in England £86, in Germany only £44, or little over half. Such calculations err in the omission of several material

[1] Supra, ch. I. § 2.

[2] Geffcken in Schönberg, 53.

circumstances. The rates of wages and salaries in the two countries are not on the same level. Under any system a given number of German soldiers would cost less than an equal number of English ones. Next, though the compulsory service in the former country reduces considerably the amount of direct outlay by the State, it inflicts a tax on those compelled to serve, whose amount could be measured only by what they would pay in order to escape it. A third influencing condition is the indirect effect on the productive powers of the country.

'The military service,' says a favourable critic of the German army, 'postpones to a relatively very late period the productive use of the productive power of the country. . . . The waste of skilled labour . . . is enormous. The future artisan or mechanic has not learned his business when he enters the army, nor can he practise it until he leaves the regiment. . . . Half the lifetime of the flower of the population is thus unproductively spent. Even in the case of unskilled labourers or peasants, who can go to work from the day they leave barracks, a considerable loss is sustained [1].'

None of the foregoing considerations are taken into account by Geffcken. It may, indeed, be argued that the habits of discipline and order acquired during service should be placed to the credit of the German system, but this questionable item would not much affect the general result, more especially when we add the probable loss of originality and initiative, which is another result of discipline. The national army system further involves a supervision of the movements of all the members of the potential war force, and such regulation must in some degree restrict the free flow of labour to suitable markets.

The difficulties in the way of any estimate of the financial merits of different army systems, already evident enough, are enhanced by the special circumstances with which each

[1] Leslie, *Essays* (1st ed.), 143. See Wagner, i. 426, for a directly opposite view.

country has to deal, and which render the complete adoption of a foreign system almost impossible. Thus England has to provide garrisons for many places very distant from her own territory, and service of this kind in India or the Crown Colonies could not be made compulsory. Separation of the home and foreign (or Indian and Colonial) armies appears a retrograde step[1], and in any case the supposed home force might, in time of pressure, be required for service abroad. A great power, whose foreign possessions are insignificant, has not this problem to face.

§ 5. A partial solution of the difficulty of procuring sufficient military force without compulsory service, and at the same time keeping expenditure within due bounds is presented in the English Volunteer system. By this method the public spirit of the citizens leads them to give a portion of their time to acquiring the rudiments of military training and sufficient dexterity in the use of weapons. Competent military opinion seems, however, to hold that a considerable degree of organization is necessary in order to make volunteer forces of any real service in time of war. The endeavour to combine the strict discipline essential for the soldier with the freedom naturally claimed by the volunteer is not an easy one, though the object is eminently desirable. Besides its great advantage in fostering the national sentiment of the members, and impressing them with the conception of their duties to the State, the volunteer corps would, by taking charge of the home fortresses, probably allow the regular troops to be drawn off for foreign service, and would also be a valuable source for recruiting.

It may further be remarked that a very general enrolment of the active population in such bodies, under proper discipline, would be equivalent to the national army system, and at the same time avoid the evil of compulsion. In this as in other cases of volunteer assistance for public service,

[1] This plan has recently been advocated by Sir C. Dilke, *Problems of Greater Britain*, 380.

the chief difficulty is to enable the two agencies to fit in to each other without friction or waste.

§ 6. The navies of the various powers do not present as much difficulty, for they are far less costly so far as the supply of their personal service is concerned, and that supply is taken from a special class already trained to a life of hardship, and accustomed to constant supervision and control, though here, too, the question of obtaining the necessary force without undue outlay is a serious one.

§ 7. The best and most economical mode of supplying equipment and material for both military and naval forces has been for some time recognised as a grave problem. The extraordinary rapidity of inventions soon makes the most costly and best-devised appliances antiquated. It seems a hopeless task to provide all new agencies of attack and defence, owing to their great expense and their certain replacement by later improvements, so that it might appear that the wisest course was to await the outbreak of war, and then procure the best existing weapons. Unfortunately such a course is not practicable. Ships and ordnance cannot be speedily produced and distributed. The stock, the 'fixed capital' of destruction as it may be called, like that of productive industry, takes time to create, and in warfare delay is fatal. A steadily progressive course seems the most advisable in this respect, even from the purely financial point of view, as the pressure is more evenly distributed, and by adopting this policy there is, on the whole, the best chance of security.

Against the undoubted evil of the great increase of outlay on armaments, it is satisfactory to be able to point to some compensation, or at least alleviation. One result is to favour the wealthier, and therefore the most industrious nations. A rich State can obtain the best ships, rifles and cannon, and so gains the same advantage over its poorer rivals that civilized peoples generally gained over barbarians by the invention of firearms. Then, as Mr. Giffen and Cohn have suggested, the increased cost of warlike equipment is accompanied by an immense expansion of industrial production ; if the burden be heavier the bearer is stronger, and is not so much oppressed as we might at first suppose ; and finally, though this is problematical, the skill developed in aiding the work of destruction is also of service for industry [1]. The best method of procuring arms and supplies is also a doubtful matter. The usual alternatives are: purchase in the open market, or state manufacture, and in the former case the contracts may be given privately or by public tender; but the advisability of state manufacture may be reserved for a more suitable place [2].

§ 8. The cost of actual war presents problems very similar to those already considered. The national army, when in the field, is a very expensive agency. 'An army composed of such materials as the Prussian, cannot be employed in war without immense loss and suffering both to the soldiers and the whole nation [3].' The ordinary standing army, on the other hand, is often unfavourably criticised as being composed of the refuse of the population [4]. Were this true it would be rather an advantage in the event of war, except in so far as it detracted from military efficiency. In any case it is difficult to measure the cost incurred in war apart from the direct outlay and the loss of men and material in the conflict. There is, besides, the disturbance in the economic system which is a necessary result, and which may injuriously affect, not merely the national well-being, but the state revenues. Such consequences are hard to foresee, and vary widely in different nations. With regard to England, for example, the outbreak of war would materially injure her shipping trade, which forms so important a part of her industry; the diminished profits in that trade, and the innumerable dependent and connected

[1] Giffen, *Growth of Capital*, 145; Cohn, § 390. For the stimulus to industry, Sir F. Abel's presidential address to the British Association at Leeds, *Report* (1890), 25.

[2] Bk. ii. ch. 3. 'The Industrial Domain.'

[3] Leslie, 140, who adds some striking instances.

[4] Cairnes, *ut sup.* 223.

occupations would soon be shown in the reduced income-tax returns under Schedule D, and would so far affect the state receipts at a time of extra pressure. It is needless to add that the revenue would almost certainly be acted on by other results of war, and not beneficially. A continental State would suffer perhaps in a different way. Some of its territory might be occupied by the enemy, and its contributions suspended, or under the most favourable circumstances the productive powers of the community would be reduced by the withdrawal of so many men from their usual employments, with the natural result of diminishing the yield from taxation[1]. All such elements form part of the financial considerations appropriate to the subject.

To make the estimate a fair one, it is further desirable to take into account the possible advantages so forcibly stated by Wagner[2] and others. They are: the ennobling effect of warfare on men, and even its value as an economic discipline; its tendency to bring about a better grouping of nations (as in the recent cases of Germany and Italy); and finally the fact that successful warfare may allow of the cost being placed on the vanquished. It might be added that some periods of war have been seasons of high profits, as was the case in England during the French wars of 1793–1815. But after all these supposed gains are not a set-off against the certain losses. There is no evidence that war promotes higher social or economic training[3]. Under given conditions, capitalists may gain by it, but only at the expense of other classes. The power of placing all the expense on the conquered party is not a diminution but simply a shifting of the burden, as happened in the Franco-German war of 1870–1[4]. And the redistribution is not always purely beneficial to the

[1] Leslie, 141. [2] i. 416 sq.

[3] For an admirable statement of the evils of war see the essay on 'The evolution of peace,' in Lawrence, *Essays on Modern International Law*, 234 sq.

[4] Giffen, *Essays in Finance* (1st Series), 1-55, gives an estimate of the cost of that war.

winning side, while it intensifies the suffering of the defeated State.

§ 9. In conclusion it may be said that war and preparation for war are by far the heaviest charges on the resources of modern States [1]. An enormous sacrifice of labour-power and of commodities is inevitably caused by its persistence as a usage among modern nations. The uncertainty and indefiniteness of the requirements of States for this end is a perturbing element in financial arrangements. War has been the principal cause of the great state indebtedness so general in Europe, and of the severe pressure of taxation. It is consequently beyond reasonable doubt that peaceful methods of settling disputes, or limitations of the present rigour of belligerent rights [2], are not merely social, moral, or even economic reforms: they are further of the greatest financial importance. Arrangements for disarmament, if possible, would belong to the same class. But while strongly insisting on the great advantages that are certain to result from the maintenance of peace, and the reduction of military and naval expenditure, it is quite as essential to assert that so long as present conditions last, a well-organized and effective system of defence is a necessary part of state expenditure, and one that amply repays its cost by the security that it affords for the political independence as well as the economic interests of the nation. To maintain a due balance between the excessive demands of alarmists and military officials, and the undue reductions in outlay sought by the advocates of economy, is one of the difficult tasks of the statesman. In endeavouring to attain to the due mean, many specially financial considerations have to be noticed. Among these are: the relation of state to national revenues; the risks to which unsuccessful war would expose the country; and the comparative urgency of the other claims on the State. The application of the amount judged

[1] See note at end of chapter.

[2] The exemption of private property at sea from capture is the most obvious and desirable reform in this direction.

necessary is also difficult to determine. It has to be distributed between services (*Personalbedarf*) and commodities (*Realbedarf*), so as to secure the maximum advantage, but this latter question lies, strictly speaking, outside the limit of Finance, and belongs to military administration.

NOTE.

The growth of expenditure for military and naval purposes is very plainly shown in the following tables:—

TABLE I.

Expenditure of England and France on Army and Navy at different periods.

England. *Year.*	*Amount.*	France. *Year.*	*Amount.*
1775	£3,810,000	1774	£4,880,000
1823	14,350,000	1830	12,960,000
1847	18,500,000	1847	19,320,000
1857–8	23,500,000	1858	19,960,000
1868–9	26,891,000	1868	26,320,000
1878–9	30,252,000	1878	29,240,000
1889–90	32,781,090	1890	37,640,000

TABLE II.

Military and Naval expenditure of—

(*a*) The German Empire. *Year.*	*Amount.*	(*b*) Italy. *Year.*	*Amount.*
1873	£19,200,000	1862	£8,500,000
1876	21,900,000	1869	6,800,000
1883–4	22,750,000	1875	8,760,000
1888–9	41,900,000	1880	10,120,000
1890–1 (estimate)	35,450,000	1886	13,120,000
		1890	14,500,000

TABLE III.

Total Military and Naval expenditure of the Six Great Powers[1].

Year.	*Amount.*
1868	£104,250,000
1873	124,450,000
1882	146,460,000
1888	180,200,000

Whatever qualification may be requisite in consequence of the above figures being obtained from different sources, it cannot affect the general conclusion that they are adduced to support—the increase of expenditure for the purposes of defence and aggression.

[1] Austria, England, France, Germany, Italy, and Russia.

CHAPTER III.

JUSTICE AND SECURITY.

§ 1. IN tracing the gradual development of state functions, we found that the maintenance of internal security, the protection of each member of the society against 'the injustice or oppression of every other member of it,' or in more modern phrase the establishment of law and order, was a task that was attempted in the early stages of social evolution, and one that became more fully emphasized as political institutions grew in strength. The necessity of the function is admitted by all except the most advanced anarchists. In fact the extreme urgency of the claim for public activity in this respect, has frequently led to a comparative neglect of other sides of state duty. Both in its social and economic results the establishment of security is of the utmost importance; but there is the danger of limiting its range too narrowly. All institutions and legislative measures that tend to increase the power and resources of the State so far conduce to the preservation of order, and this wider point of view should never be ignored, though it is necessary to give the most prominent place to the agencies directly employed in promoting the end.

An instance of the disposition to unduly confine the subject is found in the *Wealth of Nations*. The section of the work devoted to this topic deals solely with the administration of justice. Adam Smith appears to have believed that the one matter of importance for the State was to decide disputes, though his account of the introduction of law courts shows that it is just as essential to suppress disorder. The sovereign does certainly discharge a most useful function in settling controversies about the precise nature of private rights and duties ; but besides the claims of individuals, there is the whole body of public law, and even individual rights have to be determined in respect to their orbit and incidence by the State. The ultimate aim is the promotion of social welfare by the establishment of security which may be secured in two different ways, with very dissimilar financial effects. 'The Legislature may pass laws which give certain rights and remedies to the persons interested, and may leave it to them to enforce the law by taking their own proceedings, according to their own interests, in the courts of law. In this case the courts are the organs through which the State exercises its power. Or, again, the Legislature may intrust the duty of enforcing the law to an executive department which then becomes the organ of the State for the purpose[1].' The former method would come under the head of 'justice' ; the latter under that of 'police' or 'administration,' and it is a significant fact that it is not noticed by Adam Smith. His whole economic system on its practical side (in this respect in strict agreement with the Physiocratic position) was a protest against the older paternal policy. He had no conception of the development of administration and supervision for social and even economic ends, which is so characteristic of the modern State, and consequently his work presents a gap in regard to this important subject.

The modern student of Finance is, however, compelled to take the different elements of justice and administrative police into account when seeking to estimate the cost incurred in guarding the rights of private persons, and the security of the community which is an essential condition precedent to the former object. The growth of expenditure in this direction has been very large, and presents some serious financial problems.

[1] Farrer, *State and Trade*, 6.

§ 2. Though many of the details of legal development are as yet obscure, its broad outlines have been sufficiently elucidated by the labours of the historical jurists[1]. In the primitive community custom is binding; violations of its prescriptions are offences, but any disputes as to the fact of a breach of the customary rule have to be decided by the opinions of the tribal or village assembly. As soon as the chief comes into existence the decision of controversies becomes one of his tasks—or privileges, the submission of the parties is, notwithstanding, voluntary, at least in appearance, and the Judge is entitled to a 'fee' for his services[2]. Under such conditions, justice is a matter of special bargain. The chief as judge or arbitrator, gives his time and attention to the decision of disputes, and like any labourer is 'worthy of his hire.' Very many legal systems afford evidence of the existence of this dealing out of the commodity, justice, and of the slow process by which voluntary submission became compulsory.

At a far later stage of growth and even when the coercive power of the sovereign State was fully established, this idea of 'service for service' was retained. The financial significance of such a view is apparent. As long as the suitors paid fees for the services of judges there was no need for including the item in the public expenditure. Even if entered it would only be a matter of account, the receipts balancing the outlay[3].

First appearances are in favour of this arrangement. The public revenue is exempted from charge; the persons, who are supposed to gain, have to pay for a service rendered, and judges are stimulated to diligence by the hope of reward. The operation of individual interest has produced a satisfactory result. So plausible is the view that it was maintained by Adam Smith. But before his time the

[1] Maine, *Ancient Law*, ch. 10; *Early Institutions*, chs. 9 and 10.

[2] Cp. Maine, *Early Law and Custom*, 185 n.

[3] If the fees were so large as to leave a surplus after paying salaries and other expenses, 'Administration of Justice' might have to appear in Bk. ii. as one of the departments of 'State Industry.'

practical weakness of the system was so apparent that the abolition of all law charges was advocated, and Bentham had little difficulty in showing the mistake of the older view. It based its case on a series of false comparisons. The judge—and every judicial official—is indeed a labourer discharging a most useful service even in a strictly economic estimation; but his toil is for the interests of the society at large, and he ought to be paid out of the fund created indirectly through his work, that is, the increased wealth of the society owing to an exact administration of justice and the consequent increase of security. If lawsuits always arose from mistakes there might be something to be said for compelling the parties in fault to pay for the correction; such is not a usual case; far more often they arise from intentional wrong-doing by one party, or in many instances through the difficulty of knowing the law. The innocent suitor is not a special gainer by the action of law: he is in rather a worse position than those who, by the restraining effect of justice have been saved the necessity of asserting their rights. The great advantage that a legal system sustained by fees gives to the rich is an additional argument against it, as is also the tendency of payment by fees to foster judicial corruption. A court supported by charges on suits would be likely to work so as to increase those charges, and might not be strictly scrupulous in the methods adopted.

The theory besides is only applicable to civil courts. Suppose the criminal courts are to be sustained by the parties—one of those parties is the State, and it must draw its contribution from the public revenue. A possible source of revenue may be suggested in the penalties inflicted on wrong-doers. Unfortunately this, which so far as it goes is very suitable, proves insufficient. In many cases there is not enough to compensate the individual sufferers. The offender—either civil or criminal—may have no available property, and we therefore find ourselves forced to the conclusion that the cost of justice should be defrayed by the State. Nor so long as due care is observed in scrutinizing the outlay is there any form of public expense that is more amply justified. On the due administration of justice depends in a great degree the prosperity of a country. The outlay incurred for it ought not to be regarded as a deduction from a definite and pre-determined fund; it is more correctly a percentage levied on wealth, that but for it would never have existed [1].

§ 3. In regard to justice as to defence it is possible to adopt different methods of supplying the state requirements consisting in this case chiefly of services. As Germany has given the world the greatest example of forced military duty, affording a model that has been widely imitated, so has England supplied the most striking and impressive instance of compulsory civic service. The jury system of the United Kingdom, though it does not enter into the national accounts, is, notwithstanding, a heavy tax on those who are subject to it, and should be taken into account in estimating the national burdens.

Continental legal systems economize in another direction. By placing judicial salaries at a lower scale the work is done by an inferior class of men [2], but then they are enabled to employ a larger staff and can secure a quicker disposal of cases. In this they are aided by the superiority *in form* of their laws. A less skilled judge can deal successfully with the definite rules of a Code, when he would fail under the English method of case-law.

Whatever mode be adopted the total cost of the legal system is not light as the figures show, and it tends to increase with the growth of population and industrial intercourse [3].

§ 4. Voluntary service contributes towards the perform-

[1] The statement in the text does not exclude the levying of fees for various legal acts. This side of the question is considered *infra* Bk. ii. ch. 4 and Bk. iv. ch. 8.

[2] Promotion on the Continent is said to be from the bench to the bar, a complete reversal of English ideas.

[3] See table at end of chapter.

ance of judicial work. As England has a volunteer army so she possesses a volunteer judiciary in the unpaid justices who discharge the lower tasks of courts of first instance and are rewarded by the consideration that attaches to their office, and by the reflection that they have 'done their duty.'

The Germans, and Gneist in particular, place great weight on the advantages of 'Self-government' as it exists in England and is being gradually introduced into Prussia. It is nevertheless of doubtful efficiency ('justices' justice' has long been a byword), and from the financial point of view the gain is not great. At all events, the system of unpaid magistrates is only suited for thinly peopled districts, where small offences are comparatively few in number, and where the administrators command respect by their social position. Civil cases, above the lowest, have to be referred to a paid official—the county-court judge; and the criminal jurisdiction over large cities is given to well-trained and salaried magistrates, since the work would be beyond the power of volunteer service.

Thus self-help, or rather free public service, turns out to be a valuable aid, but impracticable as a sole or even a chief resource.

§ 5. Next to the cost of law, the outlay on 'police' requires notice. The general term 'police' has been used in a wide sense [1]; we may, however, limit it to its modern meaning. In this application it is of very recent growth. Formerly each citizen was in some degree prepared to defend himself, or belonged to some body or group that would protect him more or less effectually against aggression. All difficulties finally came to the tribunals. Now the State is held bound to have a force on hand to suppress disorder and bring criminals to justice. The absence of a police force from any scene of disturbance is regarded as a grievance, the support of order being supposed to

[1] Thus we find 'Police of commerce,' and even the 'Police State,' for a system of paternal legislation.

concern it solely. A series of causes has tended to produce this remarkable change in public feeling; they are:—(1) The increase of population and its great density in certain areas affording naturally a greater facility for escape to offenders; (2) the alteration in manners that has abolished the custom of carrying arms; (3) the modern industrial system with the consequent accumulation of valuable commodities, many of them incapable of being identified; (4) the development of agencies for locomotion and the facilities for escape thereby obtained, while pursuit though difficult to an individual is still easy for an organized body. The financial outcome of these normal forces has been a great increase both in central and local expenditure for the purpose of maintaining police forces engaged in supporting and facilitating the action of courts of justice as also in preventing outbursts of disorder [1].

§ 6. The penal system stands on the borderland between 'police' and administration. When the judge and policemen have dealt with the criminal, he is handed over to the jailor, and in this department of state outlay also there has been a noticeable change during the last century. Ancient societies treated offenders in a summary way. They were executed or reduced to slavery, so that the problems of prison expenditure or management did not arise. The mediaeval idea was quite as barbarous though not so efficient. Criminals who escaped death were the objects of great cruelty as well as at times of undue lenity [2].

The more humane spirit of the eighteenth century brought about a salutary change. Under the influence of the teachings and practical work of Beccaria, Bentham, and Howard, continued by their many followers in their various lines of exertion, the whole system of criminal legislation and penalties was remodelled. Punishment, instead of being regarded as the vengeance of the State or the

[1] See note at end of chapter.

[2] See Du Cane, *The Punishment and Prevention of Crime*, chs. 1–3.

individual, was transformed into an agency for prevention and reformation. Executions became few in number, and prisons, from being purely places for confinement, were used for purposes of discipline and instruction.

The necessary financial result has been a considerable increase of expenditure. Prisons and convict stations are formed on an elaborate scale, with careful provision for the health of the inmates. The comparative leniency of sentences has further tended to perpetuate the class known as 'habitual criminals.' This small body—for such it really is in all civilized countries—is yet responsible for the greater part of the outlay on 'crime and police.' Any effectual method of dealing with proven 'habituals' would be a financial as well as a social benefit. Even under the present arrangements the outlay on the 'penal system' is in the strictest sense productive or at least preservative of wealth.

NOTE.

The following table shows the increased cost of the maintenance of internal security in England and France.

Year.	*Amount expended by Central Government in England on Justice and Police.*	*Year.*	*Cost of ministry of Justice in France.*
1825	£ 217,000	1822	£ 746,600
1837	357,000	1840	834,000
1853	2,220,000	1850	1,077,000
1868–9	4,650,000	1860	1,204,000
1880–1	6,600,000	1880	1,422,000
1889–90	6,800,000	1890	1,498,750

To these amounts various local expenses should be added for England; and to get the cost of police for France the outlay for *Gendarmerie*, which is charged under the account for 'war' and in 1888 reached almost £1,600,000, should be included.

CHAPTER IV.

ADMINISTRATIVE SUPERVISION. POOR-RELIEF.

§ 1. THE modern State has in some respects added, if not exactly to the classes of objects under its care, at least to the complexity of the tasks connected with those classes. It is still possible to stretch Adam Smith's description of state functions so as to include the subjects of the present chapter, but the extension, though conforming to the letter, hardly agrees with the spirit of that well-known statement. In this instance we have a good example of the way in which public tasks are conditioned by the circumstances of time and place, and of the impossibility of using an inflexible formula to guide the course of social action. The expansion of administrative supervision in the last fifty years has placed a fresh series of duties on public authorities. A century ago there was little of the kind in England, and the older French and German systems of regulation were in a state of decay. The French Revolution of 1789 was believed to have removed these checks on individual liberty, and to have secured by its influence their ultimate abolition in other continental States. The passage from the *Ancien Régime* was regarded as definitely accomplished.

Such expectations have proved unfounded ; old methods of control and supervision have indeed for the most part disappeared[1] and no one advocates their re-establish-

[1] E.g. the restraints so forcibly criticised in Turgot's *Éloge de Gournay* could not exist now. Turgot, i. 266–270.

ment. In their place we have a newer body of arrangements for the regulation of various parts of social life. Under an elaborate system of legislation a large official body has been created for the purpose of regulating the free movement of the ordinary citizen. There are inspectors of mines, factories, shipping, railways, tramways, hackney-carriages, &c. The soundness and purity of articles of food are tested by public agents. Many trades are placed under special rules, and local authorities are entrusted with wide discretionary powers in their dealings with the habits and occupations of the communities under their charge[1]. The foregoing account, applicable in all points to the United Kingdom, holds true generally of all modern States; there may be differences in detail; the power which exercises supervision may be local in one country, and central in an other, nevertheless, the broad fact remains that both in Europe and America the department of 'administration' is increasing in extent[2]. Opinions may and do differ widely as to the merits of this movement[3], but on the point most pertinent for our present inquiry there can be no dispute, viz. the increase of expenditure that necessarily results from it. The budget of every civilized society is swollen by the charges needed for the salaries of agents engaged in the work of inspection and regulation, while the total cost can only be ascertained by combining the general and local outlay.

§ 2. Some of the causes of the great increase in administrative outlay have been noticed when dealing with 'police.' They, however, deserve a more precise statement:—(1) The great growth of centres of population makes organization

[1] Farrer, *State and Trade*, and Cunningham, *Economics and Politics*, both describe this movement, but with divergent sentiments.

[2] For the United States, see Bryce, *American Commonwealth*, ch. 91. For the English Colonies, Dilke, *Problems of Greater Britain*, 508.

[3] Farrer and Cunningham, as above. For a vigorous protest against the tendency see H. Spencer, *State and Man*, the recent work *A Plea for Liberty*, and the publications of the Liberty and Property Defence League; also Léon Say, *Socialisme d'État*.

and control more necessary, e. g. to employ a body of police to regulate the traffic in a country road would be absurd ; in the Strand or Regent Street it is indispensable. The inspection of dwellings in order to prevent overcrowding is another prominent instance. (2) The moral sense of the community stands at a higher point now than it ever previously did, and as a consequence the public power is invoked to remove any evil that shocks public opinion. The legislation as to unseaworthy ships affords an illustration. (3) The democratic movement makes interference with the owners of capital or property generally, as also with large dealers in commodities, acceptable to the holders of political power. (4) The establishment of bodies of officials is carried on so gradually that the total expense entailed by the system is never realized ; the special gain hoped for in each case is, on the contrary, distinctly conceived. (5) Finally, the influence of the prevalent political and economic theories should be added. Most cases of actual state regulation would come under the exceptions to *laissez faire* as discussed by J. S. Mill and Dr. Sidgwick, they also have been powerfully advocated both in Germany and America on theoretical grounds. It is therefore not unreasonable to assume that this tendency of speculative thought has in some degree influenced the conduct of statesmen [1].

§ 3. The difficult question remains. How far is this outlay financially justifiable? It may at once be conceded that many of the ends sought are eminently praiseworthy, and that no supposed principle of abstract right ought to hinder the adoption of measures of general utility. The final test must be expediency, but expediency in its broadest sense. It is only possible here to indicate some of the general considerations applicable to the problem, and which have to be used as guides in each particular case. (1) The pressure of taxation, and the probable sacrifice that its

[1] For a statement of these causes, Goschen, '*Laissez faire* and Government Interference,' *Addresses*, 59–84.

increase for a proposed new end would cause or the advantage that would result from its remission. (2) The possibility of voluntary agencies undertaking the work now carried out by the compulsory power of the State. Thus it should be a matter for deliberation how far Trade Unions could insist on sanitary provisions in factories, and associations of consumers guard against adulteration and fraud generally. The danger of weakening the spirit of association by hasty state intervention is not to be overlooked; all the more that it is inobtrusive and cannot be readily weighed. (3) The extent to which administrative action is really effectual in meeting evils, though of extreme importance, is not easily determined. Sweeping general propositions, to the effect 'that individuals do things better than the State,' or that 'the State does things better than individuals,' will not carry us far, but the inertness of human nature when relieved from the stimulus of direct self-interest, and the danger of official corruption, both suggest a presumption against state interference, a presumption it is true of very different force according to the case in which it is used. The solution of the problem belongs to the statesman, who will not form a less sound judgment by taking general principles into account.

It seems perfectly certain that administrative expenditure will continue to increase more rapidly than the cost of justice or police. These latter move with population; the cost of inspection and regulation grows much faster; it is, too, more divided and not so definitely ascertainable, and may therefore be regarded in common with military and naval expenditure as presenting the principal difficulty for the Finance of the future. Growing expenditure implies increased revenue or additional debt, and either means extra pressure on the subjects of the State. The duty of seeing that all outlay is productive of compensating advantage to the community is more than ever imperative.

§ 4. The relief of indigence is now in most countries one of the charges on the public revenue, and has even become at times—as in England under the old poor-law—a heavy burden; it has not however been assigned a prominent place in the estimates of outlay given by financial theorists. The reasons of this comparative neglect are not hard to find, for (1) it has generally been a local charge and has not found its way into the national budgets, which used to occupy most attention, and (2) the question of state relief of pauperism has been one of the contested questions of economic policy It is probable that Adam Smith, who does not mention poor-relief in his examination of public expenses, disapproved of any form of compulsory aid to distress, and his followers would in most cases take the same view[1]. But though we can thus explain the omission of poor-relief we cannot accept the reasons as sufficient. From the point of view of Public Finance it is immaterial whether the State acts through general or local authorities, e. g. in England before the Act of 1877, prisons were maintained by the counties, since the passing of that measure they are under the Prisons Commission, but in either case they involved a public charge. In regard to the second point Finance is engaged in dealing with facts, and therefore the existence of state aid to those in distress is a valid reason for examining the subject. We may at the same time admit that the question of expediency in this respect is a most difficult one, involving as it does reference to a number of political and economic considerations.

The problem presents itself in the following way. In all modern societies there are persons who, by reason of physical or moral causes, are unable to—or at least as a matter of fact do not—provide themselves with the means of subsistence. The question then arises what is to be done with this class? Ancient societies relieved themselves from the difficulty by the rude expedients of infanticide and slavery. The Middle Ages met it by the inculcation of private charity by the Church, and by the monastic institutions. In

[1] Ricardo, *Works* (ed. McCulloch), 58–9; Malthus on *Population* (8th ed.) 428 sq.

modern times the insufficiency and irregularity of private relief has led to state intervention. The break-up of the mediaeval system and the resulting economic disturbances made it an urgent matter of public policy to deal with distress. The greater power of the principal European monarchies also furnished the means in the shape of legislative action, prescribing and limiting the conditions of relief. The growth and expansion of the system of public relief is of itself an argument in favour of its expediency as meeting an evil common to all communities that have reached a certain stage of development [1].

This simple and obvious ground for the policy has been supported by several arguments of a more theoretical character. (1) Thus it has been urged that the State is 'bound' to relieve distress. The methods in use in ancient times for the suppression of indigence are happily impossible: private charity is not sufficiently regular, the State cannot with safety so far outrage the sentiments of its citizens as to allow even the poorest to perish by starvation, it therefore has an imperative duty to discharge in the relief of actual destitution. (2) Another contention appeals to justice rather than sentiment. If the relief of distress were left to voluntary exertions it would in fact amount to an extra tax imposed on the charitable, who would have to pay more than their due share; the niggardly escaping the payment of anything whatsoever towards what ought to be a common task. (3) In addition to justice amongst taxpayers, the plea of justice to the indigent may be advanced; it may be said that the real cause of destitution is the appropriation of the agents of production by private persons, and that consequently those in distress may fairly claim at least that minimum of subsistence probably attainable in a state of nature, or—to vary the

[1] 'Every society upon arriving at a certain stage of civilization finds it positively necessary for its own sake . . . to provide that no person . . . shall perish for want of the bare necessaries of existence.' Fowle, *Poor Law* (1st ed.) 10, who regards this as the 'general principle' and 'cause' of poor-law legislation.

argument slightly—the holders of property may justly be called on to pay the amount required for the relief of actual want in return for the benefits that they obtain from the present social organization, i. e. they are asked a 'ransom' for their possessions [1]. (4) To these somewhat abstract arguments, a more direct and practical one may be added. Under the present penal system [2] criminals are supported in a way that secures them a tolerable and healthy existence: now to deny to the pauper what is thus guaranteed to the criminal amounts to an inducement to crime.

The force of these several arguments, and the fact of the almost universal existence of public relief, would appear to leave no room for doubt on the subject, but we find to our surprise that a formidable list of arguments may be brought forward on the other side. The opponents of poor-relief contend (1) that to give support to the non-worker is essentially 'communistic' and that any such system has 'communism' as its logical result; (2) that aid to distress tends to act on population; that therefore an increasing number of applicants for assistance would present themselves, until at last the whole revenue of the community would be absorbed in their support; (3) that the state method of relief demoralizes the recipients, while (4) it interferes with the beneficial action of private charity and injuriously affects the moral sentiments both of givers and receivers. The more extreme foes of relief, public or private, would add (5) that all relief (and therefore public relief) discourages providence and saving. Almsgiving is —as Professor Newcomb puts it—'a demand for beggars [3].' The industrial and economic virtues are, it is said, weakened by every attempt at distributing aid. Finally (6) evidence has been adduced to show that poor relief lowers wages, since it allows the lowest sections of the population to work for less than the amount needed for

[1] Sidgwick, 'Economic Socialism,' *Fortnightly Review*, Sept., 1886.

[2] Bk. i. ch. 3. § 6.

[3] *Political Economy*, 526.

subsistence by the amount of relief that they get from the public authorities [1].

§ 5. To strike a true balance between the opposed arguments that have been just stated is indeed difficult, but for financial discussion it is possible to arrive at a satisfactory result. In the present position of most modern societies a methodised system of public relief is indispensable, and therefore forms a legitimate part of public outlay; nor is it hard to fix approximately the standard of relief. If the treatment of the pauper should be better than that of the criminal, it should on the contrary be worse than the standard of living of the poorest self-supporting labourer, and unhappily the limits as thus determined are very narrow. For financial as well as for social and moral reasons all relief should be given in the form prescribed by the State, i. e. generally 'indoor maintenance.' Assistance from public funds is not 'charity,' from which it should be clearly and distinctly separated, and in no way can this be better accomplished than by confining the action of the public agents engaged in relief to a definite sphere. It may be further said that in the administration of poor-relief the reformation of the habits of those who are indigent should be aimed at. What the habitual criminal is in the prison the hereditary pauper is in the poor-house. Expedients calculated to improve the *morale* of the destitute would powerfully affect the productive power of the nation.

The relations of private charity to the system of legal aid are of extreme importance. The absence of any connexion between the two classes of agency is a blot in most poor-law arrangements. We can hardly doubt that the contributions of private persons properly utilized would go very far towards meeting the necessary outlay on those in distress, with the double advantage of economizing the public funds for other objects, and preventing the evils that result from the existing abuses of almsgiving. Discrimination as to the causes of distress and consequently the amount of relief

[1] See J. E. T. Rogers, *Economic Interpretation of History*, 487.

can be properly applied only through the operation of private beneficence.

§ 6. In addition to the direct method of assisting actual distress the State has been often called on to meet the difficulty indirectly, either by a system of public works or by compulsory insurance on the part of the workers. The assertion of the 'right to obtain work' supplied by the State is distinctly of French origin[1]. It has never obtained full recognition in practice, as the difficulties it would cause are evidently insuperable. The provision of work, the mode of supervision, the rate of pay, and the disposal of the products, are each and all so many obstacles in the way of its adoption. The economic effect on the whole working class would moreover be surely evil; the expenditure would be indefinite and not capable of easy control. 'Compulsory insurance,' as advocated in England and in some degree carried out in Germany, presents greater advantages, and seems a more hopeful idea, but it, too, is open to the grave *financial* objections that the collection of the insurance charges is likely to be ineffective in a country where labour is allowed full freedom of movement, while it involves the State in serious financial operations, and at the same time weakens the action of voluntary effort. The English friendly societies insure a large number of the more provident artisans, and have been favourably contrasted with the foreign state insurance bodies by Mr. Goschen[2]. A strict administration of public relief encourages the habit of insurance or other provision against distress, and the development of such methods of self-help makes it easier for the State to adhere to the rigid policy of relieving nothing except absolute indigence.

[1] *Droit au Travail* quite different from the *Droit du Travail.*

[2] *Addresses*, 113 sq.

CHAPTER V

EDUCATION. RELIGION.

§ 1. THE recognition of education as one of the tasks of the State was a natural result of the decline of the influence of the Church. The innumerable religious institutions and endowments of the Middle Ages had provided instruction for youth as they had provided sustenance for those in need, and when their endowments were in great part seized by the different European sovereigns some provision in their place or by their diversion to the supply of education was obviously suggested. Even the theorists of the eighteenth century hesitated to exclude the duty of assisting education from the sphere of state operations. The Physiocrats and Adam Smith agreed in recommending state aid to education, but only under such conditions as would encourage efficiency in the teachers with industry and application in their pupils[1]. Since their time the tendency has been towards the extension of public effort in all the departments of education. The question presents itself in connexion with each of the three forms of teaching, primary, secondary or intermediate, and university.

§ 2. In respect to primary education we may note the distinct expression of opinion by Adam Smith in favour of

[1] The attitude of the Physiocrats on the subject of education is remarkable, and helps us to understand their general conception of state policy. It was not so much *interference* as *injurious interference* that they opposed, but they felt that all state action had elements of evil in its disturbance of voluntary action, and its expense. Turgot, ii. 502–551, *Mémoire sur les Municipalités*, said to be the composition of Du Pont de Nemours. Cp. Schelle, 362 sq.

state facilities for this form of teaching. The success of the Scotch parish schools had evidently impressed him, and he contends with great force that the increased division of labour due to economic progress tends to weaken the faculties of the workman—and that this evil can only be counteracted by education. The State has, moreover, he thinks, a direct interest in the education of the bulk of the people in order to secure political tranquillity [1]. A mild form of compulsion is even allowable, since he suggests that passing an examination should be a necessary preliminary to entry into a trade. Adam Smith does not advocate free education, but his reason is curious, viz. that the teacher's diligence is stimulated by the receipt of fees, an aim that would be otherwise reached through the present result-fees' system.

During the present century the state-guided system of primary instruction has become definitively established, as an examination of the details of expenditure will most clearly show. The development of this system has brought out the existence of several difficulties imperfectly recognised at its commencement. Among those are:—(1) The problem of religious teaching; denominational schools, are offensive to one section, undenominational ones to another; and both the amount and application of state funds is hotly contested by the different parties. (2) Distinct from the foregoing, but connected with it is the relation of state to voluntary schools. If no fees are charged, the private schools, in competition with the public ones, complain of the unfairness, which indeed is manifest. On the other hand, fees—especially if education is compulsory—press heavily on the poorer parents. (3) When, to avoid some of the foregoing puzzles, payment by results is made, there is a danger of superficial preparation, and yet without some test of the kind, efficiency cannot easily be measured. The only complete escape from such difficulties would be the abandonment of instruction to voluntary effort, a solution which

[1] *Wealth of Nations*, 329–30. An argument also urged by Malthus, *Essay on Population* (8th ed.), 437 sq.

is forbidden by the importance of education both socially and economically, as also by the practical impossibility of securing it without state aid in the case of the very poor.

§ 3. Secondary education is in a very different position. The older economists would abandon it to the action of individual and family interest. There is, it would appear, no pressing ground for state exertion in order to supply instruction superior to that enjoyed by the whole population. It may, therefore, reasonably be left to private initiative or to voluntary effort, more particularly in the form—too often disregarded by economic and financial theorists—of endowments by gift or bequest. The modern tendency is here, too, in favour of an extension of state action, generally directed rather to supervision and readjustment of existing resources than to the supply of additional funds. In some instances special agencies for testing the quality of secondary education, either by inspection or examination, have been created [1]. From the financial point of view it must be said that outlay of this kind is not to be placed in the same rank with that in aid of the primary instruction of a country. At best it belongs to the class of useful outlay, and is very likely to be supplied by private funds. It, moreover, is open to the objection of benefiting but one, and that the most independent, section of the population. Against these weaknesses it may claim to be of a moderate character, and not likely to seriously affect national finance.

§ 4. Universities or, more generally, institutions for higher education have to be judged on special grounds so far as their claims for state aid are concerned. It is quite true, as Adam Smith shows, that the higher education in many cases is not a necessity but rather a luxury or ornament that may very well be paid for by the wealthy, if they desire it for themselves or their families. In most of the remaining instances it is a legitimate investment in immaterial or personal capital, a point of view that pre-

[1] Provisions of the kind were made for Ireland in the Intermediate Education Act, 1878, and for Wales in its Act, 1889.

dominates in the minds of the professional and commercial classes, so that on either supposition there is no call for public intervention. State or other endowments have, besides, the injurious effect of checking the easy remodelling of the system of higher instruction in accordance with the inevitable changes in scientific and literary studies [1]. There is unfortunately a tendency on the part of highly paid permanent teachers to take their work in a mechanical manner, and expend their energies in other directions. The result of such considerations leads to the suggestion of thorough reform in the mode of higher education rather than complete surrender on the part of the State of its regulating functions, more especially when some less obvious parts of the working of Universities are taken into account.

The modern University has very different elements and may be looked at from different points of view. In the *first* place it is a grouping of professional schools, and here the tendency towards extended administrative action almost compels the State to form closer relations with the larger teaching bodies. The increase in the number of professions, entry into which is granted only on supposed proof of competence as evidenced by examinations and courses of study obtainable solely by means of attendance at a University College, affords a strong reason for offering facilities towards getting the necessary instruction. When the State imposes on candidates for various offices or professions the obligation of having a University Degree or something similar, it is in fairness bound to supply them with reasonable opportunities for acquiring that needful badge. Moreover, many parts of administrative work

[1] 'The improvements which in modern times have been made in several different branches of philosophy, have not the greater part of them been made in Universities. . . . The greater part of Universities have not even been very forward to adopt those improvements after they were made, and several of those learned societies have chosen to remain . . . the sanctuaries in which exploded systems and obsolete prejudices found shelter and protection after they had been hunted out of every other corner of the world.' *Wealth of Nations*, 323.

could hardly be carried on without the aid of the scientific skill maintained by the teaching bodies.

Secondly, the importance of scientific research in its effects on the production of wealth and in dealing with many social problems is now abundantly recognised. Even literary and historical inquiries are found in many cases to be of practical service and to powerfully aid in the advance of culture. The 'endowment of research' is a matter, if not of practical politics, at least of discussion. A University, however, is, or at least ought to be, the home of research, and its support by the State may be claimed on the ground that it discharges this most valuable function. Possessing these two departments which may reasonably expect aid from public funds a University naturally adds to them a third in supplying to the richer members of the society the ornamental education or 'culture' that they demand and are willing to pay for. By this combination it is further possible to stimulate the teachers by fees that will largely depend on the reputation and credit of the institution where they are placed.

§ 5. The question of 'technical' as opposed to general education presents itself in all the stages of instruction and in each it raises the same problems. The evident economic advantage that a nation obtains through the skill of its producers is a *primâ facie* ground for state aid being given towards the attainment of suitable training. Expenditure for such an object is productive even in a financial point of view, and it may be further argued that individual or family interest will not suffice to accomplish the end desired. On the other hand the sturdier individualists urge that self-interest, if good for anything, should surely be good for inciting men to learn in the most efficient manner the trades or occupations by which they have to earn a livelihood. The same general result is reached here as elsewhere, viz. that the true test is experience, and it shows that public outlay may be of advantage in promoting industrial training though it is subject to the inevitable drawback of all state interference in its tendency to reduce private exertion, and in the difficulty of duly regulating the supply of skilled labour called out by its action. The acquisition of training for unprofitable employments is no slight evil and under the rigid system of regulation inseparable from official management it is not unlikely to occur. Even general education may produce a *surmenage scolaire*, as the example of France shows.

§ 6. Under the same head the cost of museums, libraries, picture galleries, and institutions for promoting science and art generally should be placed. They come in to supplement the more directly educational agencies and are often quite as effective in promoting the ends aimed at. The modern development in this domain is remarkable (especially in England and the United States). Central and local authorities have both made considerable efforts in the direction of meeting the wants of the population for opportunities of acquiring information and culture. Few large towns are without appliances that were unknown a century ago or confined to national capitals. We have to add this expenditure to the cost of schools and colleges before we can say what is the total sacrifice incurred by a nation in its public capacity for the object of culture.

§ 7. Voluntary action may be expected to relieve the revenues of the State from a great deal of this charge. Not only are the expenses of education largely met by the normal economic process of payment for advantages obtained; the donations and bequests of the wealthy have supplied, and we may hope will continue to supply, a good many of the less profitable fields of instruction and research with sufficient endowment. The splendid example set by American millionaires may produce good effect in Europe by attracting attention to the benefits of supporting the educational and investigating bodies to which civilization owes so much [1].

[1] Cp. Cohn, § 150.

In any case it must be said that no modern State is likely to suffer financial embarrassment through its outlay in promoting education and culture. Measured against the cost of war and preparation for war, this form of expenditure is modest and inconspicuous in the total amount, and taken with its probable advantages it is the least questionable of the many secondary heads of charge.

§ 8. The relations of Church and State have been at different periods the principal problem of rulers. The earlier sentiment rather included the State in the Church than the Church in the State. Modern societies are practically agreed in reversing this position. Excluding the polemical sides of the subject we can see that for the financier the religious wants of the community need the supply of particular forms of services and commodities, and the question arises whether the public authority should provide these needed objects or leave them to private effort. Historical conditions have determined the actual solution in each country, while the prevalent theoretical view is derived from the doctrines of the last century. Adam Smith, who approached the subject under the influence of Hume [1], regards the clergy as a particular form of police attending to spiritual interests. His ideal is complete non-intervention on the part of the State. The probable result would be 'a great multitude of religious sects' whose fanaticism might be kept in check by the two remedies of: (*a*) 'the study of science and philosophy,' and (*b*) 'the frequency and gaiety of public diversions.' Where, however, there is one predominant religion the State ought, he thinks, to regulate and control or, to use his significant term, to 'manage' it—a process that is best carried out by the skilful use of the power of bestowing preferment. Religious endowments are regarded as a part of

[1] See his quotation from the latter (*History of England*, ch. 29) whom he describes as 'by far the most illustrious philosopher and historian of the present age,' 331.

state wealth withdrawn from the more pressing end of defence[1].

The circumstances of the case have, it need hardly be said, been profoundly altered since 1776. The United States now afford a remarkable example of the actual working of the policy of *laissez faire* in respect to religion[2], and they are imitated by the English colonies. Continental nations show a different set of changes: the 'Established Churches' with their numerous independent and private funds have given place to bodies directly chargeable on the state revenues. The 'enlightened absolutism' of the eighteenth century commenced the work of disendowment, which was further carried out by the revolutionary movements since 1789. Later reaction has made the clergy pensioners of the State. As regards the United Kingdom, the American example has for special reasons been followed in Ireland and seems likely to be extended to Great Britain.

Viewing the question as one of Finance it appears that the expenditure on religion, though not large, can be easily supplied by voluntary contributions, and therefore is not an urgent call on public resources which can be better used for other objects. When the State for political motives undertakes the supervision of religion and its supply, concurrent endowment is a necessity in modern societies, as otherwise an evident injustice would be inflicted on the non-endowed sects. Such is the policy of most States at present, but it is more expensive owing to the greater number of ministers, buildings, &c., that have to be provided.

The provision for religious teaching has a rather close affinity to that for education proper. Modern budgets

[1] 'The revenue of every established church . . . is a branch, it ought to be observed, of the general revenue of the State, which is thus diverted to a purpose very different from the defence of the State,' 341.

[2] 'Congress shall make no law respecting an establishment of religion,' *First Amendment to U. S. Constitution.* Some State constitutions contain a similar provision. Bryce, *American Commonwealth* (2nd ed.), ii. 570–1.

often combine the two charges under a single head. There is also an historical connexion between them, and it is noticeable that in countries, such as the United States and the English colonies, where state endowment of religion is given up, educational bodies take the vacant place. Public expenditure for *denominational* education is a near approximation to State aid to religion.

CHAPTER VI.

EXPENDITURE ON INDUSTRY AND COMMERCE. CONSTITUTIONAL AND DIPLOMATIC EXPENDITURE.

§ 1. EXPENDITURE for directly economic objects has often occupied a large place in public outlay. To foster industry and commerce was long regarded as a leading function of the State. In fact, it is to this conception that we owe the origin of Finance and Political Economy[1]. The great object of the *Cameralwissenschaft* of the 18th century was to give instruction as to the right direction of national resources, and most of the earlier economic writers of France and England held that it was very important to encourage economic enterprise.

The complete revolution wrought by the combined labours of the Physiocrats and Adam Smith exonerated the State from this difficult, indeed impossible, task ; but it is a vulgar error to suppose that the advocates of industrial liberty did not recognise certain definite duties of the State in economic matters. Apart from the exaggerations inevitable in so violent a change of opinion, we see that the sound sense of Adam Smith and Turgot fully understood that in several directions the Government could beneficially aid the efforts of producers[2]. The necessities of practice have made it incumbent on States to undertake a series of duties intended for the advantage of industry and commerce.

[1] Introduction, Part ii.

[2] *Wealth of Nations*, Bk. v. ch. 1. part 3. art. 1. 303 sq. Cp. Turgot's statement of Gournay's views in the 'Éloge,' i. 279.

There is, however, a distinction to be made at the outset. In one sense all state expenditure may be said to be for the benefit of industry. The armies and navies of modern States are productive of the security needed for the protection of industrial effort. The administration of justice and the maintenance of an efficient police have the same effect. A great deal of administrative supervision has, or is supposed to have, considerable influence in increasing production. One of the strongest pleas for aid to education is based on its economic value, and writers of the School of Hume would regard the inculcation of honesty and frugality as the most useful function of the clergy. So close is the *consensus* of social phenomena that there is no part of public expenditure that may not aid the progress of economic production.

§ 2. Besides this more general action of the State on industry, there is a special one. Portions of the public revenue are devoted to objects either solely or principally economic; and it is the employment of this part that we have now to consider. It again may be divided into expenditure on industry and commerce generally, and that on special trades or employments. Of the former we may notice the following as the most usual:

(1) The cost of maintaining a monetary system, as in the case of the English gold coinage.

(2) The establishment and preservation of a system of weights and measures.

(3) The enactment (as in some countries) of a commercial code with possibly a special tribunal or tribunals.

(4) Agencies for facilitating communication and transport, viz. post offices, telegraphic communication, roads, railways, and canals. In the same group may be included lighthouses, surveys of coasts or new countries.

(5) Consular and diplomatic establishments chiefly for the benefit of foreign trade, but with an indirect action on home industry.

The slightest glance at the above list at once suggests a

criticism. Some of the agencies included will, under proper management, yield a profit to the State, and therefore more fitly belong to the domain of state industry. The English Post Office and the Prussian railways earn large net revenues for the States to which they belong, and the currency system may, by the imposition of a seigniorage be made to cover its cost, and probably leave a surplus. The answer to this difficulty is not hard to find. Granting the truth of the assertion on which it rests, the fact remains that in many cases the State has to incur cost for the objects mentioned. The gains of post offices and railways will be noticed in the proper place [1]. There are, however, some that have a recurring deficit [2], which has to be met out of the funds derived from other sources. We get but one more illustration of the difficulty of drawing 'hard and fast lines' in social inquiry. What is in one country a cause of expenditure, is in another a source of gain as a state industry, while in a third it yields revenue through taxation.

§ 3. State aid to special branches of industry presents much greater opening for objections; but here, too, suitable cases present themselves. Among these are:—

(1) The introduction of new and profitable industries. In modern times this part of state action has been usually carried out by means of protective duties. The so-called 'infant industry' argument is one of the best of the protectionist pleas, and its theoretic force has been recognised by most economists, but the question is really a wider one. The problem before the statesman amounts to this: How far is it expedient to incur a present loss for a future gain? And on the financial side the balance of the different public wants, as also the percentage of the national income absorbed by the State, are elements to be taken into account in the actual solution. In its simplest form encouragement is given by means of bounties on production or premiums

[1] Bk. ii. ch. 3; Bk. iv. ch. 8.

[2] E. g. the Indian and Canadian Posts and most of the continental state railways.

for the establishment of new industries. A protective duty may be regarded as a tax on the consumption of the protected article with an equivalent bounty to the home producer; it is, therefore, in reality more complicated than a simple bounty. This aspect of the matter may be reserved for a later stage of our inquiry[1]; but here we have to note the difficulty of escaping corruption and favouritism in the application of a policy of encouragement. In an undeveloped industrial system such aids, if applied with wisdom, may afford a beneficial stimulus, as was probably the case with some of the measures of mediaeval sovereigns. They, in some degree, occupy in economic policy the place that despotic government holds in political evolution, but appear quite unfitted for a progressive system of industry[2]. The direct support of special branches of production from the public revenue is sure to be a diminishing item of charge in modern countries.

(2) The promotion of inventions, by the inducement of state premiums, or even the encouragement of a higher standard of excellence in production by the same means, has been regarded without disapproval by Adam Smith. Their effect is not to disturb the natural distribution of employments; besides, as he remarks, their cost is insignificant[3]. A good patent law will, however, be the most effectual way of facilitating invention[4].

(3) The periodical holding of exhibitions of industrial products under state auspices, and in fact at the state's expense, is now an established custom, though it is probable that the need of agencies of the kind is at present less than it formerly was.

[1] Bk. iv. ch. 7.

[2] The fact that the Anglo-Indian government has adopted a policy of non-intervention so far as industry is directly concerned is the more remarkable, since, if ever there were a case where rulers might be supposed to be fitted by superior wisdom and insight to direct their subjects, this would be one.

[3] 213.

[4] See *Quarterly Journal of Economics*, Oct. 1890, 44–69 ('A Century of Patent Law,' by Chauncey Smith), for the effects of the United States patent laws.

(4) Model institutions, such as agricultural schools, &c. are also frequently formed.

(5) State subvention of railways and means of transport for the improvement of the poorer districts of a country.

(6) Outlay on the administration of forests and drainage is, in many countries, an important part of the *economic* expenditure of the State. The former seems more properly to belong to the subject of the 'public domain' as it usually gives a surplus.

(7) The support of credit institutions and assistance by loans is also more fittingly discussed in a later part of our inquiry.

§ 4. Finally, we should remark that the State may find itself called on to act in relation to any economic interest of the society that it regulates. There is no strict and universally binding rule that can mark off the area of its action. The protest of *laissez faire* was directed against the policy of continual interference. The intervention of the public power should, however, be only admitted on clear and definite proof of its advantage. The best safeguard against excessive state action is to be found in insistence on a careful calculation of all the elements entering into each case, and more especially of the financial relations that it necessitates.

The actual figures of modern budgets do not indicate much danger from the purely economic action of the State. Some exceptional cases occur where the zeal of politicians has led them to develop the system of public works beyond legitimate limits. Thus the several States of the American Union at one time engaged in a reckless policy of internal improvements that culminated in the repudiations of 1840–50[1]. The plans of the French Minister, De Freycinet, for railway extension were also arranged on too extensive a scale, as their subsequent abandonment proved. The public works of India have furnished a ground for bitter controversy; but the opponents of the policy have not

[1] H. C. Adams, *Public Debts*, 317–342.

made out their case, though under the special circumstances of the country greater moderation might have been advisable[1].

§ 5. We have kept one of the most essential parts of state expenditure for the last—that incurred for the maintenance of the central organs of the State itself. No matter what be the form of government, the head of the State, 'the Sovereign' in Adam Smith's phraseology, must be supported. Round this personal head are grouped the various branches of the executive, and in some relation to it the legislative body also exists. In a so-called constitutional or 'limited' monarchy—the prevalent European form of this century—the head of the State may possess a private income, but is far more likely to be paid out of the Civil List. The royal or crown lands are generally absorbed in the public domain, and in any case they must in strictness be regarded as a portion of public property set apart from the general funds for a specific public object. This application of public revenue is necessary, though it often excites an amount of popular irritation that might be more advantageously exercised in other directions[2]. The head of the State is frequently called on to discharge ornamental functions requiring a good deal of expenditure, and has, moreover, to hold a higher position than the wealthiest of his subjects.

§ 6. A republican State is partly relieved from this expense; its head, usually elected for a short term, receives the salary of a minister in monarchical States. There is, however, a counterbalancing cost in the expenditure on the numerous members of the corporate sovereign[3]. Nearly

[1] Cp. Fawcett, *Indian Finance*. For a vigorous defence see Strachey, *The Finances and Public Works of India* (1869–1881).

[2] For the position of the King's revenues, *infra*, Bk. ii. ch. 2. Cp. Roscher, §§ 9, 117; Wagner, i. 401 sq.

[3] A comparison of the cost of the English Monarchy and Parliament with that of the United States President and Congress, shows that the latter is on the whole more expensive. This curious circumstance is the consequence of the non-payment of the members of the English Houses. Admirers of the American

all democratic societies approve of payment to legislators in order to reduce the chances against poor men being elected. The inevitable result is an increase in the cost of the legislative body, and when the same principle is applied to subordinate legislatures, a further increase has to be faced. The belief that legislative efficiency is improved by reward does not appear well-founded so far as Finance is concerned. We must remember, too, that historical conditions, and particularly the way in which wealth is distributed, have considerable effect in determining the wisest course. Thus the English colonies that possess responsible government are perhaps justified in departing from the English method of unpaid legislators. At the same time, there is an unquestionable advantage in the development of public spirit produced by the English system. One point is certain, viz. that the least satisfactory method of all is the granting of small payments which do not attract the best men, while they discourage those who would serve without any salary. The danger of corruption and jobbing is also brought to its highest in the case of ill-paid legislators who are inclined to supplement their official incomes by less honourable means.

The expenditure on diplomatic agents and ambassadors may perhaps be best placed under the present head. Such outlay is hard to classify. It might be plausibly regarded as incurred for the sake of securing peace, and so be added to the cost of the military and naval services. Or again, it might be regarded as expenditure for economic objects, viz. the promotion of trade, as the consular service undoubtedly is. But on the whole the diplomatic staff is really representative of the sovereign, and is entitled to its present position.

§ 7. In nearly every civilized country the charge of interest on debt has to be considered. We shall have to

system would remark that British peers and M.P.'s obtain indirect rewards, that are still less to the advantage of their country.

examine fully the theory of public credit and debt, and therefore need only mention it here as an item of outlay.

When dealing with the mechanism of the financial system, we shall have to distinguish carefully between gross and net revenue, the former being the total receipts, the latter the net result deducting the cost of collection and the expenses necessary for obtaining the required resources. Here we have simply to note these charges as one of the parts of public expenditure, and to see how large an item they are. In England the Customs, the Inland Revenue, and the Post Office are mainly earning departments. The mere mention of these establishments will suggest the remarkable differences in the relation of revenue to cost of collecting or earning it. Savings in this respect are as important as those made in connexion with outlay on other state functions, but any reduction of cost which impairs the efficiency of the fiscal service is as imprudent as over-retrenchment in other directions.

The cost of collection or earning of revenue in the leading English Departments is as follows:—

TABLE (000's omitted).

	Customs.			Inland Revenue.			Post Office.		
Year.	*Receipts.*	*Cost of Collection.*	*Percentage.*	*Receipts.*	*Cost of Collection.*	*Percentage.*	*Receipts.*	*Cost of Collection.*	*Percentage.*
	£	£		£	£		£	£	
1875	19,289	1,022	5·3	44,681	1,672	3·7	6,885	5,077	74·
1880	19,327	973	5·	48,500	1,810	3·6	7,874	5,212	65·
1890	28,424	905	4·5	53,768	1,749	3·2	11,774	8,303	71·

In 1806 a gross revenue of £58,255,000 cost £2,797,000 to collect or 4·8 per cent., while in 1826 the charge for collecting £54,840,000 was £4,030,000, i. e. 7·3 per cent.

In France the total expense of collection for the last ten years has averaged about £13,000,000, but of this amount £5,000,000 should be charged to the postal and telegraphic service and nearly £3,000,000 to the expenses of the tobacco monopoly, leaving a balance of £5,000,000 for the cost of collecting the direct and indirect taxes[1].

[1] Leroy Beaulieu, i. 267 sq.; Wagner, iii. 432–4, 607–10.

Having concluded our brief survey of the forms of state expenditure, we have now to summarize the results, as also to develope some points that could not be properly treated until the several heads of the public services had been duly noticed. There is, however, one topic that must be first discussed, viz. the distribution of state outlay between the central and local powers.

CHAPTER VII.

CENTRAL AND LOCAL EXPENDITURE.

§ 1. UP to the present we have taken no notice (except incidentally) of the division of duties between the central and local organs of the State. For the object that we had in view, this mode of treatment was quite legitimate. In order to bring out the fact that all expenditure by public bodies is really one in kind, and that any differences are subordinate and secondary, it is advisable to set forth the leading forms of that expenditure in a general and comprehensive manner. The principles that determine the distribution of public functions between central and local powers, or even between federal and state governments, though highly important and influential on financial policy, are yet immaterial when we are considering the broad grouping and effect of the cost of maintaining those compulsory agencies that we place together under the title of 'the State,' and the expediency of extending or contracting their field of operations. It is, besides, impossible to draw a precise and definite line applicable to all or most countries between general and local expenditure. What is retained in one country or period in the hands of the central authority is in other places or times delegated to subordinate bodies; or to regard the subject from a different aspect, which is in some cases more in accordance with historical fact, the older and smaller groups have reserved from the encroachments of the State very different amounts of power in different ages and nations.

Examples of this diversity in usage are abundant. The transfer of the English prisons from local to central management has been already mentioned[1]. The older system of poor-relief in England was purely local. The great reform of 1834, though it did not go the length of making the aid of the indigent a national charge, yet accepted, and was based on, the recommendations of the Poor Law Commission, in favour of complete and efficient regulation of local administration by a specially formed central board. The treatment of primary education affords another example; in England and Wales it is largely under local management, while in Ireland the national school system is strictly centralized. The police systems of the United Kingdom also show like differences in administration.

On extending our view to other nations we find that this absence of uniformity is general. The powers of a Swiss Canton or an American State are far greater than those of an English County or a French Department. Even limiting the comparison to countries with substantially similar constitutions there still is much variety in the actual division of duties.

§ 2. Such remarkable differences have arisen from more than a single cause, but undoubtedly the most powerful reason is to be found in the peculiar historical conditions under which States have been formed and developed[2]. To explain e.g. the diversities in the distribution of public duties in France and Germany, recourse must be had to history. In no other way is a full interpretation possible. The centralized system of French administration goes back to the Revolution of 1789; it is a product of the absolute monarchy and of the consequent impossibility of developing local authorities[3]. The greater division of state power in

[1] *Supra*, Bk. i. ch. 4. § 4.

[2] 'Es ist vor allen Dingen der Reichthum historischer Veranlassungen und historischer Besonderheiten, welcher diese Verschiedenheiten erklärt.' Cohn, § 115. Cp. Thorold Rogers, *Economic Interpretation of History*, chap. 22.

[3] Tocqueville, *Ancien Régime*, Livr. ii. ch. 2 (Eng. Trans. 40 sq.).

Germany is one result of the unhappy conflicts that prevented its attaining to national unity till the present century. In order to comprehend it we must know the history of the Holy Roman Empire and its many changes. Exactly similar is the case of Switzerland or the United States; each is the product of special conditions. The nature of American state and local governments is affected by the circumstances of the colonial institutions from which they have sprung. At all stages of formation this influence is powerful. It is due to the particular events of the time that Italy at almost a single step reached the full unity of France or England, while Germany as yet retains so many traces of the process by which it has been formed. There is nothing of rigorous necessity in the course of development; circumstances that may be regarded as accidental have had most effect in deciding the result, and there seems, consequently, little place for the employment of scientific explanation in so purely empirical a matter.

Historical conditions are, however, often the result of deeper forces; the political destiny of a nation is not altogether at the mercy of events. The physical features of its territory, the character and sentiments of its members, go a long way in determining its constitution. We cannot doubt that the mountains of Switzerland and the enthusiasm of its citizens for independence have contributed towards the great vitality of its local institutions, but then it is also true that circumstances somewhat analogous have not hindered Holland from becoming a centralized state.

§ 3. The most complete recognition of the preponderating influence of historical and physical agencies in determining the actual division of state duties between the central body and the local ones ought not to prevent us from endeavouring—as far as possible—to disentangle from the mass of material any ascertainable general principles. There seem to be—quite apart from national peculiarities—some tendencies operative in all societies which assign particular duties to the central agency and place others under local supervision. An examination of the several public wants will we believe confirm this view, showing that some of them can be best satisfied by local management, and that others should, in order to attain the desired object, be supplied through the central organization of the State.

In making this distribution by reference to general principles it is necessary to take into account the historical influences that we have previously noticed. They partly determine, not only what are, but what should be general and what should be local tasks. What has been for a long time confided to local administration ought not without good reason to be transferred to the general government, as on the other hand where, from any cause, little has been left to local action, the devolution of tasks by the central administration should be gradual and cautious.

§ 4. Additional light is thrown on the leading principles and present position of the distribution of powers between local and central organs by consideration of the fact that two different tendencies have been in operation during the course of history. Political evolution is not a direct movement towards a definite goal; it is rather a series of efforts following the line of least resistance at any given time. Early societies do not exhibit the opposition or distinction between central and local powers. All government is local, either in the tribal system as found in Germany, or in the city states of Greece and Italy. War—and its result conquest—is the introducer of centralization. The smaller groups are unable to withstand the successful military chief and have to submit to his rule. The municipal governments of the classical age—for such they were in fact—passed at last under the dominion of Rome, which gives us the picture of a vast administrative organization employing local authorities as the instruments of its working. The autonomous city was in practice reduced to take commands even as to the smallest details from the Emperor and his officials. Some place for local co-operation was allowed under the earlier Empire, and up to the last the expenditure of towns was distinct and separate from that of the Imperial government[1].

Mediaeval society shows a movement towards the revival of local privileges. In all European countries the cities succeeded in acquiring a large amount of freedom in dealing with their own affairs. In some countries—as Italy—they almost reached independence, and in all they were enabled to apply their resources to objects of local interest. One of the principal features of the steadily growing consolidation of states in modern times has been the reduction in power of the various semi-independent bodies within the state[2]. Provincial liberties were curtailed, and particular immunities, whether of towns, districts, or associations, had to give way to the rule of uniform rights and duties. With great varieties in the process in different countries the same general result was reached, viz. the absorption of all independent political forces in the single organ of the State. This point was sooner attained in England than in France, and in France than in other continental states, but, except where a federal system has preserved the authority of one group of bodies, it is now accomplished in all civilized societies.

The establishment of a controlling and legally omnipotent government, though it marks an important stage in political growth, is nevertheless accompanied by some disadvantages. However desirable it may be that the powers of a nation should not be weakened by the existence in its midst of powerful bodies in a position to frustrate the attempts of its rulers to act with vigour and decision in a given way, and however much society may suffer from the absence of political cohesion, it is not conducive to the interests of the nation to concentrate all administrative power in a single centre. The gains from centralization may be great, but to obviate the evils that accompany it

[1] For the division of expenditure between the state treasuries and the towns, see Humbert, *Essai sur les Finances*, i. 208, 389–401, 411–417.

[2] Roscher, § 156; also his *Ackerbau*, §§ 5 sq.

a wise decentralization is also requisite. Having secured political unity, it becomes the task of the statesman to so distribute the powers of government as to obtain the best political and financial results. The earlier historical movement that has led to combination needs to be supplemented and corrected by the rational process of division of duties. All modern societies have to see whether their present institutions strike the mean in this respect, and if not, how they can best attain it.

§ 5. The relations of the administrative organs become more complex as States increase in size. A small society has no need of intermediate political forms between the lowest unit and the State, but in countries with the area and population of the great European powers or the United States something more is wanting. Between the 'parish' or 'township'—the 'primitive cell' of the political organism—and the central government there are found one or more bodies essentially subordinate to the latter, but of greater range and larger resources than the former. Thus France has the canton, arondissement, and department; Prussia, the district, the circle, and the province; England, the union and the county; the United States, the county and the state or 'commonwealth'; and in each nation a different class of duties is assigned in proportion to the size and importance of the particular body.

The complexities of local government and Finance have in some countries been increased by the irregular and almost haphazard method of expansion adopted. Instead of following a definite and orderly plan, each special need has been met by a special creation. This natural but unfortunate method of procedure is characteristic of English and in some degree of American legislation. Where a new local duty has been marked out, a new area with a separate board has been formed, ideas of uniformity or co-ordination being almost ostentatiously disregarded. The outcome in England has been, according to Mr. Goschen's often-quoted phrase, 'a chaos as regards authorities, a chaos as regards rates, and a worse chaos than all as regards areas[1].' Something similar is the case in a few American States. 'In many of our commonwealths,' says Professor Seligman, 'there are separate local taxes for almost every purpose of local expenditure. In New Jersey, e.g. we find no less than forty such separate taxes[2].' The reason for this confusion is only discoverable by considering the usual conception of local governing bodies; they were regarded rather as associations for a particular end than as delegations of the public power, and it is in fact true that the smaller subdivisions do approximate more closely to private groups in proportion as their sphere of action is reduced. The generally unsystematic character of English legislation also favoured this extreme multiplication of local functions arranged on no definite plan.

Political organization developed on perfectly logical principles would offer a decided contrast to the multiplicity of arrangements just described. It would be symmetrical and convenient to a degree that no country—not even France—can lay claim to at present. In actual political life, perfectly-adjusted plans of the kind are inapplicable. Constructive legislation is hindered by the nature of the materials that are at hand. The correct and well-fitted plan will not work by reason first of all of the varying circumstances of different districts. Rural areas are suited for a simple kind of local government that would utterly fail if applied to towns or cities. The latter require a more elaborate and careful system; their expenditure is sure to be much greater, and even if part of it be what is called 'productive' and likely to afford counterbalancing receipts, there is still a greater amount of energy and toil required in working their Finances, and special provisions are needed to prevent abuses[3]. In many countries, however, backward

[1] *Local Taxation*, 190.

[2] *Finance Statistics of the American Commonwealths*, 108.

[3] Rules limiting expenditure, and so raising a barrier against abuses, are in such cases very useful, and seem to be growing in favour both in the United Kingdom and the United States.

agricultural districts are often transformed in a few years into seats of manufactures and commerce, making alterations in the form of local government essential[1]. Some particular interests are also so important as to need special treatment. The management of harbours, river navigation, and drainage, or of great public works created at the cost of the State may have to be placed under bodies formed to represent the interests chiefly concerned, and they must be kept apart from the general system, and so far mar its completeness[2].

The necessity for attending to geographical boundaries tends to prevent even an approximation to divisions with equal areas or population, and special local habits and customs act with the same effect. But the greatest check in this direction arises from constitutional restraints. Perfectly unified governments such as those of France and England are seemingly free from this defect. There is nothing in English law to prevent Parliament from abolishing the divisions into counties and parishes and substituting a new one in its place. The whole machinery of municipal administration might at the same time be handed over to a central board with an official staff[3]. The federal countries—Germany, Switzerland, the United States—are differently situated. The power of constitutional legislation is distributed in a more complex manner, with the intention and result of checking its frequent exercise. Such 'rigid' constitutions —as they have been happily called—give a permanence to particular local divisions that prevents the powers of administration being divided in accordance with theoretical conceptions. A Swiss Canton or American State claims a

[1] The number of new towns that have sprung up in England, Germany, and above all in America, during the last fifty years, makes this point important.

[2] The Harbour and Dock Boards very common in England, elected under special franchises and with powers to levy tolls, are a good example.

[3] Every one knows that Parliament will do neither of the things mentioned in the text, but the limitations on its action are *moral*, not *legal*, and consist in the fear of exciting opposition on the part of the people, and in its own sentiments, i. e. they are external and internal. Cp. Dicey, *Law of the Constitution*, Lect. ii.

legal position essentially different from that of a County or Department. It is prior in order of time to the central government, towards whose creation it may be said to have contributed, and it is entitled to object to measures affecting its existence[1]. Whatever be the reasons in favour of this system—and we need not undervalue them—it is a fatal barrier to orderly and proportionate distribution of functions. Delaware and Rhode Island, insignificant both in population and area, hold the same place as the great States of New York, Pennsylvania, and Texas; Berne, with more than half a million of people, is only equal to Uri, with less than one-twentieth of that number.

Difficulties of the kind just noticed are not in reality so serious as they at first appear. To begin with, the intractableness is found in one only of the minor groups or subdivisions; the others can be easily adjusted. Congress cannot indeed re-distribute the areas of New York and New Jersey without the consent of both of those States, but either State can re-arrange its counties and municipalities as it pleases; the important cities of New York and Brooklyn are absolutely dependent on the legislature of their State for corporate powers. Therefore within each State a re-organization of local government is possible. Again, by taking extreme cases an unfair impression is produced. The average State or Canton (say Wisconsin or Freiburg) is a convenient body to interpose between the national government and the smaller local groups. There is besides a tendency towards adjustment between the habits of a people and its indigenous institutions. The Americans and Swiss have by usage become fitted for their particular systems, which therefore work with greater ease. The distribution of the several German States is more irregular,

[1] 'No new State shall be formed or erected within the jurisdiction of any other State, nor any State be formed by the junction of two or more States or parts of States, without the consent of the legislatures of the States concerned as well as of the Congress.' *Constitution of U. S.*, Art. iv. section 3. Cp. Art. 78 of the German Constitution for an analogous provision.

and illustrates, as noticed before, the powerful influence of historical conditions. The principal anomaly is due to the preponderance of Prussia compared with the very small States that form part of the empire. The internal local government of Prussia is however based on a well-proportioned system[1].

§ 6. Applying our results to the financial question of expenditure and its proper division, we commence with the central government. Its claims to disburse the larger part of the total public revenue are unquestionably strong. It is the representative of the nation. Other bodies exist under it and to relieve it of undue toil, but 'the State' in the popular sense of the term is *primâ facie* the agent in charge of all public duties. It is at once clear that all general interests ought to belong to its province. What concerns the whole community may indeed for other valid reasons be delegated to localities, but the fact that a public function concerns all is a weighty reason for intrusting it to the central government. No smaller body can take the same ground, no matter how liberal its constitution may be. Even an absolute ruler is in most cases more likely to regard the welfare of all than the representative assembly of one part of the nation's territory, while the highest security for due attention is obtained by the representation of all districts in a national legislature. This attitude of the central government is partly the consequence of the wider view that it is almost compelled to take, but it is also partly due to the higher intelligence and skill that it has at its disposal. For tasks in which these elements are of importance the superiority of the central administration is generally apparent. A third circumstance in many cases favours the centralization of certain classes of state duties —those namely in which unity and co-ordination are required. Though division of labour is beneficial, combination of labour is no less so, and public duties that need

[1] See the instructive articles on 'Local Government in Prussia,' by F. Goodnow, *Pol. Science Quarterly*, iv. 648–666, and v. 124–158.

combination will naturally be placed under a single control. It would be too much to assert that these conditions have completely determined the actual sphere of the national government in modern countries; it would be a grosser exaggeration to say that they have done so consciously. There is however much truth in the doctrine that the actual forces which they describe have generally had a powerful effect.

The sphere of local agencies in directing expenditure can be indicated by reference to conditions strongly contrasting with those just described, that make it expedient to call into play the administrative energies of the smaller territorial bodies.

As the central power guards the general interest, so do the representatives of localities best attend to their particular interests. 'That people manage their own affairs best' is not universally true, but it has sufficient truth to justify the intrusting of local matters to the several localities affected. A second case in which local is superior to central administration occurs wherever minute supervision is required. Central authorities with superior skill and intelligence may often fail through the difficulty of regulating from a distance operations that need unfailing attention and watchfulness. It is to this circumstance that we must attribute the almost universal devolution of the smaller parts of economic administration, as it is to it that we probably owe the origin of the attempts at decentralization on the part of the general government. Finally, it is expedient to place the charge of public duties in the hands of the smaller bodies when diversity rather than unity is needed. Some of the forms of state action are not suitable for being conducted on a uniform pattern. Special conditions and habits have to be taken into account, so that the very tendency to adopt different methods becomes a benefit instead of an injury. In fact, as the result it appears that if attention to the general welfare, the command of higher intelligence and skill, and the power of unity in action are advantages possessed by the central government, regard to local interests, attention to details, and possibilities of judicious variety in practice will be best secured by local management.

The same conditions help to determine the functions of the intermediate public organs. A county administration has the same advantages over a parochial one that the national one has over it, and it is inferior in the same respects. An American State holds the same position in respect to the smaller local divisions. Its sphere of action has to be limited in both directions by reference to the general principles already noticed. When we come to such important divisions as the State of New York or the newly-formed administrative County of London, the restrictions on their functions are dictated rather by considerations of national unity than by defects of organization. The position of the larger German States, Baden and Saxony, and still more Bavaria and Würtemberg, in the distribution of power can hardly be settled by reference to principle. Their claims to national independence are strong, but are tending to be reduced.

§ 7. Taking up in order the different forms of public expenditure, we find it easy to understand the reasons for making the military and naval forces a national charge. Security is the greatest general interest of a society; the appliances and organization necessary for successful defence tax severely the highest powers of human intelligence; and unity of management is of great advantage in warfare. Consequently the cost of war and preparation for it always comes from the national budget. Germany and Switzerland still preserve some traces of the older independence of their component parts, but the German forces are in fact completely under imperial control and their cost is defrayed from imperial funds[1]. One of the most

[1] Bavaria and Würtemberg are the only States that keep an appearance of independence, but in war the allegiance of the Bavarian troops is due to the Emperor, and her contribution towards expenses is compulsory. In Switzerland,

decisive marks of union between hitherto independent States is the formation of a common army.

The cost of Justice also seems most fitly to belong to the general expenditure. It figures in all national budgets, but some of the charge may be thrown on localities. In a Federal State the subordinate courts are usually reserved by the separate units, but the Judiciary of the Union becomes a general charge. The reason of this division is plainly historical, and as there is no pressing necessity for complete unity in the judicial organization it is allowed to continue. The importance of distinguishing between federal and state law is a further ground for separating the central and local courts. Uniformity in law and in its administration is such a benefit to a society that, unless under special circumstances, it is advisable to place it in the hands of the national government. Efficiency, too, is increased by removing the judges from the distracting influence of local feeling that is sure to affect them when they are appointed and paid by the district in which they act.

Police, and the treatment of criminals, cannot be definitely assigned to either department. On the one hand it is certainly advantageous to have these matters arranged on general principles. All members of the nation are interested in the preservation of internal order in every part of their country. No district should be allowed to so relax its prison administration as to offer inducements to a criminal class to congregate within it[1]; but on the other hand, the benefits in closer supervision and greater economy when

though part of the forces are cantonal, the first claim on their services belongs to the Federal Government, and the principal outlay is by it. In 1876 it was about six-sevenths of the whole.

[1] 'It would not be a matter personally indifferent to the rest of the country if any part of it became a nest of robbers or a focus of demoralization, owing to the maladministration of its police, or if, through the bad regulations of its gaol, the punishment which the courts of justice intended to inflict on the criminals confined therein (who might have come from or committed their offences in any other district) might be doubled in intensity or lowered to practical immunity.' J. S. Mill, *Representative Government*, 116.

the duty is intrusted to localities are a considerable set off; besides, the principal interest of good order is found in the case of those resident in the district. A practical solution is generally discovered in a division of the duties, combined with regulations as to the distribution of the burdens imposed.

Administrative duties have also been divided, and, though in most countries no attempt has been made to settle the partition on intelligible principles, usually in conformity to the guiding conditions indicated above. Where wide, general interests, requiring a high degree of skill from those who control them, are involved, the central government has been the acting body. In smaller and more detailed matters the local governments have undertaken the task.

The relief of distress is primarily a local duty. During the development of the English Poor Law, previous to 1834, the whole system of management was left to the small unit of the parish, and though this arrangement led to much irregularity, it afforded examples of the best method of administration, which were utilized by the reformed system [1]. Local administration and charge does, however, give rise to difficulties; in particular the question of the domicile or 'settlement' of those relieved becomes a constant subject of disputes. 'The birthplace and dwelling of the foremost peer,' says Mr. McNeil-Caird, 'the birthplace and dwelling of Newton, Shakespeare, Milton, or Burns were never investigated with half the eagerness, or a tenth of the expense, that is freely spent as to the birth and residence of a pauper' [2]. The injustices attending the distribution of the cost are always perplexing, but local direction and management under central regulation presents, on the whole, the least objectionable method.

In dealing with education it is at once obvious that

[1] See *Report* of the Commission of 1832, 232–260.

[2] *Local Government and Taxation*, Cobden Club Essays (3rd Series, 1875), 143.

elementary teaching has a closer relation to separate localities, resembling, in this respect, poor-relief. Particular circumstances so far affect it that there is reason for making it, at least in part, a local charge ; but it is also a general interest affecting the well-being of the whole society and requiring for its proper working a great amount of trained intelligence, which can be best supplied by the central government. The higher grades of education do not admit of the same degree of localization. Universities in especial bear a distinctly national character, and are therefore, so far as they receive public aid, rightly a national charge. Other appliances for instruction and the promotion of culture are provided both from general and local sources, though it is hard to determine what should be the exact position of each in the matter.

Wherever the support of religion is a public function it is met from the national budget or at least by national endowments, the cases where local bodies pay for religious services being simply compensation for work done, as in the case of prison chaplains, &c.

The principle of general or particular interest explains the division of the economic duties of the State. What affects the whole society is done by the central government; what is specially needed by a locality or minor division is usually done by it. Here, however, there are exceptions. Works too extensive for the resources of a district are undertaken by the central administration, or aid is given to the subordinate authorities who direct and manage them. In this department of expenditure the smaller bodies are more likely to become embarrassed than is the central state authority. Their available funds are not of such vast extent, and change more speedily in amount owing to their limited area. Local administration, besides, in reference to public works is more liable to suffer from the private interests that affect all public economy[1]. The modern credit system, moreover, affords facilities for

[1] Bk. i. ch. 1. § 2.

expenditure based on a pledge of the property of the district that will not be felt at once, but will prove a continuous charge. It is in respect of this so-called 'reproductive' outlay that the difficulties of local finance at present are most serious.

Finally, with regard to what we have called constitutional expenditure, the boundary line is plain and simple. Each part generally pays for its own outlay. Members of the central executive and legislature are paid from the central budget. The officials and subordinate legislators of States, cantons, or municipalities are paid from the budget that they are connected with. As an exception, the charge of all elections is sometimes a local one, but it is so on the ground that it is really a local interest.

§ 8. It thus appears that on a broad view and with full allowance for the influence of previous history and special circumstances in each case, there is a tendency to distribute functions, and therefore expenditure, in accordance with the principles that we have seen in operation. Some additional reasons for particular forms of distribution may be noted here: they are really expansions of those already pointed out.

First, particular duties are often given to, or withheld from, local bodies on the ground that they are well suited, or unable, as the case may be, to bring the cost of the service home to those who benefit by it. This, however, is merely an application of the principle that particular interests belong to those concerned in them and a further reason for that policy. The division of control over outlay so as to secure justice in the apportionment of the burden can be realized in another way, viz. by a readjustment of receipts between the central and local governments. A further ground for limiting local duties is sometimes found in the existing division of general and local taxation. When, as in some countries, local revenues are rigidly restricted in amount, it is evidently impossible to place duties needing much extra cost on them. Here, too, the true explanation is found in the narrowness of the local interest that has led to the limitation on its taxing power, and it can be remedied either by removing the restraint, or, as in recent English legislation, by a transfer of part of the general revenue. By dexterous use of the latter method it is possible to combine the great aim in expenditure—the maximum return for outlay, with that in the collection of revenue—a just distribution of burdens.

§ 9. Some further characteristics of local Finance in relation to expenditure require attention. We have seen the classes of duties that local bodies deal with, and that they are mainly of an economical character, at least in so far that advantage and cost can be somewhat definitely measured. This feature suggests, as we saw, a comparison with private economic associations ; and though the resemblance is closest in the industrial domain [1], it also appears with regard to expenditure. There is, however, one essential difference. The private company is formed on a voluntary basis. No one is compelled to enter it against his will ; a local governmental body has compulsory powers, and is therefore more particularly in need of being kept within bounds in its action, and of being compelled to act when circumstances require it. Some of the duties in its charge are general state tasks, delegated for motives of convenience. These it cannot be allowed to neglect. Otherwise provisions for poor-relief, education, or police of the highest value might be rendered utterly useless by hostility on the part of the local administrators. In other cases, where the task is purely of local interest, as e. g. water-supply, a minority of the inhabitants may suffer from the ignorance or carelessness of the majority when also there is ground for interference by the central power. Such cases make supervision and regulation of the various divisions a necessity of good government. To insist on the discharge of certain functions, to prevent an undue extension of others, and, finally, to protect the interests of individuals against

[1] As in the case of municipal gas or water-works ; Bk. ii ch 3.

encroachments by local authorities, becomes an important state work[1]. An organization connecting the local and central bodies is needed, and has been developed in most countries. The English Poor Law Board—becoming later on the Local Government Board—is a good example. So are the many Commissions in the American States; while similar results are attained in another way by the bureaucratic systems of France, Germany, and Italy. The need of securing due discharge of duties imposed, avoidance of expenses in directions not allowed by law, and moderation in the exercise of expenditure, even on lawful objects, has brought about a system that shows in the clearest way how all expenditure, local as well as general, is really one, and has to be combined in order to judge correctly of the pressure of the State and its organization on the national resources.

The value of this conception of the unity of state services in helping to form a true idea of public expenditure, will be better realized by reference to the following table:

TABLE (000's omitted).

EXPENDITURE.

	Central.	*Local.*	*Total.*	*Percentage of total expenditure by Local Government.*
	£	£	£	
United Kingdom (1887-8)	87,423	67,451	154,874	43·
France (1886)	131,740	53,400	185,140	28·
Italy (1885)	69,220	27,300	96,520	28·
United States (1886-7)[2]...	53,600	21,460[3]	75,060	28·6

[1] Roscher classifies duties of local bodies as (*a*) State, (*b*) compulsory local and (*c*) optional local, § 157. Cp. Wagner, i. 96 sq.

[2] Some of the State returns are for 1886, others for 1887.

[3] "State" expenditure only has been given owing to the difficulty of obtaining returns of municipal outlay, but it is beyond doubt that the inclusion of county and city expenditure would more than double (probably treble) the sum given in the table. Thus the expenditure of the five cities—Baltimore, Boston, Chicago, New York, Philadelphia—for 1887 was in round figures £24,000,000. The total local (i. e. State, county, and municipal) expenditure for 1880 has been estimated at £62,550,000. Cp. Ely, *Taxation*, 453, 478; Seligman, *Finance Statistics*, 108.

§ 10. In some discussions of Finance two other kinds of combined expenditure have been included [1]. They are, first, the Finance of 'State confederations' (*Staatenbünde*), and second, the Finance of colonies. Neither of these seem entitled to a place. There is a clear distinction between a Federal State and a confederated group of States. The former is a unity, and one of its points of unity is financial; the latter is easily dissolved into its component parts. The resources of a confederacy are always derivative, and come from the separate units. A comparison between the old German Bund (1815–1866) and the present German Empire brings out the difference in Finance, as in other points, with the utmost clearness.

The same reasoning applies to colonial Finance. It is perfectly correct to combine the Imperial and local Finance of the United Kingdom into a single whole. To add together British, Canadian, and Indian Finance would be a transparent error. The conditions are different, and the interests affected are independent. Even the Finance of different colonies, e. g. Victoria and New South Wales, could not be amalgamated. The conditions of unity do not exist. The whole conception of a financial system rests on the oneness of the State, and any departure from that guiding rule is sure to lead to confusion.

[1] As by Stein, i. 64, 76–81. Wagner, i. 79, includes the first, but not the second head (Colonial Finance).

CHAPTER VIII.

SOME GENERAL QUESTIONS OF EXPENDITURE.

§ 1. THE outlay of the State, like that of the individual, may be distinguished into normal or 'ordinary,' and abnormal or 'extraordinary.' These terms almost explain themselves, but may be thus contrasted. Normal expenditure is that which recurs at stated periods and in a regular manner; it is accordingly capable of being estimated and provided for. Extraordinary expenditure has to be made at indefinite times and for uncertain amounts, and it cannot be reckoned for with any approach to accuracy. The distinction is not always applied in the same way [1], and indeed the boundary line is not to be quite sharply drawn. Most heads of outlay vary from time to time, and any increase may so far be regarded as extraordinary, the 'ordinary' charges being those that, like the English Civil List, are fixed for a long term. In practice, however, very close estimates can be made of probable expenditure, small increases in some directions being compensated by savings in others [2]. To use the distinction to the best advantage, we shall confine it to marking the difference between the usual expenditure and unanticipated extra demands, arising in most cases from fresh calls on the State. We should describe the usual annual expenditure on military and naval forces, the cost of justice and education as normal or

[1] For the different uses see Wagner, i. 135 sq.; Cohn, §§ 157–9.

[2] The English budget estimate of expenditure for 1889–90 was £85,967,000; the expenditure for that year was £86,083,000; an error of less than one-seventh per cent.

'ordinary.' The cost of a war, or expenditure for the relief of distress in a sudden emergency, is on the other hand plainly 'extraordinary' or abnormal. No French financier could have foreseen the burdens that the Franco-German war of 1870–1 would impose on his country; nor, though the probability of disturbance was recognised in the United States for some years before the Civil War, could there be any calculation of its expense [1]. In like manner it is not open to the English Government to provide beforehand for Irish distress, or for Indian administrators to say whether their Finances will be disturbed by famine. War and—in backward countries—distress approaching to famine are events that do recur, and though it is not possible to forecast their effects on public expenditure for short periods, they ought to be taken into account in the general scheme of Finance. The famine fund of the Indian Government is a recognition of the correctness of this principle, and though the cost of war does not admit of the same mode of treatment, it is sound policy to reduce liabilities in time of peace, so as to secure some relief in the extraordinary charge in the time of war [2].

It thus appears that, by taking a sufficiently lengthy period into consideration, the separation between normal and abnormal outlay may be so attenuated as almost to disappear. The conception is a vague one. 'It indicates,' as Cohn remarks, 'an undeveloped stage of economic thought' [3] to be replaced by the more careful estimation of the future. State economy expands both in bulk and duration. The expenditure of e.g. England under the

[1] The direct cost of the war of 1870–1 to France has been estimated at £234,000,000. Giffen, *Essays in Finance* (1st Series), 1–55. That of the American Civil War at £1,800,000,000. Wells in *Cobden Club Essays* (2nd Series), 488. Mr. Bolles gives £1,238,000,000 as actually paid out up to 1879, *Financial History of U.S.*, 241 sq.

[2] 'The amount of revenue raised in time of peace, ought to be greater than the expenses for a peace establishment, and the overplus applied to the discharge of debts contracted in former wars.' Hamilton, *National Debt*, 7.

[3] § 157.

Tudors was likely to show 'extraordinary,' i.e. unusual elements in matters that are at present well within the prevision of the Chancellor of the Exchequer. When the outlay is measured by thousands, a variation in hundreds is serious, but when it reaches millions changes of thousands are trifling, besides being balanced through savings in some other parts of expenditure. There is also in modern States a greater facility for foreseeing and, so to say, 'discounting' the future. The refined financial mechanism by which public borrowing is carried out, enables 'extraordinary' expenditure for a short period to be transformed into 'ordinary' expenditure for a long one.

Still, the development just noted does not remove completely the dividing-line between the two classes of expenditure. We shall find later on[1] that both on financial and political grounds it is eminently desirable to have the estimates and results of national Finance set forth fully and in unity at short intervals, usually in practice annually. But during such a period it must sometimes happen that the amount to be paid out of the National Exchequer will be much above the average, and it follows as a matter of course that the expenditure is then 'abnormal.' What modern Finance can accomplish is to secure a more even distribution of the pressure.

Another point for consideration is found in the fact that what is at first extraordinary, may soon become ordinary, expenditure. At the outbreak of war the cost of the army and fleet will be greatly increased, giving rise to abnormal outlay, but after a time, say after the first year, a probable estimate of the expenses to be incurred in the prosecution of the war will not be so difficult. The financial history of England affords several illustrations. During the century and a quarter from 1688 to 1815 there were the following war periods, 1688–1697, 1702–1713, 1718–1721, 1739–1748, 1756–1763, 1776–1783, 1793–1802, 1803–1815. At the commencement of each period expenditure was greatly

[1] *Infra*, Bk. vi. ch. 3.

increased, but when the state of hostility became a settled one, it was possible for, and therefore incumbent on, the Minister in charge of the Finances to present the outlay on war as part of the ordinary expenditure. Under such conditions the charge for war became the normal charge of an abnormal period.

Abnormal expenditure also frequently occurs in a somewhat different way, as in the case of durable public works or other improvements. It may be a part of state policy to erect extensive public buildings; to carry out a system of fortifications, of railroads, or canals; to drain and plant waste lands; to promote colonization, or to develope an industry that requires the aid of fixed capital. Innumerable examples of such forms of expenditure are found in connexion with local government: the acquisition of the industries engaged in supplying large towns with water and light, will at once occur. Outlay of this kind is in mercantile phraseology 'chargeable to capital, not to revenue,' and is clearly abnormal. The method almost invariably adopted is to meet the abnormal outlay by an abnormal receipt, viz. borrowing; or, to put the point in another way, to turn the extraordinary expense of a given year into the ordinary one of interest on debt[1].

Much ingenious argument has been advanced in favour of borrowing for all such extraordinary expenditure, on the ground that it is in substance a creation or investment of capital, which is an asset to be placed against the new liability[2]. The plausibility of this doctrine in its extreme form arises from failing to notice the different effects that may follow from different forms of State expenditure.

§ 2. For understanding the point it is necessary to separate State outlay into 'productive' and 'unproductive,'

[1] The theory of public debts and borrowing is treated in Bk. v. ch. 5. In local Finance we shall see that borrowing is in such cases the only course open, as otherwise the funds could not be obtained owing to the restraints on local taxing powers.

[2] See on this point Bk. v. ch. 5. C. Dietzel appears to be the originator of the theory. He is followed by Stein and partly by Wagner.

using these terms in the sense given to them by Adam Smith[1]. The former does in fact secure a return in the shape of material goods possessing value, and it may be said that expenditure of this kind is admissible even by the aid of loans. The general category of productive expenditure will however be found to need further analysis. It is not at all difficult for the central and local governments to expend a great deal in obtaining articles that possess value but yet will not yield revenue. For instance, the many buildings existing in the United Kingdom for the meetings of legislative bodies, sovereign and subordinate, from the houses of Parliament down to the smallest town-hall, are certainly embodiments of value, but do not, except in very rare cases, bring in a return. They are 'consumers' capital,' and their cost must be supplied from other sources. In contrast to the foregoing are those forms of wealth that return a revenue by their use as 'producers' capital.' Municipal gas and water works belong to this class; so do the continental State railways. The policy of expenditure on such works is plainly to be judged, partly at least, as a question of investment. Public bodies may succeed in realizing good value for their outlay. It is perhaps on the whole best to divide expenditure into 'economic' and 'non-economic' rather than into productive and non-productive; outlay for the purpose of securing future revenue being 'economic,' while that which will not have this result is 'non-economic.' The expediency of economic outlay is really a question closely connected with the formation of State property and the (so-called) 'private revenue,' and has to be treated under that head[2]. Non-economic outlay includes the procuring of material goods that are not productive capital as well as the cost of those public services that take no tangible form. It may be, and often is, more necessary than pure economic expenditure, but it cannot be regarded as a creation of capital. National security and honour, the

[1] *Wealth of Nations*, Bk. ii. ch. 3.

[2] Bk. ii. ch. 3.

promotion of culture and education may be better than wealth, but they are not wealth, and their cost is so far a deduction from the stock or accumulated wealth of the society. They belong to consumption not to production, and the outlay on them has to be limited by economic considerations. Thus this case is closely parallel to that of the individual whose expenses for enjoyment, general education, &c. reduce his economic resources and have to be limited by the amount of his income.

Some expenditure, both of individuals and of public bodies, may prove to be indirectly productive. What a person spends on recreation may so improve his health, both physical and mental, as to make his labour more efficient. The State may likewise by its maintenance of a powerful army and navy or an active police increase the production of wealth, and in practice all public expenditure has this amongst other aims in view [1].

§ 3. Though public and private expenditure have so many points of resemblance, there is one very important difference. The individual's income is formed by the returns on his property and the reward of his exertions. Public income or revenue is to some extent composed of similar constituents, but in modern times it is mainly derived from contributions levied compulsorily on the members of the society ; that is to say, state income or revenue is derivative, and is dependent on national income; local public revenue is in like manner derived from the revenue of the community in its locality.

This connexion of public and national revenue has been recognised from the earliest days of Finance : it is to it that we owe in great measure the commercial policy of Europe in the sixteenth and seventeenth centuries. The Physiocrats also accepted it, as Quesnay's famous maxim '*pauvres paysans, pauvre royaume; pauvre royaume, pauvre roi*' shows. It is an essential doctrine of modern theory, though there

[1] *Supra*, Bk. i. ch. 6. § 1.

is not perfect agreement on the question whether it is on 'net' or 'gross' national revenue that State income depends[1]. There can be no doubt that a small nation with little accumulated wealth cannot adopt the same scale of outlay as a larger and wealthier one, and one of the rules of good Finance is to observe moderation in the demands of the State on its citizens. Beyond this general precept no definite result has been reached. Some writers have suggested a percentage limit for State outlay. Justi regards 16 per cent. as the average, 25 per cent. as excessive. Hock states 15 per cent. as the upper limit. Leroy-Beaulieu, who confines his discussion to the amount of taxation, arranges the charge on national income for State ends in grades: 5 per cent. he thinks light, between 5 and 10 per cent. moderate, over the latter figure heavy, and when 15 or 16 per cent. is reached it is almost impossible to increase it[2]. Any attempt to settle once for all the proper proportion of public expenditure to national income is necessarily vitiated by the different elements to be taken into account; such as (1) the object of the outlay; if it has an economic end a larger amount may be taken, since it is expected to yield a direct return, and even if not for economic ends, no decision can be made until the urgency of the want is known. A nation engaged in a conflict perhaps involving its national existence is justified in expenditure that would in ordinary times be imprudent. (2) The amount of the national income is also a factor to be considered. Expenditure requiring 10 per cent. of the annual income of India would be much more burdensome than if 30 per cent. were to be required in England or the United States. (3) The distribution and the forms of wealth, though less in importance, have some effect on spending power. The bounds of outlay in any given case can only be ascertained

[1] Schäffle and Schmoller have both suggested that 'net income' is not the only source of public revenue.

[2] For Justi see Roscher, *Geschichte*, 463. See also Hock, 35; Leroy-Beaulieu, i. 127 sq., esp. 133.

by trial, though it is plain that the agreement of the writers referred to above supports the belief that 15 per cent. of the national income is too large an amount to appropriate for State objects, unless in very exceptional cases.

§ 4. Other methods of measuring the proper amount of State expenditure are still more doubtful. We might take the proportion to area as a guide, were it not for the fact that the extreme differences in the value of land in different countries, as also the varying proportions that other forms of wealth bear to land, make this test fallacious. The amount of accumulated wealth as estimated in modern statistical inquiries[1] might be used, but we shall find that income (not property) is the fund out of which in ordinary cases expenditure has to be met, and the relation of income to property varies. A very commonly-used index is the charge per head of population, though for this purpose it is far inferior even to the amount of property. An attempt to measure the comparative pressure caused by expenditure in India and in the Australasian Colonies based on taking the charge per head, would give the astonishing result that it was about nineteen-fold heavier in the latter[2].

Such considerations lead to the belief—which indeed ought to be obvious—that there is no mechanical mode of judging the sufficiency or the legitimacy of public expenditure, a belief that is strengthened by remembering that local expenditures must be added to that of the central government before the full pressure can be known, and that a series of complicated calculations is needed to apportion the combined charges over the several districts.

Fortunately the question of expenditure in all its forms does not present itself as a single problem. It would be quite hopeless to attempt to prepare a budget of outlay for

[1] Such as those of MM. Giffen, De Foville, and Pantaleoni, for England, France, and Italy, respectively.

[2] *Victorian Year Book*, 1887–8, i. 203, where a table of comparative taxation is given. In India and Australasia the proportion of tax to non-tax revenue is almost the same (40 per cent.), and the rate per head in India for 1885–6 was 3*s*., while averaged over the Australasian colonies it was £2 17*s*.

any country without the aid of the material collected during previous experience. The great mass of expenditure is taken as settled, and it is only the particular changes that have to be anxiously weighed in order to estimate their probable advantage. This method of treatment simplifies the issues very much. In the language of modern economists it is 'final' rather than 'total' expenditure that needs the financier's attention. Though the increments dealt in are not of inconsiderable magnitude, a further reduction can be made by taking increments of those increments into account.

§ 5. The usual form that deliberation has to take is that of considering the advisability of increased expenditure. Theoretically it is of course equally possible to debate the benefits of retrenchment, but in nearly all modern States outlay is steadily increasing. The older doctrines of economy and frugality have disappeared, and in nearly every direction proposals for new exertions on the part of the State are put forward [1].

First as to the facts: we may take a few typical examples. English expenditure in 1833 was 48¾ millions, in 1889–90 it was over 86 millions, or an increase of over 37 millions. As 1833 marks the lowest point of English general expenditure, it will be fairer to take another set of examples given by Mr. Gladstone.

'The gross expenditure of the State was in 1842-43 £55,223,000, and the local expenditure in the three kingdoms was £13,224,000, making a total in round numbers of £68,500,000. In 1853–4 the total State expenditure was £55,769,000, or very nearly the same amount as in 1842–3, and the local expenditure £15,819,000; making together in round numbers £71,500,000, instead of the £68,500,000 which was the amount in 1842–3. In the year 1859–60 the gross State expenditure had grown from £55,769,000 which it was in 1853 to £70,123,000. The local expendi-

[1] During the Parliamentary Sessions 1880–2, out of 576 financial proposals, 556 were for increase of expenditure, only 20 for reduction.

ture, no doubt actuated by a spirit of honourable rivalry, had increased in the same period from £15,819,000 which it was in 1853 to at least £17,458,000, and probably something more; the total expenditure for the year 1859–60 thus reached £87,697,000 [?]. Accordingly it appears that in the eleven years from 1842–3 to 1853–4 the expenditure of the country under the two comprehensive heads which I have mentioned increased at the rate of 4½ per cent., nearly the whole of the increase being local, while in the six years which have elapsed between 1853 and 1859 it became much more mercurial and increased at the rate of 22½ per cent., by far the larger part and greater rate of increase being now imperial[1].'

To complete the illustration, we may state that for the year 1879–80 the national expenditure had risen to £82,184,000, and the local expenditure to £61,174,000, making a total of £143,358,000, or an increase over 1859–60 of over 60 per cent.; and finally, that in 1886–7 the national expenditure was £89,996,000, and the local expenditure £65,974,000, giving a total outlay of £155,970,000, or in round figures 156 millions, being an increase of 87½ millions over the expenditure of 1842–3, i. e. 127 per cent.

France presents a similar movement. In 1820 the general expenditure was 906 million francs, by 1860 it had reached 2084 million francs, or much over double; more precisely, 130 per cent. The budget estimate for 1890 is 3769 millions, giving a growth since 1860 of 80 per cent.

The Italian expenditure of 1861 was 812 million lire: the estimate for 1889–90 is 1857 million lire, an increase of 1045 million lire, giving a growth in 28 years of 128 per cent.

The Prussian budget in 1849 was 282 million marks, in 1865 it had grown to nearly 507 million marks. Since the formation of the North German Confederation (1866) and the German Empire (1871) the increase has continued,

[1] Budget Speech of 1860 in *Financial Statements*, 119.

the actual expenditure in 1885–6 being 1376 million marks, and the estimate for 1890–1, 1591 million marks.

The smaller German States exhibit like features. Bavaria spent thirty-two million marks in 1819–20; the estimated expenditure for 1889 was 260 million marks.

In Austria, Russia, and even in small States like Belgium, we find the same general tendency towards increased outlay. In the last-mentioned country, whose administration has been well-conducted, the expenditure in 1835 was 87 million francs, the estimate of ordinary expenditure for 1890 is 321 million francs, making (with the usual extraordinary expenditure) a fourfold increase.

So well-established is the general fact of increasing outlay—and whoever doubts it need only run over the examples just given—that even conservative writers on Finance, such as Roscher and Umpfenbach, lay it down as a general law of progress[1]; and they explain it by reference to the increasing demands made by society on the modern State. 'What judgment should we pass,' asks the former, 'on a government that, after the manner of the Middle Ages, did not trouble itself about the health, mental training, maintenance, or enriching of the people?' And so far there is no doubt that the intensifying of State duties is one cause of the almost universal increase. In previous chapters we have seen how the cost of defence, of administration, and the minor needs of civilization have gone to swell the growing totals of modern budgets, and in each case special causes have appeared that went far to explain the final result.

Before collecting these, it may be well to correct to some extent the impression that increasing figures of outlay are apt to produce. Leroy-Beaulieu remarks[2] that one cause of the general increase is to be found in the depreciation of the precious metals. As expenditure is estimated in terms of money, any change in the value of the circulating medium should be taken into account, and the application of some

[1] Roscher, § 110; Umpfenbach, 38. [2] ii. 159.

test as to the reduced purchasing power of money would considerably alter the figures for the earlier part of the period that we have taken, i.e. from 1820 to 1870, but for the last twenty years the correction would act in the other direction. Increases in outlay since 1873 would certainly mean more than the amount as measured in money, so that we cannot place much stress on this part of the explanation of increase. Another element is however important. In most countries population is growing, and national income grows with it; and in the exceptional cases where, as in France, population is stationary, income is increasing. It therefore is not certain that the proportion of public outlay to national income has become greater. Moreover, and this is the most important consideration, the extension of the economic activity of the State in certain directions has been accompanied by a passage of special industries from private to public management. As a necessary consequence, public expenditure and income are both increased without the real pressure on the people becoming greater. It may be that in this tendency there lies in Roscher's phrase '*ein communistischer Zug*,' and it is plain that the transfer in this manner of all industries means the establishment of socialism pure and simple. But apart from its economic reactions, financial theory is not entitled to absolutely condemn this movement. Its duty is however to point out that comparison between the expenditure of a State with large industrial enterprises in its charge and one without them is illegitimate unless due correction is made. To take a simple illustration, it is plain that if the State purchased the English railways, and the accounts entered into the national budget (as they should), both expenditure and income would be largely increased. This has actually happened in Prussia, and explains a large part of the increase in outlay in that country [1].

[1] The estimated expenditure on the Prussian State railways in 1890–1 was 522 million marks, besides the part of the total debt which was due to their purchase. The receipts however were estimated at 851 million marks.

Notwithstanding these extenuations, there has been we believe an increase in expenditure that is not balanced by receipts from the property of the State, and this larger outlay may be attributed to the following causes :—

(1) The cost of war and preparation for war. We need not repeat the details already given on this subject[1], but we ought to emphasize the general fact. The annual military and naval expenditure of Europe is £140,000,000, and the disturbance to industry, the apprehension of hostilities, and above all the interest on debts incurred for the most part for the pupose of war, considerably increases the burden[2]. As if to enable us to judge of its effects, a test case has been provided in the condition of the United States, which further shows that it is not war, but the necessity of constant readiness for it, that affects most injuriously the economic interests of nations.

(2) A second cause is to be found in the extension of administrative action. To maintain a large staff of competent officials considerable outlay is needed, much of it necessarily wasteful. It may be that a great deal of official work does with advantage to society what men are too busy or too careless to do for themselves. Perhaps also it checks some moral and social evils, but, financially speaking, it is undoubtedly costly, and if the end could be otherwise gained it would be an economic benefit.

To these causes many would add a third, viz. the progress of democracy[3]. It is argued that a widely extended suffrage lowers the standard of the legislatures, and that under the influence of socialistic ideas the expenses of the State are increased. There is probably some truth in this doctrine. The 'new radicalism' is not desirous of economy in expenditure[4], and it may be freely conceded that

[1] *Supra*, Bk. i. ch. 2.

[2] Neymarck, *Les Dettes Publiques*, 89.

[3] Leroy-Beaulieu, ii. 169 sq.

[4] The contrast between the doctrines of *The Radical Programme* (ch. 8, 'Taxation and Finance'), and those of Cobden, Bright, and George Grote, is very extreme.

'democratic Finance' is remarkable for its disregard of principles and its utter incapacity to measure financial forces; but on the whole it cannot be said that Russian Finance, which is certainly not democratic, is much superior in these respects. Nor is it plain that English Finance before the Reform Act of 1832 was worthy of commendation. The socialistic element in modern democracy has an injurious influence on Finance, but it is not an essential part of it. The technical administration of revenue and expenditure is also likely to suffer while under the control of an untrained democracy. But allowing all this, the real enemy of sound Finance is ignorance whenever it attains to power, an event which is unfortunately too common under all forms of government.

§ 6. Any discussion of public expenditure that neglected to notice its influence on national and social economy would be incomplete. The State through its central and local organs is by far the greatest purchaser of goods and employer of services; it can in this way powerfully influence prices and wages, and through that influence affect the distribution of wealth. The sum of £150,000,000 annually disbursed (after allowing for the amount that goes as interest on loans which operate on the money market) must both by its great amount and its changed direction alter the structure of the British national industries. Demand for commodities determines the direction that production will take, and consequently the form of labour in many cases depends on the policy of the State; so also do the rates of remuneration and the conditions of employment[1]. The economic systems of Germany and the United States owe their different features largely to the special direction of state activity in each country. The technical arrangements for the supply of commodities for public requirements are a serious consideration for administrators owing to their ulterior effects. Government manu-

[1] Hermann, *Staatswirthschaftliche Untersuchungen* (2nd ed.), 465, indicates this very clearly.

facture is liable to the evils of expense and inferiority in quality of products, but the alternative method of purchase in the open market, necessarily carried out through agents, is not free from similar evils. In particular, the result of giving contracts at the lowest tender has been vehemently assailed by reformers as tending to lower wages[1]. The direct employment of services or labour by the State gives rise to further complications. Hiring on the ordinary system and at the market rate is impossible in the case of the higher officials, while for military and naval services special conditions of engagement are needed. The great extent and variety of the general Civil Service makes the determination of its proper remuneration a question of much difficulty. To avoid the political evils that short tenure—as in the American system—causes, its members ought to be permanently employed. Permanence in state service soon affects private employers, who will have to give either like security of tenure or better pay[2]. In every part of national life this influence of state expenditure is felt, and it is becoming greater.

The great and increasing importance of state outlay does not however afford a presumption that the movement is advantageous. The current of modern sentiment runs as strongly at present in favour of state action as it did fifty years ago against it, but neither tendency can be its own justification; both have to be judged on the grounds of reason and experience. Some popular arguments for state expenditure may be at once dismissed. Perhaps the crudest is that which regards the State as affording employment, and imagines that if war and the other conditions which call for state services were to cease, there would be no field for the labour of those now employed as soldiers, policemen, and officials. This obvious

[1] C. Kingsley, *Cheap Clothes and Nasty*.

[2] On this point cp. Prof. Foxwell's article in *Claims of Labour*, 254. For further observation of state dealings with labour, see Bk. ii. ch. 3.

fallacy arises from entirely overlooking the previous existence in private hands of the funds collected by the State as its income, and which would afford like employment, but on other lines: the best practical refutation is however found in the ease with which the enormous expenditure of the United States during the Civil War was reduced at its conclusion, and the military forces absorbed in various industrial employments [1]. Expenditure of itself is plainly not a good, it has to be judged by its object, i. e. by the benefits obtained in return for the sacrifices made. By taking this view we avoid the opposite fallacy that all state outlay is bad, or at all events that the less the expenditure the better. This doctrine, though accepted by Say and Ricardo [2], is palpably incorrect, since it takes no account of one of the two factors in the problem. It is not true that the cheapest article is the best, nor is 'the cheapest State' the most serviceable. That state organization is the best and really the cheapest which, all elements of the question being taken into account, gives the greatest amount of benefit to its citizens and provides best for the future progress of the nation.

[1] Wells in *Cobden Club Essays* (2nd Series), 491.

[2] 'The golden maxim of M. Say "that the very best of all plans of finance is to spend little, and the best of all taxes is that which is the least in amount."' Ricardo, *Works*, 145.

BOOK II.

PUBLIC REVENUE.

THE ECONOMIC OR QUASI-PRIVATE RECEIPTS.

CHAPTER I.

THE FORMS AND CLASSIFICATION OF PUBLIC REVENUES.

§ 1. A SYSTEM of public expenditure such as has been examined in the preceding book requires as its necessary basis a corresponding public revenue. State economy is in nowise exempt from that condition of all private economies, which makes it essential to provide that consumption shall be balanced by production and that effort must be put forth in order to procure satisfaction. In respect to the public power there is a wider field, but no change in the nature of things; the correlation of exertion and enjoyment holds here as elsewhere, and if temporarily disturbed is certain to be sooner or later re-established. All financial systems are in fact compelled to recognise the relation, though political exigencies may sometimes make it inconvenient to adopt a line of conduct completely in accordance with that recognition. Every Parliamentary Government has arrangements for raising funds as well as for granting supplies. In England the Committee of Ways and Means is quite distinct from the Committee of Supply [1]; and in the United States the small House Committee on Ways and Means is composed of different members from that of the Committee on 'Appropriations.' There seems to be an instinctive feeling that

[1] Though each is simply the House of Commons sitting under a special name.

the raising of revenue should be formally separated from the more agreeable occupation of applying it for the public requirements.

Public revenue, then, being the counterpart or obverse of expenditure, it becomes our duty to consider its forms and sources, and to see how far they admit of logical grouping and arrangement.

§ 2. This, like most financial questions, needs to be studied at first from the historical side. The early tribe shows us expenditure and revenue in combination; the services and commodities required for public use are directly levied and applied to the particular end[1]. When once this primitive stage is passed, revenue as distinct from expenditure emerges, and its collection and administration become matters of vital concern to the growing state organization. It is true that for a long time contributions of goods are levied in kind, but their employment is more complicated, and involves redistribution of the different forms of wealth obtained by the State. With the introduction of money the divorce between the revenue collected and the expenditure undertaken is finally established, since public agents can directly buy what they need for the public service, while the revenue is brought in under the form of the general medium of exchange. What strikes the observer most forcibly in contemplating this development is the extreme variety of the forms of revenue or state receipts. Dues levied on land, on goods of all kinds, on the performance of different acts, in addition to all the kinds of individual revenue, are enjoyed by the State. The Roman Finances received contributions from very many and diverse sources, and so did the Exchequers of mediaeval sovereigns. When we run over the long lists that appear in legal and historical works treating of this side of mediaeval law and economy, the greatest difficulty is to reduce them to some manageable

[1] *Supra*, Bk. i. ch. 1. § 7.

form[1]. This complexity seems to have puzzled the earliest scientific students of Finance. Bodin, as noticed before, arranged the sources of revenue under seven heads, but Klock, who fairly represents the German views of the seventeenth century, gives a far more extensive list. The 'chamber science' writers were more successful in grouping the forms of revenue under (1) those from the domain of the sovereign, (2) the so-called '*regalia*' or prerogative rights, and (3) taxes. In Adam Smith's hands the double aspect of the State became the basis of classification. Regarded as an artificial personality or (in the language of modern jurisprudence) 'juristic person,' it might hold property and engage in trade. Revenue obtained in such ways 'peculiarly belonged to the sovereign.' It was his quasi-private income. In another aspect as sovereign or supreme power he was able to impose charges on the revenues of his subjects, and these contributions or 'taxes' formed the second group of state receipts. The simplicity and clearness of this classification commended itself to English and French writers, who have almost universally adopted it. The greater political development of France and England, by making taxation the most important part of the state income, favoured its acceptance. The remains of the feudal system were more numerous in Germany, and its methods of Finance in particular, with all their variety and confusion, were slow in disappearing from that country. Consequently German *Finanzwissenschaft* aimed at so arranging the forms of revenue as to give harmony and consistency to the existing systems. The '*regalia*' or prerogatives were always regarded with particular attention, and it was sought to place them alongside of taxation as a head of revenue.

Rau is in great measure responsible for another addition

[1] Thus Blackstone (i. 281–337) gives twenty-one different rights as composing the 'ordinary' revenue of the King, from which enumeration taxes are excluded. Cibrario describes twenty-four heads of revenue in mediaeval Italy, *Economia Politica del medio aevo*, Lib. iii. cap. 6.

to the main groups, viz. that of 'fees' (*Gebühren*). He noticed that in many cases public institutions gave special benefits for which they charged an equivalent; e.g. in law proceedings fees were asked from the litigants. It was natural to regard this class of objects denoted by a special name as a separate and independent form of revenue, giving as a final result that state receipts were distributed under four heads: (1) 'Private' industry of State, (2) Prerogative rights, (3) Fees, (4) Taxes. On this classification of public revenues most of the controversies as to arrangement in German financial works turn. It is too plain for dispute that the first and fourth of the above-mentioned heads must be kept apart, but in the endeavours to bring the two intermediate divisions into some form of combination with them, great difference of opinion is to be found. One set of writers oppose 'Taxes' to the three other forms of revenue, which are joined under some more general term [1]. Others place Taxes and 'Fees' under one head and oppose them to the 'quasi-private income' and prerogative dues, or with greater wisdom eliminate the latter from the division altogether [2]. There is even a decided tendency in the latest inquirers to come back by a somewhat devious route to the plainer position of Adam Smith, and to recognize only the two great divisions of state revenue into (1) quasi-private and (2) public, though distinguishing, as he has done, between the cases of extra payment for special services [3]. A detailed examination of the many points raised in the controversy on this subject of classification would lead us too far, but some of the results are too important to be passed over and must be briefly noted.

[1] This is the course followed by Stein and Roscher: the former (i. 138 sq.) speaks of 'economic' income; the latter of 'whole or half private economic state receipts,' Bk. i. chs. 4, 5 (69–107).

[2] Umpfenbach, who substitutes the term 'Fiscal prerogative rights' (*Vorrechte*) for '*regalia*,' takes the former course, 78; Wagner, i. 487 sq., ii. 33, the latter.

[3] This is the case with regard to Cohn (see e.g. § 107), who declines to discuss the question of state property, as being economic rather than financial.

§ 3. First, it is abundantly established that much of the difficulty of classification arises from the historical peculiarities of different countries. The whole doctrine of the *regalia* is an instance in point. It was the result of attempting to apply the special German forms of revenue, due in part to rudeness of the financial system, as general categories suited for all times and places. A particular kind of state rights was opposed to the general state right to raise funds of which it was but one part.

A second result of the discussions on arrangement is that the many and varied shapes of public revenue do not always admit of sharp and clear-cut divisions. Just as in Economics we pass by a series of steps from the purest form of productive capital to what could not by any straining of terms be regarded as such, so do we find many transitional forms between what is the State's private income and what it gains by pure taxation. The attempt to create a co-ordinate class composed of 'fees' parallel to taxes is the outcome of this circumstance, as also of the want of analytic power in the originator of the classification. If Rau had recognised the frequent combination of the double elements of state industry and taxation under an apparently simple and independent form of revenue he would have aimed at separating and assigning to its proper place each of those elements, while he duly noted the intermediate forms that presented most difficulty. The department of fees or *Gebühren* at one end touched the private income of the State and at the other (as in the case of 'taxes on commerce') the field of taxation, but it has no central point possessing well-assigned and definite features and enabling us to give a definition that is at once rational and useful in practice.

A third conclusion is also warranted, viz. that it is easy to overrate the value of very precise and correct classification. We need not deny that a good and natural grouping (i.e. a grouping in accordance with the real affinities of the objects) is very helpful both for exposition and investigation.

Features of resemblance and of contrast are in this mode most easily perceived, and new and hitherto neglected relations are often suggested; but notwithstanding these undeniable advantages, the most essential matter after all is to give adequate and proper treatment to the material of study, and even with a somewhat faulty arrangement this end can be attained. And not only so, the merits of any particular classification depend partly on the end in view. In a purely historical inquiry the class of *regalia* is entitled to a prominence to which it has no claim were a scientific exposition of principles most desired. So in descriptive and statistical works the terms and divisions adopted by positive financial legislation have to be followed, subject to whatever qualifications scientific arrangement may necessitate. In an investigation of general Finance, the grouping of topics ought to be based on the underlying economic and social conditions and aim at bringing out their relations as clearly as possible[1]. Besides, different arrangements naturally tend to place different parts of the subject in prominence, and thus study of a new, even if on the whole inferior, system of grouping will suggest novel points of view to the inquirer.

§ 4. We have already shown in the preceding criticisms the arrangement that appears to be best. It has now to be more fully stated. The widest division of public revenue is into (1) that obtained by the State in its various functions as a great corporation or 'juristic person' operating under the ordinary conditions that govern individuals or private companies, and (2) that taken from the revenues of the society by the power of the sovereign. To the former class belong the rents received by the State as landlord, rent-charges due to it, interest on capital lent by it, the earnings of its various employments whether these cover the expenses of the

[1] Cp. Wagner, i. 474–5. For the *regalia* cp. Sax: '*Die Regalien gehören der Wirthschaftsgeschichte und dem positiven öffentlichen Rechte an, die volkswirthschaftliche Theorie . . . hat mit ihnen nichts zu schaffen,*' *Staatswirthschaft*, 480.

particular function or not, and finally the accrual of property by escheat or absence of a visible owner. Under the second class have to be placed taxes, either general or special, and finally all extra returns obtained by state industrial agencies through the privileges granted to them. This method seems best to satisfy the conditions of scientific accuracy and practical convenience. It places together distinct and well-defined parts of public revenue, and it separates the economic from the compulsory receipts of the State.

To test it in its relation to other divisions we may consider the place it assigns to (1) the prerogative dues, and (2) 'fees.' If these classes can be fittingly placed, then the arrangement may be said to be justified. A very slight examination shows that many, if not most of the prerogatives or *regalia* are really special property-rights. Roscher has noticed that they originated in the mixture of landed property and sovereignty[1]. They are thus in their right place when classed along with other economic sources of revenue. In some instances, however, an element of monopoly created by law comes in, and where there is an additional receipt from this condition it is certainly a tax and must find its place in the compulsory revenue of the State.

Fees admit of a somewhat similar analysis. Usually they are but a small return for the expenses of the state agency to which they are paid, and find a position among the private economic receipts as a deduction from the expenditure. It may even be best to deduct them from the expenses and charge the balance as net outlay, though in practice the wisdom of bringing all expenditure and receipts (not merely balances) into the Budget is well-established. In some cases it happens that fees just cover all expenses, and then the public office or agency is a state-industry that pays its way. Up to the point at which ordinary profit is obtained the same title is justified, but

[1] § 18.

when (the institution being exclusively a public one) ordinary profit is exceeded, the monopoly possessed by the office is employed for taxation. It therefore follows—and this is perhaps the greatest difficulty that our classification raises—that one and the same public institution may occupy different positions in this respect at different places or times. The Post Office, for example, may be a purely public function involving expenditure, as the earliest government Posts probably did ; it may in another country or at a later time just cover its expenses, or even pay fair interest on whatever capital it employs,—such has been at times the position of the United States Post,—or, lastly, it may, as in England at present, give a large surplus to the general revenue, when its charges become a tax on communications, though, as we shall see, sometimes admitting of full justification. In truth, this apparent defect is a reason in favour of our grouping of the forms of revenue. Such institutions as the Post Office are in this respect different in different countries, but in all, they are capable of presenting the three elements of expenditure, industrial revenue, and tax revenue. In treating of economic expenditure we have already noticed the first aspect[1]; in the present book we shall consider the second, reserving the last for its appropriate place.

Some classes of fees, e.g. law fees, are closely connected with the primary functions of the State. They then approach so nearly to taxation as to be best classed with it. There is an appearance of straining the conception of state industry by including them under that head. Here acquaintance with the historical development is of use in establishing that in their origin such fees were strictly payment for service done, and even when this element has been obscured by the increase of state power, it gives place to that of special as opposed to general advantage, a distinction on which so much of local taxation turns,

[1] Bk. i. ch. 6. § 2.

and which can be applied to the class of fees under consideration.

§ 5. So much suffices at present with reference to the general classification of public revenues. We have now to arrange the sub-divisions of the public 'economic' income in their natural order. The great importance of this part of the receipts in less developed societies made it a subject of greater attention formerly than it is now, and led to those long lists of the heads of revenue above referred to. The modern student of Finance gains little from these enumerations, made in all cases from the legal or administrative point of view, but he is impressed by the fact that such receipts are regarded as the 'ordinary' revenue of the State, taxation being merely an occasional resource. This idea survives in Blackstone's chapter on 'The King's Revenue,' where the tax revenue is regarded as 'extraordinary.' Even such recent writers as Mr. Dicey have to notice this division, and the fact that the change in circumstances has made the old terms seem incongruous [1]. A classification of the quasi-private funds of the State must, it would seem, have to follow the lines of the analysis of individual incomes made by economic science. One of the most valuable of Adam Smith's investigations was that presented in his chapter on 'the component parts of the price of commodities' since it not only gave a starting point for all later analyses of cost of production, but it afforded in outline a scheme of economic distribution, and it is on it that the discussion of taxation in the *Wealth of Nations* is based. Its main point consists in showing that all incomes can be separated and referred to one or more of the three categories of rent—the return on natural agents; wages—the reward of labour; and profit—the gain on capital. The

[1] For the view of taxation as an occasional resource, Neumann, *Progressive Einkommensteuer*, 1, 2, and the references there given. Also Blackstone, Bk. i. ch. 8, and contrast Mr. Dicey's view. 'We may therefore, putting the hereditary revenue out of our minds, direct our whole attention to what is oddly enough called the extraordinary, but is in reality the ordinary or Parliamentary revenue of the nation,' *Law of the Constitution* (1st ed.), 316.

State's economic revenue must be capable of being put under the same heads, but the general doctrine, as it appears in the work of its originator[1], requires two corrections before we can use it in this connexion: for firstly, the massing together of the interest on capital and the earnings made by its productive use is now perceived to be inaccurate. The function of the capitalist is distinct from that of the 'undertaker' or 'employer,' and is so distinguished in all later economic work[2]. Another correction is needed for the present application. The category of 'wages' cannot enter into the public receipts; the State often pays but never receives a reward for labour. Any apparent exceptions really come under the head of 'undertaking' or 'management' of industry. We thus get three broad divisions of the public industrial revenues, viz. (1) the receipts of administrations, central or local, from rent of land or similar natural agents; (2)—and this is obviously a less important source—the gains of the State as capitalist or lender of funds; and (3) the returns to the industrial activities of the public power. Such a grouping would appear to be clear and logical, but it needs some further modification to bring it more into accordance with the realities of actual Finance. Instead of confining our attention to the State as a landlord in receipt of rent, we shall find it more convenient to consider all its dealings with its agricultural property, whether retained in its own hands or let out to tenants. In like manner the treatment of mines may most suitably be placed along with the state's action as employer or undertaker of industrial operations. Two additional topics will also have to be brought into the list. The many and various fees and dues may be combined with the rent-charges and other

[1] Though the analysis can be traced back to the Physiocrats, yet Adam Smith originated its form and applications.

[2] The text-books of President Walker, Dr. Sidgwick, and Prof. Marshall are instances. The separation between capitalist and entrepreneur is made both by J. B. Say and Rau.

settled sums payable to the State, and also with the interest on loans made by state authorities, the whole class being connected by the common idea of fixed payment, that is for the most part capable of capitalization. And finally to the revenue-yielding industrial domain we ought to add those state institutions that either give no direct returns, or whose expenses may exceed any receipts that they may bring in.

In short, to sum up, the public economic revenue may, partly on grounds of logical arrangement, partly for practical convenience, be classed into (1) returns from land, including forests, (2) payments which either represent or can be converted into a capital charge, with much administrative revenue, (3) industrial revenue, and (4) a discussion of those industrial forms of property that yield not revenue but utility in a less distinctly measurable form.

CHAPTER II.

THE STATE DOMAIN. LANDS AND FORESTS.

§ 1. THE oldest form of public property undoubtedly consists of the territory on which the society is situated. There is a great body of evidence to show that communal holding of land is far more persistent and enduring than other kinds of common enjoyment. The witness of history is moreover supported by all the probabilities of the case. Until agriculture has extended and improved with the growth of population there will be a large part of the tribal land lying waste or only used for pasture. It remains under the control of the community or, at a later time, of the chief. Public land is increased by the action of war; the land of the vanquished becomes the property of the conquerors and goes to swell their public domain. A counter-process is found steadily operating in the allotment to individuals of parts of the domain. The Roman *ager publicus* dwindled in extent under this influence and the territory of the Provinces [1]—in technical law the property of the Commonwealth—was 'possessed' by individuals with the substantial rights of ownership. A public domain was notwithstanding retained and some of the local revenue was derived from the letting of land, though largely supplemented by other sources. The earlier Middle Ages regarded the royal domain as the basis of public income. The Feudal King was the greatest landholder and was expected to discharge the necessary public duties by aid of the

[1] Cp. the statement of Gaius '*Provincialia praedia usucapionem non recipiunt.*'

revenue that he obtained from that source. The same opposing forces that were operative in earlier times affected the royal lands. They were reduced by lavish grants to royal favourites, and increased by resumptions and forfeitures. The position of the domain depended very much on the strength or weakness of the individual monarch, improving in extent during vigorous reigns and shrinking considerably in feeble ones.

The later history of the domain varied in detail in each European country, but one very general result is found in the transformation of what had been the King's estate into public property. In the few cases where royal or princely estates have remained in the possession of the reigning family, they are nevertheless, in substance, public, inasmuch as they supply the ruler's official income, and by rewarding his services relieve the treasury from an equivalent charge [1].

§ 2. The disintegrating forces that tended to break up the great state domains as well as the other parts of mediaeval Finance did not everywhere act with the same intensity. Owing to peculiarities of situation, and in some degree to differences of policy, the proportion of state domain is at present hardly the same in any two countries. England is remarkable for the almost complete alienation of its Crown lands, the revenue derived from that source being one of the most insignificant in the budget of receipts [2]. 'It was in the fifteenth century that,' according to Thorold Rogers, 'the great impoverishment of the Crown estate

[1] The distinction between the property of the ruler as a private person, and that which accompanies his office is now of little interest. It was emphasized in the Roman Empire—*res privatae* opposed to *res fiscales*—(Humbert, i. 187 sq), and was of much importance in Germany in the case of mediatised princes, who naturally tried to stretch the private element as far as possible. In practice the same end is reached by different means in modern States, as in the cases of Baden and Würtemberg, noted by Roscher, § 9.

[2] The net receipts in the year 1888-9 were £430,000, the gross £506,828, or less than ½ per cent. of the total (£88,472,855). The revenues of the duchies of Lancaster and Cornwall should in strictness be added with a corresponding item of expenditure for the sovereign's support, Bk. i. ch. 6. § 5.

began,' and though increased by the dissolution of the monasteries by Henry VIII, it was again reduced by his successors until it reached its present position at the commencement of the eighteenth century[1]. In France there has been also a series of losses which has reduced the public lands held by the central government to a very small amount, with the exception of forests, of which it possesses 1,070,477 hectares (about 2,650,000 acres). There is, however, a remarkable difference as compared with England in the large quantity of land held by the *Communes* or local units. These bodies in 1877 had 2,058,707 hectares (or, in round numbers, 5,000,000 acres) of forests and 2,258,310 hectares (or 5,600,000 acres) of other land, most of it being of very poor quality. The productiveness, however, as distinguished from the extent of this property, is not considerable; in 1877 the receipts from communal goods, including other items than land, was only 51,702,694 francs, or little over £2,000,000, and showing less than £40,000 increase since 1862. These figures need some further correction, since a large amount of communal land has been sold and in some cases timber has been freely cut down. Thus in 1877 over 24½ million francs were obtained from those extraordinary resources that had for the earlier year 1862 yielded over 34 million francs. It accordingly appears that a sum of about £3,000,000 was the contribution from immovable property for 1877 towards a total communal expenditure of about £27,000,000[2]. It is plain that neither England nor France can hope for much financial advantage from public lands, either general or local. The policy, or at all events, the desire of alienation has been too strong, as the speedy disposal of the confiscated estates of the clergy and the emigrant *noblesse* shows in regard to France[3]. Nor are the cases of Italy and

[1] *Economic Interpretation of History*, 417 sq.

[2] Say, *Dictionnaire des Finances*, s. v. 'Budget Communal.'

[3] The most careful estimates place the amount of immovables disposed of during the revolutionary period at £220,000,000, i. e. £120,000,000 for Church and Crown lands, £100,000,000 for those of the *émigrés*. Stourm, ii. 461.

Spain substantially different. The heavy expenditure that the unification of Italy necessitated was partly met by sale of the state lands, and at a later time by confiscation and sale of the possessions of the ecclesiastical bodies so numerous in that country. By 1886 over £33,000,000 had been realized through those sales, and by far the greater part of the lands had been disposed of.

The countries of Eastern Europe are differently situated. Germany, Austria, and Russia all possess large public estates—a circumstance that may be fully explained by the later growth of constitutional government in the former and its absence as yet in the last named. A State that cannot rely on taxation as a resource at need must provide other financial support, and taxation is productive only on the condition of general willingness to contribute. States, therefore, in which royal power has not been completely displaced by popular government will probably retain a larger amount of public land. The position of Prussia illustrates this proposition. The budget estimate for 1889–90 gives a gross receipt of 87,000,000 marks, and after allowing for the working expenses of nearly 40,000,000 marks, there is a net revenue of about 47,000,000 marks, or £2,350,000. The Bavarian domains are, in proportion, larger and more valuable than those of Prussia. The biennial budget estimated the yield for each of the years 1888 and 1889 at 33,500,000 marks. Würtemberg, Baden, and Saxony also have large domains, chiefly forests.

Austria and Hungary have each state lands and forests, the estimated revenue in the former country from that source being over 4,000,000 florins, and in the latter 2,500,000 florins [1]. Russia is a more remarkable case: it illustrates the statement that the less the development of the society the greater is the proportion of public land. At the time of the great reform usually known as the emancipation of the serfs an amount, estimated at from two-fifths to one-

[1] The estimate for the Austrian domains and forests for 1891 was less than 500,000 florins (net revenue).

half of the land of Russia was held by the State. About eighty years earlier 10,500,000 serfs were found on the state lands, and in 1861 this number had increased to 23,000,000. The measures of emancipation—so far as the state domain was concerned—consisted in a re-adjustment of the dues that were payable which henceforth, in many cases, assumed the form of taxation either imperial or local. Economic inquiries are said to show that rent has been evolved from taxation, but it is equally true that in many cases taxation has passed into rent, or rent-charge. In some parts of Russia the state charges on the former imperial serfs are higher than an economic rent, in others they are lower, and in the latter case they may be looked on either as a reserved property or as a land tax. It appears in this way that the income of the State as land-owner may approach very closely to the tax revenue that is imposed on land, and that the line of separation can only be fixed with reference to all the circumstances of each particular case. In addition to this wider form of state domain the Russian government received, in the year 1888, nearly 25,000,000 roubles from lands and forests, though the expenditure on the same objects has to be deducted to arrive at the net gain[1].

The Indian land tenures present the same features even more forcibly. Under all the varying forms of assessment the principle that the State is ultimate owner has not been, in practice, completely lost sight of, except in the settlement of Bengal. Nothing appears more equitable than that this head proprietor should receive a share of the increasing value of the soil. On the other hand, the machinery of assessment and collection is compulsory; it is far more akin to the processes of the tax-collector than of the landlord, and the difficulty recurs of saying whether the receipts are taxes or rent. The best solution of this question is arrived at when we see that in strictness they belong to neither class. They differ most markedly from the rent,

[1] For the position of the state serfs, see Wallace, *Russia*, 105, 473, 553.

either customary or competitive, of a modern landowner, and more nearly resemble the dues of the feudal lord. They are just as distinct from the ordinary tax, and are not governed by the canons to which it ought to conform; at the utmost they might be assimilated with the taxes on special advantages or monopolies, of which class the possession of land is one example. Where the state dues are frequently revised in accordance with the movement of land values the approximation to rent is very close; where they are changed in order to suit the needs of the State they are practically taxation[1]; but where, as is most common, they are fixed for long periods, or in perpetuity, they are really charges that may be capitalized at the market rate of interest. The Indian Land Tax with its great net return of nearly £20,000,000, has, at different times and in different provinces, shown each of the three features, but on the whole the rent-charge element has preponderated over the others. The lengthening of the period of settlement, and the disposition to keep the assessment under the value, have both tended to this end.

§ 3. European colonies and more particularly the English settlements in North America and Australasia contrast remarkably with the preceding cases. The most prominent economic features in a new country are abundance of land with scarcity both of labour and capital; land is consequently the cheapest of commodities, so much so that it is freely offered in full ownership as an inducement to fresh settlers. The progress of cultivation soon changes this state of things. The more fertile land is taken up, and acquires value from the growth of population. At first sight it seems that the State might derive important resources from a reserved charge on its land, or, by adopting the simple expedient of leasing it out instead of giving it away,

[1] 'It seems to me that the distinction between a tax and a rent is merely a matter of amount; and that if a land tax is so high as to absorb the rent it becomes in fact rent,' Campbell in *Cobden Club Essays* (1st series), 130-1. Cp. Marshall, *Principles*, 681 n.

would obtain a share of the increase in its value. The Wakefield system, though not designed for financial ends, sought to secure a higher capital return for land that was sold, at the same time applying the funds so derived for the promotion of immigration; in fact, increasing both colonial receipts and expenditure. The advantages of free access to land are however so great in a new country; the effect on economic development of a speedy growth of population is so considerable and so easily perceived, that no effectual method of limiting the occupation of the soil in full ownership has been continued. The United States, the various English colonies, and the South American Republics have all found that nothing is such a stimulus to immigration as full liberty of acquiring vacant land. For this reason the revenues of those States from land are comparatively speaking small, and for obtaining the necessary funds recourse must be had to other forms, principally indirect taxation. As examples it appears that in 1889 the United States obtained over £1,600,000 by the sale of public lands, but against this the expenses on the same account have to be set off, and the result seems to be that on the whole there is a loss on the state lands: they really are an item of expenditure not of receipts [1]. For the financial year 1886–7 the Canadian land receipts were a little over £40,000, though it is hoped that in future years the return will be greater. In the same year the Australasian colonies received over £3,500,000, about two-thirds of which was from sales and the remaining one-third from rents on leases [2]. Thus neither in new nor in old countries are the lands of the State one of the main

[1] 'Except for the period 1830 to 1840 the lands have been a drain upon, and not a resource of our government,' *Quarterly Journal of Economics*, i. 174.

[2] The precise figures are

United States land sales, 1888–9		$8,038,651·79
Canada land revenue, 1886–7		$213,459
Australasian colonies, 1886–7,	sales	£2,279,769
ditto.	rents	£1,280,528
ditto.	sales and rents combined	£3,560,297

supports of the financial system. It requires an extraordinary combination of circumstances, as in the case of India, to create an exception to this general rule.

§ 4. The apparent advantages of a large state revenue from land and the peculiar nature of the income received from the use of superior natural agents has suggested the advisability of dispossessing all private owners and reverting to the primitive system of public ownership. Whether under the name of rent or of the single tax, this plan of imposition involves the confiscation of all existing rights in land. Its bearings, when regarded as a form of taxation, belong to the theory of that part of our subject, but we may notice it in so far as it advocates an extension of state property. And here there is an evident distinction to be made. In one form of the proposal, existing owners are to be compensated, when it simply amounts to an extension of the state domains by purchase. In the other and more drastic form no compensation is to be allowed. Owners of land, no matter how acquired, are to be compelled to surrender their incomes from this source to the State. It is not necessary to characterize the morality of this scheme, but its financial attractiveness, at first sight great, is much diminished on closer examination. The disturbance of economic relations and the general feeling of insecurity that the adoption of such a measure would produce, even on the assumption that it would be carried into effect without a revolution, would go far to reduce the productiveness of land to the State, and to lower the incomes of other classes of the society in whose interest the measure is advocated.

The proportion of land revenue to the total receipts in each of the last mentioned colonies is as follows:—

Western Australia	26·87 per cent.
New South Wales	21·65 ,, ,,
Queensland	21·25 ,, ,,
South Australia	11·50 ,, ,,
Tasmania	10·99 ,, ,,
New Zealand	9·17 ,, ,,
Victoria	8·72 ,, ,,
Average	14·98 ,, ,,

In another way, too, the gain would be reduced. The large amount of general and local taxation at present raised from land, as also the necessary expenditure for keeping it in proper condition, must be deducted before the net advantage to the Exchequer can be known. Besides, all the difficulties attendant on state management of land would exist in at least equal strength if it were acquired without paying its fair value[1].

§ 5. From these far-reaching and unsafe theoretical plans we may now turn to the actual questions connected with the public ownership of land. They are divided into two groups, the first of which considers the advisability of the State retaining its domains, and the second, taking the retention as desirable, investigates the best methods of administration. As the former comprises the already noticed question of land nationalization with full compensation, we shall find it convenient to commence with it.

At the opening of scientific economic inquiry the treatment of state lands was a subject for discussion. German writers e.g. Justi, favoured their retention as being a better source of income than taxation, but the tendency of the new doctrines of the Physiocrats and Adam Smith were in the opposite direction. Taxation in the form of a direct charge on the net revenue of land was regarded by the former as the proper support of the State, and the latter has unequivocally pronounced in favour of the alienation of the public domain. 'The revenue which in any civilized monarchy the Crown derives from the crown lands, though it appears to cost nothing to individuals, in reality costs more to the society than perhaps any other equal revenue which the crown enjoys. It would in all cases be for the interest of the society to replace this revenue to the Crown by some other equal revenue, and to divide the lands among

[1] The idea of state ownership of land, based on an application of the economic theory of rent, first appears in James Mill's *Elements*. He was probably led to it by his study of India. J. S. Mill, in the later years of his life, maintained a like opinion, which in recent years has been urged with much enthusiasm by Mr. Henry George, and in Australia by Mr. Syme.

the people, which could not well be done better perhaps than by exposing them to public sale[1].'

The reasons given in favour of this policy are clear and simple. Firstly, the lands held by the State are managed so badly that the revenue of the society would be increased by their alienation, since the produce obtained from them would be larger. The price obtained by the government would go to discharge liabilities, and therefore the amount of receipts, if not larger, would certainly not be less; and, finally, the improvement of the alienated lands, under the management of private individuals, would by adding to the source from which taxes are drawn, make their yield greater. The case as so presented is a strong one, and, in the main, convincing. Nevertheless, the German writers on Finance have regarded this view of Adam Smith's as one-sided and exaggerated. His condemnation of state property is, it is said, too absolute, and various arguments in favour of the retention of state domains have been put forward. Thus, the advantage of such property as a security for public loans is suggested as a reason for their retention; also the advantage of model estates on which improvements may be introduced as a means of instruction to agriculturists. The political gain to the Crown from possessing an independent source of income, and, too, the prospect of the value and return of land increasing through the progress of society are given as further reasons in favour of retention. Most of these pleas are unfounded: if public lands are a security for loans their sale would prevent the need of borrowing. The royal income is just as secure when settled on the civil list; no matter what be its form a revolution will disturb it. The value of model estates is a distinct and separate question,

[1] 347a. cp. the opinion of Burke 'A landed estate is certainly the very worst which the Crown can possess. All minute and dispersed possessions, . . . which require a continued personal attendance are of a nature more proper for private management than public administration.' 'Speech on Economical Reform' (1780), *Works*, ii. 79.

and belongs rather to expenditure than to revenue, so that the only valid argument remaining is that derived from the growth of rent or unearned increment. The question, however, remains, whether this very growth is not in great measure due to the incentive that private ownership of land gives, and which is removed by state occupation. Still it must be admitted that in the case more especially of land suited by position for building sites there is a decided advantage in reserving the constant increments of rent for public use ; and that any equitable mode of accomplishing this end is deserving of approval. The retention of state or crown lands is of itself by no means sufficient for the purpose. Even in Germany or Russia the proportion of public land really at the full disposal of the State is only a fraction of the whole, and the part of it that is situated within urban districts is much smaller, so that it appears that under actual conditions the difficult question of unearned increment in connexion with ground rents must be solved, if solved at all, by special taxation. The contention of Adam Smith therefore holds good, that in general, from a purely financial point of view, the sale of lands in order to clear off debt or meet extraordinary expenditure is expedient. Underlying the discussion in the *Wealth of Nations* there are, it should be noticed, some assumed conditions that did really correspond to the facts in Adam Smith's time. These are (1) the existence of debt on the part of the State. While it is financially wise to dispose of property yielding small returns to meet obligations paying a high rate of interest, it is not equally clear that alienation of property to meet current expenditure is justifiable. Expenditure of the normal kind should be met by equally normal receipts, and the sale of land is not of this nature [1]. Unfortunately, the case is rather conceivable than actually existent, as every

[1] The Australasian colonies, incorrectly as it seems, place sales of land among current receipts, a partial exception is found in Victoria, where a small sum is carried to the Railway Construction Account, *Victorian Year-Book* (1887-8), i. 140.

country has its public debts to a larger amount than the sale of its domains would meet. (2) The expediency of selling the state domain also depends on the available market. In most European States in the eighteenth century there was no difficulty in finding an open market for the amount of land held by the sovereigns. But under other circumstances it would be hopeless to expect that large masses of land could be sold at their normal value owing to want of capital and enterprise on the part of individuals. Such is plainly the position of India in those cases where the land tax is really a rent [1]. In addition to the political and social evils there would almost certainly be a financial loss from forced sales. The same statement would hold good for all new countries where the sale of land depends on the demand of fresh settlers, and where the amount disposable in any one year is limited.

The evident conclusion seems to be that the function of the State as owner of agricultural land is sure to decline in importance with the advance of society. The proportion of the quasi-private income of the State to tax revenue becomes smaller in the course of time, and as the industrial domain has in certain directions a tendency to expand, the falling off in the yield from rent must be very decided. Though this will be the probable final result, it is also true that for a long period the management of state lands will be of practical interest in some countries, and will always remain as a problem of financial science. If the State, through its central or local organs, is the owner of landed property it is desirable that property so held should be wisely managed.

§ 6. The methods of administering state lands may be reduced to the same classes as those existing in the case of a large private owner. As in the latter instance the estate may be worked by the proprietor or let out to tenants, so may public property be either directly under state adminis-

[1] The sale of fee-simple estates to European settlers is emphatically one of those exceptions that prove the rule.

M 2

tration or be leased to private individuals. The former system is probably the earliest. The celebrated capitulary of Charlemagne, entitled *de villis*, contains a set of regulations for the management of his manors, and in Germany several parallels are to be found [1], but the same influences that caused land-owners to abandon farming by bailiffs affected the royal estates. A direct financial gain was procured by letting the lands to tenants. To work effectively a large area of land requires a good deal of capital applied with intelligence, under diligent supervision. All these conditions were wanting in public or royal management, and therefore the economic advantages of the tenancy system were so great as to be easily recognised. The method of direct state administration as a financial policy has no supporters [2].

The dealings of the State with agricultural tenants ought, it is plain, to be modelled on the system of a prudent landlord. There is no possible reason why the treatment of state domains should differ from that applied by private owners to the management of their properties. In two respects, indeed, the nature of the public power has peculiarities that affect its dealings with land. It is of longer duration than the individual owner, and it has necessarily to act through agents. A result of the former is the possibility of longer agreements and a more continuous policy in the system adopted: the latter makes the use of definite rules desirable to prevent corrupt action on the part of officials. Even as regards these special features there is not much difference between the state property and those of the largest class of English owners where the method of estate management is handed on unchanged for generations, and most of the administrative work has to be done by paid representatives [3].

[1] Roscher, § 11.

[2] Not even Wagner, cp. i. 540–1.

[3] An interesting description of estate management is given in Escott's *England*, ch. 3. The following passage bears out the view in the text, 'The Crown and the Ecclesiastical Commissioners are at the present moment the

The earliest agricultural tenants are probably to be found in the serfs who cultivated the soil and paid rents in labour, or produce, or both. The advance in personal liberty freed these cultivators from many of the more degrading incidents of their tenure, and by degrees they became established as free tenants paying money rents. In another way a larger class of tenants was created. Officials in charge of land were bound to account for a certain return, the surplus, if any, going to them, and this function of collecting dues with the obligation of giving a fixed quota to the sovereign, became in many cases tenancy, passing later on into ownership.

The application of what are called 'commercial principles' to the letting of land is of comparatively recent introduction, but it is only at this stage that the idea of conscious choice between different systems, hitherto followed through the blind influence of custom, comes prominently forward. Three forms of tenure are possible, viz. tenancy from year to year, or in popular language 'at will,' leases for years, and heritable, extending to perpetual, leases. The first form has been almost universally condemned, though under the fair and impartial guidance of a public department it would be free from some of its most objectionable aspects. The undue increase of rent and the discouragement to improvements characteristic of the tenure would neither of them be likely to happen under state management. Leases for years are, however, free from even the chance of such evils, and it is perhaps wise to adopt this system, as otherwise the example of the public estates might be put forward to justify the conduct of private owners in adhering to yearly tenancies. The exact number of years to be given in the state leases can hardly be decided on general principles. It should be long enough to give full room for

most extensive land proprieters in England, having the management of properties with a rental of upwards of £400,000, situated in all parts of the United Kingdom. These are administered upon practically the same principles which obtain in the cases of the large landed nobility,' 37.

the application of the tenant's industry and capital, while in the interest of the public it should not exceed the time during which a large increase of the natural value of the land takes place. Provided that full allowance is made for the tenant's improvements, thirty years seems a fair term, and sufficient to eliminate the effects of casual disturbances.

Older than leases for years is the system of hereditary lease (*Erbpacht*) that has from early times been connected with public property. The *emphyteusis*—the form that it takes in Roman Law—was originally developed on the estates of municipalities, and in the Middle Ages ecclesiastical bodies were foremost in granting similar tenures [1]. The advantages to a corporation of obtaining a settled rent without the trouble of supervision and calls for expenditure are greater than in the case of a single owner who hopes to gain extra rent by his attention and outlay, and when combined with fines for change of possession the revenue obtained is generally satisfactory. Nevertheless the hereditary lease is in reality a step towards alienation. The tenant holding by this tenure is part owner and in course of time tends to take the position of full owner subject to a rent charge [2]; more especially is this true when the fines, as usually happens, are redeemed by a fixed payment. The head landlord—i. e. with regard to public lands the State—is substantially a creditor entitled to certain remedies if his obligation is not paid. What seems the most prudent policy, alike on financial and social grounds with respect to state management of property, is to follow the system adopted by the best individual landowners, and the forms between which choice will generally lie are the lease for a sufficient term of years and the hereditary lease; the former is financially the wisest, but special circumstances may make the *emphyteusis*—to use

[1] For the origin of the *Emphyteusis*, see Gaius, iii. 145; cp. the *Aforamento* in Portugal described by Laveleye, *Cobden Club Essays* (1st Series), 241.

[2] Thus the *Emphyteuta* had for his remedy the *utilis actio in rem* closely analogous to the *Vindicatio* or owner's remedy.

the old title—more convenient, when we must remember that the land revenue is practically converted into a fixed charge. Leases for lives are open to the objection that they are uncertain, but by judicious regulations as to renewals much of the evil of insecurity can be avoided.

The modes of setting vacant farms, the duty of supplying buildings and permanent improvements, and the form in which rent is to be received, have all been carefully discussed in the older financial treatises. Most of these questions belong to practical administration and are, moreover, not of great interest in modern times. Certain plain rules may, however, be stated. The claims of successors to the late tenant should not be overlooked; it is better for the tenure to be continued without break, and therefore the question of new letting ought rarely to occur. When it does, the best mode of disposal will depend on the circumstances of the particular district; with capitalist farmers letting to the highest bidder is admissible and it excludes all chance of unfairness. But where, as notably was the case in Ireland, there is exaggerated competition for land, the amount of rent payable over a series of years by a solvent tenant should not be exceeded. In such cases a sale of the interest subject to a fixed rent seems the best course. The supply of suitable buildings, and the institution of permanent improvements must, under a system of short leases, be carried out by the State, but the modern plan of advancing public funds for improvements could be easily applied, the interest on loans being added to the rent and paid at the same time. Hereditary leaseholds may be safely left to the tenant as he gains all the benefit of improvements. The form of rent ought clearly to be, as far as possible, in money. Special conditions may make payment in kind more convenient, but this mode of receiving rent should be only temporary and all possible efforts be tried to introduce the more definite system of money payments. Even where for practical convenience the rent is a fixed part of the total produce, the actual payment had best be in money, the various articles being estimated at their money value.

§ 7. We are now in a position to deal more fully with the expediency of extending the state lands. In their extremest form plans of this kind aim at the acquisition by purchase of all private landed property. More moderate proposals seek to increase those possessions in a smaller degree. Any plan of the kind even limited in the most careful manner is open to overwhelming objections. It amounts to the creation of a new public department engaged in countless dealings with what is the most intricate and complicated form of property; arrangements as to valuation, the renewal of leases, allowances for improvements, abatements for unexpected losses, the maintenance and audit of innumerable accounts would all fall to the lot of the department. It would, on the supposition of purchase, have to pay interest on a large amount of debt. There would be little hope of a favourable financial result under such conditions. In short, we may say that if land-nationalization without purchase is palpably unjust, land-nationalization with purchase is as evidently inexpedient. The same arguments apply to smaller acquisitions of land. They have little chance of being remunerative, while they so far contract the supply of a much desired commodity and they necessitate a class of administrative duties that are of exceptional difficulty. If the alienation of state lands should only be carried out with due care and deliberation, the acquisition of new estates can only be justified on non-financial grounds. Practical politics clearly conform to this rule of prudence. State lands are often alienated and seldom acquired, and in these latter cases there is generally some social or political reason as the actuating cause. We may look on the slow decline of the state domain as one of the permanent facts of financial development.

§ 8. So far we have confined our attention to the case of cultivated land—of 'farms' as Carey would say—where the ordinary economic motives operate with considerable force. The State, it seems, had best avoid entangling its interests with the difficult questions of land tenure, and can hardly expect any financial advantage from retaining its ownership of land. It does not follow that with regard to other closely allied forms of extractive industry it may not be expedient to retain or even extend public ownership. The principal example is afforded by forests, and in their case the wisdom of alienation is far less clearly established. Individual self-interest is not in the same general agreement with public advantage as with regard to ordinary agriculture. The creation of a forest is a work of time and technical skill which can hardly bring in recompense to the originators, and existing forests are a ready resource for the embarrassed owner. Moreover, forestry is only applicable to large tracts of land, and is most profitably carried on where the soil is of little use for other purposes. The estate of the large owner is, as we saw, not very differently managed from the state domain, and therefore some of the usual arguments against public ownership lose their weight. There is, besides, the important effect of suitable plantation on climatic conditions, and in some countries the need of wood as the only available fuel. There is here a striking example of failure in that harmony of individual and general interest which was so enthusiastically set forth by Bastiat and became a 'watchword' of what was supposed to be 'Political Economy.' The case against not simply state owership, but even direct state management is accordingly deprived of its foundation; while the promotion of his own interest had best be left to the individual, the interest of the community cannot always be safely entrusted to his hands. The real questions at issue are to be decided by estimates as to (1) the influence of other than purely self-regarding motives on the proprietors, (2) the amount of general interest that is jeopardized by the possible action of individuals, and (3) the probability that public management will secure the desired results.

In reference to the first it has been universally remarked that large proprietors are in many cases willing to give up a portion of present wealth for the future advantage and beautifying of their estates, while peasant proprietors show no such disposition, but, on the contrary, seek immediate gain by the removal of valuable timber[1]. The inattention of the State to forests in England compared with continental conntries is partly explicable on this ground. English proprietors have done at their own cost what foreign countries have to secure at the public expense. Another reason is to be added. The supply of fuel in England is not dependent in the smallest degree on the cultivation of timber, and the recent developments of naval architecture have destroyed the importance of forests as a source of shipbuilding material, the object to which the Woods and Forests Department principally attended. Considerations of climate are besides of less weight in the case of islands subject to the equalising influence of the sea. We can thus easily understand the peculiar attitude of England and the reasons for the very different policy of the Indian Government where the circumstances are in all essential points reversed. The chance of success in state administration of forests depends on the application of the best scientific and technical ability to the work which can only be attained by effective organization. Among examples we may mention the Indian forests department and the Prussian organization. The objects of a sound method of dealing with this part of the public domain are not mainly financial, though good management may make them yield a surplus. But, as appeared in dealing with expenditure[2], it is quite possible that the general revenue of the State may have to con-

[1] '*Presque partout le paysan n'aime pas la forêt, dans le Midi il n'aime pas l'arbre; il n'a qu'une faible idée d'utilité indirecte des choses. Les grandes et les moyennes propriétés, les parcs, auxquels s'attaque la frivolité démocratique, rendent à ce point de vue de réels services à la communauté,*' Leroy Beaulieu, *État Moderne*, 124.

[2] *Supra*, Bk. i. ch. 6. § 3.

tribute for the maintenance of the requisite plantings, when the policy has to be judged on the grounds of expenditure in general.

§ 9. The necessities of practice have led States to a recognition of the special advantages of directly controlling forests. In all nations they form the largest part of the public land, the figures for France have already been given, and the same general features mark the position in other countries. The broad result is that about one-third of the forests of Germany are held by the States; about one-sixth by communes and quasi-public bodies; very little over half remaining in private ownership. In Austria one-fourth belongs to public bodies, and in Norway one-eighth.

The excess of forests over other state land is easily explained when we call to mind that they are the last remnants of the old common property. To a primitive community land with timber is of little service. When, at a later time, wood rises in value the one aim is to clear the soil as speedily as possible, and land still under trees is waste. The fact that poor soil is often best suited for planting tends to confine it to land of this kind, since more fertile land is turned to other and better uses. The recent movement towards reafforesting is for the same economic reason directed towards inferior land, and it is only by adopting this policy that new forests can be made even tolerably remunerative. There is almost a consensus of competent opinion in favour of state action for the purpose of increasing the area under trees, and directly administering those areas by a skilled and well-organized staff[1].

Most European countries have a considerable area of uncultivated land which would be particularly suitable for planting and a well-considered system of purchase by the State, perhaps accompanied and facilitated by the sale of the other parts of public landed property is likely to be

[1] Leroy Beaulieu, i. 46–66, 91–2; Wagner, i. 571 sq; Roscher, §§ 16, 17.

advantageous. The financial results cannot be of much importance. Prudence and judgment may, however, save a good deal of unnecessary expenditure and combine the two ends of public economy—utility and saving of effort.

§ 10. The division of control over landed property between the central and local governments can hardly be arranged on general principles. Historical conditions and the special features of each case are the principal factors in the settlement. Management by a central department is open to the dangers of laxity in administration along with pedantry in the application of inflexible rules. Public estates so placed have all the defects attributed to the absentee proprietor. Local bodies have a different but not less serious draw-back, viz. the danger of jobbery and intrigue in the administration of what ought to be applied to the best advantage of the community. This evil is of varying magnitude according to the size of the body. Among the larger German States as, e. g. Würtemberg or Baden, it disappears completely. In a small French or Swiss *Commune* it is at its maximum. The dealings with public or quasi-public property by small corporate bodies need to be carefully controlled and regulated, and this necessity has been recognised. Thus the French *Communes* are unable to sell or grant a lease of their lands for more than eighteen years without the sanction of the Préfet in the council of the Préfecture[1]. The property of British corporations has in former times suffered from the want of such control, as has also that of the Swiss communes. When local government is applied to a sufficiently large area and public spirit is operative, landed property is generally better managed than it would be by a central department. The concessions to tenants are more liberal, but except where the land is within an urban district, its sale is probably advisable if there is a local debt sufficient to absorb the purchase money: where this is not so there is

[1] Say, *Dictionnaire des Finances*, s. v. 'Communes,' 1120; see also 'Alienation,' 117–8.

the danger of the price, which is really capital, being treated as current revenue. The retention of building sites by corporations is, where practicable, the happiest solution of the vexed problem of taxation of ground rents, and their alienation should not, unless in the exceptional cases of extraordinary pressure or special encouragement to small proprietors be sanctioned.

The above considerations are in some degree modified with regard to forests. So far as the inhabitants of rural districts obtain fuel from the communal possessions there is no reason to object to local management. But in modern times the need of husbanding and developing the national forests has become too important an end to be surrendered to the care of persons whose views are from the nature of the case certain to be limited to a particular district and the present advantage. The result has been a very general centralization of management in this respect. France, Italy, Switzerland, and the United States have all dealt with the matter as one for the central government. The Swiss cantons, so jealous of their autonomy, have not refused to surrender the control of forests to the Federal government. All the conditions that we noticed in a former chapter as tending in favour of central management are in operation here. General interest, need of trained intelligence, and of unity of control make it expedient to continue the policy of centralization.

CHAPTER III.

THE INDUSTRIAL DOMAIN.

§ 1. IN the preceding chapter the gradual decay of state revenue from landed property has been considered. Special circumstances may preserve a comparatively large amount of agricultural possessions in the case of some nations, but so long as the present system of private ownership and free competition continues—and it is only to societies resting on that economic basis that attention need be directed—no large part of the State's resources can, speaking generally, be obtained through the rent of public lands. The universal tendency exhibited in countries so widely separated in all respects as England, the United States, and India is towards a relative, or even an absolute decline in the revenue derived from this form of receipts.

Another class of public property does not show so clearly the same movement. The industrial domain, if it has been contracted in some directions, has been enlarged in others, and its position in state aud public economy is deserving of the most careful examination. For this purpose it is best to take the leading groups of industrial activity beginning with that which belongs to extractive industry, and is consequently nearest to agriculture and forestry.

§ 2. Besides the retention of agricultural land and forests, the State has in most societies regarded mines as belonging to itself. Thus the famous silver mines of Laurium were an important source of revenue to the Athenian people who let them out on lease. Rome retained its salt mines and monopolized the sale of the product. As the Roman dominion extended by conquest the mines of the provinces came under its control. The modes of management applied were different in respect to the various minerals, gold and silver mines being directly worked by the state slaves, and other mines conceded on lease or abandoned to private working subject to a tax proportional to the produce.

The mining laws of mediaeval Europe were affected by feudal ideas; they placed the right over minerals in the 'Lord' or '*Seigneur*,' and the influence of this system can be traced at present in the English law as to gold and silver mines. The desire to encourage mining industry, and the need of gaining revenue for the sovereign, both tended to restrict the rights of landowners with respect to what lay beneath the surface. Hence the system of 'free mining,' under which the discoverer was entitled to open a mine against the landowner's wish subject to the payment of royalties to the State (*Bergregal*) became usual[1]. Notwithstanding this growth in continental States of a separate property in mines, some countries retained much of their mineral wealth as public property, more particularly where the landed domain also was extensive. The various parts of the German Empire are noticeable for their state mines, though the distribution of these sources of wealth is far from uniform. Prussia owns coal, iron, lead, silver, and copper mines, which (including the value of the partially worked-up products) contributed in 1884–5, 102½ million marks *gross* revenue. Austria, Russia, Spain, and India also possess some mines as state property, though they are practically conceded to private owners. The financier is not much concerned with this part of the public possessions as the *net* revenue obtained is small. The mines and mining works of the Prussian government in 1884–5 gave only 17½ million marks (about £875,000) as their *net* yield. Salt, which in many countries contributes very largely to the public resources does so through taxation.

[1] Roscher, *Handel und Gewerbfleiss*, § 180.

Whatever be the net return from mines it should—economically considered—be divided into two parts, (1) the rent of the mine and (2) the profit on its working including the gain of elaborating the raw material obtained from it, where this is done at the mine. The former is essentially the same as the rent of land, though possessing some peculiarities due to the exhaustible nature of mineral products and is generally levied in proportion to the gross product. Without state ownership it might be applied as a special tax on private owners of mines [1]. The second element is plainly the result of the employment of capital and should therefore comprise both ordinary interest and employer's gain. The use of capital in mining is a highly speculative one being most uncertain in its returns. The receipts from the Prussian mines have varied much between 1870–1880, and of course are dependent on the prices of the minerals produced [2]. It therefore seems desirable to give up this source of revenue by selling the mines to private individuals or companies, and applying their price to the reduction of debt, and from the financial point of view, the wisdom of the policy of sale is indisputable. The continuance of mines as state property is due partly to the survival of the older forms of public economy in which taxation was subordinate to quasi-private receipts, and partly to views of economic policy. The danger of mineral supplies being worked in a reckless and extravagant manner without regard to the welfare of future generations, and the dread of combinations by the producers of such commodities as tin, copper, and salt, with the aim of raising prices, have both tended to hinder the alienation of state mines. There are fortunately other and more effectual methods of warding off these, by no means imaginary evils [3]. The dis-

[1] On the value of mining rents see Sorley, *Mining Royalties*; also Marshall, *Principles*, i. 491.

[2] Wagner, i. 609.

[3] Jevons' *Coal Question*, 354 sq. The recent 'rings' in the articles mentioned in the text illustrate the danger, but in the case of the two former the originators have suffered heavily.

posal of state property does not carry with it a surrender of the right of state regulation where public interests require it. It is also possible to retain the ownership or *dominium* in the State, giving long leases to the capitalist workers by which system the risk of marked fluctuations is in a great measure avoided ; or, finally, the net receipts from mining industries may be specially taxed.

In one case, the policy of sale may not be a wise one. When the particular product of a mine is taxed, the necessity for supervision compels the public officials to watch the processes closely, and under such conditions to place the whole business in the hands of the administration or of a powerful company may be the best course and prove the least inconvenient to all concerned. The principal example is in the case of salt which is taxed in most countries, and monopolized by the State in some. Where the supply is obtained from mines there is an obvious advantage in keeping them in the hands of the State[1].

§ 3. The modern State has not confined its activity to extractive industries. In the 17th century, France started some of those model manufacturing establishments which continue to the present, and possess so varied a character[2]. The German States followed a similar course, and during the 18th century many artistic industries were founded under official management. The object was not financial ; it was rather to supply a standard for private producers and to discharge the functions now supposed to belong to exhibitions. The more costly products were intended for court use or as gifts to foreign princes[3].

This class of state factories has preserved its original

[1] See Bk. iv. ch. 6 for the salt tax.

[2] '*On ne se fait pas une idée de tout ce que fabrique l'état en France ; il fait de tapis (les Gobelins), des porcelains (Sèvres), des cartes au Bureau d'état major, des gravures (au Louvre), de l'imprimerie (à l'Imprimerie Nationale) : il fait des boîtes d'allumettes, des cigarettes, il élève des chevaux et des poulains dans ses haras ; il fait du vin à l'école d'agriculture de Montpellier,*' Gide, *L'École Nouvelle*, 18.

[3] Wagner, i. 623.

type and is important only as giving examples of superior work or supplying some state need for a certain commodity. But though financial aims are not prominent in this department of public economy, there are opportunities for realizing a moderate revenue by careful management and securing a superior class of products.

The latter consideration becomes of great importance when we pass to the method of supplying the larger public services such as the military and naval forces. The difficulty of deciding on the best mode of meeting the manifold needs of modern armies and fleets is chiefly due to the conflict of financial and technical reasons. As we shall see, there are strong economic and financial objections to direct manufacture by the State. But in some cases it is essential to secure a high standard of excellence in the products. Guns that will not go off at the right time and bayonets that bend under pressure are dear at any price: and state establishments for the production of these articles are defended on the ground that in no other way can goodness of quality be guaranteed. The state clothing-factories and flour-mills have been supported by like arguments, since it is assumed that complete supervision of private contractors is practically impossible. On purely financial grounds state industries of the kind are open to serious criticism owing to the very defective system of keeping accounts which is characteristic of such establishments. The amount of invested capital is hardly ever properly estimated; receipts that should go to capital are assigned to revenue, and expenditure that ought to be met from revenue is defrayed from other state funds or by borrowing[1]. To

[1] This defect in state industrial management is very forcibly exposed in Cobden's last speech in Parliament (July 22nd, 1864): 'Throughout the inquiries before Parliamentary Committees upon our Government manufactories, you find yourself in a difficulty directly you try to make the gentlemen at the head of these establishments understand that they must pay interest for capital, rent for land, as well as allow for depreciation of machinery and plant,' *Speeches* (popular ed.), 301–2. 'The accounts rendered of this clothing department are most fallacious. I find that about £15,000 a year for fixed charges and interest of money have never been brought into the accounts at

meet this evil it seems best in a developed industrial community to trust to private enterprise for the supply even of warlike implements. The growth of such factories as those of Elswick and Essen ought to enable Government to dispense with the troublesome institutions that require so much attention and vigilance to prevent the grossest abuses. Where there is not a fully grown system of industry it may be necessary to keep up state arsenals, dockyards, and factories, to supply wants that would otherwise remain unsatisfied, and it is, perhaps, partly to this earlier condition that we owe the erection of the state industries in question. Moreover the possibility of keeping down prices, by having an alternative source of supply in the not unknown case of there being only one private factory in existence, may be allowed in favour of state industry, though against it there is the risk of political corruption in towns that are largely supported by public outlay. Admitting then that the State's manufactories for its own use are necessary only in the earlier stages of development, and ought to diminish as society advances, we may go on to assert that the same proposition is true of public industry in general. The Government of a backward country may rightly undertake works that would be quite uncalled for in more advanced nations. British India gives us numerous illustrations. The most promising agricultural industries have been taken under state management, and costly experiments have been tried. The best available evidence, however, leads to the conclusion that the greater part of these well-meant efforts have been unsuccessful, and have in some instances been abandoned[1].

§ 4. Though any very large system of state-directed

all, and that there is no allowance for rates and taxes,' *ib.* 304. Cp. Parnell, 'Although the victualling and other offices that carry on manufactures produce accounts by way of showing that they make them cheaper than they can be got by contract, this does nothing towards supporting their case, because their accounts are all kept in so imperfect a manner that they cannot be relied on,' *Financial Reform*, 162–3.

[1] Hunter, *Imperial Gazetteer of India*, vi. 515–6.

industries is not likely to be a financial success, and is besides open to other weighty objections both social and political, there are some exceptions to the general statement. There is no validity in a plea of *laissez faire* set up in opposition to special cases of state industry, when it can be shown that the interests of the community will be furthered by interference. The rule of non-intervention is nothing but a generalization from experience, and holds good so far only as experience supports it. Where special reasons justify the action of the public power there is no ground for objecting to its employment. To avoid the opposite and more dangerous extreme, we should add that the advantageous conduct of certain industries by the State is no argument in favour of extending its activity to other and dissimilar cases.

In addition to the direct supply of the needs of the public services, which in some cases is a good ground for the State undertaking industrial functions, there is the important class of cases in which the production of certain articles is subject to heavy taxation. In such cases the placing of the absolute control of the process of production in the hands of a state department may be a financial necessity, as the only effectual remedy against fraud and evasion. The French tobacco manufacture is probably the best example of this system, to which the Bengal opium regulations may be added. The large receipts obtained from these industries are not in reality industrial. Scientifically speaking, they are a part of the revenue raised by taxation of which state monopoly is a particular form[1]. The ordinary gains of a business are all that should be credited to it as 'earnings,' unless the extra amount is due to the superior efficiency of public management.

§ 5. The remaining cases, where the industrial action of the State may possibly be useful and has in practice been largely applied, may be grouped under two heads, according as they exhibit specially one of two characteristic features;

[1] Bk. iv. ch. 6.

viz. (i) those industries in which there is a tendency to the creation of monopoly, or in which the establishment of monopoly is likely to prove economically advantageous, and (ii) the large and important industries that deal with communication and transport. This classification is unfortunately not completely distinctive, since the last group in many instances exhibits the features of the first-mentioned one; but it is sufficient as a guide in discussing the principal points of interest.

(i) The first group is not easily characterised and separated, but there are some general marks that may be taken as common to all the industries in question; they are:—

(1) The products are much required, and in some cases absolute necessaries or of high sanitary importance. (2) They are connected with special localities, and situation is an element in their advantages. (3) They are usually subject to the (so-called) law of 'increasing returns,' and thus concentration and unity in management tend to cheapen the product. (4) Competition is not steadily operative even when no legal restrictions are imposed[1].

On coming to collect the industries that belong to this group, we further notice that they in great measure fall within the domain of local rather than that of general government, and are moreover chiefly due to the conditions of city life.

The oldest, and one of the most important, is the supply of water. Under ordinary circumstances this indispensable commodity is valueless in the economic sense, and has usually been the stock example in economic text-books of objects that possess utility but are not wealth. The growth of population in certain confined areas at once creates a greater demand than can be supplied from natural sources, and at the same time pollutes that limited amount. Fresh supplies must be obtained from a distance, and often

[1] The nature and characteristics of these industries are discussed by Farrer, *State and Trade*, 68 sq. Cp. H. C. Adams, *Relation of the State to Industrial Action*.

necessitate heavy outlay. In earlier times this of itself made it incumbent on the State to do what no private individuals' association could accomplish, a policy extensively carried out by the Romans. In the modern period, the business of water-supply to cities has been placed in the hands of private companies, who have invested large amounts of capital for the purpose. The rise of the sanitary movement of the present century and the danger of monopoly on the part of the holders have led to an extension of public activity, and to the purchase of waterworks by the municipalities. This tendency has been clearly shown in the United Kingdom during the last quarter of a century. Of the larger towns, London, Bristol, and Newcastle only are supplied by private companies, and the purchase of the London water-companies is already debated. The receipts for water-supply by English local bodies in 1887–8 were over £250,000. In the United States there has been a like movement. Out of 135 towns of above 10,000 inhabitants, 91 had municipal waterworks, the remaining 44 being supplied by companies. Continental cities also in many cases have acquired full charge of this industry: this is true of Berlin, Paris, and Vienna, not to mention smaller towns [1].

The business of lighting has not as yet been so largely entrusted to public agency, but several leading British towns have acquired their gasworks; Manchester, Birmingham and Leeds, Glasgow, Edinburgh and Belfast may be mentioned as examples. The United States have hardly entered on this branch of state industry. Philadelphia and Richmond are the only important towns that have public gasworks, and some smaller towns have public stores for

[1] For the position of English municipalities see the annual *Reports of Local Government Board*. For the United States, *The relation of modern municipalities quasi-public works* (American Economic Association, ii. no. 6); also Ely, *Taxation in American States and Cities*, 47 sq. For Germany, Wagner, ii. 160–4; Roscher, § 158. Also Leroy Beaulieu, *État Moderne*, 228 sq.; Say, *Dictionnaire d'Économie politique*, s. v. 'Eau dans les Villes.'

electric light. Most German cities own their gasworks, while Paris is supplied by a privileged company[1].

Drainage and the removal of refuse, as well as other sanitary arrangements, are usually regarded as a public function involving expense, though scientifically these operations are on exactly the same plane as the supply of water and light, and might be carried on as a private business; but in practice, as the service is a general one, its cost is defrayed from taxation.

The actually existing forms of these public industries, and the line of development that they are following, are easily explicable. The rapid increase of public waterworks is due to the great importance of a pure supply of that necessary, to the large quantity of it that is required for public purposes, and finally to the absence of invention in the industry. Lighting, while it possesses some of the features just mentioned, is very different in the last respect. Until the contest between gas and electric-lighting is closed, the acquisition of either of these industries will be a financial risk that no prudent body will care to incur[2].

§ 6. Without dwelling on further details, or considering the politico-social aspect of the movement, we need not hesitate to say that a new public domain, yielding large gross returns, has within the last fifty years become established in most civilized States. The gas and waterworks of the United Kingdom under municipal working give an estimated yield of about £7,000,000, and the similar German industries afford a considerable net return to the local budgets. It is quite possible that in the next century such industries will give substantial aid towards meeting the heavy expenditure that town administration requires[3].

On the other hand, there are some financial aspects of the case which reduce this apparent gain to much more

[1] In addition to the works given in the preceding note see James, *The Modern Municipality and the Gas Supply*, and Farrer, *State and Trade*, ch. 11.

[2] 'Waterworks are generally owned by our municipalities and gasworks rarely,' Ely, 48.

[3] Leroy Beaulieu, i. 110.

moderate dimensions. The purchase or construction of the needed public works has involved municipal governments in heavy debt. Thus the latest returns of English municipalities show that forty-six leading towns had an outstanding debt for waterworks of £28,000,000, while thirty-one owed £10,330,000 for their gasworks; further, that forty towns had a debt of over £1,500,000 for market buildings. Adding these figures together we get over £40,000,000 of debt remaining, besides what has been already paid off. According to the United States Census of 1880, about £29,000,000 of local indebtedness was incurred for waterworks. The cost of these loans has to be deducted from the gross receipts of the industries before a full estimate of their financial position can be made; and though the actual debt charge is enhanced by the sinking funds attached[1], there is on the other side the cost of renewing the works after a period. Another deduction has also to be made. On the assumption that the different public industries were left open to private enterprise, it would be possible to tax their profits, or, as most of these industries are monopolies, to levy a special charge on their gains. The right of supplying a large city may be sold to a company or let for a term of years, and the revenue thus obtained without risk or trouble applied to the services of the municipality. By granting a long period, with the ultimate reversion to the local governing body, a large revenue would be provided for the future, and the difficulties of public management escaped.

As in the case of mines and their products, any excessive charge for municipal services must be regarded as taxation. The profit of capital expended on public works is a part of the earnings or industrial receipts; so is any further amount gained by the low interest at which well-managed towns can borrow, or the savings that monopoly, with the consequent check to waste in competition, may cause; but any additional charge for the supply of water, gas, or other

[1] See Bk. v. ch. 8. for an examination of local indebtedness.

services is in fact a tax on the consumers or users of that service [1]. We have noticed before this mingling of earnings and taxes in public economy. Another financial evil may possibly result from municipal industries. Instead of taxing the consumers by heavy rates, the administrators may reduce the charges below the profitable level, and so give what is in fact a bounty on the commodity at the expense of the tax-payers. Where the article is required by the poorer members of the community the temptation to adopt this course is very strong, but it really involves the transfer of the industries so dealt with to the head of expenditure; from being a source of revenue they become a charge on the municipal budget, and their development only adds to the public burdens.

§ 7. (ii) The second group of industries leads us back to the Finance of the central power, and includes amongst its ranks the best known and accepted of all state employments. The Post Office has been regarded, even by the older economists, as an exception to the general rule against state interference in trade and industry. 'It is perhaps,' said Adam Smith, 'the only mercantile project which has been successfully managed by, I believe, every sort of government [2],' and his opinion has been accepted by all his English followers, none but the extremest advocates of state abstention ever questioning the public management of this department.

State postal service originated in the claim of the sovereign to monopolize whatever affairs closely affected public interests, and in the need of communication between officials. Its development has been the same in its general features in all European countries. At first the service was rendered by private persons, or by some specially privileged body (e.g. in France the messengers of the University of Paris), and was finally taken by the State, though in most instances it was farmed out to a company.

The English Post dates from Charles I (there being little

[1] Cp. Cohn, § 458.

[2] 344.

evidence for the earlier dates of Edward IV and Henry VIII), and became a strict monopoly during the Commonwealth. After the Restoration it was bestowed on the Duke of York, who retained it on his accession to the throne as James II in 1685. The net annual revenue was at that date about £50,000[1]. The growth of revenue during the 18th century was steady, and various improvements, such as the introduction of mail-coaches in 1784, improved its position. The invention of railways and steamships further aided the expansion of the postal service, until in 1840 the introduction of the penny letter-post, on Rowland Hill's proposal, widely distributed the advantages of cheap communication. Without in the least denying the wisdom of this reform, its real financial result was not what is popularly believed. So far from improving the net revenue of the service, it actually lowered the *gross* revenue, and so far reduced the already deficient income of that period. In 1839 the gross revenue had been £2,390,000, and the net revenue £1,630,000. In 1840 the former fell to £1,360,000, and the latter to £500,000, showing a loss of over £1,130,000, and this loss continued for several years: the gross receipts did not exceed those of 1839 till 1855, and the net revenue did not recover its losses till 1864. Taking into account the growth that would have taken place even under the older system, it is plain that the immediate adoption of the penny post involved a sacrifice of financial resources[2].

The French post office was instituted by Louis XI in 1464, and carried on irregularly, till in 1627 the service was better organized and improved. The business was farmed out in 1672, and the competition of the agents of the University of Paris was prohibited; the yield increased

[1] Macaulay, *History of England*, ch. 3.

[2] The reform is described by one of the most sober of English statesmen as 'A measure of undoubted social and general advantage, but extremely inconvenient in a financial sense,' Northcote, *Twenty Years of Financial Policy*, 9. It was opposed at the time by J. R. McCulloch; see his *Taxation and Funding*, 327–32. For an examination of the uses of the Post Office as an agent for taxation, see Bk. iv. ch. 8.

from 100,000 livres in 1661 to 1,220,000 in 1677, and 1,400,000 livres in 1683. In 1699 the postal income was 2,800,000 livres, in 1750 it had increased to 4,500,000 livres, and in 1788 it reached 12,000,000 livres. The method of farming, so common under the *Ancien Régime*, made it in fact a monopolized private industry, on which the State levied a gradually increasing rent.

The Revolution separated the carriage of letters from the other duties of the old '*Poste*,' and in 1792 placed the former under the direct management of the State. The great financial pressure and the general mismanagement of the revolutionary period caused a great increase in the charge for letters, destroyed the receipts from the business, and even left a deficit on the working. The postal service did not gain much during the Consulate and Empire, but several improvements were introduced after 1815. The rates were better adjusted, and the increased facilities of transport allowed of a better service. The example of England, whose adoption of the uniform penny post attracted much attention and was eulogized by Bastiat, led to the establishment in 1848 of a charge of 20 centimes (2*d.*), which has been raised to 25 centimes in 1850 and again in 1871, restored to 20 centimes in 1854, and finally reduced to 15 centimes (1½*d.*) in 1878 [1].

The same fact of financial loss through reduction presented itself in France in 1848 as in England in 1840. The gross revenue fell from 45,000,000 francs to 32,000,000 francs in the first year after the change (1849), and only recovered the earlier amount in 1855.

The postal history of other States is very similar. Germany, owing to its political disorganization, was in part served by the house of Thurn and Taxis, who managed the carriage of letters for several of the smaller States. The Prussian post began in 1646, and was under direct state

[1] For the French Post before 1789 Vignes, *Traité des Impôts*, i. 476 sq.; Clamageran, ii. 658; iii. 43, 232, 293, etc. For its later history Leroy Beaulieu, i. 645 sq.; De Parieu, iii. 287 sq.

administration. Its net yield in 1685 was less than 40,000 thalers; by 1740 it had increased to 220,000 thalers. The financial necessities of the government caused an increase in the tariffs, and in 1806 there was a clear surplus of 667,000 thalers. The amount in 1856 had risen to nearly 1,760,000 thalers, and in 1862 to over 2,200,000 thalers. The events of 1866 and 1870–1 changed the Prussian post into that of the German Empire—Bavaria and Würtemberg only retaining separate establishments. The net revenue of the imperial post was, in 1874, 5,000,000 marks (1 thaler = 3 marks); in 1879, 17,500,000 marks; and in 1888, 28,000,000 marks.

The postal systems of Austria, Russia, Italy, and those of the smaller European States need not be examined in detail. Nor does the postal development of the United States, India and the Colonies present any special features of interest. One general fact is the smallness of the revenue obtained. England, France, and Germany are the only countries that derive a substantial amount from the post[1].

§ 8. The so-called 'Post Office' is in fact a collection of different, though connected, industries. The earliest state posts in both England and France carried passengers as well as letters, and this function lasted in the latter country till the Revolution, when the state passenger-service became a separate organization, and endured till 1870. But the conveyance of patterns, books, newspapers, and small parcels forms an extensive part of the postal service, and is the least profitable side of its endeavours. The rates for these separate classes are below the ordinary letter charges, since otherwise the amount of business would be much reduced. The State is compelled to adopt the principle familiar to railway-managers of charging what 'the traffic will bear,' but it necessarily obtains very little over the cost of its operations. So far as the conveyance of parcels and newspapers is concerned, the English Post Office does not possess a monopoly, and is therefore a true

[1] Wagner, ii. 142; Cohn, §§ 293–6.

industrial agency whose earnings contain no tax element. The German post has specially developed the conveyance of parcels, a part of the business which is left entirely to private companies in the United States, and is a recent addition in England (only since 1882)[1].

To secure a proper adjustment of rates on the many classes of articles, and to duly apportion cost and service to the several items, is beyond doubt a most complicated problem. Such solutions as have been reached are for the most part empirical, and are the outcome of innumerable changes. The mere recapitulation of the diverse charges of the various state letter-posts would fill many pages with figures that could hardly be explained on any definite principle. There are, it would appear, three elements that might be taken into consideration, two of which depend on definite physical facts, viz. (1) the weight of the communication or document; (2) the distance over which it has to be carried; and (3) its nature; to which (4) the mode of conveyance might conceivably be added. The first is at present the basis of the charge for letters, which increases with the weight, but in a reduced proportion, and there is a disposition to raise the lowest weight. The second element has lost most of its importance. Since 1839 the question of distance has entirely disappeared in the postal charges of the United Kingdom. A letter from Penzance to Wick pays the same as one posted to a person residing in the same street as the sender. France has with one exception adopted the same policy since 1848, and the United States have also a uniform rate, practically the same as that of England (2 cents). The reason for this at first sight curious system is found in the fact forcibly urged by Rowland Hill, that the actual cost of carrying letters is small enough to be ignored. At the rate of one penny per ounce a ton of letters all up to the full weight would produce almost £150, while the mere cost of conveyance would certainly not be

[1] Another side of the Post Office, its dealings with money, belongs to 'Banking' and will be considered under that head, Bk. ii. ch. 4. § 2.

£5 or one-thirtieth of the receipts. The real charges are those of collection and distribution and the maintenance of offices, the cost of which is equal on all letters. The uniform charge irrespective of distance and the lower charges on additional weights are thus easily explained and proved to be sound as well as equitable. It is in the extension of this principle to international postage that the greatest advance in the future may be expected [1].

The character of the articles transmitted is now one of the principal distinctions. Circulars and post-cards would not bear the same charge as ordinary letters. The transmission of newspapers and books gives a yet smaller fund of utility on which to levy a tax, and the result is a series of differential charges not very logical or simple, but in its essence expedient in the interests of the postal revenue. The mode of conveyance might be used as a measure of the relative value of the service, speed in transmission being a very important part of the advantage of communication, but in fact this test has been little used.

§ 9. The question of the retention of the postal business by the State is hardly an open one. Long experience seems to have decided altogether in its favour. No country has adopted the method of private industry as regards letters, though the extension to parcels is not so general. The reasons for this remarkable unanimity are to be found partly in the facts of governmental administration, partly in certain special features of the employment. Before the rise of the economic schools that opposed industrial action on the part of the State, the method of public postal service was firmly established, and was seen to give, on the whole, sufficiently satisfactory results. It therefore escaped the hostile criticism that economists freely bestowed on the less efficient public departments. Mr. Herbert Spencer

[1] The Berne Convention of 1875, by which the uniform rate of 2½d. per ½ oz. was settled as the International postage charge for most civilised nations, and gradually extended to others, has been a great advance. India and the Australasian Colonies have since the opening of 1891 obtained the same rate with England.

himself has hesitated to condemn the continuance of the English Post Office. The peculiar nature of the service supported the evidence of facts. It requires as a first condition that the agency shall cover the whole territory to be served, or be universal. Next, it must be uniform and regular, and conducted on a definite routine; and, thirdly, the necessary capital is very small in proportion to the recurring expenditure and receipts. All these conditions favour state management, while its close connexion with everyday life secures a constant supervision on the part of the public who are the consumers interested in the efficiency of the service[1]. It is, therefore, expedient as a matter of policy to place the work in the hands of the State, and the bestowal of a monopoly is justified on the double ground that otherwise private agencies would compete for the more profitable parts of the business, leaving the supply of sparsely peopled and backward districts to the official post office, while the waste involved in rival establishments would hinder the reduction of rates below their actual level.

On the purely financial side the gain from the service must generally be a small one; the return for capital employed is little, and the only remaining element would be the economy that results from the application of monopoly, and the consequent unity of the service. Any further charge is really a form of taxation and requires to be tested by the rules applicable to that mode of procuring revenue[2]. The resources to be obtained are in any case not important, though good management may easily prevent a deficit, and unduly high charges will by their

[1] Adam Smith noticed these conditions: 'The capital to be advanced is not very considerable. There is no mystery in the business. The returns are not only certain, but immediate,' 344; cp. the fuller account of Jevons, *Methods of Social Reform*, 277–80; also Wagner, i. 654–5.

[2] This combination of different elements in the postal revenue has led to a curious diversity in the classification made by financial writers. Adam Smith considers it under the head of 'Funds which peculiarly belong to the sovereign. Leroy Beaulieu (Bk. ii. ch. 12), De Parieu (iii. 285), and Cohn (§ 77), place

reaction on industry prove seriously detrimental to other financial resources.

§ 10. The telegraph as a state business forms a natural appendage to the postal system. It is invariably connected with it owing to the resemblance in the work to be done. There are, however, some serious differences. Unlike the letter post, telegraphic work has been successfully carried on by companies, and international telegraphy is still largely in their hands. The capital expenditure is much greater in the case of the telegraphs, and therefore leaves room for that tendency of official bodies to confuse capital and revenue which we have already noticed [1] and which is so detrimental to sound Finance. Not only is the original cost of establishment or of the purchase of pre-existing rights comparatively speaking large, but incessant renewals and extensions are required in order to meet wear and supply new demands. The saving by unity of management is, besides, not so great, and the cost of transmission forms a larger proportion of the expense, which increases with increased work more rapidly than in the letter-post.

All the circumstances suggest that state telegraphy is not likely to prove financially successful, and such is apparently the result as shown by experience. The intermingling of postal and telegraphic business makes it hard to establish this proposition, but where a strict separation is kept up the telegraph balance is generally on the wrong side. The English state system has suffered financially, first from the excessive purchase money given to the companies who held the business, and secondly, through

it under Taxation. Roscher (§ 28) practically follows Adam Smith. Stein (ii. 315 sq.) places it in the list of prerogative rights (*regalia*); while Umpfenbach (§§ 61–3) and Wagner (ii. 141 sq.) regard the postal revenue as being derived from 'fees' (*Gebühren*). These differences are due to the attempt to reduce to simplicity what is in its nature complex, and are therefore necessarily failures. J. S. Mill distinguishes, as in the text, between the industrial and tax elements.

[1] § 3, *supra*. A grave oversight was committed with regard to the English telegraph account, by which £800,000 was spent without sanction.

the pressure on Parliament for lower rates, as shown in the adoption of sixpenny telegrams.

If full power to regulate its rates on economic principles be given to the department, there seems to be no reason why it should not at least meet expenses, including interest on capital, or perhaps give a small surplus sufficient to clear off the first charges in a series of years. Behind the fiscal question there remains the more difficult one of the effect of state management on the development of improvements. To retard the progress of the most essential of modern auxiliaries to commerce for the sake of adding a sum to each side of the national budget is not a desirable achievement. The dealings of state agencies with new inventions are the worst blots on public administration, and it seems that there is this risk in the State telegraphs, that though they are quite up to the standard at their inception, they almost insensibly fall behind as it advances with growing knowledge. This consideration belongs to economic policy rather than Finance, which, however, suffers from any hindrance to commercial expansion and is certainly not likely to gain by state telegraphy.

§ 11. The agencies of transport and the different facilities for the movement of goods have in modern times acquired much greater prominence and have to some extent come to occupy a different financial position. Adam Smith regards the maintenance of roads and canals as one of the duties of the State, requiring expenditure that ought to be defrayed out of the special receipts obtained from the users. His recognition of the so-called 'fee-principle' (*Gebührenprincip*) is qualified by his discussion of the taxes on communication, and is further weakened by the modern development of the transport system[1]. To understand the financial position of the industries in question, we have to separate the different forms and examine them in order.

[1] 303 sq.; cp. 379.

The maintenance of ordinary roads can hardly be regarded as a quasi-private industry. It is a part of the functions of the State, and preferably of the local governments. The principle of particular interest assigns this task to the smaller divisions, unless in the case of great main lines of traffic, but in no way does it fall within the industrial domain, unless the antiquated method of tolls is employed, and even then such charges have more resemblance to taxes.

The canal system has better claims to treatment under the present head. Private companies have in many instances reaped large profits from this form of investment, and there seems to be no reason why the State should adopt a different policy when it is the owner. In practice the usual tendency has been to keep the rates down to the amount necessary to cover expenses and meet the interest on the capital charge. The introduction of railways has put an additional strain on the canal finances, since rates have to be kept under those of the more rapid competitor, until finally in many cases all charges have been abandoned, and the canals have been maintained at the public expense. Such has been the position in France from 1880, when, contrary to the opinion of experts, the last remnant of the canal dues was abolished. The Erie canal constructed by the State of New York, which at first gave very large surpluses, had to be relieved from all tolls in 1882. The German rates have also been lowered, so that it appears that no assistance to the national or local revenues can be derived from this source, so long as present industrial conditions continue. The system of purely gratuitous service is certainly unjustifiable. A canal ought at least to pay its working expenses, otherwise its maintenance is a direct loss. The charges needed for this purpose would come from the utility that it affords, and the assumed impossibility of levying them is a proof of the uselessness of the service.

With regard to capital expenditure the case is different.

The tendency of all improvement is to displace fixed capital previously in use by newer and better forms, and state agencies cannot expect to escape this influence. But the existence of this danger is a good ground for seeking to get the maximum net revenue in the earlier years, in order to wipe off the capital charge, and in the period of decline for keeping the rates at the highest profitable level.

Much stress has been laid on the indirect benefits likely to result from the abolition or lowering of dues on waterways by encouraging industry. This claim really amounts to the advocacy of a bounty, and should be judged on that ground [1].

§ 12. In social and financial interest and importance railways far surpass the other agencies of transport. The creation of the present century, they have contributed largely to promote its special characteristics. Existing political and economic arrangements depend for their successful operation on the modern railway system, supplemented by steamboats and telegraphs. We need not accordingly be surprised to find that the principal financial problems of the public industrial domain centre in the treatment of railways. Every country has had to consider in what mode it might best utilize the invention, and in each the influence of national peculiarities and historical conditions has produced different effects. The railway legislation of England, France, Germany, and the United States affords many interesting examples of this statement.

Confining our attention to the financial aspects of the subject two divergent modes of treatment are broadly contrasted [2]. The policy of England and the United States has been to regard railways as merely one particular form of industry taking a place alongside of Banking, Insurance, Shipping, Mining or other Companies, but dependent for

[1] Bk. i. ch. 6. For the economic and financial position of canals, De Foville, *La Transformation des Moyens de transport*, ch. 7.

[2] For a clear statement of the opposed methods see Cohn, § 437.

any special privileges on the direct exercise of the legislative power. The railway company on its first appearance was regulated by enactments curiously similar to those devised for the earlier turnpike trusts and canal companies. The liberal laws of the various American commonwealths with reference to the formation of companies, while giving certain advantages to promoters, were based on the same principle. Such a policy reduced the public financial interest to a minimum. Railway companies were indeed taxed for local purposes as any other proprietors of land and buildings. A passenger duty intended to balance the older stagecoach tax was imposed on them. Various corporation taxes were raised by the American States, lavish grants of land were given to new companies, but in all other respects the public powers and the railways were separate. The various changes of English and American legislation have not infringed on this complete isolation. The restraints of the Intestate Commerce Act and the Railway and Canal Act (1888) have had no financial aim or effect. They are confined to the field of economic policy [1].

Continental countries have started from a different condition of things, and have all been willing to recognise a much closer connexion of the State and the railways. The earlier transport agencies had been under state direction. The carriage of passengers was one of the branches of the French post before the Revolution, and the administration of both roads and canals had been carried on by a state department. The German States had the same general conception without the centralized organization of France. There was thus a predisposing cause for the recent movement towards state railways, which has been encouraged by the ablest theoretical writers. The direct action of the State in the construction and working of railways has been restrained by econo-

[1] An admirable account of the variations of American and English railway policy in Hadley, *Railroad Transportation*, chs. 7 and 9.

mical conditions too potent to be set aside by legislation. England was the birthplace of the railway, and its mode of procedure had some effect on other countries, but the principal check was found in the absence of sufficient capital for the work. It was only by severe pressure on the English middle classes that the rapid progress in railway construction of the years 1845–50 was accomplished [1], and the motive power was the extravagant hope of gain. No such force assisted continental governments in procuring funds, and they were therefore compelled to fall back on the support of private companies whose shareholders were actuated by the ordinary economic motives.

§ 13. The different circumstances of the different countries affected the railway system. France with its strongly unified government aimed from the first at establishing a well-arranged series of lines on a systematic plan, with the reservation of the ultimate property in them to the State. This course had much to recommend it when considered *a priori*. It preserved the routine policy of the administration as to the older communications, and it promised at the end of the periods of concession to the companies to add a valuable property to the public domain. The earlier concessions under the legislation of 1842 were for short periods not in any instance exceeding forty-five years. The result was, however, to hinder the investment of capital, and to gradually force more favourable terms from the Government. To encourage the construction of new lines a guarantee of interest was given to the older companies who opened them, and the time of the concessions was extended. Special legislation was applied to induce the construction of local railways either at the expense or with the aid of the local governments. The war of 1870–1 and its effects made the improvement of the service a matter of great interest. In 1878 some railways were acquired and worked

[1] Tooke-Newmarch, *History of Prices*, v. 367–9.

directly by the State, and a plan for the creation of state railways on a large scale was proposed. Owing to the impossibility of procuring the necessary capital a new arrangement was made with the companies in 1883, by which the state railways became only one, and that the least important, of the seven groups into which the main lines are divided.

The financial results are decidedly unsatisfactory. The surplus from the government group after the working expenses are paid is small (for the year 1885, 4,257,000 francs), and by no means equals the interest on capital, which for the same year (1885) was over 40,000,000 francs. The local lines are a further charge on the central and local governments, as they have been proved to possess little earning power. Under the various conventions between 1859 and 1883 large advances have been made in the form of guaranteed interest, amounting for the eight years 1867–74 to over 290,000,000 francs. As these charges are repayable out of the future increments of value, they have under the newer system been separated from the annual Budget charge [1]. To shortly state the outcome of French railway policy on its financial side, we may say that as yet the expenditure of the State has been considerable, for which the returns so far have not been a sufficient recompense, but that the method of limited concession which checks the development of railway enterprise, and almost forces the State to give subsidies or guarantees, has the advantage of creating a large state property in the future. The terms of the six great companies who possess the main lines of France all expire between 1950 and 1960, when nearly 16,000 miles of railway will revert to the State, besides the new lines amounting probably to about 6000 miles for which public money is by the arrangement of 1883 to be gradually advanced. The net revenue of the French lines for 1887 was over 500,000,000 francs, so that

[1] Say, *Dictionnaire des Finances*, 991, s. v. 'Chemins de Fer'; Stourm, *Le Budget*, 257.

without taking the prospects of increased revenue into account there would be an addition of £20,000,000 annually to the state resources. Whether undue sacrifices have been made for the sake of this distant benefit is a difficult question to answer. We may conjecture that a simpler and more consistent method would have been better for French Finances[1].

§ 14. The earlier German railways were developed chiefly by state assistance or in some cases by state construction, but on no uniform plan. Each of the smaller territories formed its own railway system to meet local needs, without paying attention to the through lines of communication. Prussian railway policy was somewhat exceptional. Private companies were allowed to take part in the work of supplying needed lines, and guarantees of interest were given as encouragement. On military grounds several railway lines were constructed and worked by the State, and thus a basis was laid for the later policy.

The creation of the German Empire and the unification of its monetary and banking legislation could not fail to influence the position of the means of communication. State ownership and management were decided on; the only question of difficulty being the determination of the bodies who were undertake the duty. At first the central or Imperial government was to have been the owner. When, in deference to the sentiment of the smaller States, this plan was abandoned, the Prussian administration proceeded to buy up the chief private lines and work them by state officials. The magnitude of this process, which commenced about 1870, may be judged from the fact that in the year just mentioned thestate-owned railways were about 3,000 miles against 8,000 miles owned by private companies. In 1889 the lines owned or worked by the State had 13,200 miles against 1260 miles owned and worked by private companies. The smaller States have also purchased most of the few private lines

[1] For French railway policy Hadley, ch. 10, and the articles 'Chemins de Fer' in Say, *Dictionnaire des Finances* and *Dictionnaire d'Économie politique*.

in their territories. Hesse alone has a greater length of private than public mileage[1].

So far as Prussia is concerned the financial results have been extremely favourable. The prices paid for the purchase of the several lines were high, but nevertheless there has been a good surplus in each year after meeting all expenses and paying interest[2]. The services given to the imperial post by the railways form another gain, which is hardly ascertainable since it is mixed up in the postal receipts, which are thereby increased. To obtain a clear revenue of over £5,500,000 is an undoubted proof of financial success, though it may partly be derived from limiting the facilities for goods and passengers, and be in fact a tax on industrial activity. The great amount of public debt contracted as the purchase money of the private lines should be taken into account in considering the policy of Prussia. All pre-existing debt makes the terms of future loans more onerous, even when there are assets sufficient to meet the earlier charges, and it may be that Prussia's railway debt will injuriously affect her credit should she need it for war.

In the smaller German States the advantages of owning the railway lines are not so great. In Baden the estimate for 1890 assumed a surplus over working expenses of 14,341,000 marks, while the interest and sinking fund on the railway debt was taken as 17,091,000 marks. Württem-

[1] For the history and present position of the German railways, Wagner, i. 707–13; Hadley, 203–8.

[2] The surplus over working expenses, the interest on debt, and the net gain for each since 1881–2 are as follows:—

	Surplus over working expenses.	*Interest on debt.*	*Net gain.*
	MILLION MARKS.	MILLION MARKS.	MILLION MARKS.
1882–3	138·1	98·7	42·4
1883–4	147·8	112	35·8
1884–5	186	140·5	45·5
1885–6	193·8	158·6	35·2
1886–7	225·2	157·6	67·6
1887–8	273·3	164·3	109
1889–90	278·5	165·5	113

berg is in a similar situation. The net revenue for 1889–90 was estimated at 14,500,000 marks ; the interest on the railway debt being 15,861,000 marks. The Bavarian railways hardly meet the interest of their debt, and the lines of Saxony just balance. The reasons for this relatively inferior position are not clearly established. The greater activity and the wider area covered by the Prussian railroads probably allow of more economical management than can be applied to the smaller lines. The system of state management is of longer standing in the other States, and it is possible that sufficient time has not elapsed for a proper judgment on the merits of the state railways of Prussia.

§ 15. Both Austria and Hungary have in recent years increased the number of their state lines. In consequence of the financial troubles of 1873 and to avoid the heavy payments for guaranteed interest several leading lines were purchased by the State, though more than half remain in the charge of private companies. The surplus of the Austrian railways for 1891 is estimated at 8,300,000 florins, which does not meet the interest on the railway debt. The Hungarian state railways also have been in an unsatisfactory financial condition, the surplus for 1891 being taken as 20,200,000 florins, against a much larger debt charge [1].

Belgium illustrates perhaps better than any other European country the operation of state and private railways. The earlier lines were created by the State with the object of developing the transit trade, for which the country was so well suited. Additional lines were afterwards constructed by private enterprise, which competed with the state railways and with each other. To avoid this struggle a large part of the company-lines has been purchased by the government, but with the unfortunate result of reducing the receipts below the profitable point. In 1870, before the era of purchase, the surplus was nearly 20,000,000 francs, and the interest on debt nearly 13,000,000 francs,

[1] The new zone tariff policy of Hungary has improved the net receipts, but it is too soon to say whether the improvement will be permanent.

giving a net gain of almost 7,000,000 francs. Ten years later the surplus had risen to 45,750,000 francs, but the debt charge had reached 45,795,000 francs, giving a deficit of 45,000 francs, or, speaking broadly, the total receipts and expenses balanced. By 1883 the surplus was 48,500,000 francs, the debt charge having grown to 52,000,000 francs, thus making a deficit of 4,000,000 francs. Higher rates were imposed as a remedy for this evil, but in 1888 the surplus was only 51,700,000 francs, still leaving a deficit.

The experience of other European countries in regard to the financial effects of state-owned railways does not materially alter the conclusions that the cases already examined suggest. Holland and Italy (since 1885) have preferred to lease the state lines to private companies. Russia has some state railways, but for the larger part of her system gives guarantees of interest to private companies. Roumania, Norway, Sweden, and Denmark have most of their lines under state ownership, which in the former countries does not give sufficient surplus to pay interest on capital charge. Spain, Portugal, and Switzerland have as yet substantially adhered to the system of private enterprise [1].

§ 16. Outside Europe the railways have been mainly an item of state expenditure to the various governments. Both in North and South America large grants of land and guarantees of interest have been given as inducements to the undertakers of railways. Brazil and Chili possess some state lines which do not pay the interest on their capital. The government lines of Canada in some years have not even paid working expenses; the deficit in 1886 being 185,000 dollars, and 1887, 311,000 dollars, with the interest on $50,000,000 capital.

The Australasian colonies have entrusted the work of railway construction to their governments, who have borrowed largely for the purpose. In the year 1887 the total receipts from the Australasian state railways were £7,200,000 and the working expenses £4,540,000, giving a surplus of

[1] In addition to works already referred to, Von Scheel in Schönberg, 94–104.

£2,660,000. The debt contracted for railways amounted to £95,300,000, the interest on which is about £4,000,000. £1,340,000 would therefore represent roughly the expense of the Australasian railways for the year under consideration[1]. The Victorian railways, however, show better results than the other colonial lines, especially since the appointment of a special board of commissioners, and the growth of population will in the future largely increase the receipts in all the colonies.

The Indian railway policy is financially interesting as a further proof of the readiness of English administrators to adopt a system quite different from that of their own country. As in Australia, the State has taken a great part in the extension of railway communications. The first method was that of securing or guaranteeing interest to private companies, under which stimulus some of the main lines were constructed. Then came the pressure of military necessities and of famine relief. A number of smaller and less important lines were established and for the most part worked by the government. Finally, financial conditions have made it desirable to return to the guarantee system, but at a lower rate of interest and for a limited time. Though the receipts from the state railways are large (166,865,000 rupees for 1889–90), the expenditure is still larger (187,131,000 rupees for the same period), so that if the net balance only be taken into account, there is an annual outlay for the service.

§ 17. The statistics of state-railway Finance have been given at some length in order to facilitate the formation of

[1] *Victorian Year-Book*, 1887–8, iii. 141. The following table gives fuller and more precise figures for each Colony:—

	Receipts.	*Working Expenses.*	*Surplus.*	*Debt.*
	£	£	£	£
New South Wales	2,285,836	1,457,761	828,075	29,989,750
New Zealand ..	990,395	653,363	337,032	13,362,424
Queensland ..	710,458	534,381	176,077	13,127,799
South Australia ..	674,419	409,128	265,291	10,891,728
Tasmania	53,074	80,752	−27,678	1,771,928
Victoria	2,453,345	1,363,587	1,089,758	25,413,206
Western Australia	41,104	47,712	−6,608	816,147
Total	7,208,631	4,546,684	2,661,947	95,372,982

a correct judgment on the system. Within the last twenty years the movement towards 'railway nationalization' has been increasing in force, and though the grounds on which it has to be decided belong mainly to economic policy in the widest sense, financial considerations cannot be altogether neglected. The one conspicuous success of state-managed railways is found in Prussia, of which the minor German States, as Cohn allows[1], fall very far short. France and Belgium in recent years have not profited financially from their state lines. Those of Australasia and Canada afford on the whole no direct addition to the public revenues, a statement which is also true of India.

If the question be determined on these definite facts the conclusion ought, we believe, to be against state property in railways. Many other considerations are however to be taken into account. Advocates of state property dwell on the future increases from the growing movements of both persons and goods, and regard construction or purchase as a profitable investment for the future. Transport agencies act powerfully in the promotion of industrial and commercial development, and hence it is argued that even unremunerative lines may so benefit the community as to increase the productiveness of other sources of revenue. Again, unity of management, only to be obtained under the State, would reduce working expenses and leave a larger surplus as net profit. The superiority of state credit is alleged as another reason for believing that its ownership would be financially successful. The English government could some years ago borrow at $3\frac{1}{4}$ % (and now at less than 3 %), and buying up the railway shareholders' interests at their market value would, it is supposed, secure for itself the difference between the return on railway shares and that on Consols. By an extensive investment of borrowed capital a margin of profit would be obtained for the discharge of other public services.

[1] 'Die anderen deutschen Staaten sind Preussen (sofern sie nicht vorangegangen) in der Richtung der Staatsbahnpolitik gefolgt, haben freilich nicht ebenso günstige finanzielle Ergebnisse aufzuweisen,' § 439.

The objections to such a policy are obvious enough. There is no financial reason for investment in railroads that might not be applied to other forms of industry. If the advantages of unified management are important, the dangers of attempting to deal with a varied and complicated business are grave. Railway nationalization as a financial measure is open to the risks that attend similar proposals for land nationalization. Without accepting Jevons' view that the supposed gain from purchase through the higher credit of the State is wholly a fallacy [1], it is certain that it depends on a series of events which are uncertain and incalculable. Depression in trade, appreciation of the standard of value, or new inventions, would reduce very much the value of the fixed capital of the railway system. The policy of state acquisition exposes the public finances to all the chances of loss that these possibilities open up. At best the system of state-owned and managed railways thus appears to be a speculative employment of financial resources, and judged in the light of experience to be of more than doubtful advantage to the Exchequer. The general difficulties of state industrial enterprise are besides likely to occur in this as in other cases. The defective accounts of capital and revenue, expenditure and receipts cannot be escaped any more than in the dockyards or arsenals. With the best intentions it is not easy to distinguish clearly between the source and application of the different funds that railway administration has to deal with, and yet to get a perfectly trustworthy statement of the financial position of state

[1] 'If the State manages the railways just with the same degree of skill and success as the Companies there would then be no gain or loss; if better, there would be gain accruing, not from good credit, but from good management; if worse, there would be certain loss. Thus, in theory, the use of the public credit proves to be a pure fallacy, and if it were not so there would be no reason why the Treasury should not proceed to invest money in many kinds of industrial enterprises besides railways and telegraphs,' *Methods of Social Reform*, 371. The fact that the chance of loss is usually overestimated is here neglected. Jevons would be right if the same *income* as formerly were to be secured to shareholders, but the suggestion is that only the *market value* of the shares should be given.

railways is essential for a correct judgment on the policy that has created them.

§ 18. What the railway system is to the nation, tramways are to the town, and therefore it is quite in accordance with the general course of policy that there should be an effort to 'municipalize' these means of communication. English legislation places local governments in an exceptionally favourable position, either for establishing tramways themselves, or, after the expiration of a period, purchasing the rights of companies. Several leading British towns own their local lines, but are obliged to lease them to a contractor for working. Nearly £3,000,000 of capital has been applied to this object by about thirty towns. In the United States 'a few municipalities manage their own street-car lines'[1], but the number is small.

Though classed in accordance with their nature among the industries of transport, the tramways resemble in their economic and financial aspects the other industries discussed in an earlier part of the chapter.

§ 19. The proper administration of the railway system, assuming it to be owned by the State, is a further problem. Shall the lines be leased to a company, as in Holland, or be managed directly by state officials? The former seems the solution that offers the greatest financial advantages. The full value of the line can be obtained and the chance of loss in a great measure avoided. Unfortunately the objects for which state railways are often desired cannot be accomplished in this way. The lessees will doubtless use their privilege to gain the highest possible returns, and the evils of competition and unfair rates will continue.

State administration is so much desired by the opponents of private companies that, as in Germany, private lines are leased to the State. In this way the great outlay of capital is not required, and as the management of a railway line may be reduced to a system of routine, there at first appears to be a fair analogy with the post office. This resemblance

[1] Ely, *Taxation*, 270.

is only apparent. Instead of the simple tariff and limited classes with which the Post Office deals, there must be very elaborate classes and frequent adjustment to new conditions. The management of a great railway is an industrial 'undertaking' of peculiar difficulty, and is almost certain to suffer from the want of capable direction. The financial success of state-managed railways will be affected by the efficiency of the management of so complicated a business, and it is more than doubtful whether the gain through unity of direction and system will compensate for the lack of energy and zeal that state industries display.

A great deal will depend on the particular constitution and situation of the country. The good financial results of the Prussian railroads are attributed to the skill and care of the trained officials in the service of that State. Countries where the public service is not so well organized and with Governments more subject to popular control cannot hope for equal success. 'I tremble to think,' said Jevons, 'what might be the financial results if a property exceeding the national debt in nominal value and requiring in every part of it constant repairs, renewals, and extensions were in the hands of a Parliamentary minister who might find some day that he had been illegally and ignorantly signing away great sums of money at the bidding of his subordinates[1]'.

The financial working of the system would be particularly exposed to danger; for in addition to the risk of of errors in management there would be the pressure of opinion in favour of low fares and rates. If a substantial surplus were realized in any year it would be impossible to escape reductions that would effectually prevent its recurrence. Victorian experience is instructive on this point. Any increases in the gross receipts of the Colonial lines have been 'absorbed by the additional working expenses' due to extra facilities and lower rates. The Railway Commissioners declare that 'No department controlling state-

[1] *Methods of Social Reform*, 359.

owned railways can expect to be allowed to realize more than a small margin beyond the amount required to pay the interest upon the capital invested, as immediately that point has been reached the public request and insist upon concessions in rates or increased facilities, both of which are practically an amelioration of taxation.'[1] It remains to be seen whether Prussia will succeed in maintaining her high revenue from railways when once a movement for remission of taxation sets in. Cohn, for example, justifies the railway surplus on the ground that it is derived from the well-to-do classes, and makes the distribution of public burdens fairer, but if the duties on commodities of general use, which are so heavy in Germany, were modified, the claim for lower railway charges could not be met in this way[2].

The question of compensation for loss is another of the financial points in railway administration. State post offices escape the difficulty by repudiating all responsibility, no matter what the loss they inflict, but railways could not follow this most objectionable method. Over a large system it is probable that the cost of accidents and other losses could be averaged from year to year, though some variation would still occur. Smaller countries would not have this refuge from loss. A single heavy accident would damage the balance and turn profit into loss. The Victorian railways had for a single accident to pay claims to the amount of £128,988; but the total expenditure under that head for the year in question (1887–8) only amounted to £142,562, while for the preceding year it was but £6655. It is moreover highly probable that if the amount of compensation was assessed, as at present in England by juries, their bias would be altogether against the railway administration and to a greater extent than it is at present against private companies.

§ 20. One difficulty common to most forms of state industry arises from the necessity of dealing with large numbers of employees. The tasks of the modern State are

[1] *Victorian Year-Book*, 1887–8, ii. 139.

[2] Cohn, §§ 440–1.

sufficiently varied and comprehensive to take up all the ability and time of administrators without adding unnecessarily to their duties. Public industries, however, require for their efficient working a body of organized hands, obtained by free contract. The unavoidable consequence is the possibility of disagreement between the State and its helpers, culminating perhaps in the last weapon of industrial war—strikes[1]. The position of the public powers is in such cases a trying one. The agency that is bound to enforce order and fair-play is one of the parties to the dispute; the natural disposition of an administrator in a popular government is to make things smooth by yielding to the demands of the discontented, a course that involves additional expense and injuriously affects the financial position. The pressure of the consumer—that is the community—for low rates, and that of state officials for better conditions of service, is the most serious financial risk that the industrial activity of the State is likely to encounter. The Prussian railway service controls its 80,000 employees on an almost military system, aided by the organization of the national army. But any attempt to direct the railway system of the United Kingdom on a similar plan would be hopeless.

§ 21. But whatever be the judgment that we form as to the expediency of the policy, there can be little doubt that it has had important effects on public Finance. In most European States a new branch of the public domain has been called into existence, with very large gross receipts. The weight of public indebtedness has moreover been increased, and the real nature and results of that burden have been obscured[2]. A large section of private industry that would otherwise contribute to the public resources through taxation has come into the charge of the State. The broader social and political results do not concern us

[1] That this is not an imaginary danger is proved by the fact that in July 1890, there were 'strikes' at the municipal gasworks in Leeds, at the London Post Office, and in the Metropolitan Police, and also a 'mutiny' in the Guards!

[2] Bk. v. ch. 5 on the so-called 'reproductive' debt.

here. But the purely financial consequences of a continuance of the movement have much interest. One inevitable result will be the comparative reduction of tax-revenue as contributing to the gross receipts. The addition of English railway expenditure and receipts to the National Budget would nearly double its already portentous sum [1].

Under such conditions the ordinary method of interpreting financial returns would prove defective. At present the Post Office unduly affects the balance of the Budget, but its effect is insignificant compared with accounts of the magnitude of the railways. The Indian Budget, as Fawcett very clearly showed [2], is open to misinterpretation on this ground. Until the *gross* and *net* figures are separated and arranged, there are no correct data for discussing the financial situation.

Of more weight is the fact that this great increase of gross receipts and expenditure would leave the real power and burdens of the country almost unchanged. The

[1] The railways of the United Kingdom show the following results for the year 1889:—

Receipts from all sources	£77,025,017
Working Expenditure .	£40,094,116
Net Receipts . .	£36,930,901
Paid-up Capital . .	£876,595,166

The gross public revenue for the year ending March 31st, 1890 was £89,304,316

The total expenditure	£86,083,314
The National Debt at the end of the year was . .	£684,954,150
The charge of the debt for the same year, including redemption	£24,749,659

The inclusion of the railway accounts in the Budget would raise the receipts to over £166,000,000 and, taking the present railway net receipts to be capitalized at 4 per cent., the total expenditure to £163,000,000, and the Public Debt to about £1,600,000,000. If the now standard 2¾ per cent. stock were to be given, the capital should be proportionally increased or severe loss inflicted on the shareholders who had invested in the assurance of being undisturbed. The establishment of a sinking fund in the same proportion as that applied in various forms to the present debt would necessitate increased taxation unless state management proved very much more economical.

[2] *Indian Finance*, 17–25.

Finances might be a little better or a little worse according as there was a net gain or loss from the new state domain, but in substance the public wants would still have to be met from taxation, and the pressure would fall on private income, since the large revenues from quasi-private possessions would have corresponding charges against them.

The system of creating a state industrial domain by the policy of granting long concessions with ultimate reversion to the State is by far the most plausible. It appears to be a form of saving by securing advantages in the distant future at a small present sacrifice. For we cannot believe that the concessionaries do not endeavour to compensate themselves for their shorter term by increased charges, the result of limitation of advantages. Such is apparently the case in France, where the railway companies, if their tenure is limited, derive a counter advantage from the very high dividends guaranteed to them.

From one point of view the formation of a state property may be regarded as a process of saving somewhat analogous to the treasures accumulated by sovereigns in earlier times. A long-continued process of judicious investment might succeed in raising these accumulations to a very large amount, but under modern conditions it is better to trust to taxation for the needed revenues, and allow the investment of capital to proceed from the action of individuals. It may be further remarked that each extension of state ownership and management is a step in the direction of Socialism. That the growth of public industries, if carried on unchecked, would ultimately transform society into the type desired by the more thoughtful socialists, is undeniable; and whatever may be the merits of this kind of social organization, it is utterly incompatible with the continuance of the conditions which existing financial theories assume. During all changes of social life the fundamental economic and financial categories will survive, but their form may be so changed as to render entirely new expositions essential.

We are not called on to discuss socialistic proposals, but, to all who recognise their impracticability, the encouragement to Socialism that attends the extension of the industrial domain of the State may be noted as a further objection to it.

CHAPTER IV.

THE STATE AS CAPITALIST. ADMINISTRATIVE REVENUE.

§ 1. THE agricultural and industrial property of the State, though the former has lost most of its importance, and the latter is confined to particular sections of industry, have both retained a place as substantial sources of revenue in the case of at least some countries. The domain, the forests, and the railways of Prussia contribute a considerable amount to the budget and cannot be passed over. The land revenues of India are the mainstay of the Finances of that country, and England would feel the loss of the postal revenue. Very different is the position of what once might have been regarded as a co-ordinate part of the quasi-private income of the State, viz. the revenue from commerce. At one time the regulation and even the monopoly of certain branches of trade was believed to be a part of the royal prerogative. This position, which was most strongly held in the sixteenth century, gave way before the pressure of new economic forces and the criticisms of the more intelligent theorists. It is now universally recognised that, to use Adam Smith's words, 'no two characters seem more inconsistent than those of trader and sovereign[1]'. The speculative nature of commerce, the need for constant watchfulness and minute calculation

[1] 344.

of the chances of gain or loss which are its essential features, make it impossible for a State to hope for revenue by engaging in it.

The exceptions to this general rule are rather apparent than real. When a State possesses and works lands, forests, mines or factories—unless the products are used in the state service—it must find a market for what it turns out, but even this irreducible minimum of commercial transactions is the weakest part of state economy, and by its risks forms an additional objection to those already urged against increasing public lands or industries. The same necessity of course exists where an article is artificially monopolized for the purpose of effectual taxation, a process that is sometimes confined to the sale, leaving the production to private enterprise. Such revenue as is obtained in this mode is virtually taxation on the commodities so dealt with, and must be considered in that connexion. The only other exception that we need notice is that of the Dutch government trade from Java. Under the 'culture system' large quantities of valuable products, chiefly coffee, tea and spices, are received by the Colonial government and sold at a high rate. For many years large surpluses were realized, but lately the modifications of the culture system and the fall in prices have led to deficits in the colonial budget, and given still further proof of the hazardous nature of such revenues [1].

§ 2. The business of banking is in so many ways connected with the State that its public management appears to have much to recommend it. The ordinary method has, however, been that of granting concessions to privileged companies who are bound to afford facilities to the State in return for advantages enjoyed. England, France and Germany at present adopt this policy, with the various modifications that the circumstances of each country make advisable. The pure 'state-bank' in which the capital

[1] The Dutch policy in Java is too favourably described by Wallace, *Malay Archipelago*, chs. 7 and 17; cp. Wagner, i. 626–7.

of the undertaking is supplied from the public funds is found only in Russia and Sweden. In most countries banks contribute to the revenue either by the special services that they perform for the State, by taxation, or by sharing profits over a certain point with the Treasury, the last being the system of the German Imperial bank [1].

Banking may naturally be divided into (1) dealings with money, and (2) with capital. There are strong reasons for regarding the former as a state function, and it is probably from this part of the business that public revenue may best be obtained [2]. The trade in capital on the other hand seems entirely unfit for governmental intervention, though some small revenue may be gained from it by judicious taxation.

The relations of Public Finance with the banking system are not confined to questions of revenue. The public debt in its different forms, especially that of inconvertible paper issue, is mixed up with the trade in capital, and the whole mechanism of the financial system is dependent for its successful operation on the agencies of credit. We shall therefore have more than once to return to the subject [3].

Another form of state-banking has come into existence in the last thirty years, in the savings bank which originated in England in 1861, and has extended to Belgium, Italy, Holland, France, Austria and Sweden; but its financial importance is confined to the aid which the large deposits afford on the creation of terminable annuities.

§ 3. A more important but at the same time more questionable source of revenue is by many States derived from the receipts of lotteries conducted by the government. The tendency of the State to seek gain from the errors or

[1] The Imperial Bank of Germany appears as an annual contributor to the Budget, the estimate for 1890–1 being 1,383,500 marks.

[2] Cp. Ricardo's 'Plan for the Establishment of a National Bank,' where the two branches of banking are carefully distinguished, *Works*, 503–12.

[3] For inconvertible issues as a form of loan see Bk. v. ch. 6, and for the relation of the Treasury to Banks see Bk. vi. chap. 3.

vices of its subjects is very noticeable in the earlier periods of financial history. Appeals were often made to men's 'absurd presumption in their own good fortune' by the establishment of periodical lotteries, in which the contributors taken as a whole were certain to lose. In many cases the lottery became a state monopoly, and several examples still exist. The Prussian budget estimate for 1890–1 assumes a net yield of 8,291,500 marks from this source. The Austrian state lottery was estimated to give 21,500,000 florins in 1889. Italy is the receiver of the largest revenue from lotteries, the gross yield for 1889–90 being computed at 76,300,000 lire. Saxony, Hamburg, Spain and Hungary are also indebted to this system for portion of their revenues. The objections are rather moral than economic, though the virtues weakened by the prevalence of gambling are the peculiarly economic ones of prudence and willingness to acquire wealth by labour.

From the purely financial point of view, the more refined lottery systems depending on combinations of numbers are objectionable, as there is some uncertainty as to their gains. The State is exactly in the position of the banker of the gambling table. Thus 1885 was a bad year for the Italian lottery, 1886 a good one. The simple method of prizes arranged in classes is preferable, but it appeals less powerfully to the spirit of adventure, on the prevalence of which the institution depends for its continuance.

The pernicious effects of state sanction of the vice of gambling have led to the abandonment of the lottery system in England (1826), Hesse (1832), France (1836), Sweden (1840), Bavaria (1861), and Switzerland (1865), and Prussia seems likely soon to follow the example thus set.

§ 4. Adam Smith has made the institution of a 'public pawnshop' familiar by his reference to the case of Hamburg, and many similar establishments in the shape of the '*monts de piété*' in France, Belgium and some German States are in existence. The proceeds when they exceed the advances and cost of working are not applied to public use, so that the whole system is rather a charge, chiefly on municipal revenues.

A priori it would seem that the lending of accumulated wealth would be a convenient mode of securing a revenue for the public services, but, as in the case of industrial investments, the test of experience makes it plain that this is really an expensive way of obtaining the necessary supplies, since the principal has first to be raised and is afterwards less productively employed than when left in the ownership of private persons. A true conception of the relation of state income to the national income, which is the sum of all private incomes within the nation, overthrows the fallacy of state accumulation and investment.

Notwithstanding the force of this general canon, the financial accounts of modern states exhibit apparently many examples of advances of capital by the State. On investigation these cases turn out be connected with the use of public credit. For the furtherance of certain economic or social ends, as e. g. the improvement of land, or the erection of better dwellings for workmen, or municipal improvements, advances are made by the central government either to individuals or local bodies, but these loans are themselves ultimately derived from private capital by means of the public credit. The Treasury acts simply as an intermediary in supplying capital for certain desirable objects—a position made clearer in England by Mr. Goschen's separation of the local from the general debt. The repayment of the money so advanced is but the appropriate method of discharging the amount of debt that was contracted for the original loans.

§ 5. The interest on capital lent out is thus not a source of state revenue that need receive attention here since it does not really increase the public receipts. We may therefore pass on to consider those kinds of revenue that are fixed in amount and admit of capitalization, a circumstance that connects them with the gains from invested capital, notwithstanding that their origin is very different.

Foremost among such revenue is the gain from charges on land. In an earlier chapter of the present Book we found that the agricultural domain had often passed gradually from the hands of the sovereign by the introduction of hereditary leases. Permanency of tenure without limitation of rent is of little benefit, as increase in the charge can always be used to destroy the tenant's interest. Consequently the fixing for ever or for a long term of the rent to be paid accompanies the hereditary lease. The variable payments become settled and definite charges.

In another way the same form of revenue comes into existence. The servile tenures of the Middle Ages prescribed a great variety of duties to be performed by the tenants, which under the new conditions of 'money economy' were commuted into fixed sums. English legislation on copyholds, the measures of the French Constituent Assembly, and the Prussian land legislation since 1807, have all had this commutation and settling of dues as one of their objects. The tithes, so peculiarly distinctive of ecclesiastical property, have also undergone the same treatment, wherever they have not been abolished. The universality of the forces that work this change is shown by the extension of the terms of the Indian land settlements and the favour in which perpetual settlements are held. The difficulties as to the distinction between rent and taxation in India have been already noticed, as also that with a perpetual settlement the state receipts are in reality neither[1].

A still further question arises, viz. whether long-continued taxes on land should not be included in this class of receipts. Much controversy has arisen in connexion with the French *Impôt Foncier*; one party contending that its burden has ceased to be felt, since all purchasers deducted the capitalized amount of the tax from the purchase money; opponents of this view have brought forward the ever open possibility of changes in the amount so levied. The broader

[1] Bk. ii. ch. 2. § 2.

theoretical aspects of the matters at issue will occupy us in studying taxation, when we shall see reason for adopting the last-mentioned view, but some concession can be made to the advocates of the rent charge conception of land taxes. Where as in the case of the English Land Tax of 1692 (originally intended to include all property, but evaded by the holders of movable wealth) the amount is fixed on each estate, it does become a charge on the land. The system of redemption, applied first in 1798, is of itself sufficient to prove the correctness of this view. The so-called 'English Land Tax' is gradually disappearing. From its highest point of £1,911,663 in 1798, it has come down to £1,035,000 in 1889[1].

The expediency of allowing the parties liable to redeem charges depends altogether on the nature of the burden. As long as the land tax was really variable or intended to be so, the permission to capitalize the payments would necessarily be futile, since a fresh charge could always be imposed, but where fixity has been introduced the redemption is generally for the advantage of both sides, for that of the person liable since otherwise he would not consent to redeem, and for that of the State which is thereby enabled to reduce its liabilities. Whether a charge should be rendered fixed or not depends on the way in which it has been established, and is mainly determined by considerations of public policy. The conversion of taxes into fixed payments is, however, unquestionably an error in Finance, as, owing to the growth of public expenditure, provision has to be made for procuring larger sums, while the immobility of each existing tax compels the financier to have recourse to new, and on the whole, less eligible sources of revenue. The same consideration applies to commutations of rent, either of land, of mines, or of concessions for railways, canals, and other undertakings. The probability is

[1] See Dowell, *History of Taxation*, ii. 48 sq., and iii. 81–91, for the history of the tax. Movable property was exempted in 1833, and offices and pensions in 1875.

that they will give a larger return at each renewal, and this additional gain is lost by commutation for a fixed sum unless, indeed, full allowance is made in the arrangement for the value of the increments that may reasonably be expected in the future. Such transactions are not usually settled on terms favourable to the public revenue. An individual will not estimate a very distant gain at its real value to the community, and as a result the fixed payment will be but slightly raised by the inclusion of a benefit to come later on. Financially, it is best to reserve these prospective receipts for the new objects of outlay that are certain to arise.

§ 6. Besides the services attached to land, there is a miscellaneous group of receipts which may conveniently be noticed here. Historically they belong to the class of *regalia*, and are due to the Sovereign's prerogative. Amongst them we may mention charges for the privilege of hunting, or of fishing, which to some small extent contribute to the public revenue at present. Mediaeval Finance expanded this class of receipts to a remarkable extent. They acted, as Roscher has shown, as a transitional form between the earliest condition in which the domanial revenue sufficed for the royal service, and the later state economy depending chiefly on taxation [1]. Our modern customs and excises appear in germ in these feudal or imperial dues. Succession duties can also be referred to the same source, but apart from what may fairly be regarded as tax revenue in rudimentary form, there are the well-known feudal aids; the right of the Sovereign to fines; that of taking ownerless goods, and the numberless other claims that the ingenuity of lawyers succeeded in establishing.

Modern Finance has chiefly to deal with these prerogative rights so far as they help to explain the evolution of the existing systems of taxation, or in the scattered remnants which are found as survivals in every country, inexplicable

[1] Roscher, § 18. The whole chapter (Bk. i. ch. 4) is one of the best in his work.

except on historical grounds. This discussion also serves as a suitable introduction to another class of public receipts that has presented much difficulty in regard to its correct position in the financial system.

§ 7. The problem of classifying the revenues known as 'fees' (*Gebühren*) need not be again considered[1]. In accordance with the conclusion before reached no separate department for fees is requisite. Some of the so-called *Gebühren*, e.g. the postal revenue, have been noticed in the preceding chapter, others will find their place in the study of taxation, while the remainder of the heterogeneous class will be considered here as a sequel to the fixed charges imposed by the State. By this method the complications that otherwise occur are avoided and the creation of a distinct group of state receipts, co-ordinate with that derived from taxation, becomes unnecessary.

If further justification were needed for this breaking up of the topic of *Gebühren* that German financial science has laboured so strenuously to develope, it would be found in the remarkable divergences of opinion among its exponents. No two of the able and erudite workers at the subject give precisely the same interpretation and arrangement. The one fixed and definite result obtained can be and is recognised in our treatment, viz. that the 'fee' is paid in return for service done, and that it does not bring in a clear return to the State over and above the cost of the service for which it is paid.

The classification and division of the different kinds of fees is almost as unsettled as the nature and position of the whole system, but when we deduct those charges that really belong to the industrial domain, as also whatever is in fact tax revenue the difficulty is very much lessened. Special reasons apart, the State might charge for any service rendered to a determinate individual, and therefore it would seem abstractedly possible, that each public function would have its corresponding fees. State services cannot, as we

[1] See Bk. ii. ch. I. §§ 4, 5.

know, be analyzed, and their effect on each citizen assigned. The general interests of the society are a matter of importance to all; were it otherwise the whole organization of the State might be dissolved and its duties given up to individual enterprise. Fees come in only as a supplement to the other receipts of the public exchequer, and have to be confined to certain cases of measurable services where the citizen is brought into direct contact with the public power.

§ 8. The administration of justice has been the occasion for the earliest of these charges. Without returning to the previously considered position of primitive law courts[1] we need only bear in mind that the cost of law services has been more and more placed on the general revenue. From being self-supporting, the cost of justice has been steadily increasing. Nevertheless, a large number of charges are still levied in connexion with legal proceedings in every modern country. The United Kingdom shows net receipts for the year 1889–90 to the amount of £615,889 under the general head of 'Fees,' of which by far the largest part was obtained from court charges, the English Judicature alone contributing £352,356. Local governments also receive fees for police and justice which ought in strictness to be added, but the total amount was less than £500,000 for 1887–8. In France the system of court fees in the older form of *épices* was abolished at the Revolution, but the charges for documents and legal forms are still a part of the revenue under the title *Greffe*. The *Timbre* or stamp duty also affects judicial acts, but the greater part of its return is really taxation. For the year 1888 the receipts from the *Greffe* were 8,225,000 francs. The same category of receipts in Italy for the year 1881 came to 7,000,000 lire. The several German States, as well as the Imperial Government, obtain more or less revenue from the same source. So do many of the American commonwealths,

[1] Bk. i. ch. 3. § 1.

but the value of the comparative figures is very little, owing to the intermixture of fees with taxation[1].

Besides the revenue derived from contentious proceedings, or from fines on criminals, there are numerous juridical acts which require for their validity the payment of a contribution to the State, or which involve work on the part of the public officials, that can be charged for on the ordinary principle of service done. Such are entries in official registers, grants of naturalization and the supply of copies of legal transactions. One of the most important in practice is the dealing with land titles. In all countries with a proper land system owners' titles are registered and changes in the rights over land are recorded. The benefit of such a system to owners and intending purchasers is beyond question, while the cost is very moderate. A low scale of fees for the operations of the registry suffices to cover its expenses, and therefore is an eminently suitable mode of providing for them. Such charges are in principle clearly distinct from the heavy duties on the transfer of land that still exist in France, and form a part of the system of *Enregistrement*. Low fees have the double advantage of securing without difficulty a good proportion of the expense that administration entails, and of allowing transactions to be carried on without check.

§ 9. Fees for justice and juridical acts shade off almost insensibly into 'administrative fees' (*Verwaltungsgebühren*), so that many of those enumerated in the preceding section might fairly be placed under the latter head, but where the payment is made in connexion with questions of legal right it seems better to regard it as a 'law fee.' Among administrative fees those for ordinary certificates, e. g. of births, deaths, and marriages, may be included, the issue of passports, attestation of degrees and diplomas, and the

[1] Die absolute und relative Höhe des Gebührenertrages in verschiedenen Staaten mit einander zu vergleichen, ist darum bis jetzt nur höchst unvollkommen möglich, weil die Gebühren fast überall, jedoch mit sehr verschiedenem Grade, mit Verkehrssteuern verquickt sind,' Roscher, § 23, n. 16; cp. Wagner, ii. 69.

many other payments for special official relations. Most important, however, are the charges which are more or less connected with economic transactions, such as fees for testing the quality of articles that now exist chiefly as survivals of the older system of regulation, as e.g. the English hall-marks on gold and silver, or have been introduced on social grounds, as in the case of testing for adulteration.

In this somewhat miscellaneous collection, whose indefiniteness results from the wide extension of state functions, may be placed the revenue from seigniorage. The function of coining money is undertaken by every civilized government, and in most cases a small amount of the metal sent for coinage is retained in order to meet the expenses of the process. Where the deduction is limited to the amount necessary to cover the cost it is substantially a fee for guaranteeing the fineness and weight of the currency. The English mint does not do even this in respect to the gold coinage, which is a cause of expense to the State. It is more than recompensed on the token coinage of silver and copper which gives a varying surplus amounting for the year 1889–90 to the unusually large sum of £774,000. A receipt of so considerable an amount, if normal, would not be treated under the present head. If it could be shown that the seigniorage charge pressed on any class or classes it would be a special tax levied on them; if it was the result of state monopoly it would be a gain of the State from the industrial undertaking of coinage. As any large gain is very rare—the receipts of the English mint for 1889–90 were described by Mr. Goschen as 'a windfall which cannot be expected to recur[1]'—and as some mints do not cover their working expenses it is best to regard seigniorage as being one of the class of 'fees.'

Charges for testing weights and measures make another item in the list, so do light-house dues and dock charges. In almost every case of administrative action there will be

[1] *Budget Speech*, April 17th, 1890. The receipt for 1890–1 was £200,000 over the estimate.

some receipts owing to the definite services that are rendered to individuals or the commodities supplied to them. The sale of official publications may be given as an example.

A comparatively important head of revenue from 'fees' is found in the school payments that excite so much hostility on the part of reformers. The promotion of education has become a public duty, involving extensive outlay, which must be supplied either from taxation or from the fees paid by those who avail themselves of instruction. There is no valid reason why a part of the expenses of the system should not be borne by the parents, unless in the case of actual destitution. The policy pursued is very varying. The United States, and France since 1881, have no fees for primary schools. England and Germany retain them as yet, though there is every probability of their speedy disappearance in the former country. The receipts from school fees in the United Kingdom for 1889 came to almost £2,230,000. The fees obtained in Prussia in 1886 to nearly 11,000,000 marks [1].

The higher educational institutions also produce fees in small amounts, as e.g. in England the University of London almost covers its annual working expenditure by the fees of candidates for its degrees and certificates.

§ 10. Looking back on the list of receipts that may fairly be classed as fees, we see the absence of any harmonious or

[1] More precise figures are :—

		£
England.	Fees in School Board schools	635,255
	Fees in other schools receiving grants	1,207,695
Scotland.	Fees in Public Schools	249,155
	In other Schools	46,164
Ireland.	School Fees in National Schools	110,592
	Total	£2,245,861

In Germany the School Fees were in		
	1871	10,498,794 marks.
,, ,,	1878	12,975,527 ,,
,, ,,	1886	10,926,085 ,,

Cohn, § 190, n. *. The Education Act of 1891 can hardly be said to have abolished fees, though it has made their ultimate removal certain.

logical arrangement. There is no branch of the public power to which they can be attributed ; they are spread over the local and general budgets, and sometimes never come into account, being the perquisites of the officials who receive them, as is not uncommon in the United States. Much of the law that regulates them is only of interest in administration ; they are often inextricably mixed up with the public industrial receipts and with taxes, especially 'taxes on commerce' (*Verkehrssteuern*)[1], and finally the aid they give to the financier is not considerable. They may indeed be regarded as *incidental* products of state action. Just as in manufacturing processes certain by-products are formed which are sold for what they can bring, or as the labourer disposes of his spare hours for any wages that will overcome his desire for leisure, so the mechanism of the State, while aiming at the efficient discharge of the tasks set to it, nevertheless does not refuse to collect revenue that can be acquired without neglect of the primary object in view, and such revenue is that from fees.

There is thus complete justification for regarding them as an appendage to the quasi-private economic receipts as we have done in the present chapter.

[1] Cp. 'Bei dem engen Zusammenhang von Rechts- und Verwaltungsgebühren mit Verkehrssteuern in der Praxis und bei der für beide vielfach gemeinsamen Erhebungsform im Stempel ist die bezügliche Einnahme daraus ebenso wie die Gesetzgebung darüber nicht wohl zu trennen. Die Gesetze betreffen meist beide Abgabearten in bunter Vermengung,' Wagner, ii. 69.

CHAPTER V.

STATE PROPERTY.—GENERAL CONSIDERATIONS ON QUASI-PRIVATE REVENUE.

§ 1. WE have now examined the different classes of public receipts that can be fairly classed as 'quasi-private' or 'economic'; what the practical financier would describe as 'non-tax revenue.' The component elements are somewhat heterogeneous, a necessary result of the variety and complexity of public administration. Some of the categories shade off indefinitely into the other great class of contributions obtained through taxation, and thus deprive the technical groupings made for practical purposes of the logical consistency needed in scientific inquiry. In another respect the nature of things presents difficulties in the way of precise classification. The 'economic' revenue of the State is the product of property held, or payment for services done, by it. Great masses of public property are however, not productive of revenue in the ordinary sense. From the Houses of Parliament down to the smallest court-house, from Epping Forest to the village green, there are buildings and lands that bring in no return to be entered in any budget, local or general. They are, nevertheless, a constituent part of the public domain, the loss of which would be seriously felt even financially. They contribute not wealth in the strict sense but utility, and the problem of determining their financial advantage is therefore a difficult one. It seems that the best mode of framing an approximately correct estimate is to take the sacrifice that their loss would impose. The destruction of the public buildings of this class in the United Kingdom would place a considerable charge on both national and local resources, and this sum gauges the value of the existing buildings. The same test applies to the land devoted to general use, such as parks, commons, and roads when free from tolls[1]. The last-mentioned case shows how revenue-yielding property can pass into the class under discussion, and the French canals previously noticed afford another instance. Strictly speaking, the policy of charging fees only equivalent to the cost of maintenance or less than it is an intermediate stage between using state possessions as a source of economic revenue, and abandoning them to gratuitous use.

The extension of this 'unproductive' public domain is one of the remarkable features of the present century. The movement, usually described under the title of 'State Socialism,' has made the public powers owners of museums, picture-galleries, libraries, baths, gardens, and the other appliances of a civilized society. No *data* are at present available for forming an adequate conception of the extent of the movement, but of its reality and importance there can be no question. It is not limited to any particular country, and it is as prominent in local as in central government. Though commonly placed under the head of 'State-*socialism*,' it is really *communistic* rather than socialistic, since it implies the gratuitous supply of certain advantages

[1] Other but less satisfactory measures have been sometimes suggested. Instead of the cost of restoration the original cost of production or acquisition would, it is said, show the amount of public advantage obtained from the outlay. This method is certainly easier and more definite, but it overlooks the fact that mere cost, as such, does not determine value, and that all fixed forms of wealth change their values, generally in a downward direction, in the course of time. Land is the only part of the national possessions that is likely to increase in value. The measure of present exchange value is also inapplicable, as much of the property forming the public domain is not of a kind that is demanded by private purchasers.

that may be wholly unearned by the receivers. The classes who benefit directly are not those who contribute, even in labour, to the work of society. The public domain applied to either state or general use also influences the financial position by the outlay that is needed to keep it in efficient working. The existence of numerous public buildings, of large areas of land devoted to the service of the community, of works directly supplying state needs might give a very considerable sum of assets to be entered in the national ledger if an inventory of state property were taken [1]. It must, however, be remembered that the State is in mercantile phraseology 'a going concern.' Its property cannot be realized without suspending the processes of political life, and so long as these continue further expenditure is unavoidable. This part of public property resembles the mansion, demesne, coinage, plate and furniture of a rich man, which are only productive of wealth on the breaking-up of his establishment, and otherwise involve him in additional outlay. Each is in the language of modern economists the 'consumers' capital' of the proprietor, affording utility but not revenue in the narrower sense of the word.

These various points of connexion are quite sufficient ground for noticing the unproductive possessions of the State, and their suitable position is plainly in immediate sequence to that other section of public property which does contribute to the resources of the Budget. Between land earning profit and land that merely affords enjoyment there are so many intermediate gradations, that we pass almost insensibly from one to the other; and the same statement is applicable to some other forms of fixed capital.

There is an evident convenience in the use of separate terms for these two classes of public property. The language of French administration describes the revenue-giving part as *Domaine privé de l'état*, while the remainder

[1] As pursued in Italy under the system of M. Cerboni.

is the '*Domaine public*,' though the latter term is sometimes used in a wider sense to include all the possessions of the State. The phrase *Domaine privé* has often a legal rather than an economical or financial meaning, and denotes the property held by the State as a juristic person. Stein has proposed the terms '*Staatsbesitz*' and '*Domänen*' for the 'unproductive' and 'productive' parts of the public property, and perhaps the best English equivalents would be 'property' and 'domain,' though the former is rather too vague unless qualified by some limiting term [1].

§ 2. All the sources of revenue described in the present book possess one common feature that differentiates them from the tax receipts. Their amount has no essential connexion with the public wants. No matter what may be the demands on the public treasury the various parts of the national domain will continue to give the returns that the economic conditions establish. State lands will afford rent, state investments interest, and state industries profit under the normal form of those divisions of income. They will not increase in times of pressure, nor will they diminish when funds are abundant, and they therefore deserve the epithet 'mechanical' as opposed to 'organic' which has been given to them [2]. This feature of itself makes recourse to taxation a necessity in times of increasing expenditure. Even on the supposition that England had sufficient returns from its economic revenues to meet the expenditure of 1790, the French wars would have disturbed the balance, and it would never since have been restored. It might appear that the proposition just stated is not strictly exact. Fresh state wants might lead to more judicious management of the domain. Rents might be brought nearer to the economic limit. State industries might be worked with a closer eye to profit, and fees, notably, might be made higher. This qualification is only apparent. The

[1] Leroy-Beaulieu, i. 28; Say, *Dictionnaire d'Économie Politique*, i. 719; id., *Dictionnaire des Finances*, i. 1482–85; Stein, ii. 144 sq.

[2] Umpfenbach, 78.

previous low receipts were either the result of bad management or of a particular line of policy, and if the former, could have been rectified apart from the new needs; if the latter, would involve the loss of the object previously aimed at. Increased rents may retard agricultural advance; higher railway charges injuriously affect commerce, and increased fees tend to limit the transactions on which they are charged. Assuming then that pre-existing receipts have been arranged on correct principles, no increase can be obtained without a corresponding loss to the community, and in many instances it will be really taxation, as may easily happen with regard to any economic source of income. It is further probable that new demands will act injuriously on the economic revenues, e. g. a war retards social progress.

The antithesis between 'mechanical' and 'organic' revenue is thus shown to be based on the natural conditions of the two classes, and to indicate the place of each in a developed financial system.

§ 3. The division of the mechanical sources between central and local authorities is in general determined by the history and situation of each particular country. Land may, it would seem, be held either by the State as representing the sovereign of mediaeval times, or by the parish or *commune* which is the descendant of the old village community, but peculiarities in legal development have influenced the actual position. The English parish is very different from the French *commune* with its juristic personality, and separate property. The *commune* and the State are in most European countries the only public powers that have had enough continuity of existence to acquire the ownership of land. The crown and church possessions have passed to the latter, the 'waste' of the district to the former.

Intermediate bodies under unified governments, e. g. the English 'County' and the French 'Department' have little economic receipts, and what they possess is of recent origin. Federation naturally supplies the principal subdivisions with larger possessions, or rather it leaves them the wealth which they held before union, though in certain cases the tendency is towards placing land, and especially forests, under the central government[1].

With regard to industrial undertakings the general rule, confirmed by practice, is in favour of placing them in charge of the State. Local bodies cannot be expected to deal wisely with the complicated and involved questions that must arise. The principle of 'particular interest' is the reason for a class of exceptions. Just as those public functions that principally concern a town or district should, generally speaking, be entrusted to its authorities, so should the industries connected with those functions or services. It is on this ground that municipal gas and water works, main drainage systems, and tramways are to be justified. Such undertakings are most prominent in urban districts, but, if needed, rural bodies may fitly carry them out. Local railway lines (e.g. the *Chemins de Fer d'intérêt local* of French Finance) may be, and sometimes are, owned by the appropriate local body. The railways possessed by the various German States would probably be more successful if they were in the hands of the imperial administration, and such was the original design of the promoters of state purchase, only defeated by the jealousy of the smaller States.

Postal and telegraphic administration and industries monopolized for the purpose of special taxation are best suited for administration by the general government. As regards the various receipts capable of capitalization no general rule obtains. Where they are received by local bodies supervision by state officials is desirable in order to prevent mal-administration or redemption for insufficient value, but there seems to be no reason for depriving a town or district of any resources of the kind that it may possess.

[1] Cp. the recent Swiss legislation on forests already mentioned (Bk. ii. ch. 2. § 10), and the surrender of public lands by American States to the Federal Government.

Its taxation is so far reduced, and the nation as a whole has no claim to the funds.

Fees have to be distributed according to their source. Local administration is fairly entitled to what may be called its 'incidental earnings.' On the other hand all administrative revenue that is gained by agents of the central government is justly due to it. By this simple rule much confusion is avoided, and there is the best chance of effective control.

A like consideration ought to guide the division of unproductive property. Whatever land or buildings subserve the wants of local administration should belong to the authority so administering : the general government should retain the remainder. Thus buildings for the local courts, parks, or baths for a town are best put under local control. National museums or libraries, or the principal courts of justice, belong rightly to the State.

§ 4. The necessity or advantage of general rules on the subject of division is, however, much reduced by two circumstances, viz. first, the variety of conditions in different countries, and the numerous modifications in the structure of local government. Much more depends on the character of the particular people, or even the particular body, than is usually the case in Finance. Thus the devolution with benefit of powers to the Corporation or to the County Council of London is no argument for a similar course with the municipality of Paris. Nor can inferences be safely drawn from both those bodies to the proper position of the Corporation of New York. At present the duty of the inquirer is rather to note the actual phenomena, avoiding hasty generalization. The other qualifying circumstance is the interaction of the central and local bodies in respect to Finance. Not to touch as yet on taxation, we can, even at present, see that land belonging to the *communes* may for financial reasons be managed by the State, and the receipts paid over to the owners. Again, local bodies may for convenience or economy take charge of public property which is essentially that of the State. So also general fees may be received by local officials or *vice versa*. The consequence is that the two agencies, or rather the two sides, of the public power are so interlocked that systematic distribution of revenue cannot be made without a comprehensive survey of the whole position, and full allowance for the many influencing conditions.

§ 5. A final question now presents itself, viz. what is the proportion of revenue contributed by the 'mechanical' sources? Or in other words, how much is left to be supplied by taxation? The answer, it need not be said, will vary according to the time and the country to which it applies. In some German States, at the end of the Middle Ages, taxation did not exist save as an exceptional resource. The present English or French revenue is almost wholly made up from this 'extraordinary' aid, as it was anciently called. And many intermediate positions are to be found.

Before entering on these particulars we must recall a distinction noticed already for another purpose, viz. that between *gross* and *net* revenue. Modern Finance has accepted as correct the policy of bringing all sums received and expended into account, so that the Budget shall conceal no defect in the operations carried on. For scientific analysis it is just as necessary to eliminate certain elements from each side of the accounts. To take the nearest example. In the English budget statement of 1891, Posts and Telegraphs figure on the revenue side for £12,180,000, and add roughly about 13 per cent. to the receipts. The expenditure was, however, taken as £7,950,000, and this, deducted from the former sum, leaves the more modest item of £4,230,000, or 5 per cent. If all the component parts of revenue were equally affected by this diminution there would be no difficulty in comparing amounts; but the nature of the quasi-private state revenue makes the gross largely exceed the net receipts, while in respect to taxation the existence of any remarkable difference between the two is of itself a strong objection to the particular form so affected as showing undue cost in collection. Nor are these differences confined to the tax as opposed to the non-tax receipts; within the latter class the relation of net and gross revenue is not in every, perhaps hardly in any, case exactly the same. The Indian land revenue gives a very high proportion of net return; in 1888–9, about £19,500,000 out of £23,000,000. The Prussian mines on the contrary give very little net receipts, and some purely industrial enterprises have often a balance on the wrong side.

What is most important at present is to recognise that in estimating the financial merits of the various sources *net* revenue is the only sound basis of calculation. No matter what are the gross incomings, if there are equal outgoings the exchequer does not benefit. Taking this view we are led to reduce very much the importance of the economic receipts. Except in the case of rent the net returns are small. Even the Prussian state railways, the most profitable of public undertakings, do not produce much revenue when compared with the total net receipts of the budget. Besides the intrusion of the tax element tends to deprive some of the most important public industries of their purely economic character.

§ 6. The intermixture of economic and tax revenues as well as the complications of net and gross receipts, and the involved relations of capital and revenue accounts, prevent a precise and definite answer regarding the proportion of public expenditure defrayed out of taxation. It is, however, possible to give approximate results that are not without value. In the English financial year 1890–91, the taxation receipts were £73,663,000. The cost of collection was £2,645,000, leaving a net return of £71,000,000. Non-tax receipts came to £15,911,000; expenditure to £9,450,000; and the net receipts to £6,460,000.

Passing over the various readjustments that the questions of fees, and the distribution of interest on capital charges, might in strictness necessitate, 92½ per cent. is obtained from taxation against 7½ per cent. from other sources. Local Finance in England and Wales, for the year 1888–9 (the last available), gained by taxation almost £28,000,000 directly and £4,750,000 from contributions of the central government. Industrial undertakings yielded over £9,000,000; while their cost was somewhat less than £5,000,000. This balance of over £4,000,000 has to be further reduced by the interest on debt incurred on the industries in question, or about three millions, the net gain being brought down to £1,000,000. Fees, fines, school money, rents, and dividends, came to about £4,750,000, from which the uncertain cost of collection has to be taken. The broad inference from these figures is that about 70 per cent. of the gross local receipts come from taxation, the balance of 30 per cent. being otherwise obtained, but that in the *net* receipts taxation stands to other sources in the ratio of 6 to 1[1].

Germany shows a somewhat different position. Nearly all the German States have a good percentage of their gross receipts from economic revenue, but when the cost of gaining that revenue is taken into account there is very little surplus left. Thus the estimated net revenue for the year 1889–90 from the Prussian lands, forests, and industries (other than railways), was less than 56,000,000 marks (£2,800,000), the railway earnings (part of which is perhaps taxation) contributed 113 million marks (about £5,680,000), or a total of about 169,000,000 marks (or £8,450,000). The gross receipts would convey a quite different impression. They for the same year were estimated at 965 million marks, the corresponding outlay, including interest on railway debt, being 796 million marks. The gross receipts from all sources were taken at 1,513 million marks, the net

[1] The returns of local Finance for Scotland and Ireland fail to distinguish between tax receipts and payments for gas and water. Nor are the English accounts as yet quite clearly separated. For earlier periods they are almost useless for the present purpose.

receipts at 839 million marks. The conclusion consequently is that while the domain and industrial undertakings were over 63 per cent. of the gross, they were only slightly over 20 per cent. of the net receipts[1].

The inclusion of fees and administrative revenue would increase the proportion of economic receipts, but the tax element is so prominent in them (especially in the law fees) that the correctness of this course is doubtful[2].

The other German States resemble Prussia, though in their case the proportion of net receipts by taxation is probably larger, as their net income from railways and mines is lower. Austria and Hungary, too, gain much less than Prussia from the economic sources of revenue. The estimated net product of the Austrian state domains, forests and mines, is only 1,830,000 florins (£183,000). The railways, as stated before, do not meet their debt charge.

India is the only other country whose proportion of economic revenue is deserving of attention. One of the noteworthy features of Indian finance is the contrast between its most productive sources, and those of European countries, especially Great Britain. Its financial mainstay is in the rent charges on land which, together with the parts that are truly either rent or taxation, supply close on £20,000,000 annually. Other sources of the same class are unproductive. Postal service, telegraphs, and railways lead to expenditure rather than profit. Forests produce a small surplus. The tax revenue is just as sharply contrasted with that of England. Salt and opium are the chief contributories, and fiscal monopoly is a prominent

[1] The contributions (*Matricularbeiträge*) of the States to the Empire and the assignments from the imperial revenue to the States further confuse the statistics. In 1889–90 the Prussian contribution was 114,000,000 marks; the assignment from the imperial revenue 170,000,000 marks, showing a net gain to the Prussian revenue of 56,000,000 marks, £2,800,000). The budget should be reduced on each side by the sum of 114,000,000 marks, which is really a matter of account.

[2] The German law fees (*Rechtsgebühren*) are so high as to really amount to a tax on litigation. For estimates of the proportion of taxation and industrial receipts cp. Von Scheel in Schönberg, 68–69.

agent in the collection. The ordinary excise, customs and stamps are comparatively unimportant, so is direct taxation which is of such importance in England. On the whole we may say that even in India less than half the net receipts are derived from quasi-private sources of revenue.

§ 7. The preceding facts sufficiently support the general proposition that the economic revenue of the State is financially inferior to that gathered by the tax-collector, and it also seems to hold good that the greater the economic development of a country, the less important is the former. Whether the statement will be applicable to the future is perhaps doubtful. Modern tendencies are in the direction of creating an industrial domain that may rival in value the agricultural domain of earlier times, but the net revenue to be obtained from it will probably be less than would at first appear likely. The cost of constructing the modern state domain and the pressure on the administration to reduce the cost of service to the lowest point that expenses of working will allow, are both hindrances to the use of state industries as an effective relief from the charge of taxation. There is no probability that in the near future the proportion of the public charges to be met by direct levies from the citizens of the State will diminish, more especially when the rapid growth of public expenditure is taken into account.

Taxation will, therefore, next claim our attention, and as the main support of the State's economy will need fuller and more critical investigation than has been necessary with other forms of revenue.

BOOK III.

PUBLIC REVENUE.

THE PRINCIPLES OF TAXATION.

CHAPTER I.

DEFINITION AND CLASSIFICATION OF TAXATION.

§ 1. THE subject of the present book is undoubtedly the central part of modern Finance. Its importance has led English and American writers to treat it as almost the sole topic for discussion. Though this is not true either of England or the United States, and is still more erroneous when other countries are taken into account, yet the existence of such a view proves the preponderating influence of taxation in the modern financial organization. Another reason for the great prominence of this source of state revenue is perhaps its close connexion with Economics. State expenditure may be looked on as a question of public policy to be decided by the practical judgment of 'that crafty and insidious animal vulgarly called a statesman or politician'; the quasi-private receipts may be treated as almost a part of private economy, but taxation raises a series of fundamental questions which involve refined ethical and economic considerations. The effect of any given tax system is a strictly economic question requiring for its solution frequent reference to the conditions both of production and of distribution. What ought to be the system adopted in each special case must be decided by reference to both moral and economic conditions. Assuming that the partition of the burden should be a 'just' one, we must estimate its true weight and the share really borne by each citizen before we can come to a conclusion for or against any proposed arrangement.

The necessity of constantly appealing to the theorems of economists has made the study of taxation almost a part of applied political economy; but, notwithstanding that this is the favourite English method of treatment, it is far better to discuss it as a part of the wider subject of Public Finance, since its origin and growth are in this way better understood, and the unquestionably close relation between the several departments of Public Finance, can only thus receive due recognition.

§ 2. At the commencement of our examination questions of definition and classification present themselves in embarrassing number. Administrative practice and economic theory are both in part responsible for this difficulty. Terms, apparently of the utmost simplicity, have been and are used with a variety of meaning that is all the more confusing because of the strong points of connexion between the different uses.

Discussions as to the meaning of terms are, it need not be said, hardly ever purely verbal: they in almost every case turn on different conceptions of facts, or different modes of grouping the objects under notice. The literature of Finance, especially in Germany, is rich in examples, and some of the best known doctrines derive a great deal of their authority from some particular application of an ambiguous word. To clear up our terminology, or at least to explain the use of the terms we employ, is an indispensable step in the investigation.

§ 3. First of all we have to settle the meaning of the word 'Tax.' This term, so clear and simple to the ordinary citizen, has been very variously defined, sometimes at astonishing length, and often with the, it may be unconscious, design of aiding a particular theory as to the character of the facts denoted by it. The following definition is, we believe, correct and quite in accordance with the realities of Finance and Politics: it has the further advantage of not implying unfairly any special view respecting the nature or justice of taxation.

A tax is a compulsory contribution of the wealth of a person or body of persons for the service of the public powers.

Each term in this definition is significant, and helps to explain the object defined. First, a tax is 'compulsory.' This does not mean that all tax revenue is paid unwillingly, but merely that the will of the payer is legally immaterial. The amount, the mode and time of levying, the persons affected are all determined by the sovereign or its delegate, and individual preferences or dislikes are allowed no place in the act. It thus appears that so-called voluntary taxation is not true taxation, which is plainly the fact; for in the rare cases in which it has been tried, society is either in the pre-political stage where the public economy exists only in a rudimentary form, or the system is one of self-assessment supported by the social rather than the legal sanction. Gifts may indeed be made by individuals to the State, a circumstance not without importance in the history of Finance, but they are at present so few as hardly to need mention.

Next, a tax is a 'contribution,' that is to say it involves a sacrifice on the part of the contributor. It is quite possible that some persons may gain through the operation of a tax of which they themselves pay a part; but it is rather the operation of the tax than its payment by the person affected that produces this result. Every tax necessitates a deduction from the wealth of the contributor, even though compensation may be indirectly brought about through its action.

Thirdly, the term 'wealth' has to be understood in a wide sense, including 'services' as well as commodities. Military service or forced labour for, say, repairing roads (*corvées*) is taxation quite as much as payment of money or goods. These may be good or bad forms of taxation, but they must be reckoned in the category of taxes.

Again, all taxation is imposed on 'persons.' This necessarily follows from the circumstance that the payment of taxation is a duty, and persons only can be liable to duties. The proposition is apparently inconsistent with the division of taxes into 'personal' and 'real,' and also with the taxation of commodities so often mentioned. There is, however, no opposition between the different uses. The term 'real' taxation refers to the 'object' of taxation; the owner or ultimate bearer is the 'subject' of the tax, and he is a person. Taxation of commodities falls on the consumers or other persons connected with the taxed articles, and a similar analysis will apply to other forms of taxation. The truth, though often forgotten, yet always holds good that a tax must ultimately be paid by someone.

Fifthly. Taxation is levied for the 'service' or 'benefit.' The public economy requires the supply of its wants, and taxation is the mode of meeting whatever proportion of those wants remains unsatisfied from other parts of the public revenue. The produce of taxation has unfortunately been only too often misapplied, and resulted in injury rather than gain; but the tax-imposing body must be regarded as the final arbiter of the justice of its wants. That some requirements are evil makes them none the less requirements in the case either of individuals or of States.

Finally, taxation is for the 'public powers,' i. e. it has to meet the wants of both central and local governments. A rate raised by the smallest parish is as much a tax as if it were levied by the Imperial Parliament. All contributions to the various organs of government are taxes in the view of Finance, whatever be their administrative name. Special kinds of taxation have been often denounced as being for the benefit of classes or individuals, not for that of the State. Protective taxes, e. g. have incurred this reproach. Such forms of taxation are, however, imposed in the interest, or supposed interest, of the nation, and if they yield any revenue are so far productive of gain to the State. The advantage obtained by the protected producers may be regarded as equivalent to so much public expenditure in their favour. It is generally incapable of being estimated, but this circumstance is of practical, rather than theoretical importance. That all taxes of equal pressure are not equally advantageous, either to the State or the community, is too evident to need formal assertion. Otherwise there would be no reason for the selection of any particular forms.

§ 4. The foregoing definition, with the accompanying explanations, conveys all that is essential in the idea of taxation, but the numerous efforts to explain the term deserve some further notice. Many of the ablest writers on the subject have given definitions which substantially agree with that stated in the preceding section. Thus De Parieu defines taxation as 'the charge levied by the State on the property or labour of the citizens, in order to provide for the public expenses;' Roscher asserts that taxes are 'the contributions which individual economies must pay, in consequence of their dependence, to the State province, commune, &c., or, generally the particular collective compulsory economy placed over them in order to assist in satisfying the financial needs of the receivers. According to Cossa, a 'tax is that part of the wealth of private individuals which the authority of the State, province, or municipality appropriates in order to provide for the public expenses incurred for the advantage of the general body of tax-payers [1].' To these definitions it is not here desirable to add the many others that generally agree with them; but we ought to consider some of the doubtful variations in the formal statements of the nature of taxation. One of these is suggested by the last clause of the definition just quoted from Cossa. 'Incurred for the advantage of the general body of tax-payers' contains a reminiscence of the once-established, and still generally popular, doctrine that taxes are the price paid for the services of the public authorities. This way of looking at the facts was quite in harmony with the political doctrines of the seventeenth and eighteenth centuries. Belief in a

[1] De Parieu, i. 5; Roscher, § 33; Cossa (Am. Trans.), 50.

compact between the ruler and his subjects led naturally to the contemplation of taxation as simply a payment for service done. The citizen received security and paid its price in taxation. The immediate advantage of this doctrine, as placing a limit to arbitrary exactions and tending to increase security is apparent, and there is accordingly no reason for surprise when, in some form or other, the idea of exchange is associated with the payment of taxes. In Montesquieu's opinion 'the revenues of the State are the portion of his property that each citizen gives in order to have security for the remainder, or to enjoy it in comfort.' Here the conception of payment to escape further demands is combined with that of return for services rendered. The French National Assembly gives still another variation in its reference to taxation as 'the common debt of all citizens, and the price of the advantages that society affords them.' From this it is not far to the assertion of Proudhon that 'Taxation is an exchange in which the State gives services and the contributor money[1].' Hardly distinguishable is the belief that taxation is the insurance premium against the risks of social disorder set forth in Mirabeau's proposition that 'Taxation is only an advance to obtain protection for social order.' The desire to present a ready justification of the arrangements of society finds an illustration in these attempts to depict taxation as a *quid pro quo*.

To show that this way of explaining taxation is incorrect is not difficult. The assertion that taxes are purely a return for services rendered is plainly untrue. We shall see that there is no possibility of measuring precisely the most important of the benefits rendered by the State. Security against aggression is, literally speaking, an 'incalculable' good. Social order cannot be sold by retail like tea or sugar, and so is it with the other state functions, even the purely economic ones. Indeed, it would be very

[1] Montesquieu, Liv. xiii. ch. 1; Stourm in *Dictionnaire d'Économie Politique*, art. 'Impôts,' ii. 3; cp. Leroy Beaulieu, i. 113.

near the truth to say that the difficulty of applying the normal method of purchase makes a given form of activity suitable for state management; if defence and justice could be readily bought and paid for, we might trust to private enterprise for a sufficient supply. Wherever the benefit to the individual can be even approximately estimated there is a strong presumption in favour of levying the cost incurred from him and converting the tax into a 'fee.' Special reasons may make it desirable that this charge should be compulsory. The citizen may be so neglectful of his true interest as to omit obtaining the best appliances for the purposes of health or education, but even in these cases there is also a general interest which furnishes the principal ground for the intervention of the State.

The opposition between free payment and taxation is a marked one not to be evaded by the introduction of a vague idea of exchange of services as including both, and any definition of taxation that implies or expressly states this combination is so far erroneous. Like the general doctrine of the social contract its practical convenience as a weapon on the side of liberty cannot conceal its scientific weakness. The equivalence between the amount of taxes paid and the benefits obtained is rather to be found in the case of the community as a whole than of any special part of it. Looking at the public agencies from this point of view, it is well to consider whether the advantages of government are a compensation for its cost, and this test should be steadily applied in judging the merits of any proposed expenditure. The question in truth belongs to that department of Public Finance. Once expenditure has been incurred the imposition of taxation in order to meet it is a matter of course. We have accordingly considered it in its fit connexion [1]. In any case, to introduce what is at best a highly disputable doctrine into the definition of so important a term is altogether a mistake.

[1] See Bk. i. ch. 8. § 4 sq.

§ 5. Other definitions of taxation fail through excessive vagueness. We gain little by being told that taxation is 'a public charge, a duty imposed on certain things'[1]. Very, often one or more of the essential elements is omitted. Thus the fact of taxation falling solely on persons is neglected in the definition of taxes as 'the enforced proportional contribution of persons or property levied by the authority of the State for the support of government and for all public needs'[2]. Besides the error of including 'property' as a subject of taxation, this definition brings in the unessential principle of 'proportionality,' and would therefore, exclude large groups of what are universally regarded as taxes. This is a very common defect in the definition of the term due to the desire to give an exhaustive account of its attributes, or to bring some favourite theory into its general conception. Professor Ely's elaborate account, like those of many German writers, illustrates this danger[3]. The real function of a definition is to give a clear idea of the nature and limits of the phenomenon denoted by the term, not to convey in a formal statement all that is known about it, still less to prejudge the questions that may arise in the course of further inquiry.

§ 6. The etymologies of the words employed in different languages to denote this class of public contributions are full of instruction. The English 'tax,' as also its equivalent in local Finance 'rate,' suggests the estimation or fixing of the amount of charge. So does the German '*Schätzung*.' The assistance or advantage to the State is foremost in the

[1] The definition of the dictionary of the French Academy.

[2] Quoted from Cooley by Ely, *Taxation*, 4.

[3] 'Taxes are simply one-sided transfers of economic goods or services demanded of the citizens, and occasionally of those who are not citizens, but who nevertheless are within the reach of the taxing power, by the constituted authorities of the land for meeting the expenses of government or for some other purpose, with the intention that a common burden shall be maintained by common contributions or sacrifices,' *Taxation*, 6–7; cp. the definition given by Wagner, ii. 210, which brings in the complication of a distinction between 'pure financial' and politico-social taxation; also i. 499–500, where 'taxes' are marked off from 'fees' (*Gebühren*) by their 'general' character.

French '*aide*' and the German '*Steuer.*' The idea of compulsion is primary in '*impôt*' and '*Auflage.*' The surrender by the payer is connoted in '*tributum*' '*dazio*' and '*Abgabe,*' while finally the root of taxation in voluntary payment is evidenced by the words '*donum*' and '*benevolence.*' Minute investigation may show that there are differences in the charges described by these several names, but speaking broadly they all cover what we regard as taxation, and help to justify the definition given above [1].

§ 7. Having determined the meaning of 'taxation,' it is necessary to understand its chief classifications and the technical terms employed respecting it. First, we may notice the term 'subject,' which is conveniently used to denote the person who bears its burden, and who must be distinguished from the immediate payer, e. g. the importer of wine in England pays the duty on it, but the 'subjects' of the wine duties are the consumers so far as the charge is really a pressure on them. The 'subject' and the payer may or may not be the same according to the particular circumstances.

As the 'subject' of taxation is the person affected, so the 'object' is the thing or fact on which it is imposed, thus in the example just given of the wine duties, the commodity wine would be the object of the duty. Even where taxation is said to be 'personal' it is assessed on some object as 'income' or 'produce,' or in the extreme instance of a capitation or poll-tax on the person as a physical body. Confusion between the 'subject' and 'object' is the cause of the belief that some taxation does not fall on persons [2].

The 'source' of taxation has somewhat the same relation to its 'object' as the ultimate bearer or subject to the immediate payer. The fund created by taxation is derived from the resources of the community, i. e. as we shall see from the income, or in special instances the property, of the

[1] Cp. Roscher, § 33; Wagner, ii. 223.

[2] This mistake is somewhat like that committed by Blackstone in speaking of 'the rights of things' (*Jus rerum*).

'subjects.' There has been much dispute as to the real 'source' of the tax-revenue that will need consideration later on, but there is no doubt as to the proper use of the term 'source' in respect to taxation. It is, perhaps, unnecessary to mention the terms 'unit' and 'rate' which are employed, the former to describe the quantity of the objects taken as a standard, the latter the amount of taxation per 'unit.' Where commodities are taxed the unit will be a measure of weight, e. g. the lb. as in the British tea duty, or contents as the gallon in the wine duty, or length as in the old duties on cottons. A sum of the standard money is the commonest, as in the system of *ad valorem* duties [1].

§ 8. A much more important set of terms is that connected with the classification of taxation. The division and grouping of the several kinds of taxes have been varied to suit particular financial systems, and much of the general discussions on the subject is concerned with the comparative merits of these arrangements, and the extent to which they conform to the natural order so far as it can be said to exist. A preliminary notice of some of the more common distinctions is desirable at the present stage.

One of the most widely known and frequently used divisions of taxation is that into 'direct' and 'indirect'; unfortunately it is used in different senses, though with several points of connexion. That most familiar to English readers is stated by J. S. Mill in the following terms:—

'Taxes are either direct or indirect. A direct tax is one which is demanded from the very persons who it is intended or desired should pay it. Indirect taxes are those which are demanded from one person in the expectation and intention that he shall indemnify himself at the expense of another [2].'

The difference is here made to turn on the mode of

[1] Cp. Roscher, § 33; Wagner, ii. 226–8; Schäffle, *Steuerpolitik*, 52–3, for the use of these terms in German Finance. The use of 'subject' in the text differs from that of the above writers, as they apply it to the person legally responsible for payment.

[2] *Principles*, Bk. v. ch. 3. § 1.

incidence, a matter often very difficult to determine, and changing with the special circumstances of each case. Whatever be its economical importance, it is evidently useless for administrative purposes, and probably owes its origin to the peculiar theory of the Physiocrats respecting the 'source' of taxation.

A natural result has been that practical financiers have adopted a different basis of distinction, and regard those taxes as direct which are levied on permanent and recurring occasions; while charges on occasional and particular events are placed under the category of indirect taxation. On either method the income tax would be 'direct,' and the excise and customs 'indirect': the 'death duties' would be 'direct' from Mill's point of view, and 'indirect' in the administrative sense[1].

Another division is that into 'taxes on revenue' and 'taxes on capital,' or, perhaps better, on 'property.' The former are paid out of the annual national production; the latter encroach on the accumulated wealth of the society. But in qualification of this statement it must be added that most of the actual property or capital taxes are so only in name, being really paid out of the income of the persons subject to the charge. There is thus a discordance between the practical and scientific use of these terms as great as in the case of direct and indirect taxation.

Taxes are often said to be either 'real' or 'personal,' and attempts have been made to distribute them into two classes on this basis. Personal taxes are those in which the person is taken note of in assessment. They require lists of the tax-payers (*rôles nominatives* in the language of French administrators). Real taxes are assessed on objects other than persons, and without direct reference to the owners or possessors. Capitation and income taxes are 'personal'; taxes on land, houses, or goods, are 'real.' The use of these terms has the inconvenience, already noticed,

[1] For further discussion of the questions here raised see Bk. iii. ch. 4, 'The Tax System, its Forms.'

of obscuring the fact that all taxation is in the last resort on persons, and further raises a particular form of levy into undue importance. An income tax is certainly personal, but Schedule A of the English income tax is very similar to the French *impôt foncier* that is as certainly 'real.'

In respect to the mode of assessment taxes may be either 'rated' or 'apportioned[1].' In the former class the charge per unit is fixed, but the total yield is always uncertain, depending as it does on the number of units that pay. An apportioned tax is one the total amount of which is fixed, the shares being apportioned among the objects that are charged. As examples the English income tax and the French *impôt foncier* will again serve. The former is 'rated,' the latter 'apportioned,' being so divided among the departments as to make up the previously fixed amount. This method is decidedly the more primitive: it has disappeared long ago from the English system, and will probably meet the same fate elsewhere[2].

§ 9. The foregoing distinctions are too important to be passed over, but they are also too imperfect to be of much use in a scientific classification of taxes. Particular aspects of taxation, the administrative peculiarities of certain countries, and obsolete or imperfect theories have been the causes of their employment. It is accordingly advisable to consider the subject from a more general point of view in order, as far as possible, to reach a natural arrangement.

In choosing the principle of grouping we have to make a selection between two contrasted systems which may be distinguished as (1) the economical and theoretical, and (2) the empirical or fiscal modes.

The first mentioned depends on the economical theory of the distribution of wealth, and can be traced back at least to Adam Smith. He opens his discussion of taxation by

[1] These terms seem to be the least unsuitable equivalents of the French *impôts de quotité* and *impôts de repartition*.

[2] The old English 'tenths and fifteenths' and the later 'subsidies' were apportioned. Dowell, i. 88. The recent change in the French house duty is an illustration of the tendency to abandon the system.

asserting that 'the private revenue of individuals arises ultimately from three different sources—rent, profit, and wages, and proceeds, 'every tax must finally be paid from one or other of those different sources of revenue, or from all of them indifferently. . . . The particular consideration of each of these different sorts will divide the second part of the present chapter into four articles [1].' Nothing can be plainer and simpler in appearance than this arrangement. The economic shares in distribution are regarded as so many sources of revenue on one or more of which every tax must fall. The later analysis of profit into the component parts of 'interest' and 'employer's gain' would add one further source, but would not otherwise disturb the treatment [2]. The great attraction of this method is its simplicity and the facilities that it affords for employing the propositions of Economics in deducing the effects of taxation. To reduce the subject into 'four articles' even with 'several other subdivisions,' promises a welcome abridgment of labour. English economists in treating of taxation have, therefore, intended, as far as possible, to follow this course. Ricardo and J. S. Mill are the most prominent examples. But on closer examination it appears that neither of them, nor even Adam Smith himself, could adhere consistently to this over-simple grouping. In Ricardo's hands the subject requires eleven chapters, several of which consider the effects of taxes on land, houses, raw produce, and gold, in addition to those on the primary sources of rent, profit and wages. Mill goes further, and formally limits the division of taxes according to the economic source on which they are imposed to direct taxation on income [3]. The taxation of commodities and

[1] 347.

[2] It is noteworthy that Adam Smith makes this separation in his account of taxes on profit: 'The revenue or profit arising from stock naturally divides itself into two parts, that which pays the interest and which belongs to the owner of the stock, and that surplus part which is over and above what is necessary for paying the interest,' 357.

[3] Bk. v. ch. 3. § 1.

such taxes as those on contracts and on communication are quite outside it. But the *Wealth of Nations* affords a stronger proof of the insufficiency of the ground of division selected by its author. Sections devoted to taxes on produce of land, on the profit rent, and the ground rent of houses, to capitation taxes, and taxes on commodities, break up the compact order that the introduction holds out. It is evident that the subject-matter refused to fit into the limited groups that the economic classification required, and the sound common sense so characteristic of Adam Smith is shown by his deviations from the theoretic lines previously traced out by him.

The difficulty arises from the fact that taxation always has persons for its 'subjects,' and they frequently derive their income—the normal 'source' of taxation—from more than one of the different economic shares. The citizen is not a pure rent, interest, or wages receiver, he often combines all three in his annual receipts. Again, the most prominent external feature of taxation is the 'object' on which it is levied. These are, however, very many, and it is often beyond the power of analysis to decompose the charge on some commodity or form of receipt into its economic constituents, e. g. the produce of land may be due to the co-operation of natural agents, capital, labour, and directing ability, but to say how much of the taxation imposed on the result is due to each factor is quite impossible.

The obvious conclusion is that the classification is unsuitable. It is often convenient to use the economic theorems respecting rent, wages, &c., in our investigations of the effects of taxation, even though we should never meet in fact with the pure taxes on those parts of the product. For the problems of Finance it is also necessary to remember that these preliminary inquiries are but steps towards the final result which must deal with realities, and not with imaginary and hypothetical cases.

§ 10. The defects of the economical mode of classification lead us to turn to what we have entitled the 'empirical' or 'fiscal' one, which takes the actual kinds of taxation, and arranges them in the most convenient way. To this procedure it may at once be objected that as each country has its own tax system, varying from time to time, we cannot attain to a *general* arrangement valid in all cases. The classification of taxes suited for ancient Rome would be inadequate in modern England, and even confining attention to the present day, the Indian and British tax systems cannot be easily reduced to the same classification. This effect of temporary circumstances in limiting general principles has been already noticed [1], and it does at first sight raise difficulties in the effort to prepare a natural grouping of taxes. The mode of escape is, however, obvious on a little consideration. The names and minute details of taxation vary greatly at different times and places, but this does not preclude the existence of large categories of taxation possible in all countries and found in somewhat different forms in many. The Indian land revenues differ from the English land tax, and also from the French *impôt foncier*, but in all three countries there is 'taxation of land,' which offers a general title, under which they may be placed in company with the Roman provincial tax and several others. A like mode can be applied to different forms of taxes on the produce of industry, and so in other cases.

The question next arises, How far should this process be carried and what general categories can we form? Rau has boldly grouped all taxes under the two heads of 'estimated taxes' usually charged on goods (*Schätzungen*) and 'taxes on expenditure' (*Aufwandsteuern*) which does not carry us much beyond the rude divisions mentioned in § 8. Hoffmann prefers the division into taxes on possession (*Besitz*) and taxes on acts (*Handlungen*), while Cohn accepts the tripartite arrangement of Wagner, into taxes on (*a*) acquisition (*Erwerb*), (*b*) possession (*Besitz*) and (*c*) con-

[1] See Introduction, Part i. § 8.

sumption (*Verbrauch*) [1]. De Parieu carries out the division more minutely, and forms five classes of taxes, viz. (1) on persons, (2) on wealth, (3) on enjoyment, (4) on consumption, (5) on acts. In defence of this arrangement he argues that, like all natural classifications, it allows of an indefinite margin between each adjacent group, and that it further harmonizes with the administrative division between direct and indirect taxation, classes 1, 2 and 3 belonging to the former and classes 4 and 5 to the latter category [2].

All the preceding classifications appear to have at least two defects: for (1) they simply deal with certain external features of taxes, and do not take note of their essential characteristics, and (2) like the otherwise very different arrangement of Adam Smith, they are too simple for the complexity of the facts to which they are applied. Hock has attempted to avoid this defect. He starts from the untenable position that taxation is a compensation for state services. These services are, he thinks, of three kinds, to wit; (1) protection of person, (2) of property, and (3) the performance of special services. To each corresponds a 'primitive tax' (*Ursteuer*): these are (1) personal taxes, (2) income taxes, (3) taxes for special services rendered [3]. The practical difficulties in levying these taxes in their pure form leads to the use of other taxes as substitutes (*Surrogate*) in the form of taxes on (*a*) consumption, (*b*) product, (*c*) customs, (*d*) special income taxes, (*e*) fees and charges on occupations [4].

Though it is plain that the ground idea of Hock's

[1] Rau, i. § 292; Hoffmann, *Lehre von den Steuern*, 69; Cohn, § 332; Wagner, ii. 233 sq., 515.

[2] De Parieu, i. 12–14.

[3] *Abgaben und Schulden*, 15–17.

[4] *Ib.* 82 sq. Stein's classification of taxes into (1) direct, (2) indirect, and (3) income taxes—the first falling on capital, the second on labour, and the last on individual economic activity—is decidedly unsatisfactory; nor are the subdivisions better. Thus the direct taxes are divided by him into those on (*a*) produce, (*b*) acquisition, (*c*) commerce, but the land tax comes under (*a*) and the industry taxes under (*b*), though the latter are evidently produce taxes. Stein, ii. 495 sq., and iii. *passim*.

division is unsound it yet has the merit of suggesting the best way of reaching a truly natural arrangement. The distinction between primitive and derived taxes is a valuable one, and can be used to combine the economical and empirical methods of grouping in our arrangement.

§ 11. The position of Adam Smith that taxation must be derived from the constituents of private income is undoubtedly sound. Where it falls on property there is a diminution of the national wealth which, if continued, must prove destructive. A true instinct therefore prompted him in his effort to analyze taxes into those on rent, on wages, and on profit. On the other hand it is equally true that the 'objects' of taxation do not easily allow of this analysis. Between the taxes of economical theory and the taxes of actual Finance there is a gulf that appears hard to bridge over, and one that has retarded the progress of financial science.

This difficulty is at all events extenuated by the circumstance that though the abstract economic taxes are not met with in fact, they are not wholly imaginary. The economic tax on rent has some, and often considerable resemblance to a land tax, or to put it the other way, a land tax often tends to become a tax on rent. The 'tax on profit' of the economic text books bears a like relation to the taxes on business, of which Schedule D of the English income tax, the Prussian *Gewerbesteuer* and the French *patentes* may be taken as specimens. So with the wages tax, in relation to actual capitation taxes, or the late *Classensteuer* of Prussia. If now we regard taxes on the factors of production, and therefore on the shares in distribution as 'primary,' we have a basis from which to proceed to the investigation of those secondary taxes that are placed on other 'objects.' By grouping together the various taxes on land we can consider the play of financial forces in the case of rent. The industrial taxes will similarly enable us to see the working of charges on interest and profit, and finally poll and capitation taxes will perform the same service for taxes on wages.

The economic mode of arrangement assigns a place to taxes on income or revenue which we regard as a combination of all the primary forms. It might in certain cases be admissible to break up an income tax into its component parts, just as it might, on the other hand, be well to combine a series of taxes that together make up an income tax. Thus the five schedules of the English income tax or the four of the Italian one might be separately treated, or again the 'four direct contributions' of the French system might be taken in combination as nearly equivalent to a general income tax[1]. Still it is necessary to consider the fiscal bearings of general income and property taxes, and this discussion most fitly follows the examination of the taxes on component parts of income.

When the 'primary,' and if the phrase be admissible, 'quasi-primary' taxes have been discussed, there remains no small number of other charges. The whole elaborate system of taxation on commodities that has so large a place in every country must be dealt with. It may be regarded as taxation of consumption or of expenditure, but for practical purposes it includes the two great departments known to English Finance as 'excise' and 'customs.' So far the taxes enumerated have appeared to fall on the production, the distribution, or the consumption of wealth; those that directly affect the remaining economic process of circulation must also be noticed. Taxes on transport and communications come under this head; so does the yet more important class of taxes on the transfer of property and the transactions of commerce, i. e. the 'taxes on acts' of De Parieu's arrangement. The taxation of succession after death may be treated as a particular case of transfer, but it also has affinities with property and income taxes which must be carefully considered. In like manner taxes on necessary commodities often resemble in their effects a tax on wages as Ricardo with some exaggeration urged. The

[1] They are (1) *Contribution foncière*, (2) *Contribution mobilière*, (3) *Contribution des portes et fenêtres*, (4) *Patentes*.

other secondary taxes have similar reactions on the constituents of income, but, nevertheless, their separate treatment is desirable and indeed unavoidable.

§ 12. We have now obtained what appears, on the whole, a satisfactory distribution of the several taxes. Briefly recapitulated it is as follows. The main division is into 'primary' and 'secondary.' The primary taxes comprise those on land, on business and capital, on persons and on labourers' earnings. The combination of these primary forms gives us the general income and property taxes which come next in order. Passing to the secondary forms of taxation we find (1) taxes on commodities, including both excises and customs, (2) taxes on communication and transport, (3) taxes on transfer of property, (4) succession duties, (5) the remaining taxes on commerce and legal transactions.

But the discussion of the several taxes in the foregoing order must be postponed until we have studied the operation of taxation in general and the conditions required for its satisfactory working. No single tax can be rightly appreciated without reference to the financial system of which it forms a part. The chapters immediately succeeding will be devoted to a study of the characteristics of taxation in general and the principles that should regulate its application. In this part of Finance we meet with the most difficult theoretical and practical questions which require the utmost attention for their proper understanding. On some points opinion is sharply divided, and consequently, while endeavouring to reach a definite judgment on each disputed question, we shall aim at putting the views of both sides in their strongest form before the reader.

CHAPTER II.

THE GENERAL FEATURES OF TAXATION.

§ 1. THE increasing importance of taxation as the mode of supplying the public wants is a conspicuous feature in financial development. It is partly attributable to the decline of the earlier forms of revenue, but far more to the great and continuous growth of expenditure. The modern state is dependent on taxation to an extent unknown in mediaeval times. Hence all questions connected with this department of Finance have an enhanced interest. Errors on the subject or mistakes on the part of practical financiers tend to become more and more serious. The need of a careful study of the general features of the tax system is greater. Without a true appreciation of the conditions under which it works, it is hopeless to expect the adoption of a wise policy or determination in applying it. Practical sagacity has its part—and no small one—in successful financial management, but it is all the more effective when enlightened by the study of principles. The complications of modern financial systems make it advisable to note their chief characteristics before discussing the comparative merits of the rules proposed for their regulation. The phenomena are not so simple as to admit of regulation by a single mechanical rule, and the real bearing of the different propositions will be best understood after some acquaintance with the subject-matter to which they are applied and the difficulties that surround them. The interaction of state and national economy brought about by taxation produces further complications that will not allow of hasty treatment. We shall therefore begin by a study of some of the general features of the tax-system, a knowledge of which is essential for forming a correct judgment respecting its regulation.

§ 2. Looked at in a broad general way the first circumstance that strikes the observer is the fact that taxation means the subtraction of so much wealth from individual enjoyment or use. The definition given in the last chapter expresses this clearly by pointing out that taxes are contributed by persons from their wealth for the public service. State expenditure is devoted to the supply of certain wants of the community or nation by the action of the public powers. These, like all other agencies, cannot be obtained without cost partly met by the economic or quasi-private revenue, but leaving a balance to be supplied by taxation. It thus appears that there is an element of truth in the description of taxation as 'the expenses of production of the State'; the phrase, however, suggests too close an analogy with industrial enterprises, in which the expenses are repaid out of the product. In respect to public services the benefits will in normal cases largely exceed the cost, but the method of calculation is not so easily applied, nor is the object in view the attainment of profit.

The proposition that taxation is a form of cost or expense proves that it is so far an evil in the sense that every sacrifice is such. It may be necessary or advisable, but could the object be otherwise accomplished it would be still better. Any saving in the expense of working the State enables a larger amount to be left in the possession of the tax-payers, and to that extent improves their economical position. The formal statement of this very plain fact might appear superfluous were it not for the existence of strong popular prejudices in favour of the expenditure of funds derived from taxation. 'Government expenditure gives employment and benefits the labourers' is the commonest form in which this belief is asserted. Without entering into the question how far such expenditure does really reach the labourers, it is sufficient to reply that the persons from whom the funds have been taken by the tax-collector would have certainly made use of them, either in the employment of labour, or the purchase of commodities. The belief that taxation returns in 'a fertilising shower' was rightly regarded by Bastiat as one of the errors arising from defective observation[1]. Hardly worthy of refutation as a theoretic doctrine, its evil effect, particularly in democratic societies, in producing extravagant expenditure is not to be overlooked.

The idea that 'taxation is the best form of investment' is placed by Bastiat in the same category as the gross fallacy just refuted, but it admits of a more favourable interpretation. If it be said that the taxation required for the national defence, the maintenance of justice, and the necessary functions of the State, has been invested in the best manner and yields a good return, the assertion is substantially true, though perhaps expressed in a misleading way, as the State cannot be regarded as a mere industrial concern. Further, as Leroy Beaulieu points out, the proceeds of taxation, if employed in public works, may yield a satisfactory return, and thus be 'a good investment' in the literal sense. The expediency of such investment belongs rather to the subject of expenditure than to that of taxation, but we may remark that, if public works are likely to be profitable, it seems better on the whole to raise the requisite funds by a loan to be repaid through the agency of a sinking fund. To use taxation for this purpose is almost equivalent to a 'forced loan [2].'

§ 3. The consideration of taxation as reproductive in

[1] Bastiat, *Œuvres*, v. 344 sq.; cp. Leroy Beaulieu, i. 118.

[2] Leroy Beaulieu, i. 125–6. See above, Bk. i. ch. 8. §§ 2, 3. Also Bk. v. ch. 5, for a discussion of the expediency of public borrowing for this object.

the way of investment suggests the further question of the possibility of its productiveness through reaction on the national economy. If the use of the funds raised by taxation can prove beneficial, may not the effect of taxation itself on production be sometimes good? This view is expressed in the maxim discussed by Hume, 'that every new tax creates a new ability in the subject to bear it, and that each increase of public burdens increases proportionably the industry of the people,' which, he thinks, 'must be owned, when kept within certain bounds, to have some foundation in reason and experience[1].'

Natural disadvantages sometimes stimulate industry, why then should not artificial ones have the same effect? Economic progress has been most remarkable in countries where man has to exert himself in consequence of the parsimony of nature, not in the richest and most fertile lands. A judicious use of the engine of taxation would, it might be thought, have a similar effect on the disposition of the people. Such was the opinion of McCulloch who maintained that the heavy taxation of England, during the French wars (1793–1815) was one of the causes of the growth of wealth at that time, since it stimulated industry and the spirit of enterprise and invention[2].

The doctrine in this rather extreme form is open to an easy refutation, for if taxes create a new ability on the part of the payers there can be no determinable limit to their useful employment. A wise government would increase taxation indefinitely, and thereby augment the national possessions. The process of creating fresh wealth by simply taking it from the producers is so evidently impossible that its advocates hesitate to carry their view to its logical outcome. In truth there is a two-fold fallacy in the argument. In the first place natural obstacles do not, in general, stimulate exertion; economic development is

[1] Hume, 'Essay on Taxes.'

[2] McCulloch, *Taxation and Funding*, 7 sq.

not greatest among the Eskimos, or the Fuegians, as it ought to be on this hypothesis. Some natural difficulties urge man to action, but others reduce him to torpor, and check the first steps towards civilization. The influence of natural disadvantages in promoting the growth of wealth is rather by their indirect effect on the physical and mental qualities of those subject to them, not by the economic loss that they occasion. Secondly, the analogy between natural and artificial obstacles is unsound. It does not follow that because men work more strenuously (and this is doubtful) to till a barren soil, that, therefore, they will exert themselves the harder the more they suffer from the incursions of marauders. The greatest promoter of industry is security, and protection from arbitrary taxation is but one form of that 'protection against the Government' on which Mill justly insists as more important even than 'protection by the Government[1].'

Later on, however, Mill appears to adopt a milder form of McCulloch's view. When examining the effect of a tax on profits, he declares that 'It may operate in different ways. The curtailment of profit, and the consequent increased difficulty in making a fortune, or obtaining a subsistence by the employment of capital may act as a stimulus to inventions, and to the use of them when made. . . . Profits may rise . . . sufficiently to make up for all that is taken from them by the tax. In that case the tax will have been realized without loss to anyone[2].' Such a result, though possible, is extremely unlikely, as the additional production in consequence of the tax would itself be subject to taxation. A low rate of profit may lead to the introduction of economizing expedients, but the expectation of a high rate is far more effective in increasing production. There is just as much and just as little truth in the belief that low profits encourage industry, as in the similar beliefs that low wages make the workman and high rents make the

[1] *Principles*, Bk. i. ch. 7. § 6. [2] Ib. Bk. v. ch. 3. § 3.

farmer industrious [1]. Some special examples have been brought forward in support of the position that certain forms of taxation stimulate invention. McCulloch cites that of the Scotch distillers, who, under the influence of a spirit duty assessed according to the contents of the vessels, so improved their processes by economy of the time spent in distilling, that instead of taking a week they, in a few years, required only three minutes, and thereby were able to bear a duty nearly forty times as great as at first. Somewhat similar improvements have been introduced into the continental beet-root sugar industry in consequence of the method of imposition, which assumes a certain yield and charges duty only on that amount leaving any excess free [2]. In these cases what is really striking is the fact that invention has been stimulated, not by the duty but by the possibility of escaping it: the imperfect form of assessment has encouraged efforts in this direction that would cease if the true return were brought under taxation. They do not show in the slightest that the progress of invention in a taxed industry is greater than that in one free from taxation. All antecedent probability, and all actual experience go to prove the opposite [3]. One great impediment to the use of new processes is the surveillance that taxation renders necessary.

The result of the preceding discussion is, briefly, that any compensating effect of taxation in increasing production is extremely doubtful, and is at best so small, and occurs in so few cases as not to form an element worthy of entering into the rational calculations of the financier. The raising of compulsory revenue means so much loss to

[1] For a good refutation of the idea that low wages make workmen active see *Wealth of Nations*, 34. Arthur Young approved of high rents as promoting industry, *Northern Tour*, ii. 80–83; and Sir J. Caird deprecates under-letting, but wisely remarks that the opposite error of over-letting is much more hurtful, *English Agriculture*, 477.

[2] McCulloch, 151–2; Leroy Beaulieu, i. 258–260.

[3] For further discussion of this point see ch. 4 of the present Book, also Bk. iv. chs. 6, 7.

the payers and to the community for which the only return obtained is the benefit resulting from the efficient execution of state functions. Any doctrine that removes attention from this cardinal fact is erroneous in principle and may lead to serious practical evils.

§ 4. Nor does taxation only mean the withdrawal of the amount required by the public powers from the disposable funds of the subjects of taxation. It may, and often does, take much more. In all countries the cost of collection is no inconsiderable item, which must be added to the actual amounts needed by the state departments, unless it be regarded as an additional state function. In either view it increases the burden to the payers. Consequently one of the most generally recognised maxims of Finance is that which prescribes that 'Every tax ought to be so contrived, as both to take out and to keep out of the pockets of the people as little as possible over and above what it brings into the public treasury of the State[1].' This rule, declared by Wagner[2] to be simply the application of the general principle of economy to Public Finance, has two distinct applications: (1) As regards the State itself, the aim of securing the best return in amount of taxation for the expense incurred in collection is very plain, but even when this is realized there is (2) the still more important object of not inflicting indirect loss on the subjects, either by the obstruction of industry that taxation causes, or by the inconvenience that the regulations of the system of collection may produce. Some forms of taxation are much more oppressive in these respects than others, and one of the principal tasks of financial practice is to discover the least burdensome modes.

The public economy depends ultimately on the national economy; anything that reduces the economic power of the individual citizens is an injury to the State. A system of

[1] *Wealth of Nations*, 348. The fourth of Adam Smith's 'classical' rules. See appendix to the present Book on 'The Maxims of Taxation.'

[2] Wagner, ii. 467. In Jevons' phrase, 'The maximisation of utility.'

taxation that diminishes the revenue of the subject without a corresponding return to the public treasury is certain before long to show its effect in reduced receipts from taxation.

A comparison of English taxation as it existed in 1820, with that now in force proves how much may be gained by a determination to conform to the rule of 'economy[1].' But even in the best existing systems of Finance there is a large amount of waste, some of it unavoidable. The raising of such a sum as £70,000,000 in the course of a year cannot be accomplished without much interference with industry and trade, and a great deal of annoyance to individuals. From the purely material point of view the canon of economy is probably the most important in Finance, and no efforts should be spared to secure the closest observance of it that existing conditions permit.

§ 5. The supply of state wants by taxation is then, it is plain, a charge on the collective resources of the community. In Finance, as everywhere else, there is no method for obtaining something out of nothing. Prudent management may make the available resources go further than they otherwise would. The financier, like the mechanician, proves his ability by the direction not by the creation of force, and especially by reducing to a minimum the loss through friction. But having decided that taxation is a charge on the national resources, there is room for further inquiry as to the precise fund on which it falls. We have already mentioned Adam Smith's opinion that it must be derived from the shares of revenue. Ricardo declares that 'Taxes are always ultimately paid either from the capital or from the revenue of the country[2],' and expands his statement by pointing out that the proceeds of a tax must curtail consumption, increase production, or reduce capital, i. e. 'impair the fund allotted to productive con-

[1] See on this Dowell, ii. 249, 261, who quotes Sydney Smith's humorous account.

[2] *Works* (ed. McCulloch), 87.

sumption.' From this he concludes that taxation should be imposed on revenue rather than on capital, since the latter form of tax tends to check future production. Some writers have even raised this into a maxim of Finance[1]. The danger of hindering the growth of capital is apparent, though as capital is derived from revenue it is not easy to avoid taxing it to some extent. 'To provide that taxation shall fall entirely on income and not at all on capital is,' says Mill, 'beyond the power of any system of fiscal arrangements[2]. In actual economic life the line between capital and non-capital is not so fixed and rigid as the text-book definitions would make us believe. Any tax is certain to take some wealth that would otherwise have been devoted to the aid of production, and also some that, if left to the taxpayers, would have been consumed unproductively. How much will come from each source is not always easily determinable.

The distinction between capital and revenue is, besides, not quite the same when considered from the national instead of the individual point of view. Much of individual capital is not national capital, and this is likewise true of revenue; now for the financier it is the national capital and revenue that need attention. Any pressure on the most important auxiliary of production is so far as possible to be avoided; but where capital is rapidly increasing a tax that appears to trench on individual capital as e.g. the English Death Duties, is not open to the objection of reducing national capital in the same degree as it would be in a poor and unprogressive country. Taxation is drawn from the total stock of wealth, including at any given time both capital and revenue. The real aim should be to so direct it, as to interfere to the smallest extent with the action of the forces that promote accumulation. Heavy taxation will always be injurious in this

[1] '*Tout impôt doit porter sur le revenu, et non sur le capital*' is the *first* of Sismondi's maxims. *Nouveaux Principes*, Liv. vi. ch. 2.

[2] Bk. v. ch. 2. § 7.

respect. If imposed on revenue it reduces the fund from which capital comes, and may even lead to direct encroachments on individual capital: if on capital it leaves revenue free to partially fill up the gap that it has made. There is no impassable barrier between the two categories of wealth; any action on one must extend to the other.

In addition to the productive capital and annual new production, all civilized societies possess a large mass of wealth in process of use, 'Stock reserved for immediate consumption' as Adam Smith calls it, 'consumers' capital' in Dr. Sidgwick's phrase. There is in this 'stock' a further source on which taxation may fall without injuriously affecting the productive powers of the community. In fact we can fairly say that no less comprehensive term will suffice to describe the source of taxation than that already employed, viz. 'the collective wealth' of the country. But in actual societies in their normal condition taxation is derived from the national revenue, some of which would have been transformed into capital. Nothing but a national crisis would justify taxation so heavy as to absorb the free income of the society and reduce the sum of its accumulated wealth.

§ 6. A celebrated doctrine has carried still further this limitation, and maintained that all taxation should be levied on the net, as opposed to the gross, income. The net income is asserted to be the only disposable fund for the purpose. Gross income includes the necessary expenses of maintaining the citizens, and replacing the national capital. To touch on that part of the gross receipts would be a blow to the industrial organization, inasmuch as it is an essential requisite for the society being continued in its full efficiency as 'a going concern.' A tax that takes away a part of the labourer's necessary subsistence, or lowers profits below the minimum for which men will consent to take the risk of investment is indefensible and in the long run defeats its own object.

The earliest appearance of this doctrine is with the

Physiocrats. Their theory of the '*Produit net*' has its chief application in respect of taxation. The fifth of Quesnay's maxims lays down 'that taxation should not be destructive, or disproportioned to the sum of the national revenue; that its increase should follow the increase of revenue; that it should be imposed immediately on the *net product* of land.' According to Du Pont de Nemours, 'the portion of the returns called the net product is the sole contributory to taxation, the only one that nature has prepared to meet it. It is of the *essence* of taxation to be a part of the net product of cultivation.' Mercier de la Rivière is, if possible, clearer, 'Taxation is nothing but a part of a net product, and can be levied only on a net product[1].' The conception of the net product as consisting of nothing but the rent of land appears to a modern absurd, but the way in which Quesnay and his followers reached that startling result is not hard to follow. The labourer requires a definite amount of commodities for his subsistence, more than that he will not receive, and so much he must get under penalty of starvation. This 'subsistence theory' of wages was fully accepted by the Physiocrats[2], and fairly accorded with the fact in the France of the *Ancien Régime*. Precisely analogous is the position of the capitalist. The rate of interest is just sufficient to keep up the existing supply of capital. The interest on capital advanced is, Turgot tells us, 'the price and the condition of that advance, without which the undertaking could not continue. If that return is diminished, the capitalist will withdraw his money, and the undertaking will cease. That return ought then to be sacred and enjoy an entire immunity[3].'

[1] Quesnay in Daire, *Physiocrates*, 83; Du Pont, *ib.* 351; Mercier de la Rivière, *ib.* 474.

[2] The often quoted passage of Turgot, '*En tout genre de travail il doit arriver et il arrive en effet que le salaire de l'ouvrier se borne à ce qui lui est nécessaire pour lui procurer sa subsistance*' (i. 10), shows this.

[3] Turgot, i. 63.

When wages and profits are removed by the nature of things from the tax-collector's power, it goes without saying that rent is the only remaining source on which he can draw, and we are compelled, their premises being given, to accept the Physiocratic conclusion. Adam Smith declined to follow this seemingly rigorous deduction. He holds that both wages and profits may contribute to taxation, though the amount to be obtained from the former is very small. Ricardo takes the same view. While asserting formally that it is only from profits and rent 'that any deduction can be made for taxes,' wages 'if moderate, constituting always the necessary expenses of production,' he qualifies his statement by the admission that labourers may receive more than their necessary expenses, in which case the surplus is a part of 'net produce [1].' J. S. Mill emphasizes the share of the labourers in 'net produce,' and seems to desire to amend Ricardo's doctrine on this point [2].

§ 7. The doctrine of net income as the sole source of taxation, whose history we have just traced, has met with strenuous opposition in Germany. For the last thirty years the fact that taxation is a duty incumbent on the citizen and to be paid by him, not by the pure abstraction called 'net income,' has been loudly proclaimed. Hermann's theory of 'use capital' (*Nutz-capital*) has been employed to show that there is an enjoyment revenue to be added to the economic revenue derived from production in the strict sense. 'It is,' says Cohn, 'undoubtedly income that the owner of a house enjoys from his residence in it, the owner of a park from his enjoyment of the park, that a third enjoys in his own hunting-ground, in his own picture gallery. It is income in the specific form of enjoyment of property [3].' Such an extension would give a larger fund on which to draw, though it seems preferable to regard these forms of wealth in the way adopted in a

[1] *Works*, 210. [2] *Principles*, Bk. i. ch. 11. § 1.
[3] § 241.

preceding section of the present chapter, as property or capital, and so far liable in exceptional cases to taxation. Of greater force is the argument that the cost of maintaining the State is itself a part of the necessary expenses of the society. 'The protection of person and property,' the duty of the public powers even in the opinion of the extremest individualists, is almost as indispensable as feeding or clothing. So far then from taxation being dependent on the surplus produce of the community it may with justice be looked on as one of the first charges on the gross production, coming next to that minimum of food and covering that is needed for the preservation of life.

The apparent contradiction between two such plausible opinions can, we believe, be escaped by taking a broader view of the subject than the disputants on either side have done. Necessary expenses are in no case a fixed amount. Each standard demands a certain minimum outlay, but the standard can be varied. The necessary subsistence of the English labourer has always been higher than that of the Hindoo. What is true of labour is equally true of the other factors of production. The amount of capital can be reduced to suit a less intensive method of production, and the smaller the quantity needed the less *caeteris paribus* will be the rate of interest. And so is it also with state wants. Their amount and cost can and must be adjusted to the general position of the society. The difficulty of laying down any definite rule as to the proportion of national income, gross or net, that ought to be devoted to the public service has been shown at an earlier stage of our inquiry[1]. Here it will suffice to distinguish between that part of taxation that conduces directly or indirectly to the production of wealth, and that which produces non-economic advantages. The former is beyond dispute a part of the cost of production ; without it the amount of wealth would be smaller, and the payment of this part cannot be

[1] Bk. i. ch. 8. § 2.

said to come from the net income or surplus after necessary expenses are met. The latter, like all other forms of enjoyment, can be dispensed with, and yet leave the amount of production as great as before. It may, therefore, be said to come out of the net produce in the wider sense given to that term by Mill. This separation is, however, very hard to carry out. All forms of public expenditure have some effect in promoting industry[1], and some retrenchment might be made in all without economical loss to the society. Still the principle of the separation is intelligible, and within limits can be usefully employed[2].

§ 8. Inquiries respecting the derivation of the tax revenue from gross or net income, or from the sum total of the national wealth, may appear at first a piece of unnecessary subtlety. They have, however, important practical bearings. Until the normal source of taxation has been determined, it is impossible to estimate the pressure that it places on a community. The taxable capacity of India would be very different, according as the gross or the net revenue is taken as its measure; and in a comparison between Great Britain and the United States, the test of income would probably give the first place to the latter, while that of property would assign it to the former[3]. In another important question of Finance the problem of the true source of taxation becomes of moment. The justice of any particular system of taxation cannot be estimated without a knowledge of the fund from which the tax revenue is derived. According as taxation has its source in net or in gross income our view of the equity of existing systems must vary.

[1] Cp. Bk. i. ch. 6. § 1, for the relation of state expenditure to industry and commerce.

[2] On the whole question cp. Wagner, ii. 315 sq.; Cohn, § 236 sq.; Roscher, § 35; Held, *Einkommensteuer*, 66 sq. For Hermann's theory of income see *Staatswirthschaftliche Untersuchungen* (2nd ed.), 582-598. Professor Marshall has developed Hermann's view, *Principles of Economics*, i. 139 sq.

[3] Giffen, *Growth of Capital*, 124–139.

CHAPTER III.

THE DISTRIBUTION OF TAXATION.

§ 1. FROM an examination of the general, and what may almost be called the necessary features of the tax system, conditions that are beyond the direct influence of human agency, we have now to pass to a problem of a very different character, viz. the determination of the proper distribution of that burden inevitable in the levy of taxation among the persons or 'subjects' liable to it. Instead of studying 'what is,' we ask 'what ought to be.' The distribution of taxation may be said with far more justice than the distribution of wealth in general to be 'a matter of human institution solely[1]'. Like all questions, into which the conception of 'ought' or rightness enters, it is an ethical one; but its correct solution is so bound up with economic and financial considerations, that it must remain within the field of financial inquiry. Without a knowledge of the surrounding conditions, and the effects of any given tax system, the attempt to form a judgment respecting its justice is hopeless. Moreover, the, at least approximately, correct answer to the question is of great importance to the practical financier. Any error, wilful or otherwise, on the subject is apt to show itself in political difficulties, that may in some cases reach an acute point. Nor is it sufficient that a tax system shall be substantially just: it ought to

[1] J. S. Mill, *Principles*, Bk. ii. ch. 1. § 1; cp. Marshall, *Principles of Economics*, Bk. vii. note to ch. 3.

be generally recognised as such. The prevalence of even an unfounded belief that the public burdens are not fairly divided among the different classes and individual members of a society, is a seriously disturbing force. Finance touches on the domain of general politics, and no method of fiscal administration, however successful in other respects, can be worthy of approval, unless it seeks, so far as existing conditions allow, to realize the idea of an equitable division of the public charges.

The establishment of general principles on this point for the guidance of financial policy and their recognition by the people in general, is, then, eminently desirable, so that the investigation of the grounds on which taxation should be distributed is a work of utility in the narrowest practical sense.

The difficulties of the inquiry are increased by several distinct circumstances. First, they are due to the changing nature of the public economy. The city state of Greece or Italy, the mediaeval kingdom on a feudal basis, and the nation of modern times, have so many points of contrast, their several functions are in outward appearance so different, that it seems impossible to assign a single law of distribution that can include them all, and yet be more than a truism. Will it not be necessary to take each stage of political evolution and deal with it separately? Next, even confining our attention to a single type of State, it is not easy to bring the numerous public charges, and the equally numerous functions whose cost they defray, to the test of a common calculation. It is not clear on the surface that all citizens should bear all charges in an equal degree, or that all expenditure should fall on a common and indivisible fund. The text-book writers have, it must be said, created a third difficulty that is an illustration of the preceding ones. They, in too many cases, have supplied us with formulas that allow of a convenient laxity of interpretation, and give an appearance of information without the reality.

Under such circumstances it will be expedient to examine

the various rules of distribution, and to note their historical application. While thus engaged we shall see how misunderstanding has often arisen from neglect of changes in public economy, and of the gradual development of the State, as well as from attempts to stretch a particular rule beyond its legitimate limits.

§ 2. The first and, in one sense, the simplest principle for the distribution of taxation is that which would treat it as a payment for public services. We have already seen reason for rejecting this mode of explaining the *nature* of taxation [1], and thereby implicitly its value as a *measure* of its amount. There was, however, much in the mediaeval economic system that tended to foster the belief. Private economies admittedly sold their services, but the royal economy was nothing but the largest of private economies. The King lived by his domain and by the fees that he obtained for the performance of duties. The whole feudal system was based on the idea of contract. Defence against enemies was the payment for the vassal's homage and dues. Justice was bought, and so were the few economic services rendered by the sovereign. Under such conditions the doctrine that taxation should be measured by service supplied was but the formal expression of an existing fact. The growth of the state economy made this no longer true, and the doctrine thus became a survival from earlier times. It is still more important to note that the method of specific payment for public services was never a realization of justice in the distribution of burdens. Neither in respect to national defence, nor to legal administration, nor finally to general economic activity, is it possible to distribute the advantages among individuals, and to charge in proportion. The introduction of general taxation was in part a result of the defects of the older mode, and it was undoubtedly a step in advance, particularly in the direction of securing a fairer allocation of the expenses of the public powers.

The theory that taxation is the price of the State's

[1] Bk. iii. ch. I. § 4.

services, and finds its measure for each citizen in the amount of benefit received is, as regards the latter part, quite unsupported by history. The system of direct purchase applied to the State's tasks was so far from being equitable, that justice was only made possible by its abandonment.

The plausibility of this view of the measure of taxation arises from the apparent support that it gives to the individualistic theory of the State. If the services of government are the standard by which to regulate taxation, there appears to be no essential difference between the payment of taxes and the purchase of commodities. The assimilation of the two forms is in reality a forced one. In the case of taxation the advantage given is indefinite, and the payment for it is compulsory; the modern upholders of the doctrine are consequently forced to have recourse to some other standard, which, they declare, brings about a substantial equality between the benefits received and the taxes paid[1]. That usually suggested is the rule of taxation in proportion to revenue. It is, however, quite impossible to establish any such connexion. Limiting state functions to the minimum, viz. the protection of person and property, there can be no doubt that the former would in general require equal payment from all. It costs quite as much, 'perhaps on the whole more,' to protect a poor man's person as it does to perform the same service for a rich man. Again, as regards property, there is little ground for the belief that the cost of guarding it varies directly as its value. If security is to be sold like tea or sugar, there ought on the strictest commercial principles to be some allowance made to the purchaser of a large quantity! The natural conclusion therefore appears to be that the rate of taxation should, on the theory of purchase and sale, be lower on large than on small incomes; but even this result does not rest on very solid ground since any change in the quality

[1] For a statement of this theory see Thiers, *De la Propriété*, 348, who compares taxation to an insurance premium.

or quantity of state services would alter the relations of the parties concerned.

§ 3. The evident weakness of the theory just discussed, makes the adoption of some other and more precise criterion necessary. Retaining the idea that taxation should be equal, but giving up as hopeless the attempt to measure the respective services performed for each person by the State, we might conceivably abandon all efforts at differentiation between individuals, and hold that equality was realized by taxing all persons (or all families) at the same rate. Such a method might be admissible in a primitive community. All are dependent on the State for certain essential conditions of social life. Why should not all pay equally for these advantages? Military service is rendered by all alike, and the same principle might seem as applicable to the contribution of commodities as to that of services. Civilized societies have, however, almost forgotten the existence of a state of things in which such an arrangement would be feasible. The annual tax revenue of the United Kingdom may be put roughly at £75,000,000, and the population at 37,500,000. Under a system of equal contribution the rate per head would be £2, or £10 for a family of five. The labourer's family, with a weekly income of £1, would be taxed about 20 per cent.; a middle class family, with £500 per annum, would be taxed 2 per cent.; where the family income was £50,000 per annum the charge would be an insignificant fraction. The method of equal contributions per head would be impossible politically, besides being extremely unjust.

Dismissing then the idea of equal taxation of persons as utterly impracticable, we come to what is the best known and most widely accepted doctrine, viz. that which takes 'faculty' or 'ability' as the measure for taxation. This view, which is found as early as Bodin [1], has been em-

[1] 'Sunt igitur ea vectigalia . . . probanda quae in omnes ordines pro singulorum facultatibus exaequantur,' Bodin, *De Rep.* Liv. vi. ch. 2. See Neumann, 'Die Steuer nach Steuerfähigkeit,' in Conrad's *Jahrb.* 1880, for a history of the doctrine.

bodied by Adam Smith in the *first* of his classical maxims; 'The subjects of every State ought to contribute towards the support of the government, as nearly as possible, in proportion to their respective abilities [1].' For the last twenty years it has been the doctrine accepted by the majority of German financiers. One reason for the readiness with which 'ability' has been adopted as the measure of taxation, is perhaps its convenient vagueness. The mere statement that taxation should be proportioned to 'ability,' does not afford much practical guidance. A measure of 'ability' is further wanted, and in fact different criteria have been put forward with equal sincerity and equal confidence. Property, revenue, net revenue, have each been selected as the test of the tax-payer's ability.

All of these are more or less measurable, and present, so to speak, objective standards, but the measure of 'ability' has sometimes been transformed into that of 'sacrifice,' and this test has been widely approved of. 'Equality of taxation,' says Mill, 'as a maxim of politics means equality of sacrifice [2].' It is apparent that the rule of equality of sacrifice is but another mode of stating the rule of equality as to ability. Equal ability implies equal capacity for bearing sacrifice. An equal charge will impose equal sacrifice on persons of equal 'faculty,' and where abilities are unequal a corresponding inequality in the amount of taxation will realize the aim of equality of sacrifice. There is, however, a shade of difference in the two terms. Ability suggests the positive element of power to contribute; sacrifice the negative one of loss by contribution: the former is most naturally measured by some objective standard; the latter refers primarily to the sentiments of the people concerned, and is, therefore, rather subjective. The use of sacrifice incurred as the measure of taxation is probably due to a disposition to place weight on the element of privation felt by those who are taxed,

[1] *Wealth of Nations*, 347; cp. 342. See Appendix.

[2] *Principles*, Bk. v. ch. 2. § 2.

instead of the external marks that evidence ability to pay.

But whether 'ability' or 'sacrifice' be taken as the standard, it is possible to reach very different practical results according to the amount of weight assigned to the different elements. We accordingly meet with three different forms of distribution, all avowedly based on the criterion of ability, and all claiming to realize true equality. These are: (1) pure proportional taxation, in which income is taken as the standard, and the amount of public burdens regulated by it; (2) qualified proportional taxation, where income is still the test, but is subjected to certain modifications, either by deduction of necessary expenses or by analysis of its component parts; (3) 'progressive' or graduated taxation, which places a heavier rate of charge on large than on small incomes since the ability of the 'subject' is supposed to increase in a more rapid ratio than the increase of his income.

§ 4. The rule of proportional taxation has been undoubtedly the doctrine of the classical political economy. Connected on its political side with the liberalizing movements of the 18th century, its representatives protested against all exemptions and privileges, and against none more than those granted in respect of taxation. The assertion of the justice of taxing in proportion to revenue carried with it a condemnation of the very common freedom from all personal taxation enjoyed by the privileged classes of the Continent. 'There is,' says Vauban, 'a natural obligation on the subjects of all conditions to contribute in proportion to their revenue or their industry. . . Every privilege that tends to exemption from that contribution is unjust and abusive [1].' If taxation should be proportional it follows necessarily that it must also be general. The French Revolution, and the changes that it led to elsewhere, so completely abolished the objectionable privileges that this side of the doctrine is often ignored, and its refer-

[1] *Dîme Royale* (ed. Daire), 48; cp. Meyer, *Principien*, § 2.

ence to the income possessed alone considered. Adam Smith completes his statement that taxation should be adjusted to the abilities of the subjects by adding 'that is in proportion to the revenue which they respectively enjoy under the protection of the State[1].' And since his time the rule has been quoted and adopted by most of his English and French successors[2]. At first put forward as a protest against the injustice of the old system of privilege, the maxim of proportional taxation is now employed as a weapon against the newer Radical socialism[3].

One great advantage of the rule is its simplicity. As M. Say puts it, 'Proportional taxation does not need definition, it is the rule of three. . . When it is said of a tax that it will be levied proportionally every one understands it[4].' The problem of taxation is reduced to its least complex form. Given the amount that must be raised by taxation, and given the sum of individual incomes, the rate per cent. can be assigned, and applied to each case. It is true that there are certain practical difficulties in the way. The ascertainment of individual incomes is not a perfectly easy work, and where, as is almost universally the case, it is necessary to specialize the tax system and have a number of duly arranged charges, it is difficult to measure the exact amount paid by each citizen to the public treasury. But any other principle must either meet or evade these embarrassments besides those that are peculiar to itself. Simplicity and easy application, though desirable in Finance, are not the sole objects to be attained, and, therefore, the rule of proportional taxation has been vehemently opposed as failing to give a just distribution of the public charges. The question has, in fact, been mainly

[1] *Wealth of Nations*, 347.

[2] '*Nous l'avons adoptée et nous devons la défendre*,' is the expression of Leroy Beaulieu, i. 139.

[3] See for a full exposition of this point of view Léon Say, *Les Solutions démocratiques de la Question des Impôts*.

[4] *Ib.* i. 167.

debated on the issue whether proportional or progressive taxation should be the system adopted.

§ 5. What is known to continental writers as progressive—but more familiar in England as graduated—taxation includes, as we have said, any system in which the rate of taxation becomes higher, or progresses as income increases. In this consists the essence of the principle; the grades into which incomes are divided, the initial rate of charge, and the increases at the several stages of advance, though very important, are yet matters of application.

The reasons that have led to the popularity of progressive taxation are obvious enough. The loss of a portion of wealth by a rich man is generally regarded as a very slight evil or as none at all; while to a poor one it causes curtailment of real enjoyment. The deduction of £10 from an income of £100 will in most cases prove a serious pressure, sweeping away perhaps the savings of the period, or compelling the sacrifice of all relaxation, that of £100 from £1,000, though still heavy, would not trench upon the conditions of a comfortable life. £1,000 taken from £10,000 would leave a balance sufficient to support a luxurious existence, and £10,000 from £100,000 would hardly, so popular sentiment imagines, be perceptible by the owner. Yet it is precisely these deductions that proportional taxation carries out, without recognition of the real gradations of ability and capacity for bearing sacrifices. So regarded, the levying of equal rates on all incomes has an appearance of unfairness that has given much support to the plan of graduating charges according to different scales.

Though the general current of economic opinion has till recently been decidedly against the idea of progression, the system has secured the adhesion of some eminent authorities. A passage of Montesquieu's has been often quoted in its favour, in which, speaking of the Athenian property tax, he says, 'it was just though not proportional; if it did not follow the proportion of goods, it followed the proportion of wants. It was thought that each had equal physical necessities, which ought not to be taxed; that what was useful came next and should be taxed, but not so highly as superfluities [1].' Rousseau and the elder Mirabeau took the same view. In the present century J. B. Say and Joseph Garnier have approved of a system of moderate progression. The former 'did not fear to declare that progressive taxation was the only equitable form'; the latter held that taxation ought to be progressive without spoliation [2].' Still the weight of authority was on the other side. 'Progressive taxation,' like 'protection' or 'a double standard,' was an heretical tenet opposed to the true economic faith. Alike in England, France, and Germany, it was rejected by such representatives of competent opinion as J. S. Mill and McCulloch, Levasseur and De Parieu, Gneist and Hermann [3].

The recent change in opinion on this subject has been due partly to increased popular influence over government. The shifting in the centre of political gravity that the growth of democracy has brought about has, as one of its consequences, a tendency to alter the distribution of taxation in favour of the most powerful classes, i.e. the numerical majority. This can only be accomplished by putting a heavier burden on the wealthy. The diffusion of socialistic ideas assists in this movement. Progressive taxation is one of those agencies that seem likely to facilitate the transition from the capitalist to the socialist *régime*, and it consequently has the support of the various sections of that party. Among the counts of the indictment that the French economists bring against the system one of the weightiest in their view is its socialistic character.

Modern developments of economic theory have also had

[1] *Esprit des Lois*, Liv. xiii. ch. 7.

[2] Garnier calls his system 'progressional'; see J. B. Say, *Traité*, Bk. iii. ch. 9; Garnier, *Traité des Finances*, 68.

[3] 'This doctrine seems to me too disputable altogether, and even if true at all, not true to a sufficient extent to be made the foundation of any rule of taxation,' Mill, *Principles*, Bk. v. ch. 2. § 2; cp. McCulloch, *Taxation*, 65; De Parieu, I. 38; Levasseur, *Précis*, 343; also Neumann, *Progressive Einkommensteuer*, 112.

their share in the work. The members of the 'historical' school have not been bound by any undue respect to the opinions of their predecessors, and their greater sympathy with semi-socialist ideas made them inclined to favour what seemed to be a mode of relieving the poorer classes from the pressure of excessive taxation. Some moderate form of progression has generally been approved of by them.

Another and apparently opposed school has tended in the same direction. The more accurate study of the variations of utility which forms the common starting point of the researches of Jevons, Menger, and Walras, has among its other important effects given a new mode of measuring the pressure of taxation. The final utility becomes the measure of sacrifice, and if, as is plain, 1*s*. is more to the possessor of an income of £100 than it is to one of £1,000, it does not follow that it is exactly ten times as great. The assumption that equal percentages of income are of equal utility is a rough 'first approximation' admissible, perhaps, in the earlier stages of inquiry, but certain to give place to the more accurate results of later investigation. It is noticeable that Sax and Wieser, who represent the financial studies of the Austrian school, have both declared for progressive taxation [1].

§ 6. A system of progression may be realized in different ways as, e. g. by heavy taxes on luxuries consumed by the rich [2], or higher duties on the finer kinds of all commodities. The taxation of inheritances, and duties on the transfer of property, as also on commercial transactions generally, could be so adjusted as to reach the same end, but the mode usually employed is that of progressive income and property taxes. This is obviously the most direct way, since it places the increased charges at once on the larger incomes, and has not to trust to the less certain and calculable operations of taxes on 'consumption' or on 'acts.' In form the tax may be on property, or on income, or on

[1] Sax, *Staatswirthschaft*, 508-513; Wieser, *Natürlicher Werth*, 229.

[2] The English assessed taxes might have been thus employed.

both; but, as in any case, it must normally be paid out of income, the assessment on property is simply a particular mode of fixing the rate of charge.

Whatever be the form, the policy of progressive taxation is open to serious objections, of which the following may be noticed as the most important.

(1) Progressive taxation is entirely arbitrary. The possible scales are infinite in number, and no simple and intelligible reason can be assigned for the selection of one in preference to its competitors. The statement of some suggested scales will illustrate the truth of this remark.

Professor F. W. Newman has proposed the following system of progression. Incomes under £100 to be free; those between £100 and £1,000 to pay 3 per cent. on the excess over £100; those between £1,000 and £2,000 to pay 4 per cent. on the excess over £1,000; those between £2,000 and £3,000 to pay 5 per cent. on the excess over incomes in the preceding class and so on, the rate increasing 1 per cent. for each additional £1,000. This scale at first sight seems moderate enough: an income of £600 would pay only £15 (i. e. 3 per cent. on £500) or $2\frac{1}{2}$ per cent.; one of £1,700 would have to pay £55 (i. e. 3 per cent. on £900 and 4 per cent. on £700) or less than $3\frac{1}{4}$ per cent. When, however, the higher incomes are considered, its aspect is changed. In an income of £97,000 the last £1,000 would be taxed 99 per cent., leaving but £10 to the possessor, and any higher amount would be altogether absorbed. Therefore, the maximum income possible would be £47,533[1].

[1] The following calculation shows this:—In an income of £97,000 the first £100 is free; the next £900 will be taxed at 3 per cent., or £27, leaving a balance of £973 out of the £1000; of the second £1000, taxed at 4 per cent., the owner will have £960; of the third, £950; and so on, decreasing by £10 for each additional £1000. The maximum income will therefore be £973 plus the sum of the series

$$(10 + 20 + 30 + 40 \ldots\ldots 960) = 973 + 10\,(1 \,.\, 2 \,.\, 3 \,.\, 4 \ldots\ldots 96):$$

$$973 + 10\left(\frac{96+97}{2}\right) = 973 + 46560 = 47533.$$

Again, take that mentioned by M. Leroy Beaulieu, in which the tax triples as the revenue doubles, the rate at starting being 1 per cent., and the lowest grade up to 500 francs. This will work out as shown in the following table[1]:—

Income in Francs.	*Amount of Tax.*	*Rate per cent.*
500	5	1
1,000	15	1·50
2,000	45	2·25
4,000	135	3·375
8,000	405	5·06
16,000	1,215	7·6
32,000	3,645	11·4
64,000	10,935	17·1
128,000	32,805	25·6
256,000	98,415	38·4
512,000	295,245	57·6
1,024,000	885,735	86·5
2,048,000	2,657,205	129·7

In both cases, after a certain point is reached, the total additional revenue is taken by the tax-collector, and at a much lower one the rate becomes oppressively high. Actual examples of progression are, as will appear, much milder. The highest rate of charge is fixed at a comparatively low percentage. The fact, however, remains that there is no self-acting principle by which to determine the scale of progression. We must perforce agree with M. Say when he declares that 'progression is naturally arbitrary[2].' Opponents of the system will naturally hold that the most moderate form is the least evil, and try to attain that result (unless they prefer to have an extreme measure in the hope that its hardships may cause a reaction). Reasonable supporters will recognise that a rapidly increasing rate is both unjust and economically injurious. But beyond such vague

[1] Leroy Beaulieu, i. 148–150.

[2] *Impôts Démocratiques*, i. 172. It may be suggested that the scale that would give the maximum revenue should be chosen, but this is (*a*) extremely difficult to determine, and (*b*) is not consistent with the aim of proportional sacrifice. It is besides quite possible that several different scales should satisfy the condition.

propositions nothing can be stated. All depends on the will of the Legislature, i. e. in most modern societies on the votes of persons who will not directly feel the charges placed on the higher incomes, and will probably believe that they will be gainers by them.

(2) A serious obstacle is the danger of evasion. No empirical law is better established in Finance than that which states that high taxation leads to efforts to avoid it. Duties on luxuries are in part escaped by the smuggler's aid; special duties on the better kinds of goods lead to false declarations; progressive income and property taxes cause false returns on the part of the contributors. For this latter fact there are several reasons. The increased charge on higher incomes offers a special inducement to understatement on the part of those liable, as thereby they obtain a lower rate, a proceeding the more readily excused to their consciences by the plea that the exaction escaped is itself unjust. Another reason is the impossibility of employing effective measures for collection. With a uniform income tax a great deal of income can be taken at its source where evasion is impossible; with progression, as the rate varies according to the *sum* of income, the ascertainment of that fact is required for fixing the charge, though it is undoubtedly very difficult to get a proper answer to inquiries respecting it. Thus the motives for evasion would be stronger, and the means of prevention less effective in the case of a progressive than of a proportional tax. It is the intrusion of the personal and arbitrary element that raises this difficulty which is accordingly unavoidable.

(3) A powerful argument against progressive taxation is derived from its probable effect on the accumulation of wealth. One of the motives to providence is the desire of gaining a large fortune, but a system that in its extreme forms prevents, and in any case hinders the attainment of this desire must, it is argued, check the growth of capital. The imposition of special taxation on the larger incomes is,

in fact, a fine on saving, and consequently an impediment to the supply of one of the auxiliaries of production. If the legislator is to interfere at all he ought rather to encourage the formation of new stores of wealth that will, in the vast majority of cases, be used to assist industry.

The discouragement to capital may operate in two different ways. There will naturally be a movement of wealthy persons from a district in which they are subjected to special penalties. Any existing outflow of wealth will be increased and the influx of other wealth so far checked. Such is a very probable and serious danger in a small district from which movement is easy, and with the modern tendency to an international movement of capital it may occur even in large areas. But for countries with a highly developed system of industries, another effect is more to be dreaded, viz. the stoppage of saving at an earlier period. Capital may not emigrate readily from such a country as England or France, but the annual increment may become smaller and finally cease. Considering the dependence of industry on the facilities for obtaining new capital it would seem that any artificial check to its growth would be a grave evil and likely to react on the Finances of the State.

In mitigation it may be urged that progressive taxation is not in fact likely to weaken the disposition to save. It will only affect those who possess a good deal already, and such persons save as much from habit as from conscious motive. There is, too, the further fact that the heavier taxation on the rich will leave the poor a larger disposable sum, part of which they may save, and to that extent increase the store of wealth. But, though in both those ways, the loss to capital under a moderate progression may be reduced, it seems clear that some loss there will inevitably be, and it is incumbent on the supporters of any measure tending in this direction to show what compensation will be gained through fairer distribution.

(4) The productiveness of a progressive tax on incomes is not as great as is popularly supposed. This failure to

reach expectation is due partly to the evasions that have been noticed as incident to the tax, and also to the various devices not absolutely illegal that are used to escape the extra pressure. If vigorously collected the tax causes much capital to emigrate, discretion is therefore very often employed in enforcing claims, and in either case the revenue suffers. Another reason is found in the fact that in most countries large incomes do not form a large proportion of national revenue. Taxation, to be productive, must draw on the resources of the middle and working classes. The unproductiveness of progressive direct taxes is paralleled by the small yield of taxes on the luxuries of the rich as compared with duties on articles of general consumption [1]. To obtain the funds needed by the State pressure must be placed on all classes of society, not merely on the well-to-do.

§ 7. The foregoing objections, which may be distinguished in their order as political, moral, economical, and fiscal, are so weighty that nothing but a very clear proof of injustice inflicted by any other system than progression would permit its use. The injustice of proportional or regressive taxation, if established, goes to show that for the realization of equity progression in some form must be adopted. In support of this contention, we have nothing but the appeal to equality of sacrifice as the standard, and the alleged failure to conform to it by taking equal proportions from different incomes. The deduction of £10 from A's income of £100, and of £10,000 from B's of £100,000 will, it is maintained, inflict greater suffering on A than on B. Such is the assumption of the upholders of progression, and their view accords with popular sentiment. There is, nevertheless, room for doubt. Is it really certain that A, whose income is reduced from £100 to £90 is worse treated than B whose £100,000 is brought down to £90,000? There can be no dispute as to the wants which the latter will have to leave unsatisfied being very much slighter than those of A,

[1] Cp. *Wealth of Nations*, 375.

when looked at from the same point of view. But the point of view is not the same, B's system of life on its material side is so differently constituted from A's that any comparison of the kind is absurd[1]. £10 from A's income may mean the loss of a certain amount of alcoholic drinks; B, by having to give up £10,000 may lose the chance of purchasing an estate, or may have to abandon some social scheme that he could otherwise have carried out. The economic calculus is not at present competent to deal with such comparisons. The complexity of the problem is admittedly great, and not to be solved by simple methods[2]. The weightiest difficulty that the theoretical advocates of progression have to meet is the essentially subjective nature of their standard. Its translation into an objective rule of taxation can be accomplished only by the aid of assumptions as to the relations of enjoyment in different classes that must contain a large element of conjecture. The modern developments of the theory of utility fail to supply any definite practical basis on which to frame a scale of progression.

Progressive taxation has been supported by a very different line of reasoning in Cohn's brilliant *Treatise on Finance*[3]. Proportional taxation is asserted by him to be the logical result of the 'contract,' or assurance theory of the State. In accordance with that belief, it was fitting that all should pay the same proportion of income in exchange for the stipulated services. The modern, or 'higher' conception of the State, abandons altogether this theory of the social compact, and therefore its corollaries in which is included the rule of proportional

[1] See Wicksteed, *Alphabet of Economic Science*, for a clear statement of the general principle applied in the text. Signor M. Pantaleoni argues that the richer person (B) may even suffer more if (1) the additional wealth happens to be of special importance to him, or (2) if his sensibility be keener.

[2] Cp. Sax, 'Die Progression ist keine vollständig regelmässige. Je nach der Beschaffenheit der einzelnen Bedürfnissgruppen kann sie bald geringer sein, vielleicht zum Stillstand gelangend, bald in raschen Sprüngen emporsteigen,' *Staatswirthschaft*, 512.

[3] §§ 210, 211.

taxation. Writers, who like Rau, De Parieu, and Leroy Beaulieu reject the older view of the State's relation to its subjects and yet maintain the justice of proportional taxation are guilty of inconsistency explicable only by their dread of the often described evils of progressive taxation.

To this ingenious contention, the answer is, that granting the deduction of proportional taxation from the 'assurance theory,' the refutation of the latter does not upset the former since a true conclusion may result from false premisses. But even this concession need not be made. It has been argued in the present chapter that the exploded doctrine of 'assurance' would logically lead not to proportional, but to what has been called 'regressive,' taxation, i.e. to a lower percentage on large than on small incomes [1].

§ 8. Experience of the actual working of progressive systems might be expected to throw light on the reality of the evils attributed to them and their real operation. A large amount of evidence has been collected with this object by very competent inquirers [2], but, unfortunately, the results are not decisive. Most of the cases discussed are those of Swiss cantons or the smaller German States. (The short-lived income tax of the United States, and the apparent progressive income tax of Prussia are the only exceptions.) Now, the financial arrangements of small political bodies are undoubtedly full of instruction and deserve attentive study, but they belong to the domain of *local* rather than general Finance. The conditions of working are therefore different, and there is to some extent, room for the use of a different principle of distribution [3], since the public services rendered by local bodies do often allow of an estimation of their value to individuals, and, besides, have to be considered in connexion with the taxation of the State.

[1] The *progression à rebours* of French economists.

[2] Neumann, *Progressive Einkommensteuer, passim*; Léon Say, *Les Impôts Démocratiques*, i. 203–258; ii. 225–264; Leroy Beaulieu, i. 152–156, 160–168; Cohn, §§ 213, 214; Palgrave, 'Progressive Taxation in Switzerland,' *Journal of the Statistical Society*, li. 225–267.

[3] See § 12; also ch. 6 of the present Book, 'Principles of Local Taxation.'

The peculiar economic conditions under which progressive taxes have been applied are shown in the discussions respecting their merits which are chiefly concerned with the danger of forcing capital to emigrate and that of undue discrimination against particular persons. Both are real and serious in a small area; within the wider boundaries of a nation their probability would be smaller. It is hardly conceivable that the English Chancellor of the Exchequer should arrange his scheme of taxation with reference to any small number even of the wealthiest tax-payers; nor would the emigration of capital be caused by even a fairly heavy tax. On the other hand, the facilities for assessment are much increased by having to deal with a limited district in which the income and property of each resident can be ascertained with a close approach to the truth, and as incomes are in no case very large, there is not the same room for injustice. Progressive taxation would not be easily applied in national Finance. The forms of wealth are very numerous, and can be so placed as to escape the tax-collector's notice, when he has to deal directly with income as a whole. We have, therefore, no evidence sufficient to modify the unfavourable conclusion reached on general grounds respecting progressive taxation[1].

§ 9. The idea of securing equality of sacrifice while escaping the dangers of unregulated progression has led to the adoption of what is known as 'degressive' taxation; a system in which a uniform rate of tax is levied, but incomes under certain limits are either altogether exempt, or rated only for a part of their amount. Some of the so-called progressive taxes in Switzerland are really of this kind: thus in Zürich, 500 francs are free, the excess up to 1,500 francs is rated at only one-fifth, the next 1,500 francs at two-fifths, the next 3000 at three-fifths, and the next 4000 at four-fifths, anything beyond being rated at its full amount, e.g. an income of 12,500 francs (£500) would only pay on 8,300

[1] Particular instances of progressive taxes will be considered in Bk. iv. ch. 4, 'Taxes on Property and Income.'

francs[1]. By this method the confiscation of the higher portions of income can never happen, but there is still an arbitrary power of fixing the several scales which is inconvenient, while this form of progression is particularly open to the charge of unproductiveness, and is somewhat hard to work owing to the minute sub-divisions that are usually made.

Degressive taxation may, however, like the more moderate forms of progression, be employed rather to secure, than to destroy proportionality of taxation, as it affects only one part of the tax system, and may correct inequalities in other directions. When the articles consumed by the poorer classes are heavily taxed they would contribute more than their share to the maintenance of the State were they not relieved through the income and property taxes. This is one of the reasons for the exemption of incomes under £150 from income tax in the United Kingdom, and the abatement on those under £400. The duties on tea, tobacco, and spirits, which chiefly affect the smaller incomes are thus balanced, and a substantial equality (or what is believed to be such) attained. The rule of proportionality is applicable only to the whole tax-system, and it may be necessary to have several partial inequalities in order to establish that final equality that is one of the principal merits in Finance.

§ 10. Another ground for modifying the rule of proportional taxation exists in the doctrine that net income is the sole available fund for social objects. If certain kinds of expense be necessary and unavoidable, it seems that any income which only suffices for meeting them must be exempt from taxation. On the supposition that the labourer's wages are just enough to keep him alive, the

[1] I. e.

500	Free	0
1000	$\frac{1}{5}$	200
1500	$\frac{2}{5}$	600
3000	$\frac{3}{5}$	1800
4000	$\frac{4}{5}$	3200

slightest extra charge will lead to his death unless he is relieved from some other quarter. Taxation on the minimum of subsistence must, by the nature of the case, be paid by somebody else. The Physiocrats, as we saw[1], extended this argument to the interest on capital, but their successors have not accepted this extreme view. However, the doctrine known as 'the exemption of the minimum of subsistence' is widely spread. Among its supporters in one form or other may be reckoned Justi, Bentham, Sismondi, Hermann and J. S. Mill, and it has received recognition in the English system of taxation, since there are no duties on the necessaries of life, and, as mentioned, incomes under £150 per annum are free from direct taxation[2]. The different interpretations put on the doctrine need to be distinguished. The primitive and most natural meaning is that which limits it to the absolute necessaries of existence, though here there is room for doubt as to the correctness of including the expense of maintaining a family under this head. The wider use of the term to cover 'the sum of the means of support which, according to the standard of a given period, is required for the conduct of an existence worthy of man[3]' would extend the exemption far beyond the limit of physical necessaries, and would almost approach to the exclusion of whatever expenditure is necessary for the earning of the person's income from the amount to be taxed[4]. By regarding the outlay requisite for the support of each grade of income as its expenses of production, we might bring the fund available for taxation down to a very small amount.

[1] Bk. iii. ch. 2. § 6.

[2] The effect of local rates and the repercussion of taxation do in fact put some of the pressure on the very poor, but the statement in the text is generally true of the immediate effect of Imperial taxation.

[3] Schmidt, *Steuerfreiheit des Existenzminimums*, 4, 5.

[4] The criterion of 'necessaries' varies according to the class concerned. 'We may say that the income of any class in the ranks of industry is below its necessary level, when any increase in their income would, in the course of time, produce a more than proportionate increase in their efficiency,' Marshall, *Principles of Economics*, i. 122.

Such a construction of the doctrine may be dismissed as impracticable. The subject's outlay is determined by himself and is directed for his own advantage. The only ground for doubt would be the possibility of expenditure on these 'necessary' items being curtailed in consequence of the tax. This effect would be very improbable unless the rate of taxation were so heavy as to show bad administration, but even in the limited case of physical necessaries the argument for remission is not so clear as might be thought. The danger of relieving the lowest class of labourers from nearly all the burdens of the State, while it holds preponderating political power is apparent. Again, there is much force in the view that public expenses are a part of necessary expenditure. 'The State,' argues Cohn, 'belongs as much to the life of every civilized man as his daily food, or the air; without the State a civilized existence is not thinkable. The minimum of every moral existence includes the blessings of the State. It follows that the minimum of outlay for existence must also include the necessary expense of the State[1].' Why should not the poorest citizen pay something towards security as well as purchase the bread that supports him? The practical side of the question seems rather to favour the existing English policy. So far as the argument from ability is concerned it is plain that those who barely possess the means of subsistence have little or no ability to contribute. In any country where legal provision is made for poor relief it would seem that to tax those at the point of subsistence would be simply driving them into the ranks of pauperism, and taking with one hand to give back with the other. The cost and trouble of raising money by direct taxation from the poorer classes, added to the foregoing consideration, strongly supports the method of exemption from direct taxation of the smaller incomes with the employment of

[1] In *Political Science Quarterly*, iv. 64-5; cp. 'Der Staat ist für alle ein Bedürfniss, seine Existenz ist für die Gesammtheit nothwendiger als das Leben eines Einzelnen,' Held, *Einkommensteuer*, 103.

moderate taxes on the luxuries of the poor. When exemption is claimed for the minimum it can only be on the ground that it will be employed in buying necessaries; any other application of this amount fairly brings it under the weight of taxation[1].

§ 11. The question of justice may also be raised in respect of incomes that differ, not in amount but in origin. As usually debated the point is confined to the case of an income tax, but it is really wider and applies to all forms. To put the issue in the simplest way let us suppose that of two persons one, A, obtains by his exertions £500 per annum, the other, B, obtains the same sum from the rent of land or interest on capital. Is it just or expedient that A should pay the same sum in taxes that B does? The most natural answer is, perhaps, a negative one, and many persons have proposed that the capital values of the two incomes should be taken as the basis of taxation[2]. A little reflection will show that under certain conditions there is nothing unjust in the arrangement. A's income it is true is less durable, but then so is its chance of taxation. The permanence of B's receipts involves likewise permanence of taxation. So long then as the public charges are uniform, there is no reason for complaint. Special occasions will sometimes occur in which extraordinary expenditure actually is, or is deemed to be, necessary, and then it seems that as there is an extraordinary call it ought to come from the capital rather than the income of the community. A convenient mode of realizing this end would be the imposition of an additional property tax, which, being met out of the income of the holders, would accomplish the end of taxing permanent incomes at

[1] Mill's view on the subject, though his conclusion is the same as that in the text, appears to be inconsistent with his views on population and his criticism of allotments (*Principles*, Bk. ii. ch. 12. § 4). Would not taxation of the minimum tend to check population, and remission of it tend to increase it?

[2] See the Reports and Evidence of the Parliamentary Committees on the Income Tax 1852–3 and 1861, especially the evidence of Newmarch, Farr, and J. S. Mill.

a higher rate. Another mode would be to meet the increased outlay by loans to be repaid in a series of years.

In practice the difficulty is not so great; the distribution of burdens can never be accomplished with mathematical precision. The avoidance of real and serious grievances is all that can be expected, and the actual working of the financial system meets these in a tolerably satisfactory manner. Necessity compels recourse to loans whenever there is any large extraordinary outlay, and thus the particular holders of incomes from labour do in fact escape. Again the two categories are not so sharply divided as is supposed; they shade into each other at many points; and, moreover, the return on property (as distinct from 'unearned increment') is itself the result of saving and entitled to as liberal treatment as any other form of revenue. The technical difficulties that any attempts to differentiate incomes would lead to belong to a later part of our inquiry[1].

The foregoing considerations help us to meet a very different proposal also aiming at a departure from the rule of taxation in proportion to income, viz. that which asserts that expenditure alone should be taxed, what is saved being entirely exempt. The reasons given for this privilege are (1) that saving is not enjoyment, but a useful social process that deserves encouragement; and (2) that unless exempted savings would pay twice over, viz. first at their origin, and again when they yield a further return after investment. It may be freely allowed that to encourage providence is desirable, but it does not follow that exemption from taxation is the proper mode for so doing. If income be the normal fund from which taxation comes, and if it is on its amount that the measurement of the burden is to be taken, an arbitrary separation of a certain part is obviously objectionable. The line between saving and expenditure is besides a thin one; the true distinction should rather be between productive and unproductive

[1] Bk. iv. ch. 4, 'Taxes on Property and Income.'

expenditure, i. e. the result of outlay ought to be the test, a plainly impossible course in practice. Further it may be said that many forms of productive outlay are just as enjoyable as any non-productive one, and some forms of the latter are sociably preferable to others. There is in reality no reason for a sharp division into two classes, whether we take enjoyment or social advantage as the basis. Practical Finance could not deal with such shades of difference as would be the apparently fair course. The same consideration may be applied to the case of temporary and durable incomes, the former of which are very variable in character.

To the plea of double taxation it may be replied that taxation is imposed on income as such, that the wealth which is taxed as income is not identical with the extra produce that is the result of its application, and the charge on each is distinct. The income out of which savings are made cannot be the same as the subsequent income produced by those savings [1].

There is it should also be noticed a direct opposition between the proposal to relieve temporary incomes, and that to exempt savings from taxation. What is the net advantage of getting a premium to save only to discover that the earnings which result from that saving will be subject to heavier payments? The broad and simple principle of taxing all incomes alike and of taxing all that is income (allowance being made for the action of taxes on consumption in the case of the smaller incomes) appears to attain the result of just distribution quite as well as the more refined discriminations so often suggested. Should any further adjustment seem necessary in a particular system it may be reached by a nominal property tax [2] or by duties on inheritance.

§ 12. The principal theories and contentions on the subject of the just division of taxation have now been

[1] See Vocke, *Abgaben*, 471–2.

[2] I.e. a tax assessed on amount of property, but really paid out of income.

considered, and it remains to state the general results which seem to be warranted. The attempt to measure taxation by service rendered has been recognised as hopeless and due to an erroneous theory of the State's nature, but it contains a small element of truth. Where specific and measurable advantages are rendered to individuals or groups direct payment for those services ought to be obtained, either in the course of exchange or by the payment of fees or, if either method cannot be employed, by a special tax. Cases of the latter are very rare in general, but they hold a more prominent place in local Finance. Indeed, as we shall see, the division between local and general taxation is itself a case of making those interested pay for special services, and in the detailed division of local charges the same principle can often be carried out.

The use of 'ability' or 'faculty' as a measure is encumbered by the necessity of defining its true meaning. We have seen reason, chiefly on practical grounds, for rejecting that interpretation which issues in the system of 'progressive' taxation. Its fiscal productiveness is slight while its economical effects are likely to be injurious. Between the system of payment as recompense for state services which would naturally lead to regressive taxation and the system of progression resting on the idea that sacrifice should be equalized, the intermediate method of taxation in proportion to income is on the whole the best standard for regulation. Its true foundation needs to be carefully appreciated. It cannot claim to be a realization of exact distributive justice; it is rather to be accepted as a convenient and fairly definite working rule of Finance, or at the utmost as supplying a measure of what may be called the objective side of ability. Income, when the lower grades are passed, is, we may hold, a fairly good mark of power to contribute, provided we make abstraction of individual circumstances.

In the same spirit we can solve the problem raised by the existence of incomes at the minimum. Financial convenience combines with economic conditions to make it desirable to exempt the smaller revenues from direct taxation where the duties on articles of common consumption are productive. Where it is possible to relieve necessaries from taxation the minimum of existence is in fact free; where the needs of the Exchequer prevent this being done the pressure placed on the lowest class is of a kind not much felt by them unless the rate of taxation is excessive. To tax the very poorest is a sad necessity, but where the want of revenue is urgent, not inconsistent with justice: there is a real advance when national wealth has reached so high a point that the lowest class are called on to contribute only through their luxuries, but the highest stage is that in which the improvement of society is such that all classes are in a position to pay their share as citizens for the common services of the State.

The distinction between temporary and permanent incomes, as also that between expenditure and savings, may, it appears, be disregarded as involving subtleties unsuitable for fruitful application and to a great extent cancelling each other. The result is therefore that on the whole, and speaking broadly, taxation should be proportioned to revenue, by which a fair approximation to justice and a convenient basis of working are supplied.

§ 13. One class of revenue is so peculiarly situated that its position deserves further notice, viz. that which arises from 'unearned increment' in the widest sense of the term, including the growth of rent from land, monopoly profits and the gains of speculation [1]. The characteristics of this class seem to have marked it out as specially suited for taxation. The physiocratic tax on land was not, indeed, due to this idea of it as yielding a monopoly gain, but the practical result was just what it would have been in that case. Adam Smith distinctly notes the fitness of unearned gains for special taxation. 'Ground rents and

[1] All included in the German '*Conjuncturgewinn*'; cp. Prof. Marshall's explanation of '*Conjunctur*,' *Principles of Economics*, i. 656.

the ordinary rent of land are,' he holds, 'perhaps the species of revenue which can best bear to have a peculiar tax imposed upon them. . . . . Nothing can be more reasonable than that a fund which owes its existence to the good government of the State should be taxed peculiarly[1],' while later on he widens his view by declaring that 'the gains of monopolists whenever they can be come at,' are 'certainly of all subjects the most proper' for taxation, a doctrine the truth of which as a general statement can hardly be denied. When regarded by itself unearned wealth seems, as it were, designated to supply the public wants of the community[2], and there is no reason for surprise at the popularity of any proposals in that direction. But the imposition of taxation must be studied not simply with regard to a single general fact, but to the whole economic and financial constitution of the society. The obstacles in the way of this form of special taxation are serious enough. To begin with, it is not always easy to say what gains are 'unearned.' The rent of land and the receipts from pure speculation are the first examples, but the line that separates pure rent from profit rent is not so readily determined. As Adam Smith remarks in this connexion, 'The ordinary rent of land is in many cases owing partly at least to the attention and good management of the landlord[3].' The gain from land is in a new country profit rather than rent[4], and as society advances the investment of capital in land improvements complicates the problem. In the case of commercial speculation it is not pure accident that determines gain. Speculation is rather, as Cohn well describes it, the struggle of intelligence against chance[5]. To tax the profits of specu-

[1] *Wealth of Nations*, 356, 378.

[2] For a forcible statement of this view see George, *Social Problems*, 205–208.

[3] *Wealth of Nations*, 356.

[4] Cp. Sumner, *Life of Jackson*, 184–5; Marshall, *Principles*, 494–5.

[5] '*Die Speculation ist nicht bloss, wie Lassalle behauptet, "ein Rathen auf die Wirkungen, welche die unwissbaren Umstände hervorbringen werden." Sie ist mehr als das. Sie ist der Kampf der mit Kenntniss der wissbaren Umstände ausgerüsteten Intelligenz gegen die rohe Uebermacht des Zufalls,*' Cohn, § 343.

lation would check the operation of the economizing force of competition. Monopoly gains are better fitted for extra burdens, and where excessive profit is obtained through natural or legal monopoly there is a fair case for obtaining at least some of the advantage for the public. But these cases are so few as to form but a trivial financial resource. Railways, banks, and some other companies are the principal examples of possible monopoly, and among them the amount of excessive profit is not considerable. Two further circumstances diminish still more the importance of this extra source of tax revenue, viz. (1) the existence of losses that counterbalance unearned gains. If individuals engage in a venture, be it cultivation of land or industrial enterprise, they can hardly be called on to give up their surplus gains unless they are guaranteed against possible loss. A landholder will not care to open up his property with the certainty before him that his accruing 'producer's surplus' will be appropriated by the State, while he has no security for ordinary interest on his outlay. The like sentiment will be even stronger in industry and commerce than in agriculture. Just as weighty is (2) the fact that with a system of private ownership and a developed economic organization the claims to these 'unearned gains' are in a constant process of transfer, and future values are estimated in the prices given. The anticipated future movement of rent is registered in the price of land. Premiums on shares measure the gain from speculation or monopoly. Justice could therefore be attained only by taxing each increase immediately on its existence being noticed, an evidently hopeless endeavour. For these reasons it is desirable to narrowly limit special taxation of monopoly values to the clearest and best established cases, and for the rest to rely on the increased productiveness that this unearned wealth will give to the ordinary taxes. This conclusion it may be added does not apply to any existing land taxes which may be plausibly regarded as reserved rents, nor does it cover the specially interesting case of ground rents in towns where the effect of public expenditure introduces a new and difficult element, and which strictly belongs to the domain of local Finance[1].

§ 14. So far we have dealt with taxation as if it were applied to a single country or district in complete isolation, and have sought to arrive at the rule of just distribution among its inhabitants. Modern societies and *a fortiori* limited districts are not so placed. Many of their inhabitants draw income from outside the particular area. Foreigners hold property within it, and there are sure to be complex legal relations between residents and non-residents. Hence it is necessary to examine the difficult class of problems usually described under the title of 'double taxation.' We have not to consider the case of different taxes imposed by a State on the same object in different ways. Taking the rule of taxation to be proportionality to income, any taxation that attains that end is right; what fails to reach it is so far imperfect. Nor need we trace the operation of the corporation tax. Juristic persons are, for Finance, but intermediaries by which the individual members can be reached. The taxation of corporations is the taxation of their members, and the pressure of the tax on them is to be taken into account along with the other taxes in estimating the total burden. This elimination of so many of the points usually treated[2] allows us to direct attention at once to the international relations. These cases are three in number and may be arranged as follows—(1) Where a citizen emigrates with all his property. Here it is plain that he is only amenable to the laws of his adopted country; there is no power on the part of his native land to levy taxes on him and no justice in doing so. (2) A citizen may reside abroad and derive

[1] For state ownership of land see Bk. ii. ch. 2. § 4. On the Land Tax see Bk. iv. ch. 1; and for taxation of ground rents ch. 6. § 5 of the present Book.

[2] For a full and able discussion of the questions referred to see E. R. A. Seligman, 'The Corporation Tax,' No. iii. *Political Science Quarterly*, v. 636-675.

his income from his original home. In this case double taxation may exist. The country of residence may tax all the income and the country of birth may tax all the property situated within it. (3) The remaining case is the converse of the preceding. A resident native may possess property abroad, and be taxed on it in both countries. This too would be plainly double taxation.

What principle of justice should be applied to Nos. 2 and 3? The old protection theory would say that the country of residence should be paid for guarding the person, and that where the property lies for watching over it. The more modern solution would be that where there was a judicious arrangement of taxes the income tax should be levied by the country of residence, the land or property taxes by that of situation. Local rates would clearly belong to the latter, while the former would have the benefit of the indirect taxes on the subject's consumption. Were the cases of conflict numerous the best solution would be found in international agreements on the basis just indicated, and where, as in the German States and Swiss cantons, there is a central power it would seem that the determination of the adjustment should be given to it. The solution for like cases in local taxation is to be differently reached[1].

§ 15. Our judgment as to the equity of any particular distribution of the pressure of taxation will depend on the view that we take of the objects to be attained. Even when taxation is limited to the supply of the public wants the proper division of its weight may vary according to the amount and character of the services supplied by its employment. Where state functions are confined to the narrowest possible field the poorer classes may claim to bear a smaller share than if—as in many modern societies—they were largely benefited by public expenditure. But from the difficulty of discrimination it seems better to adhere

[1] On this question cp. Cohn, §§ 223–228; Roscher, § 63; Wagner, ii. 406 sq.

to the general rule of distributing taxation without direct reference to the results of expenditure on the different classes. Injustice of this kind ought to be corrected not by redistribution of taxation but by alteration of outlay.

There is a tendency in recent years to take a wider view of the functions of taxation than the purely financial one. Its agency is regarded as valuable not solely for the resources that it brings into the State but for the effect that it produces on the distribution of wealth. By the use of a properly adjusted tax system the inequalities of wealth may, it is thought, be reduced if not entirely removed, and one of the aims of Socialism approached without revolution. Such is Wagner's position when he declares for the 'politico-social' conception of taxation in opposition to the 'pure financial' one. This change in standpoint must of necessity change the mode of estimating the justice of taxation. What is wise and prudent when we aim simply at supplying the requirements of the public powers in the fairest and cheapest way ceases to be such when it is sought to bring about a supposed better distribution of wealth. Proportional taxation, caution in taxing unearned wealth, and moderation in expenditure, may be admitted to be the logical results of the 'financial' conception: progressive taxation with a high rate of increase, rigorous fiscal supervision of all gains except those from labour, and bold attempts at improving the condition of the poorer classes by state outlay in various directions will be the natural outcome of the 'social' attitude[1]. There is a change of aim which necessitates a corresponding change in the appropriate methods.

The general arguments on the subject of socialistic interference do not concern us here, but the results of financial experience are of some value in respect to the use of taxation for other than fiscal purposes. The taxing power has

[1] See Wagner, i. 47, 500; ii. 381 sq., 455–459, for a statement of the 'social' view.

been often employed to encourage industry, to improve taste, to benefit health, or to elevate morals, but in none of these applications has the desired success been obtained. There is, therefore, a presumption against its use in remedying the inequalities of wealth. Its definite and universally recognised function is the supply of adequate funds for the public services. To mix up with one very important object another different and perhaps incompatible one is to run the risk of failing in both. It is within the power of financial skill to so select the forms and rates of taxation as to secure the requisite amount without unfair pressure on any class, but if the ulterior effects on the distribution of wealth have to be considered, and the adjustment made to attain particular ends in that respect, the difficulties of the task are enormously increased. If the socialistic *régime* is to be the goal aimed at, there are more direct and more effective modes open than the manipulation of taxation.

§ 16. At the opposite pole to the doctrine that Finance should aim not solely at preserving justice, but at remedying injustices already existing in the social system is that which refuses to see anything of justice in financial problems. For the upholders of this view the distribution of taxation is reduced to placing the burden where it will give the least trouble and friction in collection. McCulloch's often-quoted statement that 'the characteristic of the best tax is not that it is most nearly proportioned to the means of individuals, but that it is easily assessed and collected, and is at the same time most conducive to the public interests'[1] is a sufficiently clear expression of the view which is a very natural feeling among practical administrators. An escape from the difficult questions that the problem of justice must always present is a pleasing prospect, though unfortunately based on illusion, since injustice in distribution is certain sooner or later to show itself in the difficulties that the practical financier wishes to avoid. All the conditions of a good

[1] *Taxation and Funding*, 18.

system of taxation are interdependent, and the breach of one reacts on the other. The observance of the mere technical rules at the expense of justice will not be successful any more than the utmost straining after fairness without regard to the other conditions which we proceed to examine in the next chapter.

CHAPTER IV.

THE TAX SYSTEM: ITS FORMS.

§ 1. THE construction of a system of taxation, like all works of art, is the result of a combination of materials derived from different quarters. To attain success it is necessary to bear in mind certain general facts respecting the economic structure of society: the important aim of realizing substantial justice in the apportionment of burdens must never be lost sight of, and in addition the financial and constitutional conditions require to be duly considered. It is to this latter class of problems that the present chapter will be devoted, and we shall see what form the tax system ought to take in order to satisfy these various requirements and be at the same time effective for what is after all its primary function—the supply of adequate resources for the public service.

The facts of past and existing financial institutions, when compared with the general principles discussed in the preceding chapters, present at first sight a curious contradiction. Taxation we discovered was normally a deduction from the national income, and ought to be divided among the citizens in proportion to the share of that income possessed by each. Though some qualifications of this statement were made [1] such was the broad general result: from which it would seem to follow that the amount

[1] See Bk. iii. ch. 2. §§ 6–7; ch. 3. §§ 10–11.

needed should be levied from the tax-payer in a single payment in proportion to his ascertained income. In fact the single tax would, we might think, be the necessary deduction from established principles.

On turning to the facts of practical Finance the state of things is very different. No country possesses this simple and logical arrangement. Instead of a single tax there is a prodigious number of imposts varying according to place and time, and very hard to reduce to any reasonable classification. Taxes on every form of production, on nearly every commodity, and on most of the transactions of life, may be found in the history or statistics of Finance.

One partial explanation is that which regards the complexity of the public charges as due to ignorance or love of routine on the part of practical financiers. The beginning of the tax system, obscured as it was by the other forms of state receipts, was due to fiscal necessity. The extraordinary levies of the sovereign were made on the wealth most easily reached and owned by the feeblest members of the community. 'To raise the largest sum of money with the least trouble'[1] is an inadequate description of the functions of a modern finance minister, but it was the sole aim of his mediaeval predecessor. It may then be thought that the immediate pressure of the public wants has led to this undue complication in the collection of taxation.

Such, however, is not the case. There is no doubt an element of truth in the assertion that it was want of funds that led to the creation of so many different forms of taxation. A war period is usually a time of financial pressure, and most new taxes owe their introduction to occasions of this kind[2]. But when the pressure is removed and the work of financial reform made possible, though great consolidations of duties are effected, there is no example of recourse to that simple method that appears so natural and appropriate

[1] A dictum credited to Sir G. C. Lewis.

[2] The war period (1793–1815) affords a good illustration of the disposition to impose fresh taxes, Dowell, ii. 208–245.

in the light of some elementary principles. It is, therefore, necessary to examine the grounds on which a multiple system of taxation is retained notwithstanding the apparent advantages of the single tax system.

§ 2. In the face of the general, indeed universal, policy of employing diverse forms of taxation, there has been at times a strong disposition on the part of students of Finance to propose some particular kind that should tend to supersede all others and be the principal resource of the Exchequer. Prominent among these plans is that promulgated by the famous engineer Vauban in his *Dîme Royale.* He does not, as has been sometimes supposed, advocate the complete abolition of all other charges. Among the duties to be retained were a moderate salt duty, the customs, and some of the taxes on acts: but the *taille*, the capitation, the *aides* (internal duties chiefly on drinks), the provincial customs and the miscellaneous sources of revenue classed as 'extraordinary' were to give place to a single tax—the 'Royal tithe'—imposed on the product of land, industry and, in short, all revenue, its amount to be five per cent. or ten per cent. according to necessity[1]. His contemporary Boisguillebert, with whom he had so close an intellectual affinity, put forward the same idea of a single tax of one-tenth of the product of land and industry.

A similar tendency is shown in Sir M. Decker's plan (referred to and criticised by Adam Smith) of a license for the consumption of commodities as a substitute for the excise and customs, a scheme which, in spite of its obvious difficulties, has been reproduced in a modified form in later times[2]. The popularity of duties on consumption favoured

[1] Vauban, *Dîme Royale*, 50–98. A remarkable proposal was placed before the States-General of 1577 at Blois. Besides the duties whose repeal was advocated by Vauban, the salt tax and the customs on wine were to be removed, and a graduated duty on households, called *taille égalée* was to be employed, Clamageran, *Histoire*, ii. 217–219.

[2] For Adam Smith's criticism see *Wealth of Nations*, 371. The idea of a general consumption tax was defended in Revans, *A Percentage Tax on Domestic Expenditure*, and by Pfeiffer, *Staatseinnahmen*, ii. 538–554.

the growth of plans like this. Still more significant was Vanderlint's scheme for a single tax on land and its products, perhaps suggested by some remarks of Locke. The pamphlet, in which Vanderlint stated his plan, is a distinct anticipation of the physiocratic idea as to the true system of taxation [1].

§ 3. The proposals already described came from individual thinkers, and had little or no influence on competent opinion or on financial practice. But in the circle of economists, who regarded Quesnay as their master, the dogma of a single tax—the *Impôt unique*—became an accepted article of belief. This doctrine was the natural result of their theory as to the limits of net produce. The rent of land was, they thought, the only 'source' of taxation, and it was therefore convenient that it should be its only 'object.' Vauban's idea of a Royal tithe was good so far as simplicity went, but it was unequal [2], inasmuch as it fell on capital employed in cultivation which, in the physiocratic dialect, was not 'disposable.' In the application of their principles the Physiocrats were more inclined than is sometimes believed to admit modifications. The elder Mirabeau was prepared to raise two-thirds of the requisite revenue by an income tax, leaving only one-third for the land tax, and Turgot frankly concedes that the time had not come for an abolition of *octrois* [3].

Besides the plan of a single tax on land rent, which has recently received support on different ground from that of its originators, other forms of single taxation have been suggested in the present century. One is the general income tax, which would directly attack the normal source

[1] Vanderlint's *Money answers all Things* appeared in 1734. See Ricca-Salerno, *Dottrine Finanziarie in Inghilterra*, 23–26.

[2] See Turgot's advocacy of the single tax on land. He declares: 'Cette proposition est contraire à l'opinion de ceux qui avaient conçu le système de la dîme royale . . . Ce système peut effectivement éblouir par sa simplicité, par la facilité du recouvrement, par l'apparence de la justice distributive. . . . Il pêche cependant par différents inconvénients,' i. 404.

[3] Mirabeau, *Théorie de l'Impôt*, 316; Turgot, ii. 114.

of taxation, and secure whatever adjustment seemed desirable to the legislator. In the form suggested by some economists it would be proportional to receipts, and might be so framed as to cover acquisitions by gift or inheritance[1]. Radical democrats would prefer that the single tax on incomes should be more or less rapidly progressive.

The plan of a single tax on 'realized property' has also received much support. It would be confined to property not engaged in production 'as land, the public funds, money lent on mortgage, and shares, ... in joint-stock companies'[2], and was believed by its advocates to escape the inequalities of the income tax, and to present greater facilities for collection, since the objects of assessment would be definite and open to observation.

Of rather wider scope is the plan for a single tax on capital, put forward by De Girardin and Menier, and approved by M. Guyot. Under it taxation is to be imposed on 'fixed' capital, i. e. on 'all such utilities as yield their products without changing their nature,' to wit, 'land, mines, buildings, machinery, implements, ships, carriages, animals employed productively, furniture, and works of art[3].' Raw materials and goods for sale would be exempt from charge. The basis of assessment proposed is the selling value of the taxable capital, one per cent. of which was believed by Menier to be sufficient in the case of France to meet the public expenditure.

§ 4. These several plans have certain elements in common and appeal to the very natural desire to secure a simple and inexpensive form of taxation. Were there no obstacles in the way it is plain that direct imposition on the source of taxation would be preferable to the complicated methods actually employed. The cost of collection would be materially diminished, and the immediate incidence on the

[1] An ingenious plan of this kind was proposed by W. N. Hancock under the title of 'A perfect Income Tax.'

[2] Mill, *Principles*, Bk. v. ch. 2. § 3.

[3] Guyot, *L'Impôt sur le Revenu*, 222. See Menier's various works, especially his *L'Avenir Économique*.

several individuals and classes precisely determined. Moreover, the society, as distinct from the State, would gain by the removal of restraints on industry, and it could measure definitely the cost of the public services.

Against such plain and obvious advantages there are weighty considerations to be set, which militate against the adoption of the single tax in any form. (1) The danger of a single tax, no matter how skilfully estimated not being duly proportioned to revenue is a serious one to which any other proposed base, e. g. capital or expenditure, is equally open. With a combination of different taxes the errors in any one case will be small, and probably compensated by the operation of other taxes, but with a single tax there is no possible room for correction. Experience shows that what is in appearance a perfectly fair tax may be practically very unequal in its operation. Evasions and false returns destroy the proportionality of the best arranged income tax. (2) The pressure of taxation in most modern States is by no means a slight one. On the average it exceeds ten per cent. of the national revenue. Now it is evident that 'the ignorant impatience of taxation' would prevent this amount being raised without much irritation through any single tax. To disguise the burden is, so far as sacrifice is concerned, to reduce it, and the breaking up of the system into several distinct forms undoubtedly has this advantage. (3) The use of a single tax would remove the advantage that is obtained at present by reaching the different *forms* of taxable capacity. Consumption, income as stated, property inherited are all so many indications of the capacity arising from the possession of revenue, which, when duly considered enable a better proportional rate of taxation to be maintained. Besides, in certain cases it is, as we saw, necessary to separate the tax-payer's contributions and treat some as given for special service, or to assign the total amount between different countries and districts. A single tax would faii altogether in this respect. (4) It is, moreover, important to note that a so-called single tax is not so in reality.

Thus a general income tax is nothing but a combination of several special taxes, and may often prove just as troublesome and complex. A tax on fixed capital would be in fact a tax on land, mines, factories, furniture, works of art, &c., which would be so many separate categories for distinct assessment. A general tax on consumption or expenditure would be even more involved. The simplicity of such plans is therefore often only apparent, and covers a real complexity. (5) The results of the shifting of taxation increase the force of the preceding argument. A proportional tax in assessment may, in the ultimate incidence, be a very one-sided charge. Taxation in the simplest shape introduces a complicating element into the economic system the effects of which are hard to follow and often very far removed from what first appearances would suggest.

§ 5. The foregoing considerations and actual fiscal practice have given countenance to the directly opposite doctrine which has been perhaps most precisely enunciated by Arthur Young. 'The mere circumstance of taxes being very numerous, in order to raise a given sum, is a considerable step towards equality in the burden falling on the people; if I was to define a good system of taxation, it should be that of bearing lightly on an infinite number of points, heavily on none. In other words that simplicity in taxation is the greatest additional weight that can be given to taxes, and ought in every country to be most sedulously avoided [1].' This passage has at least the merit of placing the issue in a clear and definite form. To attain equality in distribution there ought on this theory to be an almost universal system of taxation touching the people at every point. Property, income, consumption, transactions, inheritance should all be moderately taxed to make the burden as even and as light as possible. Young's views were, beyond question, produced by repulsion from those of the Physiocrats, and went even farther in the opposite

[1] *Political Arithmetic.* A statement quoted with approval by Sir G. Lewis. Northcote, *Financial Policy*, 309.

extreme, but they do not inaccurately describe the characteristic feature of the Finance of the eighteenth century. As a standard for modern times they are evidently inapplicable and opposed to the most important and valuable reforms of the present century. To secure the placing of pressure 'on an infinite number of points' would require the interference of the revenue authorities in most of the industrial processes and the private life of the community. Taxes on all commodities, on transfers of goods, and on the different forms of production would be extremely prejudicial to the development of industry, irksome and inconvenient to the payers, and very costly in collection. Financial history affords abundant examples of these evils. The *Alcavala*, or duty on all sales, has been regarded by Adam Smith as the cause of the ruin of agriculture and manufactures in Spain [1]. The English customs before the first reforms of Huskisson exemplified the evils of undue multiplicity in one branch of taxation, and the United States revenue system during the Civil War was an even more striking instance of the same defect [2]. To properly arrange and combine a great number of duties is too difficult a task to impose on administrators, who are sure even with the utmost care to inflict much injustice and cause heavy losses.

§ 6. The defects of the opposed systems of single and of multiple taxation tend to countenance what has been called 'plural taxation,' in which the revenue is not on the one hand collected by a single form of duty, nor, on the other, divided into a great number of trifling charges. Under the existing conditions of society this is the course that has most in its favour as being at once the most productive, least inconvenient, and on the whole approaching nearest to justice. But it is necessary to remark that this conclusion is limited

[1] *Wealth of Nations*, 381.

[2] For the English tariff, Dowell, ii. 249–261; Buxton, *Finance and Politics*, i. 18, 19. For the United States, Wells in *Cobden Club Essays* (2nd series), 479.

to present circumstances. It does not follow that it may not be possible at some future time to adopt a single tax system, or at least a very close approach to it. Among the arguments urged against the single tax is the actual weight of taxation and the risk of exciting discontent by raising the required sum in a single payment. Suppose, however, that public expenditure were greatly reduced, so that instead of eight, ten, or fifteen per cent. of national revenue, only three or four per cent. were required ; it might well be that the relief to industry and the facility of collection would make an income tax advisable as the sole agent for raising revenue. So large a reduction of expenditure is not to be expected. When dealing with that part of our subject we saw that the tendency was towards increase, but it is not difficult to conceive how a very different state of things might have come into being. Let us suppose that England had never engaged in the Revolutionary and Napoleonic wars, and that her foreign policy had been for the past century that of rigid 'non-intervention,' the financial results would certainly be (1) the entire removal of the national debt with its charge of £25,000,000 and whatever surplus may actually exist; and (2) the reduction of the army and navy estimates to less than one half of their present figure. Moderate reductions in the Civil Service would allow of a curtailment of expenditure to the amount of at least £50,000,000, leaving in round numbers £25,000,000 to be provided by taxation. An income tax of 9*d.* in the pound (including as it should the smaller incomes now exempt) would be the most direct mode of procuring that sum. The position of the United States, if the Civil War had been obviated by prudent statesmanship, would be even more favourable. A very moderate income tax would have met all the expenditure of the years 1850–1860, as the low customs duties actually did[1].

It thus appears that the form of taxation depends in a great degree on the amount of expenditure. With modera-

[1] Cp. Leroy Beaulieu, i. 179–185.

tion in outlay it is possible to have simplicity in taxation, and the difficulties of the problem of expenditure, already hard enough, are increased by the need of weighing the greater difficulties of heavy taxation. It is eminently true that wise policy is essential for sound Finance[1].

§ 7. Financial necessity makes the retention of different forms of taxation, if not an absolute necessity, at all events advisable both in the interests of the State and of the payers. And this being so we have next to examine the comparative merits of the different forms in use. The first broad distinction—that between direct and indirect taxes—has some connexion with the controversy as to single against multiple taxation. The most popular forms of the single tax are direct, while most of the charges in a multiple system are indirect. There has been accordingly a not unnatural tendency to confuse the two separate issues by identifying single with direct and multiple with indirect taxation. The confusion is helped by the fact that the great advocates of the single land tax laid particular stress on its being direct. 'The essential form of taxation,' says De La Rivière, 'consists in taking taxation *directly* where it is, and not wishing to take it where it is not. . . . To change that *direct* form of taxation in order to give it an *indirect* one is to reverse a natural order from which we cannot depart without the greatest inconvenience'[2]. The idea that taxation should not lead to shifting and repercussion was one of the strong points of his school. The original conception of direct taxation as being that which is imposed immediately on the ultimate source from which it comes was, as we saw, altered for administrative convenience, and applied to cases where recurring payments were made and lists of tax-payers kept[3]. But this use of the term, whatever its technical advantages, obscures the broad line of division that the

[1] Cp. the well-known saying of Baron Louis, '*Faites-moi de bonne politique et je vous ferai de bonnes finances.*'

[2] *Physiocrates*, 474. The italics are in the original.

[3] See Bk. iii. ch. I. § 8.

older meaning gave, and which really possesses so much scientific importance. Whether a duty is assessed directly on the ultimate bearer or is passed through various intermediaries before reaching him, may not be capable of being precisely known in all cases. There are no hard and fast lines in fact, and the instances on the margin may be numerous, but if we take the terms, not as giving a complete classification of taxes, but as marking the presence or absence of a certain characteristic, they may be employed with advantage, but rather to suggest reasons for discrimination than to definitely settle results [1].

The expressions 'direct' and 'indirect' have received a further alteration which makes it more difficult to employ them without careful explanation. Taxes on property and income form a very large part of the direct taxes; those on commodities collected from the producer or dealer an equally large part of the indirect ones. These are, besides, the special forms of the two kinds of taxation that are usually selected as types in discussions about them, so that it is not difficult to understand how the comparisons between direct and indirect taxation have become for the most part an inquiry into the relative merits of taxes on income and property as against taxes on commodities.

This employment of the terms is supported by the distinct origin of the two forms. 'Taxes' on property and persons (*Steuern*) present a marked contrast to the 'duties' on goods and commerce (*Abgaben und Auflagen*), and especially in the fact that the former were direct, the latter indirect. A feeling of this original separation is at the

[1] 'The classification of taxes as direct and indirect it may be as well to premise has been objected to on the ground that it cannot be consistently applied. . . . But this objection applies only to the wording of the ordinary definition of direct and indirect taxes, and we may safely continue to employ the terms to denote the radical distinction intended; namely between taxes on the one hand levied either directly from the contributors themselves or from funds on the way to them; and taxes on the other hand on producers or dealers in the intention that they shall recover them in the prices finally paid by consumers,' Cliffe Leslie, in *Cobden Club Essays* (2nd series), 192.

root of much of the discussions on the merits of the two classes and helps to make the issue more obscure[1].

Still the contrast between the two groups of taxes that are usually regarded as being direct and indirect, quite apart from the question of incidence, has a sufficient value to make it convenient in estimating the merits of a given system. The peculiarities of the separate taxes that a more scientific arrangement exhibits may fitly be treated in dealing with particular taxation, but the broad general separation that is so familiar in financial discussion serves better for the purpose of showing the requisite conditions of taxation as a whole.

§ 8. Starting, then, with the conception of direct taxes as those levied immediately on the 'subjects,' and therefore embracing taxes on income and property, or on their component parts, in opposition to duties on commodities and on exchange, where there is a shifting of the burden from the immediate payer to the subject which justifies the name of 'indirect,' we have to consider the merits and defects of each class, and the most desirable mode of combining them.

At the outset the advantages of direct taxation seem to predominate. As income is the ultimate source of taxation its immediate imposition is the most obvious and rational way of claiming a share in the produce for the State. The taxes on the different components of income have the same merit. Rent, interest, and earnings, are the natural objects on which to place the charges of the State. Where it is thought desirable on grounds of justice to tax property, the direct mode of doing so seems the simplest and least involved. As a single tax appears better than a multiple system so does direct taxation seem superior to indirect, and for much the same reasons. There is the greater facility and lower cost of collection, and the power of knowing the exact amount paid by each person liable. The drawbacks are also of the same kind. The greater

[1] See Dowell, *Hist. of Taxation*, *Pref.* xii.; Vocke, *Abgaben*, 1-6.

dislike to direct levies of taxation is notorious; the demand for payment is more disagreeable than the fact of paying, as it brings home the existence of the charge without any possibility of escaping notice. Formerly financiers were too anxious to escape popular resentment to have recourse to this form unless in extremities, and in modern days taxation must be suited to the taste of the voters. Another difficulty is the necessity of assessment in all direct taxes. If imposed on income, on property, or on any separate part of produce, there must be a valuation of the object which is charged, affording opportunities for evasion and for arbitrary official action. It is true that the progress of society may be expected to reduce these objections. As acquaintance with the operation of taxation becomes greater the payers form a juster estimate of the amount that they pay, and will feel that direct levy is really no worse than taxation through the enhanced price of commodities.

Moral progress may also diminish the disposition to evade payment by creating a higher standard of social duty, and the better organization of the financial service will limit the risk of undue official pressure. Still these evils actually exist, and the extent to which they are likely to occur must limit the employment of direct taxation [1]. Again, under a system of pure direct taxation it is very difficult to obtain their due proportion from the poorer members of society. The attempt to carry the income tax at a high rate down to the lower incomes now exempt would be both costly and irritating, and the only produce tax that would much affect them—that on wages—would be still more obnoxious. No doubt with moderate expenditure and an improved standard of social morals the difficulty would become manageable, but we cannot assume the existence of these favouring conditions without adequate proof [2].

[1] Cp. Vocke's remarks, *Abgaben*, 624–5.

[2] See Cliffe Leslie's forcible argument in *Cobden Club Essays* (2nd series), 252 sq.

It is moreover alleged that direct taxation is inexpansive, in that it does not grow in proportion to the increase of national wealth. This, however, is not altogether correct, and so far as it is true can be accounted for without difficulty. The growth of so important a direct tax as the English income tax since its re-establishment in 1842 has been very remarkable. The yield per penny for the first year was only £730,000; in 1890–91 it reached £2,200,000, or a three-fold increase[1] in less than fifty years. Indeed the only explanation that can be given of a lower increase in an income tax than in income is that of evasion by the payers, an objection already considered. But in fact there are special reasons for the slow growth of certain direct taxes. A tax on rent will not increase in proportion to the growth of income, as it is generally fixed for a period of some length. The French land tax cannot increase since it is apportioned and therefore fixed in amount, and in all cases of valuation it is not easy to keep the assessments up to the actual gains[2]. The counter-advantage that, in a progressive society, these taxes tend to become lighter while yielding a definite amount ought not to be overlooked. It is a benefit to have one part of the revenue that can be depended on, even in times of crisis. Taking the defects and merits together we may believe that direct taxation ought to be a part of every modern financial system, and that the extent to which it can be carried will depend on the particular conditions.

§ 9. The weak points of direct taxation are the strength of the opposed form. Indirect taxes are not felt by the payer in the same degree, and therefore cause him less annoyance. A tax mixed up in the price of wine, tea or tobacco, is not brought so clearly to his mind: it seems to be a part of the expenses of production and to be due to

[1] Ireland was not included till 1853, but the abatement limit was raised, which probably compensated for this addition.

[2] E.g. in Ireland Schedules A and B of the income tax so far as land is concerned are taken on a fixed valuation, and therefore cannot expand.

purely economic causes. If 'the best tax is that whose forms most effectually disguise its nature'[1] there can be no doubt of the superior merit of indirect ones. A second advantage is the facility that they supply for taxing the smaller contributors. Duties on articles of general consumption touch all classes, though if necessaries are exempt they leave the minimum of subsistence unaffected, but only on the condition that the minimum revenue is confined to that object. Thirdly, they are both productive, and in times of prosperity elastic without undue pressure. The growth of the English excise and customs, in spite of great reductions, has been remarkable. Again it has been often pointed out, that taxes on commodities are collected at a convenient time, since the contributor 'pays them by little and little as he has occasion to buy the goods . . . he is at liberty too to buy or not to buy, as he pleases[2].' This remark of Adam Smith's has been extended to the assertion that indirect taxation is preferable as being 'voluntary.' There is no necessity to pay unless the tax-payer is willing. This, if true, would be a disadvantage, but, as Mill has shown[3], it is an obvious fallacy. A citizen can escape a wine duty by not consuming wine. That course, however, has the double disadvantage of depriving the State of revenue and of diminishing his own enjoyment. In the case of a direct tax of equal amount the same saving would be made by giving up the use of wine, by which the revenue would not suffer. This possibility of checking consumption is a bad, instead of a good, feature in taxes on commodities. Other defects are easily discoverable. The rule of equality appears to be frequently violated. Articles of general consumption are used in much larger proportion by the poor than by the rich, so that in any modern fiscal system the pressure of direct taxation comes chiefly on the working classes. Expedients may be suggested to diminish this evil. Articles of luxury may be subjected to

[1] Gaudin; cp. De Parieu, i. 121.
[2] *Wealth of Nations*, 348.
[3] *Principles*, Bk. v. ch. 6. § 1.

heavy taxation, and the rates of duty may be fixed according to the quality of the articles taxed. Such measures, however, give rise to further difficulties. Duties *ad valorem* lead to evasion, and articles of luxury are easily smuggled. In spite of any possible alleviations the remaining inequality must be considerable. The elasticity of indirect taxes has its unfavourable side. At times of depression their yield cannot be relied on; as they grow in prosperous years so do they shrink in bad ones. Nor are they easily extended. Increased duties may possibly give stationary or even diminished receipts[1]. Reliance on indirect taxation alone will therefore sooner or later cause financial embarrassment.

Expenses of collection are probably somewhat larger in the case of indirect taxes, though the difference is not so great as is often asserted. The cost of collection of the English Inland Revenue (about one-half of which is direct) is less than that of the customs, but so much depends on special conditions and the amount of revenue to be raised, that a general conclusion on the subject would be misleading.

By far the most formidable objection to the indirect taxation of commodities is the loss to the society through disturbance of industry. The evils of both customs and excises in this respect have been forcibly shown by Cliffe Leslie[2]. The former close some ports altogether on the ground that there is not trade sufficient to justify the expense of maintaining custom houses at them, and limit the imports of taxed articles at others. Towns without bonded warehouses are at a disadvantage in competing with those who possess them. Industries are either prevented from coming into being, or have their development retarded by such regulations and restrictions. The excise system is injurious to the industries under its supervision, as it

[1] The increase of duties in 1840 by Baring is an instance; 5 per cent. extra all round did not give increased receipts, Dowell, ii. 313.

[2] 'Financial Reform,' in *Cobden Club Essays* (2nd series), 189–263; also reprinted separately.

controls the processes to be employed, and hinders the introduction of improvements. Routine is necessary for effectual regulation, but it is fatal to the spirit of enterprise that is the cause of industrial advance. The various items of this indictment are supported by specific allegations[1], and there can be no dispute as to the gravity of the issue raised, and as to the existence of the grievances stated. None the less are we compelled to hold that the retention of taxation on commodities is at present a necessity in most societies, and that by judicious measures it is possible, not indeed to remove, but to reduce the evils complained of. There are considerations other than those noticed by the assailants of these duties. All taxation is, it must be remembered, evil in its deduction of wealth and in the restrictive measures that must be used to make it effective. Direct taxation has its own inequalities and injustices, and is, besides, often vexatious and inquisitorial. A presentation of the faults of one particular form of tax-revenue is impressive, but should be qualified by considering the difficulties of any alternative method. In Economics and Finance we must be on our guard against the 'fallacy of objections.' Again, it is not clear that the taxation of a small number of articles has the very serious influence ascribed to it. Most of the instances of interference with processes are taken from cases that no longer exist. The duties on salt, glass, and sugar, may have hampered invention, but they are things of the past. Apart from intoxicating drinks and tobacco the industry of the United Kingdom may be said to be free from control for fiscal purposes. A further point may be noticed. The customs staff is not purely a revenue agency; inspection and supervision of the shipping industry is, or is generally assumed to be, needed for sanitary and police reasons. It is but one part of the system described in an earlier chapter[2], and its whole cost should not be ascribed to the need of revenue.

[1] Leslie, *ut supra*, 204, 205, 207–8, 219, 225–231.

[2] Bk. i. ch. 4, 'Administrative Supervision.'

So far as the duties on stimulants seek to repress consumption, whatever hindrances they cause to the industry cannot be looked on as evil, since they conduce towards the object aimed at. The value of industrial liberty is doubtless great. What represses or diverts the economic forces that tend to increased production of wealth should not be allowed without adequate reason, and should be carefully watched; but on striking a balance it seems that the advantages outweigh the evils wherever a large revenue has to be obtained, and where the system of indirect taxation is kept within narrow limits.

§ 10. On the borderland between direct and indirect taxation lies a large class, or rather several classes, of taxes such as those on transfers of property, on ordinary contracts, on communication and transport, and in short the numerous charges on acts. All of them belong to the category of indirect taxes in the administrative sense as do most of them in any sense of the term. They stand on somewhat different ground from duties on commodities, inasmuch as they sometimes approximate to fees for special services rendered, and in others are directly levied from the ultimate payers. They do not so much interfere with industry as with commerce in the strict sense, but they are open to the same kind of objections as those urged against the taxation of commodities. To hamper exchange is to prevent the passage of productive agents into suitable hands: a tax on communications is a check on commercial intercourse, and duties on legal transactions, if widely extended, prove very troublesome and annoying to the most active and intelligent members of a community. For these reasons it is desirable to keep taxation of this kind as a subordinate resource applied only to a moderate amount, and chiefly with the aim of completing gaps in the financial system. The difficulty of making the pressure of these taxes at all proportional or even of analyzing, their incidence ought of itself to prevent their being made a principal source of revenue. But when used partly as fees for special services, partly as affecting forms of wealth that are very likely to escape their due share of taxation in other ways, and finally as affording valuable tests of the correctness of the returns to direct taxation, they have a good claim to continue as a subsidiary means of revenue, and as a relief to the pressure on visible income of the purely direct taxes, and on the general consumption of the community from taxation of commodities. The extent of their application must be decided with reference to the particular circumstances of the country, and the opportunity for employing direct taxation.

§ 11. The system of Finance best adapted for a modern society is accordingly one in which the objects of taxation are judiciously diversified in such a manner as to realize the ends desired. The usual source of taxation is national income, the mass of fresh production during the period under notice, and one most desirable part of the revenue system is that which directly receives from the shares of this fund a contribution towards the maintenance of the State. The rent of land, the interest on capital, the earnings of management, and the wages of labour, may all as the component parts of income, be rightly made contributory. Whether they should be imposable in their separate forms, or simply as income, is in principle immaterial, but the method of distinct taxes on each share seems to belong to a lower stage of development than the general income tax. To escape the difficulties, partly technical partly political, that direct taxation by itself creates, the taxation of various 'objects' on which income is expended, must generally be adopted. Instead of attacking wealth as it is acquired, its use is made the object of charge. The method of taxing producers and dealers, in order that they may pass on the charge to consumers, is a recognition of the tendency of certain taxes to shift their weight, and an effort to utilize that tendency in facilitating the collection of revenue.

Taxation of income and of commodities are the two great forms of revenue receipts, whose importance overshadows all others; but while this is apparent in every budget, it is equally true that a certain proportion of revenue can be obtained by the operation of other charges, that cannot easily be brought under either of the leading categories. Some transactions are well suited for the imposition of moderate duties. Communications may be made to yield no inconsiderable resource to the State, and above all the inheritance of property is at once a means of testing the accuracy of returns as to income, and an opportunity for taxing masses of accumulated wealth.

These ingredients of a well ordered system require to be combined in very different proportions at the several stages of development. In a new country, with sparse population and little capital, a direct income tax would be a very defective instrument. Where there is little foreign trade, and most commodities are produced and consumed at home, taxation of commodities is not, and cannot be, productive. Peculiarities of social organization have, too, considerable influence. Taxation of inheritances is unsuited for a community where the family is the unit of society, and property is really held by corporations, not by individuals.

How important the special circumstances of social life may be in this respect can be better realized if we reflect how much of existing English taxation rests on the circumstance that wine, tea, and tobacco, are not native products[1].

§ 12. We thus get a well-defined system of taxation comprising the three departments specified in the preceding section, and it seems beyond question that this will for a long period be the prevailing type. So far as any general course of development can be traced, the movement is towards a greater use of direct taxation. The income tax —a product of the present century—is on the whole increasing in favour, and the imposition of higher duties on inheritances is also probable. The great importance of

[1] The last-named only through the legislative prohibition, slightly relaxed in the past few years.

both excises and customs is nevertheless a prominent feature. We cannot see how the existing outlay of any modern State could be maintained without their aid. We shall indeed discover that they are confined to one branch of Finance, and are unfitted to be local resources[1]. Still the general conclusion is clear, that the great divisions of the tax system are likely to remain in active use, partly no doubt in consequence of their suitability to the existing financial organizations, but far more on account of their serviceable qualities.

A further advantage of this combination should be noticed—its elasticity. In modern Finance it is desirable that the receipts shall be capable of easy adjustment to the expenditure without undue inconvenience to the contributors. The employment of the different forms of taxation tends to realize this object. The steady growth of the receipts from commodities in times of prosperity, the definite yield of direct taxes, and the power of altering the rate of the income tax, taken together, provide the conditions for securing a growth or contraction of receipts as may be thought best.

[1] See ch. 6. § 3.

CHAPTER V.

THE INCIDENCE OF TAXATION.

§ 1. UP to the present we have avoided all but the most incidental mention of the difficult problems connected with the real as opposed to the apparent pressure of taxation. This course has the great convenience of allowing an acquaintance to be made with the leading features and general guiding rules of the system free from the complications that are inherent in any discussion of the question of incidence. The omission must now be remedied; we have to consider the nature and consequences of the series of processes usually known as shifting or repercussion of taxation, and to study the effects produced by them on the financial organization. A correct solution of the problem is indispensable for full knowledge of the subject. Our judgments on every part of the tax system will be affected by our theory of incidence. Take, e.g. the question of justice. How can we say that any given arrangement of taxation is fair unless we know its real, not merely its apparent incidence? The extent and limits of the shifting of taxation are elements in estimating the expediency of exempting the minimum of subsistence, of imposing a progressive income-tax, or of taxing articles of consumption. Instead of confining our attention to surface appearances, we must examine the underlying conditions, and estimate in their entirety the effects of fiscal regulations.

This complicated investigation will occupy the present chapter. We shall seek to establish the general laws of repercussion and their most important results, reserving the treatment of the several taxes for the appropriate place[1].

§ 2. Popular discussion of financial matters has always given a large place to this special topic. The real incidence of tithes, of import duties, or of local rates has been hotly debated at many a dinner-table and in many a tavern, and very positive conclusions have been reached in entire ignorance of the grave difficulties that surround any attempt to determine accurately these and similar points. It takes some training to see that confident decisions as to the division of rates between landlord and tenant, or of duties between producer and consumer, cannot be made in a ready and off-hand way. Such is however the case. The complications are too great; the subtle modes in which pressure applied at one point is diffused over a wider area are too hard to be followed without a clear appreciation of the general conditions and a careful use of the slippery instrument of abstract deduction. In dealing with the problems of incidence we are at that part of Finance that touches most closely on economic theory in its hardest form.

Scientific students have long recognised the fact, and the earliest efforts of financial inquiry have been directed to the question of the incidence of taxation. In some instances it was apparent that duties temporarily paid by the seller of a commodity were only advanced by him, to be obtained later on from the buyer in the form of increased price[2]. The extension of this result to all cases of taxation on producers or dealers was so plausible that it became an accepted doctrine of practical Finance before passing into a theoreti-

[1] See the sections on incidence in the several chapters of Bk. iv.

[2] Tacitus notes the fact in the case of slaves: 'Vectigal . . . venalium mancipiorum remissum, *specie magis quam vi,* quia cum venditor pendere juberetur in partem pretii emptoribus accrescebat,' *Ann.* xiii. 31.

cal form. This particular position dealt only with readily observed facts, and was confined to outward and apparent effects of taxation. A far more important step was made when the fruitful idea of a single source from which all taxes must, in the last resort, come suggested itself. The doctrine found a definite expression in Locke's statement, 'that taxes however contrived, and out of whose hands soever immediately taken, do in a country where their great fund is in land for the most part terminate upon land [1]. Put forward tentatively by Locke in connexion with his controversy as to interest the conception of land as the true source of taxation was made the basis of a practical plan by Vanderlint, and more fully developed by the Physiocrats as a part of their view of the 'net product.'

This earliest scientific theory of shifting rested on certain general assumptions, some of which we have already noticed [2]. They are (1) that wages are at the minimum point of subsistence; (2) that taxation of profits will drive capital out of industry, and by thus reducing the supply raise the rate to its former point, the tax excluded; (3) that expenditure for consumption is simply the employment of income, and that increased prices through taxation will compel a compensatory increase of money wages and profits. By aid of these propositions it was easy to establish that taxation of wages or profits or their outlay must be passed on to some other class in society. The gains from commerce and professional avocations were brought under the same principle by the ingenious argument that they also were necessary to secure the continuance of the trade or profession [3].

We thus obtain a rigorously complete theory of incidence accompanied by a description of the mode in which the shifting is carried out from the points of initial pressure to

[1] 'Considerations on the Lowering of Interest,' *Misc. Works*, 595.

[2] Bk. iii. ch. 4. § 2.

[3] See Turgot, i. 442–4, for an application of this argument to the case of Holland, which had been brought forward to refute the doctrine of Quesnay.

the ultimate resting-place. The equalizing agency of competition and the necessity for normal wages and profits are the forces that push the burden of taxation on to the landowners' revenue. The conception of society as a mechanism in which strains were distributed in obedience to general laws, quite independent of legislation or intention, was thoroughly grasped by the physiocratic school and was applied by them to this as to other questions [1].

The contrast between Adam Smith and his French contemporaries, so often noticed, appears clearly in his treatment of the question of incidence. The sharp and definite theory that regards all taxation except that on rent as necessarily shifted is changed into the broader doctrine that transference may or may not take place according to circumstances, and may fall on any one of the three constituents of income. In the application of these general positions several qualifications are introduced. Taxes on wages are always, Adam Smith holds, transferred partly to the consumer in higher price, partly to the landlord in lower rent. The employer must have his ordinary profit, and he recoups himself for his larger wages' bill by increasing his sale price, or if a farmer, by giving his landlord a smaller amount of produce. The share of profit known as employers' gain is also unamenable to taxation, as being merely the necessary reward of the entrepreneur. Interest, though capable of bearing some of the public charges, is difficult to estimate, and its root, capital, is apt to emigrate under exceptional charges. Taxes on necessary articles of consumption tend to raise the wages of labour, and therefore are, like direct wages taxes, passed on to the consumer or the landlord. A house-tax tends to fall partly on the occupier, partly on the ground-landlord, the builder always in the long run receiving his normal profits.

The result of the inquiries on incidence in the *Wealth of Nations* is a modification of the *Économistes*' view. The

[1] For the physiocratic doctrine of incidence see Quesnay, *Second Problème* (ed. Daire), 127 sq.; Turgot, i. 392–444.

landlord is still the chief bearer of public charges which are shifted on to him from various points, while his special burdens are not transferable ; but he is not the sole bearer : the capitalist has to contribute a share, and the vague class of consumers has to pay on the taxed forms of expenditure, and that expenditure may come from rent, profit, or even (in the case of taxes on luxuries) wages. The landlord has nevertheless, as Falck remarks, the 'lion's share of the payment of taxes,' and therefore in part Adam Smith occupies the physiocratic position [1].

The title of Ricardo's treatise marks taxation as one of its subjects, and it may be said that the space devoted to that topic is altogether occupied with the question of incidence. Adam Smith's positions are corrected in the light of the newer theories of population and rent. In fact Ricardo's doctrine of taxation is a development of his theory of distribution. Notwithstanding the generally loose form of his writings, there is an amount of precision about his statements as to the movement of taxes that has made him the leading representative of economic orthodoxy on these points. Reduced to a definite form his views are represented in the following propositions, resting, it must be noted, on the assumptions of (1) self-interest as the motive-power of action, and (2) the universal mobility of labour and capital.

(1) A tax on economic rent is not transferable; it remains on the landlord. (2) A tax on ordinary labour is transferred to the employer, and is in reality a tax on profits. (3) A tax on profits in general is not transferable, and must remain on the capitalist; but (4) a tax on the profits of a particular employment will be transferred to the consumers of its product. (5) Taxes on commodities paid by the producer are passed on to the consumer, as in the case of taxes on particular profits. (6) In the case of commodities

[1] See *Wealth of Nations*, Bk. v. ch. 2. pt. 2. For exposition and criticism of his views see Kaizl, *Überwälzung*, 3–8, and Falck, *Steuerüberwälzung*, 30–48.

consumed by the labourers there is a further shifting from the consuming labourers to the capitalists who employ them [1].

The main outlines of this theory of incidence reappear in J. S. Mill's *Principles*, with some not unimportant amendments. For example, the higher classes of wage-earners are admitted as possible bearers of taxation. In their case a tax on wages may or may not be shifted. The results as to tithes and profits are somewhat altered, and greater emphasis is laid on the tendency of profits to a minimum. But these are special points: speaking broadly, there is no part of Mill's work which so fully deserves the description 'a readable Ricardo' as that which deals with taxation [2].

§ 3. The very general adoption of the Ricardian theory in its developed form as the sole and exclusive scientific doctrine makes it advisable to note some of the objections that prevent us from accepting it as a complete interpretation of the phenomena of incidence. Some of these criticisms have been forcibly urged by Cliffe Leslie and Held, but they may be put in a more general form. The first weak point in Ricardo's position is his ambiguous treatment of consumption and consumers. In his general scheme of distribution there is no place for the consumers as a class, but we often find him asserting that a given tax does fall on 'the consumer.' How are we to explain this apparent discrepancy? The most natural answer is that landlords and capitalists make up this class, the labourers being normally outside it, as their consumption is a part of the expenses of production. This explanation is not completely satisfactory, for it is plain that *all* landlords and capitalists are not affected by particular taxes falling on consumers, and yet no criterion of separation is available. The necessity for studying the forms of expenditure as a

[1] On Ricardo's doctrine of incidence see Falck, 48–70; Kaizl, 8–11.

[2] On J. S. Mill's differences from Ricardo see Falck, 71–90. He points out that 'Mill's doctrine of the operation of taxes differs but slightly and only on special points from that of Ricardo,' 71.

department of Economics seems clear from this consideration. Besides the pressure that falls on the primary divisions of income there is the additional one on the employment of that income, and differences in employment produce differences in pressure. A doctrine of incidence that is confined to the receipt of income without regard to its expenditure is so far defective. A second objection to the theory is its dependence on a few unduly simplified conditions. Social forces are regarded as definite and precise in their action, and very positive statements are made on the strength of this insecure foundation. Thus taxes on wages and on labourers' necessaries are regarded as being always transferred to the capitalist, a proposition true only on the assumption that wages are at the minimum, and that any change in them will at once act and act proportionately on population. In the same way the equality of profits and the complete dependence of rent on the margin of cultivation are made to support very sweeping propositions as to the incidence of taxation. If we allow that the economic forces of population and competition in regard to the employment of capital and the movement of cultivation are not quite so regular in their action the deductions made from them must be qualified.

Thirdly, the theory exaggerates the simplicity not merely of economic forces but also of the forms of taxation. Taxes on rent, on profits or on wages are not all the same, and the particular modes of imposition often affect the incidence. There is need for much care and discrimination in using those results of deduction that depend on the identification of so many different taxes.

Finally, there is far too little notice taken of the actual facts and of the unavoidable limitations in the application of theoretical principles. The orthodox theory of incidence professes to explain what will happen in the long run, 'but taxes,' as Leslie remarked, 'are paid immediately under the real conditions of life and out of the actual wages and profits or other funds of individuals, not out of hypotheses or abstractions in the minds of economists[1].' Knowledge of what will happen when the limit is reached is desirable, but what takes place during the process of adjustment is also important.

The existence of these imperfections does not destroy the great service of the doctrine as a preliminary or introductory inquiry (*Vorstudium*). Without some such attempt the intricacies of incidence could never be explained, and it is by expansion and correction of the Ricardian procedure that advance can best be made in the explanation of these problems. As an intellectual exercise the abstract theory of the shifting of taxation has a high disciplinary value. The root-error of its followers lay in taking a part for the whole.

§ 4. The course of development in the preceding theories is clear enough. From the first suggestion of Locke to the compact exposition of J. S. Mill there can be traced a series of connecting links and alterations in consequence of wider knowledge. Adam Smith has the French theory constantly in mind, as Ricardo in turn has the ideas of the *Wealth of Nations*. All have in common the recognition of certain points on which the pressure of taxation ultimately rests, and all, it may be added, suggest the wisdom of adapting legislation to the conditions of incidence in order to secure a fair distribution, or at least to prevent unnecessary waste through friction.

Another group of doctrines has a quite different tendency. In place of investigating the complicated shiftings that settle the ultimate incidence, it either denies the possibility of ascertaining them or assumes that they bring about a general diffusion of the burden over the whole society. The natural conclusion is that the particular forms of taxation are altogether immaterial, as, whatever be the immediate charges, the burden is finally distributed in an equitable manner.

The first scientific statement of this view is ascribed to

[1] *Essays* (2nd edition), 384.

N. F. Canard, whose essay, attacking the theory that all taxation must fall on the owners of land, obtained a prize from the French Academy. The gist of his argument is that there is surplus product in labour and commerce as well as land, and that taxation falls on all of these 'net products.' The process of diffusion is carried out by exchange, buyer and seller in each transaction dividing the amount of tax imposed, and at every fresh exchange a division of the part of taxation transferred takes place until ultimately the charge is spread over all the parties concerned. Extending this conception to the whole society, taxation comes to be regarded as *after a time* diffused equably among all its members. The qualification of time is important, as the process of diffusion is not complete at first, consequently old taxes are the best, and all new taxes, or even changes in existing ones, are to be deprecated as disturbing this beautiful and harmonious distribution, which relieves the legislator of any trouble respecting the apparent merits or demerits of existing taxes[1].

The comfortable nature of this theory makes it a popular one with statesmen. Without adopting Canard's peculiar explanation of the mode of diffusion, Thiers asserts the general diffusion of the public charges; Stein, from a still different point of view, reaches what is practically the same result. In his opinion the whole theory of shifting is an error arising from imperfect comprehension of the real nature of the process, which in reality contains two different parts. For, first, a tax is a part of the cost of production similar to the expense of raw materials or labour, and like other expenses must enter into price, and taxation is through this medium diffused 'from one to another' until it extends to all. Again, from a higher point of view, the portion of product paid in taxes is a surplus product, the result of the services of the state administration, which pays back at least what it receives. The conception of incidence of

[1] Canard's *Principes d'Économie politique* appeared in 1802. See Kaizl, 11-15, for a clear summary.

taxation has to be replaced by that of the 'production of taxes[1].'

Closely allied to the negative doctrine of incidence is the disposition on the part of some writers to regard the problem as insoluble, and at the same time to treat all questions of taxation as if it were non-existent. To deny that the incidence of taxation is discoverable seems to be the first step towards believing that it is unimportant[2].

No lengthy criticism of the negative theory of incidence is needed. Facts speak for themselves: if the incidence of the public burdens be really so settled that legislative action has no effect, how comes it to pass that some forms of taxation are much more oppressive than others? It is impossible to escape entirely the weight of a load by judicious arrangement of it, but it is quite feasible to diminish the fatigue it produces. Canard's doctrine is contrary to experience, and is not established by abstract reasoning. There can be no doubt that taxes are not always a part of cost of production, but in any case the real question is whether they can always be shifted by the immediate payer, and to this the answer must be a decided negative. The desire to pass on the burden may be universal, but the capacity to do so is limited. Even in the special case of taxes on commodities it is not always open to the producer to shift the duty to the consumer. As regards other taxes, the very idea of cost of production is quite inapplicable.

§ 5. Proceeding to examine the conditions of incidence, it is well to remember that the total denial of the existence of shifting and the assertion of its universal existence are both unfounded. That e.g. taxes on commodities are sometimes transferred by the immediate payers is an obvious fact. No one can believe that the distillers bear

[1] Stein, ii. 550–591.

[2] A prominent representative of this attitude is Held, who declares: '*Die Überwälzung ist gewiss kein reines Phantom, aber sie ist noch weniger im einzeinen Falle nachweislich,*' *Einkommensteuer*, 145–6.

the whole burden of the English spirit duties. On the other hand, it is just as incredible that a landlord could entirely shift a tax on rent to his tenant or any other class, or that the payers of income-tax could completely relieve themselves at the expense of others. The existence and the extent of the process of transference must depend largely on the conditions of the case, and it is these conditions that a general theory of incidence has to consider and explain.

The course of transference may be in different directions, and according to its starting-point and direction it is necessary to distinguish. Where the shifting is from the producer to the consumer, or more generally from the seller to the buyer, there is 'forward incidence'; where the movement is from the buyer to the seller, there is 'backward incidence'; where the process of shifting affects more than two parties, it may be called 'diffused incidence[1].'

The simplest instance of shifting is, as more than once mentioned, that in which the producer of a commodity passes on the charge in increased price to the consumer. A closer examination of this familiar case will suggest some important conditions. Why does the buyer submit to this additional charge? An increase in price tends to reduce demand, and will not the falling off bring about a return to the old level? The usual reply would be that the dealer or producer had been obtaining normal profits before the imposition of the tax, and that without an increased return proportional to his new charge he would not or could not continue in the business. The doctrine of average profits resulting from the perfect mobility of capital is thus the foundation of the proposition that taxes on commodities levied on the producer are shifted to the consumer. The reason for the proposition also shows

[1] The terms in the text are the nearest equivalents of *Fortwälzung*, *Rückwälzung*, and *Weiterwälzung*, which are used by German writers, but with various minute differences. The process called 'Abwälzung' by Hock and Wagner should not be regarded as belonging to the subject at all. See Hock, 96; Wagner, ii. 346–8.

its limitations; wherever an industry is yielding such exceptional gains that taxation will not reduce them below the supposed normal level, the motive for abandoning the employment not being present, the force that produces shifting will not be in operation. It may therefore be allowed, that so far as producers' gains are at all of the nature of monoply, taxation will remain on them. But here a further qualification is presented. Exceptional gains may be made by some producers, but not by others; in fact in nearly every industry some of those engaged in it can barely hold their ground. This unfortunate class must, on the increase of taxation, either raise their price or leave their business; if they can succeed in the former attempt, their successful competitors will gain by it, and shift their charge to the consumer; if they fail, the margin of pure profit is raised, and the burden will remain on the producers. It is quite possible that the actual result may be a compromise. Some of the weakest producers may be driven out, but the price may also be somewhat raised, in which case there will be division of the charge. Therefore the true conclusion is, that with perfect mobility taxation will be shifted from producer to consumer, with strict monopoly it will remain on the producer, and that in the various intermediate positions either result is possible, but a compromise is most likely. Again, the possibility of shifting taxation of the kind under notice does not depend simply on the elasticity of supply, the effect of changes in price on demand must be considered. If increased expenditure has to be devoted to taxed articles, there is less to be applied in the purchase of others; the consequent reduction may lower prices in other industries from which withdrawal is not economically expedient, and accordingly diffuse the indirect incidence of the tax to a different set of producers. Further, it must be remarked that as all industrial processes are really complex, it is quite possible that a tax may not affect the holder of floating capital who is ready to seek other investments, but may fall entirely on the owners of land, or specialized capital suitable for the production of the article. Both land and fixed capital are indeed capable of different uses, but the alternative ones are necessarily less profitable than that in which they are actually engaged. Hindrances to mobility are hindrances to shifting of taxation. The very application of a tax of itself produces disturbing effects. Additional capital has to be employed, restrictions which mean the sacrifice of time and money come into force, both tending to reduce the number of producers and to concentrate industry. The production approaches to a qualified monopoly, and thus the weight of taxation falls so far as actual receipts are concerned on the consumers, with a further loss to the small producers excluded from the business.

The precise method of taxation employed will have an important influence; whether the duty be imposed at an early stage or allowed to lie over till the article is ready for the consumer, whether the measure adopted is supposed capacity of production or actual product, are very material circumstances in deciding the exact incidence.

The apparently simple case of taxation of commodities thus appears to be really surrounded with complications that need close and careful study. The same questions would arise if the tax were levied directly from the consumer; there would be the possibility of a backward incidence, just as there is of failure of the forward one. In fact, as the position is sometimes explained, there is a struggle between producer and consumer, each striving to throw the loss on the other, and much will depend on the economic strength of the parties. As a rule, producers are a smaller and better organized class, and therefore have the chances in their favour, though where they possess a monopoly or any differential gain, this advantage is lost to them. Fresh increases of taxation are more readily passed on to the consumer than reductions are restored to him. This element of friction has another effeet. Small additional amounts of taxation are not easily shifted; a few pence on or off the gallon of spirits cannot directly influence retail price. The initial shifting always implies an effort, which however very readily takes place in industries accustomed to alter prices as the various expenses of production change. Additional taxation and a rise in the price of hops are events of exactly the same kind to the brewer, and their final result is distributed in the same way.

The diffusion of the burden may be still more complicated. In modern society products pass through the hands of several distinct classes before reaching the consumer, and the struggle of buyer and seller will be repeated at each separate stage. The existence of monopoly or of some form of limitation at any point may prevent the shifting passing any further. An economically strong intermediate group may throw a charge back to the producer, send it forward to the consumer, or divide it between both.

The foregoing analysis of the actions and reactions that may accompany or result from the imposition of a tax on a commodity shows the general conditions that are influential. They are (1) the presence or absence of mobility; in the former case, the normal shifting to the consumer will take place; in the latter, it is retarded: (2) the law of demand, on which depends very much the extent to which there will be a reflection of the burden either back to the producer or to other industries: (3) the method of taxation as affecting the preceding conditions: (4) the organization of the industry and its division, and (5) the amount of taxation. In regard to this last circumstance, it may happen that additional taxation will increase the force of competition. The new element may be just the last thing wanting to break up the existing settled conditions. This will be easily understood by considering the effect of successive *very small* additions to the duty on a given article. Each of these will tend to remain on the the payer, but as soon as the additions are sensible or easily distributed the shifting movement will tend to act.

The most rigid and gainful monopoly must, if taxation be carried sufficiently far, either pass on the weight or abandon the undertaking.

§ 6. The comparatively easy case of a tax on goods enables us to perceive the general character of the changes in incidence produced by the process of shifting. We have now to deal with the more important and interesting question of the movements of incidence in respect to the incomes of the different economic classes. The whole tendency of modern Economics has been in the direction of emphasizing the fundamental similarity between the departments of exchange and distribution[1]. Rent, wages, interest, and employers' earnings are exhibited as the prices of the respective services of land, labour, capital, and business ability. Might we not say that a tax on any of these commodities would be amenable to the same reasoning as that already applied to material goods, the consumers of each of the factors of production being those other factors that need its co-operation? This mode of treatment is, we believe, inconvenient, owing to the distinguishing peculiarities of the shares in distribution. Their production is not in the same form or subject to the same conditions as that of ordinary commodities. Nor is the nature of demand the same in respect to them. To reduce them to a common heading would be an undue straining of the analogy that undoubtedly exists. A better mode of dealing with the question is rather to consider it in the light of the theory of distribution, while availing ourselves of whatever is applicable in the case of taxation of material commodities.

There is no need for attempting here to re-state the economic theory of distribution. The work of Ricardo has been filled in and placed in closer relation to actual conditions by the ablest workers of the past and present

[1] 'The theories of the values of labour and of the things made by it cannot be separated; they are parts of one great whole,' Marshall, *Principles*, Preface, viii.

generations [1], who have carefully elaborated the originally fragmentary doctrines on the subject. The main conditions affecting changes in distribution must however be noticed: for the effect of taxation is plainly a deduction from the total produce, i. e. so much loss to be re-distributed among the parties concerned [2].

Assuming competition, the main circumstances on which the amount of rent depends are the position of the margin of cultivation, and the several qualities of land that lie above it. Change either the worst land in cultivation, or the relation to it of the superior soils and the quantity of rent will be altered [3]. In estimating the incidence of a tax on rent, its effect on these conditions is the first consideration. The usual way of showing that a tax on rent cannot be shifted is to point out that it does not affect that particular land that pays no rent, and consequently leaves the determination of the total amount, including the tax, as before. Ricardo and some of his nearest disciples differed as to the incidence of tithes or proportional taxes on the raw produce of land. The former maintained that such a tax must fall on the consumer, since in the case of products from the worst land in cultivation there was no rent on which it could be placed, and it was the production from this land that determined price; as the cultivator would need his average profit, the shifting to the consumer was necessary. Senior and McCulloch held that the rise of price would cheek demand, and therefore by changing the position of the margin in an upward direction would reduce

[1] See Ricardo, *Principles*, chs. 1–6; J. S. Mill, *Principles*, Bk. ii; Sidgwick, *Principles*, Bk. ii. chs. 6–9; Walker, *Political Economy*, pt. iv; Marshall, *Economics of Industry*, Bk. ii. chs. 6–12; *Principles of Economics*, Bk. vii. chs. 4–11.

[2] The increased produce that wisely expended taxation provides is not a determinable quantity, otherwise it would perhaps be well to meet the loss out of it, as the older theory of state services would suggest.

[3] The facts that land may vary in productiveness either from fertility or situation, and that cultivation may be either extensive or intensive, make the statement more complex, but do not alter its essential nature.

rent[1]. Without discussing the special point at issue, which belongs to the group of land taxes[2], we see that the criterion used by both is the effect on the general condition of agricultural industry. That on the hypothesis of perfect competition a tax on rent must remain on the payers is an indisputable truth, but for the cases of actual taxation it is important to bear in mind that economic rent is mixed up with other elements. The investment of capital in land yields a return in many instances indistinguishable from economic rent, but at the same time it is 'really the profits of the landlord's stock[3].' So far as no discrimination can be made between these components, the incidence of a tax will fall to some extent on the return to capital, and, if sufficient to discourage its investment, will tend to be passed on to the consumers of agricultural products, since land of inferior natural quality must be cultivated in order to supply the required quantity.

The opposite case of taxes imposed elsewhere falling on rent is much more probable. The class of differential gains of which rent is one very conspicuous instance is peculiarly liable to be affected by taxation. The influence of competition is, speaking generally, effective in distributing special burdens on a particular industry; but where special gains have been obtained an equivalent tax is the restoration not the destruction of equality. This is the kernel of truth in the Physiocrats' belief, and on it their exaggerated doctrine was based. No kind of actual tax can be imagined which might not under certain conditions diminish the fund that goes to the landowner. Wages, interest, employers' receipts, duties on goods, or on acts, all supply such examples, and they all accomplish their effect by operating on the margin of cultivation in the widest sense. The complicated working of the tax system is very well shown by this circumstance. It is, as we discovered, very difficult to single out

[1] See Ricardo, *Works*, 104; Senior, *Political Economy*, 123; McCulloch, note 30 to *Wealth of Nations*

[2] See Bk. iv. ch. 1.

[3] Ricardo, 102.

differential gains for exclusive or extra taxation, but the ordinary agencies of economic life are tending to that object, though of course in a very limited and imperfect way. They strike as well the earned and the unearned increment, the investment profitable through the foresight of the prudent employer and the lucky chance of the rash speculator, the rents of careful and improving as well as of inattentive and tyrannical landlords.

§ 7. Taxation of the capitalist's share of the national income gives rise to more difficult problems than those connected with rent. Between the doctrine of Turgot that a tax on profits is always, and that of Ricardo that it is never shifted[1], we have to take an intermediate position. A general tax on interest as it affects all employments equally would appear certain to remain on the payers. The mobility of capital cannot here, so long as we confine our attention to a single country, have any effect. Where the tax does not extend to capital invested abroad it is evident that it would discourage home investments and lead to the emigration of wealth to other places. 'The proprietor of stock,' as Adam Smith tells us, 'is properly a citizen of the world, and is not necessarily attached to any particular country[2]'. Even within a limited area another feature of capital will affect the incidence of special taxes imposed on it. Unlike land, it can be indefinitely increased by human foresight and providence, having as a chief inducement the return to be obtained by investment. Taxation on interest lowers that return and is therefore a direct discouragement to saving. So far as it is effectual, the diminution in the supply of available capital tends to raise the rate of interest and transfer the incidence to the consumers of capital, i. e. the other factors in distribution, and as rent is not likely to be much affected, in reality to the producers, including both employers and labourers. How far the check to production will show itself in a higher cost of production and therefore fall on the consumer is not easily

[1] Turgot, i. 63; Ricardo, 122. [2] *Wealth of Nations*, 358.

determinable ; if there were to be a substantial check to the investment of capital this would be a probable result, causing a diffusion of the incidence, some of it returning to the capitalist in his capacity of consumer.

For most purposes of economic reasoning there is an advantage in neglecting the differences between the different forms of capital and dealing solely with the characteristics common to all. But in handling the problem of incidence it is necessary to see that there are two broad classes of reproductive wealth, the one free and capable of being turned in any direction ; the other fixed in some particular industry. It is primarily to the former that the arguments from the mobility of capital apply. Once invested, the difficulties of withdrawal place the possessor for the time in the same position as the landlord. A tax on fixed capital would then seem to resemble in its effects a tax on rent, and to be equally untransferable. One instance—that of land improvements—has been already discussed, and in considering it we saw that the mode of relief to the capitalist was simply by reducing future investments. The single tax on fixed capital in the sense used by Menier and his followers would be at first a heavy burden on the owners of those forms of wealth, that would later on show itself in reduced investment and retarded production.

Free capital, if separately taxed, has much readier modes of escape. Employment outside the particular tax area makes it very difficult, even if the law enacts it, to enforce collection, consequently the chance of placing a tax on movable capital is much reduced by both economical and technical circumstances.

The chief condition then on which the incidence of a tax on interest depends is the effect on the accumulation and investment of capital, including the action on the saving propensities of the inhabitants and their disposition to move their wealth to escape taxation. If the rate of interest is determined by what Jevons calls the 'final utility' of capital, it is plain that the possibility of shifting the tax will depend on the effect produced on this margin of investment. If it is forced up the weight will be transferred from the recipients of interest to that indeterminate class who gain by the cheapness of capital [1]. A tax on the returns of fixed capital will at first rest on the payers, and only be transferred with difficulty, but it will ultimately, when the old supply is sufficiently contracted, come under the same influences.

Mixed up with the interest of capital in Ricardo's treatment of taxes is that element of profit variously described as 'wages of superintendence,' 'earnings of management,' or 'employers' gain.' It has, however, strong claims to separate treatment. The profit of the entrepreneur has some points of resemblance with wages as it has others with rent, and we must therefore be prepared to find that the movement of taxation is different in its case from that of ordinary interest. The analogy of rent would lead us to believe that a tax on the gains of the employer would not be transferred, since there would be no opportunity for escape on the part of the immediate bearers. A tax on this very indeterminate element of the gross profit of business would, however, be certain in practice to trench on the other constituents. Limited as the gains of employers are by the competition of inferior rivals the effect of a tax in driving out the weakest of those engaged in the business would help to shift a part at least of the weight from the survivors. Taxation of this kind would operate somewhat as taxation of commodities. The objection may occur that when the gains of all industries are taxed there is no motive for the weaker employers giving up business. They can, however, pass on to the class of labourers as others by taxation may be hindered from leaving it [2]. The position

[1] 'Either the labourers themselves or the public generally as consumers' is Jevons' statement, *Theory*, 278.

[2] 'It is laid down that taxes on the profits of all employments fall on capitalists only, and cannot be shifted on any other class. But there is in

of the marginal employer appears as the condition determining the shifting of taxes on the employer's gain.

This share of national income may also suffer through the operation of taxes on commodities. When a duty of this kind is not transferred to the consumer the burden is likely to fall on the differential element in profits; the tax has to be paid without the compensation of a rise in price, and there is no way of shifting the burden unless in the case of raw materials where rent may be curtailed. It is quite in accordance with the analogous case of rent that taxes should be shifted to the peculiar gains of the employer. It is, besides, possible that a tax on interest may be transferred to profit in the limited sense. When the rate of interest is raised, as we have seen that it may be, by taxation, the employer has to pay dearer for his borrowed capital, and, so far as what he works with is his own, loses on one hand what he gains with the other. On the whole we may confidently say that the broad and simple statement that taxes on profits fall on the capitalist, who can in no wise transfer them to others, requires to be very much limited before it can be accepted as correct. We must separate the two essentially different elements of interest and employer's gain and recognise that while the one is affected by changes in the point of final utility of capital, the other is connected with the opportunity for profitable industrial effort.

§ 8. If the older theories on the subject of incidence assumed too hastily that rent and profits had to bear their own immediate burdens and under certain conditions those of others, they made amends when dealing with wages. The transference of taxes on this part of revenue was asserted in the most positive manner. The landlord, the capitalist, the consumer might all be affected by a tax on wages, but the labourer himself was always exempt from contributing to the requirements of the State. This immu-

reality a perpetual migration along the borders between capital and labour, as there is also an intermediate class who individually may be regarded as capitalists or workmen,' Leslie, *Essays*, 390–1.

nity extended to the higher kinds of wages and salaries since they had a fixed relation to the ordinary rate[1].

The historical explanation of this belief is afforded by the evolution of the system of hired labour from the earlier condition of serfdom. The slave as an instrument of production received what was needed for his maintenance; any reduction in its amount would reduce his efficiency. Taxation was paid only out of his master's income, it did not concern the living machines engaged in the creation of wealth. This conception survived in the earlier period of free labour, and gained support from the doctrine of a 'natural' rate of wages common to the French and English economists. Any reduction in the rate would, it was held, act on population, and by diminishing its number restore the former real reward of the labourer. In spite of occasional concessions such was the opinion of Turgot, of Adam Smith, and of Ricardo[2], and given the premiss the conclusion was sound enough. It is also true that in the France of the eighteenth century and the England of the Napoleonic war wages did seem to have touched the subsistence point and to give a direct verification of the economical doctrine. But strange to say there was no notice taken of the fact that one of the causes of this deplorable situation was the heavy and unequal pressure of taxation. The French peasant and the English labourer were the greatest sufferers by the fiscal systems under which they lived and financial reform was one of the means of their relief.

No account of the incidence of a tax on wages can be satisfactory that does not fully recognise the existence of varying standards of comfort, even among the lowest unskilled labourers at different times and places. Beside and above the physical minimum there is what Mill calls a

[1] 'The recompense of ingenious artists and of men of liberal professions . . . necessarily keeps a certain proportion to the emoluments of inferior trades,' *Wealth of Nations*, 366; cp. Turgot, i. 444. The salaries of state officials are the only exception allowed by Adam Smith.

[2] See the passages already quoted.

'moral' minimum. The conditions must be exceptionally unfortunate that do not allow the labourer something above mere subsistence, and when that minimum point is exceeded there is something on which taxation may fall. To judge the incidence of taxation we must know its effect on the standard of comfort. If that is retained unaltered there will be a transference of the tax to the capitalist or employer; if it is lowered the labourer bears the tax himself. This consideration applies to each industrial grade, but it is evident that the higher the usual scale is placed the less the probability that it will be readjusted to suit taxation. When a group of labourers possesses a monopoly it, in common with all holders of differential gains, has no power of throwing off the burdens imposed on it, and as most skilled labourers have more or less special advantage the shifting of taxes in their case is beset with difficulty.

As in the case of rent, interest, and profit we find that the ultimate incidence of a tax on wages will vary according to its effect on the standard of living usual in that class and, so far as the higher kinds of wages are concerned, the extent to which their receivers are privileged through natural or artificial causes. Special gains of labour are just as much at the mercy of fresh taxation as any other differential advantage. The process of shifting requires the actual exertion of force to carry it out, and those forces can only be the agencies that work through supply and demand. If the same supply of labour of any particular kind is forthcoming with an unchanged demand then direct taxation of labour will not be transferred. The great difficulty of adjusting the supply of labour is a reason for believing that any shifting of taxes imposed on it must be a slow and uncertain process.

A similar conclusion applies to the case of taxes on the labourer's consumption. We do not find that duties on food produce higher wages; they only bring the starvation point nearer, as the history of the English Corn Laws shows. When Ricardo argues that taxes on articles of the labourer's consumption are exactly the same as a tax on profits he assumes far too rigid a connexion between the cost of living and the supply of labour. A tax on the food of animals used in production would increase cost because the food so given is regulated to secure efficiency, but the labourer seeks to procure the best terms for himself. The element of free contract present in the latter case entirely alters the position. For completeness of statement it is desirable to add that a great deal of wages is really the return on capital invested in the education of the workers, but in reality this does not produce as much practical effect as might be expected. A tax on wages unaccompanied by an equivalent tax on the yield of material capital would apparently discourage expenditure in the formation of personal or immaterial capital and turn it towards the production of goods. This check to the supply of trained workers would tend to raise the price of their services and shift the pressure to the consumers of the goods produced by them or to the employers. In practice the calculations of parents and others who make the investment in the education of the young are not so carefully worked out as to be influenced by the existence of a tax on the wages of the higher employments. Still, even with the actual imperfect estimates, some effect would probably be traceable if the tax were a heavy one. The necessary expenses of living in a suitable way and the cost of training are the two agencies that give some justification for Adam Smith's doctrine of a balance not to be disturbed by taxation between the different employments.

§ 9. Our examination of the general conditions that help to determine the true incidence of taxes on the different constituents of income though necessarily brief at least makes it plain that the theoretical explanation of the subject is not the simple process sometimes imagined. The movement of a given tax is not invariably in the same direction: its course will be guided by the surrounding circumstances. Without knowing what these are we cannot tell the direction much less the precise extent of its incidence. To pretend to say where e. g. a tax on profits will fall without possessing further data is as vain as to seek to determine the space traversed by a moving body whose initial velocity and period of movement are both unknown.

The difficulty of estimating the incidence of taxation is increased by the complementary alterations that take place in the economic system. A change in rent implies changes in the amount and probably in the relations of the other shares in distribution ; a rise or fall in the price of one article leads to other changes of price, and we may therefore expect that even in the most precise and determinate cases of incidence some additional diffused effect will be produced.

At the best and after the exercise of the utmost care, there will remain some obscurity as to the exact extent to which shifting takes place, owing chiefly to the difficulty of employing statistical verification. Deduction from general propositions cannot overcome this obstacle: special vigilance is therefore necessary to avoid errors arising from the want of a check such as the process of verification provides. The earlier theories are so many warnings of the danger of hasty deductions from insufficient premisses.

But, subject to these cautions, the use of the theory is by no means slight. We may not be able to give confident answers to general questions on the subject, but in dealing with particular instances we shall have the advantage of knowing what conditions we ought to notice and what effects we may reasonably look for. So understood, the theory of incidence is an indispensable part of financial doctrine.

CHAPTER VI.

THE PRINCIPLES OF LOCAL TAXATION.

§ 1. BESIDES the system of taxation intended for the support of the central government, and therefore usually described as 'general,' or 'imperial,' the compulsory revenue needed for the due maintenance of local authorities requires to be considered. This latter class of charges is just as much entitled to the name of taxation, and in many respects exhibits the same features as the imperial tax revenue. Local and central government are simply different forms of the state organization and show this fundamental resemblance in Finance as in other respects. The need of revenue, the general characteristics of that revenue in respect to its origin, and the influence that it exerts on individual and national wealth are the same in the case of central and local bodies. It might almost seem that no necessity existed for a separate treatment of the tax receipts of those smaller units that historical circumstances or the needs of social life have called into being.

But, notwithstanding this general similarity, there are certain peculiarities in the methods of local Finance that make it desirable to consider the forms of taxation used by it in a separate chapter. Without in the slightest abandoning the conception of the unity of all taxation, we may examine those aspects of local taxation that give it in some degree a distinct and common character, and enable us to contrast with advantage the two categories of revenue belonging respectively to the supreme and the subordinate political bodies.

One very obvious, though rather superficial reason is found in the great magnitude of each class. The English Imperial revenue for 1886–7 was, in round figures, £90,000,000, that for local purposes was £66,750,000. In other countries there is the same possibility of opposing the two sets of charges without finding any such difference as to warrant us in regarding one as entirely insignificant. When we add that local charges are on the whole increasing more rapidly, it is easy to understand the interest that has been excited respecting them.

There are other and deeper reasons. Local institutions have a special function as representing the interest of particular districts; they are confined to a somewhat narrow range of duties and as a consequence their revenue system is simpler and less involved than that of the State. A rural *commune* must have a comparatively primitive form of financial organization, and even in the case of the largest sub-divisions the absence of military and naval expenditure and the large portion of other public duties discharged by the agents of the central government keep down their requirements. The expenditure of a great municipality, or a large American State is no doubt considerable and for very varied objects, but cannot compare in extent or in comprehensiveness with any national budget. Moreover, the restraint imposed on their financial action, either by legislation, or (in federal States) by constitutional limitations, is a serious check on the power of local bodies [1].

Another reason may also be assigned: the subjects with which local administration has to deal are mainly of an economic character and very often admit of rather definite

[1] In such governments as England or France the legislature can completely control the fiscal expedients of municipalities and other smaller territorial administrations. The powers of the American 'State' are limited (*a*) by the federal constitution, (*b*) by the state constitution. Cities are controlled by state legislation, cp. Bryce, *American Commonwealth*, i. 498.

measurement. Water-supply, lighting, drainage, and the care of roads are instances. The conduct of such matters, if it has some resemblance to the duties of the national government, has others no less strong to the management of an industrial company. The propositions that 'contributions should be proportional to advantage received,' and that 'political power should depend on the amount contributed' are much more plausible when applied to local than to general government. The extent of this resemblance will, of course, depend on the special character of the sub-division. A rural parish, or *commune*, is in this respect very different from London or Paris, but the prominence of economic interests in the widest sense is traceable in all forms of subordinate governments.

§ 2. The history of local institutions has already been briefly noticed in connexion with expenditure [1], and it throws light equally on their receipts. One prominent class of these bodies is really a 'survival' of what were orginally sovereign powers. The 'States' of Germany and America, and the 'cantons' of Switzerland are well-known examples. Lower down in the scale the *commune* is the primitive political 'unit' whose importance has also decayed with the growth of the State. In all of them the taxing power has been limited by the pressure and competition of the national government, and in the earlier forms by the slow development of taxation. The manor, or 'village community,' depended on economic revenue, not on taxation in the modern sense. One striking feature in state development has been the absorption of the more productive forms of compulsory revenue by the central financial system. It was only natural that the monarchical State with its hostility to feudalism and to local privileges and immunities of all kinds should endeavour to take into its own hands the customary taxes of districts and municipalities. The centralizing movement of the sixteenth and

[1] See Bk. i. ch. 7. §§ 2 sq.

seventeenth centuries was specially noticeable in respect to taxation.

Motives of convenience assisted in promoting this change. Some of the principal forms of revenue were manifestly unsuitable for small territorial divisions. The taxation of commodities or of income was far better fitted for the control of the central government. Thus, both political and economic reasons existed for the breakdown of the older tax revenue of towns and localities.

The existing systems of local administration have, in many cases, a quite different origin; instead of being older than the State they are its direct creation. In France, for example, the whole tax system of the 'departments' and 'communes' rests on legislation not a century old, and though English institutions have a longer history, they are equally the expression of the State's will[1]. Thus local institutions are not always survivals, or even revivals, of the past; they are often entirely new formations, so arranged as to satisfy the needs for which devolution of authority has been deemed expedient.

In such instances their power of taxing is a concession strictly limited by the terms of the grant. The adoption of new expedients is precluded so that very often it is merely the amount of one particular tax that has to be settled and that only within definitely fixed limits. Local taxation becomes, in fact, a kind of supplement to the general system admitting of little independent movement. The two opposing tendencies that affect local administration are also in operation here. On the one hand, there is the desire of skilled financiers to keep the errors and mistakes of the smaller bodies under supervision. Party spirit and class-interest are intensified when confined to a small area and are but too ready to employ taxation as an engine of oppression: even when no injustice is intended the ignorance

[1] The great measures of legislation on local government are (1) The Poor Law Act, 1834; (2) The Corporation Reform Act, 1835; (3) The Local Government Act, 1888.

of the real working of taxation that is so common among local administrators would, if unchecked, prove disastrous to the national interest. Hence the limitations on the form and amount of taxation as well as on its application. The citizen who is unfairly burdened by his local taxes has as legitimate a claim to relief as if the general charges were too heavy in proportion to his income.

Side by side with this idea of more careful control there is the disposition to extend the sphere of action of local authorities. It is felt that political education is promoted by inducing citizens to manage their common affairs in an independent manner. To awaken or to strengthen the feeling of responsibility is impossible, unless power to act is also bestowed. A local body cannot be expected to feel any great interest in its work if all the important parts of the system are determined beforehand. To secure a vigorous municipal life there must be a good deal of latitude given to the corporations engaged in its management. Wider taxing powers and new forms of local revenue are, therefore, often suggested as indispensable steps in reform. To understand the position of the question we must bear in mind the existence of these apparently contradictory sentiments both, in some cases, vehemently urged by the same persons.

§ 3. The first step in an examination of the principles of local taxation is the determination of the proper line of division from the general state revenue. We have seen that the distribution of duties between central and local administration conforms on the whole to certain general principles[1], and the most natural course would be to apportion the charges on a similar system, but, in fact, there is no real correlation between the two: the division of duties is quite independent of the division of taxes, just as both are distinct from the distribution of public property and quasi-private receipts. The partition of taxes between

[1] Bk. i. ch. 7. §§ 6, 7, 8.

the two classes must depend on, or at least be guided by, financial and economic considerations.

Some important taxes are at once on sound principles shut out from use as local resources. The customs are only levied at the national frontier, any attempt to restore the provincial customs-boundaries that hampered the trade of France before the Revolution, and in the present century that of the German and Italian States, would be a retrograde, as well as an unpopular, step in Finance. The taxation of commodities *in transitu* is only legitimate, when exercised in a way calculated to cause the smallest amount of delay and inconvenience. To regulate trade between small areas for fiscal purposes would be at once costly and unproductive, and therefore uneconomical. The earliest step towards federation between independent States has been the abolition of custom houses at their frontiers, and there is no probability that a reversal of this salutary process will be witnessed. The *octrois* are an exception, but admit of explanation. They are confined to towns and, therefore, are regulated with comparative ease, having, in fact, some resemblance to the market dues once so common in British towns. They make as near an approach to direct taxes on local consumption as can well be devised, with some additional incidence on the surrounding country through their effect on demand. Besides, they are unquestionably a decaying form. France and Italy are the only countries where they are in full force, and even in these they are looked on as a necessary evil. It is almost certain that in the progress of reform they will before long disappear. On the same grounds local excise taxes are practically prohibited. To impose a duty on an article without having the power of levying an equivalent customs duty would mean the sacrifice of local producers, unless they had a strict monopoly up to the amount of the tax; such a tax would be easily evaded by moving outside the boundary. Thus the two great forms of indirect taxation on commodities are withdrawn from local resources. Direct duties on consumption might be used, but, as will appear, they are objectionable in either general or local Finance owing to the difficulties of estimation [1].

The income and property taxes are as unavailable though for a different reason. Both are essentially personal and belong to a given individual. Now to tax a person on his income for the service of the locality in which he resides is open to the double objection that it is likely to be evaded and is grossly unfair. Local authorities have no efficient machinery for detecting concealed income: they are in a worse position than the English revenue officials in regard to foreign investments where failure is admitted. The mere moving from the area for part of the year would upset the arrangements. As to the unfairness Mr. Goschen's view seems conclusive. 'It appears to be impossible to devise an equitable local income tax, for you cannot localize income. An attempt was made in Scotland, and it broke down when an English Lord Chancellor, who drew his £10,000 a year in London, but had a small place in Scotland, was made to pay income tax on the whole of his income in that country as well as in this [2].' No real correction could be made without exempting all income earned outside the district, i. e. in fact, changing the income into a partial produce tax. No matter how large the local division may be the same objection lies. The American States and Swiss cantons are as little suited for the application of separate income taxes as England, Ireland and Scotland. Owing to the variety of modern incomes and the trouble of following them to their sources the income tax should always be a general tax. A general property tax is in much the same position in local taxation, though its defects as a part of any tax system are so great that it is doubtful whether it can be admitted even into the list of good national taxes. It appears to have the two great faults of injustice in distribution and liability to evasion. On both these points the American evidence respecting the

[1] Bk. iv. ch. 5. § 6.

[2] *Local Taxation*, 204.

state property taxes is overwhelming. Large categories of property escape altogether, and others are sometimes taxed in two different places. Personal property is either not returned for assessment at all, or is scandalously underrated. Stocks, bonds, and various immaterial forms of wealth are easily removed from the tax-collector's notice. Efforts at reform have proved ineffectual, and competent students seem agreed that the system must be abandoned[1].

The reasons for the removal of taxes on income, property and commodities from the list of local resources are in a great degree technical, and rest on the difficulties of their fair or economic application. But it is further plain that there must be a large body of productive taxation reserved to the central government. Even if all the taxes mentioned were eminently fitted by their nature to contribute to local revenue, they would have to be reserved for the still more important services of the national administration. So much depends on division of duties between the two sets of organs and their relative cost, that it is hardly possible to lay down any general rule on this part of the subject. We may fairly assume that at lowest one half of the total sum collected in taxes will have to be taken by the central government.

§ 4. On the other hand there is a different class of taxes that appears well fitted for local treatment. Such are those that are levied locally on fixed property and permanent occupations carried on in the locality. First in natural order is the land tax. Both abstract reasoning and experience tend to show that a large proportion of local taxation must be obtained from this important 'object.' In rural

[1] See the *Local Taxation Report* of Mr. Wells and his colleagues made in 1871; Prof. Seligman's article on 'The General Property Tax,' *Pol. Science Quarterly*, v. 24–62; and Prof. Ely's *Taxation*, 146–201, in which a mass of evidence is collected showing the grievances that arise from the property tax. Prof. Ely, however, fails to notice that the same arguments may be urged against the state income taxes advocated by him in a later part of his valuable work (287–311).

districts there is little else to be taxed, and in the case of towns the value of land is so much increased by the action of social conditions, that it forms a most suitable mark for the larger taxation that the wants of urban societies make necessary. The theory of incidence also supports this view. Other charges are often shifted to rent, while it can hardly ever transfer its peculiar burdens. As a land tax tends to become a tax on rent, and can generally be so regulated to take that shape, it has the definiteness of incidence in its favour, and its pressure falls on a form of wealth that is likely to grow without effort on its owner's part. The doctrine of taxation in proportion to service, though untenable in general, has here some force. The chief gain of local expenditure accrues to those who own property in the district. Some advantages may be more evident in their effects than others, but in a broad general way the advance of a locality means an advance in the rent of its area. There are no doubt exceptions: unfortunate proprietors have sometimes had to pay for 'improvements' that lowered the value of their land, but on the whole the opposite effect is more common [1].

Next to the land tax we may place the house tax as a convenient form of local impost. It is, indeed, somewhat more complicated in its operation; its incidence, which, by regarding houses as a particular manufactured commodity, would appear to be on the occupier, really varies according to local conditions, and it has the disadvantage of affecting one of the most important elements of necessary expense [2], but on the other hand it is easily collected, tolerably proportional to income, and does not touch those unconnected with the district. If houses are to be taxed the revenue thence derived should, we believe, go to the local, not to the general revenue. The same reasons that have been noticed in the case of land apply, but with less force, to that of houses. This form of property gains in value by expendi-

[1] Cp. Report of Town Holdings Committee (1891), Questions 176–180.

[2] See Bk. iv. ch. 2. § 5 for a discussion of the incidence of house taxes.

ture, but it also deteriorates through use, and therefore the indeterminate portion of the tax that falls on the house-owner should be kept within moderate bounds.

A third form of local taxation is discovered in the taxes on the exercise of occupations known as 'licenses.' These are far better suited for local, than for general, taxation. They can be collected readily, and, if properly selected, do not hamper industry. The system of low license duties on most trades and employments has the chief attributes of a fair local tax. The English method of appropriating the spirit licenses to the local bodies might with advantage be further developed.

Very similar in outward appearance are the licenses for direct enjoyments, and, though they differ in their essential character, they also may without impropriety be assigned to the several localities. Certain difficulties do indeed arise in this connexion. A license taken out in one place may be required for use elsewhere, or may even be exercised in several different localities. In practice the right of transfer may be allowed, or better still, such cases may be reserved for the central revenue, leaving only the localized privileges to the smaller bodies. As a further resource some of the taxes on acts may be usefully employed by localities. Thus the transfer of property, registration of companies, and other charges on legal transactions, would provide a fund for the payment of the expenses connected with these administrative functions. Those taxes that closely resemble fees will come under the same rule as to their division[1]. Each administration will take for itself what it collects.

The foregoing suggested distribution must necessarily be modified to suit the needs of particular financial systems. Thus the house tax forms a part of general taxation in several countries: its complete surrender to the local authorities when proposed in England was made contingent on the position of imperial Finance, and has not yet been

[1] Bk. ii. ch. 5. § 3.

carried out[1]. We cannot imagine the Indian Government yielding up a part of the land revenue to the provinces. The line of division has to be varied, but it is nevertheless well to know the general principles that should assist in determining it.

§ 5. But given the partition of revenue between the two forms, we have next to see whether the rule of justice that we accepted for general taxation can be applied without reservation in local Finance. Taxation in proportion to income gives a substantially just division of general burdens, but in the case of smaller districts the burden is not a general one. Most local services are specific, and can be dealt with on the rule of payment for service. A large part of the so-called English 'rates,' such as those for water supply, lighting, cleaning, drainage, &c., may best be measured for each payer by the benefit, or rather the quantity of the service. The citizen in fact pays for the supply of so many useful commodities. The local authority is performing a strictly economic duty. Taxation so far should be in proportion to advantage. Difficulties, however, soon arise in the attempt to apply this principle. In addition to the direct service rendered there is a margin of advantage accruing to the whole society, and part of the service is not done for specified persons. The necessity of investing capital, the repayment of which is spread over a long period, complicates the case. To get a fair division of the charge between owners of land, possessors of fixed capital, including houses, and the immediate users of these public services, is no easy task. It involves (1) a determination of the real incidence of the different modes of taxation, and of the extent and rapidity of the process of shifting; (2) an estimation of the truly equitable division between the several interests; and (3) a full recognition of the practical limits that any effective system must observe.

[1] Goschen, *Local Taxation*, 205: 'It may happen that owing to events at present unforeseen, it will be impossible for the Imperial Exchequer to part with so important a source of revenue as the house tax.'

As regards the first it depends partly on the general principles of incidence, and partly on the special incidence of land, house and capital taxes. For convenience we may here so far repeat and anticipate the results elsewhere stated[1].

The immediate consumer, i. e. the occupier of a house or the user of other taxed convenience, looks on local taxation as simply a part of the price of the utilities he receives. So far as the outlay benefits him directly, he bears it as payment for increased advantage, and taxation is only shifted by him when the sacrifice it imposes reduces demand. Heavy local taxation, unaccompanied by corresponding increase in utility, would tend to diminish demand for the services so charged, and give a backward shifting on the producers, i. e. the house-owners or other holders of the articles. The check to these particular forms of industry would ultimately reduce the capital and labour employed in them, and thereby pass the pressure on to the landowners in the shape of lowered ground rents so far as land entered into the supply of services. Such seems to be the process by which the 'orthodox' views on the incidence of rates were arrived at, the burden being ultimately distributed between the owner of land and the consumer. In respect to taxes on agricultural tenants the same train of reasoning would suggest that the incidence would be ultimately on the landlords, as outside competition would hinder any forward movement to the consumer of produce[2]. It is hardly necessary to say that this doctrine assumes a uniformity in the course of shifting that has no real existence, since it omits some circumstances that are essential elements in the problem. Amongst these are: the long duration of the arrangements between owners of land and of capital; the

[1] See Bk. iii. ch. 5. §§ 5, 6, 7; Bk. iv. ch. 1. § 6; ch. 2. § 5.

[2] On the question of incidence see Goschen, *Local Taxation*, 163–168, and the *fifth* Report of the Committee on Town Holdings, No. 341 (1890), especially Questions 41–5, 88–101, 331 (Sidney Webb); 1804–32, 2024–26 (Munro); 1243–46 (Farrer); 2714–22 (Rogers).

position of qualified monopoly that owners of land in towns possess, and which with its advantages has the disadvantage of exposing them to the action of shifting; the slowness with which adjustments are made, which hinders much reliance in matters of legislation being placed on the operation of shifting in securing a proper division of the burdens.

The second difficulty as to the true interpretation of equity is partly the result of the complicated interests, some present, some future, that modern society is ever creating. In apportioning taxation between occupier, houseowner and ground landlord, we may discover that each of the two latter interests is divided into three or four parts, all in equity bound to share in the burden for the common advantage. Far more is it due to the multiple duties of local government, some of which are merely delegated for convenience, not because they are solely of local interest. Police, prisons, poor relief, and education, may be cited as examples. We cannot with any reason maintain that owners, whether of land or other property, and ordinary householders, are alone interested in the efficient management of these important matters. The policy of defraying all these charges out of particular funds with the practical exemption of others no less liable is a grave injustice. The cost of expenditure that is in essence for general purposes should follow the same distribution as that of general taxation.

An opposite case is that in which outlay is incurred for the benefit of particular owners. They may fairly be called on to pay for this special advantage. The 'betterment' principle has thus a foundation in justice. The community charges for the service it has performed, but its action requires to be carefully controlled; the proof of benefit bestowed must be very plain and well established, and the indirect benefits to others must be taken into account. The owners of building plots and houses in an improved street gain largely, so however, in a less degree, does the general community. The rule then of taxing according to interest affected is not a complete and absolute principle for the distribution of local Finance. Certain forms of direct public services can be so dealt with as well as the special improvements of private property. Another portion may be fairly placed on the owners of durable property as those who benefit most by an active and judicious local administration. A third and not inconsiderable share may be placed on the community generally by the agency of local licenses and taxes on transactions, and still more by a tax proportional to house rent which is a good rough measure of taxable capacity [1].

§ 6. After all these different expedients have been carried as far as circumstances will allow, it may be necessary to readjust the balance between the central and local governments by a transfer from the funds of the former, or by the employment of its taxes as a base on which to raise additional local resources.

Most systems of Finance have adopted one or both of these expedients. To begin at home: for many years it had been the established practice to pay local authorities various sums for special objects to be applied in the manner prescribed by Parliament or some branch of the central administration. In common with other expenditure these grants increased in amount till they reached six millions in 1887. The result was a confusion between the two classes of revenue and expenditure: what was outlay in one case was income in the other, the same sums being counted twice over. The method of assigning particular taxes or portions of them to local authorities is plainly a great improvement. Under the new plan introduced by Mr. Goschen various duties have been directly marked off for local revenue, and thereby removed from the imperial

[1] 'It is one of the fairest and most unobjectionable of all taxes. No part of a person's expenditure is a better criterion of his means or bears on the whole more nearly the same proportion to them,' Mill, *Principles*, Bk. v. ch. 3. § 6. Supported by Engel's researches.

budget [1]. The advantage of a distinct line being drawn, and of making the local receipts depend on the product of the duties, not on the pressure brought to bear on the government, is undoubted. The same policy has been tried elsewhere. Belgium removed the *octrois* in 1860, and replaced them by parts of several indirect taxes [2]. This method receives an extension by making the local taxes merely additions to the general ones. Thus the French *communes* and departments draw their principal tax revenue from the '*Centimes additionnels*,' i. e. charges added to the four direct contributions. The same plan is used in Germany and Austria, though independent communal taxes are found in various cases in the former.

Some high authorities approve of this policy of making local taxation a mere appendage to general taxation. 'It is rightly asserted,' says Leroy Beaulieu, 'that the French system of movable additional charges on the existing direct contributions, of uniform accountability, and the collection of direct local taxes by the agents of the State, makes the management of local Finance simpler, clearer and less costly, and gives the taxpayers much greater security against peculation and exaction. We do not hesitate for our part to declare for that system [3].' But notwithstanding this weighty judgment we are forced to believe that there is an advantage in having a separate system of local taxation. The aims of the two classes are so different, and the rule of distribution varies so much, that a decided boundary between them is rather desirable. Both will naturally avail themselves of such material in the shape of valuations and officials as exist, but this does not necessitate the treatment of local taxes as merely added percentages to established general taxes.

[1] These are (1) the license duties; (2) a proportion (one-half) of the probate duty; (3) *6d.* per gallon on spirits and *3d.* per barrel on beer, i. e. taxes on acts, property and commodities.

[2] 75 per cent. of the coffee duty, 25 per cent. of the spirit duties, the excises on sugar and wine, and 40 per cent. of the postal receipts. See De Parieu, iv. 386 sq. for a full discussion.

[3] i. 712.

The success of local government depends on the energy and vigour with which it is worked, not on restraining its action within the narrowest limits. 'The ideal condition of Finance in a perfect system of local self-government' has been described as 'one in which each local authority levies its own taxes upon its own subjects within its own area; in which it has the power of applying the proceeds of these taxes, within certain limits fixed by the general law, for the local advantage of its own citizens; and in which it has power to increase or diminish its taxes, at its own discretion, according to its means and its wants[1].' The benefits of fiscal autonomy may perhaps not be so great as in certain conditions to compensate for the want of harmony and regularity that state intervention secures; they are, however, sufficient, in conjunction with the reasons already given, to justify strenuous efforts for securing a distinct tax system, and this is possible without any sacrifice of the guarantees for good government. At the same time we may fully recognise the convenience of supplementing local revenue from general taxation with the double object of securing sufficient funds and more equitable distribution of burdens, though, while granting this, we must also insist that the extent to which the process is applied ought to be confined within the narrowest limits consistent with attaining the end in view. The allotment of part of the taxation available to meet the general expenditure is a measure that always stands in need of justification; it has a presumption against it only capable of being rebutted by sufficient evidence.

§ 7. The relations of local and general Finance suggest another closely related point, viz. the extent of the fiscal liberty to be bestowed on the local financial powers. Between the extremes of complete regulation and almost complete independence we may discover a series of steps corresponding to the size of the bodies and the political

[1] Sir T. H. Farrer, *Mr. Goschen's Finance*, 54.

training of the people. The national government may fix the particular taxes and their amount, or it may, as with the French *communes*, let the latter be varied if its permission is sought. Again, it may lay down the forms of taxation and place bounds to its amount, either definitely determined or variable. Or, finally, the duty of selecting both the taxes and determining their amount may be given up to the local government. The first mode means the reduction of the local authority to impotence so far as taxation is concerned; it simply executes the Sovereign's orders. The other extreme approaches closely to independence. The taxing power is always an attribute of sovereignty; a body that had full taxing power would have got very near that position. Accordingly we find that the customs duties in all federal States come under the control of the central government. The extent to which the right of independent taxation has been restrained is a mark of the progress of the State towards unity. Co-ordinate fiscal authorities have to be kept within bounds by constitutional rules, but we may safely conclude that in a durable State the supreme power in financial matters will sooner or later be vested in the central government.

The extent to which the liberty of experiments in taxation should be conceded to the subordinate bodies must, we believe, be carefully limited. For the smaller units the taxes should be absolutely laid down, and also the maximum to be raised, but the opportunity of economy should not be denied them on the condition that they duly discharge their necessary functions[1]. The larger circumscriptions are fairly entitled to greater latitude. A higher standard of intelligence may be expected from their representatives, and their economic resources are more varied. But even with them the need for supervision cannot be said to be absent. They may impose taxes that press heavily on unpopular sections in their district; they may deal unjustly or ignorantly with important economic and social interests,

[1] Bk. i. ch. 7. § 9 for these duties.

or they may go counter to the financial policy of the State. For these reasons the unitary form of government is in its financial aspects superior to the federal one, even though the larger liberty of levying new varieties of taxation is a certain advantage in the latter.

APPENDIX.

THE MAXIMS OF TAXATION.

THE recurring needs of financial practice would naturally suggest to those concerned with the collection of public revenue the advisability of framing general rules by which to guide their policy. Art usually precedes and is the parent of science, and Finance is hardly an exception in this respect. Unfortunately the limitation of the administrators' views to the object of securing the largest immediate return, their ignorance of the simplest economic principles, and the immature condition of the early state economy, all made the process a slow one. The most famous financiers of so relatively modern a period as the seventeenth century—Sully and Colbert—left little in the form of applicable general rules. The first really meritorious collections are those of the students of economics and administration in the eighteenth century. In Germany, Italy, and France this work was performed with more or less acuteness, but the writings of the cameralists and Italian economists have chiefly an historical interest, while the doctrine of the net product vitiated the physiocratic conclusions [1].

Adam Smith's fortune has been very different in this respect. His canons were accepted in his own day by theorists and statesmen, and have been so worked into the texture of financial science that no work on the subject can rightly omit them. Fully in harmony with the spirit of the last century, they have survived

[1] For the maxims of earlier writers see Roscher, § 44, note 1. Those of Justi in his *System*, and Verri, *Meditazioni*, are the most noticeable. As to the anticipations of Adam Smith's first rule see Held, *Einkommensteuer*, 121 sq., and Meyer, *Principien*, 3–21.

in the development of the present, and, in spite of much hostile criticism, bid fair to hold their ground in the future[1].

These famous maxims—to once more repeat them—are four in number and run as follows:—

(1) 'The subjects of every State ought to contribute towards the support of the government as nearly as possible in proportion to their respective abilities; that is, in proportion to the revenue which they respectively enjoy under the protection of the State.'

(2) 'The tax which each individual is bound to pay ought to be certain and not arbitrary. The form of payment, the manner of payment, the quantity to be paid ought all to be clear and plain to the contributor and to every other person.'

(3) 'Every tax ought to be levied at the time or in the manner in which it is most likely to be convenient for the contributor to pay it.'

(4) 'Every tax ought to be so contrived as both to take out and to keep out of the pockets of the people as little as possible, over and above what it brings into the public treasury of the State[2].'

The most obvious comment on these rules is that which notes a difference between the *first* and the remaining ones. The former is a rule of taxation; the latter are rules respecting taxes. The first canon is applicable only to the tax system as a whole, while the second, third and fourth should be observed in the case of each separate tax. Mill, therefore, has some justification when he declares that they belong to 'the discussion of particular taxes'[3] since every tax must be separately tested by them, though of course this circumstance does not remove them from the category of general rules.

Another feature that has been often noticed is the mixture of different classes of considerations. Thus they have been

[1] Between the view of J. S. Mill, who calls the Smithian maxims 'classical,' and the undue depreciation of President Walker and Cohn, the former is much nearer the truth. According to President Walker 'These maxims have been quoted over and over again as if they contained truths of great moment, yet if one examines them he finds them at the best trivial, while the first and most famous cannot be subjected to the slightest test without going all to pieces,' *Pol. Ec.* 489. Cohn, § 333, is quite as severe.

[2] *Wealth of Nations*, 347–8.

[3] *Principles*, Bk. v. ch. 2. § 1.

described as 'partly ethical . . . and partly economical in the strict sense'[1]; and it seems unquestionable that the second has chiefly a constitutional significance, as prescribing the taxpayer's immunity from arbitrary exactions, but more generally the three last may be regarded with Wagner as 'administrative precepts'[2].

The suggested separation of the Smithian rules according to their character, though in form correct, has the effect of obscuring unduly their really compound basis. The first maxim is, it may be said, undoubtedly ethical, since it refers to the justice of taxation. Granting this, it should be also remembered that inequality in taxation diminishes its productiveness and tends to impair industrial energy; from this point of view the canon is an economic one. Violations of the rule of equal treatment are, again, offences against constitutional liberty quite as much as absence of certainty. In like manner each of the remaining rules has an economic side; the certainty, the convenience, and the economy of taxation, like its equality, are highly promotive of a well-filled treasury and a prosperous industrial system. The true point of view for understanding these maxims is to regard them not as economic, ethical or constitutional, but as essentially *financial*; they therefore rightly combine the different elements that must enter into problems connected with that subject.

With reference to the first maxim it is plain that Adam Smith regarded revenue as the index of ability to contribute, and it may be conjectured that the words 'under the protection of the State' refer to the case of persons having property in different countries, and therefore imply a prohibition of double taxation[3]. The consideration of the tests of justice finds its place in the general exposition, not in an historical appendix.

Next to Adam Smith, Sismondi deserves mention as the propounder of rules that have a real value; they also are four, and assert :—

(1) 'Every tax should fall on revenue, not on capital.'

(2) 'In the assessment of taxation gross produce should not be confounded with revenue.'

[1] Nicholson, note 45 to *Wealth of Nations*, 418.

[2] Cp. Sidgwick, *Pol. Ec.* Bk. iii. ch. 8. § 6; Wagner, ii. 292.

[3] See Bk. iii. ch. 3. § 14, and the works there referred for this discussion.

(3) 'Taxation should never touch what is necessary for the existence of the contributor.'

(4) 'Taxation should not put to flight the wealth on which it is imposed[1].'

These rules are the practical application of the ideas of net produce, and the relief of the minimum of subsistence, and they prove that in Finance Sismondi had not deviated from the Ricardian position.

The succeeding writers in England, France and Germany employed the maxims of Adam Smith as the basis of their discussions: the particular variations in expression of different authors need not be noticed.

Among French expositors of Finance the series of rules given by Joseph Garnier[2] is the most elaborate. Of his sixteen rules the third and fourth correspond to Adam Smith's second and fourth. The first and sixth together deal with distribution of taxation, which ought, he holds, to be 'progressively proportional.' The remaining rules are chiefly political or technical, as e.g. the ninth which declares that taxation should be voted by the representatives of the taxpayers, and the fifteenth limiting indirect taxation to a small number of articles. Far superior in arrangement and clearness is the grouping of Hock who lays down that taxation should be: (1) just, (2) logical, and (3) economical, developing each of these chief heads in special subdivisions.

The newer financial literature has not sought so much to formulate short general rules of universal validity, as to analyse and consider the conditions suitable to the several stages of the tax-system. But analysis and discussion must, if fruitful, be the foundation of general precepts, and accordingly we find that in some cases the attempt has been made. Held's very careful discussion of the sources of taxation leads him to the assertion of three principles of distribution; viz. '(1) Generality, i.e. all who have incomes should pay. (2) Equality, i.e. income should be taxed without reference to its source. (3) The greatest possible care of the national well-being and its increase[3].' The

[1] *Nouveaux Principes* (2nd ed.), Livre vi. ch. 8.

[2] *Finance* (4th ed.), ch. 13, 156–165.

[3] *Einkommensteuer*, 121,

last includes the maxim of economy. A re-statement of the canons of Finance according to the latest view is supplied by Wagner. Rejecting the idea of a single class of rules of co-ordinate authority he divides the chief principles (*oberste Grundsätze*) into four classes arranged in the order of their importance, and distinguished as (*a*) financial, (*b*) economic, (*c*) ethical, (*d*) administrative. Under (*a*) come (1) taxation should be adequate to meet expenditure, (2) it should be elastic; under (*b*) are placed (3) the sources of taxation should be rightly chosen, (4) the kinds of taxes should be selected with reference to their effects; class (*c*) includes rules (5) taxation should be general, and (6) it should be proportional; while, finally, class (*d*) contains the rules that taxation should be (7) determinate, (8) convenient, and (9) collected with the smallest cost, in fact Adam Smith's last three maxims [1].

The economic rules are somewhat vaguely expressed, but (3) refers to the taxation of income and of capital, and (4) draws attention to the incidence of taxation. The sixth rule is regarded as varying according to the conception taken; from the pure financial point of view it is proportionality to income, from the politico-social one it is in proportion to capacity.

In reality Wagner's principles are not so much rules in the older sense, as indications of the points to be considered: he particularly dwells on the need of careful discrimination of particular cases [2].

[1] Wagner, ii. 304.

[2] 'Hier muss die Finanzwissenschaft vielmehr specialisch und casuistisch verfahren, als sie bisher gewöhnlich gethan hat,' ii. 305.

The latest English statement of the maxims of taxation is that by Mr. Devas who lays down *ten* conditions, *Pol. Ec.* 516.

BOOK IV.

PUBLIC REVENUE.

TAXATION. THE SEVERAL KINDS OF TAXES.

CHAPTER I.

TAXES ON LAND.

§ 1. IN the preceding book we have dealt with the subject of taxation under its general aspects as the most important element of the financial system. We have now to complete our inquiry by examining the characteristics of the different kinds of taxes, and we may begin this discussion with one of the oldest and most widely employed forms of compulsory contribution—that levied on land. The interest and importance of this kind of taxation need not be insisted on. Perhaps some capitation taxes or a rude form of the property tax can claim a higher antiquity, but in ancient, mediaeval, and modern times, in backward and in progressive societies, we meet with something in the shape of taxation on land as one of the primary agents of production. The economic nature of the impost and the particular methods adopted vary: the existence of some form of public charges on land is almost universal, and shows no sign of decrease. Greater financial knowledge and more efficient regulations produce important changes. Indeed, it is this development that chiefly needs our attention. From the first feeble attempts up to the elaborate processes of modern administration, we can trace progress through a series of stages which illustrate the historical movement.

§ 2. Regarding land itself as the 'object' to be taxed the most obvious 'unit' in a new community would be that of a given area. Assume that none but very fertile land is cultivated and that only in a simple manner, and the tax by area will be also the just one. Each unit is of about the same value and employs about the same amount of capital and labour. The early taxes on *Jugera* in Rome and on 'hides' in England, were probably at first based on this system, though they soon departed from it, and at present a few of the English dependencies retain it[1]. As soon as differences in quality of land and in mode of cultivation become noticeable, the method ceases to be fair.

Another form of land tax, that in proportion to the produce, is of greater antiquity. Eastern Sovereigns received their revenue usually in this manner. One-fourth, 'as in India,' one-fifth, 'as in Egypt,' or one-tenth of the yield was claimed by the monarch. This 'tithe system,' as it may be called, arose out of the ruler's part-proprietorship of the soil. The proportional tax was closely analogous to a *métayer* rent. It was partly adjusted to the productiveness of the land and did not press so heavily on the poor soils as the area tax. Under a competitive system its immediate burden would fall on the consumers of agricultural products through the rise of price, though the ultimate effect would be to check cultivation, and therefore to lower rent. As the system has been generally applied to societies in the customary stage the pressure came on the cultivator, who is at once the producer and the chief consumer of those commodities.

These primitive methods are improved, either by arranging land in classes according to its fertility and applying a different rate to each class, or by altering the proportion of produce taken according to the method of cultivation. As soon as the elements of fertility and proximity to market begin to tell, it is evident that a uniform rate falls with undue severity on the poor and distant lands, either hindering their cultivation or raising the value of all produce. Consequently we meet efforts at differentiation in various countries. Under the Roman Empire land in

[1] Dowell, i. 8, for the 'hide.' For the *Jugerum*, Mommsen, *Hist. Rom.* i. 95. St. Vincent and British Guiana have the uniform tax, Parl. Papers (1891), 181, *Taxation of Land*.

some provinces was divided into that of first, second, third, or other fertility, and the rate was adjusted accordingly; in others one-fifth or one-seventh of the yield was taken [1]. In later times the Duchy of Mecklenburg had its land graded into three classes, with a different rate on each, and some of the Indian assessments have a like idea as their base [2]. These modifications show some consciousness that the real value of the agent, land is not to be measured either by its surface area or its gross produce. They are, however, but imperfect attempts at reaching the true aim of a land tax, the value embodied in the object. A tithe or other proportional produce tax does not allow for the expenses of production: as equal amounts of produce are often due to very different quantities of outlay, it discourages the employment of capital and is practically inconvenient in the form of assessment [3]. A classification of soils gives some, but insufficient recognition to the influence of natural fertility. Far more is required. The effort to get at the true value of the 'object' is attained in respect to the land tax when it is levied on the net 'yield.' The capital of the cultivator and the profits due to it have to be estimated in order to get the income derived from the soil itself. Political equity and financial expediency have both contributed to this result; the fairest and most productive land tax is, on the whole, that which takes the net return as its standard. Fiscal practice tended in this direction. The financial reform of Diocletian seems to have adopted a unit of value, not of area (*Jugum*), as the base for taxation of land. The English 'hide' came to be regarded as the 'carucate' of variable area but constant value [4].

[1] Clamageran, i. 16.

[2] 'Land (in Ohio) was divided into three classes, according to quality, and there were three rates of taxation per 100 acres; one for land of the first quality, another for land of the second quality, and still another for land of the third quality,' Ely, *Taxation*, 134.

[3] Restraints must be placed on the sale of crops until they are inspected by the tax-collector and his share settled.

[4] Wagner, iii. 26; Clamageran, i. 19. Seebohm, *English Village Community*, 290 sq. For England, Seebohm, 40; Dowell, iii. 67.

The mediaeval land taxes are so much mixed up with rent and the incidents of tenure that little stress can be placed on their form: they are often parts of the older property tax, and only disentangled from it by degrees. Early English taxation 'reached the landowner through his cattle, farming stock and corn and other produce of lands [1],' and the later subsidies had a rate on land as one of their component parts. In France the *Taille* was developed from the feudal dues and became permanent in 1445. But wherever the system of taxing land had to be applied, the idea of taking its value as the real object of taxation came to the front, though the difficulties in carrying it out caused the frequent adoption of the 'apportioned' tax, as in the case of the *Taille*, both the English 'tenths and fifteenths,' and the subsidies, as, too, the German and Italian land taxes [2]. The defects of these systems, with their exemptions and inequalities, made a reform essential.

§ 3. It is far easier to point out the conditions of theoretic justice than to overcome the obstacles to arriving at the true net yield. The land tax system requires as its basis a valuation, and in the attempt to furnish this requisite various methods have been tried. Perhaps the simplest is that which follows the indications of the market, and uses as its guide the rent at which land is let. There is an obvious advantage in keeping close to the facts, but there is also great difficulty in ascertaining them correctly and following their successive changes. Adam Smith approved of the use of registers of leases, which he would make compulsory, and by their aid assess the land of occupying owners [3]. The selling value is another possible criterion; it is evidently related to rent as principal to interest, and for short periods the proportion is steady. A tax directly based on the sale value of land is, however, a tax on property rather than income.

The difficulties in ascertaining the actual rents, and in

[1] Dowell, i. 59.

[2] Vignes, i. 11; Dowell, i. 88, 154.

[3] *Wealth of Nations*, 349–50.

some countries the large proportion of occupying owners have popularized the system of determining the value of land for taxation by official assessment based on survey and valuation. This method is evidently the older. The Roman provincial land tax had a survey as its foundation, followed by valuation [1]. Domesday Book is a less perfect example of the same kind in England, and in one form or another valuations were common enough in the Middle Ages, but were in general used only for the ruder forms of land taxation, and dealt with the gross produce from the soil or its supposed capital value.

Refinements in fiscal methods require a corresponding elaboration in the valuation or, to use the serviceable French term, the *cadastre* [2] on which they depend. Most of the controversies about the land tax turn on the method of cadastration and the expediency of its revision at stated periods. For the completion of a *cadastre* a series of processes is needed: there must be the measurement of the surface and its delineation by maps, with the boundaries of properties marked, and the ownership specified. To this technical work the economic task of valuation succeeds. Estimates of produce and prices and of the cost of cultivation form the *data* on which the 'net annual value' is arrived at. Each of these steps involves much labour, and is liable to error, more particularly in the economic part of the work. Produce must depend on the method and skill employed in cultivation, prices on many different conditions, and both, especially the latter, are fluctuating. Besides, to be really useful, a fiscal survey must deal with minute portions of the soil; each distinct piece (or *parcelle*) should be valued and revalued after an interval. Such an inquiry takes a long period to accomplish for any country, and by the time it is completed the results for the districts first treated have become antiquated [3]. However perfect

[1] Wagner, iii. 25–6. [2] Said to be derived from '*capistratum*.'

[3] 'The survey and valuation of Bohemia is said to have been the work of more than a hundred years,' *Wealth of Nations*, 351. The French *Cadastre*,

when first started, a valuation must soon fail to represent the actual position of the land it deals with. The opening of new lines of communication, the adoption of a different style of farming, and the growth of towns will completely alter the old results [1]. The imperfections of the *cadastre* are grave enough from a theoretical point of view, but they also entail much hardship and injustice. Some persons and some districts are unduly favoured, leaving to others to make up the amount that they have escaped paying. For example in France (where the land tax is apportioned) some proprietors are taxed four times as heavily as others. The differences in Italian taxation were still greater, owing to the use of different cadastral bases for different districts [2]. Between the difficulties that adherence to an old valuation causes and those due to the expense and confusion of incessant renewals of the *cadastre*, it appears that the safer course is to keep the original valuations checked by the actual letting values of land. Apart from the expense of continual revaluation, it is also true that the 'net annual value' or the 'net income' of official estimations is in a sense hypothetical, as it depends on the accuracy of the assumptions made for the purpose. There is, however, the qualifying fact that a well-executed *cadastre* is of use for other purposes. A careful survey is essential for facilitating the transfer of land, so that it is merely the economic part that could in any case be dispensed with. There seems to be no great obstacle to a gradual revision of the general valuation supplemented by local valuations strictly on the letting value. In this way the former would

begun in 1807, was not completed till 1850. In Madras we hear that 'in 1855 the work of survey and re-settlement was begun. This work will be accomplished in or about 1895, but certain districts of the Presidency will then have seen this very re-settlement expire,' Goodrich, *Economic Journal*, i. 451.

[1] Three valuations of Lancashire made in 1790, 1840, and 1890 respectively would have few common or even proportional results.

[2] Leroy Beaulieu, i. 343. For Italy, Alessio, i. 224–5; Fournier de Flaix, *Traité* 498. According to the former land was taxed in Lombardy at 25 per cent., in Liguria at 7 per cent.; the latter gives 79 per cent. for Modena and 17 per cent. for Sicily.

be a slowly changing norm, while the latter would recognise the actual movements of land value.

§ 4. But whatever may be the hindrances in the way of a perfectly adjusted land tax, there is no doubt that most financial systems use it as a substantial resource. The English land tax, so-called, has really been converted into a rent charge[1]; but Schedule A of the income tax comprises land and houses, the former in 1888–9 being £58,755,134 in value, yielding at the rate of *6d.* less than £1,500,000. To this sum has to be added the portion of local rates that fall on land. Using the proportion of land to houses under Sehedule A as a guide to the division of rates between the two classes we would get slightly under 30 per cent. for the share of land. As the rates may be taken at something under £28,000,000 this method would give £8,500,000 as the local charge on land for England and Wales[2]. Scotland and Ireland show a larger proportion; 50 per cent. would in their case be the share of land, and allowing for the other elements mixed up with rates in the accounts for those countries, we may say that of the total £6,500,000 under £3,000,000 would fall on land. The extent to which the taxation of houses falls on ground rent is an insoluble problem, at least for statistical purposes, but omitting it for the present, we get a total taxation of £13,000,000 on land for the United Kingdom. How far this represents a charge on pure land value, as distinct from that on investments of capital is questionable. We need not in any case hesitate to ascribe the greater part to the

[1] Bk. ii. ch. 4. § 5.

[2] Schedule A—

	Land.	*Houses.*	*Land.*	*Houses.*
1887–8	61,253,522	134,739,670	31 per cent.	69 per cent.
1888–9	58,755,134	136,922,904	29½ per cent.	70½ per cent.

Local Rates for 1887–8—

England and Wales	27,804,298
Scotland	3,050,385
Ireland	3,468,149.

In the two latter countries the returns from gas and waterworks are included in the rates.

value of the land, not to the improvements. When we add to the above the tithes and tithe rent charges, so far as they are devoted to ecclesiastical or other public purposes, the total reaches £15,000,000. Allowing for considerable under valuation in the figures of Schedule A, it is nevertheless beyond doubt that land contributes very largely to the public requirements.

At the same time we must remember that a great deal of this burden is of long standing; the income tax has been for almost fifty years in continuous operation, and in the early part of the century the poor rate was excessive. There is no evidence of new and oppressive charges being imposed. The growth of local taxation, as Mr. Goschen has shown [1], has chiefly affected the towns, while until recently the rent of land was rising.

§ 5. On passing to France we meet with a very different system of land taxation. The old *Taille*, whose defects were universally recognised, was supplemented in 1710 by the *Dixième*, and from 1748 a *Vingtième* was levied. These 'tenths' and 'twentieths' were rather income than pure land taxes, but were abolished at the Revolution along with the *Taille*, and the modern system was inaugurated.

The decree of December, 1790, established the *Impôt foncier* which was to be apportioned on all landed property in proportion to its net revenue. This phrase is evidently due to physiocratic influence, and was explained to mean what remained over after all expenses were deducted from the gross produce. The tax was to be a fixed sum apportioned among the contributories, and to be payable in money. It was not to exceed one-sixth of the net revenue, and on the loose estimate that 240,000,000 francs would be one-sixth, the contribution was fixed at that amount with an additional 60,000,000 francs for local taxation. The disturbances of the Revolutionary period hindered the collection of this impost, and the unequal pressure owing to the absence of proper valuations was

[1] *Local Taxation*, 17, 50.

the ground of successive reductions, by which the total amount, from being 240,000,000 francs in 1790–6, fell to 150,000,000 in 1821. In 1835 the increased value of house property, which is included by the law of 1790, was taken into account. The additional *centimes*, really an increase of the tax, were given up in 1850, and by 1880 the total amount was almost 174,000,000 francs (£7,000,000). The extra *centimes* for the departments and *communes* were very nearly trebled in amount since 1820; in 1880 they were 94,000,000 francs and 82,000,000 francs respectively[1] The loud complaints of the agriculturists as to the inequalities and unjust pressure of the *Impôt foncier* have been the cause of the late reform by which the house tax is distinctly separated from the land tax, and the latter, which was 118,000,000 francs, reduced to 102,000,000 francs. The result has been that by the budget estimate of 1890, even with an extra charge of 8 per cent. on the original general tax, the total taxation on land stands at 255,000,000 francs or less than £10,400,000. The increase of house property and buildings has supplied a new object for the heavier taxation as in the case of England. The land tax remains one of apportionment, while the house tax, or more strictly that on land with buildings (*Propriété bâtie*), has become rated, and is fixed for the present at 3·20 per cent. The next step in reform will probably be the abandonment of the apportioning of the land tax in favour of the more suitable rated system[2].

[1] More precise figures are—

	1820 *Francs.*	1840 *Francs.*	1860 *Francs.*	1880 *Francs.*
Principal Amount .	168,225,220	155,669,805	163,837,194	173,827,511
Additional centimes for general purposes.	42,899,677	33,936,017		
Ditto for departments.	36,568,634	47,629,611	70,238,036	94,077,070
Ditto for *communes*	28,518,003	24,820,985	45,683,257	81,904,095
Ditto for relief, &c.	3,768,747	3,601,486	4,476,168	5,350,874
Total	279,980,281	265,657,907	284,234,655	355,159,550

[2] For the French Land Tax, Stourm, i. 124–220; Vignes, i. 25–39. *Dict. des Finances* s.v. '*Foncière.*'

§ 6. The Italian land tax is a development from the taxes of the several Italian States. As the simplest course, 110,000,000 lire was the amount fixed for apportionment among the different divisions. Measures of reform have been since attempted. The tax on buildings was separated in 1865 and made a rated tax, and redistributions of the total charge among the provinces were carried out. The defective scheme of the old *cadastres* has led to the enactment of a law prescribing the preparation of a new and uniform one for all Italy. The variations in amount of the land tax have been from 125,000,000 lire to about 96,000,000 lire, i.e., speaking generally, from about £4,000,000 to £5,000,000, but the local taxation has to be added. Thus for the year 1886–7 the provincial tax was 53,000,000 lire, and the communal one 76,000,000 lire which, with 110,000,000 lire, the general land tax for that year, made a total of 240,000,000 lire (£9,200,000); a much higher charge than that of France. In qualification it must, however, be noticed that the whole taxation of Italy is far heavier. The most serious grievance is found in the instances of heavily taxed *communes* where the greater part of the value of land is absorbed in taxation. So far has this been carried that there have been many cases of evictions by the State [1]. Inequality in distribution and excessive weight in amount are the gravest possible defects in any tax. The new valuation, though costly, will remedy the former, but the latter is a question of policy as well as Finance.

The Spanish land tax, which in its present form dates from 1845, includes stock, and is therefore more primitive. Owing to the want of a correct valuation the charges are imperfectly distributed. The proportion fixed for 1890–1 is $15\frac{1}{2}$ per cent. on those places that have given a satisfactory

[1] '*En* 1876, 6,614 *propriétés étaient expropriées par le fisc pour le recouvrement de* 936,774 *francs d'impôt et en* 1877, 6,644 *propriétés pour* 662,722 *francs. Le fisc dévore la petite propriété trop obéré. De* 1873 *à* 1878, 35,074 *petits propriétaires ont perdu leur avoir par l'expropriation forcée,*' Laveleye, *Lettres d'Italie* (1880), 160-1. For the Italian land tax, De Parieu, i. 205–218; Alessio, *Sistema Tributario*, i. 88–232.

declaration of value, for others 17½ per cent. The estimate for 1890–1 is nearly 115,000,000 pesetas (£4,600,000) with over 17,000,000 pesetas (£680,000) for local purposes.

The Portuguese land tax is closely on the lines of the French *Impôt foncier*. It was originally rated, but since 1852 has been apportioned; it is, however, proposed to return to the rated method. The yield is nearly 3,000,000 milreis (about £650,000) after paying assessment expenses.

Belgium has a rated tax based on an elaborate valuation. Up to 1867 the method of apportionment was employed. For national purposes the annual amount is about £500,000 with additional *centimes* for local government of over one-half that sum (£300,000[1]).

Greece, which possessed the tithe system till 1880, has now a rather primitive but yet complicated group of 'land taxes' on labouring animals, on area and certain products, yielding altogether about £500,000.

§ 7. The land taxes are as yet confined to the several States of the German Empire, the imperial revenue being derived mainly from indirect taxation. With numerous differences in detail there is the general system of basing the tax on official valuation. The Prussian land tax, inherited from the 18th century, was reformed in the period 1810–20; a new valuation was arranged, and inequalities in the distribution between the different provinces modified; but the survivals of the older system of privilege prevented complete success in this object. In 1821 its yield was under £1,500,000. These inequalities were dealt with by the legislation of 1861. The house tax was separated, and for the land tax the amount was fixed at 10,000,000 thalers (£1,500,000) from 1865, and a fresh valuation carried out. The new Prussian provinces, acquired in 1866, added 3,200,000 thalers (£480,000) to this fixed sum, giving a

[1] More accurate figures for 1891 are—

For the State, 13,103,000 francs.
For Provinces, 1,926,000 francs.
For Communes, 5,621,000 francs.

total of £2,000,000. The additional local charges are not easily arrived at, but for the year 1880–1 the communal and provincial extra land taxes were equal to those of the State in amount (£2,000,000), giving a total burden on land of £4,000,000, independent of the action of the income tax.

Each of the smaller German States employs some form of land tax. Bavaria shows a less developed form in its reference to gross produce as the basis of calculation. The cadastral surveys are in most cases elaborate, and serve other than fiscal purposes, such as facilitating the transfer of land. The *communes* of the several States also receive contributions through additions to the land tax[1].

Austria has developed a land tax on a similar type. By the reform of 1817 the valuation of the 18th century was to be replaced by a new one completed in 1856. The house tax was separated in 1820. In 1879 a law for revision was passed, and in 1881 the annual amount was fixed at 35,190,000 florins for fifteen years, a new valuation to be then made. The Hungarian land tax was almost the same sum (35,000,000 florins), and the local charges in Austria levied on land were believed to reach the like amount. Thus the burden on land in Austria proper is under £7,000,000.

Taxation of land in the United States is imposed through the general property tax, which, as we shall see, presses with undue weight on real property, but its discussion belongs to a later chapter[2]. Nor need the Indian land revenue be again considered.

§ 8. The foregoing notices of the land taxation of the principal countries bring out its characteristic features. Specially worthy of observation are: first, the considerable amount contributed on the whole, and to both general and local revenues. The absolute amount is highest in England, but everywhere a good percentage of the net annual returns is taken for public use[3]. Another very common

[1] For the German land taxes, Cohn, §§ 303–6; Fournier de Flaix, 393 sq.

[2] Bk. iv. ch. 4. § 3.

[3] Probably lowest in Saxony.

circumstance is the employment of the system of apportionment. A total fixed sum is thus secured, and as each district must pay its part, it has a manifest interest in making all contribute fairly; nevertheless, the method has the great defects of rendering an important part of the tax revenue inelastic, and it is likely to reduce the land tax to a rent charge as happened in the case of England. The 'rated' or percentage system is free from these faults, and is therefore the best suited for modern Finance. A third question intimately connected with the land tax is that of valuation. If the 'rated' system be used, it is necessary in the interests of justice that the basis on which the estimate of value is made should be uniform. Thus e.g. the English valuation of land is believed to be closer to the true value than the Irish one, from which it follows that the income tax in its A schedule is not the same in the two countries. The Italian land tax is a more extreme instance of the same evil. In all countries this inequality must in some degree exist between individuals and smaller districts, but this fact only strengthens the claim for all practicable efforts to secure the removal of proven injustices. Even if it be impossible to alter quickly the particular forms of the tax, there is an advantage in knowing the amount of inequality, which can then be compensated by the adjustment of other taxes.

Finally, the land tax is what has been called a 'real' tax; it deals with the object, land, and takes no note of the position of the proprietor. When properly developed it is proportioned to 'net produce,' and therefore allows for the expenses of working the soil. For the same reason it should not take indebtedness into account. Charges on land are a part of the net return and have no claim to deduction. A variable land tax may therefore press with great severity on encumbered proprietors who have to pay the tax on the interest of their debts. Any attempt to remedy this evil has the necessary result of creating a partial tax on interest of capital, and if unaccompanied by taxation of other forms of capital, would either discourage loans to owners of land or raise the interest on mortgages. The conclusion suggested by these facts is that the land tax had best be absorbed in a general income tax, when part of the burden would, as under existing English arrangements, be paid by the creditors. If, on the other hand, the distinct land tax be retained, two courses are open; either to retain it at a fixed amount when it becomes a rent charge, an undesirable proceeding, or to give it up to local bodies. We have seen that taxes on real property are a good form of local revenue [1], and both in France and the United States this treatment which is in accordance with British practice has been proposed. The actual condition in Germany with its numerous smaller States partly realizes this object [2].

§ 9. The incidence of the land tax is a final question for consideration. In its ruder forms the pressure fell chiefly on the actual cultivators, though the ultimate effect of heavy taxation must have been felt by the proprietors in the check to agricultural improvement and the diminution in their dues. Under the competitive system, a proportional tax on produce tends to raise prices and therefore comes on the consumer, but the inevitable reaction on rent is found here also. As soon as net return is taken as the standard for taxation, rent is the element affected. A land tax, therefore, in its developed form, may not inaccurately be regarded as a tax on rent, and the general principles of incidence applied to it. In actual working, however, various complications arise. The action of competition is not always found in full force, and so far as any portion of the pure economic rent is held by the immediate payer—tenant or other—he has to submit to the burden [3].

[1] Bk. iii. ch. 6. § 4.

[2] The proposal has been made by M. Léon Say in the recent debates on the *Impôt Foncier*, and by Professor Ely, *Taxation*, 251–3, who would exempt land from even state taxation.

[3] 'As a matter of fact it appears that a great portion of the farms in England are not rack-rented. If so, it is clear that any increase in local burdens must

A land tax may also affect the interests of labour. If investment of capital in agriculture is checked, and if the rate of wages is easily affected by the action of employers (as has been often the case) taxation on the cultivator may be shifted, not to the landlord by lowering rent, but to the labourer by lowering wages, or in a time of rising prices by preventing their proportional increase in money [1]. Again, the fact that the land which is the object of taxation often owes its value to the capital sunk in it, makes the burden fall on the yield of fixed capital, but we need not again consider this point [2].

A more difficult and disputable point arises in connexion with the incidence of a long continued land tax. Here it is said that the tax is really a deduction from property. As land is sought for its revenue, what lowers its revenue lowers its selling price, and therefore a land tax falls altogether on the possessor *at the time of its imposition.* Subsequent acquirers take the land subject to the burden and pay a lower price in consequence. This process of 'amortization,' as it has been called, makes the subsequent removal of the tax undesirable : the persons who have lost by its establishment are not the same as those who gain by its remission. A purchaser has got land cheaper and gains a further advantage by escaping the tax ; in fact he is allowed for it twice over, once at the time of purchase and again at that of remission.

The element of truth in this theory, which has received much favour, appears to be the following : (1) as previously pointed out [3], when a land tax becomes definitely fixed, so that it can be foreseen, or even capitalized and redeemed, there is no inaccuracy in speaking of it as a charge on land

fall on the margin between the actual rent and the rack-rent, and so far diminish the advantage derived by the farmer from his actual rent being below a rack-rent, and till that margin were exhausted it would naturally be useless for him to apply to his landlord to readjust his rent,' Goschen, *Local Taxation*, 165.

[1] See Leslie, *Essays*, 395–7, for an illustration.

[2] See Bk. iii. ch. 5. § 6.

[3] Bk. ii. ch. 4. § 5.

which lowers its selling price; it is just the same as a mortgage, and is taken into account by purchasers. (2) A stable tax of any kind has some of the advantages to which Canard gives such exaggerated importance. Its pressure is more regular, and therefore less felt. An invariable land tax, undoubtedly, has this in its favour. On the other hand, there is no reason for regarding the modern land taxes as perfectly stable and fixed. In transactions with respect to land there are not merely the existing, but the prospective burdens to be taken into account. To assume, e. g. that the French '*centimes additionnels*' or the English local rates have been 'amortized' would be an obvious error. We cannot foresee the future movement of taxation in respect to land, and we cannot expect that the present systems will always continue. Another important consideration is the relation of land taxation to the other forms. If it should happen to be unduly heavy there would be a tendency to depress the value of the land so taxed; just as if it were too light its effect would be the opposite, but this is characteristic of all taxation. Tea, sugar, or any other commodity will have its value for the time being affected by the creation or remission of a special tax on it. But where, as we may expect, there is a due proportion of taxation to the several forms of income, the investor in land will only receive the same proportional return as he would obtain in other directions. An alteration in the land tax ought to have as its motive the effort to secure a more equal distribution of burdens, and to this there can be no valid objection. At the same time, where a tax has been recognised as at once special and definitely fixed, it seems to pass out of the ordinary category of taxes and into that of charges, a transformation only possible in the case of durable productive wealth, and most prominent in respect to land.

CHAPTER II.

Taxes on Capital and Business.

§ 1. For fiscal purposes durable capital has the closest resemblance to land—the two are indeed sometimes inextricably mixed up together—and of its different forms, houses and buildings generally are the most important from the same point of view. Sometimes as an integral part of the land tax, but more often with a distinct position, we find the charge on houses used both for local and general purposes. The reasons for its employment are to be found, partly in its connexion with land, partly in the universality of the use of houses, which extends taxation to all classes, partly in the convenience and readiness of assessment, and finally in the belief that the value of a person's house was a satisfactory test of his income. These considerations have very different weight at different periods. In early times the one object was to secure receipts, and for this purpose houses, or something connected with them, were convenient objects of imposition.

As in the case of land, the precise form adopted varied; at first houses were taxed simply as part of the land on which they stood, being treated as a particular kind of improvement. The hearth or chimney tax was in use in the feudal period, under the name *foaticum*. The substitution of windows for chimneys made another variety, to be succeeded by taxation according to the class of house, or proportioned to the letting value. The problems and course of development of the land tax reappear with modifications in the case of the house tax.

§ 2. England shows this development. The hearth tax, established in 1662, was so unpopular that it was abolished in 1688, but soon replaced by the window tax, under which a scale of payment was fixed—ten windows and under, 1*s.*, increasing at a higher rate for a larger number. With several changes in the rates, and with additional stringent provisions to check evasion, the tax continued all through the 18th century. In 1815 its yield was about £2,000,000. Sounder ideas of taxation led to its repeal in 1851. Adam Smith's suggestion that inhabited houses should be taxed on their annual value was adopted in 1778, in addition to the existing window tax. Houses under £5 value were to be free; those between £5 and £50 to pay 6*d.* in the pound ($2\frac{1}{2}$ per cent.); those over £50, 1*s.* (5 per cent.). Several increases of the tax were made for war purposes, till in 1808 the rate on houses of £40 and over was 2*s.* 10*d.*, or nearly 15 per cent. By a curious selection the house duty was repealed in 1834 instead of the window tax, but on the repeal of the latter in 1851 it was reimposed. Houses under £20 were exempted, and business premises paid only two-thirds of the rate on ordinary houses, i. e. 6*d.* and 9*d.* per pound respectively. The last change has been made in 1890 when Mr. Goschen restored the old system of grading. Houses between £20 and £40 pay only 4*d.*, and those between £40 and £60, 6*d.*, the corresponding rate on business premises being 2*d.* and 4*d.* The yield of the tax was by these changes reduced from £2,000,000 to £1,450,000[1].

To arrive at the total pressure of taxation on buildings we must add, (1) the income tax in schedule A, amounting at 6*d.* to about £3,500,000, and (2) the great mass of local rates. Taking the figures in the last chapter, if the balance of rates can be assigned to buildings, we would get

[1] On the English house and window taxes, *Wealth of Nations*, 355-357; Dowell, iii. 165-192.

the enormous sum of £23,000,000 as their local taxation[1]. The occupier, the ground landlord, and in the case of business establishments, the consumers of the commodities, are all participants in the burden, but we must again note that a great deal of this expenditure is economically reproductive, so that the taxes are paid out of a fund created by their employment.

§ 3. France has not reached the same stage of development as England in regard to this form of taxation. The separation of the land and house taxes has only just been accomplished, and the door and window tax still exists, in addition to the *Mobilier*, or tax on letting value. The latter, suggested under the monarchy as a substitute for the personal *Taille*, was in its origin, as established by the Constituent Assembly in 1791, a tax on income based on the presumption that house rent was a measure of its amount, but owing to the belief that income increased more rapidly than the cost of housing, the tax was on a progressive scale so calculated as to be proportional to income, and some qualifications were made by using other elements. In 1798 these refinements were abolished, and the *Mobilier* became a house tax. The tax (which is combined with the personal tax, to be discussed in the next chapter) is apportioned, and amounts to about £3,000,000, of which at least three-fourths comes from the house tax part[2]. The contributions to local taxation through the additional *centimes* are of very nearly the same amount.

The door and window tax was established under the

[1] Bk. iv. ch. 1. § 4.

[2] The yield of the *Personnelle mobilière* has been as follows—

FRANCS (000's omitted).

	Principal.	*Additional Centimes.*
1830	27,161	14,100
1870	46,004	44,337
1880	52,161	64,382
1885	57,846	74,240
1890	75,055	
1891	81,640	

Directory in 1798. At first a rated tax, it was apportioned in 1802, and with the exception of 1831–2, it has so continued, with a steady increase in amount. From a little over £500,000 in 1830 it rose to nearly £1,600,000 in 1885, while the additional *centimes* that were only £100,000 at the former date, had come to equal the principal at the latter. The total may therefore be regarded as about £3,000,000, obtained by an inconvenient and vexatious method [1]. To the foregoing the building tax, now separated from the pure land tax, adds a sum of £2,500,000 for the principal, with additions coming very close to £3,000,000 (£2,600,000 of that amount being for the *communes* and departments in about equal proportion). As the tax is now a rated one the increase in value of house property, even if the present rate of 3·20 per cent. is maintained, will add to the yield. The total burden on houses is therefore, speaking broadly, between £13,000,000 and £14,000,000 [2].

Italy had, as we saw, established a distinct house tax in 1865. The amount obtained by it in 1866 was £1,300,000; by 1886 it had more than doubled, being nearly £2,650,000 Moreover the local charges, superimposed on the principal,

[1] The figures for the 'door and window' tax are—

Francs (000's omitted).

	Principal.	*Additional.*
1830	12,812	2,711
1870	33,911	23,750
1880	36,588	33,594
1885	39,703	38,320

[2] The estimate for 1890 for *Propriétés bâties* was—

Francs (000's omitted).

Principal	63,450
Additional for education . . .	5,076
For departments	32,723
For communes	32,698
Extras	3,557
Total	137,504

Taking this with the preceding notes we reach the result in the text. Consul Egerton states that 'the total tax on land and houses in France will be found to amount this year (1890) to about £15,000,000 independently of the personal and '*mobilière*' tax of £5,500,000 and of the door and window tax of over £3,000,000,' *Reports as to the Taxation of Land and Buildings* (C. 6209), 16.

came to almost the same amount. For the year 1888–9 the total for state and local taxation was close on £5,500,000, equally divided between the two branches. Though the absolute amount is much less, the pressure is probably greater than in England or France[1].

Belgium, Spain and Portugal do not separate their land and house taxes; it is therefore impossible to deal with them under this head.

The Prussian house tax, made distinct in 1861, and separately collected since 1865, is proportioned to value—2 per cent. (or 4 per cent. in the case of houses let to tenants). It has grown with the increase of wealth from £850,000 in 1878 to over £1,500,000 in 1889–90. The local charges may be less than half that amount, giving a total of about £2,200,000[2].

In most of the smaller German States the house tax is a part of the land tax. Bavaria, as in the case of land, applies the 'area' and 'productive power' principle to the taxation of houses.

The Austrian house tax, in existence since 1820, yielded for 1889 about £3,000,000, and that for Hungary, about £1,000,000, not including the local charges[3].

§ 4. From the facts (unfortunately imperfect) just given, we can see that the course of development in respect to the taxation of buildings is towards taking their value, or, if possible, their annual yield, as the basis of assessment, and at the same time towards separating them from land. The French door and window tax may, therefore, be at once condemned as a pernicious survival of an antiquated method: its abolition, or rather absorption in the *mobilier*, is merely a question of time.

The problem of assessment has usually been dealt with in the way approved by Adam Smith, but with a large allowance for expenses and repairs, varying in the different coun-

[1] For the Italian house tax, Alessio, i. 233–266.

[2] Cohn, § 306; *Reports on Taxation* (C. 6209), 31.

[3] I. e. taking the florins at 2*s*., the figures are—Austria, 31,058,000 florins; Hungary, 10,000,000 florins.

tries. On the whole, it is easier to ascertain the letting value of houses than of land, and there is besides the element of cost of construction to be used as a corrective. Some difficulties, however, certainly exist. It is not easy to deal with deterioration and the resulting loss of value, more particularly in respect to buildings employed in production. Revaluation at short intervals is the only suitable way, but it is both troublesome and expensive. The opposite case, i. e. where improvements have been made, is also complicated. The increased value ought certainly to be taxed, but the effect in checking improvements is serious. The usual course of allowing a period to elapse before rating new constructions is the best practical solution.

The taxation of expensive private dwellings, such as noblemen's mansions, has attracted more attention than its intrinsic importance warrants. In England such houses have been rated at a nominal figure on account of the supposed expense of maintaining them, which is thought to reduce their letting value. On the other hand, the cost of construction has been proposed as the basis for valuation, or again, that of reconstruction. Neither is, however, adequate. Letting value fails where the objects are not really and in fact let to tenants. Cost would give much too high a value in some cases, as expenditure is not always represented by additional value. The true test in such cases lies in the utility of the house and surroundings, which selling or market letting value would measure, but which, in its absence, must be estimated, either by reference to similar dwellings let elsewhere [1], or by the probable expenditure of the possessor on his house accommodation. The modern tendency to apply commercial principles, even to aristocratic residences and estates, will afford a means of readily gauging value in these instances.

§ 5. Far more important is the very difficult question of the incidence of house and building taxes. So many

[1] The plan adopted in the recent valuation of buildings in France, *Finanz Archiv*, viii. 193-4.

elements are combined that the assignment to each of its separate share is a task of some complication. The value of the ground on which the buildings stand is determined by the law of rent, and a tax that falls on it would, therefore, appear to be untransferable. A house itself is a particular kind of commodity, and its share of taxation may be supposed to come under the laws that determine the incidence of taxes on commodities. Accordingly, Adam Smith, Ricardo, and Mill have agreed in asserting that taxes on ground rent fall on the landlord, while those on building rent fall on the occupier. The builder must, they thought, get his fair profit. The solution is not quite so simple. First, as to ground rent, wherever there is an alternative use for land, it is plain that a tax on it, if employed for building, is strictly limited by that other use: thus until the rent of land for building exceeds that of agricultural land by the amount of the tax, no landlord will let it for that purpose. The tax on this minimum ground rent would be passed on to the builder; but when that point is reached the ground landlord has a differential gain, and cannot escape it by withdrawing his land as he would thereby lose still more. We can, therefore, accept the doctrine of the non-shifting of a tax on ground rent as generally true. The other part of the doctrine requires more consideration. The rent of houses depends proximately on the conditions of supply and demand; taxation levied from the occupier is equivalent to so much additional rent, what in the case of an ordinary commodity would be a rise of price. The consequent check to demand tends to take off part of this increase, and therefore the initial effect is to throw some of the tax on the house owner. As houses are a very durable commodity, the adjustment of supply to the altered demand may take a long time to accomplish. It will largely depend on the economic position of the locality; if it is progressing, the tax will check building until rent rises to its old level; but if it happens to be stationary or declining the burden remains on the house owners, who are the possessors of a particular kind of fixed capital. Again, even in an advancing locality the shifting may be on the ground rent. The increase of house rent that checks building thereby reduces the demand for building ground, and consequently lowers its value. It is highly probable that some at least of the burden will be so distributed.

In the case of buildings used for production or business there may be a further shifting. The taxes levied on factories and shops form a part of the expenses of the manufacturer or trader and tend to raise the prices of the commodities supplied by him; but where the taxation is uniformly distributed, a general rise of prices from this cause being impossible, the tax would not be transferred. As this uniformity is never really found there will be a disturbance of values through taxation, with an ultimate incidence on interest and employers' gains. The taxation of houses in all countries varies according to locality, and the modern improvements in transport and business organization have brought retail prices nearer to a general level. The result is that the shifting of building and house taxes to consumers of commodities is hardly possible, prices being limited by outside competition, and it must therefore be on the owners of the ground, in so far as it does not rest on the house owners, traders and manufacturers in question. Still the levelling force of competition is not universal, and shifting is not always possible, and it may be that in the influence of taxation we have at least a partial explanation of two important economic facts: (1) the curious local diversities of prices and (2) the failure of various local industries[1]. The creation of various interests makes the matter more complex. Between the ultimate owner of the soil and the immediate occupier there are often, as already noticed,

[1] Fawcett, *Political Economy* (5th ed.), 626, who gives the Thames shipbuilding trade as an instance. His argument as to the incidence of rates on the consumer is based on too rigid an interpretation of the doctrine of equality of profits.

several intermediate interests, and the house and building taxes may be placed on them in different degrees. The tenant free to leave can, if the economic conditions favour, throw back his taxes, but the leaseholder cannot. For this reason legislative provisions are urgently required to secure a due division of burdens that the process of shifting cannot fairly distribute, and the problem of devising a fair house tax is made more difficult. The policy of confining general taxation of land and houses to their contribution in common with other kinds of revenue to an income tax appears to be the soundest. Local Finance is thereby supplied with a special kind of taxes and the question of unequal valuation between localities is reduced in importance.

§ 6. The taxation of land and buildings covers most fixed capital. Many doubtful points may arise as to the treatment of machines and fittings, but they usually come in connexion with the taxation either of mines (a form of land) or of factory buildings, and are taken as part of a general property or income tax, or come in as indications to be used in the taxation of business. Proposals to tax fixed capital as such have been made, but they have not as yet been reduced to practice. Apart from the taxation of land and buildings and the taxes on particular commodities we have next to examine the taxation of floating capital.

The question of a tax on interest presents itself in practical Finance chiefly as to dividends and mortgages. They represent the great mass of wealth that is invested by its owners for gain without their direct supervision. Floating capital as such is so closely combined with other elements and is so hard to trace, that its separate taxation is scarcely ever presented. Unless this large part of wealth is reached in some way there is an undue encouragement given to it. Investments in land and industrial enterprises, are checked and the distribution of taxation is so far unfair. These reasons point towards the adoption of the general income tax, which will necessarily include the revenue from floating capital.

The separate taxation of floating capital for general or local purposes in a direct form is not found in England, but Schedule C (and part of D) of the income tax discharges this function, and loans in the form of mortgages come under Schedule A. The yield of Schedule C for 1889 came to about £1,100,000. The taxes on acts are of service as they compel these forms of wealth, so difficult to be reached by direct means, to contribute to the revenue.

France has employed a substitute for this part of the income tax in the *Impôt sur les valeurs mobilières*, introduced in 1872, by which 3 per cent. was imposed on the shares of companies either home or foreign; the yield, which in 1873 was £1,250,000, increased by 1880 to nearly £1,600,000; by 1890 to over £2,000,000. The rate has been raised to 4 per cent. for 1891, and the estimate for that year is £2,600,000 or more than double the receipts of 1873.

Italy, like England, reaches interest by means of a general income tax, and such is the usual method. In fact, one of the strong reasons for its introduction is precisely the desire to make capital contribute its due share. In some of the South German States a special capital tax has been developed. Bavaria has a capital tax besides its income tax, and both Würtemberg and Baden have somewhat similar imposts.

The great objection to a separate tax on the yield of capital is the extreme difficulty of making it effective. The necessary result of the ease with which it is escaped is injustice in its distribution. The French tax on *valeurs mobilières* falls on the shares of companies; it is a corporation tax and tends to discourage those associations. Investments abroad are much more easily kept out of the tax collector's ken, and thus the progress of home investments is checked. On the whole the reasonable conclusion is that the distinct tax on interest has no place alongside of the land, building, and business taxes that form so large a part of the fiscal receipts.

Its incidence, which in the case of a complete and comprehensive tax on interest is on the holders, (unless in so far as the supply of capital is checked by the lower returns), is affected by the partial form that it usually takes. A tax on e.g. mortgages lowers the profitableness of that particular kind of lending, and will therefore force the mortgagors to pay at a higher rate under the penalty of getting a less amount of accommodation. Then the incidence will probably be partly on landowners requiring loans, partly on capitalists in general, as some of the capital that would have gone to land will seek other outlets and lower the rate in them. The same reasoning applies to other similar cases, taxation of corporations or any special use of capital. The question, already noticed in connexion with land, of the wiping out of the tax by the sacrifice of the capital of the original holders presents itself here. Stocks or shares subject to a tax must sell for less than if they were free from it, and it may be thought that the transactions of the Stock Exchange speedily discount these public charges and estimate the taxed shares on their *net* revenue. In dealing with this case two considerations deserve notice, (1) the ever present possibility of the repeal or alteration of the tax, and (2) the extent to which other primary forms of revenue are burdened with like charges. If revenue from land, buildings, capital, and personal exertions is all subject to the same charge there can be no depression of their relative values. The so-called 'throwing off' (*Abwälzung*) of taxation means simply that taxation as a whole is a deduction from the resources of the country where it is imposed.

§ 7. The scantiness of direct and special taxation on loan floating capital is further accounted for by the greater prominence of industry as an object for the financier. Pure interest is not so readily taxed as profits ; the older English writers have in fact preferred not to separate this compound element of income. Taxation of profits takes the joint yield of capital and business ability for its object, a course justified by the close connexion that exists in reality. The financier must deal with external characteristics, and as rent has to be taxed through land, so have earnings to be selected in preference to the more refined elements of interest and employers' gains. The actual taxes on industrial receipts may indeed include the several factors of rent, interest, wages, and employers' gain, since both land and labour may contribute to the creation of what is popularly and legally described as 'profit.'

The original form of this taxation is found in the licenses for trade so common in earlier times. Traders who at first were supposed to pay the import and export duties imposed on their commodities were besides subjected to duties for pursuing their particular avocation. The whole mediaeval system of incorporations and guilds, which survived till the French Revolution, placed certain burdens on those engaged in industry, and the modern 'tax on business' may regard this as its precursor. Within the present century there has been a marked development of this form of taxation, influenced very much by the French system to be presently described.

Some very difficult questions are raised by the taxation of profits, questions that it is to be feared can in practice admit of only a partial solution. Foremost of these is the ascertainment of profits. Valuation of land and of buildings is a complicated and expensive process, but it is light compared with the task of measuring the fluctuating gains of industrial production. It would sometimes be impossible for the taxpayer himself to say what were his gains in a given year, but a greater difficulty lies in his unwillingness. The unchecked declaration of the contributor is quite ineffectual, while official assessment involves a considerable amount of arbitrary interference with private affairs. Taxes on industry and profit as distinct from a general Income Tax are usually based on certain legal presumptions. The letting value of the area occupied, the character of the business, the number of persons it employs, the population of the district in which it is carried on, may be used separately or in combination as indices of taxable capacity.

None of these tests can be expected to give an exact result, but they tend to obviate the dangers of fraud on the one hand and inquisition on the other. Productiveness and a tolerable approach to just distribution are the two essentials in taxation: the unfairness that the use of presumptions must more or less cause is perhaps on the whole a less evil than the encouragement to dishonesty that self-assessment gives. Moreover the gains of industrial occupations are now too large a part of the national revenue to be allowed to escape taxation without causing greater injustice than their exemption would remove. Profits hold the place that land revenues formerly occupied.

§ 8. The actual taxation of profits in England apart from the license duties on particular trades and occupations is carried out by Schedule D of the Income Tax. The former element is a small one and is mixed up with various direct taxes on consumption. Thus out of nearly £3,000,000 received for the local authorities in the year 1889–90 on account of licenses, £1,200,000 belonged to taxes levied on consumption, leaving £1,800,000 for industrial taxation, the similar taxes in Ireland and Scotland being about £400,000 net, and as the total return of licenses has not within the last fifteen years varied more than 3 per cent. we may take £2,200,000 as representing the normal contribution from this source, which so far as England and Wales are concerned is a local resource since 1888[1]. Schedule D, which at the present rate of *6d.* gives a yield of £6,000,000, is the main tax on profits, but to it the taxation of farmers' profits under Schedule B should be added, though the latter has some points of connexion with the strict land tax under Schedule A, since the assessment is based on

[1] More exact figures are—

Trade Licenses, £1,797,600;

Consumption and enjoyment ditto, £1,196,819.

Some small licenses on manufactures have been retained by the central government, viz. brewers, distillers, tobacco manufacturers, and medicines. The largest sum obtained by licenses (£3,622,217) was in 1879, the smallest (£3,497,636) in 1880.

the rent[1], and the real incidence of the tax is not clear. The yield from this Schedule is not more than £250,000. We thus get a total taxation of less than £9,000,000.

§ 9. The French system of taxation of profits commenced with the law of March 1791[2]. One of the first measures of the Constituent Assembly had been the abolition of the restraints on industry, and no intention of taxing it otherwise than through the general tax, which the *mobilier* was intended to be, existed. Fiscal necessities forced the establishment of the *Droit de Patente*, which, like the *mobilier*, was estimated on the letting value of the establishment, the tax to be 10 per cent. for rentals under 400 livres, 12½ per cent. for those between 400 and 800, and finally 15 per cent. for those above 800 livres. Abandoned in 1793 it was restored in a different form in 1795. Subsequent changes in 1796–7–8 established the outlines of the present system, which has however been developed by a series of later measures[3]. The tax applies to all occupations and professions not specially exempted. It is divided into a fixed and a proportional duty and, unlike the other direct taxes, it is 'rated,' not 'apportioned.' Of its four classes or 'tables' one (D) is imposed on salaries; the others embrace the various kinds of trades. The so-called 'fixed' duty is really graded. For the first class (Table A) its amount depends on (1) the kind of trade and (2) the population of the *commune* in which it is carried on, e.g. a trader in the first group of Table A in a *commune* with over 100,000 inhabitants pays £12 (300 francs), one in the eighth group only 10*s*. (12 francs). Were they in a *commune* with less than 2000 inhabitants they would pay 28*s*. (35 francs) and 1*s*. 8*d*. (2 francs) respectively, and the latter would be exempt from the proportional tax. In the second

[1] Half the rent in England and Wales and one-third in Ireland and Scotland is taken as the profit of the farmer, who however, if he prefers, may be assessed under Schedule D.

[2] Under the *Ancien Régime* industry was taxed through the personal *Taille* and the *Vingtièmes*.

[3] Most important is the law of 1844, amended in 1853, 1872, and 1880.

class (Table B) special rates are laid down, ranging from £80 to £1, according to business and population of *commune*. The third class (Table C) has a fixed duty for each trade, with additions for each workman employed.

The proportional duty is a certain percentage on the letting value of the trader's residence and establishment, varying from 10 per cent. to 2½ per cent. on the first class, 10 per cent. on the second, and in the third varying from 6·60 per cent. to 2 per cent. imposed at different rates on residences, warehouses, and factories. Thus a pin manufacturer who falls under the third group of Table C pays 18 francs, plus 3·60 francs per workman employed, 5 per cent. on his residence and separate shop, and 2½ per cent. on his factory. A Paris banker (Table B) pays 2000 francs and 10 per cent. on his house and bank[1].

The object of this very complicated system is evidently to escape the arbitrary pressure of officials. External marks supply the materials for assessment, and prevent the honest from suffering through the evasions of other tax payers. There is in addition an advantage given to the more successful producers and traders, as their extra gains are free from taxation. The State assumes that, in a given situation, so much profit will be made, and taxes accordingly; any defect or excess concerns the trader alone.

Certain gaps in the *patente* tax are noticeable, especially that caused by the absence of agriculturists. The farmer is free from this tax; his profits do not contribute to the services of the state. The *impôt foncier* is a tax on rent in the main, and cannot be regarded as counterbalancing the taxation of industrial profits.

In spite of its complication, inequalities, and failure to include agricultural profits, the *Patente* has the two great advantages of being productive, and not very unpopular.

[1] For the *Patente* see Vignes, i. 52–63, ii. 333–380; Leroy Beaulieu, i. 393–414; Wagner, iii. 468–489.

As a contribution to the State it has risen from less than £1,000,000 in 1830 to over £2,000,000 in 1860, and over £4,000,000 in 1885. The additional *centimes* for local purposes have grown from being under £30,000 in 1830 to £900,000 in 1860, and £2,500,000 in 1885. With the small extra items there is thus a total amount of about £6,800,000 obtained from this source[1]. Licenses are also used in the French financial system, but their return, under £500,000 in 1883, was only slightly over it in 1889. To these should be added the duty on mines, which does not amount to £100,000.

§ 10. Italy, as already stated, has followed England in adopting the Income tax. Profits come under Schedule B, which comprises 'mixed revenues' as distinct from those due to capital or personal action solely, and their taxation is very imperfectly carried out. Profits are taxed at $\frac{3}{4}$ only of their amount.

The German states have developed a tax on industry (*Gewerbesteuer*), probably suggested by the French *Patente*. The Prussian tax was established in 1810, and modified after the French war in 1820. Its present arrangement groups contributors into three classes: (1) traders and manufacturers, (2) hotel and inn keepers, and (3) hand-workers who employ assistants. The rate of duty varies according to the population, there being four different scales. A medium rate is fixed for each trade on this basis, and the total amount for the district (arrived at by multiplying the medium rate by the number of contributors), is redistributed by the local authorities. Some industries are, besides, specially charged, while agriculturists and the professional classes are exempt. The influence of the

[1] More accurate figures are—

FRANCS (000's omitted).

	Principal.	*Additional.*	*Total.*
1830	23,047	5,209	28,256
1860	48,508	31,621	80,129
1885	75,102	96,814	171,916.

The additional *centimes* include those for State purposes, which amounted to 27,973,000 francs in 1885.

Patente is clearly traceable, but the tax is much less important. In 1810 it returned only £90,000, by 1864 it had risen to £580,000, and in 1887–8 to £1,000,000, i. e. less than one-sixth of the *Patente*, or of Schedule D[1].

Bavaria, Baden, and Würtemberg all employ the tax on industry, modelled in the main on the French and Prussian system, but there is a decided tendency to prefer the income tax, or, at least, use it in addition.

Austria and Hungary have also the trade tax; in the former it gives about £1,000,000, in the latter about £2,000,000.

§ 11. The principal features of the taxation of profits, as actually carried out, show that two alternative methods are open. Either the taxpayer may be assessed on his (supposed) real net receipts, or certain external indications may be taken as a guide. The former is generally found where profits are taxed through a general income tax. England and Italy supply us with the leading examples. The difficulties in the way of arriving at the true net profits have hindered other countries from completely following this course. The French method has seemed, if less equitable in the abstract, yet in reality fairer. It does not in Mill's phrase 'tax conscience.' Nevertheless there is a cumbrousness and, in part, a want of elasticity about it. The long list of trades coming under the *Patente*, with the great varieties in the permanent and the proportional charges, must add to the labour of administration. Its inequalities must also be great. Neither the population of the district, nor the rent of residence and business premises, can give anything more than a faint presumption of profits. The *Patente* is very far from being a proportional tax on industrial gains. It rather resembles a charge on certain necessaries of the business, such as buildings, labour, or motive power. It accordingly marks a lower stage in the development of taxation. The fair

[1] For the Prussian *Gewerbesteuer*, Cohn, § 307; Wagner in Schönberg, 273; *Taxation of Personal Property* (Misc. No. 2. 1886, C. 4909), 8–10.

assessment of profits may be at present beyond the power of financial administration, but efforts should be made in that direction. It may be suggested that the external marks, which are now regarded as conclusive, should be used as presumptions, whose weight will be affected by other conditions, and it is probably by this method that advance will actually be made.

Another noticeable feature of the continental taxation of industry is its aid to local revenues. The £2,500,000 that the *Patente* gives to the French departments and *communes* is paralleled on a smaller scale in the case of Germany. There the local revenues are recruited partly by additions to the direct taxes, and, with some exceptions, this applies to the taxation of industry[1]. Austria follows the same method, by which a branch of income that is free in England is compelled to contribute to the public revenues of the locality in which it is situated. We have already seen reason to reject the plan of taxing income, or its separate parts, locally, and it appears better to use the license system for the purpose of recruiting local funds. Thus the *Patente* and licenses in France might be so remodelled as to create (1) a general tax on trade incomes, (2) a considerable local receipt from the 'fixed' part of the *Patente*, in combination with a further development of the existing licenses.

§ 12. The incidence of taxes on industry is not quite so definite as writers on Finance often suppose. Pure or economic profit is made up of two distinct elements, and the extent to which the receiver of interest and the earner of employer's gain can shift taxation is not the same. In the actual forms of taxation a proportional tax on profit may cut off more of one element than of the other in different cases. Thus the distribution of the burden between interest and earnings may be unequal, but as regards outsiders, shifting to them can only

[1] Cohn, §§ 461–3; Reitzenstein in Schönberg, 623; Fournier de Flaix, 401 seq.

be effected by the possible check to accumulation of capital. Where, however, taxation is not proportioned to pure profit the effect may be very different. It is not hard to understand that taxation so unequal as the *Patente* may drive out some of the producers, and enable the survivors to shift the charge to consumers. The tax becomes one of the expenses of production. Again, the local inequalities may allow of higher gains in some districts, and cause higher prices in others, in which latter case the consumer suffers. Differences between trades may, and probably will, affect the distribution of industry, and thereby cause a diffused incidence too complicated to trace. The same consequences must follow the use of taxes with different rates within a connected area like Germany. Specially heavy taxation in one State may actually, in some degree, increase the profits of producers elsewhere, by raising the price of the commodity within one district; but it is still more likely to press on the producers subject to it.

On the whole, the taxation of industry has not approached as closely to a tax on pure profit as that on land has to a tax on economic rent. This circumstance is partly due to the greater complication of the matter, but also to the less perfect development of fiscal methods.

CHAPTER III.

PERSONAL AND WAGES TAXES.

§ 1. OLDER than the taxes that we have been engaged in considering, but now of little importance, are the capitation or poll taxes, so familiar to students of mediaeval finance. Their origin is evidently found in the idea that persons, as such, should contribute to the wants of the public power. Capitation and property taxes were the two great categories of receipt in early times. When the greater part of a community possessed little accumulated wealth, the method of taxing each adult for a fixed sum was natural. What is very suitable in a rude state of society is altogether unfitted for a progressive and civilized one. No modern state could employ a capitation tax as a substantial source of revenue. Its inequality and directness combine to make it unpopular. The remains of this form of personal taxation are, however, very general, though their interest is rather historical or political than financial.

The equal taxation of persons by poll taxes, or capitations, generally develops, either by some form of graduation into an income tax[1], or, as happened widely in the 17th century, is replaced by an excise on the necessaries of life. The sense of proportion accounts for the former, as the great dislike to the capitation tax does for the latter. But several

[1] It is significant that Adam Smith discusses the income tax under the title 'capitation taxes,' 367.

countries, notwithstanding, retain a small charge on the person of each contributor.

§ 2. English history supplies us with some illustrations of the poll tax. The first was in 1377, followed immediately by those of 1379 and 1380 (the latter the proximate cause of the Peasant Revolt). The two latter were graduated according to rank. At intervals the graduated poll tax reappears, as in 1453, 1513, and 1641. Its last employment was under William III in the French war, and it ceased completely after 1698[1].

The French capitation was first levied in 1695, and continued with changes up to the Revolution. It was graduated; at first twenty-two classes were formed, but this part of the system was altered in 1701. The Constituent Assembly created the personal tax (1791), which consisted of the value of three days' labour, and added it to the *mobilier*. The price of the day's labour is determined for each *commune* by the Council of the department, within the limits of 5*d*. and 1*s*. 3*d*. No addition can be made for local charges, and where an *octroi* is levied, the personal tax may be paid out of it. So far as can be ascertained, the total yield is between £600,000 and £700,000[2].

The Italian states possessed complicated capitation taxes which have not survived the establishment of the present kingdom. So did many of the German states[3]; but, at present, the class tax of Prussia is the most noticeable. The poll tax of 1811 was replaced by the class tax of 1820, by which the mass of the population was grouped in four classes, paying various rates, from £1 16*s*. to 9*d*. The income tax and the class tax were separated in 1851, and the latter, confined to incomes under £150, was divided into 12 classes, which, under the law of 1875, paid from 3*s*. to £3 12*s*., incomes under £21 being exempt[4].

[1] Dowell, iii. 3–7.

[2] Vignes, i. 40–1.

[3] De Parieu, i. 139–151.

[4] By the law of 1891 the class tax is absorbed in the income tax and incomes

The Saxon income tax in its lower part is practically the same as a capitation tax. The poll tax also survives in Switzerland, where it is chiefly employed for local purposes, and not in all the cantons.

Russia, which had long preserved the capitation, abandoned it in 1887. The nobility had been always exempt, and, since 1866, the commercial classes. While it was in force the rate varied from district to district, and its amount was about £9,000,000 (taking the rouble at its nominal value).

In the United States poll taxes have been used from the colonial period. At present, more than half of the States have them in force, mostly for the state or commonwealth revenue, but, in some cases, for the counties, and in others for education, or road making. In four commonwealths the payment of the poll tax is a condition of the suffrage[1], Massachusetts being the best known instance.

In addition to the taxes already noticed, we should mention the services demanded by the state from its citizens. Military service is the most prominent, and it is a large part of the real, as distinguished from the nominal, cost of continental armies. The real nature of this service, as a tax, is best shown by the compensatory tax (*Wehrsteuer*), imposed on those who do not serve, and which has given rise to so much controversy in Germany.

The method of *Prestations* in France for the repair of roads is another example, and there too the alternative of working or paying is open. The mediaeval system of Finance availed itself more extensively of this direct method of procuring resources; the surviving instances, in modern times, are—with the exception of military duty—more curious than important.

§ 3. The poll or capitation tax is far from being a pure

under £60 are exempted. The account in the text is preserved as illustrating the system.

[1] Seligman, *Finance Statistics of American Commonwealths*, 53; cp. Ely, *Taxation*, 209–11.

tax on wages: the taxation of professions through Schedule D of the English Income Tax, and by the fourth division (Table D) of the *Patente*, is a nearer approach to that point. Attempts to reach the great body of wage-earners are generally made by means of indirect taxation. The enforcement of a capitation tax is certain to meet with, at least, passive opposition, and in any case its productiveness cannot be great. The method of using it as a necessary condition to acquiring full political rights may be admissible if the receipts are given to local bodies, but this regulation is political rather than financial.

The general result is that this form of taxation is decaying. Its persistence is due to the financial conservatism that is so strong in most countries. It is altogether out of place in the general financial system, and though it may for a long time survive in some Swiss cantons or American states, its importance will, we believe, steadily diminish.

The incidence of personal taxes, especially in the form of capitations on day labourers, has been regarded by many writers as wholly on the employers, or through them ultimately on the consumers of the products they turn out, but this conclusion is not by any means certain. It is far more probable that a small tax on the poorer classes will lower, or prevent a rise in, their mode of living. Its action on population is far too indefinite to be used for laying down an absolute rule. Much will depend on the exact form of the tax, whether uniform or graduated, confined to the head of the family or extended to its other adult members. No proposition in Finance has been more dangerous in its application than that which declares that the labourer cannot permanently suffer from taxation.

CHAPTER IV.

Taxes on Property and Income.

§ 1. At the opposite extreme to capitation or personal taxes are those that are imposed on property. The antithesis between 'persons' and 'things' or, in economic language, between services and commodities, is apparent in the earliest stages of society. When the period of contributions in kind is passed, the first objects of taxation are the persons and property of the subjects. The property tax is probably older than the separate charges on the yield of land, or capital, or even labour; the sum of existing wealth is an easier, though not so fair an object for imposition. Oxen, land, slaves and household goods—the *res mancipi* of Roman law—are the commodities that first fall under taxation: they are on the spot, easily estimated, and in most cases proportioned to the land under cultivation. As society advances and new forms of wealth come into existence, the injustice of the old system becomes evident, and taxation is extended to movable property, either by special taxes, or more generally by including it in the category of taxable objects. The difficulties in the way turn out to be too strong: personal property gradually escaped from the duty of contributing [1]. Such seems to have been the fate of the

[1] In Mr. Dowell's words 'personal property slipped out of assessment,' iii. 85.

property tax wherever it has been tried; in ancient Rome, in the various attempts in England, as also with the French *Taille* and the later *Dixièmes* and *Vingtièmes* of the 18th century.

This very general tendency to disintegration in the property tax is partly due to its economical defects, partly to technical difficulties in its administration. As regards the former there can be no doubt that, speaking generally, the property tax is merely a form of assessment, the payment being really made out of income. Taxation that falls on capital in the strict sense must diminish the sum of the community's wealth, a process that cannot continue indefinitely. In using property as the basis for taxation there is always a danger of trenching on the accumulated resources of the society. A second obstacle lies in the fact that property is not really a fair gauge of taxable capacity. Some forms of wealth give a lower return than others, and in special cases may even involve outlay. If, as we saw[1], income or revenue is on the whole a satisfactory standard for taxation, a property tax, unless carefully balanced by other charges, is unjustifiable. It is the result of a confused idea as to the true measure of taxation.

The technical difficulties result from the nature of property. In many cases it is only an abstraction obtained by capitalizing revenue. This is preeminently true of the great mass of property that the modern stock exchange deals in. Shares of companies and public debts are only of value in consequence of their revenue, and their capital value is reached by a process of estimation; it is besides constantly varying in a way that does not allow of precise measurement. Income is a definite receipt during any given period, and is therefore a better object for charge. The difficulty of reaching the multifarious forms of personal property is a further objection. To arrive at the

[1] Bk. iii. ch. 3. § 12.

amount of taxable wealth and to assess it fairly is quite impossible. The 'slipping away' that always takes place leads to grave inequalities and injustice. The owners of certain forms of wealth are unduly burdened by having to pay the share of those who have evaded their duty. These are sufficient grounds to justify the very general abandonment of the property tax as a leading source of revenue. Taxes on produce (*Ertragssteuern*), such as those discussed in preceding chapters of this book, take its place or survive it, while they in turn tend to develop into the income tax.

§ 2. The property tax has, however, maintained its ground in two countries. Switzerland still possesses, though in most instances with great modifications, this ancient method. The central government does not avail itself of the property tax—except in the charge for military exemption—but all the cantons employ it. The usual title 'tax on property and income' is, however, significant; it marks the connexion between the sum of wealth and its annual return, and it explains the object aimed at, viz. the higher taxation of large and permanent incomes, as well as the assessment of 'enjoyment capital.' The systems adopted are varied, complex, and often changed[1]. Their characteristics will be best understood by taking a single canton and examining its system. That used in Zürich divides property-holders into classes. The lowest, those under £800, pay on one-half only; the second, those between £800 and £2000, pay on one-half of £800, and on three-fifths of the excess. Between £2000 and £4000 taxation is imposed on seven-tenths of the excess over £2000; between £4000 and £8000 on four-fifths of the excess. For property under £16,000 only nine-tenths of the excess over £8000 is charged, while

[1] The total mass of legislation and legislative proposals is quite overwhelming. It has been collected with characteristic thoroughness in the elaborate work of Schanz, *Die Steuern der Schweiz* (over 2000 pages in 5 volumes).

any amount over £16,000 is charged at its full value[1]. Under such a scale the smaller properties escape very easily. The Zürich method is modified in other cantons. In Graubünden the lowest class is charged at the 'simple' rate; in the next class 10 per cent. additional is placed on the entire property; in the third 20 per cent., and so on till in the eleventh class the rate is double. The more primitive canton of Uri has a higher rate of progression: from $\frac{1}{20}$ of 1 per cent. on property under £1200, it rises to $\frac{3}{20}$ of 1 per cent. on properties over £16,000. The town canton of Bâle makes but three classes; $\frac{1}{20}$ of 1 per cent. is paid by estates under £4000; $\frac{3}{20}$ of 1 per cent. on those between £4000 and £8000, and $\frac{1}{5}$ of 1 per cent. on those over £8000. In some cantons there is no progression, all properties being taxed at the same rate. Communal taxation is also in many cases levied on property, but it is rarely progressive (e. g. in Zürich *communes* are forbidden to impose a progressive rate), and generally moderate in amount.

The Swiss system of property taxation suggests several points of financial interest. Though a long-established form, it has been gradually adjusted in accordance with modern ideas, and is used to supply gaps in the other kinds of taxation. The aim of taxing permanent incomes at a higher rate is accomplished by a tax that does not touch pure earnings. Non-revenue yielding wealth is also reached, and the democratic ideal of reducing the burden on the smaller incomes is in some degree realized. But notwithstanding this tendency, the rates are so moderate

[1] The following table will show the rates of charge—

Property.	*Sum chargeable.*
£	£
400	200
800	400
1200	640, i. e. $\frac{1}{2}$ of 800 and $\frac{3}{5}$ of 400
2000	1120, i. e. ,, ,, of 1200
4000	2520, i. e. $\frac{7}{10}$ of the extra 2000
8000	5720, or $\frac{4}{5}$ of the extra 4000
16,000	12,920, or $\frac{9}{10}$ for the extra 8000
20,000	16,920, the extra 4000 being all charged.

that the effect on capital is hardly perceptible. Evasion perhaps accounts for a good deal of this indifference on the part of the wealthy, and shows that the administrative system is far from perfect. Again, the very narrow areas within which the several systems are applied, and the small populations affected, make the operation of the taxes more difficult to use for generalization [1]. They are, in fact, a remarkable form of local taxation, and should be so regarded.

§ 3. One of the many points of likeness between the American States or 'Commonwealths' and the Swiss Cantons is their use of the general tax on property. But on closer examination the special differences are more important than the general resemblance. The American tax is not in any case progressive, and is rarely accompanied by anything resembling an income tax. Another feature of difference is the apportionment system adopted in the United States. A given sum has to be divided over the several counties of a state in proportion to their assessment, and the valuation of property is in consequence put at the lowest figure admissible by the county officials. The system adopted in Ohio may serve as an illustration of the general methods. By a constitutional provision all property (with some insignificant exceptions) must be taxed. To carry out this law real property is valued once in ten years by assessors appointed for the purpose, who are to take each plot 'at its true value in money.' As the assessors in each county compare results they are probably uniform, but as between different counties there is often great difference, which is corrected, though imperfectly, by a board of equalization. For personal property an elabor-

[1] The following are the areas and populations of the cantons referred to—

Canton.	*Area. Square Miles.*	*Population.*
Bâle (town) . .	22	73,749
Graubünden . .	2774	94,810
Uri	415	17,249
Zürich	665	337,183

ate series of queries is issued to each adult, who is bound to answer them, and to swear to the truth of his return. The numbers of cattle, watches, pianos, merchandise, money, stocks, lands, &c., have to be declared, and their selling value stated [1]. Nothing could apparently be more searching and effective. Other states possess tax laws quite as rigorous. In Georgia both land and personalty are included in the queries issued, which moreover contain a question as to evasion. Unfortunately the universal experience is that the greater part of personal property is not returned. Assessors' reports, Governors' messages, and reports of tax commissions all dwell on this fact. The New York report of Mr. Wells in 1871 is quite in agreement with the Maryland report of Professor Ely in 1886, while Professor Seligman declares emphatically that 'the general property tax as actually administered to-day is beyond all peradventure the worst tax known in the civilized world [2].' The reasons for this general condemnation are not far to seek. They are due first of all to lax administration. Officials elected for short terms cannot be expected to scrutinize very closely the answers of their constituents. Palpably inadequate returns are accepted with little question, and the wealthiest get off best. A second cause is the local nature of the property tax, as compared with the national, or even universal movement of the finer forms of personal property. Bonds and shares are easily moved outside a state during the time of assessment, and more obvious forms of capital have to be leniently treated to avoid their emigration. Mr. Wells has pointed out very forcibly the discouragement to capital that the New York system gave [3], in contrast with those of Pennsylvania and other adjoining states; but in practice the pressure is very slight. One fact suffices to establish the

[1] The above account of the Ohio property tax is condensed from Ely, *Taxation*, Pt. ii. ch. 4, which gives full details.

[2] *Political Science Quarterly*, v. 62 (January 1890).

[3] *Report on Local Taxation*, 17–18.

defectiveness of the property assessments. It is the decline in the declared value of personal property during a period in which wealth has beyond question increased enormously. The personal property in New York state in 1869 was assessed at $434,000,000, in 1875 it had fallen to $407,000,000, and in 1885 to $332,000,000, i. e. a decline of over £20,000,000 in the commercial centre of the Union. The similar figures for real property are, for 1869 $1,532,000,000, for 1875 $1,960,000,000, and for 1885 $2,762,000,000, or an increase of nearly £130,000,000!

The defects of the property tax are, it would appear, beyond remedy, and therefore it may be anticipated that it will in the future be transformed into a land tax with additional charges on other selected receipts, and perhaps finally into an income tax. We may, however, conjecture that a system of state income taxes will also fail owing to the difficulty of localizing income. The conclusion already reached[1] that the income tax is best suited for the national government applies fully to the United States. The most promising sources of state revenue seem to be the real property and license taxes. But whatever new forms be adopted the property tax is decisively condemned[2].

§ 4. The failure of property taxes in so many separate cases, and the clearer comprehension of income as the true normal source of taxation have made the plan of a general tax on revenue or income appear advisable. We have noticed the imperfections and dangers of the single income tax: it is now rather as the constituent of a general system of taxation that we have to estimate it. In this aspect we find that the income tax is a distinctly modern product, and one that is likely to grow in importance. A well-balanced financial system will derive a large part of its receipts from direct taxation, as otherwise an approach

[1] Bk. iii. ch. 6. § 3.

[2] On the whole subject of the property tax see the works of Wells, Ely, and Seligman referred to in Bk. iii. ch. 6. § 3, 361, n. 1, also Seligman's *Finance Statistics of the American Commonwealths*, 53-66.

to just distribution would hardly be possible. Among the objects of these direct charges the produce of land, capital, and labour must take their place, and when they have each come under contribution the elements of the income tax are present. The close analogy between the four direct contributions in France and the five schedules of the English income tax is evident, and this resemblance extends to the German 'produce taxes.' There is, however, one very important difference; the taxes on the several elements of wealth are far less elastic in yield. Thus the French, Prussian, and Italian land taxes have a fixity that is not found in the income tax; and the other produce taxes, though possessing more expansive power, are yet not at all as effective as is desirable; the *Patente* expands more slowly than Schedule D. There are besides various gaps in the most developed of the continental 'produce taxes.' State creditors in France escape taxation, while the English and Italian fundholders pay on that part of their revenue. Mortgages and other forms of loanable capital also manage to avoid their proper share, which would be impossible with the income tax. The actual institution of a tax on income is not due to refined consideration of justice: like most imposts, it is the child of necessity. When other contributions have been carried to their productive limit the financier has perforce to fall back on the direct taxation of income. This method is the more necessary in a country where taxation of the several parts of income is absent or inadequate. Both conditions were combined in the case of the first English Income tax (1798)[1], and were also present in a great degree in Italy in 1864.

The result of this originating cause is seen in the use of the income tax as a complementary receipt, to be employed in cases of pressure and to meet what would otherwise be a temporary deficit. The aim of keeping a correct

[1] 'It was in the crisis of the revolutionary war that, when Mr. Pitt found the resources of taxation were failing under him, his mind fell back upon the conception of the Income tax,' Gladstone, *Financial Statements*, 14.

balance of expenditure and receipts can be best realized by having a varying income tax adjusted to suit the special circumstances of each Budget. Thus in England the rate has varied from 1*s.* 4*d.* (if we include the earlier income tax from 2*s.*), to 2*d.* per pound. Italy has been unable to follow the same course, as the highest rate is in her case requisite in order to procure funds, but the desirability of having a movable tax of the kind is indisputable.

Another advantage of the tax on income is the opportunity that it offers for fairly distributing the burden of taxation. Indirect taxation, and particularly that on consumption, is heaviest on the smaller incomes, and lets the rich pass too easily. An income tax with a suitable scale of exemption goes far to correct this inequality, which duties on acts and inheritances also aid in remedying. Both on financial and equitable grounds there is a strong case for the use of the income tax, not as the sole source of compulsory revenue, but in due proportion with other receipts, and with close attention to the special circumstances of the country.

§ 5. The development of the English Income tax throws light on many of the problems connected with its general use. Its history is divided into two periods, (1) that of the war Income tax (1798–1816), and (2) that of the peace tax (1842–7). The former, preceded by 'the triple assessment,' consisted at first of a tax on the sum of income to be ascertained by the taxpayer's declaration. A lengthy form of return was required, and a number of deductions were allowed; for repairs, support of children, insurance premiums, &c. The yield was about £6,000,000 [1], at the rate of 10 per cent. on the national income, estimated by Pitt at £102,000,000. Repealed at the Peace of Amiens in 1802, it was reimposed in 1803, with the important change of substituting 'particular returns of particular sources of

[1] 1799 . . £6,000,000
1800 . . 6,250,000
1801 . . 5,600,000.

income' for the previous general return. Thus arose the well-known five schedules, and inquiry as to the total amount of income was avoided[1]. The rate was 1*s.* per pound; incomes under £60 were exempt, and those under £150 taxed at a lower rate. The yield for the first year was over £5,000,000. In 1806 the rate was raised to 2*s.* in the pound, and several changes in the regulations were introduced. The exemption limit was lowered to £50, and the allowance for children withdrawn, also that for repairs in Schedule A. The method of stoppage at the Bank was applied to Schedule C. With the high rate of charge the yield was at first £12,000,000; in 1815 it had risen to £15,642,000. On the conclusion of peace the Government desired to continue the tax at half the existing rate, but they were defeated and had to abandon it.

The difficulties of English Finance during the succeeding quarter of a century were largely due to this mistaken step. The retention of the income tax would have allowed reforms in other branches to have been carried out with comparative ease. Accordingly competent opinion as expressed by Sir H. Parnell and Sayer advised its reintroduction[2]. This prudent counsel was adopted by Peel in 1842. His measure—really the old system with unimportant modifications—was enacted for only three years, and the rate was fixed at 7*d.* per pound (or under 3 per cent.). The yield in the first year was over £5,600,000, the same as at the rate of 10 per cent. in 1801. At its expiry there was an extension to 1848, and again to 1851. It was voted for one year in 1852; in 1853 it was extended to Ireland, and fixed for seven years by Mr. Gladstone, who held out the prospect of its 'relinquish-

[1] They are—
Schedule A. Owners of land, including houses.
,, B. Farmers, including owners in occupation.
,, C. Fundholders.
,, D. Profits and professions and all other gains unenumerated.
,, E. Public Offices.

[2] See B. Sayer, *On the Income Tax*, 1831; Parnell, *Financial Reform*, 1830.

ment' at the end of that term. The Crimean war, during which the rate rose to 1*s.* 4*d.* per pound, prevented this result, and since 1860 it has been continued as an annual tax at varying rates, and it may now be regarded as a permanent part of our financial system [1].

In studying the English Income tax the first noticeable point is its composite character. It is, in Mr. Gladstone's words, 'rather a code or system of taxation [2]' than a single tax. The five schedules may well be regarded as so many distinct taxes, since they deal with separate kinds of revenue. The connexion between them comes out only in cases of exemption or abatement. Inequalities are, however, removed by the comprehensiveness of the tax. Mortgages pay under Schedule A by deduction; but there is no inducement to capitalists to put their wealth into the forms included by B, C, or D, as there also they will have to pay on their receipts. Another important part of the system is the extensive use of stoppage at the source. The result is that a large body of taxpayers never receive the sums due by them to the state. The public funds, dividends, mortgages, are all treated thus, and evasion and fraud are thereby reduced to a minimum. The separate sources of income are tapped, and supervision is made much easier.

Thirdly, we may bear in mind the very large yield of the tax. At its commencement it contributed £6,000,000 in a time of great pressure, while at present at half the rate it supplies close on £14,000,000 for the public revenue. The yield derived from the penny per pound is in fact an indication of national progress; from £700,000 in 1842 it has swelled to £2,300,000 in 1891 [3].

[1] The last time that its existence was endangered was by Mr. Gladstone's proposal of abolition in 1874.

[2] *Financial Statements*, 20.

[3] The following figures of income assessed are instructive—

Pitt's estimate, 1798	. . .	£102,000,000
Amount assessed, 1842	. . .	204,000,000
Ditto, 1878–9	. .	578,000,000
Ditto, 1888–9	. .	645,000,000.

This productiveness accounts for its great services both in war and peace. It supplied the means for carrying on the struggle against Napoleon, and it rendered possible the reforms of Peel, besides saving the country from deficits [1].

The extension of exemptions and abatements is a further interesting point. The original limit of exemption (£60), was soon reduced to £50, in order to include the large class who returned their incomes at £59 10*s*., and £200 was the point at which the full charge was enforced; this also came down to £150 in 1803.

Under Peel's measure the exemption limit was placed at £150, and, though subsequently lowered to £100, it has since returned to the higher figure. In 1863 a deduction of £60 was allowed from all incomes under £200; in 1873 this was increased to £80 from incomes under £300; and in 1876 to £120 from incomes under £400.

§ 6. The Italian tax on 'movable wealth' has strong points of resemblance to the English Income tax, and has been much affected by its example. It commenced in 1864, when a sum of 30,000,000 *lire* (£1,200,000) was apportioned among the several provinces, and raised by a tax on revenue (that from land excepted). In 1865 the amount was more than doubled (66,000,000 *lire*), and in 1866 the tax was changed from an 'apportioned' to a 'rated' one, and the rate fixed at 8 per cent. In 1870 it was advanced to 12 per cent., which, with the additional tenth, levied since 1868, made the total 13·20 per cent. Many changes have been made in the methods of levy and assessment. The original law of 1864 has been amended in nearly every succeeding year, until in 1877 a new and comprehensive measure was passed dealing with the whole subject. After the English pattern, the contributors are grouped under several schedules, but the arrangement is different, and used for a different purpose. Class A includes, permanent revenue, which is assessed

[1] On the Income tax see Dowell, iii. 92–120. Chailley, *Impôt sur le Revenu*, 89–218, gives a full and lucid account of the English system.

at its full value. Class B contains what are called 'mixed' revenues, or those in the production of which capital and labour cooperate: these escape with payment on six-eighths of their amount. Class C contains revenue from labour, assessed at five-eighths of its total. The incomes of public officials are placed in Class D, and pay only on four-eighths of their amount. To these four classes should be added the Metayers as forming a fifth. A complicated scale of allowances for small incomes is also part of the system. Incomes under 400 *lire* in classes B, C, D are exempt, and up to 800 *lire* the taxable sum is reduced. The declaration of the contributor is the basis of charge, but is tested by inquiry, and, as far as possible, the tax is collected by stoppage.

Notwithstanding the very elaborate provisions of the law, it is found impossible to reach a great deal of the national revenue. Incomes in classes B and C are very generally returned at much below their true amount. Like the property tax in the United States, the Italian income tax is ineffective through evasion. Thus, though the method of stoppage is only applied to a limited set of cases, its receipts are nearly as large as those from direct collection. Again, the proportion paid by companies is about 40 per cent. of the whole, a ratio quite inconsistent with all other available statistics. An analysis of the actual returns of revenue leads to the same conclusion. In 1874 only 639,302 persons made returns, and out of this number only 986, or 1 out of 640, admitted incomes of more than £1000 *per annum*. Even though the wealth of Italy is much less than that of England or France, these figures are quite inadmissible and prove the existence of fraud on a large scale.

One cause of such widespread evasion is the very high rate of taxation. The 13·20 per cent. is equivalent to 2*s*. 7½*d*. per pound[1], and so high an income tax would even in England lead to much dissimulation of income.

[1] I. e. on permanent income; the other groups pay at the lower figures mentioned in the text.

The most obvious remedy is a diminution of the tax rate, combined with greater powers of assessment, more particularly in respect to professional and industrial incomes. The differentiation of the classes of income, which originated in an attempt to apply certain theories very popular at one time in England [1], also tends to make the returns inaccurate and to embarrass the officials.

These drawbacks notwithstanding, Italian Finance has found a powerful resource in this form of taxation. The original £1,200,000 of 1865 has increased to £7,000,000 in 1875, to over £8,000,000 in 1885, and to over £9,000,000 in 1890. It must besides be remembered that owners of land are excluded from the operation of the tax, since they come under the land tax discussed in a preceding chapter [2].

§ 7. The German Income taxes are best represented by those of Prussia and Saxony. The Prussian *Einkommensteuer* was introduced in 1851 as a development of the older class tax. It was only applicable to incomes over £150, and dealt with them by groups. A sum was fixed for each group amounting to 3 per cent. on the lowest incomes in that group: thus e.g. incomes between £600 and £720 paid £18, those between £12,000 and £15,000 paid £360, and all incomes over £36,000 paid £1080, the highest sum due. Along with the reform of the class tax in 1873 the income tax was settled on a somewhat different scale, but with a general rate of about 3 per cent. The objections to this system as unequal have been so strong as to lead to the reform of 1891, by which the class tax [3] is absorbed in the income tax, and all incomes under £60 exempted. From that point the rate rises by degrees; between £525 and £1475 it is 3 per cent.; on incomes over £5000, 4 per cent. The idea of progression is thus realized,

[1] This view has received the support of Newmarch and J. S. Mill, as, too, of Leroy Beaulieu and Chailley.

[2] For the Italian Income tax see Chailley, 220-344; Alessio, i. 318-370.

[3] See Bk. iv. ch. 3. § 2.

though in a very limited way. The method of assessment is also changed. It was previously settled by official valuation based on the materials possessed by the administration, but is henceforth to depend on the declaration of the taxpayer.

It is evident that the Prussian Income tax differs in some important respects from those in England and Italy. The function of supplementing the other branches of receipts is entirely absent, as the rate is fixed, not movable from year to year. The produce taxes are not brought under the income tax, but are continued quite separately: the taxes on land and industry present, accordingly, apparent cases of double taxation. Finally, the productiveness is much less. In 1864 the amount rcceived was over £500,000, in 1876 it was nearly £1,500,000, in 1884 over £1,750,000; for 1889–90 the estimate was over £2,000,000. Under the new system (with the class tax included) the estimate for 1892–3 is £4,000,000 [1].

The Saxon Income tax is also a classified and progressive one, but, unlike the Prussian, it is not accompanied by a separate 'industry tax.' Its amount is about £750,000.

Austria has had a (so-called) Income tax since 1849, which is a tax partly on industry and partly on salaries, the former at the rate of 5 per cent. of net gain, the latter rising from 1 per cent. to 10 per cent., according to amount of income. Its yield in 1883 was about £2,000,000.

To the foregoing may be added the taxes of the Swiss Cantons. Their property taxes already mentioned are supplemented by income taxes, in many cases on a progressive scale. No two cantons have adopted exactly the same system in all details, but there are, as might be expected, general points of resemblance. The Zürich Income tax follows the pattern of the property tax. The smaller incomes are taxed on a part only of their amount,

[1] For the Prussian Income tax see Cohn, §§ 315–20, and for the recent reform, J. A. Hill, 'The Prussian Income tax' in *Quarterly Journal of Economics*, vi. 207–26.

and at each higher stage the excess over the preceding one is placed under greater pressure until the point of full liability is reached. Graubünden follows its property tax by grouping incomes in classes and by raising the percentage rate as they get higher. Switzerland is in fact the classical country of progressive income taxes, though the moderation of the rates, and still more of their application, weakens the conclusions that might otherwise be drawn.

§ 8. We have deferred a discussion of some fundamental questions relating to the constitution of an income tax until the leading facts of its use were known. Most of them have been already encountered in connexion with the general principles of taxation, but they take a different shape when the income tax is treated as but one part of a larger system, and need to be handled specially with a view to that fact.

One important question is that of progression in the rate of charge. The general conclusion that we reached [1] as to the inexpediency of any progressive system has to be reconsidered, when the income tax is used as a complementary resource. Progression in the case of such a tax may be necessary for true proportional taxation. If the smaller incomes are unduly weighted by taxes on consumption, their exemption, or milder treatment, under the income tax appears so far justified. A variation in the rate of charge is not open to the objection of arbitrariness, as it is determined by reference to the amount of other taxes. The other objections are not so readily disposed of. Risk of evasion and unproductiveness may both be urged against the graduation of even a moderate complementary tax. Where the area is a large one, the effect on accumulation and investment will not be serious, as the distribution of taxation will *ex hypothesi* be equal, but the existing attempts at progression are, it may be said, hardly worth the trouble they involve. The English

[1] Bk. iii. ch. 3. § 8.

method of exemption and abatement has great advantages from the technical point of view, since it allows the sources of income to be taxed without reference to their amount. The treatment of each person's income as a whole compels recourse to returns of a complicated kind, is disliked as being inquisitorial, and gives opportunities for escape to large masses of income. For these reasons the proportional rate is, on the whole, advisable.

The answer just given helps us in deciding as to the adoption of different rates on different kinds of income. The proposal that life incomes and those derived from industry should be charged at a lower rate has received influential support, and is illustrated by Italian practice. When considering the distribution of taxation, we noticed the general arguments as regards the income tax in England. It was for so long looked on as a temporary charge, that the idea of capitalizing incomes subject to it gained a good deal of support. The defence of the strict proportional rate rested on two admitted facts: viz. (1) that no ingenuity could avoid some injustice, and (2) that any alterations would mean the destruction of the tax[1]. Its gradual passage into a permanent charge has greatly strengthened its position in this respect, though the cry to remedy supposed grievances in its distribution may gain greater support[2].

The working of the Italian tax does not support the system of different rates. The lower scales for profits and salaries are confusing, and account for much of the loss through concealment of incomes. The single general rate would prove advantageous from a fiscal point of view, and with stricter assessment could be effectually carried out. The attempt to group incomes into 'permanent,' 'mixed' and 'temporary' is, moreover, too rough to give satisfaction or to realize justice.

[1] 'The real tendency of all these exemptions,' said Mr. Gladstone, 'is the breaking up and destruction of the tax,' *Financial Statements*, 45.

[2] A new period of assault on the alleged inequalities of the Income tax seems to be approaching.

Allowance for necessary expenditure and repairs is one of the practical difficulties in the administration of the income tax. On principle, as the tax is one on income, not on gross produce, deduction of the expenses of production of the income taxed should be allowed. Where much fixed capital is employed, this is very hard to determine, and we can understand the preference of French administrators for the self-acting rules of the *Patente*. In respect to land the English rule fails to recognise the cost of repairs; it, therefore, treats this class of revenue with unusual harshness, and gives some support to the view that Schedule A should be regarded as a distinct land tax. The exceptional treatment of farmers' profits is another fact that points in the same direction; but it may be hoped that this anomaly will be gradually removed.

The exemption of savings has been already discussed, but one method—that of life insurance—appears to be a case of capitalization; it is in fact turning a life income into a smaller permanent one, just as the purchase of an annuity is the opposite process. Up to a certain limit—one-sixth of the income—the English system allows exemption of insurance premiums, a privilege not extended to savings in general. Though the desirability of encouraging providence may be granted, it would seem that an exemption from duty on transfer after death would be a more fitting mode of bestowing the favour. It cannot be contended that an insurance premium is not a part of income, and the principal created by its use will not contribute to the payer's income in the future. The case is, as Mill puts it[1], one of concession to 'human feeling,' rather than a sound deduction from general principles.

The problem of assessment is another of the difficulties to be faced: between the Scylla of the contributor's evasion under self-declaration, and the Charybdis of official inquisi-

[1] Bk. v. ch. 2. § 4.

tion, it is hard to take an intermediate course; but the dealing with each separate part of income, the combination of declaration and official control, and above all the use wherever possible of taxation at the source of revenue, so characteristic of the English method, are undoubtedly the best. The direct contact of the citizen and the tax-collector is the most delicate part of the fiscal machine, needing care and use of the results of experience to prevent friction. Allowing for the inevitable margin of error, the results of the English income tax are eminently satisfactory.

§ 9. Any notice of the question of incidence may seem unnecessary in respect to a tax which falls on all the constituents of revenue. On whom can income receivers in general shift their burdens? Some of the suggested objects are certainly not available. Thus the vulgar idea alluded to by Mill, that the income tax falls on the poor by checking the expenditure of the rich, has no foundation in fact. Nor is there much force in the contention that in so far as the tax is paid out of capital it falls on the labourers[1], as this is no peculiar quality of the income tax, but one common to all taxation. The state must obtain revenue, and unless the income tax were specially obstructive to saving, it would produce no peculiar effect. Looking at the subject in a rather different way we obtain a better result. The income tax is composed of taxes on rent, interest, profits, and the higher forms of wages, therefore it may be said that the incidence of these several parts of the tax will, taken together, give the incidence of the whole. This, however, brings us back in a large degree to its non-transferability; for taxes on rent, on the higher kinds of wages, or on employers' gains, are not easily shifted. Even in the case of interest, unless the growth of capital is checked, a tax tends to remain on the payer. Therefore, speaking broadly, we may say that the shifting

[1] Fawcett, *Political Economy*, 538 sq.

of an income tax is not to be expected, and in the rare cases where it does happen is brought about, either by a check in the growth of capital through diminished interest, or by disturbances in the relations of the several industries and trades through its action. A progressive income tax will of course have a stronger tendency to cause the former effect.

CHAPTER V.

TAXES ON CONSUMPTION: THEIR CLASSIFICATION. DIRECT CONSUMPTION TAXES.

§ 1. THE income tax, as developed in the present century, marks the highest point attained in the methodising and skilful use of direct taxation. From the rude land, property, and poll taxes up to the existing system of charging the net receipt of the subject, regarded as a whole or its several parts, there has been an unmistakable improvement in justice, productiveness, elasticity, and that absence of irritation that is so important from the political point of view. The natural order of advance is in a great measure the historical course of financial movement. If existing direct taxation is very far from being perfect, it is, at least, better now than it ever was before. The true aims to be reached are better understood, and there is a more intelligent effort made towards their realization. In the present and immediately succeeding chapters we have to see how far another large department of taxation has received the benefits of like improvements. We have spoken of the taxes already discussed as being 'primary[1],' since they include all possible parts of the sole normal source of taxation—income. In contrast to them, the great mass of charges imposed on consumption and enjoyment, on transfers and juristic acts is secondary, since in a thorough analysis its several elements may be decomposed into taxes on some form of income. But the realities of practical Finance do not easily

[1] Bk. iii. ch. I. § 12.

adapt themselves to this mode of treatment; whatever be the 'source' of taxation, its 'objects' are many, and the mode of imposition is too important a circumstance to be entirely neglected.

The same conclusion is attainable from another direction. The classification of taxes most in favour in Germany[1] places first those that fall on wealth in the making, and next those imposed on its possession, and under either of these heads the various taxes already examined would be grouped. To these it, however, consistently adds an additional set of taxes levied on wealth in the using, and it is to the study of this form of taxation that we must now proceed. On both historical and financial grounds it is to the full as important as the taxation of income and property.

§ 2. The great body of taxes on consumption is capable of division on several different grounds. Thus the kind of commodity used may be employed as the basis of arrangement, giving the classes of (1) eatables, (2) drinks, and (3) other articles[2]. The sub-division of the second class into alcoholic and non-alcoholic drinks, and of the third into raw materials and manufactured articles naturally follows. Another mode of arrangement divides taxes according as they fall on necessaries, conveniences, or superfluities, and is supported by reference to the important differences in the economic and social effects of these different kinds of charges. From a financial point of view, however, the best grouping is that according to the mode in which the tax is levied. It may (1) be obtained at once from the consumer, in which case it is, in one use of the term, direct. It may, on the other hand, (2) be charged within the country on the manufacturers or dealers, who are expected to shift the burden to the consumers. Or again, it may (3) be realized by a state monoply of the industry or sale; while finally it may

[1] Wagner, ii. 233, 515; Cohn, § 332.

[2] This is probably the best plan in a purely descriptive or historical treatment. It has been adopted by Mr. Dowell (who gives tobacco a class to itself), and in great measure by De Parieu.

(4) be collected at the frontier. It is true that the same article may be differently treated in different countries [1], but this circumstance does not affect the general principle. In fact, it is quite safe and convenient to follow the usual fiscal practice and deal separately with (1) the immediate taxation of enjoyments and commodities, (2) the excise or internal duties, and (3) the customs.

The order just given is also the best to adopt in a scientific inquiry, as the immediate taxation of consumption is the closest to the direct taxes on property and income, the border-line being in some cases indistinct. This absence of quite precise boundaries has been more than once noticed; the difficulty that it places in the way of rigid lines of demarcation is best escaped by placing the nearest groups in close connexion with each other. The real relations are in this way best perceived, and the grounds for the actual classification are better understood.

§ 3. Historically the system of direct taxes on consumers can be traced very far back. The levies of commodities in kind by the sovereign may, where they consist of articles used by the contributors, be regarded either as taxes on produce or on consumption, though the former is the more natural interpretation. In like manner the taxation of movable property may be regarded as a charge on its use. Thus the tax on consumers' capital in the shape of furniture, plate, and works of art is plainly the same in effect as a tax on their use. Taxes on direct consumption and use seem to have originated in the sentiment to which sumptuary laws are due—the desire to repress luxurious expenditure. The first measure of the legislator was to prohibit; when that failed, the next was to tax the supposed injurious expenditure [2].

[1] Tobacco, e. g. is free in India, subject to excise in the United States and Germany, monopolized in France and Italy, and taxed by the customs in England.

[2] Cp. Cato's over-valuation of articles of luxury after the repeal of the *Lex Oppia*, and his taxation of them.

There is thus a double origin for the existing taxes of this kind; they are stray remains, either of the older property taxes, or of sumptuary enactments. With one doubtful exception their financial value is slight. No modern country derives any noteworthy revenue from their use. The reasons for this small return are to be found partly in the development of the excise, under which most commodities are taxed in the hands of the producer or trader. By adopting this method the state gains the double advantage of having to deal with a smaller number of persons who can be watched with comparative ease, and of avoiding the annoyance that direct taxation causes. Direct taxes on consumption seem to combine the defects of the two classes of taxes as described in an earlier chapter[1]. They have the unpopularity and inelasticity of direct taxes, without the equality and definiteness that are the chief recommendations of the latter. Industrial progress has further curtailed their area. They are the readiest way of reaching commodities produced and consumed at home, but this once large group of articles has shrunk to a very narrow space. The factory system has been destructive to the method of direct taxation on the consumer. Where large industry prevails the employment of an excise has very decided advantages; e. g. the concentration of breweries has made the license tax on home brewing insignificant. It may also be remarked that the system of indirect taxation through producers tends to promote production on a large scale. Heavy taxation on an industry is a grave danger to the smaller producers[2].

There is, however, another reason for the decline of the direct consumption taxes. They have been in many cases imposed on luxuries, or, at least, on the consumption of a limited class. The power of changing the direction of expenditure is here at its greatest, so that even a moderate

[1] Bk. iii. ch. 4. §§ 8, 9.

[2] Leslie, *Financial Reform*, 241–2. This is one of the many instances in which economic forces act and react on each other.

tax diminishes consumption very rapidly. This fact explains the small productiveness of the old assessed taxes in England, though a limited field of action is still left to this particular fiscal expedient.

§ 4. One important tax, which might be regarded as coming under the present head, has been considered at an earlier stage. This is the tax on dwelling houses when levied on the occupier. A very plausible case could be made out for this view. A house is as much a commodity as other more perishable articles, and it may fairly be classed among necessaries. A great part of the taxation so collected comes out of the occupiers' pockets, which lends further support to the conception of it as a consumption tax. It is, however, on the whole, more convenient to deal with it in immediate succession to the land tax, and in connexion with the taxation of buildings in general. The difficulties that arise respecting its incidence, and the undoubted fact of its falling back, under certain conditions, on ground rent seem to justify that course. We may therefore limit any notice of it in this place to a reference to the earlier discussion [1].

The other English taxes of the same character originated in the 18th century. Carriages, men-servants, dogs, and armorial ensigns were brought under taxation, and have continued in the same position up to the present. Plate, horses, watches, clocks, and hair powder have also for a longer or shorter time been made contributory. The bare enumeration of these several items shows sufficiently the character of the taxation. It is imposed on certain kinds of expenditure, which, if not superfluous, are, at least, not necessary, and only possible where a considerable amount of wealth exists. The plate tax, so long as it continued, was a tax on one part of consumers' capital. The licenses for killing game, and the later one for guns are strictly 'taxes on enjoyment,' and might indeed be placed

[1] See Bk. iv. ch. 2. §§ 1–5 inclusive.

under the taxes on 'acts,' but they find a more natural place in the present group.

The fiscal history of this group of taxes is instructive. At first separately levied by special commissioners, they were formed by Pitt into the 'assessed taxes,' and used by him as the basis of his 'triple assessment,' which was substantially a property tax. Its failure showed the defects of the system, and led to its replacement by the income tax. In the present century, after many alterations and extensions of exemption, the system of assessment has disappeared, and that of licenses been substituted, while the latest event in their history has been the transfer of the taxes to local bodies in 1888. Points for criticism abound in respect to the English consumption licenses [1], and the taxes that preceded them. In the first place they are unproductive. The most important, the carriage duty, gives an annual average of £550,000, the dog tax only reaches £340,000, and the remaining imposts make up the general average of £1,360,000. They are far better suited for the purposes of local taxation, and their transfer may be unreservedly approved of. But the further question arises as to their fitness for use in any part of the financial system. They have the great disadvantage of being very often unequal as between persons. It requires much watchfulness to prevent evasion in the case of sporting and gun licenses, and armorial ensigns, particularly the latter. The tax on male servants is so far a check to their employment, and special exemptions have to be made for occasional hirings. The carriage tax is rather complex and often presses unfairly on some classes. There is either the alternative of including all vehicles to the injury of trade and agriculture, or where, as at present, there are large exemptions, the difficulty of administration is increased. A more comprehensive tax, such as the horse and wheel tax, proposed in 1888, would avoid much of this difficulty, and as a local resource would

[1] To be distinguished from the trade licenses noticed in Bk. iv. ch. 2. § 8.

have the merit of making the users of roads contribute towards their maintenance, but its unpopularity and complicated incidence are both against it. The dog tax is perhaps, on the whole, the least objectionable, on account of its service as a measure of police, but for that very reason its rate to be effective should be so low as to deprive it of any great financial value[1]. The conclusion suggested on the whole is that which recognises the consumption licenses as a possible local contribution, but one entirely unfit for imperial taxation. It might be possible within limits to give the local authorities the privilege of selecting the particular articles to be taxed, and regulating their number and the rates of charge by the needs of the particular district.

§ 5. France has made a more sparing use of direct consumption taxes, and when employed they have had a sumptuary aim. Those established under the Directory were given up in 1807. Some, however, have been re-introduced: thus the horse and carriage tax was passed in 1862. A local dog tax was enacted in 1855, and the legislation as to game licenses dates from 1844. The tax on servants has not been restored. Among taxes that may be placed in the present category is that on societies, introduced in 1871—20 per cent. on the subscription of the members—which is practically direct.

The revenue derived from these imposts is small, being about £1,200,000[2], though as, with the exception of the horse and carriage tax, they serve as measures of police, it may be expedient to retain them.

The development of direct taxation of consumption in

[1] The Irish rate of 2*s*. (with 6*d*. additional for stamp) is for this reason better than the English one of 7*s*. 6*d*.

[2] The respective contributions are—

	£
Game licenses	450,000
Horse and Carriage tax . .	400,000
Dog tax	300,000
Tax on Societies . . .	60,000.

other countries is less marked. Taxes on dogs, servants, and carriages, are a part of the optional communal resources in Italy, but their yield is unimportant. The dog tax, e.g. was in 1883 only applied in about 1400 *communes*, and produced less than £25,000.

Prussia tried these forms of taxation between 1810 and 1814, but abandoned them at the latter date. The tax systems of the Empire present some variety in the use of these taxes, so far as they have been continued. The dog tax is a communal receipt in Prussia ; it is a state one in Bavaria and Würtemberg. The amount obtained from these direct taxes is inconsiderable.

In the United States the direct consumption taxes are assigned either to the States or smaller divisions, and they vary from State to State. The almost universal employment of the general property tax does in practice bring most of the objects of consumption taxes under charge. Some of the licenses so extensively used fall on enjoyment rather than on trade or production, but they are insignificant in their yield.

§ 6. From the foregoing (unfortunately incomplete) notice of the past and present taxation of this kind, we get a confirmation of the view already expressed that it is a decaying form of impost. No modern State has managed to raise a large revenue by its aid ; on the contrary, its relative importance is much less than formerly. There is quite enough evidence available to prove that it can without inconvenience be surrendered to the local bodies whose requirements make all new resources desirable, and who at the same time have not to meet sudden changes in expenditure. It may even be questioned whether the American or German State is not too large a division. The town or rural *commune*, or at highest the county, department, or circle (*Kreis*), is the proper area for the application of the direct consumption taxes collected within it.

There is in fact a kind of resemblance between the poll taxes and those now under discussion. Both are employed rather freely in early communities, but decay as Society advances. The causes that reduce their services are different, though the result is the same. The poll tax is both unjust and unproductive where wealth is unequally distributed: taxes on enjoyments and luxuries are too easily evaded to be of practical use in an advanced financial system.

CHAPTER VI.

INTERNAL TAXES ON COMMODITIES.

§ 1. DIRECT taxation of enjoyment or consumption is, as we have seen in the preceding chapter, of comparatively little financial significance. In this respect it presents a marked contrast to that system of indirect taxation that has now to be examined. All European countries rely on what is known in England as 'the Excise' for a substantial part of their revenue receipts[1]. Any failure in this branch of taxation would be a fiscal disaster very hard to retrieve. Even the United States, which in times of peace can dispense with internal taxation of most commodities, had, under the pressure of war, to apply this system in a particularly rigorous form[2]. Nothing but a much higher standard of morality in regard to the payment of direct taxes, or a very unlikely reduction of expenditure, will render the remission of taxes on commodities possible. Another noteworthy feature of the taxes under consideration is their modernness in their present form. The

[1] Thus in England the receipt from the Excise on commodities is, speaking broadly, 30 per cent. of the total tax receipts—£22,572,000 out of £76,387,000 in the year 1888–9. The *contributions indirectes* and the fiscal monopolies in France show for 1889 a gross yield of £47,000,000. Allowing for the expenses of working the tobacco monopoly and deducting the post telegraphs and the taxes on communications, the balance remaining is over 25 per cent. of the total tax revenue. The German Imperial excise is of less importance, but it gave a return of over £6,000,000 in 1887–8.

[2] Bolles, *Financial History* (1861–1885), Bk. i. chs. 9, 10; Wells in *Cobden Club Essays* (2nd Series), 479.

English Excise is hardly 250 years old[1], and the corresponding branch of revenue in other countries cannot claim much higher antiquity. A reference to general economic conditions supplies the explanation of their relatively recent origin. An extended and productive system of indirect taxation requires for its effective operation a large development of money transactions with an accompanying separation of employments. Any attempt to tax producers or dealers in the expectation that they will recoup themselves by charging an increased price for their wares is obviously impracticable where most production is for domestic use, and such exchanges as do take place are transacted by means of barter. Besides, the natural tendency of financial policy is to begin with customs duties, partly as being easier to collect, but also as, in the popular belief, falling mainly on foreign producers. A further prerequisite for the creation of an excise is the formation of an administrative organization capable of effectively supervising the production of the dutiable articles within the territory of the State.

The tax system is however, in all its divisions, the result of a gradual evolution, and therefore we need not be surprised at finding earlier forms of taxation falling on the production of commodities, and hence ultimately on consumers. The claim of the feudal over-lord to ill-defined prerogative rights is one source. Market fees and tolls were the foundation on which a system of indirect taxes could without difficulty be constructed, and the older import and export duties presented a convenient analogy. A charge on the sale of a domestic article did not seem a greater violation of the subject's liberty than if it were imposed on the introduction of a foreign one. The licenses on trades and occupations supplied another means for attaining the same end. When confined to particular industries they must evidently be regarded as part of the

[1] The first excise was created by the Long Parliament in 1643, Dowell, ii. 8 sq.; Sinclair, *History of the Revenue*, i. 46, 278.

expenses of production, and—unless there is a differential gain—will be ultimately shifted to the consumers of the products[1]. A license graduated in proportion to the output or amount of sales is hardly distinguishable from a tax on the commodity produced. The relations of mediaeval traders and craftsmen to their rulers and municipalities brought this kind of taxation into use as an expansion of the general property tax. Still more important was the influence of the quasi-private receipts of the sovereign, which led to the monopolizing of certain forms of production in order to increase the royal revenue. The State monopolies, of which so many examples are to be found in ancient and mediaeval Finance, are, however, so far as the price of the commodity is thereby raised, nothing but a special form of taxation. As already explained[2], the normal profit on the capital employed is a part of the economic receipts, but any excess is unquestionably taxation.

In these different ways the indirect taxation of consumption has been attempted, and the last-mentioned—monopoly—is even yet employed, as being, under certain conditions, a convenient mode of levying taxation.

§ 2. The problems presented to the financier in connexion with the whole system of indirect taxation are both numerous and important. The earlier methods were directed simply to obtaining resources for the immediate wants of the State without regard to the ulterior effects on the economic position of the nation. This irrational and almost instinctive procedure was soon replaced by attempts to use taxation as a means of guiding private expenditure in the supposed best direction. The desire to employ taxation as a moralising agency is even at present—as the duties on alcoholic drinks prove—an element of no inconsiderable weight. The proper development of the taxes

[1] Subject of course to the complicated reactions discussed in Bk. iii. ch. 5. § 5.

[2] Bk. ii. ch. 3. §§ 6, 9.

on commodities has, moreover, been hindered by mistaken views as to the true effect and operation of this part of the tax system. The earlier excises aimed at including all the various articles of consumption: it was thought that the maxim of equality demanded nothing less than this comprehensive procedure. The often described *alcavala* and *bolla* were imposed, the former on the sale, the latter on the manufacture of all kinds of goods. The excises of the 17th and 18th centuries were regarded by financiers as the principal form of taxation, destined, if not to replace all other kinds of imposts, at least to hold the principal position in the fiscal system. Dutch methods of taxation had shown how productive taxation on commodities could be made, and the greater the number of the taxed articles the more perfect was the system deemed to be. Popular sentiment by no means agreed with this idea of theorists and statesmen. The unpopularity of direct imposts has often been noticed as one of their defects, but no form of taxation has ever excited more genuine dislike than the 'general excise' which Walpole was accused of attempting to introduce into England. We have seen the weighty reasons that forbid the adoption of indirect taxation on a great number of articles[1], and here we may add that the historical movement of the 18th century made such a course impossible as a permanent system of Finance. The political revolution placed power in the hands of a class that would not tolerate it, while the less-noticed, but quite as important, industrial revolution established conditions under which it would not be endurable[2].

The influence of economic doctrines is also to be traced in the later legislation on the matter. Without at all

[1] Bk. iii. ch. 4. § 5.

[2] The hostility of the Physiocrats to indirect taxation was shared, so far as internal taxation went, by the other sections of the liberal party. It is noteworthy that this disposition is also found in the labour parties of the present day, who resent taxation on commodities consumed by the working classes as taxation of labour. Cp. Lassalle, *Die indirecte Steuer und die Lage der Arbeitenden Classen*.

asserting that modern taxation in this department is in full conformity with the prescriptions that result from economic principles, it may be said that there has been a decidedly beneficial remodelling of internal taxation, which has removed many of the objections that might be urged against its cruder forms, and there is every reason to hope that this progress will continue.

§ 3. The first problem to be faced in determining the character and extent of the taxation on commodities is the number of articles to be taxed. As we cannot with prudence bring all, or even the greater part of the commodities produced under duty, it is necessary to make a selection, and to do so on certain definite principles. The old and simple rule of taxing whatever is most easily reached can hardly claim scientific justification. It is the product of fiscal necessity, not of providence and deliberation. One very important condition is the amount of revenue required; the expediency of taxing a given article will always, in some degree, depend on this condition. If, as we have found[1], the whole category of indirect taxes is the outcome of the heavy expenditure of the modern State, it is plain that the greater the outlay the more imperious will be the calls of the Exchequer for receipts from this source. With an increased expenditure of £20,000,000 per annum in Great Britain, the exemption of sugar from taxation could hardly be continued. It is next necessary to settle the proportion that can be obtained by the various kinds of direct taxation, as well as by those further imposts that we have grouped under the title of taxes on acts and communications, before we can say what sum must be gained through the excise and customs. This, again, suggests a fresh consideration. From the economic and fiscal point of view, the existence of import duties establishes the expediency of corresponding excise ones. Any other policy is detrimental to the revenue, and therefore to be condemned. We may, however, escape the

[1] Bk. iii. ch. 4. § 6.

discussion of this question at present by regarding protective import dues as being equivalent to bounties on production, and therefore forming a part of expenditure[1]. When the amount to be raised through internal taxation of commodities has been fixed, the more difficult question of distributing the total charge among the several dutiable articles, and of saying what these shall be, arises. One very plain limit is supplied by the condition of maximum productiveness in the case of each article. The rule of charging only what 'the commodity can bear' has not always been as carefully observed as it should be, but it is now well understood that increased rates may give diminished receipts. No single class of goods could yield the amount that modern fiscal systems require. But it is not merely the need of attaining the highest productiveness that leads to an extension of the list of dutiable goods; considerations of equity also come into play. The different classes of society do not expend their incomes in the same proportion on the many articles of consumption, and even persons in the same class have very different habits and tastes. A tax that presses heavily on one individual or class may scarcely affect another. Hence it is necessary to make a judicious selection of objects, in order to secure a fair distribution of the charge in accordance with the general rule adopted as a guide. The inclusion or exclusion of necessaries will depend on the view taken as to the treatment of the minimum of subsistence. If its exemption be deemed proper, all taxation that would trench on it is to be peremptorily forbidden: where the duty of all to contribute to the service of the State is recognised, duties on such articles as corn and salt may be the easiest way of enforcing that responsibility. At the opposite extreme, the mode of dealing with articles consumed only by the rich will be affected by the amount already obtained through income and property

[1] Cp. Bk. i. ch. 6. § 3; and for a notice of the fiscal aspects of protection, ch. 7. § 2 of the present book.

taxes and duties on the transfer of wealth, and, too, by the extent to which the idea of progressive taxation is accepted. Heavy imposts on luxurious expenditure tend to press more heavily on the rich, and are in principle the same as a progressive income tax [1], though their actual operation may vary more according to circumstances.

The main brunt of indirect taxation will, in most modern communities, fall on the great intermediate class of goods that form the staples of consumption. It is one of the earliest observations in Finance that taxation on the expenditure of the working classes will yield much better results than that which is placed on the apparently more profitable outlay of the comparatively few rich persons [2]. The objects of general expenditure must be brought under contribution, in order to secure the high return that is needed as a justification for the imposition of so vexatious a system as the excise.

We thus reach rather limits within which the field of taxation has to be kept, than direct indications as to the articles and rates to be imposed. Another class of considerations will help us to make some further progress. An excise system must depend largely for its success on the technical conditions of the industries that it supervises. Where industrial improvement is rapid, the restrictions needed for the protection of the revenue are felt as a serious hindrance. The adoption of new processes, so necessary for the most effective production, is not readily carried out, and the system of taxation violates the maxim of 'economy' by inflicting loss on the community without corresponding gain to the State. The only escape is found in restricting the objects of taxation to a small number of articles, and in so choosing them as to include only those industries in which invention is not very active, or in which interference with it will not be seriously felt.

Again, it is evident that some commodities are far more closely connected with the work of production than others.

[1] Bk. iii. ch. 3. § 6.

[2] *Wealth of Nations*, 375.

A duty on manufactured silk would obviously have less effect on industry in general than one on iron. The former would—apart from its diffused effects—only concern the producers and consumers of silk goods; the latter would affect almost every industry of importance by enhancing the price of one of the most essential auxiliary materials of production. This contrast between auxiliary articles and those destined for direct consumption[1] leads to the rule that taxation of raw materials or goods that aid production should, as far as possible, be avoided. Not only are the real effects of duties on such articles harder to estimate: there is the further evil that the taxes have to be advanced by the producers for a longer period, and the ultimate increase of cost to the consumer is made greater by the interest on those advances. It is true that the State receives the money at an earlier time, but its gain is not sufficient to counterbalance the loss through interest on the locking up of what would otherwise be active capital.

The system of taxing commodities is consequently most effective when it is confined to a comparatively small number of goods, which form the typical objects of the general expenditure of the various classes and grades of the community, and which, at the same time, are not important elements in auxiliary capital. The production of these goods must, moreover, not be in a very scattered form, and in the hands of small producers, as excise supervision then becomes too burdensome to the industry and too costly to be effective. All the real objects of taxation on commodities can be accomplished without including many items in the list of dutiable goods. Productiveness, economy, and equity, are the ends in view; and they cannot all be secured without this limitation of the field of the tax collector; while equity, which seems to be violated, is really and substantially attained by a small as well as

[1] For Economics this distinction has been worked out by Menger, who grades commodities in 'orders' according to their nearness to the consumer, cp. Marshall, *Principles of Economics*, 109.

by an extensive number of taxes. One article of general consumption is a better object for purposes both of revenue and justice, than thirty or forty minor commodities on which the cost of collection would be high and the ultimate incidence uncertain.

The last important influence that affects the selection of the objects of indirect taxation is the desire to discourage certain forms of outlay that are regarded as pernicious, or, to take the mildest view, not promotive of economic or other virtues. This idea, which lies at the root of all sumptuary taxes, is represented in modern Finance by the treatment of intoxicating drinks and tobacco. In nearly every country these articles form the mainstay of the revenue from indirect taxation, owing to the two conditions of large consumption and heavy taxation. So far has this movement been carried in England, that it is quite within the limits of probability that both excise and customs may soon be confined to these commodities of doubtful advantage, as the former virtually is [1]. Though the French *contributions indirectes* have a broader basis, they are yet largely dependent on the wine and spirit duties; while the tobacco monopoly is highly productive. The United States and Russia have their internal revenue in a similar position, and the inferior yield in Germany is admittedly one of the weak points in the fiscal system of that Empire.

§ 4. One result of the preceding inquiry as to the conditions that should be taken into account in framing a system of duties on commodities is to give strong support to the position that such duties must be varied according to the country in which they are applied. The really productive objects of taxation are not quite the same in any two countries. The tastes and habits of each community have to be carefully observed and taken into account,

[1] Some license duties and that on the railway receipts from passengers are placed under the excise, but they really belong to another category of taxes (see ch. 8 of the present Book). The tea duty is the only productive part of the customs outside spirituous liquors and tobacco, and its yield is much diminished by the reduction to 4*d*. per lb. made by Mr. Goschen in 1890.

otherwise the revenue receipts will suffer. But the financier has not merely to study the direction of demand ; he must further pay attention to the agencies of supply. The system required for a wine-producing country, such as France or Italy, is not the same as that best fitted for districts in which alcohol is produced by an elaborate manufacturing process. Adjustment to the economic environment, so exceedingly desirable in the arrangement of taxation, necessitates the adoption of special taxes in different cases in order to gain the best results.

The same point is further enforced by the varying amount of revenue that is required, and the extraordinary differences in the amount of consumption on which taxation can be imposed. The exemption of necessaries from duty must be contingent on the power of obtaining the required amount from other objects. Thus salt, which is rightly free in England, has to be taxed in India owing to the absence of other resources, and sugar, released from taxation in Great Britain in 1875, would, in case of financial pressure, be one of the most eligible objects for imposition. The true test of financial competence is to be found in the application of the general principles to the varying circumstances of each particular nation in such a way as to realize the ends of a sound and prudent policy.

The modern developments of financial conditions have, it must be said, tended to bring about a greater approach to uniformity in the taxation of consumable commodities, both in respect to the objects taxed and the procedure employed. Economical and political causes have both contributed to this result. The modern industrial system with its uniform and mechanical methods of production, the general diffusion of a taste for articles of convenience, and the formation of powerful fiscal administrations have all helped to make the excise systems of European States more nearly resemble each other. Scientific investigation has also aided in producing this situation. The skilled financial advisers of a government are acquainted with, and ready to adopt, what is effective in the forms and methods of other nations.

Even greater progress in this direction may be anticipated in the future. We may not unreasonably hope that some of the anomalies at present existing will be removed, and that by due co-ordination and uniformity in method the hindrances to production and exchange that indirect taxation now causes may, if not entirely removed, be at least reduced to a minimum.

§ 5. The freedom of this country from internal taxation of commodities was one of the boasts of Englishmen so late as the seventeenth century. Under Elizabeth the granting of monopolies was the first step towards what might have become an effective system of taxation, but this encroachment was successfully opposed. The introduction of the excise on the Dutch model, said to be the proposal of Pym, was due to the needs of the Parliament in its struggle with Charles I; it included a large number of articles of necessary consumption, chiefly food and clothing. Retained during the Protectorate, with some modifications, as an important source of revenue, the excise was re-established after the Restoration in the form of a tax on beer and ale, partly as a compensation for the abolition of the feudal dues, and partly as a resource for the growing needs of the Sovereign [1]. At the close of the reign of Charles II the yield of these taxes was £620,000.

Whatever may have been the advantages of the Revolution of 1688, reduction in the burden of taxation was not one. The cost of the French war and the entanglement of England in the European disputes respecting the Balance of Power, along with the Colonial and commercial policy that resulted from the predominance of the monied interests, largely augmented the annual expenditure. During the eighteenth century the process of building up the excise by the inclusion of fresh articles and the increase of the rates

[1] The hereditary excise had the former, the temporary excise granted for the life of the King the latter object, but the distinction was only a formal one.

on those already taxed was in process. Breweries and distilleries were soon placed under charge; the malt duty was imposed (1697), and later on developed into an important tax. Several articles of necessary consumption were brought within the fiscal net. Salt, leather, soap, and candles are enumerated, and their taxation condemned, by Adam Smith[1]. The extension of the system was however carried on in a tentative way; new taxes were tried, and if they proved to be unpopular or unproductive were repealed, perhaps to be soon re-imposed under more favourable circumstances. The best known incident in this part of fiscal history—Walpole's excise scheme—was really a reform in the customs treatment of tea and tobacco, and excited prejudice rather by what it seemed to lead to, than by its actual provisions. The financial result of the many measures passed respecting the excise during the eighteenth century is best shown in the increased receipts. At the commencement of that period they had averaged £1,200,000[2]: by 1792 they had risen to £10,000,000. From the latter date the extraordinary drain of the Revolutionary war with France affected the financial policy of the country, and caused those fresh applications of taxation that have been so often described by historians. The existing rates were in nearly every case raised to the highest productive point (often as experience proved beyond it). The duty on salt was doubled, and later on again subjected to a 50 per cent. increase. Glass, tiles, and leather were also made liable to additional charges. Beer and ale, as might be expected, received specially severe treatment. At the commencement of the French war the various taxes on these articles or their constituents yielded £3,578,000: in 1815 they came to almost £9,600,000. The spirit duties were trebled during the course of the war,

[1] *Wealth of Nations*, 369.

[2] 'The revenue from inland duties had varied considerably in different years. In 1700 over a million, it was in 1702 nearly £1,400,000,' Dowell, ii. 62.

until in 1811 they stood at 10*s*. $2\frac{3}{4}$*d*. per gallon, or almost the present rate [1].

Such very great increase of taxation, accompanied as it was by corresponding advances in respect to other classes of imposts, could not long survive the return of peace, aided by the application of proper fiscal methods. Unfortunately the abandonment of the income tax and the injudicious methods of borrowing pursued by Pitt and his successors made reform a work of some difficulty. The debt charge of £32,000,000 and the heavy military and naval expenditure, not readily brought back to a peace footing, both hindered immediate remissions or exemptions. The national industries had, besides, become adjusted to this very heavy taxation, and caution was needed in the attempt to alter the situation. At first the want of revenue was so great that certain excise duties were increased, e. g. those on soap, malt, and British spirits. This extreme pressure did not, however, last long, and it became possible to carry out some moderate reforms. The salt duty was reduced, and its abolition fixed for an early date (1825). That on leather was lowered one half, and the very high tax on British spirits (11*s*. $8\frac{1}{2}$*d*. per gallon) was placed at 7*s*. in order to meet the illicit trade and in connexion with the lower duties on wine. The exertions of Huskisson were, however, chiefly directed towards the improvement of the customs, which, indeed, most urgently required reform. The internal taxes were not directly affected by the disturbing influence of the protectionist system, and therefore the changes to be carried out were of a comparatively moderate character. They may be said to consist in: (1) the elimination of raw materials from the list of goods liable to duty; (2) the contraction of that list to a very small number of articles, and (3) the placing of the weight of internal taxation on intoxicating drinks. A further aim has been to secure a complete harmony between the excise and

[1] For the details of these taxes, Dowell, ii. 208–245, and vol. iv. under the several heads.

customs systems, which has been reached by the abandonment of protection and the establishment of exactly equivalent duties in both departments. In fact, that substantial unification of the excise and customs for which Walpole vainly risked his popularity has been definitely accomplished so far as financial effectiveness is concerned.

Some of the facts of this reform of the excise are not without interest. After the disappearance of the salt tax the duties on leather and candles did not long remain. In 1830–1 they were repealed. The impost on soap—that 'tax on cleanliness'—survived till Mr. Gladstone's first Budget in 1853. Glass was released in 1845, but paper continued liable to duty till 1861. Starch and bottles were exempted in 1834, bricks and tiles in 1850. These repeals of duty, which seem so trifling, were really, taken together, a considerable boon to British industry and to the bulk of consumers. The progress of the chemical industries may be dated from the repeal of the salt duty. Bricks, tiles, and glass are constituents of that most necessary commodity—a house, besides being of use in numberless other ways. The paper tax was even more than a 'tax on knowledge'; it hindered the development of an important industry and raised the price of an article capable of many different uses. These advantages were well worth the sacrifice of the revenue obtained from the abandoned duties [1].

The treatment of alcoholic drinks stands apart from the

[1] The following were the amounts yielded by the excise taxes on the above-mentioned articles at the dates of abolition :—

	£
Salt (1825) . . .	380,000
Leather (1830) . . .	360,000
Candles (1831) . . .	476,500
Starch (1834) . . .	90,000
Bottles (1834) . . .	3,600
Glass (1845) . . .	600,000
Bricks (1850) . . .	456,000
Soap (1853) . . .	1,126,000
Paper (1861) . . .	1,350,000
Total	4,842,100

general system pursued with respect to industries. In their case there has been no remission, except when there was a prospect of increasing productiveness. The only exception to this rule—the repeal of the beer duty in 1830, by which £3,100,000 of revenue was sacrificed—had in part the aim of making the malt tax more productive, and this was in good degree attained. Besides the double system of taxing both malt and beer was recognised as inconvenient. During the half century 1830–80 the malt tax was the mode in which beer and ale were taxed, and supplied a standing grievance to agriculturists. Its large yield—£8,000,000 in 1877—made it impossible to repeal it, but in 1880 the existing duty on beer was imposed in its place, partly to relieve the depressed farmers, but also in accordance with the principle that a tax should be as near the point of consumption as can be arranged, in order that the preliminary processes may be released from excise restraints. The returns from the beer duty for the ten years 1881–90 have quite realized expectations. For 1889–90 the amount was £9,400,000.

The duty on hops, first imposed in 1710, became later on a subsidiary duty to the main tax on beer. It had the grave defects of being uncertain in its yield and pressing on the raw material, which was moreover an agricultural product. Accordingly this tax was repealed in 1862, leaving nothing of the kind, except the trifling duty on chicory, in the English excise. Its yield had varied from £86,000 in 1852 to £728,000 in 1855.

British spirits have presented greater difficulties. If the principle of fixing the duty in proportion to the amount of alcohol contained be adopted, the rate on spirits should much exceed that on beer, and the aim of encouraging temperance would lead to the same result. On the other hand the principal seats of production of spirits are in Ireland and Scotland, and the average consumption in their case is also greater. Heavy taxation of the more alcoholic drinks therefore presses unfairly on those parts of the United Kingdom. Finally, the enforcement of the revenue laws is no easy matter in wild and mountainous districts, and consequently the limit of productivity was at first rather low. Existing methods are the outcome of the efforts to meet these several obstacles.

The scale of duty, previously fixed on different principles in the three countries, was unified by Robinson (1825), the only difference being the higher rate in England (7*s.* per gallon). By a series of measures the Scotch and Irish duties were brought up to the level of the English one, itself raised by degrees, until in 1858 a uniform duty of 8*s.* per gallon was imposed. The increase in return was considerable. In 1829 the yield had been £4,800,000; by 1851 it was over £6,000,000. For 1859 the amount received was a little under £9,000,000. An increase to 10*s.* per gallon in 1860 made the tax still more productive, till in 1868 it was £10,500,000. The great prosperity of trade and the more efficient excise administration caused large annual increases, until in 1875–6 the highest return——£15,150,000—was obtained. From that date there was a decline for several years, but the yield is again elastic, and a new maximum was reached in 1890–1, when the receipts from this source were £15,475,000.

It is therefore apparent that the excise system of England, so far as it applies to commodities, is almost exclusively a tax on alcoholic drinks, and is carried out by supervision of the brewing and distilling industries, which involves a very complete control of their operations. The modern tendency to concentrate the production of both beers and spirits at a few centres makes this system less troublesome, and the heavy taxation in turn favours the larger producers. Further steps in this direction have been taken in the last few years by the extensive creation of limited companies, who almost possess a monopoly of special forms of beer, ale, or whisky, and who therefore bear the first weight of increased taxation. The whole situation is a highly artificial one; by it the State draws very large resources from the taxation of what is an instrument of luxury, in many cases one of vice. The aim of reducing the national consumption of these drinks is naturally postponed to that of maintaining so material a support of the public revenue, and the problem of adjusting the duties between the different classes is very imperfectly dealt with. There may be some reason for favouring such beverages as are believed to possess some nutritive power and to be less likely to cause intoxication; but the present scales of duty seem unfair as between the consumers of spirits and those of beer.

The trade licenses which accompany and are officially regarded as a part of the excise have been already discussed[1].

From one point of view the internal tax system also deals with the important article of tobacco; but until within the last few years it has been confined to the negative function of preventing its cultivation in the United Kingdom. This system of prohibition, which seems to be a direct violation of industrial liberty and an interference with a probably gainful employment, dates in England from the time of Charles II[2], and has been justified on the grounds of the inferiority of the home-grown plant and the great trouble of collecting a very high duty on an article of local production. At present licenses are granted for the purpose of experimental growing, though there is little probability of the cultivation extending.

The processes of the English taxation of commodities are reduced almost entirely to levies on the producers of the taxed articles, the sale licenses being rather charges on the profits of the occupations, which, however, does not prevent their being useful as adjuncts of the excise by bringing all producers and dealers under the notice of the authorities, and facilitating supervision. Duties purely on sale are not employed, though the bonding system, by

[1] Bk. iv. ch. 2. § 8.

[2] The prohibition at first applied to Ireland, but was removed in 1779 in consequence of the American war. It was reimposed in 1832.

which goods are retained under official control free of duty until withdrawn for use, nearly approximates to that form. Neither are duties on the land under cultivation for a crop of the taxed article in use. Finally the monopoly system is not a part of English policy. Spirits, beer, and tobacco would be the only objects for its operation, and each of them is treated in another way. In fact the great characteristic of this form of British taxation is the simplicity alike of its objects and its processes.

§ 6. The French methods are much more elaborate, and possess a longer history. Under the *Ancien Régime* indirect taxation had been extensively employed. The necessities of the State had led to the heavy and unequal salt tax, to the duties on drinks, on leather, iron, and other useful articles, to the monopoly of tobacco, and the costly and vexatious inter-provincial duties. The origin of the system may be traced to the fifteenth century, in which the monarchy was reconstructed after the English wars. A great expansion, however, took place in the seventeenth century, when the administration of Colbert had recast the financial system, and when such a new source of revenue as tobacco was secured.

The continuous development, apparently broken by the Revolution, soon returned to its old course, though purged of many of the defects that had previously existed. The vices of pre-revolutionary taxation arose rather from defective administration than from the inherent badness of the articles selected for duty. There were innumerable personal and local discriminations; the *noblesse* were exempt from various charges, and some districts were free from duties that pressed heavily on others. Thus salt was under six different systems, according to the particular province, not to speak of the many local privileges. Similar complexities were connected with the duties on wines and brandies. But far greater was the evil of the mode of collection, which was by the system of farming or letting out to companies, who contracted to pay a certain sum in return for the collection of the duties. This system, so characteristic of Roman Finance, recurs in the French indirect taxes, and did much to increase their unpopularity. The 'Farmers General' were objects of universal dislike, and some of the members of the body paid the penalty during the Revolution [1].

One of the first results of the disturbances that broke out in 1789 was a check to the collection of the indirect taxes. The offices for the duties on salt, on wines and spirits, and also the internal customs were attacked. Contraband salt and tobacco were freely sold, and the toll-barriers of the cities were thrown down [2]. The failure to collect the *taille* was more than paralleled by the case of the indirect taxes. This strong popular sentiment undoubtedly encouraged the Constituent Assembly, already imbued with the physiocratic dislike to taxes on consumption, to take the somewhat rash course of abandoning the greater part of the obnoxious duties.

After an ineffectual attempt to maintain it provisionally the salt tax was abolished in March 1790. In 1791 the *aides*, or drink duties, met the same fate, as did also the tobacco monopoly. The abolition of the *octrois* was decreed in Februry 1791.

So complete a break with past financial conditions could not continue [3], and accordingly we find that the work of the next ten or fifteen years consisted in building up the structure on the same general lines, but without the serious faults that it had previously contained. The salt tax was restored in 1806, but the old inequalities and the system of monopoly were not brought back. The suitability of tobacco as an object of heavy taxation made it advisable,

[1] Lavoisier, the eminent chemist, was one of the sufferers. For the system of the *Ancien Régime*, see Stourm, chs. 11–14. For the mechanism of the Finances, cp. Bk. vi. ch. 2, and the *Dictionnaire de l'Économie Politique*, s. v. 'Finances de l'Ancien Régime.' For the earlier history, Clamageran, *Histoire de l'Impôt*.

[2] Stourm, i. 295.

[3] Introd. Part i. § 8.

after a series of ineffective attempts at taxation in the ordinary way, to re-establish the State monopoly of that article in 1810. The *octrois* were gradually re-introduced, beginning with that of Paris in 1798, and soon extending to other towns. Finally the complete freedom of spirituous liquors from taxation was put an end to by the law of 1804, which imposed a tax on wine and cider when in the possession of the producer. Further taxation of this promising source speedily followed in the duties on the transport of drinks, and the tax on the amount sold by dealers. Thus in less than twenty years the system apparently overthrown at the Revolution was again in force, freed from its most objectionable features.

§ 7. The existing French system, which in its main outlines was established at the fall of the first Empire, shows when compared with that of England, a number of suggestive resemblances and equally suggestive differences. There is the same broad general treatment as respects the commodities selected for taxation and the proportionate burden placed on each class; there is also the same readiness to levy the duty at the most favourable point, and lastly there is the same prominence given to this kind of indirect taxation in the fiscal system. On the other hand the French system has a wider basis. Salt, so necessary both for domestic and industrial uses, is an object of charge. So is that very general article of consumption, sugar, whose treatment has so often harassed financiers, and which when freed from duty has grown so much in favour in the United Kingdom. The paper tax has only been suppressed in the last five years, while matches, whose taxation in England Mr. Lowe could not propose without losing whatever financial popularity he had possessed—are placed under a state monopoly, as is also gunpowder, while dynamite is taxed. Oil is another important commodity that has to suffer taxation, to which may be added candles. Acid and vinegar may close the list, which establishes that France possesses that diversity of indirect taxes, which McCulloch believed to have been too hastily abandoned in England [1].

Again, the procedure of the French administration is much more varied. The drink duties are levied partly on wine in circulation, partly on the retailers who sell it, partly on its entry into towns. Beer and spirits are taxed at the point of manufacture, in fact on the system of the English excise. Salt and sugar are similarly dealt with, but in all these cases the duty on transport may come into operation.

A more remarkable feature is the use of monopoly as a fiscal agent. It is true that in England the Post Office is under this *régime*, but ordinary commodities are quite free from it. In France, besides the small monopolies of gunpowder and matches—the latter created in 1872, and conceded to a company, but taken up by the State in 1890—there is the great tobacco manufacture, which is altogether a State concern. Experience has shown that only by this means could sufficient revenue be obtained from it.

These contrasts are to some extent due to the more rigorous administrative system of continental countries. Interference with internal trade would be much more difficult, and cause more irritation in England. But the different position of the two countries is a far more powerful cause. It is comparatively easy to watch the manufacture of drinks in the United Kingdom owing to the concentration of the industry. The problem of supervising the vineyards of the French peasantry has proved too difficult for the revenue officials of that country, and led to the repeal of the inventory duty of 1804. The insular position of Great Britain has been a further assistance in protecting her excise system from the introduction of contraband goods. Thus the price of the State manufactured tobacco in France has to be varied according to the proximity of the district to the frontier. The methods of each country are in fact adapted to meet the circumstances peculiar to its situation.

At the same time it must be said that in certain respects

[1] *Taxation and Funding*, 231.

French taxation of home commodities falls short of the highest attainable standard. Some of the duties are of too small a yield to justify their retention. The salt tax, even though it is confined to that used for domestic consumption, is too irksome and unequal a charge to be maintained when its return is only £1,250,000. The taxes on oils, matches, candles, and explosives might also be removed. The sugar duty is a more doubtful case. Its yield is very considerable—£6.300,000 in 1890—and with the heavy burdens that the country has to meet such a resource should not be lightly given up. Unfortunately the duty on sugar has become mixed up with the pernicious bounty system, which is evil alike for the treasury and the producers. Moreover, the technical problems connected with the measuring of the quantity and quality of sugar yielded are very difficult, so much so that they were some of the reasons for the repeal of the duty in England. A uniform duty on the finished product, adjusted to equal the import duty on the article, seems at present the best course. It would get rid of the bounty trouble and would not leave much opening for fraud.

The wine and spirit duties are an indispensable part of the system, and should be very cautiously treated. The exemption of wine consumed by the grower is a gap in the tax, that at once reduces the receipts and makes its incidence unfair. Nothing but the hopelessness of levying the duty could excuse this omission. A system of licenses for private consumption, such as that adopted for private brewing in England, might in some degree remedy the grievance. A further cause of complaint has been found in the comparatively high duty on retail sales. The artisan who buys his wine in small quantities is more severely taxed than the large consumer, who has only the moderate duty on transport to pay. The impossibility of raising the latter tax without provoking an extensive contraband trade, and the loss that any lowering of the duty on retailers would cause are the hindrances to reform. The duty levied on the entry of wine into towns with more than 4000 inhabitants is a further pressure on the residents in them, though its consolidation with, or perhaps more accurately speaking replacement of, the duty on retailers, where the population exceeds 10,000, carried out in 1875, is on the whole a desirable measure. The attempt to exercise surveillance over the very large number of agricultural distillers has proved a failure, compelling resort to the tax on circulation of spirits. These difficulties—which are good examples of the inevitable dilemmas that indirect taxation gives rise to—are due in a great measure to the position of France as a wine-producing country. Taxation of the cheaper wines falls necessarily on the bulk of the population, as it is imposed on their usual consumption. The cry of a 'free breakfast table,' once so popular in England, would need for its realization in France the removal of the wine duty. It is highly probable that the bulk of the drink duties will be more and more shifted to alcohol, and thus let the lighter wines escape easily.

Notwithstanding these grievances and gaps in the French system, it must be pronounced to be, on the whole, and considering the problems to be dealt with, a skilful application of well-planned administrative principles. Tried by the great test of productiveness, it answers the object for which it was planned. The various indirect contributions bring in close on £26,000,000, of which the drink duties provide about £18,000,000, and the internal sugar duty £3,400,000. The monopolies gain about £16,000,000 (95 per cent. of which comes from tobacco). When the total is taken it comes to the great amount of £42,000,000. Of this great revenue, spirits, beers and wines, tobacco, and sugar are the principal sources, the other duties forming but a trifling supplement. As in England, these articles are the support of the exchequer, while in France the drink duties further contribute about £4,000,000 annually to local Finance[1].

[1] See § 13 *infra*.

§ 8. Italian Finance has not had the same opportunities for the development of a productive system of indirect taxation as those possessed by England and France. The poverty of the people and the short duration of the present Kingdom have both prevented the creation of a complete system. Nevertheless the eminent statesmen and economists to whom the conduct of affairs has been entrusted have made great progress in this direction, and have endeavoured to apply scientific principles, so far as the difficulties of the situation would allow.

The tax system of Italy had to be built up on that of the several states out of which it was formed, and it had to supply sufficient funds to meet the growing expenses of the new Government. These conditions made the adoption of taxes, in other respects very undesirable, a necessity. The grist tax which fell on the main items of subsistence was at once oppressive and unequal, but it became one of the sources of revenue from 1869 to 1882, bringing in 83,500,000 lire (£3,340,000) in 1878, and an average of over £2,700,000 for each year of its continuance. Salt—another necessary—has been kept under a state monopoly, as it was in most of the smaller Italian states. Spirits, beers, and mineral waters have also been placed under an excise; so have cotton oil, chicory, gunpowder, and the more important article of sugar. A monopoly of tobacco has been conceded to a company, and the return from this source is one of the large items in the budget (over £7,500,000).

Italy, however, differs from both England and France in making use of the town duties on goods as a source of State revenue. The Italian *octroi* duties are notorious for their severity, falling as they do on articles of necessary consumption, as well as on the commoner enjoyments. Flour, rice, meat, butter, sugar, wine, beer and spirits, are all subjected to these local customs for the benefit of the State, with additional charges for municipal purposes. The inconvenience of this method is indisputable : it causes local variations in taxation levied for common purposes, and it is besides open to the general objections to the *octroi* system. The tax on wine may be defended on the same ground as the French entry duty, viz. that it is the only possible way of reaching an article of such general production and consumption, but this very difficulty seems to point to some other form of taxation as the most desirable solution. The total yield of £3,200,000 from *octrois* for State purposes is not large enough to justify the employment of so unfair and unpopular a method of taxation.

In extenuation of these seemingly oppressive and burdensome taxes it is necessary to remember the smaller amount of the national wealth[1] and the impossibility of limiting taxes to such articles of superfluous, or at best convenient, expenditure as alone are dutiable in England. Where good objects of taxation are wanting, the financier must perforce adopt those that are indifferent or bad. The direct taxation of the country is also heavy, and therefore the question of fiscal reform is primarily one of expenditure. Curtailment in the military and naval outlay and in the cost of administration would allow at least the removal of the *octrois*, combined with a reform of the tax on movable wealth, that would be a great relief to trade and secure a fairer distribution of the total load. A judicious reform of the drink duties might even raise their productiveness without injury in other respects. The whole position of Italian indirect taxation is a useful illustration of the modifications necessary in applying general principles to the economic system of a people at a somewhat low stage of industrial development. Such taxes as the grist tax or the existing salt monopoly would be unhesitatingly condemned on *a priori* grounds, but they were required in the particular situation.

The relation of indirect taxation to the consumption of the people is here shown afresh. It is not possible to gain

[1] The wealth of Italy has been estimated at £2,120,000,000, or one-fifth that of England. Pantaleoni, *Giornale degli Economisti*, Aug. 1890, 139 sq. Cp. Giffen, *Growth of Capital*, 153.

large returns from a southern people through the duties on the stronger alcoholic liquors. Such taxation as that of England would check the use of spirits completely. The same statement would hold true of any particular article. The theoretical doctrine that the minimum of subsistence should be exempt from taxation, however well it may sound, can only be applied in a society that has a considerable disposable surplus. When dealing with such populations as those of Italy or India, taxation must, to be effective, fall on objects that constitute a part of necessary consumption.

§ 9. The system of excises had a comparatively early and wide application in Germany. Without entering closely into the details it suffices to indicate the general fact. That the German cities should adopt a system of the kind was quite natural ; it was merely an *octroi* applied by a virtually sovereign state, but it seems that the method was imitated by the various princes, and notably in Brandenburg, where 'the general excise' was introduced in 1640 for some towns and gradually extended. This tax, which was limited to the towns, affected corn, meat, drinks, raw materials, and imported goods. It was intended to fall on the country through the process of shifting, and was undoubtedly one of the principal sources of revenue. The re-construction of the Prussian Finances after the French wars resulted in the substitution of the 'meal and meat' tax (1820), which was imposed only on the towns, as a kind of compensation for the 'class tax'[1] that affected the country districts. The yield of these taxes, which were given up in 1873, was about £400,000.

Other taxes, more in accordance with modern practice, were added. Breweries and distilleries came under excise supervision, and a moderate tax on the production of wine was imposed. The beet-root sugar was placed under duty in 1840, the old salt monopoly was retained, and tobacco

[1] Cp. Bk. iv. ch. 3. § 2 for the 'class tax.'

was made to contribute through a tax on the land given up to its cultivation.

The chief interest of this part of Prussian Finance lies in the fact that it has furnished the basis for the system of the present German Empire. Its development had in turn been influenced by the need of adjusting internal taxation to suit the regulations of the *Zollverein* as, e.g. in the cases of the sugar and tobacco duties. The advances in technical precision and productiveness since the formation of the Empire have not been as great as might have been expected. The salt monopoly was changed in 1867 into a tax on the article, which has been retained up to the present. The other objects of taxation are, it must be said, treated in an unsatisfactory way. The sugar duty which ought to be fairly productive is destroyed by the bounty system which has absorbed the greater part of the receipts [1]. Even when this difficulty has been removed—as it will be by the recent legislation on the subject—the yield of the tax will not be large, as the produce of the industry is mainly exported, and heavy taxation would be injurious to its development. The tobacco tax is suffering in a different way. At present it is levied through the inefficient excise system, and its amount is consequently low, 10,021,000 marks (£500,000). The remedy proposed in 1885 was the establishment of a monopoly, on the same system as that existing in France, Italy, and Austria, but it was defeated and no further reform has been carried out. A like attempt which was made with regard to the refining of spirits met with the same fate. However, the rate of duty has been increased considerably in the latter case with very beneficial results to the revenue, the receipts for the year 1889–90 being estimated at £6,750,000. Beer is also a source of revenue, but to a much smaller amount, owing to the lower rate, and the collection of the duties by the state governments of Bavaria, Würtemberg, and Baden, which reduces the receipts of the Empire.

[1] 114,000,000 marks out of 141,000,000 marks in 1886–7, Cohn, § 413.

German internal taxation is in some respects unfortunately placed. The separate interests of the different states hinder the most effective forms of duty being imposed, but still more the articles to be taxed are specially important products. Spirits, beer, and sugar, are all exported, and engage a good deal of the national capital and labour. Taxation is, therefore, more keenly felt, and strict supervision by the revenue officials is more injurious. The treatment of agricultural distilling is a particularly difficult matter, and one that only admits of a compromise. Fiscal presumptions, whose operation we have already noticed [1], are employed to escape the cost and trouble of more exact determination.

The economic and social conditions have, therefore, prevented as great a development of the modern excise system in Germany as has taken place in France: the duties are less productive—the total amount from the this source for 1889–90 was only £12,800,000—and they are deficient in just those articles that form the mainstay of British and French Finance. Tobacco and alcoholic drinks do not pay what might be expected from them; while the sugar duty is far under its real productiveness in consequence of the expenditure on bounties. The removal of this difficulty will be one addition to the receipts, and may be taken at £5,000,000, though production may fall off somewhat under the new regulations. An increased yield from tobacco, the end most needing to be accomplished at present, is to be reached—as a monopoly seems impracticable—by a more effective excise supervision. Beer might also be made to provide a larger revenue than it does at present. But even if these reforms were realized it is not to be expected that the revenue could equal that of more favourably situated countries. A large revenue from taxation of commodities implies either extreme rigour in the tax system or a high standard of comfort in the bulk of the population. Revenue may be wrung out of the subsistence fund of the

[1] Bk. iv. ch. 2. § 7.

nation, or it may be obtained from its comforts and luxuries. Neither condition is found in Germany, and consequently the returns of the indirect taxes are comparatively small.

§ 10. The tax systems of other countries repeat with modifications and new combinations the phenomena already described. Austria and Hungary derive a good part of their revenues from this source Salt and tobacco are monopolized by the State in both countries, and are important contributories, the net return in Austria being close on £7,000,000, in Hungary about £3,700,000. The drink duties, including spirits, beer, and wine, give £5,000,000 in Austria, and about half that amount in Hungary. Sugar is also taxed, yielding a revenue of £2,000,000 in Austria, and £300,000 in Hungary. A cattle tax is another of the forms adopted, but its productiveness is small, being less than £1,000,000 for the two kingdoms. The *octroi* duties in the larger Austrian towns are in part taken for the general revenue. In this way wine, beer, meat, and other articles are made to contribute.

The principal duties in Russia are those on sugar, tobacco, and particularly spirits. The first mentioned is the smallest; in 1888 it came to £500,000. Tobacco yielded in the same year £4,200,000, but both were insignificant in comparison with the amount of £42,000,000 obtained from the taxes on alcohol. This immense sum shows how the existence of a particular habit may affect the revenue of a country, and how it is possible under certain conditions to tax a very poor population. The contrast with the already noticed cases of Italy and Germany is very remarkable.

A further point of interest is the method employed in the collection of these taxes. Tobacco, as in the United States, is taxed by requiring stamped paper for its sale. Sugar and alcohol are subjected to a strict supervision at the factories. Formerly there were monopolies of both alcohol and tobacco, and the former continued till 1862 when it was abandoned for the present system with satisfactory financial results in the increase of the yield from less than £20,000,000 in 1862 to its present amount.

Except in the crisis of war the internal taxation of the United States has always been very restricted. Hamilton's attempt to tax whisky (1791) had led to a rebellion, and the duty was given up, to be again tried during the war with England (1812–14), and abandoned at its close. From that time till the outbreak of the Civil War (1861) there were no duties on domestic goods, not even on spirits. The war requirements of the Federal Government compelled recourse to heavy taxation; in addition to the income tax, and the customs, an extensive system of internal taxation was formed. 'Raw cotton was taxed at the rate of 2 cents per pound. . . . . Salt was taxed at the rate of 6 cents per 100 pounds; tobacco from 15 to 35 cents per pound; cigars from 3 dollars to 40 dollars per 1000; sugar from 2 to 3½ cents per pound. Distilled spirits were first taxed in 1863 at the rate of 20 cents, per gallon; the next year 60 cents; then 1 dollar 50 cents and subsequently 2 dollars[1].' Most manufactured articles were also taxed, sometimes both in the raw material and on the finished products, without any attention to the conditions of justice or productiveness. This very rigorous and on the whole effective application of taxation did not long survive the close of the war. By a series of enactments during the next five years all the duties except those on tobacco and spirits were repealed. The former, which is carried out by means of a stamp imposed on the tobacco as manufactured, has varied between £5,000,000 and £9,000,000 during the last twenty years[2]. The duty on spirits—which has changed much in amount, being reduced to 50 cents in 1868, and raised to 70 cents, and then to 90 cents—is far more productive. The amount realized in 1883 was over £11,500,000.

[1] Wells in *Cobden Club Essays* (2nd Series), 479.

[2] For the tobacco tax, Olmsted in *Quarterly Journal of Economics*, v. 193 sq.

Indian experience of direct taxation of commodities is confined to the case of salt and spirits. The former article, which next to land is the most important contributory, is taxed partly through monopoly, partly by excise. Spirits are now being placed under excise control at distilleries in preference to the old farming system. Out of a total of 120,000,000 rupees, salt yields two-thirds, spirits and drugs the remainder.

§ 11. We are now in a better position for examining some general features of the taxation of goods. Certain points have been impressed by repetition. One is the great prominence of drink duties. England, France, Russia, and the United States, regard them as the principal resource of the revenue. Improvements in the methods of German taxation will probably bring about the same result there. This circumstance suggests some important considerations. The moral difficulty of basing the financial prosperity of the State on the growing consumption of what is useless, and in many instances injurious, will be more and more felt in the future. The advocates of temperance can hardly remain contented with the present state of things in which the revenue from drink so far exceeds other receipts. But the possibility of sweeping restrictive legislation, extending perhaps to prohibition, raises the further question of the effect of such measures on the State's income. A reduction of 50 per cent. in the duties on spirits and beer would mean a grave deficit in the English Budget, hardly to be replaced by any readily available substitutes. A much higher rate of income tax or a heavy charge on land would probably have to be tried, perhaps combined with higher duties on tea and fresh taxation of sugar. The difficulties surrounding any of these courses need not be dwelt on; the limits of productiveness are reached sooner in the case of other indirect taxes, while an extension of the income or land taxes would involve a shifting of the present distribution of taxation that would need the greatest caution before it could be justly applied.

Connected in certain respects with the drink duties is the tobacco tax, which is so important a resource in France and Italy and—as a branch of the customs—in England. This impost has the advantage of falling on a luxury and affording a means of taxing the poorer classes who cannot well be made to contribute directly, but it is also open, though in a less degree, to the danger of shrinkage through a change of habits, and is, besides, in common with the drink duties, hard to levy in countries where the production is extensively carried on, as a high rate inevitably leads to illicit traffic.

It is in great part owing to a recognition of these complications that the method of monopoly has been so much employed. To place the manufacture of an article in the hands of the State is a strong measure, to be justified only by very cogent reasons; but where the need of revenue is great, this sacrifice of a particular business to secure complete freedom for the others may be desirable. It cannot be disposed of by an appeal to the principle of non-interference as a rule peremptorily binding on the State. The real point to be aimed at is to secure the needed revenue with the smallest amount of restriction, a result perhaps best attained through monopoly. This, among other considerations, has led to the proposals for a State monopoly of alcohol, which have been brought forward both in Germany and France, but which have not proved acceptable in either country. The reasons advanced in favour of such a measure are weakened by the great extent of the industry and the elaborate appliances needed for its proper working. That a State department could with financial profit undertake the production or sale of spirits is not likely, though it was confidently believed that this result could have been reached in Germany[1]. So far as the evidence goes a rigid excise system appears to be better both for the industry and the State. The progress of invention is certainly retarded by the routine that State

[1] The Swiss alcohol monopoly has given a small profit.

management sets up, and therefore, where it is desirable to secure the continual development of new processes, production should be left to private initiative, and as far as possible released from surveillance. But whatever be the form adopted, intoxicating drinks and tobacco must in the immediate future be the principal resource— so far as indirect taxation is concerned.

Among the other dutiable articles sugar holds a high place, and if revenue be needed, it is one of the most eligible objects for taxation, much more so than a necessary commodity like salt. This latter, again, is a preferable object to either corn or meat. A fiscal system that includes all these duties reaches a high degree of harshness, the addition of duties on raw materials being all that is necessary to make it attain the maximum in this respect.

The technical operations connected with the levying of duties deserve some notice. Modern appliances have made it far easier to gauge the exact product in most taxed industries; the strength of spirits or the sweetness of sugar can be ascertained with great precision by the use of special instruments, and in other cases similar aids are more or less available. As a means of checking fraud and stopping that 'leakage' and waste that has been so prevalent in the earlier attempts at taxation, they may be regarded as valuable contributions to Finance. The best devised duty from a purely economic point of view may fail in consequence of technical obstacles. In fact, the application of taxation is always dependent on a careful observance of these special circumstances. All the details of a duty are important in this connexion. Thus, the rate to be imposed must be regulated with reference to the intensity of the demand for the article, the gradations of the several qualities, and the effective power of testing that exists. The reasons for the repeal of the English paper and sugar duties were partly founded on the difficulties of discrimination: the adjustment of the American spirit duties, in order to meet the risks of illicit distilling and secure the highest return, has been shown by Mr. Wells to rest on similar grounds. The treatment of the different forms of spirits and beer in Germany has been largely conditioned by consideration of the effects of different methods of levying duties on the development of the industries and the receipts of the State.

Nor is it merely the conditions that exist within the particular country that have to be considered. With the modern agencies of transport no community can be regarded as an isolated unit. Its methods of taxing commodities will be influenced by the economic and fiscal systems of other countries. Due adjustment ought to be reached between excise and customs, and the trade relations with outside producers and consumers should be carefully studied. The greatest prospect of advance in financial arrangements probably lies in this direction. To expect uniform taxation in all European countries would be Utopian, but there is room for approximation in the selection of the articles to be taxed, and in the rates of duty imposed. Thus, the treatment of alcohol and tobacco might possibly be made the same in a good many nations, and thereby the obstruction to industry and risk of contraband traffic in great measure avoided. Even at present the monopoly system, as regards the latter article, is in force in France, Austria, Italy, Spain, and some smaller states, and may possibly be introduced into Germany. The rule of imposing higher duties on the more intoxicating spirits is now very generally adopted, though there is room for more complete agreement in both the mode of taxation and the rates fixed.

Finally, then, while it is evident that the forms and extent of internal taxes on commodities must depend on the financial necessities and the particular conditions of each country, it is also beyond doubt that what is vaguely called 'the progress of society' must lead to greater uniformity in both respects, though it would be premature to conjecture what will be the exact form of that common system.

§ 12. To complete our account of internal taxation it is necessary to notice its position in local Finance. The United Kingdom and the American Union are very markedly distinguished from other countries by their freedom from indirect taxes for local purposes. There have been some cases of 'ingate' tolls in English and Irish towns, and the London wine and coal dues were a more important instance, but with these exceptions internal trade has been altogether relieved of duties. This freedom of commerce was according to Adam Smith one of the reasons for the greater prosperity of the country. The Constitution of the United States, enforced by the resolute action of the courts, secured internal free trade over the whole area of the Union[1] and prevented the establishment of any local barriers.

In continental countries a very different state of things has prevailed. Everywhere, in one form or another, duties have been levied on goods entering into cities. These taxes, which may be traced back to the dues (*portoria*) imposed by the cities under the Roman Empire, were adopted by the *communes* as a ready means of acquiring funds. So early as the thirteenth century we find them in force in France, and their development continued till in the seventeenth century nearly every town possessed them. The ministers of Louis XIV saw in this form of tax a valuable resource for the hard-pressed Finances of the Kingdom, and accordingly a part of the *octrois* was appropriated for the use of the State, a system that continued down to the Revolution. Other countries had the same system; the German towns levied duties on the commodities entering within their walls, and both the Empire and the territory of Brandenburg derived revenue for their general purposes through the town taxes[2].

[1] Constitution of the United States, Art. i. § 10.

[2] *Supra*, § 9.

The abolition of the *octrois* by the Constituent Assembly, and their re-introduction a few years later, have been already mentioned[1]. In other countries the same popular sentiments and the same pressure of actual facts have made their influence felt. No form of taxation is more oppressive on the artisan and small trading classes, and it has, besides, an indirect effect on the rural producers. On the other hand, where direct taxation is extensively employed by the general government, it is hard for local authorities to devise any less inconvenient form of duty that will supply an equal revenue. The opposed forces are seen in operation in the history of *octrois* in the present century. There has been a disposition to, as far as possible, get rid of these troublesome imposts, while at the same time they continue in several countries as a source of local, and even of general revenue.

§ 13. France in particular possesses a carefully arranged system. Municipal Councils are empowered, and in certain cases compelled, to establish an *octroi*, which is distinctly recognised as a tax of consumption. The objects to be taxed may be food, drinks, fuel, fodder, and materials, but the power of taxing is limited by restrictions, which exclude articles already heavily taxed by the State or monopolized by it. *Octrois* on intoxicating drinks are specially regulated so as to bear a proportion to the general taxation of those objects[2].

The system applies to 1523 *communes*, or about one in twenty-four of the entire number; but as it includes all the large towns, its operation directly affects one-third of the population (12,500,000). The greater number of *communes* (887) raise the duties themselves. State-officials manage over 250, and 400 are farmed out at a rent. The city of Paris has a special *régime*, which extends to the outlying *communes* and is administered by the *Préfet* of the Seine. A considerable revenue is obtained from this source. In 1889 it amounted to £12,000,000, a little over one-half of

[1] *Supra*, § 6.

[2] Vignes, i. 205–16.

which was raised in Paris. This amount is an increase over earlier years. From less than £2,500,000 in 1823 it had risen to £3,800,000 in 1853, and nearly £8,000,000 in 1872. This growth is due to the larger population of the towns and their improved condition[1].

The Italian *octroi* duties in their present rigorous form only date from 1864: some of the smaller States had used them, but Sardinia and Tuscany were comparatively free[2]. Since the first measure on the subject several further orders and decrees have extended the system, until it has come to be productive of a large revenue as well as extremely oppressive. Without again considering that part of the duties which goes to the general revenue[3], it appears that in addition to further charges on the articles already taxed by the state *octroi*, there are duties on a large number of goods arranged into the same categories as in France, with an extra division for colonial produce. The result is that, in contrast with the French duties, foreign goods already submitted to customs taxation are taxed over again on their entry within the 'closed' *communes*, and that both the cost of living and the distribution of industry are injuriously affected. The duties vary according to the

[1] The distribution of the duties among the different articles is shown by the following figures for the year 1889—

	Francs.	*Percentage of total.*
Drinks and Liquids .	135,291,342	45·1
Food . .	85,090,337	28·4
Fuel . . .	32,565,756	10·9
Fodder . . .	16,218,211	5·4
Materials . .	25,976,552	8·7
Miscellaneous . .	4,521,778	1·5
Total	299,663,976	100·0

Of the total on drinks, 73,500,000 francs were levied on wine, 26,000,000 francs on spirits, and 17,250,000 francs on beer. Meat paid 56,000,000 francs, or two-thirds of the total on food. The cost of collection in 1889 came to about £1,000,000, which should be deducted from the gross receipts of £12,000,000.

[2] Only six Tuscan communes had *octrois* out of 246, and only one in every ten of those in the kingdom of Sardinia. 'Report on the Octroi duties in Italy,' Parliamentary Papers (C. 6206), 1891.

[3] *Supra*, § 8.

population of the town, and are levied on sales in the 'open' or rural districts. The revenue received by the Italian *communes* from these taxes in 1884 was £4,400,000, which, taken together with the part that goes to the central Government, represents a much heavier burden than that imposed in France by the same class of duties. A complete separation between the tax systems of the general and local governments would seem desirable, and might be accomplished either by the exchange of the state *octrois* for the local direct taxes, or better still by a complete reform of the methods of indirect taxation.

The various German States have gradually reduced their indirect local taxation. Some German towns retain the *octrois* as a supplemental resource. In Bavaria this method is adopted, but the list of articles is not at all so extensive as either in France or Italy. North Germany is for the most part free from *octrois*, though a beer duty is levied, as e.g. in Berlin. In any case this form of taxation is of minor importance for the German cities. Austria and Hungary use the *octroi* system more extensively; some of the funds obtained in this way are taken for the central Government, and the local taxes appear as additions to these state charges [1].

More radical measures have been applied in some other countries. Belgium, as we saw [2], abolished these taxes in 1860, and was followed by Holland in 1866, and by Spain in 1868, though the last-named country had soon to return to the old method. Denmark and Switzerland are practically without *octrois*, which are also of little importance in Portugal and Sweden [3].

[1] For the German *octrois*, see Cohn, §§ 457 sq.; cp. Schäffle 'In Deutschland sind die Octrois von geringer Bedeutung, der Bieraufschlag in Bayern und einige neuere Verbrauchsabgaben Württembergs ausgenommen. Belangreicher sind sie schon in Oesterreich; Wien zieht aus den städtischen Verzerungssteuern eine ansehnliche Summe,' *Steuerpolitik*, 452.

[2] Bk. iii. ch. 6. § 6.

[3] Isolated *octrois* may be found in all these countries, e.g. that at Copenhagen.

§ 14. When considering the general principles of indirect taxation, we concluded that its employment in local Finance was objectionable, and certain to disappear under the influence of sounder ideas on the subject of taxation. The fact that so many countries can successfully manage their municipal administration without recourse to indirect taxes is of itself a strong point against their continuance. They have the unfortunate peculiarity of combining the defects of customs and excise duties; for they hinder trade between town and country and impose heavy pressure on urban industries and consumers. Thus the materials for house-building are taxed both in France and Italy; the ordinary articles of the labourer's consumption are compelled to pay toll before they reach him, and so are many of the materials on which he works. Inequality of distribution is another glaring defect in the *octroi* system, which varies in its incidence from place to place and between different classes. The one valid argument in its defence is the plea of necessity. To surrender £11,000,000 of the French communal revenue would be a hazardous step until an assured equivalent was provided. This is the problem that reformers have to face, and the usual proposal has been the introduction of direct local taxes as a substitute. The difficulty of this plan lies in the resistance that most of the *communes* would offer to it. M. Léon Say's more fundamental method would alter the existing relations of the general and local governments, and place the direct taxes at the disposal of the latter, giving them at the same time increased functions[1]. Another, and perhaps more feasible proceeding would be to follow the Belgian precedent, and pay over a part of the general indirect taxation to the *communes* in lieu of *octrois*. One important consideration indicated by M. Say is the distinction between the fifty towns having over 30,000 inhabitants, whose net revenue from this source is £9,000,000, and the remaining 1470 communes that gain only £2,000,000. It is obvious

[1] *Journal des Économistes*, December 1891, 449–461.

that the latter class might easily replace their indirect taxes by additions to the *contributions directes*. Even the remaining towns—when Paris with its net receipt of £5,600,000 is deducted—ought to be able to furnish the £3,400,000 that would be needed by a development of the general taxation of spirits.

The case of Italy is a harder one; though the burden of the duties is greater, so is also the need of revenue; and thus for the present it seems that reform rather than abolition is advisable. Exemption of the materials of industry, low rates on articles of necessary consumption, together with greater uniformity in the different tariffs, might be carried out with advantage to the revenue; and these measures would prepare the way for further reforms.

§ 15. The last question that has to be discussed is that of the incidence of taxes on consumption. Everyone is familiar with the proposition that they fall on the consumer and are intended to be a deduction from his income when he comes to employ it. It, however, appeared that the process by which taxes are shifted is not so simple or uniform as this statement assumes[1]. That ultimately and 'in the long run' the bulk of the taxation of commodities falls on the general body of consumers is undoubtedly true, but this is in fact the case with a general income-tax, which arrests the funds previously to their expenditure. But before we assert that a tax on a particular commodity comes out of the pockets of the consumers of that commodity, we must be satisfied of three things, viz. (1) that none of the burden remains on the producer who pays the tax immediately, (2) that none of it is thrown back on other producers or owners of land or capital who contribute to the production, and (3) that the consumer has no way of passing on the burden to another set of persons. The realization of these conditions is not always found. In some cases the producer has a complete or qualified monopoly, or more accurately a differential advantage,

[1] Bk. iii. ch. 5. § 5.

and when this is so he bears the burden in whole or part. Again, the limitation of demand caused by taxation leads to a lower value of land or fixed capital or specialized labour suited for the industry, in which case some of the loss falls on the particular agent so affected. Finally, and this fact has been even exaggerated in the 'orthodox' theory of incidence, the additional cost of living may lead to a higher rate of wages, which must inevitably lower interest or employers' gain, unless indeed it is limited to certain groups of workers, when the consumers of their products may bear the burden.

Applying these general facts to existing tax systems, it is an interesting question to consider how far the abolition of the present English excise would (*a*) increase the profits of brewers and distillers as well as retail traders, (*b*) allow of higher prices for barley, hops, sugar and other materials of the kind, or (*c*) cause a lowering of wages in consequence of the smaller drink bill of the labourer and artisan. That each of these effects would in some degree be produced is, we believe, indisputable; but so much depends on conditions that cannot be even approximately estimated, that it would be impossible to offer a conjecture as to their relative strength. The effect on other industries through the sums set free from the purchase of drink, or the increased labour and capital required in the distilleries and breweries if the total expenditure on drink remained as before, would be a further puzzle. Now, if the remission of these duties would produce such effects, it is unquestionable that the development of the modern excise has caused, not perhaps quite the same, but quite as complex and important changes. When we take—as financiers and statisticians too readily do—the actual distribution of taxation as a guide to its real effects, we should never forget the far more intricate problems that the working of a set of taxes imposed on a complex economical system is sure to raise.

If this be true of the very simple and easily examined

excise of England it holds good with still greater force of the more elaborate systems of France, Germany, and Italy. Where several articles are taxed the effects are sure to become intermixed; e.g. a duty on sugar tends to combine with duties on breweries where that article is used as a material. Especially where taxation is different in different cases we may expect complicated results; the heavier duty on wines entering French towns is surely an element in the cost of living, and probably in the wages of the workmen residing in them, and hence on the price of the goods produced in such places, while this altered price may cause a redistribution of industry.

The *octrois* exhibit some of the best examples of the practical existence of these—at first sight far-fetched—positions. One of the arguments of the defenders of local taxation of commodities is that their incidence is not really on the consumer, who would not benefit by their abolition. It is pointed out that in many cases the reduction or removal of the town barriers has not lowered prices. The gain is reaped by the producer or trader[1]. So far as this argument has any truth it illustrates the proposition that we have already laid down, though it is hardly a good defence of the system[2]. In like manner it has been argued that the Italian *octroi* system has compelled manufacturers to establish their industries in agricultural districts where the cost of subsistence is not artificially enhanced[3]. But what is apparent in the limited sphere of local taxation must be equally operative, though its influence is harder to trace, in the wider field of state economy.

[1] This argument will reappear in connexion with the incidence of import duties.

[2] This has been alleged of the Belgian reform and also of the partial remission of the Parisian *octroi* in 1848.

[3] *Report on Octroi Duties* (C. 6206), 14, 15.

CHAPTER VII.

Customs Duties.

§ 1. The taxation of goods at the frontier or on passing a fixed boundary line—what is known in England as the customs revenue—is far older than the system of internal duties. Almost from the origin of commerce we can find traces of its employment, and can note its gradual development into an important source of state income. Nor has it as yet lost much of its prominence. Notwithstanding the great increase of other branches of taxation, customs are still a conspicuous part of nearly every national budget, and in some countries are regarded as the only convenient mode of levying dues on consumption[1].

The most primitive form of this kind of taxation is probably that known as a transit duty, imposed on goods passing through a district. Modern African travellers have made us familiar with the 'gifts' demanded by each petty chief in return for leave to go through his country, an exaction which in the trader's case is practically a tax on the wares that he carries. How natural such a system is its revival in the earlier Middle Ages shows. In that disorderly condition of society each lord or *seigneur* asserted

[1] The English Customs revenue for 1890–1 was £19,480,000 or nearly 22 per cent. of the gross receipts. In France the amount for 1891 is estimated at £15,400,000 or 12 per cent. of the revenue. The German Customs for 1889–90 were estimated at £13,500,000, and the Italian at £10,600,000 or 26 and 15 per cent. respectively. A much larger proportion of the United States Federal revenue (over one half) is obtained from this source, £44,000,000 out of £78,500,000 in 1890–1.

his right to charge dues on goods in passage, basing his claim on the services that he rendered by keeping the roads, bridges, and water-ways in fit condition, and by protecting the trader against violence. The collection of the tolls was, however, far more regular than the performance of the corresponding services, and therefore the first efforts of reviving commerce and increased royal power were directed towards the curtailment of such vexatious dues, which were either abolished or confined to payment for actual service done [1]. The use of transit duties was however continued in state taxation, and they have only been given up in the present century.

Next in historical order comes the export duty, levied on commodities as they leave the State's territory. The reasons for the employment of this kind of duty in early times can hardly be adequately appreciated, without considering the differences in economic beliefs and conditions. By taxing exports it was thought that the foreigner was made to pay a high price for native wares, or at worst that a more abundant supply was kept for the home consumer. Even if the burden should fall on the native producer, the article taxed was generally an important one, and its proprietors were bound to contribute to the public revenue. In fact the export duty is often a mitigation, introduced in the interests of the Exchequer, of the more rigorous prohibition of export.

The field of action for export taxes has been greatly diminished by the influence of the mercantile system [2], which, looking on exportation as advantageous, was naturally hostile to anything calculated to restrict it. The few exceptions that it admitted for special reasons [3] have since been removed by the change in commercial policy, so that the use of export duties is now on a very limited scale.

[1] For the great number of tolls and passage duties in mediaeval times, see Clamageran, i. 160–1; Pigeonneau, *Histoire du Commerce de la France*, i. 96–99, 182–3: for Germany, Zimmern, *Hansa Towns*, 102.

[2] See *Introd.* Part ii. § 5.

[3] For this side of Mercantilism, see *Wealth of Nations*, Bk. iv. ch. 8.

The decline of the older forms of customs taxation has not affected the import duties, which indeed have come to be regarded as synonymous with the customs. The complete abolition of duties on exports would hardly affect the Finances of European States, but anything that disturbed the revenue from imports would be the cause of grave concern to nearly all nations [1]. Though probably of somewhat later origin than transit or export dues, duties on imports were well established at an early period. They were employed under the Roman Empire, with separate customs lines or points for each province [2], but the rates were moderate, not exceeding five per cent. *ad valorem*. The break-up of the Empire brought back the ruder state of things already described, and it was not till royal authority became somewhat firmly established that duties on imports were effectively levied. The cities exercised the power of taxing goods, each in its local market, which was in many cases the same as an import duty, but the great agency in the development was the expansion of the King's administration. England supplies the earliest example with its 'customary' dues on wine, accompanied by the heavy tax on exported wool [3]. Other European countries followed the same course. France, e. g. adopted import taxation at a later date, export and transit dues being at first more prominent. As trade increased, and as the desire of encouraging national industry took a firmer hold, resort to import dues became more frequent. The rise of mercantilism, discernible in England from the time of the Tudors, and in France from the sixteenth century [4], supplied a fresh force in favour of this form of taxation, while it tended to lower its financial importance in compari-

[1] India is perhaps the only country in which the revenue from exports exceeds that from imports.

[2] Mommsen, *Hist. of Rome*, iii. 397–8; Merivale, *Romans under the Empire*, iv. 45; Clamageran, i. 73.

[3] Dowell, i. 75 sq.

[4] For England, see Schanz, *Englische Handelspolitik*, and Cunningham, *Growth of English Industry*; for France, Pigeonneau, *ut supra*.

son with its use in assisting native producers against their foreign competitors.

Among the great services that Adam Smith performed in the cause of sound Finance, his establishment of the true function of import duties was undoubtedly one. His vigorous attack on their employment as an instrument of economic policy helped materially to bring out their true use as a fiscal agency. To gain a large revenue and at the same time protect native industry from the entry of foreign goods was, he plainly showed, impossible[1]. The revenue duty is not protective, and the protective duty is not revenue-yielding. The influence of Adam Smith's teaching on administrators, and the need of revenue in consequence of increasing outlay have led to at least a partial recognition of the financial aims of import taxation. Even in countries that adhere to a rigid system of protection, some of the duties are solely productive of revenue, and in all, the financial aim crosses and modifies the political one. A great deal of the modern protectionist revival is really due to the need of revenue to meet growing expenditure. The general adoption of a purely financial customs system, with complete exclusion of all other aims, may be long deferred, but state requirements will always secure that the gaining of funds shall be one of the objects aimed at. The real danger lies rather in the probability of the methods employed being wasteful and unduly oppressive to the consumers.

§ 2. In order to understand the position of the customs in the fiscal system, it is essential to see that they are in reality a form or mode of collection, rather than a distinct branch of taxation. This point has been indicated before[2], but it is worthy of repetition. Whether a given commodity—say salt—is taxed directly in the possession

[1] 'Taxes proposed with a view to prevent, or even to diminish, importation are evidently as destructive of the revenue of the customs as of the freedom of trade,' *Wealth of Nations*, 191.

[2] Bk. iv. ch. 5. § 2.

of the consumer, or indirectly, either by excise supervision over the producer, by making the production a state monopoly, or, finally, by levying a duty at the frontier, is in one respect immaterial, as any of these methods secures taxation of consumption. The separate treatment of the customs is only defensible on historical and technical grounds. This fundamental unity of the various forms of taxation on consumption at once leads to the conclusion that most of the conditions governing the excise may be applied without hesitation to the customs. Thus the whole formation of the tariff should be determined by the parallel system of internal taxation, and the duties of both should be exactly the same. No one has disputed the justice of imposing a customs duty where an excise one is already in force. To allow e.g. foreign spirits to enter duty free, while native ones paid heavily, would at once reduce the revenue and divert the normal course of industry. But exactly the same reasoning applies to the case of an import duty without an equivalent excise one. Expenditure is in this case also diverted, with the double evil of forcing some of the consumers to take what is in their opinion an inferior article and depriving the State of funds.

The problems of the excise as to the number of taxed articles and their selection reappear in connexion with the customs, though some modifying circumstances also occur. As regards the first, it is abundantly established that for productiveness only a small number of commodities should be taxed. This is best shown by the fact that in all countries the really productive articles are few in number. Before the restrictive system had been seriously altered in England (1839), five-sixths of the receipts came from nine articles. Forty years later (1880), three-fourths of the French customs revenue was raised on eight principal commodities, and in 1887, corn, coffee, tobacco, and wine provided more than one-half of the German receipts from this head[1]. The lesson of the excise is repeated in respect

[1] *Report* of Import Committee (1840); Leroy Beaulieu, i. 615; Cohn, § 407.

to the customs. It is further clear that more than a single article will have to be taxed. To secure the maximum of revenue with the minimum of friction, it is expedient to get a sufficiently broad field on which to operate. By this means the stability of the revenue is best secured. A particular commodity may fluctuate in its yield from year to year, but the general customs revenue can be made to annually approximate to a certain amount for a long series of years [1]. The adoption of a pure revenue system greatly assists in the attainment of this desirable result.

The administration of the customs is relieved from one of the technical difficulties of the excise. Its treatment of all commodities is very much alike, and there is no interference with the work of production, or the development of industries; nevertheless other complications arise. The supervision of a long frontier is an arduous task, and where high duties are imposed, contraband trade can hardly be prevented. The more portable commodities are therefore not fitted to bear heavy duties, and, in fact, the limitation of taxation to products of distant countries, and to fairly bulky articles would, from this point of view, be advisable.

It has been suggested as a rule of fiscal policy, that customs duties should, as far as possible, be placed only on those goods that are not produced at home. This, however, is hardly practicable, since, even where the exact commodity is not of native production, some available substitute is, and a tax that stimulates the use of substitutes is, in principle, as vicious as a protective duty. This problem arises in connexion with the English tea and coffee duties, but is not in their case of much practical weight.

The further questions as to the treatment of necessaries and raw materials must be answered in the same way as in the excise. Both are injurious, if they can be avoided,

[1] The English revenue from this source has kept very near £20,000,000 per annum for the last thirty years. In the period 1815–1890 it has only varied between £24,000,000 and £19,000,000 notwithstanding the extensive remissions of taxation.

but the wants of the State may, as we saw[1], compel the taxation of such articles as salt and corn, in which case the customs system must levy its part of the tax. Taxes on raw materials, though they impede industry and raise prices unduly, may, on the whole, be the least vexatious mode of reaching a particular class that would not otherwise contribute its share. A tax on raw cotton might e. g. be the most effective and least irritating way of taxing the consumers of calico[2].

In fine, the customs system requires to be thoroughly adapted to the conditions of the general taxation on consumption, of which it forms a part, and has besides to conform to the technical limits imposed by its constitution and mode of working. Productiveness, equity, and economy both with regard to the cost of collection and the loss imposed on the community are the ends to be realized, and of these, the first and last are the most important, as unfairness in the pressure of taxes on commodities can be rectified by alleviations in other parts of the tax system[3].

§ 3. The English customs system is remarkable for its rigorous adherence to the principle of purely financial duties. All traces of a political aim in the imposition of customs charges have now disappeared. This result has, however, been reached only as the result of a long development during which other principles were operative. England, from its insular position and its stronger government, was more favourably situated than any continental state in respect to this form of tax. From being merely customary charges on wine and wool, the port duties expanded in the seventeenth century into a broader system. The receipts—derived from the general tax of five per cent. on all imports and exports, and the duties on wine, cloth, tobacco, silk, brandy,—rose from £127,000 in 1604, to nearly

[1] Bk. iv. ch. 6. § 2.

[2] Cp. Mill's advocacy of a tax on raw silk, *Principles*, Bk. v. ch. 6. § 2.

[3] Cp. Bk. iii. ch. 3. § 9 for this use of a progressive tax on income.

£500,000 in 1641, and nearly £1,000,000 in 1688[1]. After the Revolution they fell off, owing to the French war and the increase of duties to ten per cent., but by 1702 they came to £1,500,000.

All through the eighteenth century, war and the influence of the mercantile doctrines hindered the growth of the customs revenue; profitable lines of trade were closed, and prohibitive duties encouraged smuggling. The most prominent features were the imposition of special duties, and the increase of the general import duties. Wines, spirits, sugar, tea, and coffee, had all to pay extra charges, while the ten per cent. general charge of 1698 became fifteen per cent. in 1704, twenty per cent. in 1747, and twenty-five per cent. in 1759. The pressure of the American war of Independence brought further additions in the shape of two separate five per cent. increases on the total duties existing on each article, with further extra duties on sugar and tobacco. Far greater, however, was the effect of the French wars (1793–1815), with the enormous outlay in which they involved the country. At six different times the import duties generally were raised, besides heavy special increases on particular commodities. The final result was that at the close of the conflict in 1815, the tariff contained nearly 1400 items, and the rates were in many cases prohibitive.

In this unfortunate course of development, but two periods of mitigation occur. Walpole's long peace administration (1722–39), secured the carrying of some desirable reforms; such as the abolition of the general export duty, the reduction of the more onerous duties on raw materials, and the adoption of a new valuation of goods. The opening of the younger Pitt's ministry also promised well. The duties on tea and coffee were lowered (1784); the Eden commercial treaty with France (1786),

[1] Dowell, i. 195; ii. 34. Some of the hottest contests between the king and the people turned on questions of taxation, e. g. the currant duty (Bates' case). For the earlier history, see Hall, *History of the Customs Revenue.*

enabled an open trade to be carried on between the two countries; and in 1787 the customs laws were consolidated. These measures, however, had but a temporary effect; the need of securing revenue made recourse to bad taxes necessary, when the productiveness of the better ones was exhausted. But from the fiscal point of view it is plain that a simpler and better-regulated system would have been far more effective. In spite of the oppressive duties on almost every article, and the frequent increases of rates, the returns were not what might have been expected. In 1739 the yield was less than in 1702, and the growth up to the accession of George III. was slow [1].

In the period 1820–1860, this complicated and uneconomic tariff system was completely transformed. The old prohibitive duties were removed; so were all the surviving export taxes. Raw materials, articles of food, and finally, manufactured goods disappeared from the customs list, until the attention of the customs staff was concentrated on a small number of productive articles, taxed at suitable rates. Thus the customs system has become nearly as simple as the excise, though owing to the conditions of production it at present includes somewhat more articles. Notwithstanding this notable diminution in the number of dutiable goods, the yield has hardly declined, and by the replacement of a moderate sugar duty would now be higher than ever [2]. We are not concerned here with the history of this important reform,

[1] The following figures give the yield of the customs at selected periods:—

Year.	£
1702	1,500,000
1739	1,400,000
1760	1,824,000
1784	3,025,000
1802	8,815,000
1816	11,950,000.

Sinclair, *History of Revenue*, ii. Appendix, No. i.; Dowell, ii. 62, 109; Wilson, *National Budget*, 55.

[2] In 1872 the low sugar duty gave £3,180,000; allowing for the increase in consumption, the same rate would bring the present customs to over £24,000,000.

carried out in more logical and consistent manner than is usual in English legislation [1]. Still less have we to consider the economic issues of the free-trade contest; but it is in place to note the real cause of the financial success achieved. It was by singling out the fiscal element in import duties and neglecting other considerations, that the revenue was maintained so close to its former level. The great number of duties created or increased between the Revolution of 1688 and the battle of Waterloo had two grave financial defects, for (1) they were not really productive of revenue [2], and (2) they violated the rule of 'economy' by taking far more out of the taxpayers' pockets than they provided for the state Treasury. The successive prunings of the customs tariff removed what had little life, and gave room for growth to the branches that remained. Cheaper raw materials made industry more effective; cheaper food left a larger surplus to be spent on enjoyments, and lower duties on the productive articles stimulated consumption, while they diminished smuggling. Consequently there has been an apparently immense remission of duties without any real loss to the revenue [3]. It must, however, be remembered that the low rates of duty now prevailing—those on tobacco and spirits excepted—are dependent on the development of direct taxation, and the stamp (including the succession) duties. The emer-

[1] There were three stages in the movement, viz. (1) the reforms of Huskisson, 1823–7, which opened the way; (2) Peel's tariffs of 1842 and 1845, by which a substantial instalment of free trade was given; and (3) the measures of Mr. Gladstone in 1853 and 1860, which completed the work. For the fiscal history of this period, see Dowell, ii. 249–361; Buxton, *Finance and Politics*, i. 1–217; also Northcote, *Twenty Years of Financial Policy*. For the general character of the legislation, Wagner, iii. 300–1.

[2] Thus in 1839 crystal beads yielded 1*s*. 7*d*., starch 1*s*. 9*d*., Bruges thread 1*s*. 3*d*., extract of vitriol, 12*s*. 3*d*!

[3] Between 1815 and 1885 the amount of duties remitted was £35,861,000 against £8,063,000 imposed, or a balance of £27,800,000 remitted, Wagner, iii. 299. But there have been no remissions in the last ten years of the period, and those in the preceding fifteen years (1861–75) amounting to £14,500,000, were on purely revenue duties—tea, sugar, &c. Since 1885 the tea, tobacco, and currant duties have been lowered.

gency of a war or any weakness in the treatment of the income-tax would lead to higher rates on wine, tea, and coffee, and a return to the sugar duty.

As regards the particular objects of charge, the chief difference from the excise lies in the fact that certain exclusively foreign products are taxed. Tea, coffee, figs, raisins, currants, and wine are not British products, a position that fiscal regulations have also given to tobacco. Hence these commodities are contributories to the customs only. Beer and spirits come under both departments. An important development in fiscal expedients has led to what is practically a connexion between the two branches. The bonding or warehousing system, by which goods can be landed and stored free of duty, if they are placed under official control, is extensively used, and is now available in several inland towns, with the result that customs and excise become practically intermingled. Of the advantage of this concession it is needless to speak, but it is found rather difficult to extend it as far as traders desire, owing to the extra cost that it causes[1]. At all events, the sacrifice imposed on traders and on the community is minimised by this means, especially when the very small number of dutiable articles is taken into consideration.

The bulk of the customs revenue is made up of drink and tobacco duties, the former giving £4,800,000, the latter £9,500,000 in the year 1890–1. Tea is the only other large contributor. At the reduced rate of 4*d.* per pound it yielded £2,400,000, but a continuance of the normal increase of the last few years in the other branches of the revenue would allow of its repeal, along with the smaller duties on coffee, cocoa, chicory, and dried fruits. Were this accomplished, the whole indirect taxation of consumption in the United Kingdom would be confined to drink and tobacco, as 90 per cent. of it is at present.

§ 4. France, on the whole, shows a greater difference from England in Customs (*Douanes*) than in internal

[1] On the bonding system, cp. Cliffe Leslie, *Financial Reform*, 199, 214–6.

taxation. Not only are the dutiable articles much more numerous, but the aim of gaining revenue has never been the sole end in view. To reach the position of England, an entire recasting of the tariff would be necessary. All the points in which reform was carried out in the latter country remain for treatment. Food, raw materials, and manufactures are all subject to import duties, often high in amount. The development of this system can be traced from the sixteenth century, but its most striking period was under the administration of Colbert (1661-1683), when the old export and transit dues were diminished, and the import ones increased, especially on manufactures. The whole customs system was, however, affected by the absence of unity, the internal duties between the different provinces being just as heavy, and far more injurious to trade. These obstacles were finally removed by the Revolution, and the reform tariff of 1791, which is the basis of the present structure, was established[1]. Unfortunately the liberal provisions of this measure were not continued in subsequent legislation. From the outbreak of war in 1792 to 1860, political rather than financial considerations governed the framing of tariffs in France. The result is seen in the comparatively small yield of this form of tax. Instead of the English revenue of £20,000,000, obtained without any direct pressure on the necessaries of life, or the raw materials of industry, the highest yield of the French customs has not reached £15,000,000, though the list of dutiable articles is a long one. The smaller return may be partially explained by reference to the lower standard of living in France, the difficulties of supervision, and the different position of taxed products, *e.g.* wine and tobacco are taxed solely by the customs in England. On the other hand, the duties on salt and sugar give a large part of the receipts, and they are not in force in England. But the full explanation of the smaller return is to be found in the unproductive

[1] For Colbert, see Clamageran, ii. 599–697; for the internal customs, Stourm, i. 470 sq., and for the tariff of 1791, *ib.* ii. 61–75.

character of so many of the articles taxed. Thus, out of a total yield of £13,400,000 in 1887, but six articles produced more than £500,000 each, and they made up £9,800,000, or nearly three-fourths of the total, viz. coffee £4,000,000, corn £1,640,000, sugar £1,560,000, petroleum £1,200,000, wine £900,000, and cocoa £510,000. All the remaining goods produced only £3,600,000, or £400,000 less than the single item of coffee, the only fairly productive article being coal, with £450,000. Even of the productive duties, those on corn and petroleum are seriously inconvenient, while the former is an encouragement to the unprofitable occupation of wheat-growing. A further proof of the revenue being really derived from a limited number of articles, and having its best resource in them, appears from the fact that in 1872 the six commodities enumerated paid only £3,600,000, or little over one-third of their yield in 1887. Of these, coffee and cocoa have increased four-fold, petroleum nearly three-fold, corn and wine about eighteen-fold, while the return from all other goods has only risen from £2,200,000 to £3,600,000, or a little over sixty per cent.[1]. The duties on hundreds of small articles do, it is true, help to make the budget balance, but at an excessive cost. A small addition to the direct taxes, a readjustment of the more productive duties, or some minor retrenchments would be preferable methods.

The absence of any due relation between the customs and the internal taxes is a further blot from the financial point of view. An import duty, uncompensated by an equal charge on the corresponding native product, causes a diversion of demand that is unprofitable both to the State and the consumers. Regarding such a method as—what it really is—a bounty on home production, we can see how an unnecessary cost is incurred through the system. More

[1] The great increase in the corn duties is due to the return to agricultural protection by the laws of 1881 and 1885; that in wine to the failure of the French crops and the consequent importation. There is, however, a falling-off in sugar of £350,000 that could have been easily avoided by wiser treatment of the bounty question.

particularly is this true of the duties on raw materials, such as the various yarns, and on machinery and implements. Though such taxes have little direct financial significance, they do much to dry up the source of all taxation by retarding the development of industry and the growth of commerce.

While then the French customs could hardly be as productive as the English with their duties on tea, tobacco, wine and foreign spirits, they might yield a satisfactory contribution of at least £10,000,000, or probably more, by duties concentrated on a small number of commodities, and this revenue would further be steadily increasing as the relief to industry from the other remissions came to operate [1].

§ 5. The Italian customs system, with its comparatively brief history, shows the same faults and illustrates the same general principles as the French one. From less than £2,500,000 in 1862, the return has grown to £10,500,000 in 1889–90, but this increase is due to the imposition of much higher rates of duty, which are very heavy on raw materials and necessaries. Still the productive articles are few in number. In 1883, sugar, mineral oils, and coffee contributed more than half (53 per cent.) of the total, or £3,200,000 out of £6,000,000. Since then, by heavier rates on yarns, tissues and metals, the customs revenue has been brought up to its present point, with, however, a very severe pressure on the consumers generally, which, be it said, is only in keeping with the general system of Italian taxation. Reform therefore is not so easy as it would be in France; the high duties bring in a much needed revenue, and remissions of taxation are not likely to be compensated by rapid recovery through increased consumption [2].

The German system is specially interesting as supply-

[1] The exaggerations of the protectionist system by the tariff of 1891 will, it is estimated, add £2,800,000 to the receipts, but this is a very insufficient measure of the real cost that will be placed on the country.

[2] On the Italian customs, see the elaborate study by Alessio, ii. 346–452.

ing one of the best possible examples of the gradual absorption of smaller customs areas in a common unity. The condition of the German States, each with distinct custom-houses that were so many obstructions to trade, led the wiser financiers to promote the establishment of fiscal unions between the States. These efforts brought about the series of agreements by which the *Zollverein*, or customs union, was created, which included Prussia, Bavaria, Würtemberg, Saxony, Baden, and most of the smaller territories, and which was the forerunner of political union. The immediate effect of the removal of internal restrictions was an increase in customs receipts, and a reduction of the proportionate cost of collection by one-half. The moderate rates of duty, derived from the Prussian tariff of 1818, assisted this expansion, which was hardly checked by some partial protectionist movements.

The customs union when transformed into the German empire at first continued its moderate financial system, and even (1873) made further reductions. But the need of revenue and the stronger protectionist sentiment brought about a much higher scale of duties in the tariff of 1879. That this important measure increased the receipts is indisputable; from £5,700,000 in 1878–9 they rose to £13,500,000 ten years later. Whether the mode adopted was the best one is not so clear. The corn duties, as in France and Italy, press on the working class, and owing to the large home production are decidedly uneconomic. The cattle duties have not even the advantage of yielding revenue. Still more objectionable are the taxes on wood, iron, and machinery in consequence of their effects on industry.

The limitation of the productive articles to a small number is, as we saw, also found in Germany. If corn, coffee, tobacco and wine, were removed from the tariff, more than half of the revenue would disappear; and it is more than probable that a reform of the duties on these articles, accompanied by an adjustment of the inland taxes on commodities, would allow of a great curtailment, if not an entire removal, of the remaining items[1].

The tariff systems of Austria, Russia, and the United States are even more remarkable for their subordination of financial to political objects. Under the influence of a protectionist policy the revenue duties on tea, coffee and sugar have in the last-named country been either abolished or cut down to a very low amount, while the duties on raw materials and manufactures are many and high. There is no approach to equality between the inland taxation and the customs tariff; on the contrary the duties are designedly fixed so as to give a preference to native producers.

§ 6. The broad result of an examination of the customs systems of different countries is to indicate that the financial operations are greatly interfered with, and their effectiveness diminished, by the intrusion of politico-economic objects. We may indeed conveniently divide import duties into two classes: (1) the small number that contribute to the revenue in a satisfactory way, and (2) the far larger number that only provide income as it were incidentally. The protective duties of modern societies are in fact often rather a mode of expenditure than of revenue, since by the increased cost of collection that they make requisite, and by their indirect effects on the financial duties, they take more from the Exchequer than they bring in to it. The line is not always clearly drawn; the same duty may be at once revenue and protective, as the French and German corn duties prove; but this situation really indicates either that the protection given is ineffectual, or that a great deal of the tax is wasted on the virtual bounty given to the home producers. Whatever view we may take of the wisdom of a protective policy, we must allow that it means a certain outlay on the part of the State by the sacrifice of what would otherwise have gone to increase the revenue.

[1] For the founding of the Zollverein, see Roscher, § 102; also his *Geschichte*, ch. 34, and for the present German customs, Cohn, §§ 404–10.

Another noticeable feature is the almost exclusive use of import duties. Transit dues have been completely abandoned [1], and export duties have a very subordinate place. They do not exist in Great Britain, France, Germany, or the United States, and may be said to be confined to countries at a lower stage. Brazil has a productive duty on the export of coffee, but India takes the foremost position with its opium and rice duties. Some of the English Colonies also levy duties on the export of their staple product, *e.g.* sugar in the case of the West Indian Islands [2]. But these exceptional cases only tend to confirm the rule that for the present time imports are the most effective object of taxation. Nor is it hard to see the reasons that have made them preferred. The excise taxation of commodities almost necessarily carries with it the use of corresponding duties on imports, and some imported articles are very suitable objects for imposition. Hence their employment for revenue purposes. The desire to encourage native industry accounts for the duties on many articles that are very decidedly unfit to be taxed, and especially for the use of import duties with respect to them. We may indeed trace a general movement by which the transit duty has been abandoned, and the once prevailing export taxes reduced to insignificance, while the import tax comes to the front.

There is a further movement in respect to the customs system that is deserving of notice, viz. its extension over, or application to, wider areas. The case of Germany has been mentioned, but France in the last century, Italy in the present one, and even the United Kingdom are additional instances [3]. It is not likely that no further advance will be

[1] The Indian transit duties—the most important of which was that on Cashmere wool (10 per cent.)—were abolished by Mr. James Wilson: see his *Financial Statement* (1860), 22. But part of the opium revenue is really a transit charge on the drug from the native states.

[2] The Indian opium duty—partly monopoly, partly transit—yielded 84,500,000 rupees in 1880–1, but has sunk to 53,100,000 rupees in the estimate for 1891–2. The Brazilian coffee duty gave £1,800,000 in 1889.

[3] The English customs system was extended to Scotland in 1707, but not to

made in this respect. Proposals for customs unions of Australasia, of the British Empire, of central Europe and of all the American nations, however they may differ in practicability, are all signs of the times, and show the direction in which change is probable. To understand the real meaning of this tendency it is well to reassert a point previously noticed, viz. that, financially considered, customs duties are but one form of the taxation of commodities, and that therefore the formation of a customs union is *pro tanto* the substitution of excise for customs. How far this method can be carried at present is not easily determinable, but it may be suggested that ultimately the boundary duties on imports will share the fate of those on the export and transit trades. The taxation of goods at the frontier, in spite of the improvements in the mechanism of collection, is a serious obstruction to trade, especially under modern conditions in which rapidity and despatch are of such great importance. Just as the town *octrois* would be intolerable in England or America, so it may come to pass that a customs line between England and France will be too inconvenient to be endured. For the immediate future, however, the customs system will be a necessary element in the taxation of commodities that the heavy outlay of modern States makes indispensable.

§ 7. The problem of incidence—always a difficult one—is specially involved in the case of taxation of foreign trade. The various parties affected and the conditions that govern the course of unimpeded trade, which are themselves complicated, must be taken into account before a full interpretation can be given; it is, besides, very hard to obtain confirmation or correction of the results of deductive reasoning by appeal to statistics, as they do not throw much light on the really difficult parts of the subject.

To begin with the most primitive form. Who pays the

Ireland till 1825, when the Union duties were repealed. At present the Channel Islands are outside it, and the Isle of Man is under special regulations.

cost of a transit duty? According to Adam Smith 'duties of this kind are paid altogether by foreigners, and, perhaps, are the only duties that one State can impose on the subjects of another, without obstructing in any respect the industry or commerce of its own[1].' The loss must, he supposes, fall on the sending or the receiving country. This view, however, needs qualification. A transit duty will force trade to take another direction, or if this is impossible will reduce its volume, and thereby injuriously affect the transport industry and the *entrepôt* business. For example, a transit duty in Belgium would be disastrous to the railways of that country and to the depôt business of Antwerp. If we recognise that a transit duty is an import tax without a drawback on export, we see at once that it is unadvisable for the same reason that drawbacks have been universally adopted[2].

The export duty is, generally speaking, open to similar objections. As employed in mediaeval times, it was intended partly to tax those foreigners who used the staple product of the country, and partly as an impost on the producers, or owners of natural agents. It is evident that the incidence of the tax will vary according to the position of the article taxed. That the home traders will try to raise the price is certain, but their success in this endeavour will depend on (1) the extent to which outside competition is possible, and (2) the need that foreigners have for the article. Where several sources of supply exist, the effect of taxing one will be to turn demand to the others, and where increased price checks demand, it tends to bring about a fall. Thus it may be said that, in most cases, an export duty is chiefly paid by the country that imposes it. Unless the country has a complete monopoly of the product, and the foreign demand remains unaffected by a rise of price, the whole burden cannot be transferred to the consumers.

[1] *Wealth of Nations*, 379.

[2] The abolition of the Indian transit dues was for the object of stimulating through trade. Wilson, *ut sup.* 22.

This case is, it need not be said, rarely found [1], but any approximation to it will partly pass the tax to the foreign consumers. Still as a practical result, the bulk of the duty falls immediately on the producers of the taxed product, though it may be shifted by them to the owners of land, skilled labour, or fixed capital concerned in the business. A large number of export duties might even by diminishing foreign trade lower the rates of wages and interest generally.

The effects of an import duty have to be judged on the same principles. The usual incidence will be on the consumers of the commodity, but where no other market is open to the foreign producer and where any increase of price arrests demand, the burden of the tax will be transferred to the producing country, with of course the same ulterior effects as those found in respect to export duties. It is also true that such a case is hardly in existence. The foreign producer has other markets, and demand is not often so sensitive; besides there is always the possibility of transferring labour and capital to other employments, should the pressure be sufficiently severe [2].

The preceding considerations suggest that it is possible, in some instances, to place the weight of taxation on foreigners, and thus to levy what is substantially a tribute from them; but they also show that the probability of success in any design of the kind is very slight. It is further to be noticed that it is through revenue duties only that any advantage of the kind can be gained; a protective duty, if effective, brings in little or no revenue. That such duties are injurious to foreign countries is, we believe, unquestionable, but they are as certainly not advantageous to the revenue of the nation that imposes them. The corn duties of France and Germany may perhaps somewhat

[1] Wool in mediaeval England and opium in India at present have been given as examples, but the latter is undoubtedly open to some competition.

[2] For further discussion of this question, see Brit. Assoc. Report, 1889, 440-48, also cp. Bk. iii. ch. 5.

reduce the demand for Russian and American corn, and thus lower the price obtained by those countries, just as the English tea duty may have in part been paid by the Chinese; but in the former instance a corresponding excise duty on corn, if practicable, would add far more to the revenue with, on the whole, less sacrifice[1].

A study of the question of incidence in relation to customs duties, therefore, leads to the conclusion, that while their real operation is often complicated and difficult to follow, the main burden falls on the country that imposes them, and that it can hardly ever hope, even if it should so desire, to shift any substantial part of its taxation to another nation or nations. On the whole the duties on imports must be regarded in common with the excise and, where it exists, state monopoly, as one part of the system for taxing the consumption of wealth.

[1] For the corn duties, Wagner, ii. 359, 367; Conrad, art. 'Landwirthschaft' in Schönberg, ii. 247–260; for tea, Senior, *Pol. Ec.* 184.

CHAPTER VIII.

TAXES ON COMMUNICATIONS, ACTS AND SUCCESSIONS.

§ 1. WHEN considering the system of taxation, we recognised that, in addition to the primary taxes levied on the income of the contributors and those secondary imposts affecting the consumption of commodities, there remained a large group of charges not to be placed under either category. Communications, transfers of property, inheritances, and legal transactions have all been made to supply a part of the State's revenue[1]. The principles on which this part of the tax system should be based, and the justification for its employment, have also been briefly noticed; but there can be no doubt that very different elements have assisted in its establishment. There is, first, the close resemblance of some of the objects taxed to commodities. A charge on transport is very like a duty on goods transported, and the same close connexion exists in such cases as the advertisement and newspaper taxes: they might be called 'taxes on quasi-commodities.' Another contributing agency is the 'fee' system. Some of the taxes on acts are but extensions of fees paid for service rendered. Land transfer and other judicial acts require the intervention of state officials, for whose services a charge may be fairly made, and these payments are easily developed into taxes. In like manner, the economic receipts from public industry or possessions may, through the use of monopoly, be carried to a point at which they become in part taxation. Older perhaps than any of the foregoing is the effect of the

[1] See Bk. iii. ch. 1. §§ 11, 12; ch. 4. § 10.

sovereign's prerogative rights. That general power over the subject's property, whether expressed in the feudal forms, or in the older idea of *dominium eminens*, issued in duties on the transmission of possessions from the dead to the living, as well as in the case of transfers *inter vivos*. The fact that all these elements contributed towards the creation of the taxes under consideration, and supply the historical interpretation of their existence, does not in the least affect the positions that at present the true legal ground of such charges is to be found in the legislative power of the State, and that their financial justification depends on the place they hold in the tax-system. A valid defence can be only based on their being conducive to the ends of economy, equity, and productiveness, and it was in that light that we admitted their legitimacy under present conditions.

§ 2. The first of the sub-classes in this part of the tax-system is that levied on communications and transport. The most conspicuous part of the revenue derived by the State from this source has been already considered in connexion with the industrial domain. Post offices and railways are apparently contributors to the economic rather than to the tax revenue. Nevertheless, it is possible to find in some cases a tax-element in such receipts. At present, the net earnings of the English Post Office are declared to be £3,450,000, and of this amount the far greater part, perhaps the whole, is obtained from correspondence. The rates for circulars and newspapers are not fixed on a profitable scale. It therefore follows that the excess of postal revenue over expenditure is a tax on ordinary and commercial letter-writers, but one of a very moderate nature, though it is not easy to estimate the check that a penny as against a half-penny rate gives to trade. Regarded as a tax diffused over the community, it is on the whole defensible, though the tendency to insist that the postal profits shall be devoted to improving the service is already becoming more pronounced. That England, with its dense population and high industrial development, is very favourably situated for cheap postal working is undoubtedly true. Other countries have very little postal surplus to deal with; their difficulty rather consists in keeping up sufficient receipts to balance expenditure.

The Prussian state railways have been in an analogous position to the English Post Office. Such high net receipts as they have obtained could hardly be due to superior management: they rather suggest unduly high rates or inefficient railway service, and in the latter respect there appears to be reason for complaint[1]. A slight reduction in train service or delay in delivery of goods may reduce the cost of working, but proves very expensive and inconvenient for traders. For reasons stated before[2], it is not likely that taxation of this kind will continue. The railway service, when under public management, will usually tend to be worked simply to cover its cost, or on the 'fee' rather than the 'tax' principle.

In countries where the railway system is left to private enterprise the question of taxation takes a different form. The companies appear as the possessors of land, buildings, and rolling stock, as well as the recipients of income, and they (*i.e.* their shareholders) will naturally be taxed for both general and local purposes. Thus the English local rates and the income-tax apply to them. Many American States employ a special Corporation tax on railroads. But these charges can hardly be regarded as falling on transport, though the last-mentioned has in some degree that effect. Nearer to our present subject are the English passenger duty and the French taxes on the transport of goods and passengers. The former, which is a kind of descendant of the duty on stage coaches, used to consist of five per cent. of the gross receipts from passengers, but by a series of abatements and exemptions its yield has been lowered from £810,000 to £320,000, or more than half. The French taxes imposed after the war of 1871, have been removed

[1] See Foxwell and Farrer, *Express Trains*, 118 sq.

[2] Bk. ii. ch. 3. §§ 14, 19.

from goods of slow carriage, but are still levied on express goods at five per cent., and on passengers at a very high rate (over twenty-three per cent.). For 1890, the receipts come to £3,210,000, or about ten times the English ones. Several of the American state taxes on railways are based either on the net or gross earnings of the lines; the latter is plainly the English passenger tax in a more comprehensive form.

The questions connected with the incidence of this kind of taxation are somewhat complex. At first it might appear that the tax would simply be added to the passenger fares or goods rates, and would therefore fall on the travellers, or in the case of goods on the dealers, and finally through them on the consumers. On the other hand, it has been pointed out that railway rates and fares are not fixed by cost of service, but, on the principle of all monopolies, so as to get the maximum net return. Consequently, the rates being already at their highest profitable point will not bear any further increase, and a tax on transport will be really a tax on railway dividends[1]. The latter view, however, assumes too easily the absolute monopoly of railway business, and also that rates are in all cases placed at the point of maximum profit. The legal, and still more the moral, limits on the power of railway managers cannot be ignored, and they would compel at least the sharing with the users of the service of any gain obtained by the railways, as they would permit an increase in cases of new taxation. In countries where railway construction is still active, a tax as heavy as that in France would tend to check the opening of fresh lines, and, therefore, in the shape of diminished railway accommodation, fall on the community. Everywhere the hindrance to fresh outlay would have the same effect, but in a less degree. Thus, there is no reason to doubt that, with the high guaranteed dividends of the French railway companies, the tax on transport is shifted from them to the passengers and senders of goods, and in

[1] Sidgwick, *Pol. Ec.* 574; Fawcett, *Pol. Ec.* 628–9.

all cases an indeterminate portion falls on them. Such a form of taxation is very undesirable: like a charge on correspondence, it acts in restraint of trade, both with respect to goods and to business passengers. Even in the case of travellers for pleasure it is an impost on one of the most effective means of improvement. If railway earnings are to be taxed, it is better that they should be dealt with directly, either by requiring a price for the concession or a portion of the dividends. To trust to the uncertain action of shifting is not advisable where commercial interests may be seriously affected [1].

The same conclusion may be extended to the treatment of telegrams and parcels. Unless on the ground of financial necessity, the effort to raise revenue from these factors of trade cannot be justified. The defence of letter-post taxation is to be found in its general diffusion, and in the fact that it is hardly perceived.

The treatment of the press and advertising agencies in respect of taxation may be next considered. Arising partly out of the system of control adopted by governments with respect to news, the taxation of newspapers by means of stamps was employed in England, France, and Prussia. Both the issues of newspapers and the advertisements in them were taxed. This impost was first established in England in 1712, at a moderate rate, but raised by degrees till, in 1815, it came to *4d.* per sheet, while the duty for each advertisement was *3s. 6d.* The latter was abolished in 1853, and the newspaper duty in 1855 [2]. The Prussian tax was repealed in 1874, and the French one three years earlier. Austria, however, has retained the duty on newspapers.

The objections to such taxation are plain enough. To tax the press is to check the diffusion of information and

[1] Professor Ely advocates taxation of gross receipts in order to escape evasion, *Taxation*, 324. But where this danger exists a more thorough reform is wanted. Taxation of railways by American States on this basis is particularly unsuitable owing to inter-state competition.

[2] Dowell, iv. 338–347.

one of the means of popular education. It has the further defect of being very unequal in its pressure, and at the same time being very likely to become uneconomical, as a tax on journals hinders their sale and lowers their quality. The advertisement duty was a direct check to trade and prevented the growth of businesses relying on the custom of a large and scattered body of persons. These considerations, together with the small revenue from the duties—£500,000 at the highest (1815)—made their repeal imperative, unless where political reasons prevailed.

§ 3. We have more than once had occasion to refer to the employment of stamps as a part of the mechanism of taxation. A great many fees, the postal revenue, the Russian and American tobacco taxes, and the newspaper duty in England are or were collected in this manner. It is, however, in connexion with the taxes on acts that the form of stamp becomes particularly prominent. So much is this the case that 'Stamps' in England, and '*timbre*' in France are actually treated as distinct heads of revenue[1]. It is therefore important to clearly understand that there is no separate stamp tax as such. The term merely denotes that the mode of collecting the taxes is by the use of stamps. This particular fiscal contrivance—first introduced in Holland, in 1624—is peculiarly suited for levying taxes on acts or commercial dealings, and is on that account regarded as being their special feature. Modern European taxation uses it extensively, and sometimes combines it with the older method of registration at a public office. The great convenience of the stamp system results from the facilities that it gives for proportioning taxation to value. By grading the prices of the necessary stamps, the tax on any act or transfer can be adjusted to the amount dealt in, and the formalities are made easier and less cumbersome.

This system of stamp duties—as following English usage we may call it—covers a very wide field and is growing

[1] See the heads of revenue in the annual *Statistical Abstracts*, where 'stamps' take a place beside 'customs' and 'excise.'

in favour. Extensions to fresh business forms, particularly in connexion with Stock Exchange transactions, have been carried out both in England and Germany, and higher rates are probable in the future. The chief groups into which the system may be divided are:—(1) Taxes on law proceedings and juridical acts; (2) those on the ordinary commercial instruments, on stocks, shares, &c.; (3) taxes on the sale of property, especially immovables; and (4) taxes on gratuitous transfers, including the large and important body of duties on successions after death. This arrangement is in some respects open to criticism, for commercial transactions involve transfers of property and succession duties have certain points of difference from gifts, but it is convenient as supplying an outline of the classes of objects taxed, and need not be regarded as logically exact.

§ 4. The taxation of law proceedings is a development of the fees charged for judicial services. So far as the charge is merely a recompense for the actual expense that the proceedings cause, it may best be looked on as a fee, but if it is raised to a higher point in order to cover some of the general expenses of justice, it is rather special taxation levied on the class of litigants for the extra advantages it enjoys. Certain classes of the community make greater use of the tribunals, and such taxation compels them to contribute a part of the expense incurred for their use. More careful consideration shows the error of applying the rule of particular interest in this way. The administration of justice is a general interest, that affects rich and poor, litigants and non-litigants alike. A tax on legal process is a hindrance to the use of the tribunals, *i. e.* an obstacle to obtaining legal remedies. The arguments of Bentham on this point have never been refuted[1], and it seems that the true course is to reduce the necessary fees to the lowest point, unless in the exceptional case of commercial courts, where a small contribution towards the permanent expense may perhaps

[1] *Theory of Legislation*, 140.

be allowable. Nevertheless, most legal systems do, in effect, tax litigants. The English charges, so far as direct receipts are concerned, hardly exceed the level of fees, but there is a good deal of unnecessary cost in the methods of procedure that is burdensome to the parties, and not productive of revenue to the State. France is in somewhat the same position; its strictly tax receipts are probably somewhat less than those obtained in England[1]. The German fees from the courts of justice also contain a tax element. The annual Prussian receipts from this source have varied from £2,000,000 to £2,500,000 in the fourteen years 1875–1889, though the part inclusion of non-contentious fees makes comparison difficult. The intrusion of taxation into this part of administration should be carefully watched, which is most effectively done by revising the scale of fees at short intervals.

Taxation of juridical acts is open to objection, as in most cases they are necessary for the assertion of claims or rights, and it can hardly be graduated in proportion to value. As a matter of policy, it is unwise to put pressure on the poorer classes in connexion with what is so conspicuous a part of state action. The fee principle is the one really applicable to such cases, unless a measure of value can be found, when a proportional scale at a moderate rate may be used, if financial necessities require it. The method of stamps enables this policy to be carried out at the lowest cost, and with, on the whole, the least evasion.

The duties on juridical acts are not quite clearly separated from those on what we have called commercial transactions. The simplest relation between parties has its legal side: the giving of a receipt or the transfer of a share may be said to be an act of law, but in the great majority of cases this aspect of the transaction passes without notice, and the economic process attracts chief attention. Dealings in bills of exchange, bills of lading, shares, or stock, in the various forms that the modern money market

[1] Cp. Bk. ii. ch. 4. § 8.

presents, may be regarded as equally suitable objects for taxation with ordinary income, or the use of commodities. They have also the advantage, as it is thought, of falling on the circulation of wealth, and therefore corresponding to and supplementing the duties on the other departments of the economic process. Some recent advocates have discovered another useful function in that they are mainly levied on the gains from speculation (*Conjuncturgewinn*), which, as being 'unearned,' are evidently a fit subject for taxation; while finally, they present to the practical financier the pleasing prospect of a tolerable revenue without the social and technical difficulties that the taxation of income and commodities gives rise to.

The objections are, however, not to be lightly treated. All such duties are, it must be said, to some extent obstructive of trade. A tax on the formation of companies is so far a check to their establishment. Duties on the transfer of shares tend to keep capital from that particular form of investment, and to make these evidences of ownership less mobile. Even a small tax on cheques is a limit to the extension of banking, and a receipt duty is a charge on the evidence of an important class of transactions in which everybody is sure to be concerned. High rates are in fact an inducement to evasion, or to entire neglect of the requisite formalities, and therefore often cause injustice where claims are disputed. The problem raised by this part of the tax system is, on the one hand, to avoid undue pressure on the circulation and transference of wealth, and on the other, to derive sufficient revenue to make the maintenance of the duties justifiable. From this point of view the English method seems the best, viz. that which raises a large revenue from low duties, and escapes unnecessary discrimination and complication by uniform rates, or at most a small number of scales. Great elaboration and minute distinctions between different classes of acts are productive of far more inconvenience to the taxpayers than of revenue to the State. Where, however, *ad valorem* rates can be easily applied, it is possible to combine simplicity and proportionality to value.

One particular class of duties, that on the transfer of property, and especially on land and fixed capital, or, in legal language, 'immovables,' gives rise to still more of doubt and question. Heavy taxation on transfer has the effect of lowering the value of the articles subject to it, and prevents their ready passage from one owner to another. In the case of such important commodities as land and buildings, any result of the kind is detrimental to economic progress. One of the agents of production is hindered from reaching the possession of those who could best use it, and the total production of the country is less than it would otherwise be. High duties on land transfer are therefore forbidden by the strongest financial and economic reasons, viz. the injury they inflict on the national wealth, and by consequence on the public revenue. Fees to cover the cost of the legal machinery needed for transfer are, as it appeared, legitimate; and where revenue is urgently required, a moderate transfer duty may be employed, just as under like conditions raw materials may be subject to excise or customs duties.

On the whole, then, it seems that the place of taxation on acts, whether by stamps or other machinery, is a subordinate one. It cannot wisely be used to collect as large a revenue as either the primary taxes on income and property, or the duties on consumption. A very wealthy community with large commercial transactions may be able to bear the levying of a toll on them, provided that it is strictly kept within bounds. The yield of the penny duties in England may be taken as an illustration, but it must at the same time be remembered that any injudiciousness in the imposition will cause a loss to the trading community not easily perceived, but none the less present and real[1].

[1] Some of the 'penny' duties devised by Mr. Gladstone erred in this respect; e.g. that on packages justified by its author for statistical reasons, *Financial*

§ 5. The regular history of the English stamp duties commences after the Revolution. By the Stamp Act (1694), duties varying from 1*d.* to 40*s.* were imposed on legal instruments, which were grouped in six classes, and each sheet of a document was separately taxed. Twenty years later some of the rates were graded in proportion to the value affected, and the duties were increased. Several other increases were made as financial necessities demanded, and the yield of the duties was larger[1]. Bills of exchange and promissory notes were brought under taxation in 1782, and receipts in the next year. Fresh increases followed in the time of the great war, and a great many complicated rates were established, until in 1815 the total yield was £2,800,000, of which £1,100,000 came from bills, notes, and receipts. Some reductions and improvements were made in 1850, and the penny receipt duty was introduced by Mr. Gladstone in 1853. The further progress consisted in a wider use of the system of low duties, a closer approximation to *ad valorem* charges in the variable duties, and an extension to the new forms of documents and transactions that modern commerce had developed. The last-mentioned movement is hardly concluded, though recent legislation has left little to be done in the future, except in the task of removing anomalies. The yield from these different forms has come very close to £4,000,000 annually, of which about £700,000 is received from bills and promissory notes, £900,000 from the penny duties[2], and over £2,000,000 from the taxes on deeds, sales, and securities.

Statements, 161, 295. The French statistical duties have the same defect, Leroy Beaulieu, i. 617.

[1] The following are the figures for selected years—

1714 . . .	£117,000
1727 . . .	160,000
1760 . . .	290,000
1778 . . .	442,000,

Dowell, iii. 290-1.

[2] In 1881 the postage and revenue penny stamps were combined, so that the exact receipt of the latter is now a matter of calculation.

The French system is older than the corresponding English one. The duties at present known as *enregistrement* and *timbre* can be traced back to a series of dues existing under the monarchy [1]. This was one of the forms of taxation that was in substance preserved by the Constituent Assembly, for though it abolished the old names, it retained the regulations under the new title '*enregistrement*,' and dealt with the two comprehensive classes of 'acts' and 'transfers of property,' including under these heads gifts and successions after death. Parallel with it were the stamp duties—first used in France in 1655—which were reformed in 1791. The field covered by this system is even more comprehensive than the English one. Transactions of all kinds are brought within the net of taxation by elaborate and complicated regulations. The legislation of the revolutionary period, which at first was ineffective, owing to bad administration, became more productive as settled conditions were restored. The duties of registration were separated into 'fixed' and 'proportional,' to which, since 1872, an intermediate class known as 'graduated' duties has been added. These groups, as their several designations show, consist respectively of uniform, of *ad valorem*, and of classified rates. In the corresponding stamp system, the charges depend, either on the size of the document (*timbre de dimension*), or on the value dealt with, and for the former a scale is prescribed. Cheques, receipts, insurance policies, and other negotiable instruments of very varied kinds are brought under this charge.

As a result, the yield of the duties has been a growing one. In 1800 the total receipts were less than £2,800,000. By 1816 they came to £5,200,000, and in 1830 to £7,280,000. The total receipts in 1860 were £14,500,000, and the sum had, in 1890, risen to over £28,000,000 [2].

[1] These charges were known as *contrôle*, *insinuation*, and *centième denier*. The stamp duty was known as the *formule*.

[2] Stourm, i. 442-3, 468-9; Leroy Beaulieu, i. 528, 533.

Out of this amount successions and donations contributed over £7,500,000, and the duties on land-transfer over £6,000,000.

This great increase—tenfold in ninety years, and nearly twofold between 1830 and 1860, and again between the latter year and 1890—is due to three distinct causes, viz. (1) the normal growth of wealth and transactions respecting it; (2) the extension of the duties to new cases; and (3) the establishment of higher rates; and, so far as the stamp duties are concerned, the effect of each has been about equal. There seems to be little doubt that in many cases the rates are far too high, and the regulations too difficult. Especially in the case of land-transfer is the first defect noticeable. The duties directly imposed on sale are nearly 7 per cent., and with the stamps and fees the total charge is over 10 per cent., *i. e.* where land sells for 30 years' purchase it amounts to at least three years' income. Such a rate is open to the severest condemnation, as tending to immobilize the most important form of property and thereby to reduce the productive power of the community.

The influence of French financial legislation on neighbouring countries has been considerable, and nowhere more than in Italy. The duties on transactions in that country have been formed on the same general lines as the *enregistrement* and *timbre*, and have increased even more rapidly in their returns. From £1,400,000 in 1862 they rose to £3,600,000 in 1875, and £5,080,000 in 1888, while the succession duties, which were only £280,000 in 1862, had become £1,400,000 in 1888. Enlarged territory, higher rates of duty, and greater stringency in collection are the chief reasons for the higher revenue thus obtained.

Neither registration nor stamp duties have acquired as much financial importance in the German States. The transfer of land is not heavily burdened, and the methods of registration are devised for the convenience of the parties concerned. The succession duties are as yet confined to the separate States, but an imperial system of taxes on commercial affairs has been established. Bills of exchange, shares and credit instruments, have been by degrees brought under very moderate taxation. The total returns from the several duties were only £1,500,000 in 1886–7—very much below the English, French, or Italian receipts.

§ 6. The actual operation of the duties on transactions is not always capable of being precisely estimated, and in regard to some of the classes the question of incidence has given rise to much dispute. Very often a transaction has reference to some material commodity, and then a duty on it may be plausibly assimilated with an ordinary tax on commodities, and the same principles applied in its discussion. To levy a charge on transactions connected with production is, so far, an increase in the expenses of production, that the producer and dealer will endeavour to shift to the consumer. In most of the taxes on receipts and bills the burden, falling as it does on trade as a whole, may be regarded as a tax on business gains. Whether any of it will be represented in higher prices to the consumers will depend on the extent to which the burden is unequally imposed, but under actual conditions this effect is not very likely to be experienced. The duties are too small a proportion of the total cost to have any influence on prices.

Where transfers of property are taxed the problem becomes more difficult, and there is room for doubt as to the real incidence of the charge. From one point of view it may be held that the purchaser, like the consumer of commodities, will in the long run bear the burden, and that therefore the price of land or shares would rise in proportion to the tax. Another view, represented by Adam Smith and J. S. Mill, assumes that in transactions with respect to land the seller is the more necessitous, and has therefore to reduce his price by the amount of the tax[1]. For a somewhat different reason this way of regarding the

[1] 'Taxes upon the sale of land fall altogether upon the seller,' *Wealth of Nations*, 364; cp. Mill, *Principles*, Bk. v. ch. 5. § 1.

matter may be extended. Forms of property are purchased for the income that they yield, but the effect of a tax, so far as it is paid by the buyer, is to lower the return obtained, and besides to make the principal less saleable in the future. It might accordingly be supposed that purchasers would take all these elements into account, and place the whole weight of the present and future charges on the actual holder. The tax on transfer would in fact resemble a fixed tax on the object sold, such as the permanent land tax. There is, on the whole, good reason for believing that the incidence is divided between buyer and seller; the former gets less than he would receive if there were no tax, the latter pays more than he would on the same supposition[1], and some persons keep out of dealing on account of the tax.

Where bills of exchange and commercial instruments, as stocks and shares, are affected, another result may be found. Taxation imposed in one country will tend to drive away floating capital. A heavy tax on transactions in the London money market is so far an inducement to shift them to another country. On this ground it is very undesirable to tax international stocks at a higher rate than exists elsewhere. The utmost care is needed in limiting this form of taxation so as to avoid injurious action on capital.

§ 7. One large and productive form of taxation which actual legislation combines with the transfer and stamp duties, must now be more fully considered—the duties imposed on succession after death, in well-known English phraseology the 'death duties.' Though they are certainly

[1] Suppose for example that a property, which free of duty would sell for £10,000, is subject to 10 per cent. on transfer. If the whole tax fell on the seller he would only get £9000, if it all fell on the buyer he would pay £11,000. Is it not plain that if an exchange is to take place the probability is that there will be a division of the tax? When there are many transactions the less eager buyers and sellers will withdraw, and there will be fewer dealings at a higher price, the tax included. See Böhm-Bawerk, *Positive Theory of Capital* (Eng. Trans.), 203–13, for the theoretical basis of this position.

taxes on the transfer of property, and are usually collected by means of stamps, the points of difference are greater than the resemblances. Their relations to property, their incidence, and the absence in their case of the ordinary conditions of exchange, all make a separate treatment desirable.

The origin of these duties may be traced to the claim of the ruler to take possession of goods that had no owner, or perhaps more often to the feudal due payable at each change of hands; but we find the policy pursued at an earlier date in the 5 per cent. duty introduced by Augustus on all inheritances, except those of very near relatives[1]. Modern States have largely developed the system with very varied scales and grades of duty, so that it has come to be almost universally regarded as an essential constituent of any well-arranged scheme of Finance. But notwithstanding this general agreement, the theoretic difficulties that such taxation suggests are by no means trivial. Taxes on successions have the great economic fault of being taxes on property as opposed to income, and of tending to retard the growth of wealth. The force of this objection varies considerably at different stages of progress, and it increases rapidly as the rate of duty becomes higher. A sufficiently high tax on successions will stop accumulation in any country, no matter what its position. The scale of duties must therefore be so adjusted as to avoid this result. A more strictly financial difficulty is the risk of evasion that a high duty is sure to cause. Unless gifts and sales are taxed at the same rate as successions, various contrivances are sure to be tried by which the liability would be escaped, but so comprehensive a plan of taxation would destroy, or at least seriously diminish, trade and industrial activity. So far as the smaller successions are affected, heavy taxation is evil in another way, since it often presses very hardly on the payers at a time of need. This applies more particularly to successions on the part of wives and

[1] The *vicesima hereditatum*.

children, but even with collaterals it is a hardship. All these circumstances converge towards the proposition that strict regard should be had to moderation in the employment of this form of taxation. Carried beyond due limits, it will prove to be oppressive and economically injurious.

From the side of just distribution a further difficulty arises. Assuming that proportionality to income is the proper rule for the division of the compulsory public charges, how can we include the large and uncertain payments for successions in this distribution? The easiest mode of calculation seems to be that which regards the succession duty as a capitalized income-tax paid once for all at the close of life, instead of in small amounts during each year. This treatment would only apply to a uniform duty such as the English Probate; the varying scales for different degrees of succession depend on a different principle. The old idea that the wife and children of the deceased are in a sense joint owners of the property, or at least have a moral claim to succession, is still powerful; they moreover are often hard pressed at the time of succession, and accordingly heavy taxation would involve great sacrifice and excite irritation, while it would certainly offer the strongest stimulus to attempts at evasion. The influence of these conditions is shown in the universal adoption of lower rates for successions by near relatives; though there is much difference in the actual concessions made in different countries.

Another form of graduation has been much discussed, viz. that by which the larger inheritances are subjected to increased duties, or in other words, the system of progressive death duties. The general arguments on the question of progression need not be again considered[1], but in respect to successions the idea of promoting a greater equality of wealth has gained some opponents of progression generally to favour its use in their case[2]. Practical

[1] See Bk. iii. ch. 3. §§ 5, 6, 7.

[2] *E.g.* J. S. Mill, who declares 'The principle of graduation . . . seems to

legislation has done little in this direction. The lenient treatment of very small estates in England may be explained on the principle of exempting a minimum from taxation, and the new estate duty has been defended by Mr. Goschen as tending to establish real proportionality in taxation[1]. A few Swiss Cantons have attempted a moderate progressive tax on successions, but elsewhere proportional, or even 'regressive,' rates have been retained[2].

§ 8. The English death duties begin with the Stamp Act (1694) which placed 5*s*. on Probates over £20. This uniform charge—doubled a few years later—continued till 1779, when three scales of duty were introduced. The usual process of increase was carried on, and the *ad valorem* principle was reached by gradual approximation in 1889. The duty now stands at 3 per cent., imposed on all Probates and letters of Administration. The old arrangement, by which a maximum rate was fixed at a certain point[3], has disappeared, and estates under £100 and £300 receive special favours. This direct charge on the estate is protected by the 'account duty,' introduced to check evasions and applicable to gifts made within a year of death. These duties do not apply to real or to settled property, and therefore fail in comprehensiveness.

The legacy duty, first imposed in 1780, developed in the same way. Though a charge on the receiver of the bequest, it is, like the income-tax in many cases, to be paid from the source, that is, the estate, and deducted in the payment. Unlike the Probate duty with its practically uniform scale, it varies according to degree of relationship, and for descendants it is now absorbed in the former.

me both just and expedient as applied to legacy and inheritance duties,' *Principles*, Bk. v. ch. 2. § 3.

[1] 'On the whole, I think, it will be found that the men whose fortunes are considerable are those who pay the least in proportion to their aggregate income,' Budget Speech, April 18, 1889.

[2] Cohn, § 351.

[3] This limit was raised from £5000 to £10,000, then to £100,000, next to £500,000, lastly in 1815 to £1,000,000. It was abandoned in 1859.

Its highest point, 10 per cent., is reserved for strangers and very distant relatives.

The parallel tax on realty and settled personalty, the succession duty, only dates from 1853. Pitt had failed to establish a tax of the kind in 1796, and it was with great difficulty that the budget plan of 1853 was carried. It amounted to an extension of the legacy duty to successions hitherto exempt[1]. This undoubtedly just proceeding failed at first to accomplish what was expected; instead of the estimated £2,000,000, its average yield has been about £700,000, or roughly speaking, one-third of what was anticipated. The great number of lineal successions and the exemption of debts from the duty explain this failure.

The latest addition to this group of taxes is the Estate duty of 1889, which is a supplement of 1 per cent. to the Probate and Succession duties where the property exceeds £10,000. Regarded as a whole the system is extremely complex and presents some striking anomalies. The separation of real and personal property and the different treatment given to each[2] are at first sight a grave injustice. The heavy local taxation on land and buildings supplies a partial justification, and there is the further difficulty of requiring an immediate payment that could not be met out of the annual yield of land—the existing succession duty, if paid at once, would mean at lowest a year's income. It may even be suggested that with such a durable property as land, an annual tax equivalent to the present succession duty would be preferable, especially bearing in mind that by far the greater number of successions are by near relatives. Either this, or the inclusion of real property under the Probate duty, and its treatment exactly as if it were personalty, should be adopted. The question of settlements is still more difficult. The present system favours

[1] 'We propose to alter the law and . . . to extend the legacy duty to all successions whatever,' Gladstone, *Financial Statements*, 62.

[2] Thus real property pays no Probate duty, and the succession duty on it is not due for a year after death; it can be paid by eight instalments, and it is calculated on the life interest only, not on the full value.

the tying-up of property, a course neither economically nor financially advantageous. For this the most effective remedy will probably be found in the equalization of the charge on deeds of settlement and Probates, which would at once remove any artificial encouragement to the former course. It is true that a duty of 3 per cent. would be heavily felt, but it would be quite as fair as the existing Probate duty.

The revenue derived from the death duties has increased largely in the present century, and now stands at nearly £10,000,000; but of this sum half the Probate duty (or about one-quarter of the total) is paid to the local authorities[1]. In spite of occasional irregularities the yield is at once reliable and progressive, and takes its place along with the income tax as an important contribution to the direct taxation that counterbalances the excise and customs[2].

§ 9. By the elaborate system of registration the French duties on successions are made a sub-division of the general mode of taxing transfers. This method is most effective as a technical arrangement, but it has the disadvantage of keeping the ordinary duties on exchange at a higher rate than they should be. The duties for lineal descendants are more moderate than in England, 1·25 per cent. For

[1] The receipts for 1890–1 were £7,444,000, exclusive of £2,412,000, the local part of the Probate, i. e. a total of £9,856,000. The half of the Probate retained for the central budget is now more than the whole receipts from that duty in any year before 1879. The growth of the total duties, which has been continuous, is best seen by the date at which each additional million was reached.

Year.	£ (000's *omitted.*)
1813	1,005
1828	2,117
1856–7	3,121
1865–6	4,303
1871–2	5,360
1876–7	6,024
1881–2	7,249
1887–8	8,241.

[2] For the English death duties, Dowell, iii. 124–140; Buxton and Barnes, *Death Duties*.

brothers and sisters the tax of over 8 per cent. is decidedly too high: it hardly differs from that of the next degree. For husband and wife the tax is a little higher than in England (3·75 per cent.), and in all cases the stamps have to be added[1].

In another point the French system is inferior to the English, as the *gross*, not the *net*, value is taxed. The absence of any allowance for debts is a serious grievance in the French succession duties[2]. On the other hand the fixed estimate of land at twenty-five times its annual value is fairer than the English method of estimating the successor's interest as only a life one.

The Italian duties are somewhat higher on lineal successions than the French, but a little lighter in other cases, and deduction of debts is allowed (if proved on good evidence). The amount received from this source in 1889–90 was less than £1,500,000.

The duties in the several German States are even less effective. The Prussian estimate for 1889–90 was only 6,900,000 marks (£345,000). In nearly all the States lineal descendants pay no duty, and in Prussia ascendants and husband or wife are also free. Two per cent. is the rate for brothers, and the highest point is only 8 per cent. A complete reform of the rates would appear to be obviously suggested by English and French experience.

Some of the American 'States' have duties on successions of collaterals: the rate in Maryland is 2·5 per cent., it is 5 per cent. in New York and Pennsylvania[3].

§ 10. The problem of incidence might at first be supposed not to arise at all in this connexion. 'Taxes upon the transference of property from the dead to the living,'

[1] The absence of a Probate duty levied on the estate makes these comparisons not quite accurate. A wife in England who gets the residue of an estate practically pays 3 per cent. on its whole net value.

[2] The rule by which the *usufructuary* or 'life tenant' pays half duty and the bare proprietor the full rate in addition is a further injustice. See *Journal des Économistes*, Feb. 1892, 186–92.

[3] New York has lately adopted a direct inheritance tax of 1 per cent. on estates over $10,000.

said Adam Smith, 'fall finally, as well as immediately, upon the persons to whom the property is transferred'[1]. But this view altogether neglects the ulterior effects on the distribution of wealth that the duties may bring about. If, as Ricardo argued, they fall mainly on capital, it is evident that the whole society suffers by less efficient production, and it is also probable that the higher value of the remaining capital will lead to a rise in interest and a consequent fall in wages. Hard as it may be to trace these results in any actual case, yet, given the conditions, they must be in existence. The pressure of death duties on capital is not however so clear. The English receipts of £10,000,000, or the French of £7,000,000, are but a small part of the annual savings (not more than 6 or 7 per cent.). Even if we suppose the whole amount added to savings the effect would be almost imperceptible. This, however, could not happen, as an equal amount of taxation would have to be imposed in other directions, and it would in some degree trench on capital.

In fact we may regard the succession duties as presenting a parallel to the income-tax. The latter withdraws annually for the service of the State a portion of the new wealth created in the period; the former operate in the same way, but at uncertain intervals, on the collected wealth of the Society.

[1] *Wealth of Nations*, 364.

BOOK V.

THE RELATIONS OF EXPENDITURE AND RECEIPTS.

CHAPTER I.

INTRODUCTORY.—STATE HOARDING.

§ 1. THE preceding books have been devoted to the consideration of the various questions connected with public expenditure and revenue. We have seen that there ought, under usual conditions, to be a balance between these two sides of financial activity. Outlay should not exceed income, or—and this is more often the way in which the case is presented—tax revenue ought to be kept up to the amount required to defray expenses. The financier, so far differing from the business manager, should not aim at a surplus, but neither should he allow a deficit. Either is an indication of some defect in calculation or administrative system.

This general principle must, however, admit of modifications. Temporary deficits and surpluses cannot be avoided. In the management of a large financial organization complete equalization of receipts and expenditure could hardly ever be obtained, or, if it were, would be due to chance. The many different forms of expenditure and the varying productiveness, both of the quasi-private and the tax revenue, forbid minute agreement. All that can be claimed is a substantial approach to a balance in the two sides of the account. The safest rule for practice is that which lays down the expediency of estimating for a moderate surplus, by which the possibility of a deficit will be reduced to a minimum.

The foregoing consideration would apply to any system

of Finance in its ordinary or usual state, but the difficulty of adjustment is much increased by the operation of what has been described as extraordinary outlay [1]. Occasions, as we saw, will from time to time arise in which it becomes necessary to spend large sums for particular objects. War and the execution of public works are the great causes of this sudden increase of expenditure, and the former of these is very hard to foresee and provide against. In any case it may fairly be said that exceptional charges of the kind should not be altogether met out of current income. As the advantages realized are of indefinite duration, it seems fair that the charge should, in popular language, be spread over a number of years. Without at present criticising this doctrine, we may remark that the political conditions place limits—elastic ones it is true—on the revenue-collecting powers of the administration, and that in practice there are only two expedients for meeting abnormal outlay, viz. either the modern method of incurring debt, or the older one of storing up treasure or other disposable wealth for the time of need. The absence of equilibrium in public Finance must show itself in the creation of a surplus store of wealth, or in the formation of liabilities. In the present chapter we shall therefore examine the policy of forming public treasures or other reserves, in order to provide for the necessities of the State in times of emergency.

§ 2. The system of public treasures can lay claim to a high antiquity. Thus the Athenians in the period immediately preceding the Peloponnesian war accumulated a sum of 9,700 talents, and at its outbreak had actually 6,000 talents in store. Even earlier, the Persian sovereigns had collected the tribute of their provinces in the shape of contributions of the precious metals, large stocks of which fell into the hands of Alexander [2]. The same policy of hoard-

[1] Cp. Bk. i. ch. 8. §§ 1 sq.

[2] Thucydides, Bk. ii. ch. 13; Grote, *Hist. Greece*, xi. 498–500; Roscher, § 124. n. 1.

ing was followed by the Romans. The stores of the sovereigns conquered by them were accumulated, and the special tax on the emancipation of slaves was used in the same way. The possession of the treasury became a leading object of the rival parties in the civil wars that overthrew the Republic [1].

Like facts are noticeable in the mediaeval period. One of the first objects of the successor to the Crown on the death of a king was to gain possession of the treasure. Both in England and France there were several instances of this eagerness [2]. The treasure and the kingdom were regarded as a joint possession, each being, in accordance with the conceptions of the time, looked on as equally a form of property. The practice lasted in England till the time of Henry VIII, who speedily dissipated the savings of his prudent father. Henri IV, who in this was guided by Sully, was the last French monarch who maintained a treasure [3].

By the time of Adam Smith the practice had decayed: he notes that the canton of Bern was the only Republic, as Prussia was the only monarchy, that continued to keep a reserve [4]. The latter country has been remarkable in this respect. Thus Frederic William I (1713–1740), as Carlyle tells us, 'Yearly made his own revenues, and his people's along with them, and as the source of them larger: and in all states of his revenue he had contrived to make his expenditure less than it; and yearly saved masses of coin and "deposited them in barrels in the cellars of his *Schloss* [5]."' His successor, Frederic the Great (1740–1786), continued this system, and it affords a striking instance of the persistence of national policy when we find that the present German Empire follows what is virtually the same method.

§ 3. The reasons that induced so many States to accumu-

[1] Roscher, op. cit.; Merivale, *Romans under the Empire*, ii. 169.
[2] Sinclair, *Hist. of Revenue*, i. 76.
[3] *Wealth of Nations*, 386.
[4] *Ibid.*
[5] *Frederic*, i. 290.

late treasure are to be found in the conditions of society existing at the time. A very rude community will have no need of a store of money; weapons and provisions would be more useful in its case. The system of money dealings must have come into being before hoarding can be regarded as the duty of a wise sovereign. Once that point has been reached, the great convenience of having a stock of a universally desired article on hand is too plain to be overlooked. The efficient maintenance of an army in the field depends in a great degree on the supply of what is so often called the 'sinews of war.' Cases are not unknown where expeditions failed altogether from want of this indispensable auxiliary. The superstitious reverence for the precious metals and the force of habit may partly account for the great treasures of ancient States; but they owe their continuance far more to their felt necessity. Where credit was undeveloped, and taxes were occasional and uncertain expedients, a State that had no treasure was in a dangerous situation, unprepared either for attack or defence. The position of the sovereign in earlier times as a large property-holder was contributory to the same result. Lands, forests, mines, and various lucrative claims were in the possession of the ruler. The treasure came to be looked on as one part of this extensive class, serving a particular purpose and completing the public economy.

As the system of state hoarding was produced by the economic conditions of the periods in which it was employed, so the change to the modern economic organization necessarily led to its abandonment. The increased productiveness of taxes, and the facility with which credit could be used, relieved governments from the duty of keeping a stock of bullion for emergencies. The State ceased to be its own banker and came to rely on the instrument supplied by the growth of credit. Not only were the ultimate advantages greater, but there was an immediate benefit in the saving of the amount required to replenish the store when it had from any cause run down.

Borrowing at times of need was more pleasant than a long course of previous saving. The change was, as we have seen, as gradual as the alteration in the ruling conditions that produced it. The keeping of stores of bullion died out slowly, and has even left, as in the case of Germany, survivals to the present day. This last instance deserves some further notice. The traditional policy of storing up a reserve for the pressure of war was applied to the German Empire by means of the resources obtained through the French indemnity. A sum of £6,000,000 was held in bullion and a much larger amount was invested in high-class securities, chiefly German railways and the debts of foreign countries. The 'fund for invalids' came to nearly £25,000,000 in 1889. There is, therefore, a reserve of over £30,000,000 held by the Empire in what is practically the form of a hoard, and apparently ready for use in time of war.

German economists have defended this proceeding on the ground that it is imperatively required for military necessities. The use of the treasure in the past is dwelt on, and it is further urged that at the outbreak of war the money market is so strained that a large loan is costly, if not unobtainable. The treasure or war chest is but the complement of the fortresses, equipment, and system of speedy mobilization that constitute the safeguards of German unity [1]. On the other hand, the general argument against state reserves is a forcible one. The retention of bullion by the State involves the loss of the interest that could be gained by its productive employment, while it is quite uncalled for in any country with an efficient system of banking. What is really required is a sufficient disposable metallic reserve to be drawn on in the time of trial. The state-treasure policy thus invades the domain of banking, and is at best inadequate. Three weeks of war would exhaust the store of £6,000,000 now held at

[1] Roscher, § 124; Wagner, i. 173-7; Cohn, § 169.

Spandau[1]. It is so hard to measure the precise amount needed, and error in either direction leads to such loss, that the policy is too uncertain in its effects to be advisable. The influence of state hoarding on trade and prices should also be considered. The withdrawal of a large mass of money means lowered prices, and is so far a hindrance to the development of trade, and the ever-present possibility of its sudden use has a disturbing effect. On the whole, then, it is beyond question that in any country with modern credit facilities the formation of a treasure is a mistaken proceeding. The case is still stronger against the use of a reserve in the form of securities. They, it is true, have the advantage of yielding interest, but where a public debt exists it is better to use this available property for its redemption. To borrow with one hand, while lending with the other, is simply introducing an additional complication into the public accounts, without any corresponding advantage. The repayment of a portion of the German debt would be as much an investment as the policy actually pursued. But the method of investing in securities is not merely useless: it has direct disadvantages. If home securities are chosen, the State is drawn into the business of speculation and stockjobbing, with injurious results to trade. The interest on such investments may apparently exceed what would be saved by paying off debt; but this higher yield means less security or at least stability, a consideration that leads to another objection to such investments. The aim to be realized is the possession of a disposable fund for emergencies, but it is just at times of emergency that stocks are certain to fall in value. A large sale of securities by a government at the outbreak of war would force down their price and make the process of realization a costly one. Moreover, the funds so obtained would be equally available for taking up a loan. To come on the market as a needy seller is the worst possible mode of disposing of any kind of state property.

[1] Cohn, § 169.

Where foreign securities are held the position is somewhat different. They will not be so much affected by the commencement of war, as they possess an international market. Political difficulties are, however, greater. Should the contemplated war be with the Power whose debt is used as an investment, the question of retention of interest would arise. In any case the relation between the investing and lending States is not a satisfactory one: it brings a sovereign power into the domestic affairs of another State, and in case of readjustments respecting the debt may cause grave difficulties. These considerations fully support the opinion that, speaking generally, the system of state treasures or reserves of securities is indefensible at the present stage of financial development.

Some exceptional cases have been suggested, but even they can hardly be admitted as modifying the principle just stated. A State e.g. may have no public debt to redeem, and then the formation of a reserve may appear desirable, but there are other alternatives, viz. either (1) the remission of the less eligible forms of taxation, or (2) the increase of the agricultural or industrial domain of the State, a course which may be adopted on social as well as economic grounds. Again, the interest on the debt may be so low that its redemption may not seem commercially profitable as compared with investment. The objections to state dealings with capital already noticed[1] are too serious to be set aside on this ground. The remission of taxation, though it seems to be a sacrifice on the part of the State, may in many cases be the best course. The real source of state revenue is, need we say once more, the national income, and judicious remission of taxation has a beneficial influence on the growth of this reservoir, on which the State in the last resort depends for its tax receipts. The often-used phrase about allowing taxation 'to fructify in the pockets of the taxpayers' is here exactly applicable. The financial power of the State rests on the

[1] Bk. ii. ch. 4. § 1.

economic development of the people, and will be proportional to it. Any special resources in the form of money that may be required are best procured through the normal agency of bankers. The case in this respect is far clearer than in the somewhat parallel one of manufacture of weapons and supplies, since the question of quality, or that of effectiveness of competition, does not arise.

§ 4. Whatever be the conclusion as to special and exceptional cases of state reserves, it is at all events plain that the older policy of hoarding as a general rule of Finance is obsolete. It is, in fact, on its ruins that the modern phenomenon of public debts has arisen. From keeping a reserve to meet all emergencies States have passed to the opposite course of not paying their working expenses. The problem of public indebtedness is becoming more and more important, and giving rise to serious questions. The remaining chapters of the present book will therefore be devoted to an examination of the different aspects of this vital part of modern Finance.

CHAPTER II.

PUBLIC INDEBTEDNESS, ITS MODERN DEVELOPMENT.

§ 1. THE development of public indebtedness accompanied the decline of the older system of treasures. In its present form it is essentially a creation of the last two centuries, and even within the last fifty years it has gained more ground than in all preceding periods. The causes of its rise and immense expansion must be sought in the special circumstances, both political and social, of the time.

There is an appearance of exaggeration in the statement that public borrowing has only come into existence since the end of the seventeenth century. In all but the ruder societies credit has been more or less employed, and we can hardly believe that the governing body would altogether neglect its use in times of need. So far, however, as classical antiquity is concerned, there is hardly any trace of loans to the State. The explanation of this fact lies in the characteristics of Greek and Roman society[1]. Instead of borrowing from the wealthy citizen, the State would adopt the more drastic, but in the long run less fruitful, method of levying a special tax on him. The small amount of floating capital also prevented a ready recourse to loans. Compulsory loans or the farming-out of taxes were, in default of a treasure, the favourite methods, to which may be added the rarer one of pledging some state or

[1] *Introduction*, Pt. II. § 1.

regal possessions. Temporary credit transactions with contractors were the nearest approach to a public debt in our use of the term [1].

§ 2. The Middle Ages show little advance on—in some respects they fall below—the economic position of the Roman Empire. The strong sentiment against usury and the feeling that it was beneath the dignity of a prince to borrow from his subjects [2] both tended to check the use of the royal credit. Where it was exercised the quasi-private nature of the feudal state system comes out clearly. The King borrows on his personal credit, or on his domain, which he even gives in pledge as a security for payment. These loans were usually obtained from the Church, or from foreign bankers. Hallam tells us that 'in 1345, the Bardi at Florence, the greatest company in Italy, became bankrupt, Edward III owing them, in principal and interest, 900,000 gold florins. Another—the Peruzzi—failed at the same time, being creditors to Edward for 600,000 florins. The King of Sicily owed 100,000 florins to each of these bankers [3].' Both in England and France, these borrowings grew more common as wealth and the cost of government increased. Francis I obtained various sums through the city of Paris, which kept a list of the creditors and distributed the interest [4]. Appeals to Parliament in connexion with loans occur as early as the reign of Richard II. Forced loans were tried by Edward IV, and by the Tudors in the sixteenth century. The pledging of taxes as security is the last step in the older forms of borrowing.

A more advanced position is found in the loans of the Italian cities, especially Genoa and Venice, which raised

[1] Roscher, § 130.

[2] *Turpe est et multum regali reverentiae derogat a suis subditis mutuare pro sumptibus regis vel regni*; Thomas Aquinas (?), *De Regimine Principum*, ii. 8. The approval of state treasures by so many early writers was a disapproval of the counter-method of loans.

[3] *Middle Ages*, iii. 340. Loans by the French kings can be traced back to 1287. Vührer, *Histoire de la Dette Publique*, i. 2 sq.

[4] Vührer, i. 16–20.

money through the agency of banks established for the purpose. The bank of St. George in the latter city was the most important instance of this system. The superior commercial development of Italy contributed to the increase of state, as well as private credit, and more especially to complicated dealings in the farming of state domains and taxes.

The commercial revolution of the fifteenth and sixteenth centuries which depressed the Italian towns brought those of the Low Countries into prominence. The system of state-borrowing and of lending to foreign countries was engaged in by the Dutch, who, in consequence of the low rate of interest, were anxious to enlarge the field of investment, and therefore undertook most of the limited international business of the time, such as the carrying trade and public loans. Imitation of the Dutch methods of commerce and Finance—so powerful an influence on the English policy of the seventeenth and eighteenth centuries —was a principal cause of the creation and advance of the English funded debt, which has in its turn been an example to other States.

§ 3. It is thus plain that neither ancient nor mediaeval Finance possessed the modern public debt system. The latter contained the germs from which our present expedients have been developed, but with so many differences that it is hardly right to place two such distinct groups under a common heading. They are widely separate species of a comprehensive genus. The increase of public debt in modern times, is the result of economical and political conditions of the highest interest and importance. From one point of view, the vast indebtedness of States and smaller governing bodies is due to the transition to 'credit economy.' Money, as a medium of exchange, has been largely superseded by the use of credit instruments. In like manner, great masses of property, or more correctly the evidences of its ownership, have become freely transferable. The shares of companies, or their acknowledgments of debt are very readily dealt in. Railways, banks, and other industrial undertakings by this means increase their business and the value of their property. It would be incomprehensible if the greatest of co-operative organizations—the State—declined to avail itself of a like expedient. In fact, governments, supreme and subordinate, strong and weak, have mobilized their credit and thereby increased their immediate financial power. The mechanism of the stock exchange has remedied the weakest point in the earlier state-borrowing—the absence of any way of quickly realizing the capital lent.

The connexion of public debts with the money market is, perhaps, most clearly seen in the modern methods of contracting loans. Whatever be the particular form adopted, the substance of the operation is the same, and amounts to an investment of capital on the part of the lenders, carried out in nearly every case by the special class of dealers in stocks. To the investor, there is no difference between taking up the stocks or bonds of a railway and those of a government. In the cases in which the latter are contracted on account of a particular undertaking, the resemblance is even closer. A loan to an Australian colony for railway construction is indistinguishable from one to a company for fresh capital outlay.

Though the modern money market affords the machinery for continued extensions of state-borrowing, it does not give the motive power. The amount of loan transactions must, it may be said, depend on the conditions of supply and demand, but then this comprehensive formula stands in need of further analysis. The reasons for the expansion of demand are discoverable in the increase of expenditure in modern societies. We have remarked how both military and civil expenditure are growing, and also that some parts of this outlay are at once uncertain and productive of durable advantage. War and public works require large immediate expense, and their full benefits are not reaped at the moment. To procure sufficient funds by taxation is both disagreeable and, on the surface at all events, unjust. The financier very naturally takes what he knows to be the most convenient, and thinks to be the fairest course in appealing to capitalists for assistance. It is true that all loans have not this plausible ground: they are often due to weak or careless Finance, and are simply a mode of staving off the evil day. State-credit, in this too, is, like all modern credit, made up of both good and bad elements, and in its case the latter are often the more powerful.

As the increasing cost of the State gives us the motive for its greater borrowing, so do the development of the capitalist class and its greater influence on government explain the willingness to bring forward the needed supply. The earlier loans were either obtained by force, on the pledge of specific property or taxes, or finally on the pledged honour of the personal ruler. In the constitutional epoch, advances are made to an administration over which the well-to-do have influence. The close relation of the English debt with the Revolution of 1688 and the maintenance of the system introduced by it is well known[1], and even earlier the Italian cities and the Dutch provinces were under mercantile influence. It is unquestionable that the development of representative government and its control of the administration have helped to secure a larger supply of loans than would otherwise be forthcoming. At the same time it is easy to overrate the significance of this fact. The mere existence of constitutional rule does not suffice to create borrowing, nor its absence to stop it, as the French debt of the 18th century and that of Russia at present will suffice to prove. A powerful class in the possession of disposable wealth will be in a position to act on the most irresponsible of rulers, and a prudent absolutism will recognise the wisdom of sustaining public credit. Nevertheless, the advance of constitutional government and the increase of indebtedness have been coincident, a circumstance due to the fact that both are products of the present

[1] Macaulay, *Hist. of England*, i. 141.

stage of development, not solely because 'the monied interest has captured the machinery of government[1].' The greater attention to justice that, on the whole, characterizes popular government naturally operates on public, as on other economical relations.

Nor is there any reason to doubt that the change is advantageous. A strict observance of public faith, besides its immediate services both to lenders and borrowers, has a further influence in making the general financial administration more regular. It may be that in some cases the policy of contracting loans has been carried to excess, or the funds so obtained injudiciously used, but the repudiation of obligations would be an aggravation of the evil. When we remember the vital importance to a State of being able to secure assistance through credit at times of pressure, it is evident that anything tending to strengthen the guarantees for punctual payment is and must be for the social good.

§ 4. The powerful effect of the influences that favour indebtedness is shown by the figures of every stock exchange, and by familiar facts of statistics. Out of the, in round numbers, 1800 stocks quoted on the London Market, 340 may be fairly described as public, of which the larger part are British. Berlin has something over half that number, of which about one-third are German[2]. Paris has a still larger number. We may say that any State that pretends to be civilized regards the creation of a debt as one of the essential marks of its having reached that position. So does every colony and large city. The

[1] Adams, *Public Debts*, 9. So far as the influence of the monied class is directed to securing public credit it is decidedly beneficial.

[2] Cohn, §§ 535, 536. 'At the present time over one hundred States that possess practical sovereignty for debt purposes offer their bonds to the choice of an English investor, and if to this number were added the obligations of *quasi*-sovereignties, the London market would show over 150 sorts of public securities. There are here found the bonds of China, Japan, Persia, Siam, Egypt, Liberia, Orange Free State, Zanzibar, besides many other peoples of the Old World. The South American States are nearly all represented.' Adams, 5.

latest developments of municipal life are shown in the issue of bonds by the responsible authorities. Universality is one of the features of the modern debt system, and it is explicable only by reference to the conditions noticed in the preceding section, together with, in the case of backward States, the influence of imitation.

Public indebtedness is remarkable, not merely for its universal employment, but also for its great and growing amount. According to a careful estimate, the national debts of European States in 1870 were, in round figures, £3,000,000,000, in 1885 they had risen to £4,600,000,000, or an increase of £1,600,000,000 in fifteen years[1]. This enormous sum does not include the local debts that are, if we may judge from all available facts, increasing even more rapidly. The national debts, strictly so called, have been reduced both in England and the United States, but the heavier local debts probably leave the total burden undiminished. In other countries both divisions of debt have been growing apace in such a manner as to excite the apprehension of reflecting observers. The reality and extent of the danger will demand examination later on; the existence of the circumstances that have caused alarm is all that concerns us here, but even at this stage of the inquiry, it is well to notice the fundamental difference between the two classes of debt, the one contracted for non-economic ends, the other for purposes of reproductive employment. War and public works have been mentioned as the two chief causes of abnormal outlay, and loans for these objects belong respectively to the different classes. To take obvious instances, the great addition to the French debt from the war of 1870–71 cannot be regarded in the same light as the indebtedness of Prussia and other German States for railway purchase and construction. The former involves increased taxation; the latter, if prudently applied, does not. The same contrast appears in the case of the English National, as opposed

[1] Neymarck, *Les Dettes Publiques*, 86.

to the local debt, though this instance suggests the necessity of a qualification. Outlay on public works is not of itself, and apart from the revenue to be thence derived, different from the cost of war or other unproductive expenditure. No readier or more dangerous mode of increasing debt can be found than the execution of works that are not economically productive. Vague assertions of indirect benefits should not be allowed to conceal the fact that 'improvements' of this kind should be paid out of income, and cannot be regarded as investments in the proper sense of the term.

§ 5. To summarize the results of the present chapter: State borrowing appears to be, in its leading features, a creation of the constitutional period, built upon the decay of the older method of state hoarding and having its germs in the Middle Ages. It is the result of the credit system, combined with the increase of public expenses and the greater security for observance of faith to the state creditors. Both on account of its universal employment and its rapid growth, it is one of the most influential factors in modern Finance, and one whose tendencies and actual effects are deserving of close attention.

To form a just appreciation of the system a study of its history in the more important countries is desirable; and we shall therefore devote some space to this side of the question before passing to the more theoretical discussion.

CHAPTER III.

THE HISTORY OF THE ENGLISH DEBT.

§ 1. THE longest and in many respects the most instructive history of a continuous national debt is that supplied by Great Britain. The earlier attempts at systematic borrowing in Italy and Holland have ceased to have any practical effect, but the present English debt shows an unbroken record of 200 years. The Stuarts had not paid much respect to their obligations, and were quite prepared to repudiate inconvenient liabilities. Still, the expansion of the public economy made it impossible to avoid some floating charges. At the completion of the Revolution in 1689 the debt stood at a little over one million (£1,054,925); in 1691 it had risen to £3,130,000, bearing an interest charge of £232,000. An Act was passed in the next year which is regarded by Macaulay as the origin of the National Debt, and which provided that £1,000,000 should be borrowed on the security of the beer and other liquor duties. The yield of these taxes was to form a fund for the payment of interest, with the proviso that as each subscriber died his annuity was to be divided among the survivors until their number was reduced to seven, when as each annuitant died his share would lapse to the State[1]. The necessities of the war with France compelled further borrowing. The *funded* debt is first mentioned in 1694. In that year the Bank of England was founded,

[1] Macaulay, *Hist. of England*, ii. 398.

and lent its subscribed capital, £1,200,000, to the Government at the, under the circumstances, moderate rate of 8 per cent., which with an allowance of £4000 for management, made a total charge of £100,000 per annum. The connexion thus formed between the Bank and the Whig party continued as an influence in politics for several years [1].

At the Peace of Ryswick (1697) the debt had reached £21,500,000, which in the four succeeding years of peace was reduced to £16,400,000. The East India Company had lent £2,000,000 at 8 per cent. in 1698, but this was applied to paying other obligations. There was thus a reduction of about £1,250,000 per annum during peace, as against the increase of £2,500,000 per annum during the longer war period, a state of things that we shall find repeated at several subsequent stages of the history. During the war of the Spanish Succession the debt rose at the rate of over £3,000,000 yearly, until at the Peace of Utrecht (1713) it came to £53,680,000 [2].

During the peace period, which, with a couple of slight exceptions, extended from 1713 to 1739, the movement of the debt was not uniform. In the first ten years, owing to the South Sea Bubble, the war with Spain, and the method of dealing with taxation, the debt became £55,200,000. Then during the remaining sixteen years of peace, with the prudent administration of Walpole, some reduction was made, so that in 1740 the amount was just under £47,000,000, or an annual diminution of £500,000.

[1] Macaulay, *Hist.* ii. 479; Rogers, *First Nine Years of the Bank of England*, xiii, xiv.

[2] One curious item, the oldest of all and hence sometimes regarded as the origin of the debt, was added in 1706. The Cabal Government of Charles II had in 1671 seized on the Goldsmiths' loans to the Exchequer, a proceeding known as the 'shutting of the Exchequer,' and had simply paid interest on the amount of £1,328,000 detained. In 1683 even the interest was stopped. Legal proceedings were taken by the sufferers, and after a series of trials the House of Lords decided in their favour; but by an Act of 1699 it was provided that after December 25th, 1705, one-half of the amount (£664,000) should be added to the existing debt, to bear interest at 6 per cent.

§ 2. This first half-century of the debt's existence presents several points of financial interest. The effect of war in adding to debt, to be a little reduced in the succeeding peace, has been noticed. A more important feature is the gradual introduction of *funded* debt. Annuities, tontines, anticipations of taxes, and floating or temporary liabilities tend to be absorbed in the now established form of capital advances for interest. The various separate debt accounts become blended in one indistinguishable charge. 'The *Aggregate Fund* was established in 1715 and the *South Sea* and general *Funds* in the following year. To each of these funds a variety of branches of revenue were appropriated . . . and each of them was charged with the payment of certain annuities then due by the public. The united surplus of these funds formed the basis of the sinking fund established in 1716[1].' This is the first appearance of the system which, at a later time and in a different form, was regarded as the most effective agency for reducing debt. The primitive sinking fund usually called 'Walpole's' was really due to Stanhope. It proved of little service for the purpose it was applied to, as it depended on the existence of a surplus whether debt would be redeemed, and the contraction of new liabilities would always render nugatory the payments made towards redemption.

The first instances of the process known as 'conversion' also occur in this period. In 1714 the legal rate of interest had been reduced from 6 per cent. to 5 per cent., and three years later a like reduction was made on the interest of the public debt. Again in 1727 a further reduction from 5 per cent. to 4 per cent. was made, by which a saving of £400,000 per annum was realized. The effect of Walpole's financial management is shown by the high price that the funds had reached. A 3 per cent. loan issued in 1727 stood at *par* in 1736, and in the next year at 107. Under such conditions it is plain that the whole

[1] Hamilton, 64.

redeemable debt might have been reduced to 3 per cent. or even lower. Political expediency, which made it an object to favour the fundholders, who were strong supporters of the Hanoverian dynasty, prevented this useful measure.

§ 3. The war of 1739–48 had the usual effect on the state indebtedness. After the conclusion of peace it was found that £31,300,000 had been added to the previous incumbrances, bringing the total amount to over £78,000,000. The return of peace gave an opening for the application of financial management. Pelham in 1749 succeeded in carrying a conversion scheme, which may be regarded as the forerunner of the modern arrangements of the kind. Interest on part of the debt was reduced to 3½ per cent. for seven years, and 3 per cent. afterwards. Next year that on the remainder was reduced to 3½ per cent. for five years, and 3 per cent. afterwards. The fundholders at first dissented, but the high price of stock made it their advantage to accept the conditions. The consolidated 3 per cent. stock was established in 1751 and existed till the conversion of 1888 as the principal part of the debt. Its price in 1752 was 106¾, the highest point it ever reached. The sluggish condition of trade, and the difficulty of finding good investments sufficiently explain this high estimation of the funds.

Up to 1756 the debt had been reduced about £6,000,000, and stood at £72,200,000 when the Seven Years' War commenced. Expenditure at once rose so much as to lead to borrowing, which continued until, at the close of the war in 1763, the funded debt was £122,600,000 with a floating debt of about £14,000,000. The consequences of the war were apparent in the position of the Exchequer for some years afterwards. In 1766 the funded debt had risen to £129,500,000 with a further unfunded one of over £10,000,000. The succeeding years of peace allowed of small reductions, coming in all to about £10,000,000 in 1775, when the funded debt was £125,000,000 and the floating one £4,150,000, or a total of almost £130,000,000. As might be expected, the American War of Independence added seriously to this burden. At the conclusion of the Peace of Versailles (1783) the total debt was over £238,000,000, or an annual increase of about £13,500,000. During the latter part of the war the strain on English credit was shown by the low price obtained for the loans of that period.

Pitt's first administration dates from 1783, and its earlier part, which may be called the peace one and which ended with the outbreak of the war with France, did not accomplish much in the direction of diminishing the capital of the debt. In 1786 the new Sinking Fund was established, and by 1793 it had redeemed about £10,250,000, leaving a net capital charge of £228,000,000.

The characteristics of the second half-century of the debt history are found in the great growth of both capital amount and interest charge. After taking into account the small repayments in time of peace, there remains a net addition of £180,000,000 in the fifty-four years 1739–1792, while the annual payment for interest had risen from £2,000,000 to nearly £9,500,000 in the same period.

The terms of borrowing varied, but up to 1780 the loans were usually issued at *par*: their capital therefore represented the amount really received, though they were accompanied by small annuities for terms of years or other special favours. Lotteries were also combined with the loans, subscribers to an issue of stock receiving tickets. In 1781, however, a loan of £12,000,000 was raised at the rate of £150 of 3 per cent. and £25 of 4 per cent. stock for £100 paid, or a total capital of £21,000,000. The result of adopting this system was to add nearly £25,000,000 to the nominal capital of the debt without any corresponding receipt. It was probably due to the fear entertained by subscribers that their stock would on the return of better times undergo a reduction of interest, and also, to the preference of the government for a large 3 per cent. stock. As mentioned above, the sinking-fund policy which so powerfully affected the course of the debt was started at this time, though its influence was not as yet very noticeable.

§ 4. The protracted struggle with France, first under the Revolutionary government and afterwards under Napoleon I, is by far the most important and critical period in the development of the debt. Without the abnormal expenditure of the twenty-three years 1793–1815, the sinking fund of 1786 would have automatically wiped out the comparatively small capital liability; and the rapid growth of British industry, free as it would have been from the oppressive taxation that Pitt was compelled to impose, would have made the operation practically unfelt. The whole financial system of Great Britain has been profoundly affected, but the present debt is the most prominent of these results.

From the outbreak of war (1793) to the peace of Amiens (1802) loans were required in every financial year. The amounts, at first small, rose with the great outlay that the continuance of hostilities made necessary, till in 1797 the capital funded was over £67,000,000, the actual sum obtained for this acknowledgment of debt being £44,000,000. As nearly £7,000,000 were redeemed by the sinking fund in that year, the net increase of debt was somewhat over £60,000,000. In the other years the additional debt contracted was not nearly so large [1], but the effect of the

[1] The following was the capital funded for each year between 1793–1802:

Year.	£
1793	6,250,000
1794	15,676,526
1795	25,609,898
1796	41,303,699
1797	67,087,669
1798	30,000,000
1799	27,499,250
1800	29,045,000
1801	44,816,250
1802	41,489,438.

See Hamilton, 256.

methods pursued was shown in the debt at the conclusion of peace. It was just £500,000,000, an increase of over £270,000,000 since the opening of war in 1793, i.e. £27,000,000 per annum. The sinking fund had paid off besides £57,000,000 of the debt incurred, which must be added to the other liabilities of the time. The principal cause of this great addition was the unwillingness to impose taxes at the commencement of the war. For the four years 1793–7 the total amount raised in taxation was £70,000,000, or £17,500,000 on the yearly average, while for the four years 1799–1802 it was £134,750,000, or an increase of 92½ per cent.

The short peace did not allow of any reductions in expense, and on the recommencement of war the borrowing system was again applied, though not to so large an extent. At the opening of the year 1816 the funded debt was £816,000,000, with a floating one of £60,000,000, showing a total increase of £360,000,000, or over £25,000,000 per annum. This comparatively satisfactory result, notwithstanding the immense expenditure of the Peninsular War, is explicable by reference to the much heavier taxation imposed. The income tax was in full operation, and the tax revenue rose from £37,250,000 in 1803 to £75,500,000 in 1815. Mr. Gladstone has asserted that the early adoption of the income-tax would have saved the necessity of borrowing, since the annual expenditure apart from the debt charge would in the later years have been met by the receipts from taxation [1]. Whether this would have been possible may be a matter of dispute, but there can be no question that the system of loans was carried to excess.

The facts just noticed bring out strongly the defects in the method of Finance during this trying period. They are to be found: (1) in the dislike to impose sufficient taxation, a feeling very natural on political grounds, but indefensible from the purely financial point of view. The

[1] *Financial Statements*, 16.

instances of this error occur chiefly in the earlier years. (2) In an undue reliance on the purely illusory expedient of a sinking fund, which, taking the most favourable view, increased the expense of management and deranged the loan market. (3) In the system of borrowing at a higher nominal capital than the amount actually received, thereby preventing, or at least hindering, future conversions of debt.

§ 5. The French wars brought the English debt to its maximum point. Since that date there has been some, though insufficient, reduction of it. The whole course of treatment has been towards a sounder and more careful policy, guided in a great degree by the influence of theory. The criticisms of Hamilton and Ricardo[1] exposed completely the sinking-fund fallacy. After inquiry it was settled, in 1819, that a real surplus of £5,000,000 annually should be preserved; but after various difficulties and changes, the sinking fund as a positive institution was abolished in 1829, whatever actual surplus existed at the end of each financial year being marked off for redemption of debt. The continuance of peace enabled the method of conversion to be tried with effect, though the field of operations was limited by the mistaken policy of borrowing in a 3 per cent. stock with a high nominal capital. In 1822 £152,000,000 of 5 per cent. stock was converted into 4 per cents., and in 1830 further reduced to 3½ per cents. The old 4 per cent. stock (£76,250,000) was reduced to 3½ per cent., to which rate a small balance of 4 per cents. (about £10,000,000) was also reduced in 1834.

The period 1830–40 is one of the most discreditable in English Finance. Hardly any fiscal reforms were carried out, and the debt was increased by budget deficits. Its amount in 1841 was £792,000,000, nearly £8,000,000 more than in 1830. The firmer administration of Peel restored the Finances. A surplus was procured by the revived

[1] Hamilton's *Inquiry* was published in 1813, and Ricardo's *Essay on the Funding System* in 1820.

income-tax, and a fall in the rate of interest made it possible in 1844 to convert the $3\frac{1}{2}$ per cent. stock—£248,000,000—into $3\frac{1}{4}$ per cent. for ten years and 3 per cent. afterwards. The further effort to create a $2\frac{1}{2}$ per cent. stock, made by Mr. Gladstone in 1853, proved a failure, owing to the rise in interest and the pressure of the Crimean War. This latter event supplied another illustration of the operation of war on indebtedness; though the progress of wiser views on the treatment of extraordinary expenditure was evidenced by the increased taxation which contributed the larger part of the total war expenditure (£70,000,000). Since that time no noticeable addition has been made to the debt, while the growth of wealth has made the weight of the existing charges very much lighter. Moreover, though no heroic efforts for the payment of debt have been tried, the agencies of the reformed sinking fund, the terminable annuities, and conversion have, taken together, produced a decided effect on both the capital and interest charges. The recent history of the debt is in fact altogether concerned with them.

§ 6. When the sinking-fund theory was abandoned, there still remained the old rule by which the surplus remaining in the Exchequer at the end of each financial year passed to the Commissioners for the Redemption of the debt. If large surpluses were realized year after year, this would be a satisfactory method, but with accurate balancing of receipts and expenses it is of little service. A considerable excess of receipts over expenditure gives rise to a cry for remission of taxation that is not easily withstood. Hence the need of marking off some special funds for the payment of debt. Sir S. Northcote's sinking-fund measure (1875), by which an amount of £28,000,000 annually was permanently set apart for this end, is the most obvious course. Unfortunately it is very easy to find plausible reasons for cutting down the sum so fixed. Under Mr. Goschen the £28,000,000 became, first

£26,000,000, and now only £25,000,000, a sum which leaves a very small margin over the interest and terminable annuity payments.

The method of redeeming debt by the use of terminable annuities seems on the whole more effective. In their commencement public debts were often raised by annuities in various forms [1], and during the Revolutionary and Napoleonic wars the system of adding long annuities to the funded loan was adopted, with the arrangement that they should all terminate in 1860. By this system a considerable relief was gained when the date of expiry was reached. As an effective method of redemption fresh terminable annuities have been created, and an equivalent amount of stock cancelled. The largest creations were in 1868 and 1884. In the former year £24,000,000 of savings-bank stock was cancelled, and an annuity of £1,760,000 substituted. In 1884 Chancery stock to the amount of £40,000,000 and over £30,000,000 of Post Office savings bank stock were similarly treated, with the result that the funded debt has been brought within more moderate limits. In 1860–1 its total amount was £788,970,799. After thirty years it stood in 1890–1 at £579,472,082, or almost £210,000,000 less. On the other hand the terminable annuities had risen in capital value from £16,500,000 to £68,500,000, an increase of £52,000,000. Within the last ten years the agency of conversion has also been employed, and with success. Mr. Childers' conversion scheme of 1884, by which $2\frac{1}{2}$ or $2\frac{3}{4}$ per cent. stock might, at the option of the holder, be obtained for the existing 3 per cents., with an increased capital of 2 or 8 per cent., according to the stock chosen, failed to attract. Only £21,648,000 of stock was offered for conversion (more than half of it from public offices).

The failure of this attempt prepared the way for Mr. Goschen's success in 1888. The principles adopted were: (1) the creation of a single new stock, so that holders

[1] See § 1, and ch. 6. § 2 of present book.

were not confused by a choice, (2) the avoidance of any addition to capital, (3) the use of the most effective technical methods, such as conversion without expressed consent where this course was legal, commission to agents for the trouble imposed on them, and small concessions in the quarterly payment of interest. These contrivances, together with the persistent low rate of interest, enabled the whole mass of stock to be converted or paid off. A new stock, bearing interest at 2¾ till 1903, and at 2½ from that date for twenty years, has taken the place of the older 3 per cents., and a relief in interest to the amount of £1,400,000 annually has been secured, with the certainty of an equal gain in 1903. As an incident of the process the floating debt has become larger, and amounted in 1891 to £36,000,000, or more than double the normal level. As soon as the condition of the money market permits, the greater part of this sum will probably be funded or turned into a terminable annuity.

§ 7. Looking back on the course of the English debt, it is very plain that its growth has been altogether due to war expenditure, while its continued existence must be largely attributed to financial weakness. A comparison of the debt incurred during each war with the amount paid off in each succeeding peace establishes this. Over £600,000,000 was added in the great war (1793–1815); hardly £75,000,000 was paid off in the forty years' peace. The Crimean War added £40,000,000; it took twelve years of peace to pay off this sum. Greater vigour in the use of terminable annuities, the maintenance of larger surpluses, and above all a wider employment of direct taxation in the form of an income tax would have produced much better results. The pressure of the debt, however calculated, is too light to justify such remissness. When we remember that each million of debt redeemed means the power of permanently remitting so much taxation, we can better understand the advantage of a vigorous policy in regard to it.

CHAPTER IV.

HISTORY OF THE FRENCH DEBT. INDEBTEDNESS IN OTHER COUNTRIES.

§ 1. THE history of the French debt is naturally divided into two parts: the former of which deals with the borrowing under the Monarchy, and the latter with that under the system founded during the Revolution. The history of the various loans previous to the present century has been concisely described as 'a history of bankruptcies [1].' All forms of loans were tried; and all possible methods of evasion were used to escape repayment. The costly wars and the internal disturbances of the country partly explain this course of policy, but ignorance of financial and economic conditions was the great cause. Forced reductions of debt and debasements of the currency were frequently employed. An extensive revision was carried out by Sully in 1604, and further reductions were made by Mazarin. Colbert's administration introduced some system into this part of Finance, but after his death the older confusion reappeared. One of the effects of the Mississippi scheme was a consolidation of the diverse forms of the debt and a reduction of its amount to a sum, estimated at 1,700,000,000 livres, with an annual charge of 48,000,000 livres [2].

The reign of Louis XV (1715–1774) was marked by fresh loans and repeated forced reductions of the capital debt. In 1764 the sum of the different liabilities was 2,360,000,000 livres and the annual charge 93,000,000 livres: at his death the total annual charge was 120,000,000 livres, besides a floating debt of 235,000,000 livres.

[1] Vührer, i. 320.

[2] *Ib.* i. 181. The estimates, however, are not in agreement, *ib.* i. 178.

The increasing embarrassments of the State, which might have been overcome by Turgot had he remained in office, were at least the proximate cause of the summoning of the States-General and therefore of the Revolution.

According to the report submitted by the committee of the Constituent Assembly in November, 1789, the annual debt charge came to 208,000,000 livres, to which the floating debt had to be added [1].

§ 2. The financial difficulties that surrounded the revolutionary governments led to large issues of *assignats*, and to a consolidation of the public debt on a plan arranged by Cambon (August, 1793). By it all debt was to be inscribed in a 'Grand-book,' which was to be the conclusive evidence of the claim. The redeemable debt with 5 per cent. interest was first so treated, and the annuities were afterwards added. The result was the creation of an annual charge of £7,000,000 (174,716,000 francs), or a capital debt of £140,000,000. Unfortunately, the use of paper money and forced loans destroyed whatever benefit this systematic treatment might have conferred, and the straits of the government led to the measure of 1797 (*Vendémiaire, Ann.* vi), by which two-thirds of the debt was 'paid off' (?) in bonds to be exchanged for land, and, after some reductions for confiscations, the balance in annual interest was ascertained to be £1,600,000 (40,216,000 francs), representing a capital debt of £32,000,000. About £250,000 was added to the interest charge by the Directory, so that by the opening of 1800, 46,300,000 francs was the annual payment. The financial administration of Napoleon I, or rather of his advisers in such matters, Gaudin and Mollien, had two great merits. It resisted all temptations to issue inconvertible paper money, and it steadily refused to meet war expenditure by the method of borrowing. The result is to be seen in the position of the public debt at the close of the Empire. In April, 1814, the interest had risen to 63,300,000 francs (£2,530,000). After allowing for the

[1] Vührer, i. 336.

debts of the annexed provinces, the net increase is less than £300,000 interest, or £6,000,000 capital. In qualification of this favourable situation the immense burdens imposed on France and other countries must be taken into account. The Napoleonic system of making war support itself was a crushing one for the nations subjected to its operation, and probably far heavier than a well-managed public debt would have been [1].

The government of the Restoration had a series of difficult financial tasks to face. It had to meet the war indemnity levied on France by the allies; it had to compensate the emigrants; and it had to take up the unpaid balance of the Imperial outlay. It handled these various problems with honesty and firmness, refusing altogether to repudiate the debts of the Empire, as some of its supporters wished.

The principal feature of debt history during the period 1815–1830 is the creation of new debts to meet the indemnities and other outlay. The total amount required for these purposes represented an annual charge of over £6,500,000 [2]. The creation of other than 5 per cent. stock was a second noticeable point. The emigrants' indemnity was in 3 per cent. stock, and the conversion of 1824 was partly in 4½ per cents. and partly in 3 per cents. At the same time the policy of redemption was effectively carried on. The annual charge was reduced by 54,000,000 francs (£2,160,000), and conversion removed about 6,000,000 francs. These sums, with a few small escheats to the State, practically wiped out the debt existing in 1814, leaving that created by the Restoration government (though it was not responsible for it) as the actual charge. From another point of view it may said that in the fifteen years there was a net increase of £4,000,000 interest. The capital of the new loans amounted to nearly £132,000,000, less the sum of £43,000,000 redeemed, or a net capital increase of £90,000,000.

[1] On the debt system of the first Empire, see Vührer, ii. 31–58.

[2] Vührer, ii. 160.

The Orleanist government commenced its career by borrowing. Its first loan added £280,000 to the interest charge, and was issued in 5 per cent. stock at 84, or nearly 6 per cent. on the actual sum received. Another loan of £4,000,000 at par only brought in £800,000. Further loans were made to clear off deficits, to prepare for war, and to carry out public works, but the redemption of existing debt was also carried on, so that against £1,500,000 fresh interest created, about £1,000,000 was redeemed, leaving a net increase of £500,000 during eighteen years, but, it should be said, years of profound peace during which public credit stood high [1]. The position of the stocks over 3 per cent. would have easily admitted of conversion without any increase of capital into a 4 per cent. or even 3½ per cent. stock, but to avoid popular hostility this evidently prudent course was not taken [2].

The Second Republic, short as was its duration, added £2,120,000 to the interest of the debt, and thus brought the total charge to nearly £9,200,000. The complete disorganization of the financial system and the hazardous experiments of the provisional government sufficiently account for this state of things.

The first financial performance of the Second Empire was the conversion of the 5 per cent. stock, amounting to £140,000,000, into 4½ per cent., with a gain to the State of £700,000 per annum. Less than £3,000,000 of the capital had to be paid to dissenting creditors. Less satisfactory was the management of the war expenditure. The total cost of the Crimean War to France was £66,000,000, and of this sum £61,500,000, or 93 per cent. of the whole, was added to the debt. Further loans followed for the Italian and

[1] In 1845 the highest and lowest prices of the several stocks were :—

	Highest.	*Lowest.*
5 per cents.	122·85	116·45
4½ "	116·25	111
4 "	110·5	106
3 "	86·4	80·85

Leroy Beaulieu, ii. 498.

[2] Vührer, ii. 238.

Mexican wars, issued much under *par*. The total addition to the debt between 1852 and July, 1870, was represented by an increased interest charge of £5,160,000. Thus the annual payment had risen to £14,400,000, and the capital was a little less than £480,000,000. Even more questionable than the large borrowing was the conversion of 1862, under which, for the sake of a premium, the 4½ and 4 per cent. stocks were to be converted into 3 per cents., with a proportionally increased nominal capital. This unjustifiable measure gained a premium of £6,300,000 for the State, but on the other hand it increased the capital of the debt by almost £64,000,000, and precluded the hope of further speedy conversion [1].

§ 3. The Franco-German war of 1870–1 is as marked a period in the development of the French debt, as the war with Napoleon I was in the case of the English one. Its first effect was to throw an enormous burden on the resources of the new government. In addition to the terrible expense and sacrifice due to the military operations, there was the indemnity of £200,000,000 to the Germans. The total expense imposed on the State has been estimated at £393,000,000. Of that sum about £340,000,000 was raised through loans of one kind or other. Nearly £60,000,000 was received from the Bank of France by the inconvertible paper issues. Over £40,000,000 was borrowed in 1870, and two great loans, the first of £80,000,000, the second of £120,000,000, were raised in 1871 and 1872 [2].

The debt incurred to the Bank of France was cleared

[1] For the Finance of the second Empire, see Vührer, ii. 258–369.

[2] The loans contracted were as follows:

Date.	Amount received. Millions of francs.	Nominal capital created. Millions of francs.	Amount of interest. Millions of francs.
August, 1870	804	1,327	39·8
October, 1870	208	250	15
June, 1871	2,293	2,779	139
July, 1872	3,498	4,140	207
Total	6,803	8,496	400·8

Cp. Vührer, ii. 538; Leroy Beaulieu, ii. 573.

off by annual payments of £8,000,000, and afterwards of £6,000,000, until in 1879 the whole was discharged. In other respects the treatment of the debt has been weaker. Fresh loans have been contracted for public works and to meet budget deficits. M. Freycinet's plans accounted for a large part of this increase in debt, which was raised in 3 per cent. stock terminable after seventy-five years. Thus a new category of debt was added to the old perpetual *rentes*, with a nominal capital of £160,000,000, an interest charge of £4,800,000, and a further charge of £1,000,000 for redemption. The old 5 per cents. have been in 1883 converted into 4½ per cents. without increase of capital, but the existing charge and capital amount are very heavy. The consolidated debt amounts to £880,000,000, with annual interest of £30,500,000. When the other liabilities are added we get the enormous total of £1,295,000,000, demanding the annual cost of £50,000,000, together with about £1,750,000 applied to its redemption [1].

The French debt is by far the largest in the world, being more than double the English in annual charge, and over £600,000,000 greater in capital amount. This great accumulation of debt has been altogether the work of the present century. A comparison with the English debt will show the steps by which the latter has been approached and then passed. It is also interesting to note the widening distribution of *rentes* among the French population. In 1830 the holders of stock were only 125,000 in number.

[1] The constitution of the French debt in January, 1891, was as follows:—

	Interest. Million francs.	Capital. Million francs.
Perpetual Rates 4½ per cent.	305·5	6,789
" " 3 "	456	15,204
Redeemable 3 per cents.	120·7	4,023
Floating debt, January, 1891	21	1,077
Annuities for life	191	2,295
Terminable Annuities	111	3,000
Total	1,205·2	32,388

The guarantee of 60,000,000 francs to the railway companies brings the annual payments to over £50,000,000, Leroy Beaulieu (5me Ed.), ii. 578–81.

By 1869 they had increased tenfold, while in 1881 they numbered more than 4,000,000. The great mass of the debt is in the hands of Frenchmen, and divided among all classes of society. This, though in some respects desirable, hampers a finance minister in such processes as conversion or repayment, as the fundholders' interest is at once powerful and in immediate opposition to that of the State.

Some alleviation of the burden may in the future be reasonably expected from (1) the gradual redemption of the 3 per cent. stock created since 1878, a process to be finished in 1952, and (2) from the falling-in of the railway property, which, as we saw, will happen at about the same time[1]. But the benefits to be thus received will largely depend on the methods employed in the next sixty years. If deficits are allowed to continue, if injudicious expenditure is carried on, and if new public works are started, it is certain that a fresh debt, perhaps exceeding that now in existence, will be formed by the middle of the next century.

§ 4. Italian unity has, from the financial point of view at least, been purchased at a heavy price. Not only has the weight of taxation been inordinately increased, but a large public debt has been contracted. The new kingdom had to take up the debts of its predecessors, and from its formation up to 1875 each year's budget showed an excess of expenditure over receipts[2]. The use of loans, either openly or by the issue of inconvertible paper, was the inevitable result. The latter expedient was in force from 1866 to 1883, when it was removed by means of a loan of over £29,000,000 in *specie*. Since then, however, there have been further deficits and an increase of liabilities, so that the total capital of the Italian debt may now be estimated at £520,000,000, involving an annual charge of nearly £25,000,000. About £6,000,000 of

[1] See Bk. ii. ch. 3. § 13.

[2] These annual deficits, 'which began with £15,000,000 for 1860 and rose to nearly £29,000,000 in the war year 1866, became less than £3,000,000 in 1871, and only a little over £500,000 in 1874', amounted in the aggregate for the fifteen years 1860-1874 to £166,000,000.

this amount has been an inheritance from the earlier States, and the war of 1866 is accountable for part of the balance; but the great source has been the budget deficits in ordinary years, that have gradually accumulated in the present heavy burdens[1].

The situation of the German States is in sharp contrast with that of the countries already considered. They are not weighed down by debt charges, and they have the advantage of possessing assets against a good deal of their apparent liabilities. As appeared in connexion with the quasi-private income, the retention of the domain, both agricultural and industrial, has been more marked in Eastern Europe, and this difference in policy has affected the position of the public debt.

The use of a state treasure prevented the employment of loans by Prussia up to the French war of 1792. From that time the public necessities were too pressing and some debt was contracted, which, by 1820, came to nearly £33,000,000 with a yearly charge of £1,140,000, and a sinking fund which brought the total annual cost up to £1,500,000. During the next thirty years the debt was reduced by the sale of public property, and suitable taxation, until in 1848 the interest charge was only £650,000. Between 1850 and 1870 there were increases both for public works and war expenditure, that by the end of the latter year brought the total debt to £66,700,000. Since then the purchase of the railways has added £153,000,000 to the debt. The process of redemption has also been carried on to such an extent that there is an actual diminution of the non-productive part. Thus since 1870 the railway debt shows an increase of over £170,000,000, and as there is a valuable property in existence by its use the net result is a reduction of about £16,000,000. In fact the railway receipts have in some years more than sufficed

[1] Even for the present year Signor Luzzatti estimates for a trifling deficit (£40,000), but his view is generally regarded as unduly optimistic, as the real excess of expenditure is likely to be £1,250,000.

to meet their expenses, and the whole cost of the interest and sinking fund on the debt. Alike in the smallness of its amount and the conditions of its creation, the Prussian debt is less oppressive that that of any other European country[1].

The four important secondary states of Germany are somewhat similarly placed. The whole debt of Baden is for railway construction, as is the far greater part of those of Saxony and Würtemberg. Two-thirds of the Bavarian debt was incurred for the same object. Though the railways hardly meet the interest on their part of the debt, yet so far as they contribute, there is a relief to the tax-payers, and if liquidation were necessary, there would be a valuable asset to assist in the work.

At its commencement the German Empire took up the debt of the North German *Bund*, which consisted in loans for the war of 1870–1, amounting to over £30,000,000, and which has been almost entirely paid off. New loans have, however, been issued for extraordinary expenditure, and they have brought the debt to over £60,000,000. The various Imperial funds must be placed on the other side of the account: they, as we saw[2], come to £30,000,000 and leave only about the same amount as the net liability.

§ 5. The United States have, again, a still different debt history from any of the preceding countries, and one that suggests some points of interest. After the formation of the Constitution Hamilton prepared and carried a scheme of funding by which the debts due to France and Spain, those owed to natives by the Congress, and lastly the debts of the States, were combined. The total debt was in 1791 $75,000,000. Notwithstanding the creation of a sinking fund, the amount due increased in 1796 to $84,000,000. By 1812 it was reduced to $45,000,000. The war with England led to greater outlay, which was for the most part

[1] For the Prussian debt, see Cohn, §§ 488–94; Neymarck, 3–6.

[2] See Bk. v. ch. I. § 3.

met by loans [1]. In 1816 the debt had reached $127,000,000. From that point there was a steady reduction, till, in 1835, the total debt was only $37,000, or practically *nil*. During the following years some temporary loans were made, as e. g. for the Mexican War (1848), and the total debt stood at about $60,000,000 when the Civil War broke out [2].

The first results of the contest were a serious disturbance of industry and commerce and a great increase of expenditure. No adequate tax system was in existence, and accordingly the extraordinary expenditure was at first almost entirely met by the use of credit. Treasury notes, culminating in inconvertible paper issues, and funded debt were both employed. It was not until 1864 that the tax revenue was made a really effective contributory to the war expenses, but from that date its development was rapid [3]. Soon after the close of the war the debt touched its highest point. According to Mr. Bolles: 'On the 1st September (1865) the debt recorded on the books of the treasury reached its maximum, though a large amount of war obligations, pensions, &c., were not yet paid' [4]. This maximum was represented by the sum of $2,846,000,000, of which only

[1] Out of $70,000,000 war expenditure, $64,300,000 was met by loans, and $5,700,000 out of the tax receipts, or 92 % and 8 % respectively. Adams *Public Debts*, 124.

[2] The smallness of the debt in the period 1836–60 will be best realized from the fact that its capital amount rarely exceeded, and in several years was much under, the annual income of the Federal Government.

[3] The following table shows the relation of loans to tax revenue in the years 1861–66. See Adams, 132.

Year.	Revenue. Million dollars.	Loans. Million dollars.	Total. Million dollars.	Percentage of loans to total receipts.
1861	41·5	23·7	65·2	35
1862	51·9	433·6	485·5	89·5
1863	112·6	595·6	708·2	85
1864	264·6	696	960·6	72·5
1865	333·7	864·8	1198·5	74
1866	558	92·6	650·6	14

[4] Bolles, *Financial History* (1861–1885), 306. According to Prof. Adams, 'the interest-bearing obligations of the United States stood at their maximum in August, 1865, amounting at that date to $2,381,000,000.' *Public Debts*, 249.

$1,110,000,000 was funded debt, and about $460,000,000 inconvertible paper, the enormous sum remaining—$1,276,000,000—was in the form of floating debt, most of it immediately repayable. The cash reserve in the treasury was, however, only $88,000,000, leaving net liabilities to the amount of $2,758,000,000.

The great financial problems for the Secretary to the Treasury were therefore: (1) to pay off or fund the floating debt, and (2) to provide a permanent scheme for the future extinction of the immense liabilities created by the war. The former required immediate attention and was successfully managed. In a little over two years the floating debt was brought down to $408,000,000, and the inconvertible issues reduced by over $20,000,000, while new funded debt to the amount of $686,000,000 in 6 per cent. bonds had been issued. The temporary obligations were cleared off in 1868, leaving free scope for the repayment, and when possible the conversion, of the funded debt.

A sinking-fund law had been enacted in 1862, but as there was no real surplus till 1866 it was inoperative, and in fact the payment of debt has not been carried on in conformity with that law. It has notwithstanding been on an immense scale, as the following short table proves.

Year.	*Capital debt.* Million dollars.	*Interest charge.* Million dollars.	*Rate of interest.*
1865 (Sept.)	2756·4	151	6·34
1868 (Nov.)	2484·9	126·4	5·8
1884 (Nov.)	1408·5	47·3	3·92
1889 (Dec.)	1056·1	41	3·7

Thus in less than a quarter of a century $1,700,000,000 has been removed from the capital liability, and the annual payment has been reduced by $110,000,000. This, at first sight, extraordinary result has been attained in part by the high credit of the United States Government, which has enabled the 6 per cent. and 5 per cent. bonds, as they fell due, to be reduced to 4½ per cent. and even 3½ per cent. A more potent cause has been the receipt of large annual surpluses which were the natural consequence of the high duties on imports. The protective system has been in this way the cause of the repayment of the war loans. From the financial point of view it is plain that a like result could have been reached at much less real cost and sacrifice if moderate duties had been used; but then it is doubtful whether in that case the policy of repayment would have been so firmly adhered to.

At all events the position of the Federal debt has ceased to be a prominent element in financial questions. It is rather in connexion with the banking system, and the method of dealing with bonds whose time for redemption has not yet come, that the debt attracts notice.

One of the methods of issuing loans in the United States deserves mention here. It is that by which a minimum and a maximum time of repayment are fixed. Thus what are known as the 'ten-forty bonds' were redeemable at ten years from the date of issue, but if not then paid off, they could not be redeemed for forty years. This system is at present a serious inconvenience, as the greater part of the debt is irredeemable, and therefore the surplus revenue must either accumulate, or a premium must be paid to the holders to induce them to accept payment[1].

§ 6. The debts of other countries need not be considered at any length. They exhibit the same general features, though each group of States shows certain peculiarities. The Russian debt has been all along mixed up with the use of inconvertible paper, and is affected by the particular character of the government. The Austro-Hungarian monarchy has three separate debt accounts, one for the Empire and one for each of the parts. But one general

[1] 'With a sinking fund appropriation of $50,000,000 a year, we shall find ourselves in 1896 again without any debt upon which the appropriation may be expended. In what manner shall the machinery of debt payment be managed from 1896 to 1907?' Adams, 279. The Tariff Act of 1890 and the increased expenditure seem likely to prevent the existence of any large surplus, and this difficulty will therefore not arise.

fact is discernible, viz. the almost universal tendency to increase, with, it is to be feared, in some cases a dangerous pressure on the limits of national solvency. Any attempt to present the total amount of indebtedness at a given time soon becomes misleading, owing to the growing liabilities of the world.

CHAPTER V.

THE THEORY OF PUBLIC CREDIT AND PUBLIC DEBTS.

§ 1. THE peculiar position of the state economy and the great importance of public borrowing have both tended to obscure the fundamental truth that public credit is but one form of credit in general, and is, or ought to be, regulated by the same leading principles. Many of the most serious errors in this department of Finance have been due to the belief that the State in its borrowing was emancipated from the restrictions that prudence imposed on the individual, and that it might safely indulge in experiments that would soon land the ordinary citizen in bankruptcy.

A reference to the nature of credit shows that a national debt is no creation of wealth; that at best it can only, in Bagehot's phrase, be 'additive' and give greater energy to production. Moreover, this position is only attained where the credit is 'productive,' i.e. used in assisting the creation of fresh wealth. Where the resource whose use is obtained by credit serves merely for some object which, however important, is not conducive to economic production, then, either for the individual or for the State, there is so far a loss of material power. Present borrowing of this latter kind implies less income in the future until the loan is repaid. In like manner the limits of individual and public capacity for borrowing are determined on the same principle. Each person can only borrow on his disposable income; a State or subordinate political body must depend on its quasi-private and tax receipts, and must deduct its necessary outlay. The fund on which a public body can call is that part of the income of individuals that the tax collector is able to appropriate, and it is on its amount that, in the last resort, borrowing power depends.

With regard to the mechanism of public credit the same fact exists. The State that enters the money market for a loan stands on a precisely similar footing to the industrial corporation. It must conform to the usual course of business, and it must submit to have its solvency gauged in just the same way—by the price at which it can obtain accommodation. State credit is, then, we may fairly conclude, one branch of the modern credit system, and its general aspect is the same as that of industrial or non-industrial credit, respectively, in the case of private economies.

§ 2. But though this general conclusion is abundantly warranted, and may be usefully employed in dispelling certain fallacies on the subject, there remain for notice some special features of public economy that give a peculiar colour to its borrowing, more particularly in the case of the central government. The sources of individual wealth reside in property or personal capacity to earn; it is from them that all private income comes. But the State's revenue is mainly derivative; it can compel the taxpayers to supply it with funds. The method of borrowing is therefore naturally suggested where heavy taxation is for the moment undesirable, and is further encouraged by the fact that public credit has the advantage of resting on a broader and more enduring basis. So far as a public domain is in existence, loans may be regarded as virtually mortgages raised on its security, as many early loans actually were in form as well as in fact.

A second peculiarity of public economy is the difficulty of sudden retrenchment in its case. The individual, or even the industrial company, can cut down expenses if receipts fall below their former level. Their expenditure is more elastic than that of the State. Decline in revenue receipts will not justify the disbanding of the army, or the dismissal of civic officials. Consequently where under any given state of things a deficit is imminent, and new taxes are not for the moment available, borrowing is necessarily prescribed.

This apparent disadvantage is compensated by the greater permanence and wider field of public economy. Whatever may be the disasters of a few years [1], the normal feature during centuries is a growth of national wealth and income that it takes more than ordinary misgovernment to dissipate. We may readily explain the special forms of state loans by reference to this circumstance. The great variety of stocks and the complicated conditions for repayment could only be adopted by a body of assured continuance and growing resources, and in this respect the greater industrial corporations, who also have the prospect of long existence, present an instructive resemblance.

More important than any of the foregoing is the peculiar legal position of a debtor State. Unlike the private citizen or corporation, it rests within its own discretion to say whether or not it will meet its obligations. The creditor who wishes to enforce his claim against a State has not at his command the usual legal machinery, the necessity of which is proved by the frequent recourse to its aid. A national bankruptcy is a strictly legal proceeding, *e.g.* an Act of Parliament repudiating the National Debt would be quite as valid as any other measure. This privilege, which is inherent in any form of Sovereignty, has been further extended to—or should we not rather say retained by—such subordinate political bodies as the 'States' of the American Union, which at one period of their history extensively availed themselves of it[2]. But where no trace of supreme power remains, this exemption disappears, and

[1] Thus the situation of France in 1871 was an entirely unexpected one, and could be no criterion for judging its usual position.

[2] The 'repudiations' of 1840–50 have deeply injured the credit of the American States.

the ordinary local governments are as amenable to legal process for recovery of debts, as any other kind of corporation[1].

The Sovereign State, though released from legal liability, is in practice under very powerful inducements to honestly pay its way. In the first place, where its creditors are foreigners, a failure to fulfil its agreement lays it open to remonstrance on the part of the foreign states affected, and possibly to even more rigorous measures. The domain of international law is not yet a settled one, and it is quite conceivable that the observance of obligations to alien lenders may be one of its rules in the future. With regard to native creditors there is an obvious interest on the part of the State to do nothing that will injure them, and whatever political power they possess will surely be used in their own defence. Stronger than either foreign or domestic influence is the economic sanction that protects the security of loans. The repudiating State for the sake of a temporary gain shuts itself out from the future use of credit. A national bankruptcy is a bar to any later borrowing unless on ruinous terms. The American 'States' have never recovered the shock that repudiation inflicted on their position as borrowers. The best support to the policy of paying in full is derived from the economic advantage that a reputation for honesty secures 'in the long run,' and nations, it must be remembered, have a far greater interest than individuals in paying attention to what happens 'in the long run.'

§ 3. The earlier theories on the subject of public credit were little more than the formal statement of popular prejudices. Ideas similar to those of Law on the nature of credit were somewhat widely diffused. Thus we find the public funds described as 'a mine of gold,' and state loans as 'realized alchemy'[2]. Credit was looked on as a fresh

[1] It must, however, be remembered that the method of procedure may often be complex, and make recovery of the debt difficult, if not hopeless.

[2] The former is Berkeley's account, *Querist*, No. 233; the latter phrase is used by Pinto, a Dutch writer. Roscher, § 125, note 1.

creation of wealth, and therefore all public debts were naturally regarded as a clear addition to the national possessions. Less extreme, but just as erroneous in principle, was the assertion that the debts of the State were quite unimportant, as they were merely owed from the right hand to the left[1]. This position—an evident deduction from the cruder mercantile doctrine—was only strictly applicable to the domestic debt, and was so limited by Voltaire and Condorcet. Foreign creditors, it was thought, did take money out of the country and therefore injured it; the resident received his interest and spent it at home. There is little difficulty in exposing this fallacy, which really rests on the same ground as certain views about expenditure and taxation already rejected[2]. The action of indebtedness on the economic system cannot be altogether without influence or effect, nor can the consumption of masses of wealth be of itself beneficial. The confusion—not altogether unknown in later writers—between wealth and evidences of ownership is the reason for the belief that public debts are an addition to the material resources of the nation. Though in some respects the existence of debt may be the cause of new wealth creation, this interpretation of its effects must be dismissed as erroneous.

§ 4. The growth of debts in England and France in the 18th century produced a very different opinion on the subject in the case of the most prominent writers on political and social matters. Montesquieu did not hesitate to condemn public debts; he refutes the idea that they are advantageous, and approves of the English conversion and sinking fund[3]. Hume is even more pronounced. Though declining 'to waste time in declaiming against a practice which appears ruinous, beyond all controversy', he yet states very forcibly his objections, some of which had been

[1] '*Les dettes d'un État sont des dettes de la main droite à la main gauche, dont le corps ne se trouvera point affaibli.*' Melon, *Essai Politique*, ch. 23 in *Économistes Financiers du* 18me *siècle*, 749.

[2] Cp. Bk. i. ch. 8. § 6, and Bk. iii. ch. 2. § 2.

[3] *Esprit des Lois*, Liv. xxii. chs. 17, 18.

already given by Montesquieu. The high authority of Adam Smith is on the same side. He speaks of 'the enormous debts which at present oppress, and will in the long run probably ruin, all the great nations of Europe,' and his whole discussion of the funding system is in an extremely hostile tone[1]. Both Hume and Adam Smith prophesied that national bankruptcy would be the outcome of the continuous English borrowing. The course of events has falsified this prediction, and later writers have not hesitated to pronounce it fallacious. According to Macaulay 'the prophets of evil were under a double delusion. They erroneously imagined that there was an exact analogy between the case of an individual who is in debt to another individual, and the case of a society which is in debt to a part of itself. . . . They were under an error no less serious touching the resources of the country'[2]. The former part of this criticism is more than questionable. In all essential points the analogy between the public and private debtor does hold good, and should never be lost sight of. It is no doubt true that the material power of England was under-estimated, but then it was impossible to foresee the Industrial Revolution and its extraordinary results. The real error of Hume and Adam Smith lay in generalizing from a too limited experience, and in assuming that no new forces would come into operation; just as Macaulay has probably erred in the opposite direction when he declares that 'a long experience justifies us in believing that England may, in the twentieth century, be better able to pay a debt of £1,600,000,000 than she is at the present time to bear her present load.' The true view, which regards the debt as a pressure on an elastic body, implies the necessity of measuring both the weight and the expansive power of the object on which it presses.

The French war and the accumulation of debt that it caused brought forward Sinclair as a moderate supporter,

[1] Hume, 'Essay on Public Credit.' *Wealth of Nations*, 387.

[2] *History of England*, ii. 400.

and Hamilton as a vigorous critic, of the system of borrowing. The former maintains that public loans are the necessary result of the new method of conducting warfare, and compares their advantages and disadvantages[1]. Hamilton's work expounds with remarkable clearness the general rules applicable to the management of debt, and contains among its fundamental principles the following proposition: 'If the periods of war, compared with those of peace, and the annual excess of the war expenditure, compared with the annual savings during the peace establishment, be so related, that more debt is contracted in every war than is discharged in the succeeding peace, the consequence is a perpetual increase of debt; and the ultimate consequence must be, its amount to a magnitude which the nation is unable to bear'[2].

Now, this is merely the statement in hypothetical form of the condition from which Adam Smith and Hume drew their dismal conclusions, and, as expressed, it is absolutely incontrovertible. A nation cannot, any more than an individual, keep adding continually to its liabilities without at last coming to the end of its resources.

The influence of Hamilton's teaching, which we shall have to notice again in respect to the method of repayment[3], is plainly traceable in Ricardo's 'Essay on the Funding System,' in which he declares his preference for taxes over loans, chiefly on the grounds that (1) imprudent expenditure will be checked by the dislike felt for heavy taxation, and (2) the probability that taxation will fall on revenue, while loans usually come from capital. Thus the main current of economic opinion was decidedly opposed to state borrowing.

§ 5. A comparatively novel view of the effect of public borrowing—though the germ of the idea is in Ricardo's Essay—was given by Chalmers, who in his *Political Economy*

[1] Sinclair's *History of Revenue*, Pt. ii. ch. 2, i. 350 sq.

[2] Hamilton, 9.

[3] Bk. v. ch. 7. § 3.

(1832) argued that the loan system was economically disadvantageous and oppressive to the labourers. His contention was that, whatever method be adopted, the whole amount must be taken within the period, but that by taxation the charge is spread over the whole revenue of the society, while by borrowing it is placed on that part of circulating capital that goes to reward the labourers, and as a necessary consequence lowers their remuneration to the benefit of the capitalists. In fact, in his opinion, the system of borrowing puts double pressure on the country that adopts it: for there is the original sacrifice when the loan is contracted and the later one involved in the payment of interest so long as it remains outstanding, and finally in its repayment. The practical conclusion that follows from this train of reasoning is of course that no borrowing should ever take place, and that all expenditure should be met out of current revenue[1].

It is highly probable that Chalmers' argument, like many of the ingenious points made by the secondary writers on Economics in the first half of this century, would soon have been completely forgotten, had not J. S. Mill seized upon and repeated it in an early chapter of his *Principles*. He asserts that the doctrine is substantially correct, though it needs qualification owing to the possibility of the migration of capital[2]; and in a later part of his treatise he endeavours to assign what is clearly an erroneous criterion by which the real effect of any actual loan could be determined.

This curious doctrine is evidently based on an application of the wages-fund theory in its most rigid form, and the general abandonment, or at least qualification, of that dogma would of itself suggest serious doubts as to the soundness of any deduction from it. As we shall see in a later section, the argument is almost wholly untenable, and rests on a very partial interpretation of some

[1] Chalmers, *Political Economy*, ii. 71 sq.

[2] *Principles*, Bk. i. ch. 5. § 8, Bk. v. ch. 7. § 1.

economic conditions peculiar to the time at which it originated.

§ 6. The exigencies of practical Finance had made the use of borrowing so general that the more practical students of the subject recognised the necessity of the loan system. In Germany especially is this view to be found. Jacob, Malchus, Rau, and Nebenius, while all dwelling on the evil effects of loans, accept them as a legitimate expedient. The arguments of Adam Smith were blended with the results of positive experience, and if the combination was not always consistent, it at least had the merit of being eminently common-sense [1].

The same judgment can hardly be passed on a later German theory, originated by C. Dietzel, which regards the loan system as the true mode of defraying extraordinary expenditure. This position, which has been already noticed in another connexion [2], regards the State as being a part of the immaterial capital of the society, and any unusual outlay for its service as in fact an investment. To charge to revenue what is really due to capital is therefore a mistake in public book-keeping, and what is far worse, an injustice to the actual taxpayers. From this point of view the issue of loans becomes a normal part of the working of a progressive State. Instead of regarding the process as wholly condemnable, or at best as a necessary evil, we should, it is maintained, look on it as both just and beneficial [3]. The upholders of the theory have arrived at a diametrically opposite position to that occupied by Chalmers, and one which, if generally adopted, would produce very serious practical consequences.

§ 7. A criticism of the preceding doctrines supplies the first steps towards a true theory of public debt. The idea of

[1] On these writers see Cohn, §§ 511–14; Roscher, *Geschichte*, §§ 152, 160, 195.

[2] Bk. i. ch. 8. § 1.

[3] See C. Dietzel, *System der Staatsanleihen*, Stein, iv. 421; Wagner, i. 144 sq.; for statements of the doctrine. Cohn, §§ 515–7, supplies a pointed criticism.

Chalmers that the system of borrowing presses too heavily on the labouring class can be easily shown to be fallacious. In the first place, it is not true that all loans come from capital; they may be obtained from savings made for the purpose [1]. The prospect of a new and secure investment is a stimulus to abstinence, and so far the labourers will not suffer. But even granting this erroneous assumption, it by no means follows that loans derived altogether from capital are taken from wages. 'The loan,' says Mill, 'cannot have been taken from that portion of the capital of the country which consists of tools, machinery, and buildings. It must have been wholly drawn from the portion employed in paying labourers [2].' He, however, offers no proof, or attempt at proof, of this proposition, which is plainly untrue. The amount taken in loans comes at first from floating capital that would otherwise have been applied to fixed capital, raw material, or the payment of workers in proportions determined by the actual circumstances. Again, the effect of the employment of the loan is altogether disregarded [3]. So far as it is expended on hiring services it actually tends to raise wages, so that, reasoning from the wages-fund position, what is taken by the abstraction of capital is restored by the outlay of the borrower on labour. The utter unsoundness of the doctrine that all loans come from wages will appear from the absurd result to which it leads, viz. that where wages are at the minimum it would be impossible to borrow without starving some of the workers.

The facts that public loans are in many cases international, and that in any event capital is capable of migrating from country to country are allowed by Mill to have weakened the theory that we are considering. If loans really come from the international market, any pressure must fall

[1] This is probably true of part of the French loans of 1871–2.

[2] *Principles*, Bk. i. ch. 5. § 8.

[3] Mill briefly refers to this point in a footnote to his later editions, Bk. i. ch. 5. § 8 (6th ed.).

on the labourers of all the countries which contribute; *e.g.* South American borrowings would have injured English labourers. He is therefore led to suggest that so long as public borrowing does not raise the rate of interest, the labourers are not damnified. This qualification is again unsound; for every loan must, *pro tanto*, tend to raise the rate of interest, or to keep it from falling. There is no line or wall of separation between capital for home and that for foreign investment[1]. The growth of international relations has rendered antiquated any argument from the hypothetical case of an isolated country[2].

Such considerations as the foregoing make it difficult to understand the acceptance of the doctrine by Mill. The reasons are to be found, partly in a special case which seemed to give it support, and partly in a portion of truth that it did, in fact, contain. The great instance of state borrowing known to Chalmers and Mill was that by England in the period 1793–1815, and at that time the labourers were suffering while the capitalists seemed to prosper. The real explanation was of course different[3], but the concomitance of the two series of facts gave a plausibility to the theory that it would not otherwise have had. The element of truth contained in it was that public borrowing is a demand for loanable capital which helps to raise its value, *i.e.* the rate of interest. Higher interest leaves less for the other shares in distribution, and as the employer and the landlord were able to hold their own, the pressure fell on the labourers; but this could not be ascribed solely to state borrowing. Taxation that really fell on capital would have

[1] Mill, *Principles*, Bk. v. ch. 7. § 1. His error has been exposed both by Cairnes, *On the Best Method of Raising the Supplies for War Expenditure*, 10, 11, and by Cliffe Leslie, *Notes* (privately printed), 17, 18.

[2] For a clear statement of the modern mobility of loan capital see Cunningham, *British Association Report* (1891), 727.

[3] The labourers' sufferings were really due to the depreciated paper money, the restrictive laws against labour, the old Poor Law, the check to imports by war, and the industrial revolution. The capitalists gained by the greater use of machinery and the command that England *at times* obtained over the supply of foreign markets.

the same effect. We cannot therefore adopt, as a sweeping and absolute rule, the proposition that the State should never at any time obtain funds by borrowing.

§ 8. The opposite theory, which puts forward the loan as a normal process of meeting expenditure of the extraordinary class, is open to quite as weighty objections. The expenses of the State do no doubt vary from year to year, and any sudden increase which has to be met by taxation may prove inconvenient, but on the other hand we have to remember that so-called 'extraordinary' expenditure is itself recurring[1]. To treat all fresh claims as extraordinary, and to meet them from loans is an easy but a dangerous course. There is also the further consideration, that in the long run the revenue from economic receipts and taxation must, if the State is to remain solvent, balance the outlay. So far as debt is not redeemed it is a permanent charge on the revenue, while its redemption must come from that source. If by taking a somewhat lengthened period we find that the ordinary state revenue meets expenditure, there is no reason why—special emergencies excepted—it should not do so in each financial year. Sudden changes in taxation may be more or less inconvenient, but the arrangement should be such as to secure some elastic sources of revenue. The English income-tax is capable of discharging this function, and the duties on commodities would also allow, in case of need, of large increases. The theory that so markedly separates ordinary from extraordinary expenditure, and assigns different funds for their immediate payment, errs by unduly emphasizing a non-essential distinction.

That borrowing is justifiable to meet 'reproductive' outlay is a further part of the theory, which is at once true or false according to the meaning given to the term. Actual purchase of productive property or creation of revenue-yielding works may fairly be defrayed by loans. The

[1] Cf. Bk. i. ch. 8. § 1.

property or particular work may be regarded as the primary object of the debt, and is at hand to pay the interest on it. What we have called 'economic' outlay has a claim to be met by borrowing that does not hold in respect to other forms. Taxation imposed for the purpose of adding to the domain has the disadvantage of taking the citizens' wealth for the purpose of accumulation, and should be employed sparingly if at all. To meet the cost of the purchase of the Prussian railways, or even the English telegraphs, by immediate taxation would not, were it practicable, be correct.

This concession to the policy of borrowing should not be stretched to include the cost of works or other state action that yields no revenue. Non-economic expenditure is primarily to be met out of the annual revenue, and unless it can be so dealt with ought not to be incurred. National culture, education, the promotion of social progress are all most desirable; but their attainment is not so pressing as to need the use of borrowing by the public powers. It is, indeed, true that much of state expenditure may be regarded as indirectly productive, and as adding to the national income in the future. A loan for the purpose of extending education or for improving the housing of the workers, though it does not directly provide the interest needed, may yet so increase the income of the community, as to make the tax receipts greater, without any increase either in rates or in rigour of collection. Regarded in the abstract such a proceeding seems defensible: the real objections to it arise from the difficulty of application. The results of expenditure of the kind are hard to trace or measure, and any statement respecting them must rest in a great degree on conjecture. The cost of the loan is definite and precise, and it constitutes a real burden on the resources of the society. Prudence seems accordingly to suggest that borrowing should hardly ever be adopted except for strictly economic expenditure, and then only where the extension of the state domain is clearly advisable.

Political and social conditions come in to limit the purely financial action of the public powers[1]. With an individualistic organization of society the extension of public industries has naturally to be kept within narrow bounds, and will not comprise all possibly gainful employments.

One great objection to the use of borrowing, unless there is an equivalent revenue obtained by its application, is the necessary curtailment of future power of spending. Large immediate outlay may, as we shall see, be requisite in certain cases, but for most of the usual forms of state activity the funds obtainable by taxation are quite sufficient, and can be continually renewed. Each year meets its own expense without causing any unevenness in the employment of the fund to be devoted to the purpose. Heavy borrowing, on the other hand, if persisted in for several years, so cripples the ordinary revenue as to compel retrenchment or further borrowing on disadvantageous terms, until the limit of solvency is touched. This appropriation of resources that will surely be needed in the future is a grave weakness in the borrowing policy.

§ 9. We have now to examine the real effects of the system of borrowing, and for this purpose it is requisite to clearly distinguish between the mere mechanism of a loan, and the actual economic phenomena that are its outcome. Reduced to its simplest form, a loan is a transfer of so much of the wealth of private holders to the State or other public body. By its aid the borrower obtains the disposal of the wealth in question, and as a consequence affects, or can affect, the production, distribution, and consumption of wealth. Thus we cannot doubt that the enormous English loans during the Revolutionary and Napoleonic wars had a powerful influence on the economic condition of the country, and we must believe that other cases of borrowing so far resembled this particular one. The application of public loans is, therefore, to be taken into account when

[1] See Bk. i. ch. 1. § 2 for this peculiarity of public economy, and cp. Bk. ii. ch. 3. § 21.

seeking to estimate their effects. If contracted for a purely industrial purpose—say railroad construction—it is quite conceivable that their influence on the state economy may be almost imperceptible. It may even happen that the actual application will be the very one that private capitalists would have selected for their investment, in which case the public credit is only interposed as an intermediary between the real investors and the industry in which the wealth is placed. There are, of course, the additional complications of public management, and the special rate of public borrowing, but in essence the State is an unnecessary additional wheel in the mechanism[1]. The expediency of borrowing for reproductive purposes accordingly depends on the policy to be pursued in reference to public industries. Where, as in Australasia, there is a decided tendency to keep certain classes of works under the public authorities, the policy of borrowing is by that fact justified[2].

Turning to the opposite case of loans applied unproductively, the first effect is the diminution of capital and the resulting loss of wealth. The typical example is that of a loan for carrying on war. Its use is turned from the support of productive industry to the purchase of commodities and services to be employed unproductively. It is, however, important to note that this distinction is not the consequence of borrowing, but of the circumstances that have led to its destination: it results from the extra expense, not from the particular mode of meeting it.

But granting that the primary cause of the economic disturbance that accompanies extensive public borrowing is to be found in the forces that have produced the increased state expenditure, it does not follow that the system of meeting that outlay by loans, instead of by taxation, has not a serious influence on the economic conditions of the society,

[1] The profitableness of such a method is, generally speaking, more than doubtful, but the Prussian railways may again be cited as an exceptional case.

[2] The present depression in colonial securities is a good illustration of the danger that attends such a system, and of the need for caution in its use.

especially as there are, beyond dispute, some pointed contrasts in the action of loans and taxes respectively. The first of these has been already emphasized in Chalmers' theory. A loan, it is said, comes from the nation's capital; taxes from its annual income; the former reduces the fund that assists production; the latter curtail immediate enjoyments. By borrowing we are sacrificing the permanent interests of the country for the sake of immediate relief. That there is some truth in this position is undeniable, but it is very easy to exaggerate its importance. The sharp line thus drawn between revenue and capital does not, in fact, exist, as there is an evident reaction of each on the other. Revenue is, indeed, the spring from which capital is fed, or rather at any given time 'revenue' and 'capital' are but names for different applications of the collective wealth of the community[1]. Large public borrowing stimulates saving, and thereby checks expenditure on enjoyments: oppressive taxation reduces the fund from which new savings are made, and so far hinders the accumulation of capital. A loan for unproductive purposes is not always a pure destruction of national capital. Though the debt charged on the national wealth is increased, there may be some compensation in the larger available assets.

A second point of contrast is in favour of borrowing. A loan is voluntary, and supplied by willing givers: taxation is levied on the willing and unwilling alike, and, if heavy, is sure to cause discontent. The former has, therefore, the advantage of putting less immediate pressure on the individual citizen, though on the other side there are the future charges, and the effect on borrowers and labourers through the increased value of loanable capital.

Thirdly, the equitable distribution of heavy taxation is not easily attained. Where very high imposts are laid, some classes and persons are likely to suffer unduly. The division of the charge over a longer time by the use of

[1] Cp. Bk. iii. ch. 2. § 5, and for a discussion of the conception of revenue see Marshall, *Principles*, Bk. ii. ch. 6.

borrowing makes the proper apportionment of the burden far easier, and more especially allows of sufficient time for its full consideration. Great and sudden changes in taxation—particularly if they are increases—are always evil. Some time is needed for the definitive incidence of a tax to become settled; a truth exaggerated in the doctrine of Canard, but still having much weight in this special connexion. To avoid disturbance, it might even be said that taxation should always be maintained at a level sufficient to meet the average outlay over a long period. Excessive expenditure in some years would be compensated by the surpluses of others, and complete equilibrium between income and outgoings would be the final result. The utter impossibility of forecasting the future course of expenditure makes this method quite impracticable. The effort to carry out such a plan would end in the accumulation of debts that would not be paid off in the prosperous periods. But though so thorough an adjustment is not to be reached, the diffusion of the burden of loans, in opposition to the immediate pressure of taxes, is a difference to be taken into account in considering their respective operations.

The contrast may also be turned the other way. Just as direct taxation is often advocated on the ground that it brings the real cost of the State more clearly before the contributors, so has the policy of paying all expenses out of taxation been regarded as 'a salutary and wholesome check' on the natural disposition to indulge in extravagant outlay. To make things smooth for the present at the cost of the future is not the duty of the wise and far-seeing statesman.

Loans for war expenditure are particularly open to this objection, and it was in reference to them that Mr. Gladstone pronounced his forcible condemnation of the policy of borrowing[1]. There can be no doubt that the immediate

[1] 'The expenses of a war are the moral check which it has pleased the Almighty to impose upon the ambition and the lust of conquest that are inherent in so many nations. There is pomp and circumstance, there is glory and

increase of taxation will to some extent damp the ardour of a people for war, which, however, is sometimes a doubtful advantage. From the point of view of the administration the method of borrowing is decidedly preferable; as, where taxes have to be imposed, it is compelled to exercise economy and to keep expenditure within bounds, while by the use of loans it may even secure favour with the monied interest, and at the same time become popular among other classes by profuse outlay.

Lastly, there is, or may be, an opposition between borrowing and taxation in respect of their ultimate incidence. With proportional taxation increased to meet abnormal expenditure there is very heavy pressure on the receivers of industrial, or more generally of temporary, incomes, which may not be in existence when the burden is removed. In the succeeding period of low expenditure the same class of incomes escapes lightly, though the recipients have benefited by the sacrifices previously incurred. This failure in just distribution between different times may be met by the loan system, the interest on debt being paid by those who would otherwise have escaped altogether, but, as we saw [1], it can also be avoided by the use of taxes falling on property, such as *e.g.* the succession duties, or direct duties on realized wealth, though this course is surrounded by difficulties of its own.

§ 10. So far the contrast of the borrowing and the tax systems, as modes of meeting extraordinary expenditure, does not seem to lead to any very decisive result. Some broad considerations favour the use of taxation: others of no slight weight give support to, at least, a moderate

excitement about war, which, notwithstanding the miseries it entails, invests it with charms in the eyes of the community, and tends to blind men to those evils to a fearful and dangerous degree. The necessity of meeting from year to year the expenditure which it entails is a salutary and wholesome check, making them feel what they are about and making them measure the cost of the benefit on which they may calculate.' Hansard, March 6th, 1854. Cp. the useful criticism in Northcote, *Financial Policy*, 259-264.

[1] Bk. iii. ch. 3. § 11.

use of loans. But, in truth, there is not quite free choice. After expenditure has passed a certain point, borrowing becomes, if not necessary, at all events highly expedient. The productiveness of every separate tax has its limits, and so has that of the tax system taken as a whole. Each additional charge implies a more than proportional sacrifice by the contributors and greater difficulty in getting in revenue on the part of the State. The existence of a law of 'diminishing returns' in public receipts is a valid ground for the employment of loans, when, all things considered, they will be less onerous than further taxation. It appeared that 15 per cent. was probably the largest proportion of the national income that, under ordinary conditions, could be taken for the state services, and though the limits of productivity are capable of being expanded at times of trial, we can hardly doubt that an income-tax of five shillings in the pound would prove too much for even the United Kingdom.

This principle admits of more extended application. If, when taxation is exhausted, a loan has to be employed, it is evident that before that extreme point is reached, borrowing may advantageously be combined with taxation, and that the exact extent to which it may be used will depend on a complicated calculation of the different elements involved. The cost of taxation, varying as it does according to its forms and amount, must be weighed against the burden, present and future, of the loan. This is no easy matter, and it can only be approximately worked out, if, indeed, it has not to be decided at once by the insight and instinctive knowledge of the statesman, who will be guided by the political, as much as by the purely financial, conditions.

The practical solution is not, however, so difficult as would appear from the preceding paragraph. A good tax system requires as one of its qualities a considerable amount of elasticity, and as far as possible the first appeal should be made to taxation. The English Income-Tax is a valuable instrument for this purpose—as its employment in the Crimean War shows—and its place in this respect is with difficulty filled by other taxes. Still, the customs and excise when moderately well administered will allow of increases for a special emergency. Tea, wine, and beer would bear much heavier duties in England, and sugar would, if again taxed, be a productive object. Some of the duties on 'acts' could also be advanced in case of need, and would soon yield a larger return [1]. Thus, even if the actual expenses are at first met by creating a floating debt, the new duties will speedily pay off what has been incurred. But when the limits of ready expansion are reached, a loan is the suitable mode of obtaining further supplies. Where there is a pre-existing debt in course of redemption, the suspension of that process will add to the available funds [2], while if there is no debt, the smaller taxation previously levied will bear very large additions. This last consideration suggests a disadvantage in the existence of a permanent debt, in that it brings future borrowing nearer by imposing so much additional charge on the annual revenue and thereby reducing the disposable balance.

The probable duration of extraordinary expenditure is an important element in determining the mode of providing for it. A sudden and large demand for a single year may well be met by borrowing (unless the moveable taxes and the suspension of debt redemption suffice), as it would not be desirable to disturb the whole tax system for such a purpose. Where there is a fair prospect of continuous outlay on the increased scale, a readjustment of taxation at

[1] Professor Adams (*Public Debts*, 94) objects to the use of the income tax for the purpose described in the text, but it seems on insufficient grounds. He hardly makes due allowance for the speedy yield of new taxes. 'The financier,' he thinks, 'may hope for assistance from his new taxes within eighteen months of their levy,' *ib.* 140. The first duties would surely come in much sooner.

[2] In England, *e. g.* the suspension of the terminable annuities and the new sinking fund—as actually happened in 1885—would provide over £6,000,000 for meeting the fresh expenditure.

the outset is the prudent course [1]. Failure in this cardinal point of sound Finance was the cause of the great accumulation of debt in England at the opening of this century, and was also noticeable in the treatment of war expenditure by the United States both in 1812 and 1861, to which instances the treatment of the French expenditure on the Crimean war may be added [2].

On the whole, then, the rules applicable to the treatment of abnormal outlay for other than economic purposes may be stated as follows:—(1) Expenditure should, so far as is possible, be met out of the annual receipts, and therefore increased outlay should be balanced by heavier taxation. (2) In the case of non-recurrent expense of large amount, a loan is preferable to a serious disturbance of the normal tax system, and may fairly be employed. (3) Where the abnormal expenditure extends over a series of years, the various forms of taxation should, speaking generally, be adjusted to meet it. (4) This general principle, however, fails where either (*a*) it would be impossible to secure an equitable division of the heavy taxation necessary, or (*b*) where the limit of productiveness with regard to the several taxes would have to be exceeded, or finally (*c*) where for political reasons it is inexpedient to press heavily on the taxpayers. Under any of these conditions resort to loans as a supplement to the tax revenue even for a somewhat lengthened period is defensible.

§ 11. The fact that a good deal of the funds that are obtained by public borrowing are derived from abroad is of some weight in judging the loan policy. Not that a foreign loan is in its purely financial bearings so different from a home one as is sometimes supposed, but that the possibility of drawing on the capital of other countries weakens the argument in favour of taxation on the ground

[1] For the passage of 'extraordinary' into 'ordinary' expenditure see Bk. i. ch. 8. § 1.

[2] For the weak treatment of the English debt see Bk. v. ch. 3. § 4; for the American instances, Adams, 112–133; for the French one, Bk. v. ch. 4. § 2.

that in any event the expenditure must be met from the national resources. When taxation fails to respond to new demands, a foreign loan may supply the necessary sums, and the competition of alien with native lenders will enable the State to borrow on better terms, and with less effect on the rate of interest, and therefore to the advantage of the labouring class. But from a purely financial point of view the source of a loan is really immaterial. In any case it is an immediate relief to the taxpayers, counterbalanced by greater charge in the future. Whether the wealth to be consumed in the outlay that is the primary cause of borrowing be derived from the stores of home or foreign lenders may have some immediate influence, but when we bear in mind the close connexion of all the countries of the world, and the great mass of private borrowing from foreigners, it is evident that the distinction may easily be made too much of.

The political and economic effects of the much freer movement of loan capital in recent times are highly important and deserving of study, but they do not belong to Public Finance. The possibility of political complications in consequence of a default in the payment of foreign creditors has been previously noticed [1].

§ 12. Very important questions arise respecting the absolute amount of public debts, the pressure that they impose on the borrowing States or other bodies, and the best mode of measuring that burden. For this purpose very different methods may be used. The most obvious is that which takes the nominal capital of the debt as the basis of measurement. Thus, in 1870, France and the United States had approximately the same capital debt [2], and therefore, it might be said, an equal liability. The defect of this method is evident from the fact that it takes

[1] Bk. v. ch. 2. § 3.

[2] France had £550,000,000; the United States, including 'State debts,' £532,000,000, as their respective capital liabilities. Leroy Beaulieu, ii. 597. The French debt, so far as the central government is concerned, is probably here placed too high, but it serves as an illustration of the principle.

no account of the interest on the borrowed capital, which latter is moreover not payable at the creditors' demand. 'The public debt,' as Lord Grenville put it, 'consists not in capital but in securities [1],' and the amount of capital is therefore no guide to the actual weight. A second method might be employed by which the actual, instead of the nominal capital value, or in other words the market price of the stock would be used as the test, but this again is open to the objection that the real value is incessantly fluctuating, and at any actual time only gives the value of the small amount sold, not of the total mass of stock [2]. A third mode takes the interest charge as the measure, by which a very different result will usually be reached; *e.g.* in the case of France and the United States, as the former had most of its stock at 3 per cent., while the latter paid 6 per cent. on much of its obligations, the comparison was altogether in favour of France.

All the foregoing methods deal with the absolute amount of the several public debts, and of themselves furnish but a slight clue to the sacrifices undergone by the people of the country. For this purpose a further combination is necessary, and the most popular plan is to divide the capital or the interest charge by the number of the population, and so get the charge 'per head.' How fallacious any test of the kind must be, has been already shown in respect to expenditure [3]; and it is equally plain here, as a comparison of England, the United States, and Victoria against India, Italy, and Russia, suffices to prove. The mere population of a country is no measure, any more than its area, of its wealth and financial capabilities, which must depend on so many different circumstances.

A far better test would be the relation of debt to the national revenue or, again, to the collective wealth of the

[1] *Essay on Sinking Fund*, 29, quoted by McCulloch, Note 33 to *Wealth of Nations*, 632.

[2] Cp. Jevons' *Theory* 119, 120 for this distinction.

[3] Bk. i. ch. 8. § 4.

society. Such comparisons are, however, by no means easy. The annual income—and especially that part of it which is disposable—must be always more or less doubtful, and estimates of national wealth, whatever method be employed [1], have even less chance of approaching accurately the real position. Nevertheless inquiries of the kind give a good rough result, and in relying on them we may fairly compare the annual charge of the debt with the national revenue, and in like manner its capital value with the sum of national wealth. The annual charge of £19,000,000 for the English debt should be compared with the £1,000,000,000 or £1,200,000,000 of national income, as the £680,000,000 of capital—subject to whatever deduction may be required for its being under *par* value—should be placed against the £10,000,000,000 or £11,000,000,000 which may be taken as the sum of British wealth [2]. In this way we get about 2 per cent. as the proportion of income, and about 6 per cent. as that of capital assigned to the public creditors.

The great discrepancy indicates the omission of some important element in the capital estimate, which can be no other than the capitalized earning power of the human beings who make up the community. Wages, industrial and professional earnings are a part of the revenue, but not of the ordinary capital account of the nation [3].

For practical purposes it is often convenient to take the proportion of the total state expenditure required for the payment of the annual debt charge as measuring its weight. Thus the smaller percentage of the English expenditure on

[1] The best methods are: (1) that of Mr. Giffen, which capitalizes income, and (2) that of M. de Foville, which takes the property changing hands by succession as the base of calculation. Giffen, *Growth of Capital*; De Foville, *La France Économique* (1887), 437 sq.

[2] If we assume that the annual increase of wealth has not changed since 1885 we can add £900,000,000 to Mr. Giffen's estimate of £10,037,000,000 for that year.

[3] Cp. Prof. Nicholson's article on 'The living capital of the United Kingdom' (*Economic Journal*, i. 95–106), in which the highly conjectural value of £47,000,000,000 is assigned to this factor, or group of factors, of production.

debt in the total outlay as compared with any earlier year in the present century shows so far a reduction in the burden. The relations of public outlay to national revenue and the amount of service performed by the State are both elements to be considered before this ready test can be used with any accuracy.

Finally, in estimating the weight of public debt, it is necessary to take account of the public assets that are available for its liquidation. The property employed in the various public functions cannot be regarded in this light. The buildings and other non-revenue yielding possessions of any government could only be sold at the cost of abandoning the normal administrative duties. Such property is an essential condition of state activity [1]. Very different is that part of public property—the *domaine privé* of French administrative law—which supplies revenue. Land, forests, mines, railways, and other industrial enterprises have all a market value, and would by their sale provide funds that could be employed in paying off debt. The real value of all such state property is therefore fairly to be set off as a deduction from the debt before computing its capital amount, as for precisely similar reasons its annual yield must be regarded as a mitigation of the interest charge. The importance of this consideration comes out very strongly in respect to countries in the situation of the German States, the Australasian Colonies, and the Indian Empire [2]. The greater part of the debt incurred by all these countries has been for the creation of public works, which—be their value more or less than the wealth expended in their creation—are undoubtedly worth very large sums, and if in the hands of private individuals or companies would be regarded as constituents of national wealth. The real debt burden of the countries so situated is much less than the apparent one. It may even be altogether removed.

[1] Cp. Bk. ii. ch. 5. § 1 for this position.

[2] Its application in local Finance will appear in Bk. v. ch. 8. § 3.

For the purposes of this allowance it is quite immaterial whether the property has been created by means of loans or obtained in other ways. Revenue from the rent of land is as much an aid towards the payment of debt as receipts from railways constructed by loans. The economic revenues of the State are a compensation, more or less effective, for debt expenditure. It is in connexion with the original application of loans that the distinction between property obtained by their employment and that otherwise derived comes up for consideration.

Estimates of the real weight of public debts are, it is now plain, by no means easily formed; the considerations to be taken into account are too complex to be dealt with in a ready and off-hand manner. The only way of arriving at a satisfactory result is by the use of each of the different methods of calculation, and a combination of their results with the due allowances previously pointed out. Where all point in the same direction a conclusion is easily reached: where they differ the selection of the proper ones depends on the object for which the inquiry is made. If annual pressure is to be ascertained, interest is more important than capital; if the cost of redemption is wanted, capital or market value should be the primary object of investigation.

CHAPTER VI.

THE FORMS OF PUBLIC DEBTS.

§ 1. THE different forms that public borrowing may take affect the actual course of public debt and its development so much as to need careful notice. Nor is the method of classification quite simple. From one point of view loans have been divided into the three groups of forced or compulsory, patriotic, and voluntary business loans. The first was a favourite method with sovereigns in earlier times. Up to the reign of Charles I it was used in England, and still later—as under Mazarin—in France. Spain and Austria have supplied more recent instances[1]. Such expedients are, however, unworthy of a well-managed State. The compulsory loan is in fact rather a tax than a credit transaction, and it may be regarded as an advance of tax revenue. Its injustice and inconvenience ought to effectually exclude it from the list of fiscal contrivances. The patriotic loan is for a different reason equally inadmissible. Experience shows that an appeal to national feeling is far less powerful than one addressed to self-interest. The British 'Loyalty Loan' (1796), though fully subscribed, was one of the most unsatisfactory in its results. Other countries, *e.g.* France in 1848 and Germany in 1870, have altogether failed in their appeal to patriotism and for the same reasons; the Italian patriotic loan suggested in 1866 would also have certainly met the same

[1] Leroy Beaulieu, ii. 285–6; Roscher, § 132. For a suggestion of a forced loan by Pitt in 1796, Sinclair, *History of Revenue*, i. 344.

fate. This result is not entirely due to the mastery of self-interest over other considerations in the minds of investors. For the success of a loan certain technical conditions are required. It needs the aid of the dealers in money to be successfully 'floated,' and in this respect the sentimental loan is wanting. Judged by its fruits the appeal to national feeling is a useless effort on the part of the State.

Voluntary loans issued on strict business principles are therefore the only eligible mode of procuring funds in time of need. Just as the normal agencies of supply are more effective guards against scarcity than state supervision or private benevolence, so is the system of depending on the investors' desire of a reasonable return the right one in the case of public loans. So long as good security is offered a supply of wealth will be obtainable by any State that requires it, and the most rigid application of business methods and the strictest conformity to the usages of the money market will generally prove to be the cheapest and most convenient course.

§ 2. Another kind of distinction between loans is found in the conditions on which they are contracted. The first state debts were what would now be regarded as 'floating,' *i.e.* they were advances repayable on demand. The need of keeping the funds so advanced for a lengthened period led to the adoption of life annuities, which in the *tontine* form were a popular method both in England and France. Under this plan the share of each deceased annuitant lapsed to the survivors, until with the death of the longest liver the whole payment ceased[1]. The issue of ordinary life annuities has also been carried on, but only as a subordinate part of the debt, and in England as a convenience rather for the annuitants than for the State.

The terminable annuity has certain advantages over the less definite plan of life payments; its exact charge can be estimated, and the time of extinction foreseen. As we saw, the annuity for a term was used as an additional advantage

[1] This system was named from Tonti, its inventor or populariser.

to float many English loans, and later on as a convenient way of redeeming debt. When employed as the chief mode of borrowing it has the great disadvantage of depreciating year by year, and is therefore unsuitable for permanent investment, while to the purely selfish person it offers even less attraction than a life annuity. It is only as an agent for the redemption of debt, and when used in connexion with the available capital of public departments or banking companies, that the terminable annuity becomes effective.

The modern system of issuing bonds redeemable in sections by annual drawings is a refinement on the preceding method. To the State it is precisely the same, as it is possible, by fixing the amount redeemable in each year, to make the annual payment even all through the period of redemption, while the capitalist is sure of the principal advanced and of interest until he receives it. Still, it introduces a gambling element into the value of the stock, and makes the suspension of redemption at any time, no matter what the pressure, a breach of faith. Borrowing may even be necessary in order to keep the automatic process of repayment going on. As a means of encouraging the redemption of debt it has undoubted merits, especially when that object would otherwise be neglected; but it may often prove both costly and inconvenient when sudden pressure comes on.

We have previously seen the American mode of borrowing, with payment at a fixed term, or rather at one of two prescribed dates at the State's option. Thus the 'ten-forties' mean loans repayable either within ten or forty years, but not at any intermediate date. When a loan is only for temporary use a short term may be suitable for its repayment, while the privilege of extending the time gives a safeguard against the creditors' demand. For the United States the method may be admissible, though it puts obstacles in the way of speedy repayment; but for a European country, where redemption is very slowly carried on, it would be most undesirable, unless the stock was below *par* and could therefore be purchased with advantage. An issue of stock so calculated that it could be converted into a much lower one at the first date fixed, and then repaid at the final one might be unobjectionable, though it would be very difficult to secure this exact result, and the disposal in the mean time of the funds for ultimate repayment would be hard to arrange. A sudden call for payment at the expiration of the term might come at a most trying time and compel refunding on disadvantageous terms.

Opposed to, and simpler than, the foregoing forms is what is known as 'perpetual' debt, *i. e.* where the stock is issued without any date for repayment, but redeemable at any time at the pleasure of the debtor. Limits to this power of redemption may be introduced to add to the lenders' security or in consequence of some special arrangement[1], but the general form is as stated. On examination it appears that the real nature of the obligation is to pay a specified annuity, with the option of wiping it out by returning the original capital. Further conditions may be added which prohibit repayment for a fixed period, but this is not usual, and when the time elapses the ordinary form is re-established. It is in this shape that the bulk of European debts exist. England, France, Italy, the German States give instances, and a reference to the advantages of the arrangement will account for the fact.

In the first place the borrowing State is relieved from the risk of demands for repayment of capital, and has only to provide for the periodical discharge of the interest. Extraordinary expenditure is distributed into a series of smaller payments, which may be regarded as ordinary, and in consequence its pressure assumes a milder form. The creditor is not, however, prevented from realizing the capital value of his loan. The modern stock exchange makes the evidence of his debt a form of intangible wealth which he can always sell at the market price. This may

[1] Thus the present English 'consols' will not be redeemable until 1923.

be more or less than the original sum advanced, but it is the value of the interest claim at the time of exchange. Again, the State is always able to redeem so much of the debt as it wishes, by purchasing in the market or repaying the capital, whichever is most convenient *i. e.* the lowest in amount. The gradually improving credit of a prosperous country will allow of the reduction of the original rate of interest, as the offer of repayment will bring the state creditors to accept the terms offered. This use of conversion, as it is called, has been already illustrated in reference both to England and France, and its service as a mode of redeeming debt will appear later on[1]. It is most easily employed in regard to the ordinary perpetual debt, which is therefore so far superior to the other kinds.

§ 3. But though the simple system of contracting debt redeemable at the debtor's pleasure is, on the whole, the best, it does not follow that the total mass of liabilities should be reduced to that shape. Life annuities, terminable annuities, debt redeemable by annual payments, are all useful forms under certain conditions. As agencies for reducing debt or attracting certain special classes of lenders they have a real function to discharge, and it is the part of the trained practical financier to say how far each should be employed. Thus in England, the terminable annuities could hardly be allowed to exceed £100,000,000, as that amount is quite sufficient to operate on at any given time[2]. The French 'redeemable' debt should also be kept much below the perpetual *rentes*. The necessity of adjusting financial arrangements to the actual conditions is quite as imperative with regard to borrowing as to taxation. The great advantage of the perpetual debt is its close resemblance to the stocks and shares of ordinary industrial companies. The debt paid off by periodical

[1] Bk. v. ch. 7. § 5.

[2] The stock held by government departments does not exceed £70,000,000, and it is by its use chiefly that annuities are created, as private persons do not regard them with favour.

drawings may suit a speculative class, just as life annuities are sought after by those who desire to use their disposable wealth in their lifetime. To suit loans to the taste of the market is one of the chief duties of the borrowing government.

§ 4. This function commences at the inception of a loan. Not only have its terms to be such as will draw the required amount in the cheapest way; the mode of offering it must also be carefully attended to. At the commencement of the modern system of public borrowing in England, a group of capitalists was invited to furnish the required amount, as at the creation of the Bank of England, or a list was opened to which all persons might contribute. In this way the utmost competition of capitalists was invited. The French method of confiding the business to bankers was probably less efficient. It had, however, the merit of enlisting a powerful class in its support and making it their aim to keep up its price. Their profit, in fact, depended on the premium that they could obtain for the stock over and above the subscription price. Where capital is not widely diffused, and where the money-market interest is powerful, this may be the best way to conciliate opposition and to gain assistance. Where a loan is not peremptorily needed, the issue of bonds at a fixed price—as close to *par* as possible—which will be gradually taken up is convenient, while in cases of great and pressing need an appeal to the public is decidedly the best. Where this latter course is chosen, the issue may be at a fixed price, or better still, it may be to the highest offers, with a minimum rate below which no tenders will be accepted. By such an expedient competition brings the price up to the highest point, and those who offer the least favourable terms are not accepted. The Australasian Colonies have largely employed the method of taking the highest tenders down to the price at which the loan is covered, and the same system has been applied to some municipal loans in England. With the greater division of capital for investment the direct appeal to the small lender is the most likely to secure satisfactory results, as it is on him that any syndicate of bankers must in the last resort depend.

In many cases, however, a loan is floated abroad, and then, especially if the credit of the borrowing State does not stand very high, the intervention of a group of large capitalists who will advertise the loan cannot easily be dispensed with. But in the case of a large State there ought to be no necessity for such aid. It borrows on a sound security, and appeals primarily to native investors whose subscriptions, as in the case of the French loans in 1871–2, may often be derived from their sale of foreign stocks.

§ 5. From the form and mode of issuing loans we now come to a much disputed question in this part of Finance, viz. the respective merits of loans bearing high interest with small nominal capital, and loans with high nominal capital and low interest. At first sight it would appear that all loans should be contracted at *par*, or as close to it as the conditions of the market will allow. Thus, if £10,000,000 is the sum required, it is obviously better to issue £10,000,000 of 5 per cent. stock than £12,500,000 at 4 per cent. The interest charge is indeed the same in both cases, but when the time for repayment comes the holders are entitled in the latter instance to £2,500,000 additional, unless they sell under *par*, and the prospect of converting the debt into a stock bearing lower interest is pushed further off, as a 5 per cent. stock will be nearer *par* than a 4 per cent. one. The issue of a nominal capital higher than the amount actually received seems accordingly unjustifiable, and a departure from the plain and simple course of borrowing. So regarded, most of the English loans during the American and French wars would be unhesitatingly condemned, as they were borrowed in 3 per cent. stock at a price greatly under *par*. This method, which is one of the greatest blots on Pitt's financial administration, has been defended on the ground that the interest charge was reduced by it, since 3 per cent. stock commanded a relatively higher price than 4 or 5 per cent. stock. The proper proportion between them would be 60, 80, 100, but the actual one was more favourable to the 3 per cents. The explanation, of course, was that the lower stock offered a chance of gain through subsequent increase in value which would be stopped in the case of the higher ones by conversion[1]. A further plea is that of necessity. It is said 'that Pitt had no choice . . . he had to borrow, not in accordance with his own views, but with those of the lenders[2].' Neither defence is at all convincing. Hamilton has clearly shown that the difference in interest between the 3 and 5 per cents. was only about 9*s*. per cent., and that even this should be reduced by the advance of interest for the first year[3]. Now, such a gain is by no means enough to counterbalance the great creation of capital with its certain cost in the future. There was a small immediate saving, but on the assumption that the extra charge had been defrayed by loans, their amount would have been less than the nominal capital added to the actual sum received. The plea of necessity is met by the existence of loans to the amount of over £60,000,000 in 5 per cent., and an £8,000,000 one in 4 per cent. stock. With sufficient determination, it is plain that far larger sums might have been obtained on the same conditions.

The real explanation of this grave error is to be found in three distinct circumstances, viz. first, the belief in the virtues of the sinking fund which led to neglect of the future course of the debt; it was expected that by a mechanical process the liability would be wiped out, no matter what its amount. Next, there was the hampering influence of the usury laws which made interest over 5 per cent. illegal, and for consistency compelled the State to

[1] See Newmarch's paper, 'Loans raised by Mr. Pitt,' in *Statistical Journal*, xviii. 104 sq., for an ingenious defence of the policy.

[2] Lord Rosebery's *Pitt*, 210.

[3] Hamilton, 197–206.

keep within that limit. A 6 per cent. or 7 per cent. loan would have been readily taken up, and at the close of the war would have been converted into a much lower stock, as happened in the United States after 1868. Lastly, there was the natural desire to keep the debt uniform, and as the great bulk of existing obligations bore 3 per cent. interest, the new issues were modelled on their pattern and became an indistinguishable part of the general mass of consols.

The two former reasons were wholly bad; neither the sinking fund nor the usury laws contributed in this respect to the public benefit. The uniformity of stock is no doubt desirable. A large stock sells better than a small one, and there is less confusion and complication where a single rate of interest prevails. But the advantage may be too dearly purchased, as it certainly is by increasing the amount to be paid in the course of redemption. At the lowest point of credit that the English Funds touched in 1797, when the 3 per cents. were only 47, it might have taken 9 per cent. or 10 per cent. (or perhaps, 7 per cent. irredeemable for thirty years) to get a loan at *par*, but then, as credit improved, this load, not so much greater even at first, would have been reduced and less than half the capital sum would have sufficed for repayment.

The system of unduly increasing the nominal capital has been extensively used in France with still less excuse than the English government could offer, and with the evil result of making the capital liability much greater. Nothing but either very favourable offers for a loan under *par* at low interest, or the absolute impossibility of getting advances any other way can justify the procedure.

§ 6. There remain for consideration two other forms of state liability, that are both in contrast with the classes of debt previously described. These are: (1) the floating debt, and (2) the issue of inconvertible paper money. The former is perhaps the oldest kind of debt, and comes into being in the most natural way. In the management of so large a business as that of the public Treasury it must often come to pass that the payments for services or commodities will not be made at once, and that at some periods of the financial year the outgoings will exceed the revenue received. As a necessary consequence, either the actual persons who supplied requirements are for a time unpaid or others advance the funds. Whichever it be, there is a temporary or floating debt. As the modern State is engaged in various business transactions and is a lender of money to local bodies[1], it will always have a number of outstanding accounts against it, with corresponding assets on the other side. Should there be a series of budget deficits, the floating debt will, unless it is funded, speedily accumulate to a formidable amount, as has been the case in several countries. A failure in national credit generally drives a government to increase its floating obligations, which attract less notice than the regular issue of a loan; and in all countries war or other special pressure may cause a temporary expansion of this kind of debt.

As a general principle of Finance it is unquestionable that the floating debt should be kept within the narrowest limits possible. The ordinary working expenses of the administration can be covered within the year, and usually, with the steady influx of the duties on commodities, in a far shorter period. The special liabilities in connexion with savings-banks or advances to local bodies allow of being dealt with as distinct accounts, and the latter can be managed by a funded debt. A growth of floating charges is at best a mark of weakness in the treatment of the state liabilities. Though it may not always be convenient to fund a mass of temporary debt, and a little delay may be admitted, this case is too exceptional to qualify the general rule.

The great evil of a floating debt is its uncertainty. To be open to the risk of a sudden demand for payment is to be in the position of a banker without the securities with which he provides himself; and it is precisely in times of

[1] Cp. Bk. ii. ch. 4. § 4, and Bk. v. ch. 8. § 5.

commercial difficulties that the call is most likely to be made.

Among examples of unduly swollen floating debts the cases of the United States at the close of the Civil War, of England after the French War, when its amount was over £60,000,000, and of France at present, may be taken. Both England and the United States remedied their position by funding, and the same course is doubtless advisable in France. It might indeed be suggested that the floating obligations should never exceed a year's interest on the funded debt, but where the latter is very small this rule could hardly be applied, and that of keeping the temporary charges under one-fourth of the annual revenue might be substituted.

§ 7. Inconvertible paper issues and their effect on economic and social life have been abundantly considered in works dealing with political economy and with monetary and currency questions. The present would be no place for such topics. Here we have only to examine the use of a forced paper currency as a financial expedient. A country with a stock of the precious metals in circulation has a store of wealth which it can obtain for use by the expedient of substituting paper for metallic money and making it legal tender. A loan up to the value of the gold and silver in circulation is thus procured free of interest, and to a hard-pressed government this is no inconsiderable attraction. Actual and historical illustrations readily occur. England, France, the United States, Austria, Russia, Italy, not to speak of smaller States, have employed this agency, and have realized therefrom an immediate gain. The ulterior effects are not so desirable. The tendency to over-issue is too strong to be resisted, and therefore we can hardly find a case of inconvertible paper permanently keeping its nominal value. This almost inevitable depreciation involves a disturbance of the standard of value, and a nominal rise of prices that is on the whole injurious to the most important interests. Carried to a great height the issue of paper money is ruinous to national credit, while it makes the return to specie payments more expensive. At the utmost all that can be gained by the policy is the saving of the interest on a sum equal to the metals in circulation and reserve in the country, which can never be very large in proportion to the total revenue[1]. Excessive issues on the other hand mean a heavy tax, levied on the creditor class, and a disturbance of the tax receipts of the government, which will be in depreciated paper[2], and immense loss to all holders if the forced currency is not redeemed at its 'face' value, or expense to the State if it is.

There seems to be a great body of evidence in support of M. Leroy Beaulieu's view that the outbreak of war will in nearly every case lead to a forced currency[3], but this does not in the slightest change our belief that such a course is both unnecessary and pernicious. The modern system of international borrowing is quite capable of supplying whatever loans may be required, and these, as already argued, need not be much in excess of what is raised by taxation. An inconvertible paper currency, if it secures a somewhat paltry gain, is, on the whole, an expensive, dangerous and unjust form of forced loan.

In a work like the present there is no occasion for further considering the technical forms of loans, whether by inscription, by coupons, or other instruments. To keep in accord with the actual money-market system will be the aim of the prudent financier, who will naturally adopt all suitable expedients to make the stock as easily transferable and as secure as possible.

[1] The metallic stock of the United Kingdom has been variously estimated at from £70,000,000 to £110,000,000, the interest on which would not exceed £4,000,000. In other countries the amount would be greater, but the shock to established habits would also be more felt.

[2] Governments have to accept legal tender money in payment of taxes, unless in the case of customs duties, which are often made payable in gold under the erroneous idea of drawing money into the country. Leroy Beaulieu, ii. 692.

[3] ii. 685; cp. the statements of Mr. Goschen and Sir J. Lubbock to the same effect. *Hansard*, April 28, 1882.

CHAPTER VII.

THE REDEMPTION AND CONVERSION OF DEBT.

§ 1. A STUDY of the conditions and limitations under which public borrowing is alone admissible naturally leads to the conclusion that the maintenance of a permanent debt ought to be avoided. If loans should be contracted only under great pressure, and to prevent the exhaustion of the agency of taxation, and if, while they exist, they act as a drag on the financial power of the State, it cannot be disputed that their speedy redemption must be eminently desirable. The same reasons that make taxation preferable to borrowing give support to the policy of raising taxes in order to pay off existing debt. So far as loans are derived from capital their repayment by taxes levied out of revenue is a restoration of the wealth previously abstracted from the work of production to its earlier and more economic use. In any event the return of their wealth to the fundholders will not diminish the economic power of the community, as some productive employment will certainly be found for it, to escape the loss of income that must otherwise come on the holders. The redemption of debt is thus a mode of increasing the amount of national capital, unless on the hardly possible assumption that the whole amount of taxation raised for the purpose is drawn from capital, or in the case of a foreign loan.

§ 2. The assertion of the general position that the redemption of public debt is desirable has necessarily to be qualified by reference to the particular circumstances of each case. As it is sometimes allowable to borrow, so must it be admitted that cases may occur in which neither borrowing nor repaying is judicious. In the crisis of war or under extra pressure of any kind, the suspension of the mechanism of repayment is obviously prescribed, and it is quite conceivable that such a state of things may long continue. The utmost that English financiers could have done during the protracted war with France was to pay the current expenses of the State, and even this, as we know, they failed to accomplish. The postponement of debt redemption is in such cases a necessity, the non-recognition of which was one of the blots on the sinking-fund theory.

On precisely similar grounds should the amount of debt to be paid off in any given year be determined. Sudden demands may make it prudent to reduce the sums devoted to this purpose as a preferable course to the hasty increase of taxation. A review of the last thirty years of English financial history supplies a series of illustrations. Exactly the same redemption of debt could not be right in such years as 1868 and 1885, when large extra expenditure was incurred, as in years like 1873 and 1889, when considerable surpluses were realized. Rapid changes in the public burdens are if possible to be avoided ; indeed one of the great services of developed public credit is the assistance that it gives in escaping this evil. But here again there is a further influencing condition. A plan of redemption or reduction will generally be organized as a permanent system, and is intended to operate through a long series of years. Suspension of an arrangement of the kind for any slight cause has a disturbing effect that is as objectionable as a small increase of taxation. To stop the normal action of the English terminable annuities for a few millions' increase in expenditure would be a departure from a settled policy, and a bad precedent for the future. The increase in outlay must be large in proportion to the total amount to justify such action[1].

Debt redemption must also be affected by the position of taxation. Where inconvenient and oppressive duties are levied it may be wiser, even with a view to ultimate repayment of loans, to relieve industry and trade from their burdens and trust to the increased productiveness of the reformed system for compensation. A thorough reform in fiscal policy may prove the best sinking fund, or at least its best feeder. Between the remission of very bad taxes and their retention for the redemption of debt, there is often ground for deliberation. Still, on the whole, the reasons in favour of substantial redemption preponderate. There is no hard and fast line between good and bad taxes. Every tax is so far an evil, and any one may, if raised sufficiently high, become oppressive and unproductive. Now if we hesitate to redeem debt on account of the badness of the necessary taxes, we must remember that we are thereby retaining worse taxes in the future than would otherwise be required. For let us suppose the several forms of contribution to be arranged in the order of their eligibility as follows—A, B, C, D, E, F. Then the surrender of F—the worst tax—in preference to paying off debt means the prolongation of the existence of E, which *ex hypothesi* is worse than D, since with the disappearance of the debt the taxes appropriated to its service would also disappear. The £6,000,000 of taxation—to take an actual case—at present applied to reduce the English debt, no doubt represents the worst part of the English revenue, but were the operation completed it would allow of the remission of £25,000,000 of the heaviest part of taxation. The true adjustment is therefore more complicated, and requires for its scientific solution more refined calculations than are ordinarily recognized[2].

[1] Perhaps 10 per cent. of the total amount would represent the limit within which increased expenditure should not alter the established system.

[2] Cp. Mill, *Principles*, Bk. v. ch. 7. § 2, for a statement of the cruder view.

§ 3. In the preceding section it has been taken for granted that all payment of debt is made out of surplus revenue. That, in Hamilton's words, 'the excess of revenue above expenditure is the only real sinking fund by which public debts can be discharged [1],' is a position too evident to need much formal vindication. Any valuable property possessed by the State can be realized to pay off liabilities, but only at the sacrifice of the revenue obtained from it. Both of public and private credit it is indisputably true that repayment can be made in no way except by excess of receipts over expenditure. The only possible mode by which either the individual or the State can get rid of liabilities is by making income greater than outlay. Hence in all well-organized financial systems the surplus of each year is applied to this object, and in the continuous action of those excess receipts lies the hope of complete redemption.

So simple and obvious a fact ought to have commanded universal assent, but the phenomena of credit have always had a remarkable tendency to create misapprehensions respecting their true character, and nowhere more than in respect to public Finance. The whole history of the 'sinking-fund' doctrine is an illustration of this tendency. In its earlier form the sinking fund was simply the surplus of certain parts of the public revenue set apart for the discharge of debt, and derived all its efficacy from the excess of revenue over expenditure. But very soon the fund, from being a part of the financial mechanism, was transformed into a positive entity, and treated as if it had an independent existence. On its security fresh loans were contracted, and the absurdity of borrowing with one hand while repaying with the other was frequently perpetrated.

The theory of Price led to a new development. This writer dwelt on the great effect of compound interest. He truly calculated that a very small sum would with interest upon interest accumulate in a few centuries to an enormous

[1] Hamilton, 10.

amount. This principle, applied to the treatment of debt, would, he argued, secure its speedy repayment. All that was required was a definite capital to start with, which would increase automatically by reinvestment of the interest, until it would equal the whole debt. If to every new loan a sinking fund of moderate amount were attached, its redemption would be secured by the growth of the fund through interest[1].

This extraordinary theory was reduced to practice in Pitt's 'Sinking Fund' of 1786, by which a special board of Commissioners was created and £1,000,000 annually assigned to them for the purchase of stock, which was not to be cancelled, but allowed to accumulate, the interest being applied to fresh purchases, until the original £1,000,000 had risen to £4,000,000. Further additions were made in 1792. The surplus of that year, amounting to £400,000, and a further annual sum of £200,000 were voted to the fund; it was also provided that all future loans should have a sinking fund of one per cent. attached to them by which they would be paid off in, at farthest, 45 years[2].

The pressure of war proved too much for the strict observance of this condition, and various modifications were introduced, but the fundamental mistake of regarding the sinking fund as a separate and distinct source of wealth was still obstinately adhered to. From this error followed the simultaneous borrowing and redemption that were supposed to keep up public credit, but which really confused the accounts and increased the cost of management. Purchases of stock for the sinking fund and the issue of new loans at probably lower price meant so much loss to the State. A calculation of the differences shows that the annual charge imposed by the use of the sinking fund during the period 1794–1816 was over £550,000.

[1] Price, *Observations on Reversionary Annuities*; criticised by Hamilton, 129–48.

[2] For Pitt's Sinking Fund, Hamilton, 97–8; Ricardo, *Works*, 517. For criticisms of it, Hamilton, 149–60; and for a more favourable view, Rosebery, *Pitt*, 81–3.

So mistaken a policy could not be maintained in the face of rational criticism, which was supplied by Hamilton and Ricardo. The true principle of regarding the surplus as the sinking fund was recognised in 1819 by the arrangement that a real surplus of £5,000,000 annually should be provided for the repayment of debt; but this course was not maintained owing to the bad position of the Finances, and finally after a careful inquiry, in which it was established that the method used had added £1,600,000 to the charge between 1785 and 1829, the sinking fund in 1829 was abolished as a separate institution, and the stock held for it cancelled.

From the foregoing facts it is evident that a sinking fund could be useful only in so far as it was based on a surplus of revenue over outlay, and therefore the belief in its efficacy rested on a fiction. Its sole advantage consisted in the pressure that it brought to bear on the finance minister to supply the requisite funds, while 'its operations are scarcely perceptible to a public, justly if sometimes ignorantly impatient of taxation[1].' The effect was in practice to keep the surplus at a higher point than it would otherwise have reached, and to prevent the reductions of revenue, which, as subsequent experience amply proves, were certain to be demanded. But this benefit was too dearly purchased by the extra cost, and was always exposed to the risk of being swallowed up by fresh loans.

§ 4. The modern methods of redemption are all founded on the necessity of providing surplus revenue for the purpose; while at the same time they endeavour to secure the stability of the sinking fund, by ear-marking a special sum for the object of payment. Such is the idea common to the new English Sinking Fund, by which a specified sum is annually devoted to discharge of debt, to the 'terminable annuities,' and to the 'redeemable' debt as it exists in France. Under all these systems there is a determination of part of the revenue to the purpose of repayment, which,

[1] Lord Rosebery, *Pitt*, 83.

if steadily persisted in, will extinguish the liabilities, unless the relief so obtained is used for fresh loans.

The chief difficulty in the way of debt discharge arises from the carelessness or positive dislike of the great body of the taxpayers in respect to the adoption of vigorous measures for its attainment. The simple and straightforward policy of appropriating a large surplus, maintained expressly for the object, to the useful function of reducing the public liabilities is not regarded by them with approval. Unless surrounded by some rather complicated financial arrangement, which disguises the true nature of the process, the surplus is apt to be frittered away in expenditure, or to disappear by reductions of taxation. The English debt after 1819 suffered in this way, and nothing but very exceptional circumstances could have brought about the great repayments of the United States debt after 1866.

Nevertheless it is perfectly evident that the redemption of debt must sooner or later be faced. If in times of peace and low expenditure no surplus is raised, and if borrowing is freely resorted to whenever exceptional demands occur, then the proposition previously quoted from Hamilton [1] will certainly be applicable, and the debt will ultimately 'amount to a magnitude which the nation is unable to bear.' Insistence on this fundamental point is the duty of the wise financier who regards the future as well as the present, and is concerned for the continuous prosperity of the nation. The extent to which taxation should be carried for this purpose, and the particular arrangements adopted must necessarily be varied; but the general principle holds good everywhere.

An additional advantage of debt redemption should also be noted. All repayment tends to raise the credit of the State and to improve the basis for future possible loans. A real sinking fund—*i.e.* one based on an actual surplus—keeps up the price of stock, though a fictitious one does not. Each portion of debt withdrawn from the market

[1] Bk. v. ch. 5. § 4.

reduces the amount available for investors, and this effect, while it cannot alter the permanent conditions affecting interest, yet improves the character of the particular stock. The amount of English debt redeemed in the last thirty years is one of the elements in its high price. Where the debt is below *par*, redemption by purchase at the market rate steadily brings it up to that point, when a new agency can be brought into operation.

§ 5. This is the process known as 'conversion,' by which a stock bearing a given rate of interest is altered or 'converted' into one at a lower rate. We have seen several examples of its use in England, France, and the United States [1] from the first conversion of 1716 down to the recent one in 1888. The principle is very simple, and is applicable both to private and to public credit. A landlord who has a mortgage on his estate on which he pays 5 per cent. will naturally, if he can borrow the amount at 4 per cent., give the mortgagee the option of taking 4 per cent. instead of 5 per cent., or of repayment of the principal. Loanable capital, like other commodities, will be sought on the cheapest terms, and conversion is only a single instance of the general tendency. Indeed, we may go further and say that where it is practicable there is a duty imposed on the finance minister, who is the agent of the taxpayers and bound to consult their interest, to carry out a scheme of conversion on the best terms. Such a view does not, however, commend itself to the fund-holders, and where they form a numerous class very strong opposition to anything of the kind may be expected [2].

As the method of conversion can only be effectively applied when stock is over *par*, it requires as a condition precedent a good state of public credit. Punctual payment of interest, adequate provision for debt redemption, and

[1] Bk. v. chs. 3 and 4 *passim*.

[2] In France, for example, conversion has not for this reason been attempted, at certain favourable periods, viz. (1) under the Orleanist governments, and (2) between 1878 and 1883.

prudent administration generally will all assist in this work. It need hardly be added that the higher the original rate of borrowing the greater room there is for the employment of this agency, a fact which we found to be one of the strongest arguments against the creation of a higher nominal capital than that really borrowed, but bearing low interest[1].

Certain plain general rules hold good with reference to this part of Finance. First, the capital of the debt should not, if possible, be increased, as it amounts to an addition to the future burden. English conversions have for the most part kept free of this mistake, but in 1883 the offer of £108 of 2½ cents. for £100 3 per cents. was a doubtful step. Some of the French conversions, notably that of 1862, were tainted by it. Next, it is desirable to make the scheme simple and unencumbered with complicated stipulations in order that it may be readily understood. A simple reduction of interest, with perhaps a guarantee against further conversion for a period, is on the whole the best. The fund-holders will not of their own accord accept any plan of reduction: the motive power comes from the capital available elsewhere, and therefore the plainer the offer the better the chance of acceptance it has. Thirdly, it is well to choose the time for the operation carefully. The commencement of the period of returning prosperity that usually comes some years after a commercial crisis is the most suitable. Loanable capital is then abundant, and the rate of interest is low, so that the chances of succeeding are at their highest. Fourthly, there is an advantage in using the conversion to consolidate stock of different kinds, as has been accomplished in several English cases[2]; but this consideration should not be carried too far, as it may be essential to separate stocks bearing the same interest, but issued on different terms, and in any case the operation will deal with that part of the debt that bears the highest interest.

[1] Bk. v. ch. 6. § 5. [2] Those of 1716, 1751, and 1888 are examples.

The funds set free by conversion are of course available either for the remission of taxation or for further redemption. It seems, however, that the latter use is the preferable one. Gains from skilful management of the debt are in justice to be credited to it, and their application in this way is, unless in exceptional cases, to be recommended. The retention of the fixed debt charge at £28,000,000 would have brought the present English provisions for payment nearer to the position they should occupy.

§ 6. Among the plans proposed for getting rid of the debt, that of a general contribution by the holders of property has commanded most support. Ricardo declares that 'a country would act wisely by ransoming itself, at the sacrifice of any portion of its property which might be necessary to redeem its debt,' and Mill allows that this course 'would be incomparably the best if it were practicable[1].' The objections are, however, overwhelmingly strong. The method would place the whole burden on property-holders, as earnings could not contribute to the extent that would in fairness be required. But all property is not equally disposable, and some of it will at any given time be almost incapable of realization. As a consequence this class of wealth would be sacrificed, or its owners compelled to borrow on far more onerous terms than the State has to pay. In fact the same arguments that prove the necessity of borrowing at times of pressure, also prove the impossibility, or at all events the great inexpediency, of wiping out debt by a general contribution.

The use of capital in investments at a higher rate of interest has also been suggested as a mode of creating a surplus. Such a method really involves the action of the State as a capitalist, the danger of which appeared in connexion with the economic receipts [2], and in any event it is rather a mode of increasing State income than simply a means of debt redemption. If the policy be justifiable, it

[1] Ricardo, *Works*, 149; Mill, *Principles*, Bk. v. ch. 7. § 2.

[2] Bk. ii. ch. 4. § 1.

is so quite apart from the existence of public liabilities, and it should be judged on its own merits.

§ 7. Altogether independent of the agencies already noticed, it has been often pointed out that there are certain normal forces in operation that tend to diminish the pressure of debt, and will in the future make its redemption easier. The progress of society, so much relied on by Macaulay, adds to the national wealth, and makes a public debt, that once seemed formidable, of comparatively little importance. The progress of Great Britain in the last century would have reduced the debt charge as it stood in 1791 to a very small part of the present public revenue. Other countries show the same phenomenon, and therefore there is some apparent force in the argument that the redemption of debt should be postponed to a more seasonable opportunity. In a country like the United States the steady increase of national wealth is sure to make the debt burden much lighter as time passes on.

But though this fact undoubtedly deserves recognition, it hardly supports the inference drawn from it. The repayment of debt is not a weakening of national power, nor ought it to be a severe pressure on the existing members of the society. Its amount should be kept within the bounds set by the extent of suitable taxation, which would not press heavily on any class of taxpayers. The reduction of debt is moreover a steady relief to public credit, and by its progress affords the means for reducing taxation. Again, as each period has its own charges to meet, the neglect of repayment will make the future burden at least equal to the increased resources. Such a policy is a dangerous discounting of the future, and the tendency to adopt it is one of the worst symptoms in modern Finance. There is, it must be added, no sure ground for concluding that economic progress will continue indefinitely. Many possible causes, some of them in action at present, might bring it to a standstill. Jevons has familiarized us with the idea that England's prosperity depends on her coal supply, which must at some time be exhausted. This relation of industrial expansion to the possession of certain material agents points to the necessity of taking careful account of the potential extent of these conditions of progress, before allowing debt to be accumulated. We cannot foresee the precise line of economic change, but it is well to err on the side of safety, and provide for the liquidation of existing liabilities within a reasonable period.

Another supposed alleviation of the pressure of state debts has been discovered in the progressive depreciation of money or the standard of value. That the Australian and Californian gold discoveries had, among other consequences, the effect of making the real weight of public debts lighter is evident enough. All depreciation favours the debtor at the creditor's expense, but so does appreciation give the latter a like advantage. The mention of this possibility shows the weakness of the position of those who look to monetary depreciation as a source of relief. For the last twenty years the weight of debt has been increasing, and in that fact lies one of the bimetallic arguments. We cannot say whether in the distant future the standard of value will rise or fall, and no satisfactory conclusion can be based on its probable movement. But even on the assumption that depreciation will ultimately take place, it does not follow that the State will gain. Is it not likely that lenders will hesitate to make advances on a depreciating security, unless they receive compensation in higher interest for the risk they run? There is in addition the objection that to count on this change is really to speculate on a defect in the standard that should as far as possible be remedied. The establishment of the fact that future depreciation is certain places on the public authority the duty of providing a corrective for the faulty standard in existence. Neither on grounds of fact or equity can we regard the relief of the state debt through depreciation as well-established or desirable.

§ 8. The distinction drawn between home and foreign

loans and the error of exaggerating its importance have been previously noticed. In connexion with repayment it has been said that a public loan held by foreigners is, when productively applied, an augmentation of the country's capital, and that its redemption is not desirable. Not to dwell again on the fact that the boundary between inland and foreign loans is not so very easy to determine, it may be remarked that the service of a loan consists in its application, not in the existence of the obligation. The advances made to the Australian colonies for railways were of service by allowing those agencies of transport to be speedily built, for which purpose the continuance of the debt is not needed. The real question at issue is rather between the use of state funds for redemption or for fresh production, or again between raising loans to pay off debt and leaving that wealth in the possession of the citizens. To settle this question the rate of interest and the probable effect of the other courses open must be duly considered. When gains are high the continuance of a loan at a low rate of interest may be expedient, but effective provision for repayment is the best mode of securing loans at a low rate.

CHAPTER VIII.

LOCAL INDEBTEDNESS.

§ 1. THE rapid increase of the debts of local governing bodies has been noted in an earlier chapter as likely to give rise to serious financial difficulties in the future. A national debt, whatever be its evils, is open and conspicuous; it is under the control of the government of the whole people, and is based on the total wealth of the country. It, moreover, has usually been incurred for objects of general interest, the ultimate value of which can be measured, and its treatment can be affected by public opinion guided by judicious criticism. In all these respects local indebtedness is less favourably placed. Instead of the single State, there are many bodies of very different character and importance, and with altogether diverse requirements. Each distinct administration borrows on the security of its special revenue, which may be adversely affected by local conditions. The expenditure of the innumerable loans is very hard to follow, and intelligent criticism is almost wholly wanting. Sectional interests and ignorance of financial principles have the same influence on borrowing that they have on taxation and expenditure: they tend to lower the probability of attaining either economy or just distribution. Under such circumstances it is the more important to examine the chief features of the system of local borrowing that has spread so widely in the last fifty years.

§ 2. As regards the fact of increase there is the most positive and convincing evidence. In 1875 the local debt of England and Wales was £92,000,000. Six years later it came to £144,000,000. By 1888 the total was £192,000,000, or an increase of £100,000,000 over the amount in 1875; giving for the period of thirteen years an annual increase of nearly £8,000,000. This general growth is made up of special increases, which in such an instance as that of London are very striking. The metropolitan debt now touches £40,000,000, showing a steady advance in the last twenty years.

The Irish and Scotch local debts, though insignificant in comparison with those of the English towns, are also becoming greater, and are now over £40,000,000.

Other countries show the same tendency. The debt of the French *communes* (excluding Paris) has risen from £13,600,000 in 1862 to nearly £23,000,000 in 1869, and to £30,300,000 in 1878. The Parisian debt is by itself a formidable sum. In 1870 it was £59,000,000, by 1876 it had nearly reached £80,000,000. At the end of 1890 the various debts of the French capital after allowing for redemption were over £98,000,000.

Many of the Italian *communes* are also falling into greater debt. At the close of 1885 the total due by them was £35,300,000, and both Florence and Naples have been forced to compromise with their creditors.

But by far the greatest development of local (and particularly urban) debt is to be found in the United States. As Professor Adams has pointed out[1], the great creation of municipal debts was after the opening of the Civil War. He estimates the total indebtedness of the smaller division in 1860 at $100,000,000, of which over one-half was due by towns having over 7500 inhabitants. Ten years later (1870) this liability came to $515,800,000, and in 1880 had further increased to $822,100,000.

§ 3. The causes of this general movement are not difficult to trace. Local, like national, borrowing is dependent on the existence of favouring conditions; and these are to be

[1] *Public Debts*, 343 sq.

found, first in the greater power conceded to local bodies, or rather in the extension of their administrative functions during the present century. Another cause is the far greater amount of disposable wealth seeking investment, and the natural desire of its holders to get good security, which most public bodies undoubtedly afford. Thirdly, the needs of city life call for the creation of works involving large capital outlay. Drainage, water-supply, lighting and transport agencies, have, at the lowest, a semi-public character, that has led to their being placed in many instances under the suitable regulative body which had to employ its credit in order to procure the required funds. It is in this last respect that local and national debts present the greatest contrast, though some of the latter have been created in the same way [1]. The defenders of the modern system of local borrowing point to the valuable estate formed by its use. Waterworks, gasworks, tramway lines and market buildings, may all be looked on as sources of revenue, which, after meeting their liabilities, will in some cases give a surplus for other objects [2]. The element of truth contained in this mode of regarding debt has been already considered, but it is here desirable to indicate the qualifications to which it should be subjected. Granting the superiority of 'reproductive' over 'unproductive' debt, it does not follow that the former is in itself desirable. That public property, if revenue-yielding, is an asset to be set off against liability has been already explained. Whether either item should be preserved in the financial system is a distinct and separate question. Thus the various municipal industries are obviously a great aid in meeting the local debt charge, which, however, would not exist except for them. The real point at issue is the expediency, socially, economically and financially, of the conduct of such industries by public authorities. If public is superior to private management

[1] Prussia, India, and the Australasian Colonies may again be given as instances.

[2] See the articles in *The Times*, May 18th, 1891, on 'Local Debt in England.'

a financial gain may be looked for, though it by no means holds good that all profitable industries should be taken up by the public powers [1].

There are, however, some further considerations which tend to limit the use of borrowing for this object. The loan system involves the interposition of the credit of a public body between the lender of capital and the actual investment. Whether gas or water works be economically successful or not, the interest on the debt incurred for them has to be met. There may be a gain, but, then, there may be a loss, in which case the burden falls on the contributors to the particular revenue affected. It is in this undertaking of risk that the borrowing system appears to show its weakest side. Speculation is a task altogether unfit for public bodies. In another way the local revenue may suffer. The absorption of a class of industries in the public property reduces the amount of private wealth that remains to be taxed, and it is quite possible that the loss in this way may exceed the supposed gain on the working of the industries. The burden of proof rests on those who favour the process of forming a municipal domain, and they are bound to establish (1) the strong probability that the community runs no financial risk, and (2) the superiority of their method to all alternative ones. The control of special industries, as indicated when considering the industrial domain [2], is a less pretentious, but in many cases a more effective, method.

§ 4. But though the policy of using public credit in a systematic way for the establishment of profit-giving industries should not be hastily adopted, and, if attempted, should be kept within comparatively narrow limits, there nevertheless remains a legitimate field for local borrowing. The needs of any modern community are such as to make increased expenditure unavoidable, and that expenditure is largely devoted to the supply of educational, sanitary, and social requirements. Schoolhouses, baths, drainage, libraries,

[1] Cp. Bk. i. ch. 1. § 2 for the limitation of public activity in this respect.

[2] Either by special taxation or sale of concessions, Bk. ii. ch. 3. § 6.

and museums have to be provided by heavy immediate outlay, and as under the circumstances they cannot directly yield a revenue, it falls within the province of the public power to take them in hand[1]. The economic conditions impose the necessity of getting such works done quickly, as otherwise the earlier expenditure would be for a long time useless. Loans are accordingly the only available means; for taxation must be kept within bounds, so as not to swallow up the nett revenue of a single year. The burden is by this contrivance distributed over the time during which the works are of service, or at least over a fairly long period.

A great deal of the modern local debt has been incurred for such objects, some of which, *e.g.* waterworks, pass imperceptibly into the strictly reproductive part of local expenditure. In the case of London, for example, almost the whole of its liabilities has been so created. Paris in like manner borrowed for the 'improvements' of the second Empire, and to repair the damage of the war of 1870–1.

This process of anticipating revenue has greater justification in the case of a local, than in that of the central, government. The former deals with a smaller revenue on which any extraordinary outlay has greater effect, and it is restricted in its taxing powers, while the national government can more easily distribute its outlay from year to year, and has full control over its means of revenue. As a general rule, therefore, it is true that loans are a convenient, indeed an indispensable, part of the financial machinery of the smaller bodies.

§ 5. The forms or classes of local borrowing may next be considered, and here also its difference from that of the State is noteworthy. The absence of sovereign power brings the town or district more nearly on a level with the industrial or trading company, while its necessary sub-

[1] Even on the assumption that Adam Smith's ideas as to the limits of state action should be observed, 'The duty of erecting and maintaining certain public works' is one of those prescribed by him, *Wealth of Nations*, 286.

ordination to the central government makes control and regulation by the latter expedient. Just as local expenditure and taxation need the watchful care, and at times the restraining hand of the Sovereign[1], so does local borrowing. There is besides a financial benefit in the interposition of state credit to assist the smaller subdivisions. Local loans, therefore, fall into two classes, viz. (1) those raised directly by the borrowers, and (2) those obtained by advances from the State. The former until recently gave evidence of the undeveloped character of local credit. Mortgage loans or floating obligations were the usual kinds. Now, however, the funding system is making rapid way, and nearly every important town has its consolidated stock, modelled on the type of the national debt. Corporation stocks form a distinct class of securities in the money market, and stand at a high rate. This higher organization has the great advantages of procuring loans on better terms, and of bringing the amount of borrowing before the public. So long as a town or district debt is broken up into several separate forms its real amount is hard to ascertain, and it may be increased without attracting notice.

Local stock is sometimes redeemable by annual drawings, (like the French 3 per cents,) or more often it is automatically worked off by a sinking fund, the established method in the second class of loans—those provided by the instrumentality of the State. For very small divisions the issue of separate stock would be impossible, and any ordinary loan could only be obtained at a high rate of interest. The central government can, without inconvenience, make advances in such cases, and arrange for repayment by instalments at suitable times. In Great Britain the Treasury acts as the intermediary, and makes the advances from capital, which is really a part of the national debt[2].

[1] For expenditure and taxation, cp. Bk. i. ch. 7. § 7, and Bk. iii. ch. 6. § 9.

[2] The separation of the local debt carried out by Mr. Goschen marks this very clearly.

Belgium also has a special fund for this purpose, and in Germany the fund for invalids—one of the assets of the Imperial treasury—has lent more than £10,000,000 to the *communes*. The convenience of thus providing local bodies with advances on reasonable terms is very great, and it, at the same time, enables the central government to exercise a complete supervision over the borrowing so conducted.

§ 6. Repayment of local debt has to be regulated in accordance with its general features. As it is generally incurred for objects that are useful, or at least assumed to be such, the time of redemption may be adjusted to the duration of the utility created. Some improvements are much more speedily exhausted than others, and it cannot be well to have a debt charge which represents no present benefit. Again, local debt does not ordinarily arise from any pressing emergency. Its use is rather to get the work quickly completed, and therefore a sinking fund that will remove the charge within a definite number of years is often serviceable, since at the conclusion of the term new objects of outlay can be dealt with in the same way. The larger bodies may prefer the issue of stock, redeemable in parts or by annual sections, or even take the chance of further reductions of interest and the power of conversion thence arising[1]. The danger of this course lies in the possible neglect of the necessary provisions for repayment, and in the undue accumulation of debt. A sinking fund that makes repayment compulsory has decided advantages.

A difficult question, however, arises in connexion with the determination of the proper period for redemption. If it is very short the immediate taxpayers suffer, while their successors in after years are disburdened. When a longer time is fixed the pressure may fall chiefly on those who hold leases extending over the time, leaving the benefit to a reversioner who has perhaps contributed nothing to the payment of the charge[2]. This failure in just distribution

[1] Many of the larger British towns are favourably situated for this purpose.

[2] Cp. Fawcett, *Political Economy*, 629–31.

is, however, primarily a question of taxation. We have seen that local charges should be distributed on different grounds from those that regulate general taxation[1], and that the chief reasons for making this distinction are the predominance of the economic element in local expenditure, and the necessity of taking the several interests benefited into account. The use of loans enables a just distribution to be more closely attained, since future interests come under liability as they are realized. But at the same time their service in this respect must be subordinate to their general working. Direct taxation of reversionary property may also be desirable, though this course is limited by the practical difficulties that it gives rise to. A still better way of reaching justice is to maintain a steady policy with regard to expenditure. By so dividing outlay as to keep it in a nearly constant proportion to the rateable value of the wealth liable, it is clear that in the great bulk of cases the partition of charges between holders of property at different times will not be an unjust one, though some exceptional instances may occur. Very heavy and irregular expenditure by means of loans will be almost certain to cause serious practical grievances, which would, however, also be found if taxation were employed in the same way.

§ 7. Up to the present our attention has been chiefly directed to the urban and smaller rural divisions, and they are no doubt the most important. But the indebtedness of intermediate bodies, such as the English Counties, the French Departments, the Prussian and Italian Provinces, and on a higher scale the German and American States, deserves some notice. Special conditions have prevented the counties in the United Kingdom from coming forward as borrowers. A different reason has closed the loan market to the American States, but there are general causes for the smaller development of provincial borrowing. The works of utility for which local debt has been incurred are for the most part confined to small areas, or are of

[1] Cp. Bk. iii. ch. 6. § 5.

national importance. They fall either into the hands of the State, or into those of the *commune*. The duties of the province are such as can be, generally speaking, met out of revenue.

It would, however, be going too far to conclude that there will be no expansion of this kind of public debt in the future. In relation more particularly to transport, there is an opportunity for creating or purchasing railway lines or canals of secondary importance, as in other instances there may be one for an extension of public forests. The German States show an example of the former, which is also found to a smaller extent in the French Departments. Arterial drainage or reclamation of waste land might also be carried out in the same way, and the loans for such objects should be governed by the same principles as those applicable to municipal debts. So much depends on the future course of political movement that no prediction is possible; but for Finance it is sufficient to dwell on the necessity of applying the same rigid tests to all classes of borrowing, and to insist on the danger of its undue use.

§ 8. The great importance of adequate control by the central government has been already indicated, but it is desirable to lay emphasis on the fact. If expenditure and taxation cannot be safely trusted to administrators who may be led astray by ignorance and prejudice, still less can the power of mortgaging the property of those under their rule. For this reason a rigid supervision is exercised in most countries. Local bodies in the United Kingdom can borrow only by a special legislative act, or after a semi-judicial inquiry by officials of the State. In France authorization is in like manner needed for communal and departmental loans. The American state constitutions often place limits on both state and municipal borrowing powers, and the latter are also regulated by the state legislatures. The convenience, indeed the necessity, of some method of the kind is obvious; without it a numerical majority of the district, perhaps possessing little monetary interest in its future situation, could burden all the holders of property and future residents with a load of debt. Heavy taxation soon brings a remedy in the impatience of the taxpayers; but borrowing is for the time an agreeable process whose evils are only perceived later on. Thus the creation, the amount, and the mode of repayment all stand in need of due regulation by the supreme authority of the State. The method employed will of course vary with the particular circumstances, but it seems best to reduce the system to a set of general rules limiting the amount obtained to a certain proportion of the taxable value, requiring definite reasons for the issue of each distinct loan, and providing for a sinking fund or other effective means of repayment within no very distant time. These conditions are all insisted on by the English Local Government Board, and they seem to be necessary for the protection of those concerned. When exceptional cases arise, an appeal to the central legislature is the proper way of dealing with them.

The character and scale of the particular bodies concerned should be further taken into account. Temporary loans by a large city, repayable on demand or within a short period, must be soon met out of taxation, and they may be allowed under the same rules as those controlling the taxing power. There is no necessity for the same constant check as that essential in the case of small areas.

This power of regulation and its efficient exercise show the real unity of all public liabilities. Whether contracted by the State or by local administrations, they result from the use of the credit obtained through public property and the power of taxation. Their examination, therefore, must be conducted on the same principles, and their effects must be combined to reach the total result.

BOOK VI.

FINANCIAL ADMINISTRATION AND CONTROL.

CHAPTER I.

INTRODUCTORY. HISTORICAL DEVELOPMENT.

§ 1. WE recognised at the commencement of our inquiry that problems of administration and control form an integral part of the science of Finance. It is not sufficient to consider public revenue and expenditure with the relations that exist between them. The constitutional guarantees for the proper application of outlay and the due and moderate levy of taxes, the machinery by which those processes are effectively carried out, and, finally, the agencies by which, and the manner in which, the public accounts are prepared and verified, have important effects on both income and outlay, which need to be studied if we want to fully understand the nature and working of public economy. To the discussions of the preceding Books we have to add one on 'Budgetary Legislation' in the widest use of the term.

So long as financial topics were regarded as a part of applied political economy, there was some excuse for omitting to notice matters that seemed rather to belong to the domain of public law. But when we treat them as being a distinct branch of political science, this reason loses all plausibility. At the same time it must be said that we are not directly concerned with constitutional or administrative principles and details. Legal and political conditions are of importance only in so far as they produce financial effects, and need be considered only from that point of view. Their more elaborate and thorough investigation must be left to the jurist or political philosopher.

§ 2. It is instructive to note that this side of public economy, though often neglected by modern writers, was the part of Finance that first attracted the attention of students and practical administrators. The most important part of the financial system to those engaged in its working is the machinery by which the various state requirements are duly met, while to the contributor the authority that taxes him, the way in which it uses its powers, and the checks on its action are the really vital matters [1].

The modes of financial regulation, like the forms of expenditure and revenue, have been gradually developed in the progress of society. It is unnecessary to repeat the account already given of the primitive stage in which little special regulation is requisite. The sentiment of the tribe, or later on of the ruler, is the all-sufficient authority for outlay or contribution. Careful official organization and refined constitutional rules would, under such conditions, be as impossible as any of the other expedients of higher social life, as *e.g.* the credit or railway system, or modern constitutional government. To the earliest form succeeds the period in which the domain is the chief source of public revenue, as in the city States of Greece and Italy, and also in feudal Europe; and here the whole financial mechanism is not very different from that of any private economy. State or royal officers collect rent and administer whatever public property is under their direct care in the method usual at the time. Receipts are thus at once applied to meet the public wants according to the ruler's discretion. Along with this economic or quasi-private revenue may be placed the beginning of indirect taxation, which arises out of the fee system. The various services rendered by the ruler afford a ground for indefinite exactions, and his prerogative rights, which can easily be

[1] For the attitude in this respect of the mediaeval writers, the Germans of the seventeenth century, and Montesquieu, cp. *Intr.* pt. ii. §§ 3, 5.

stretched beyond their due limits, are enforced by his servants.

When public economy has progressed so far, methods of account and control make their appearance. The Roman Treasury was under the charge of the *Quaestors*, but complete unity of system did not exist, and it seems to have been the *Censors* who acted as finance ministers under the direction of the Senate. Even in the time of the Empire there was a separation between the distinct treasuries of the State and the *Princeps*, though the course of movement was towards fusion, and the official organization for the collection and control of revenue was minutely subdivided and graded. The method of farming out the taxes on commodities and inheritances must also be regarded as a further mark of that incompleteness of system which was inherent in the ancient state economy.

Mediaeval kingdoms and such smaller bodies as the free cities were likewise forced to devise means for the due regulation of their income and expenditure. At first rude and imperfect, they gradually improved. The English Exchequer, with its curious and picturesque methods, was an agency of this kind, to which the King's debtors had to account and his creditors to apply for payment[1]. The Carolingian empire had its check on accounts, as the rules of the Capitularies show, a system continued under the Capetiens, but essentially of the nature of a private economy.

A striking characteristic of this stage is the rare and infrequent use of direct taxation. It only appears as an occasional and extraordinary resource reserved for times of emergency, and quite distinct in its nature from either the economic revenue or the dues (*Auflagen*) on commodities. The importance of this circumstance in the present connexion arises from the need of the contributors' assent to legalize the employment of direct levies. However cut

[1] Besides the *Dialogus de Scaccario*; Madox, *History of the Exchequer*, and H. Hall, *Antiquities of the Exchequer* may be referred to.

down and reduced in later times, it was the common law of the feudal State that direct taxation required the consent of the classes who had to pay it.

§ 3. The growth of the monarchical power from the preceding condition was gradual, and is illustrated by the history, both of the later Roman Empire and of the several European countries in the 15th and 16th centuries. The collection of revenue came to assume more the aspect of a public function, the ministry of Finance was recognised as a government department, and the methods of control and accounting were further improved. This special progress is bound up with the whole course of political development, and can be fully explained only by reference to the actual historical conditions. The increase of royal authority, the greater cost incurred in the performance of public tasks, and the more frequent use of money in transactions conjoined in giving higher importance to financial administration.

One consequence of the increasing centralization of government was the inclusion of such smaller public economies as the cities and minor districts in the state organization. The resulting absorption—total or partial—of their revenues had the natural effect of making the need for full accountability on the part of those engaged in collecting or expending public funds still more pressing. The loss of popular liberties and the absence of due control on accounts explain the oppression and waste that usually mark the financial practice of absolute governments. When the salutary check imposed by the opinion of the contributors is removed, it is vain to expect the observance of those maxims of prudence embodied in the canons of taxation [1], nor can we expect a proper supervision of the many items of expenditure.

The secrecy in respect to public revenue and expenditure that was formerly so noticeable, and which has been dispelled by the extension of constitutionalism, had ex-

[1] Cp. Bk. iii. Appendix, p. 374.

tremely evil effects. On the one hand, it allowed prodigality and injustice often to escape notice, while, as an aggravation, fair and legitimate taxation and expense were through ignorance frequently regarded as grievances. Publicity and responsibility have been shown by a lengthened experience to be the necessary conditions for an efficient administration of Finance. Though every country that has any semblance of an organized government must possess some of the constituents of a financial administration, and though it is possible, as the case of the Roman Empire proves, to have a highly developed system of taxation and expenditure with an extensive official class engaged in its working without any check on the ruler's will, yet the probability of prudent management and due adaptation to the special conditions is extremely small. Sound Finance is so bound up with good government that one cannot be had without the other. Observance of the technical rules of public economy might indeed be carried out by a body of trained administrators under an absolute monarch, but unless the checks provided by the full publication of authentic accounts and the indirect influence of public opinion in some shape or other are in operation, it seems hopeless to expect it [1].

§ 4. The rise of constitutional arrangements in respect to financial matters undoubtedly originated in England, and therefore it may be said that in their present form the guarantees for proper administration are the result of her example, extensively imitated in the present century by other countries.

The principle that grants to the Crown should be freely made by the Estates of the Realm was, it would appear, definitely established in the 14th century, as was also the right of inquisition into the application of the funds so

[1] The case of France under the *Ancien Régime* is an illustration of the evils that result from concealment and the absence of responsibility. At present the Russian and Indian Finances show by their contrast the service that publication of vouched accounts and the power of opinion may be even to a subject country.

provided[1]. But the events of the 15th and 16th centuries practically destroyed this older system, which had to be reconquered from the Stuarts. The issues of the Civil War were closely connected with the right of taxation, and even on the Restoration, the supplies to Charles II were determined by the Parliament. Votes for particular purposes—*e.g.* that for the navy—were limited to the amount deemed requisite in each case, though this prudential method was in fact easily evaded. But the rudimentary character of financial control is very apparent during this period.

The Revolution of 1688 made parliamentary supervision and control a reality. By the expedient of an annual Appropriation Act limiting and defining the objects of expenditure and the amount to be devoted to each, it became impossible, without directly breaking the law, to use the public funds in any way other than those sanctioned by Parliament. The establishment of cabinet government, with the inevitably resulting dependence of the executive on the legislature, brought the details of financial management before the Lower House, which had already asserted its superiority to the upper one in respect to money bills[2]. The annual financial statement known as 'the Budget' thus arose, and the many intricate rules as to the legislative conduct of financial business were developed as occasion needed.

The preparation of the materials, and the final checks on the accounts were, as we shall see, added subsequently, and will probably undergo further change, but it is here sufficient to remark that the growth of British financial legislation and control has been quite indigenous and in full harmony with the general movement that has made the law of the constitution so peculiarly flexible and capable of being adjusted to new conditions. Budgetary regulations

[1] Hallam, *Middle Ages*, iii. 84–6. For the development of parliamentary taxation see Gneist, *Hist. Eng. Constitution* (2nd ed.), 388–93.

[2] Hallam, *Const. History*, iii. 27–32.

are really a mass of laws and conventions in which the latter are perhaps the more important[1].

§ 5. Elsewhere, speaking generally, the example of England has been followed and the rules that in her case have been left elastic and supported only by the sanction of public opinion have hardened into the rigid provisions of a written constitution. To find the neatest expression in strict legal form of the code that governs the conduct of Finance at home, we have to refer to the legislation of France, Italy, and Belgium, though of course there are variations due to special circumstances.

Historically, this remarkable result began with the revolt of the American colonies. The right of taxation was the actual cause of dispute, and the establishment of American independence involved the complete control of the representatives over the national Finances, a privilege expressly provided for in the existing Constitution[2] and hedged round by effective guarantees.

In France the Constituent Assembly at once asserted the principle that no taxes were legal except those voted by the delegates of the nation, but it did not extend the control of the popular will to the equally important matter of expenditure. As M. Stourm has shown[3], this task was reserved for the Restoration period, and indeed it is naturally later in order. The prevention of illegal exactions is a more urgent work than that of securing a perfectly correct application of the supplies voted for the public service, and it is besides much easier to deal with. The rapid growth of constitutional government has brought the questions of budgetary legislation into greater notice, and the general

[1] Dicey, *Law of the Constitution*, 328-9.

[2] 'The Congress shall have the power to levy and collect taxes,' Art i. § 8. 'All bills for raising revenue shall originate in the House of Representatives,' *ib.* § 7. 'No money shall be drawn from the Treasury but in consequence of appropriations made by law; and a regular statement and account of the receipts and the expenditures of all public money shall be published from time to time,' *ib.* § 9.

[3] *Le Budget*, 40 sq.

result has been a fuller recognition of the essential principles of popular consent and administrative responsibility as they have been developed in England. The very bitterness of the disputes on these points—specially illustrated in Prussia [1]—proves the tendency towards their more complete establishment.

The formation of a thorough system of audit and account is one of the latest steps in the attainment of a good financial organization. In respect to it England has not held the same leading position. The system in use on the Continent is rather French in its forms and methods, and moreover has a judicial instead of an administrative character [2]. Institutions of the kind have to be judged by their fruits, a test which after all may be endured without fear by the present English methods, imperfect as they may seem, when abstracted from the particular instance in which they are employed. A final characteristic of modern Finance in this department is the, at least partial, co-ordination of general and local income and outlay. Social and economic conditions have contributed to this centralizing movement by which the scattered elements of local Finance are collected and compared with those of the State. The necessity for bringing the checks of a wider public opinion and the restraining power of the central government to bear on local action is a further reason. Careful audit and strict observance of the technical conditions desirable in any body of accounts are now regarded as indispensable in the regulation of the Finances of the minor political bodies, and their natural result is to be seen in a closer relation of central and local Finance.

§ 6. The preceding historical notice was requisite in order to understand the actual condition of financial method and regulation in the civilized nations of the present day. The varieties that still exist are by no means unimportant, either in themselves or as evidences of the differences in

[1] Stourm, *op. cit.*, 23–5.

[2] Cp. Bk. vi. ch. 3. § 7 for further explanation.

political development that have produced them ; but there is sufficient uniformity to allow of a general description which will hold true in most cases and the departures will also admit of classification and explanation. It is to this object that the succeeding chapters will be devoted, though necessarily in the briefest manner.

CHAPTER II.

THE BUDGET. ITS PREPARATION—THE COLLECTION OF REVENUE.

§ 1. FINANCIAL processes are necessarily recurrent; from the initial steps for the provision of funds to the final closing of transactions certain proceedings are required that must be repeated on every similar occasion. We may, by taking an instance of each and combining them, bring together the several stages of a financial period, and thus realize the operation of the modern public economy on one of its most important sides. Such a study will naturally commence with a notice of the preparation for what is known as *the Budget*.

This term, first applied in England to the annual financial statement[1], has in other countries and in theoretic discussion come to mean the financial arrangements of a given period, with the usual implication that they have been submitted to the legislation for approval. There is therefore a combination of the idea of (1) a valuation of receipts and expenditure or a public balance-sheet, with (2) that of a legislative act establishing and authorizing certain kinds and amounts of expenditure and taxation[2]. The convenience of the term as including the several steps of financial legislation and control is so great that it is in that wider sense that we shall use it.

[1] Derived from the French *bougette*, the bag in which the minister carried the papers and accounts necessary for his statement. The term seems to have come into use about 1760. Dowell, ii. 139.

[2] For the scientific use of the term 'Budget' see Stourm's excellent work *Le Budget*, 1–5.

§ 2. The first requisite in the formation of a budget is an approximately correct account of the expenditure within the period to be considered. In order to combine efficient legislative control with regularity in payment for services and commodities, it is necessary that this estimation shall take place beforehand. Accordingly in the modern State we find that the several departments of administration have to frame what are known in England as their 'Estimates' some time previous to the opening of the budgetary period. The particular mechanism and division will vary in each country, but in all the general process must exist [1].

The task of bringing together the scattered elements of outlay devolves on the Ministry of Finance, and the head of this department has in most countries an indefinite power of control over the expenditure. It is always open to him to remonstrate against, or at least to comment on, what appears to be extravagant outlay, and in the fullest development of this power lies a useful safeguard for economical administration. The control exercised by the Treasury in England over the spending departments, though often unpopular, is yet in this respect of the utmost value. The necessity for giving a plausible reason for every new item of expense is a hindrance to new and unnecessary claims that keeps within limits the natural tendency to increase, and checks the waste so common in public economy.

English methods are probably more effective than those of other countries. In France, the system of control hardly exists, while in the United States the division of authority and the influence of the committees of Congress hinder effectual supervision [2]. Still, even in those countries a finance minister with sufficient courage and determination has been able to exercise a salutary influence, as the cases of Sully, Colbert and Villèle, as also those of Hamilton and Gallatin prove. The close connexion of the several divisions of

[1] Stourm, *op. cit.* ch. 3.

[2] Stourm, 74; Wilson, *Congressional Government*, 171-2.

the financial system, on which we have often laid stress, is very clearly seen in this part of the subject. The prudent reduction of outlay is quite as effective as the skilful adjustment of resources.

Nevertheless, it is in dealing with the latter side of the national account that the financier's function is supposed to specially consist. It lies with him to say what under the given circumstances will be the receipts available to meet the estimated expenditure, and if there be an absence of equilibrium to suggest the best mode of restoring it. For the probable yield of existing taxes and the receipts from the domain in its various forms the Minister of Finance is dependent on his advisers who direct each branch, but it is essentially his duty to propose such alterations as may be advisable, and the more definite his responsibility is made, the better is the prospect of efficient management.

The creation of the budget is therefore a work of administrative art in which the use of proper methods will very materially improve the financial position and contribute to the public advantage.

§ 3. A number of questions naturally arise in respect to the regulation of this initial stage of action. We have spoken of the budget as covering the several financial processes of a period, but we may say that in practice this rather vague term means a year. The convenience of taking stock of the public income and expenditure, and the fact that ordinary outlay is usually repeated every year, but not oftener, as well as the recurrence of the several physical and economic conditions in the same time, contribute to bring about this result. Even where the legislative sanction is not annually sought[1] the accounts are separately stated for each year. A longer term would conceal the real variations: a shorter one would fail to eliminate accidental changes and the effect of special circumstances.

But though the yearly period is always selected, there

[1] As in some of the smaller German States.

is no agreement as to the date of its commencement. January 1st, as in France, Belgium and Austria; April 1st, in England, Germany and Denmark; July 1st, as in Italy, Spain, the United States and Canada, have been chosen as the opening. The reason that has determined the latter dates is financial convenience. If the English finance year coincided with the civil one (as it did up to 1854) the budget would have to be presented either long before, or some time after, the opening of the period; but the former would make accurate calculation of receipts and expenditure almost impossible, the latter would compel expenditure without Parliamentary sanction or a recourse to 'votes on account.' The French budget has generally to be prepared 'fourteen or fifteen months before the period of its execution[1],' to the detriment both of its accuracy and unity. What particular date shall be taken in each country can only be settled by reference to its legislative and administrative habits, but the aim of bringing the preparation and execution as close as possible to each other should be the guide, and this accounts for the selection of different dates in different nations.

More important than the particular period are the form in which the budget is presented and the matter to be contained in it. Due arrangement and classification of the several chapters, or in English phrase 'the votes,' will make the nature and movement of expenditure much more intelligible, and also strengthen the constitutional check that the legislature possesses. A grouping by the several ministerial departments—good enough so far as it goes—does not suffice; the English division into 'consolidated fund' and 'supply' services, with the subdivision of the latter into 'Army,' 'Navy,' and 'Civil Service' votes, is not full enough, while the further breaking up into 'votes' which may be for 'millions' or for 'thousands' is too detailed and is open to sudden changes which vitiate comparison. Either is, however, superior to the separate

[1] Stourm, 77.

'appropriations' of the American Congress, which hinder a clear presentation of the annual expenses as a whole, and therefore make effective criticism impossible.

Next to the proper arrangement of the many heads of outlay comes the question whether the total amounts or merely the balances of the various expenses and receipts shall be presented, or in technical language whether the budget shall be a 'gross' or a 'net' one. The latter is the earlier and in some respects the more natural method. In a great spending department such as the Army it would seem that any trifling gains should be treated as deductions from the sum of expense which alone really concerns the nation. In like manner the cost of working the Post Office might seem immaterial in a financial point of view so long as the gain remains unaltered, a statement that is equally true of the Inland Revenue and the Customs. There is, too, the further difficulty that with an extensive state domain the presentation of the gross figures gives, as already noticed, an exaggerated idea of both expenditure and income[1]. The Prussian, or the Indian, budget presents a very different appearance, according as the gross or net items are taken into account. But this notwithstanding, the gross system is better, inasmuch as it brings all the details of Finance under direct review. In the spending departments it prevents irregularities in disposing of public property, and in dealing with the funds so obtained, or at the worst it gives opportunity for bringing them to light. Again, in regard to the earning departments, it is well to have their cost of working carefully watched. The expense incurred in collecting taxation is a form of outlay that may be much reduced by suitable arrangements, and the introduction of a thorough control over it is a decided improvement. Even in the industrial departments of the State a like vigilance will on the whole be useful. If the English Treasury sometimes keeps too tight a hand on the Post Office, its supervision removes the occasion of many

[1] Cp. Bk. ii. ch. 5. § 5.

scandals, though in such cases the recognition of something more than the purely financial aspect of the business should, as in the parallel instances of the Army and Navy, be secured by the concession of powers of remonstance to the minister in charge of it[1].

§ 4. Of somewhat the same character is the dispute as to the separation of the budget into distinct parts. In an undeveloped financial system the usual course was to assign a special receipt to meet each special charge. Thus 'ship money' explained its original distinction, and the 'hereditary excise' was designed to provide for the King's expenses. As the public economy advanced, this separation was seen to be inconveniently complicated. Some accounts had surpluses, others deficits, and their combination into a 'consolidated fund' was the obvious remedy for this want of balance. Compensation and elimination of chance influences were better attained by the fusion.

Recently the system of special budgets for particular kinds of expenditure has been somewhat widely employed, though the expedient is evidently calculated to confuse the public accounts and to prevent the true situation being realized. The general rule of meeting expenditure out of income should only be openly transgressed by the use of a loan. A surplus on the ordinary budget, with a deficit on one or more extraordinary ones, is a direct infraction of the principle that the finance accounts should be submitted fully, simply and in unity[2].

Another point of some delicacy is the determination of

[1] It seems plain that the head of a great industrial department, such as the English Post Office has become, should have the same weight as the heads of the Army and Admiralty admittedly possess. The great difficulty of applying the strict administrative control necessary in the case of public expenditure to industrial undertakings is one very weighty argument against extension of the state domain. The Treasury could hardly keep a Railway Department within bounds.

[2] The French method of adding four smaller budgets to the ordinary one it therefore a violation of principle and injurious in practice, Stourm, 187. It may, however, be said that the *Budget sur Ressources spéciales* is really a statement of one part of local Finance. But it is incomplete as regards the *communes*, and in fact of no service as a mode of control.

the precise items to be included in a given budget. Starting with the intention of giving the receipts and expenses of a particular year, we may either take the actual incomings and outgoings of the Exchequer, or we may endeavour to assign to the year under notice all the revenue, whenever received, that properly belongs to it, and charge against it all expenditure incurred in it, though perhaps not paid till a much later time. In the former or English method there is a simplicity and directness that commends itself to anyone who knows the benefit of those qualities in Finance, while the latter appears to have the advantage of giving a more precise account of the real result of the transactions of the period at the sacrifice of a good deal of delay. This part of the subject more fitly belongs to a later chapter, but here we must note the greater difficulty of estimating under the French system, though it again has not much substantial effect [1].

Lastly, there is the problem of deciding on the proper method of estimating the expenses and income of the approaching year. On the correctness of these estimates rests in a great degree the success of the budget, and no parliamentary majorities or use of official power can alter the hard facts of Finance. Sincerity and care are both needed for success in this operation. One very natural course in the infancy of Finance was to take the figures of the preceding or some other year, generally the last for which the accounts are made up, as the basis. Another method nearly as mechanical is to take the increases during preceding years and count on a like result in the future. In reality these facts should only be regarded as elements in the calculation. The revenue and expenditure of a State do not move in a definite course; they are acted on by many distinct causes, and it is on these that the financier should frame his estimates. In dealing with expenditure

[1] The respective merits of the French *compte d'exercice* and the English *compte par gestion* are carefully considered by Stourm (ch. 5), who is perhaps too favourable to the former.

the statements of the several departments concerned are the starting-point, but it may happen that their requirements will prove more costly than they themselves admit, a consideration that should not be overlooked. Still, the results of experience and the great extent of the modern public economy make valuation easier than it was; special emergencies apart, expenditure is well within the field of rational prevision[1]. The receipts present greater variations within the ordinary limits, though they are not subject to the great sudden changes that expenditure may show. Agricultural and industrial prosperity or adversity will leave their mark on the revenue returns. The elasticity of certain taxes has been already noticed, and the public income as a whole is sometimes liable to fluctuate. The task of estimation is therefore a work that cannot be reduced to any automatic rule. The circumstances of each country and each particular year will have to be examined on their merits. In this respect the modern development of statistics has been a most efficient auxiliary. The financier of the present day has at his disposal materials that were unknown to his mediaeval or even eighteenth-century predecessor. Population, banking, shipping, agricultural, and industrial statistics, together with the criticism to which they are subjected, are available as aids in forming a judgment on the probable course of the facts material to the growth of revenue, and as these technical instruments improve we may expect even greater accuracy in the future.

§ 5. The several processes just described are essential preliminaries to a due presentation of the budget for the assent of the national representatives. This legislative approval, however important or even vital in the modern constitutional State, is nevertheless, as we saw in the last chapter, a late addition to the financial mechanism, and therefore, before considering it, we shall deal with the more

[1] The estimates of expenditure in England for the three years April 1, 1889 to March 31, 1892, as compared with results, show an error of only £137000, in a total of £264,000,000, or a little over 1/- per £100.

general machinery by which the public revenue is brought into the Exchequer. At first the contributions in kind were delivered directly to the leader of the tribe, who also collected the economic receipts, such as they were. The State, as its organization gradually developed, dealt with its taxes on the private or 'contract' system. Thus both in Greece and Rome the great mass of the public revenue was collected by farmers, or paid in directly by the dependent cities as tribute. This method, so characteristic of an ill-organized economy, continued in regard to the Roman indirect taxes to the last, and was revived in the absolutist monarchies of the sixteenth and seventeenth centuries. The other mode, viz. that of apportioning taxation to the several cities or districts, is evidently due to the establishment of contributions after conquest, and it also is an inheritance from an earlier stage.

The use of direct taxation and the increasing power of the State brought the special tax officials into more prominence. At first the supervisors of the state domain collected whatever taxes were not let out by contract. In England this duty fell to the sheriff, who, however, often obtained his office by purchase; the count discharged the same function in the Carolingian Empire. But the great source of a special official organization is found in the customs revenue, which was more peculiarly in the King's hands. The unfortunate policy of letting out the indirect taxes was widely adhered to, as *e.g.* in France, where the *Fermiers généraux* were a power in the State. The older system of separate and privileged districts and towns continued to a great extent up to the end of the eighteenth century, so that many public levies were apportioned among the contributing groups, to be afterwards subdivided between the members of each. The farming system and that of apportionment are the most decisive marks of an imperfect fiscal system. The former puts the payment of taxes on the same footing as a private debt, while the latter interposes a distinct authority between the citizen and the State. It is not necessary here to dwell on the grievances that the farming out of revenue has produced. The Roman 'publican' and the French '*fermier*' were both proverbial instances of rapacity, and the loss to the revenue was only exceeded by the sufferings of the poorer contributors. Apportioned taxes are plainly inelastic in yield, and generally defective in distribution. Both are, however, justifiable under certain conditions. Where tax-collectors are easily corrupted and organization is backward, farming may be the only way of making duties productive and of meeting the expenses of collection. In like manner it is expedient to adopt the apportioned tax where the statistical *data* for correct assessment are wanting, or where evasion is a serious danger [1].

The recognition of the relative use of these more primitive forms does not in the least show that the collection of revenue by public officials, for the benefit solely of the public powers, is not now the right one. Fiscal practice supports this view. Every modern government has its customs department for that branch of revenue, while the internal receipts are obtained by one or more official agencies. In England the Inland Revenue Department has absorbed the several Boards that preceded it, but the Post Office necessarily preserves a separate existence. Three different departments collect the French internal revenue under the heads of direct, indirect, and stamp duties, the public industries being also separately dealt with. The Prussian finance department undertakes the main work of revenue collection, but the Ministries of Agriculture and Public Works have the management of the quasi-private receipts.

In all countries, however, the tax system must at last come in contact with the individual citizen, and it is very prudent to make this unpleasant relation as little irksome as possible. Hence have originated Adam Smith's rules as

[1] Cp. Wagner, ii. 747.

to the 'certainty' and 'convenience' of taxation[1], as also the very general preference of administrators for indirect taxation in which the number of persons dealt with is reduced to a more manageable figure. Where direct taxation is largely used, the local authorities or their officials may be utilized for the purpose of collection, but it appears that on the whole centralization is more effective, though the same person may conveniently be the agent of both administrations. Simplicity and rapid action are not the most conspicuous qualities of 'self-government,' but they are those most needed in the collection of revenue.

§ 6. The actual process by which the funds find their way from the taxpayer's pocket to the central treasury of the State, must depend on the economic condition. In earlier times contributions in kind would be moved by the collectors to the place where they were needed. Taxes paid in money have to be brought to the public treasure-house, and stored up for future use. The development of credit enables the whole proceeding to be carried out by the agency of banks. Thus the old English Treasury has been superseded by the Bank of England, into which the receipts flow from the various points of collection. The French system of 'sub-treasuries,' which keep separate accounts and transmit their surpluses either in coin or by the aid of the Bank of France, is more complicated and costly. There can be no doubt that centralization, not merely of the staff but of the receipts, so easily accomplished by the aid of credit, is the best course. Backward countries must, however, make use of branch treasuries, and provide for the storing of coin at convenient points in order to reduce the expenses of its transmission; but whatever be the treatment of the actual material of revenue, its combination in the public accounts into a single body to be dealt with at the pleasure of the Sovereign is one of the processes needful for the establishment of a proper budget.

[1] See as to these rules Bk. iii, Appendix.

CHAPTER III.

THE VOTE OF THE BUDGET. CONTROL AND AUDIT.

§ 1. THE first stage in the life-history of the budget is finished when the administration has laid its proposals before the Legislature. It is highly desirable that the scheme of Finance so presented should possess the several qualities indicated in the preceding chapter, which may be concisely summed up as consisting in economy, timeliness, intelligibility, completeness, unity and accuracy. In other words, the estimates of expenditure should be carefully framed, and kept within the smallest amount consistent with efficiency; the period dealt with should be that about to commence; the arrangement and grouping of the items should be logical and easily followed; the full amounts to be received and expended, not merely the probable balances, should appear; the several sections should be brought together and treated as a whole; while the valuations should be real, and based on the best evidence attainable.

But though the observance of these rules will materially assist the deliberations of the Chambers, they will not of themselves suffice to secure a good result. The parliamentary treatment of the budget, which apparently belongs to the subject of public, and especially constitutional law and usage, has important financial bearings. The method by which expenses and taxes are voted will often account for the good or bad working of a particular system, since the checks imposed on governmental action may either be insufficient or too severe, as on the other hand the legislature may be too careless or unduly active in regulating financial matters.

§ 2. The consideration of the budget is one of the principal tasks of a legislative session. It involves the study of a great number of detailed points which must occupy a good deal of time, and in certain cases may give rise to keen political controversy. The way in which it is approached will have something to do with the merits of the final result. In most countries the ministerial estimates are submitted to a preliminary examination by a committee supposed to be specially suited for the work, and this body reports on—in effect very often re-casts—the proposals of the executive. The United States go the farthest in this direction by placing the initiative in the hands of distinct committees. The financial measures in fact come from the legislature itself, though they are partly conditioned by the requirements of the public departments. A consequence is the loss of all unity of plan, and a failure in almost every year to even approach equilibrium[1]. England is in the other extreme: the 'estimates' and the proposed annual taxes are placed at once before the whole House sitting as a committee, and examined without any previous inquiry[2]. Ministerial responsibility is thereby increased, as the measures that make up the *ensemble* of the budget are altogether the work of the Cabinet, whose liability is undivided. The committees of continental countries, though they appear to secure fuller deliberation, are really a screen for the original preparers of the financial proposals, and divide that liability which should be definitely fastened on the administration.

Another peculiarity of the English system goes far to explain its general economy, viz. the ancient rule that all

[1] Wilson, *Congressional Government*, ch. 3.

[2] M. Stourm is in error in supposing that the attendance in Committee of Supply is smaller than in the case of ordinary sittings. *Le Budget*, 273.

proposals for expenditure must come from the Crown, *i. e.* at present from the Ministry. No addition can be made to the estimates submitted, and anything that even indirectly violates this rule is opposed to the stricter constitutional doctrine [1]. All expenditure therefore originates with those who have an evident interest in keeping it within bounds, as they will have to suggest the taxation required to meet it. A stronger check on the natural tendency towards increased expenditure could hardly be devised, and it is at once curious and characteristic that it should be the result of a now departed condition of things [2].

The evil effect of the absence of such a rule is seen in the increased expenditure often proposed by the French budgetary commission, and also in the Australian colonies, where though the limitation exists it is evaded [3]. It is particularly noticeable in the United States, where members of Congress are more interested in securing expenditure desired by their constituents than in maintaining the character of the national Finances, and therefore indulge in the operation known as 'log-rolling,' in which representatives agree to support each other's schemes.

§ 3. The most serious constitutional disputes have arisen respecting the rights of the different chambers with respect to the budget, which, however, seem to have a very slight financial importance. Usage in England has given to the Commons what is practically the sole power in this department, but in other countries the Upper House retains the right to reject or amend financial legislation, and the American Senate extensively avails itself of this privilege, chiefly in the direction of increasing the appropriations of 'the House' for the public service. Regarded as a ques-

[1] Todd, *Parliamentary Government in England*, i. 690 sq.

[2] 'This principle is commonly involved in mediaeval metaphysics as to the prerogative of the Crown, but it is as useful in the nineteenth century as in the fourteenth, and rests on as sure a principle,' Bagehot, *English Constitution*, 146.

[3] Hearn, *Government of England*, 378. Cp. Leroy Beaulieu, ii. 113.

tion of *technique*, it would seem that if the two Houses are to consider the budget the discussion should be a joint one, as otherwise the work of detailed examination has to be done twice over, and unless there is some restraining rule, the ultimate outcome will be greater confusion and less conformity to any settled plan. If the legislative authority of the second chamber must be recognised, it may best be secured by confining its action to the actual laws necessary for validating the budget, leaving the examination of the separate items to the popular house, where they are first presented.

But whether the discussion be principally conducted in one House or separately carried on in each, the grouping of the several heads to be considered deserves attention. In this respect the general course of progress has been towards greater specialization. From the early period in which the supplies were voted *en masse*, to be applied at the ruler's will to the public services, we have come to a time in which the separate heads may be numbered by hundreds. Thus the French budget, which in 1831 had only 164 chapters, has been steadily subdivided until that for 1890 has come to contain 807; and since 1831 each chapter has been separately voted [1]. The English Civil Service 'votes' have at times reached 150, to which must be added the smaller number for the Army and Navy. A thorough sifting and re-arrangement, especially of the former, would be a great improvement. The votes for each civil department might be taken in a group, with further discussion of the leading items by a grand committee. No large assembly can possibly control each of the branches with effect, though its criticisms on the larger heads may be most useful. It is even possible that each group of votes might be thoroughly examined by a separate committee, and afterwards discussed on general grounds in the House [2].

[1] Stourm, 295.

[2] The 'Committees' of the American system have this advantage, but in their case there is no real unity.

From the method of separate votes or chapters, together with the principle of legislative control follows, the rule that no transfer can take place from one vote to another. A surplus on the votes for justice cannot be transferred to meet a deficit on those for education, or *vice versa*. Moreover, in England each of the Civil Service votes is separate and cannot be transferred, while those for the Army or Navy may be used for other votes in the same department, but subject to re-examination in the next budget. As the votes for these departments are few in number and the total amount is usually very nearly spent, the possibilities of excessive outlay under this rule are not great. By a better arrangement the same method could if needed be applied in other departments, but the rigid limitation to the amount voted under each head is doubtless a check on useless expenditure. A reserve fund, to be employed only on the responsibility of the government, and to be replaced in the next financial period, is perhaps a better arrangement, as it draws more attention to over-expenditure[1].

§ 4. The difficulty of exact adjustment and the occasional necessity for meeting unexpected demands tend to impair that unity of the budget which is one of its good qualities. In the actual management of so complicated an organization as that of any modern State, mistakes in calculation and sudden calls that no prudence could anticipate will from time to time occur. English usage has provided the agency of 'supplementary estimates,' by which additional amounts are voted to meet the extra requirements. This process, which has been made more frequent by the prompt closing of each year's accounts and the stoppage of transfers, is nevertheless, according to competent opinion, 'one of the greatest financial evils.' 'To render parliamentary control effectual it is necessary that the House of Commons should have the money transactions of the year presented to it in

[1] As in the two English funds of the 'Treasury Chest' and 'Civil Contingencies,' amounting to £1,300,000 and £120,000 respectively.

one mass and in one account[1].' A system of applying for frequent additional votes would completely destroy the single budget or at least deprive it of any value. This expedient should therefore be confined within the narrowest limits consistent with efficiency, and such is the established English policy.

In some cases, however, the amount required may exceed the funds at the disposal of the government or be wholly indefinite, as in the case of actual or threatened war when the recognised expedient is a 'vote of credit,' which amounts to an authorization of expenditure and secures the control of Parliament, though it breaks the unity of the budget, but in the least dangerous way. The technical rules of financial management ought to be sufficiently flexible to meet such emergencies, and a special vote at once satisfies this condition while it indicates that the proceeding is irregular and exceptional.

In other countries a like restraint has not been observed. 'As regularly as the annual session opens there is a Deficiency Bill to be considered' is what we hear from the United States[2]. The additional credits in France for the seven years 1879–85 came to £66,200,000, or, deducting savings on other heads, to £43,400,000, an average net excess of £6,200,000[3]. Belgium, Prussia and Italy, under the form of a qualifying budget, also transgress the normal bounds of additional votes. It would seem that a long constitutional discipline is needed to secure due attention to this point as well as a proper budgetary system. The unity of the budget may apparently be infringed in another way. It might seem that all the expenditure and revenue should be annually voted in order to preserve complete legislative control. In fact, however, this course is neither necessary nor desirable. So long as a substantial part of

[1] Gladstone, quoted by Todd, *Parliamentary Government*, i. 740–2.

[2] Wilson, *Congressional Government*, 159.

[3] Stourm, 369–70. His figures do not quite agree with those given by Leroy Beaulieu, ii. 104.

the outlay is subject to the discretion of Parliament and the mode of paying out the funds is under strict legal arrangement, there is no danger in making permanent provision for the greater bulk of the public demands. Certain heads of expenditure—particularly the interest on debt and the salaries of the judiciary—are best removed from the field of party disputes. The general revenue system will not be annually changed, and it can be most conveniently fixed by permanent legislation. Such is the *rationale* of the English 'Consolidated Fund,' into which by far the largest part of the revenue comes by virtue of permanent Acts and out of which one-third of the annual expenditure is drawn by the same authority.

This distinction between 'permanent' and 'annual' outlay and income is useful in more ways than one. It reduces the already too heavy work of voting supplies, which might indeed be further reduced by placing all absolutely needful expenditure on the Consolidated Fund. It also helps to separate the stable from the moveable taxes. The income-tax performs, as we have more than once stated, a useful function in supplying unexpected demands, and it is therefore rightly an annual tax of varying amount. So, too, are some of the customs, *e.g.* the tea duty. The separation between the two classes of taxes might be even more strongly emphasized, though the position of the income-tax is probably sufficient for the purpose. There is besides an advantage in retaining the greater part of the public expenditure under the annual scrutiny of Parliament, so that until an item is unquestionable and its amount very definitely settled, it should not be transferred to the 'Consolidated Fund' charges.

For a very different reason the German military expenditure is voted for a period of seven years and is therefore removed from annual debate, by which arrangement the Imperial government is relieved from dependence on the *Reichstag*. Some of the smaller German States have biennial or even (as in Hesse) triennial budgets, an impossible system in any country with active constitutional life, and one which will be abandoned when the popular element becomes stronger.

The permanent settlement of some sections of income and expenditure does not really infringe on the principle of unity. For England the annual financial statement—'the Budget' in the English sense—brings together all the heads of expense and receipt as well as the movement of the national debt. The Consolidated Fund charges are definitely known and the estimates supply information as to the remaining expenditure. The votes in committee either of 'supply' or 'ways and means' give the basis for the budgetary legislation of the year, which is in a sense supplementary to the existing laws, and combined with them, makes up 'the budget' in the wider use of the term[1].

In other countries the adaptation of the English system has led to a greater formal strictness and a stronger emphasis on 'the law of the Budget.' Convention and usage have however, been on the whole more successful in keeping up a high standard than definite constitutional enactments, as a comparison of English with continental Finance will amply prove.

§ 5. The general efficiency of English financial management is largely due to a feature of its budgetary system already referred to; viz. that which prescribes the closing of accounts at the end of each financial year. Only the actual money paid out is included in the expenses: all balances on votes lapse on each 31st of March, and if required must be voted afresh. Only the tax receipts are credited to the year; unpaid arrears going to the next budget. This system secures an accuracy in the accounts and a facility in presenting them which makes their speedy presentation at the end of each year a feasible measure. The consequence is that in his financial statement the Chancellor of the Exchequer is able to deal with the

[1] Thus the tedious process of 'supply,' calculated to take thirty-five working days of the session, is, in the French sense, a part of the budget.

results of the year just closed or closing and the prospects of the opening one. The position of the Finances is distinctly known at the end of the year, and no need for amended returns can arise.

The French method, in which the financial year is invested with a kind of personality, and its arrears of receipt and expense come to its account at any later time, has an appearance of completeness, since it assigns to a given period all the consequences due to it. Delays in collecting taxes or postponement of expenditure may affect the English accounts [1], but by separating to each year what is really to be attributed to it this danger is avoided. On the other hand there is the fatal objection of delay. To make criticism valuable it must be speedy. The French budget of 1880 could hardly excite much interest in March, 1883—the date of the presentation of the final law relating to it—when the Chamber would be more engaged by that of 1884 which had been just laid before it for the first time. It is hopeless to expect that long past transactions will be carefully examined, and therefore the adoption of a quick, even if less precise, method is by far the best. But the superior accuracy of the French system is more than doubtful. The arrears both of expense and income will normally be about the same from one year to another, so that what is lost at the opening will be made up at the close. Besides, it must be remembered that the arrears are at best a small part of the total amounts [2]. To gain somewhat greater precision in the small balance of a small proportion, the whole mass of accounts is surrounded by

[1] Peel, for example, miscalculated the yield of the income-tax for 1842 by not taking into account the fact that only one-half of the tax would come in during the financial year. Northcote, *Financial Policy*, 41. Mr. Lowe increased some of his surpluses by manipulating the collection of the income-tax. More generally, there is no doubt that a surplus could be manufactured by starving the permanent part of the public services and throwing the additional cost of replacement on succeeding years.

[2] In France, for each of the years 1883, 1884, 1885, the uncollected receipts were about 2½ per cent., and the unpaid expenditure 11 per cent. of the total figures. Stourm, 123-4.

the obscurity that lapse of time must produce. Accordingly we are not surprised to find that Italy and Germany have on this point followed England rather than France.

§ 6. From the legislative methods of dealing with the financial condition, we have now to pass to the regulations under which the outlay of public funds is authorized and verified. The most admirable provisions respecting the preparation and vote of the budget will be useless unless there is adequate machinery to secure conformity to the determinations of the Legislature. The mechanism by which the revenues are drawn from the contributors to the Treasury of the State has been already noticed[1]; it remains to see how the collected public income is applied to the proper objects. The supervision of issues in England originally belonged to the Exchequer, which kept a careful but rather clumsy system in operation. With the growth of expenditure and income its methods proved defective. The accounts were many years in arrears, and a great deal of the expenditure was misapplied. The final audit of accounts was in a still more backward condition, and large sums were held by the Exchequer officials, while the different spending departments had unapplied balances in their possession. The first reforms of this evil were prepared by Burke, and carried into effect by Pitt in 1785 when he created the Board of Audit[2].

Fresh abuses could not fail to arise during the long war period, and these in turn led to the reforms by which the Exchequer as a substantive institution was abolished and a better system of accounts adopted[3]. Various committees of inquiry disclosed further weaknesses in the machinery of control and audit, particularly in the influence of Parliament over the testing of the accounts. The final reforms consisted in the appointment of the Committee of Public

[1] Bk. vi. ch. 2. §§ 5, 6.

[2] Cp. Burke's great speech on 'Economical Reform' particularly, *Works*, ii. 81 sq.

[3] Sir H. Parnell vigorously attacked the methods of control existing when he wrote (1830), *Financial Reform*, ch. 11.

Accounts (1862), and in the combination of Control and Audit in 1866 by the appointment of a Comptroller and Auditor-General[1].

The system in use at present affords valuable guarantees for the legal issue and due application of the revenue that the earning departments bring into the treasury, *i.e.* the Bank of England, where it lies to the account of the Comptroller and Auditor-General. For every payment there must be the following steps: (1) a requisition by the Treasury to the Comptroller-General having as its ground an Act of Parliament; (2) a grant of credit by the Comptroller-General, who is bound to satisfy himself as to its accordance with the terms of the law on the faith of which it is issued, and which lasts only for the current year; (3) a treasury order to the Bank to transfer the specified sum from the Comptroller's account to that of the Paymaster-General for the particular service. There must therefore be the clearest legal sanction for both the object and amount of every grant. The Bank of England is the sole receptacle for the collected revenue, and the Comptroller-General's order the only key that unlocks its coffers[2].

In France the terms of disbursement are affected by the existence of the subordinate local treasuries, from which payments are made, and whose heads profit by the public funds that they hold. The responsibility for grants rests on the particular department requiring them and on the Ministry of Finance; but though a number of distinguished financiers have laboured to make the system of control effectual[1], it is as yet defective in the absence of any external preventive authority over issues.

[1] The occasional 'committees on Finance' became the annual Committee of Accounts in 1862. The Act reorganizing the control and audit department was 29 & 30 Vict. c. 39.

[2] The Bank of England by its management of the debt and its practical custody of the revenue is, in a sense, a government bank, but not a state one. Cp. Bk. ii. ch. 4. § 2.

[3] Mollien, Baron Louis, and Audriffet may be mentioned.

The Italian system has here followed the English one by requiring an authorization from the 'Court of Accounts' before any payments can be made from the Treasury[1]; and the Prussian 'Curators of the Treasury' discharge a like function in that country.

§ 7. Distinct from the control over issue and quite as necessary is the audit of accounts. There is little advantage in preventing unauthorized payments to departments if they afterwards misapply the funds received for specific purposes. To guard against this danger another duty has been placed on the Comptroller and Auditor-General, who in this second capacity is bound to discharge the duties of the Board of Audit whose place he has taken, as it superseded the inefficient audit of the ancient Exchequer. The work consists of two distinct parts: viz. (1) the verification of the accounts in order to see that no improper expenditure in the ordinary sense has been incurred; and (2) the appropriation audit, which inquires into the application of the funds and its conformity with the directions of Parliament.

This latter check, first applied to the navy expenses in 1832, was extended to the army accounts in 1846, and became general in 1866[2]. The Auditor-General is bound within a limited period to report to Parliament on the results of his inquiry, noting any irregularities that he has discovered, and as a final barrier to misappropriation the Committee of Public Accounts goes over the expenditure again in a close and critical manner. Under such conditions no great departure from the line of expenditure marked out by the budget can escape notice, though petty errors and small illegal payments are not unknown. The weakest points of the system are (1) the fact that the Auditor-General is only an administrative official, and (2) the absence of any sufficient sanction to support the rulings of the auditing bodies, who can only report to Parliament

[1] So have also Belgium and Holland.

[2] Todd, *Parliamentary Government*, ii. 57 sq.

the outcome of their investigations and the errors that they have discovered.

The United States Congress had long preceded England in this line by appointing in 1814 a Committee on Public Expenditure, to which other committees for separate departments were from time to time added. Owing to inefficient book-keeping and the undue extension of credits the detection of erroneous applications of funds was not easy, and a good deal of entirely illegal expenditure escaped notice. The absence of unity in the financial administration shows its effects even in this apparently mechanical part of the system, by complicating the forms of the public accounts [1].

The control of the Finances in France is assigned to an independent body, the *Cour des Comptes*, which examines the accounts judicially, and also reports to the legislature on any infractions of the law of the budget. The former power was bestowed on it by Napoleon I at its creation in 1807; the latter was given in 1831. The two functions broadly correspond to the two duties of the Comptroller and Auditor-General, but the French court differs in being a judicial body, not an administrative official, though its independence is perhaps less solidly guaranteed. When combined with the internal audits of the several ministries and the legislative control that the final law of the budget gives to the assembly, it would seem that the mechanism of the French system is hardly susceptible of much substantial improvement [2].

Other continental countries have followed the French model, but with certain useful modifications due to English example. The Prussian 'Court of Accounts' holds inquiries on the spot and is not limited (as in France) to the examination of documents submitted to it. The position of its President nearly resembles that of the Auditor-

[1] Wilson, *Congressional Government*, 175; also Bolles, *Financial History* (1861–1885), 523 sq.

[2] Stourm, *Le Budget*, chs. 28 & 29.

General, and its procedure is often administrative. Several countries give their 'Courts of Account' a preventive control over issues of money and greater latitude in dealing with cases. Such variations do not at all affect the general truth that the conditions of a proper audit have been established in all civilized countries, and only require the existence of a sound constitutional sentiment in the legislature to make them effective.

§ 8. With the verification of the public accounts and the establishment of their conformity to the law concludes the cycle of processes relating to a financial period. In this and the preceding chapter we have shortly noted the working of the financial machine without entering into questions of constitutional law or administrative practice, and regarding simply its effect in securing the best application of revenue to expenditure. It but remains to again lay emphasis on the fact that good Finance cannot be attained without intelligent care on the part of the citizens. The rules of budgetary legislation are serviceable in keeping administration within limits; but prudent expenditure, productive and equitable taxation, and due equilibrium between income and outlay will only be found where responsibility is enforced by the public opinion of an active and enlightened community.

www.ingramcontent.com/pod-product-compliance
Lightning Source LLC
LaVergne TN
LVHW102006210926
848483LV00009B/102
9781932512120